Confessions of a Francophile

and other essays from
The Kevorkian Newsletter

aram j.
kevorkian

Confessions of a Francophile

and other essays from
The Kevorkian Newsletter

1980 to 2000

Taderon Press
Reading, Berks.

TO Esther Harcott.

A new and discriminating reader of my newsletter - these essays will help you to "catch up" on France and discover the wanderings of an Armenian from Philadelphia

A J Kevorkian

Paris 17 VI 2003

Illustrations by Marguerite Fatus

Cover photo by Jean-Baptiste Huyhn

Published by Taderon Press, PO Box 2735, Reading, RG4 8GF, UK

ISBN 1-903656-25-7 – Printed in France

Please address inquiries to: Garod Books Ltd. PO Box 2735, Reading, RG4 8GF, UK, Email: books@garod.co.uk

This work is dedicated to the memory of my parents,
who lived by the written word.

Karnig Kevorkian (1895-1972), born in Chunkoush, Turkish Armenia,
founded in 1919 an Armenian-language weekly newspaper called Groong,
which he published in Philadelphia for 43 years.

Hripcimée Hovaguimian (1899-1962), born in Smyrna,
wrote articles for my father's paper while living in Marseille,
and then became his wife and collaborator.

Together, the Groong was their life work.

To them I owe thanks for whatever proclivity
I have in the realms of writing and seeking truth.

AJK

Table of Contents

Thematic Table of Contents

Personal Tributes

Personal Vignettes

Comparisons: France and USA

Clinton scandals

Preface

I had been practicing law in France for 17 years before the idea came to me to do a "Legal Newsletter from France," which I sent to about 100 clients and correspondents, mainly in the United States. The first Newsletter, of September 1978, was about a new French consumer warranty law, and throughout 1999, subsequent issues were all about French law. The Newsletter was produced on one of the early word-processors and photocopied onto the salmon-colored copy paper (with punched holes on the left) that we used in our office for certain files.

It was only in October 1980 that I dared approach a broader subject – the French mind. That Newsletter, called "A Word about the French Spirit," earned me more "fan mail" that all the prior ones combined, and encouraged me to believe that an American in Paris could share his experiences as a student of French culture, in the broadest sense, with a number of discriminating readers around the world, many of whom have become my friends.

As the years went by, my readership expanded considerably, mainly by word of mouth. By 1990, I was mailing my Newsletter to more than a thousand persons, and the subjects I treated were increasingly non-legal, so much so that I decided to call my publication simply "The Kevorkian Newsletter," while keeping its former name on the masthead as a sub-title. Fortunately, the Internet came on the scene in the '90s, and I began E-mailing the Newsletter to a handful of readers in 1994. Now, the Internet is the main medium of transmission. While I made no effort to increase the readership, the demand for the Newsletter increased every month, as readers sent them to relatives, friends and colleagues, who often ended up asking to be on the mailing list. Today, it is sent by me to about 3,000 persons (and probably read by four or five times that number), located in 72 countries.

In the beginning, and even now, readers would ask me how I found the time to do a Newsletter while practicing law full-time. (One lawyer even asked me, matter-of-factly, "Who writes them for you?") The answer was, and is, that I write them myself mainly on the weekend at home, and never start writing until I have worked out the theme and the beginning paragraph on my morning walks to the office. As William Saroyan told me in 1961, when I met him on arriving in Paris: "There's plenty of time; most people don't know the usage of time." In the early years, I would produce four or six Newsletters a year, but in more recent years the pace has been virtually monthly.

So many readers have urged me to make a collection of Newsletters that I have been able to overcome my natural tendency to consider these essays ephemeral. Let me confess, nonetheless, that in the course of reviewing the proofs for the book, I have myself enjoyed re-reading many of the 79 essays, which I have selected from the 145 that I wrote until December 2000.

Readers will, of course, find some repetition in this collection, such as comments on Cartesianism and the role of *ENArques*, simply because over a period of two decades these have been inevitably recurring themes. Keep in mind that as the number of readers steadily increased, these themes were new to new readers. I would not urge anyone to read this volume as he would a novel, but rather to browse through the book and simply fasten on whatever attracts his attention.

While I have my own sentimental favorites among these Newsletters, it would be more objective for me to designate a score that have aroused the most reader responses. They include, in chronological order:

"A Word about the French Spirit"

"Confessions of a Francophile"

"Report on Armenia"

"Montaigne and Descartes"

"L'Affaire Gregory"

"L'Affaire Dreyfus"

"Feudal France; Serial Justice"

"Golden Rule: French Style"

"Paranoid Alley: from Paul Valéry to Pizza Hut"

"Catholic and Protestant Justice"

"The Gold and the Silver Rules Revisited and Platinum added"

"The Free Lunch, the State and other French Fictions"

"Ethics à la Française"

"In Memoriam: Howard Goldfarb"

"Kosovars, Serbs: The Agony of Little Nations"

"My Life With Computers"

"Quantitative and Qualitative Truth"

"Lucky Jews, Lucky Arabs"

"Bach the Healer"

Of course, the most recurring theme has been France itself and the French, since I have been living in Paris throughout the life of the Newsletter. I will resist the temptation to summarize in this preface what it has taken me 20 years to tell in these periodic essays, which in large part chronicle the foibles of the functionary-political class that has taken control of the Fifth Republic, founded by Charles de Gaulle. But it may be useful to mention what a Los Angeles judge wrote me after reading a number of my Newsletters: "What makes it special is that you are both an insider and an outsider; you know France, yet you approach it with the perspective of an outsider."

The reader is entitled to know something about me from the start, since it has long been my belief that "objective writing" is an impossibility, and that any writing reflects the author's nationality, origins and background. Born in Philadelphia on December 31, 1928, of Armenian parents who fled Turkey to avoid being massacred in the first genocide of the 20th century, I am the proud product of wonderful public schools that turned children of the melting pot into Americans. Let me record the names of these schools: Andrew Hamilton Elementary School, located at 57th and Spruce Streets; Oliver Wendell Holmes Junior High School, then located at 55th and Chestnut Streets; and, finally, West Philadelphia High School, located at 48th and Walnut Streets.

My father, Karnig Kevorkian, devoted most of his life to producing a weekly Armenian-language newspaper, called *Groong* – after a bird of the heron family which is credited by the Armenians for bringing news. The *Groong* became a family endeavor when my father married Hripcimee Hovaghimian, a brilliant woman of letters, of Smyrna and Marseilles. Later, my brother Andrew and I worked in the printing shop in our spare time to help with all the tasks that make up the publishing of a small newspaper.

After getting my B.A. at the University of Pennsylvania and my J.D. at Harvard Law School, I first came to France in 1953, on a Fulbright scholarship, for which I am ever grateful to the visionary Senator from Arkansas. Shortly after returning to the States, in 1954, to practice law in New York, I again found myself in France, in July 1955, this time with the U. S. Army, as an officer in the Judge Advocate General's Corps, for a stint of 30 months. In 1958, when I returned to a Wall Street law firm, I thought that France was far behind me, but my French wife convinced me otherwise and so, in April 1961, I arrived again in France, this time, apparently for good, as the saying goes. I have been practicing law ever since in Paris and consider myself primarily a lawyer, even though many readers have been kind enough to describe me as a writer. It took several years for it to dawn on me that perhaps some atavism had led me to produce a newspaper of my own, following in my father's footsteps.

The hardest practical issue in preparing this collection was to choose between ordering the Newsletters by subject or chronologically. I chose the latter, because it would better show the development of my thought as well as give the reader a clearer vision of contemporary French history. However, to help the reader who wants to follow certain themes, I have prepared a thematic table of contents which can be found after the table of contents.

In closing I wish to offer special thanks to my brother Andrew Kevorkian who, for years, has reviewed my draft Newsletters, corrected errors of usage, grammar and spelling, and provided valuable comments concerning the contents. Recognition is due to Christophe Boutin who first participated in the makeup of this book and to Marguerite Fatus, a Parisian artist whose illustrations add sparkle to it. Finally, Simone Damotte and Richard Takvorian, of Press & Design, put the last touches on the work and saw it through publication.

Paris, July 2002

Vol. II, N° 4, October 1980

A Word about the French Spirit

As many Americans and other foreigners profess to be mystified by the way the French mind works, it occurs to me that it might be useful to devote a few pages to this subject. After a few weeks in France I realized, not without irritation, that my years of high school and college French did little to prepare me to comprehend the French spirit. Even though most of the words were recognizable, students and professors, I discovered, were at home with a level of abstraction that was over my head. And when I got involved in a discussion that I thought I could grasp, I was constantly being told "*mais, il y a nuance*." If "nuance" there was, I was surely missing it. So, gradually it dawned on me that the French spirit is itself one of the fine arts. Without claiming to have mastered the subject, I would like to pass on to the reader some insights I have gleaned over the years.

Let us start by delimiting the subject. If you want to understand the mind of a French *paysan* you could profitably study a Maine farmer (assuming you can get near him). If you wanted to know what makes a French shopkeeper tick you could analyze the psychology of "Mom and Pop" who run the store down the street. Even a self-made French businessman would not strike you as far different from the "rags to riches" captain of industry in the United States. But when it comes to an intellectual, a professional or a high-level company executive in France there are probably no models from which you can draw comparisons. The reason is that the French educational system forms a particular type, which for want of a better word, we will call Cartesian. This word is of course, derived from the name of Descartes, the celebrated 17th-century mathematician and philosopher, who invented analytical geometry and is known even in America for his *"Je pense, donc je suis"* ("I think, therefore I am.").

This phrase epitomizes the good and bad in the French spirit. The good: pithy, direct, and clear expression; the bad: confusing a truism for reasoning. When a Frenchman uses the word *donc*, be careful, for he may be about to beg the question in guise of drawing a logical inference.

Descartes is the patron saint of *a priori* reasoning. His essay *Le Discours de la Méthode* is to French intellectuals what the *Sermon on the Mount* is to Christians. For a country that produced Montaigne, Pascal, Voltaire, Diderot and Montesquieu, to mention only a few, Descartes' *Discourse* has no competition as a molder of the French mind. You will rarely, if ever, hear a Frenchman say *"Je suis Montaignien"* or *"Je suis Voltairien,"* but virtually every day you can hear one proclaim *"Je suis Cartesien."*

The heart (if I may use this term) of Descartes' dogma is this statement, which is the first principle of his method: *"The things that we perceive very clearly and very distinctly are all true."* For a non-French person this appears to be a dubious assertion. An "Anglo-Saxon" would likely retort: *"A lot of things that I once thought to be very clear and very distinct have turned out to be false."* But for better or worse, this one statement is the key to understanding the Cartesian mind. If an American says: *"that's clear"* he means only that he has understood your point. If a Frenchman says: *"c'est clair,"* he means it's true. Voilà! That's what Descartes has done for the French intellectual tradition.

The Method is the 17th century version of what Dale Carnegie might have called *"How to Think Clearly and Influence People."* Descartes, having had great success with mathematics, professes to explain how one can solve problems in the same methodical way. He makes an eminently sensible point: divide the problem up into sub-problems and then solve them one at a time. Of course, as many people have found out since the 17th century, this doesn't always work, for how can you divide the problem into parts if you don't know where to start? Few French intellectuals like to be reminded that in the essay Descartes illustrates how his Method can be put to use, by examining the circulation of blood, and concludes that it is the circulation which makes the heart beat! He also uses the method to "prove" the existence of God, beginning with the "clear and distinct" principle and concluding, very piously, that it is thanks to God that truth is perceived clearly and distinctly.

Why, despite these unimpressive demonstrations, has Descartes' essay enjoyed such a mind-boggling success in France (and nowhere else)? To answer that I would have to write a book, but the beginning of an explanation is that there is something very appealing in the notion that by applying a simple method one can think straight and solve all problems. Like other dogmas, this one clings to people despite the refutation that experience and science may provide.

If you comprehend the importance to the French mind of the term *clarté* (clarity) you'll go a long way towards understanding the intellectual French person. (I use "person" so as not to appear sexist, but I defy anyone to understand a French woman!) Let me illustrate this point by a personal anecdote. I was chatting with a distinguished French lawyer one day about the differences between American and French law. The lawyer said as nicely as he could, "I know you have a great legal system but there is one criticism I must make of it: *"Ce n'est pas clair"* (It's not clear). As I had read Descartes, I knew that this was the ultimate put down: if a system is not clear it cannot be true.

Comparison of an American contract with one drafted by a French lawyer generally shows the importance given by the latter to logical sequence of ideas. The American is pragmatic and wants only that his contract "work," *i.e.* to have all the basic points. For the French lawyer or businessman the points have to be lined up in a "logical order." I once was asked by an American parent company to have a license agreement executed by the President of its wholly-owned French subsidiary. The President refused to sign the American contract because it was not "logical" and "clear." He insisted on redrafting it, but not a single change was made as to substance. You'll have to admit that Descartes is not forgotten in the 20th century!

Another product of the method is the French attachment to form. Paul Valéry, one of the greatest 20th century exemplars of the French intellectual, wrote this of his own country: *"France is perhaps the only country where considerations of pure form, a concern for form in itself, have persisted and dominated in the modern era. The sentiment and the cult of form are... accompanied, in fact, by a particular freedom with regard to content, and often coexist with a kind of sense of generalized irony."*

Every school boy (should I have said "school person"?) in France learns to make a *plan* (an outline) of everything he writes, including examination papers. Even in college and law school, the *plan* counts as much as the contents of the paper. You could have the "right" answers and still get a bad grade because your *plan* is not logical or well presented.

Here are some actual examination questions that were used in the June 1980 Baccalaureat examination in philosophy for high-school seniors. Answering just one of these questions constitutes an entire four-hour examination: "Is appearance a falsehood?", "Can one speak of legitimate violence?", "Is respect for law a guaranty or an obstacle for liberty?", "To what extent does man make history?"

Not only do these questions illustrate the French penchant for abstraction, but also they require considerable skill in organizing one's thoughts. During the first hour the student is expected to work out his *plan* on scrap paper; then he spends three hours writing his best prose. A consequence of this system is, of course, that once the *plan* is established his creative thinking ceases, for he is now merely carrying out a pre-established outline. That is the blueprint of an *a priori* thinker; you do your thinking up front, so to speak.

The importance of the *plan* to the educated Frenchman was impressed on me once when I gave a talk to an audience of French lawyers on the practice of law in New York. As is my wont, I did not have a prepared speech but I had made a list of points that I wanted to cover and the connections between the points were more or less chronological and personal. My talk was well received by the audience. Later, one of my close friends congratulated me in this manner: *"Your speech was most interesting but I was not able to perceive your 'plan'."* What he meant was that the right way to have made the speech would have been to announce the outline in my introductory remarks (which are themselves an indispensible part of the *plan*), subsume all the points under two or three main headings, and end with a "conclusion" which summarized the whole. The fact that my points were interesting would get me only half credit.

These habits have a profound effect on French government and business life. If you read a speech of President Giscard d'Estaing or Prime Minister Barre you'll detect, without fail, faithful adherance to the principles learned in elementary school and perpetuated by the teaching of all the elite schools in France (known as the *Grandes Ecoles*). They explain why, for example, so many original laws and decrees rarely have any practical effect: the author feels that his job has been done by thinking up the law or regulation; making it work is a mere detail. During my first year in France a law professor told me: *"Some of our laws are the most marvelous works of the human spirit; if only we would follow them up in practice, we would not have so many problems."* He gave as an example the *loi cadre pour l'Algérie* which was a beautiful plan on paper for giving the Moslem majority a greater voice in government. A few months later the Algerian rebellion began.

Whatever one might think of this intellectual tradition (and there is a lot to say for it when one recalls the proliferation of machine-graded multiple-choice exams in the USA) I believe it vital for anyone dealing at a high level with French professionals and business executives to know how their minds work. If you are negotiating with a man who was graduated from one of the *Grandes Ecoles* such as "X" (Ecole Polytechnique), HEC (Hautes Etudes Commerciales), ENA (Ecole Nationale d'Administration) or *Sciences Po* (Institut des Sciences Politiques), you should have no doubt that he knows how to make a *plan* and will be looking for *clarté* in your position. Understanding this can not only save you money but also endear you to your French counterpart.

As I stated at the outset, not everyone in France is a Cartesian. The majority of people – particularly in the provinces – are hardworking pragmatists who know what it takes to earn a franc. They are the silent majority, for they permit a small elite established in Paris to make the laws and regulations as well as the speeches that are an inevitable concomitant of French public life. It is this tolerance of leadership by the Cartesian "egghead" which distinguishes the French majority from the American majority. Americans expect their leaders to be "just plain folks" who have trouble with punctuation marks and dangling participles. The French expect their leaders to have done well in school and to know how to make a *plan* at the drop of a cork. Giscard d'Estaing graduated at the head of his class at not one, but two, of the *grandes écoles*, ENA and Polytechnique! This is like graduating *summa cum laude* from both Harvard School of Government and Massachussets Institute of Technology. Michel Rocard, the up-and-coming Socialist leader is also an *ENArque* (an ENA graduate), as is Jacques Chirac, the Mayor of Paris. The difference between an *ENArque* on the left, like Rocard, and an *ENArque* on the right, like Chirac, stems not so much from ideology, as from early choices based on political opportunities.

The influence of the *ENArque* is overwhelming in France. Starting out as bright young lads who know how to make a *plan*, they get into ENA through a competitive exam, upon graduation go into Ministerial Cabinets, where they have power disproportionate to their experience, then often enter politics at the local level and get elected to Parliament. (One of the remarkable things about France is that you can have a full-time job in Paris and still be elected mayor of a small town or village in the provinces as well as member of the National Assembly.) And those who eschew politics often hop into top management positions in big companies owned or controlled by the ubiquitous French state.

In W.S. Pierce's essay, "How to Make our Ideas Clear," he gives this famous definition of pragmatism (although he doesn't use the term): "Consider what effects which might conceivably have practical bearing we conceive the object of our conception to have. Then, our conception of these effects is the whole of our conception of the object."

Paradoxically enough, the concept of Cartesianism in France becomes eminently pragmatic when this definition is applied, for it is a system that leads to jobs and power.

But enough of politics. Let me conclude by noting that the antipode of Descartes' "clear and distinct" ideal is this line from Baudelaire: *"J'aime les nuages, les nuages qui passent... là-bas... Là-bas, les merveilleux nuages."*

"I love the clouds, the passing clouds up there
up there, the marvelous clouds." (l'Etranger)

Between these two extremes, the one yearning for mathematical solutions in the human sphere, the other revelling in the nebulous unknown, lies the full range of the French spirit. If one were to classify contemporary French figures in two columns, according to their relative proximity to one pole or the other, there would be some strange bedfellows; De Gaulle and Sartre might be in the Baudelaire column and Giscard d'Estaing with Michel Rocard in the Descartes column. But of course it would make more sense to have a middle column headed by my favorites, Montaigne (the first relativist of modern times), Pascal (as good a mathematician as Descartes but who knew, as Marianne Moore once said, that "there are some nuts that diligence can't crack,") and Voltaire, who demonstrated that laughter can be a potent weapon in the battle against injustice.

Ah yes, the French spirit is one of the fine arts.

The French Spirit

Vol. III, N° 3, May 1981

William Saroyan

Born Fresno August 31, 1908 - Died Fresno May 18, 1981

One day in the Spring of 1967, when my firm was in its first year, and we were located on rue Galilée, a middle-aged woman whose name I have mercifully forgotten was just leaving my office when a dark-haired man walked in whom I introduced to her as William Saroyan. "Oh, Mr. Saroyan," she babbled out, "I thought you were dead." Chuckling graciously but without losing a beat, Saroyan replied, "That's all right, Madam, sometimes I feel that way myself."

So now Mr. Saroyan is really dead, not the one who is mistaken for John Steinbeck, but the real Bill Saroyan, the one who wrote *My Name is Aram*, *The Human Comedy*, *The Time of Your Life*, and some books you probably never read like *Not Dying* and *Chance Meetings* and others you have never heard of because they're lying in his trunk – dead of a cancer that started in his prostate and spread around, not being cared for, as Bill was not a believer in medicine or hospitals, until even his battling brain could not ward off the inevitable, as the saying goes (to use one of his phrases).

Why relate a writer's death in a legal newsletter? Because the writer was a client of the firm and a friend ever since my arrival in Paris 20 years ago in April, except for a period beginning almost six years ago when, as with everyone who was ever close to him, relatives, children, agents, lawyers, publishers, doctors and accountants, he got mad at me. By this time, I knew him so well that as he stood in my office roaring in white rage, I sat there smiling and said "That's O.K. Bill, nothing you say or do can possibly get me mad at you." This made him even angrier and he stormed out. He kept away for six years and then, in what seemed out of the blue, wrote to me a few months ago to resume relations. It was only when I visited the West Coast, last month, and called him to arrange a long-awaited visit to his home town Fresno, that I learned that he was dying of cancer. On that day, April 8, my first visit to the city that had seemed so incredibly suited for boyhood when described in *My Name is Aram*, I finally saw the two tract houses on West Griffith Way which Bill had bought in 1964 when he unexpectedly returned to Fresno to live and die. Unexpectedly, I say, because he had told me that he hated the place, particularly now that the builders and city planners had destroyed so many of his childhood haunts.

Thankful I am, nevertheless, for having made the visit, because Bill came to life during the afternoon. With Bob Damir, his San Francisco lawyer and a former Fresnoan, we ate *Kharpoot kefte* at Stanley's Armenian restaurant, tried to buy a lemon-cream pie at Rosa Karsh's bakery, a pie that Bill suddenly had a craving for, and then drove around Fresno and the neighboring farm communities, with Bill in the front seat pointing out landmarks of his childhood. At my request, Bill managed to guide us to the place which had inspired one of his most poignant stories, "The Pomegranate Trees," a work of art that becomes even more astonishing when one contemplates the barren field where his impractical, inept, impoverished uncle imagined that he was going to grow pomegranate trees.

Yet, I could understand why his uncle had chosen this field, for lifting his eyes to the east he could perceive the distant highlands which reminded him of his native Bitlis in Armenia.

That afternoon drive, it turned out, meant even more to Bill than to me because he knew it was to be his farewell glimpse of the boyhood which had spawned his art. Bill inscribed in the book that he gave me at the end of the day: "April 8, 1981, an immortal day."

Appropriately enough, this book was his last published work, *Obituaries*, a typically Saroyan *tour de force*, the form of which is built around 130 short chapters taking as theme the necrology list of *Variety* magazine for 1976. Most Americans with whom I have discussed Saroyan in recent years assume from their not having seen any of his books lately that he had stopped writing. Saroyan never stopped writing, for writing was as necessary to him as breathing. What stopped was his being in "style" and being acceptable to the reviewers in the *New York Times* and *Time.* To this obsolescence he certainly contributed greatly by being so intransigent in his business dealings, by refusing to use agents, by fighting with publishers, in a word, by not accepting that the world of business control the artist's world. Back in 1940, when Bill was awarded the Pulitzer Prize for *The Time of Your Life* – a play, incidentally, which he wrote in six days – he ostentatiously turned down the prize on the ground that "business should not subsidize art." He once told me that he would refuse the Nobel Prize if it were offered. Doubtless the Committee was well aware of this as he never got the chance to refuse it.

This is not the time or place for an appreciation of Saroyan the writer. For years, I have been predicting that Saroyan's death will bring forth a Saroyan renaissance, just as occurred for Eugene O'Neill, some of whose plays were first performed after his death. I consider Saroyan to be one of the great writers of our time, one of the few who excelled in three genres: the short story, the novel and the theater, but as he once confided to me, "The fact is, Aram, I'm a poet." How many contemporary writers can you name who have his range? *The Beautiful People* was the title of one of Bill's plays. Now the phrase describes a totally different class of people. To do justice to Saroyan's works, the critics are going to have to re-read him with a fresh eye and get rid of some of the clichés that used to infuriate him: that he was sentimental, fuzzy and a mere lover of humanity. Saroyan was as much a hater as he was a lover. His wraths and resentments were volcanic. He never forgave the world for taking away his father when Bill was three, nor his mother for putting him in an orphanage, nor the Army for drafting him at the height of his creative powers, nor the fates that broke up his marriage and estranged him from his children, Aram and Lucy, when they grew up. No, a new vocabulary is necessary to deal adequately with Saroyan the writer.

In all my years, I have never met anyone who was as alive, as vibrant, as hilarious, as seeing, and as sensitive as Bill Saroyan. In 1966, when problems in the firm where I was working led me to contemplate leaving and establishing my own office, Bill told me: "Aram, there is no need to be anxious. When the time comes to make the move, go with joy in your heart." Those words had an electric effect; they kindled my soul. I knew immediately that he was right, that the courage to make the big step must be mingled with joy.

In the last letter I wrote to Bill, I could think of no more fitting words to wish him courage on his last voyage than to remind him of what he had told me: "When the time comes to make the move, go with joy in your heart."

I know that Bill got the message. He replied on April 19 with a handwritten note that may well be the last thing he ever wrote, for he was found unconscious the following morning. His final words to me were "With deepest thanks and love."

Vol. III, N° 6, December 1981

The Rights of Privacy and Publicity in US and France

On November 10th, I was invited to address the Copyright Society of Los Angeles, consisting mainly of lawyers having a special interest in matters affecting the entertainment industry. The subject was "The Right of Publicity, a Continental View." As I represented the old continent, I felt a keen duty to bone up on the subject. While it is still fresh in my mind, I believe it might be of general interest to give a brief summary of the presentation I made.

Everyone knows something about the right of privacy, but the meaning of the "right of publicity" is not self-explanatory. In fact, I don't think it is a particularly apt title, but it does seem to be with us, until someone comes up with a better one. A good definition of the "right of publicity" was given in the dissenting opinion in *Lugosi v. Universal Studios:* "The right of publicity has been regarded as the right of each person to control and profit from the publicity values which he has created or purchased. The distinctive aspect of the common law right of publicity is that it recognizes the commercial value of the picture or representation of a prominent person or performer, and protects his proprietary interest in the profitability of his public reputation or Persona."

In this case, the heirs of Bela Lugosi, who was the most famous portrayer (but not the author) of the fictional character Dracula, claimed that Universal Studios had illegally exploited Lugosi's image in selling commercial objects without obtaining their authorization. The lower court held that they were entitled to damages, but the intermediate court and the Supreme Court of California ruled against Lugosi's heirs on the ground that the right to exploit one's name or image is personal and, unless it is exploited by the famous person in his lifetime, the right cannot be passed on to his heirs. As this is indeed a strange ruling, it warrants some further explanation. This is the way that the higher courts reasoned:

1) The right of privacy is personal, that is, you can invade someone's privacy only while he is living.

2) The right of publicity is an extension of the right of privacy, since it is the right to profit from what would otherwise be the invasion of your own privacy.

3) Therefore, the right of publicity is also a personal right.

4) If the individual exploits it in his lifetime, he has in effect created a business which can be passed on to his heirs. Otherwise, he has nothing which can be passed on.

I hope my readers will agree with me that this is a pretty silly conclusion. For the California court, if a famous person (query if it is not a famous person?) respects his own privacy so much that he does not pose for tooth-paste ads, then on his death his name and face fall in the public domain. If Abraham Lincoln were President today and got shot tomorrow, before he could found a savings bank, then anyone could put his name and image on toilet paper. chewing gum and the like, while his heirs stand by helpless to prevent the cheap exploitation of their deceased family member's reputation.

I have deliberately chosen the example of Lincoln because his name and face have often been used for commercial ventures like banks and insurance companies. That does not seem particularly offensive after a century has elapsed. The time when commercial exploitation seems offensive is immediately after the person's death, while his family is still around. As lawyers are fond of saying: *"Where do you draw the line?"* Well, Chief Justice Bird, who dissented in the *Lugosi* case, made a proposal that makes sense to me, that the "right of publicity," by analogy to the new US Copyright law, would survive the person for 50 years, after which the name or image would fall into the public domain. But, many lawyers would object to such judicial legislation. They would say, *"It took a statute to provide for copyright protection; let the legislature do the same for the right of publicity."* As long as the California legislature abstains from such legislation. it would seem dangerous for a famous person to do nothing about exploiting his publicity right in his lifetime.

Now, you may be wondering what the law of France is on this subject. Unfortunately, there is no decided case similar to *Lugosi* (or the Marx Brothers case in New York, which went the other way, but on the ground that they had exploited their publicity rights – and how! – in their lifetime). The closest French case is that involving the great actor Jean Gabin. When he died, a newspaper published a photo of him on his death bed, and the family convinced a French court that this was wrongful. The court was nevertheless troubled by the fact that the protection against invasion of "*la vie privée*" is also considered personal in France. But, it held that to publish without authorization such an intimate photo is, in effect, an invasion of the family's right of privacy. As with Antigone, the family is entitled not only to bury the corpse, but also to look at it alone.

In my opinion, the French courts would, in an appropriate case, extend the Gabin rule to the commercial exploitation of the famous person's image, at least a short time after his death. To illustrate, if someone had come out with a perfume called "Gabin," without authorization of the heirs, I would suppose that the French courts would prohibit it, not on the ground that the family name is entitled to protection (because his real name was Moncorgé) but that to exploit the name is an invasion of the family's privacy. A distinguished French avocat, whose reaction I solicited on this question, followed the line of reasoning opposite to that of the Lugosi court: *"If the deceased was so fussy about his privacy as not to permit commercial exploitation of his image, that would be all the more reason to respect his wishes when he is dead."*

In the last analysis, the difference between the likely French approach and that of the California judges seems to me to reflect a profound difference in cultural attitudes. As a US President once said: *"The business of America is business."* So, if you build a business around your name, your heirs are protected. In France, business is considered a necessary evil, like going to the toilet, but it is not the sole source of personal rights. Privacy and the family mean a great deal here.

While we are comparing cultures, let me mention another French case which deals with the rights of privacy and publicity. Many readers will be surprised to learn that it is a criminal offense in France to insult the head of State. General de Gaulle, while President, often prosecuted offenders under this law, including a Frenchman who had the misfortune to be standing next to a plainclothes policeman when giving a "Bronx cheer" as the General passed by in a parade! Under President Pompidou, there were also some prosecutions, but it is to the credit of Giscard d'Estaing that he never prosecuted anyone for insulting him. Nevertheless, during his presidency, he brought a civil action to enjoin a card manufacturer from selling a deck of playing cards called "Giscartes" in which Giscard was presented in the guise of 52 historical characters. The court ruled that the cards violated Giscard's privacy, as an individual, since they were sold for commercial purposes. The decision was criticized by a well-known specialist in this field of law, Raymond Lindon, on the ground that caricature is an established form of expression (even Daumier sold his lithographs).

When in California, I visited Gerry Gunther, one of my old friends and law-school classmates, who is now a leading constitutional-law professor at Stanford. I asked him how a "Giscartes" case would be decided in the States ("Jimmycards," for instance). My friend opined that the result would depend on whether the cards were put on the market as a form of political expression or merely for commercial purposes. If the former, the "utterance" would be protected under the First Amendment to the Constitution ("Freedom of Speech"). If the latter, the cards would be considered, as in France, an invasion of privacy. What I find fascinating is that the analysis is quite similar to that of the French court made, even though the French Constitution does not (alas!) have a "First Amendment." But freedom of expression is considered a basic right, so long as you do not abuse it by giving a "Bronx cheer" to a passing President.

Vol. VI, N° 5, October 1984

Cold and Wet

I mentioned in the June issue that no one was saying this year, *"La rentrée sera chaude."* Now we know why: September was the coldest and wettest in France's recorded history (that is, since 1877). And October must have come close to equalling the feat.

French politics are also cold and wet. The Communists are now more or less in the opposition, having refused to join in the new government headed by Laurent Fabius. And Mr. Mitterrand admitted defeat in his attempt to hold a "referendum on the referendum." The issue is now forgotten like a bad dream. Instead of hammering away at this ignominious defeat, the opposition has been wasting its time in a Jesuitic debate over the question whether, in the likely event that the Socialists lose control of the National Assembly in 1986, the new majority can "cohabit" with President Mitterrand, whose term does not expire until May 1988.

This burning issue separates Jacques Chirac from Raymond Barre. The former says, in essence, "Why not?" and the latter, that the new majority should do everything in its power to force Mitterrand to resign.

Among all the politicians in the world, only the French kind would not find it ridiculous to make a fuss over this academic question two years before the election is to take place. One understands that monks in the middle ages debated over the number of angels that could dance on the head of a pin.

Mitterrand suffered another severe setback when the Constitutional Concil held unconstitutional a key provision of the new press law. It will be recalled that this statute, purporting to be an antitrust measure, was carefully framed to break up the powerful press empire of Robert Hersant, publisher of the *Figaro.*

The Court emasculated the law by holding that it could not be applied retroactively. Thus, the Socialists, having toyed with the freedom of the press, have concocted a grotesque result: Hersant's empire stands but no competitor can ever become as powerful as he!

Laurent Fabius, who at 37 became the youngest Prime Minister in French history, is showing his age. He has done absolutely nothing to speak of, except speak. It is universally acknowledged that Fabius was chosen by Mitterrand only because he was a yes-man. Accordingly, it is evident that the Elysée Palace wants to run the show even more directly than during Mauroy's term as Prime Minister.

During Fabius' first television appearance, he was asked how he might differentiate himself from the President. All he could reply was, *"Lui c'est lui. et moi c'est moi"* (*"He is he and I am I."*) Even this reply seems to have displeased some of the sycophants in the Elysée Palace, perhaps because the *"lui"* was not capitalized.

At any rate, Mr. Fabius is doing his best to give the impression that things will change for the better. A man very attentive to his image, he works hard to avoid being identified with troublesome issues. In 1981, he was Minister of the Budget, and thus responsible for some of the most infamous tax measures that the Socialists enacted, *e.g.* the retroactive income tax increase for 1980 high earners, a 72% maximum income tax rate, the 30% non-deductible tax on restaurant expenses, and of course, the so-called "Tax on Great Wealth." Yet somehow, Fabius has managed to avoid being too closely identified with high taxes. It is perhaps this quality that Mitterrand appreciates the most in him, after, of course, obedience.

Fabius has wasted no time in nurturing his image. The French press reported that Fabius had pressured a State-owned television channel to appear once a month on the 8 pm news roundup, which has the

He is He and I am I

highest audience rating. The "High Authority," which is supposed to guarantee the independence of the television networks, put its foot down. Mr. Fabius could not appear regularly on the news program, but only in a separate slot immediately after. And to prove that France is still a democracy, the High Authority (headed by Michèle Cotta, who was chosen by Mitterrand as *his* journalist in the 1981 television debate with Giscard) declared that there would be a rebuttal program the next day. Guess how the time is divided during the rebuttal program? One third for the opposition (including the Communist party), one third for the Socialists and, yes, one third for the government! The High Authority, to justify this strange arithmetic, professed to discover a tradition along these lines. Can you imagine a situation where President Reagan gets 15 minutes free time on CBS News, and then a rebuttal program is organized, consisting of five minutes for the Democrats, five minutes for the Republicans, and five minutes for Edward Meese? The more I live in France the more I am persuaded that the monarchical tradition dominates French political and social attitudes. After the Franco-Prussian war, when Napoleon III had been ousted, a majority of the French Parliament was in favor of restoring the monarchy. It was only because they could not agree on which pretender to make King that the Third Republic was created. In more recent times, it has been reported that de Gaulle was seriously considering the possibility of inviting the present pretender, the Comte de Paris, to succeed him. As for President Giscard d'Estaing, his monarchical propensities became more obvious with every day that passed. It is well known that when he dined at the Elysée Palace, the chair opposite him was kept vacant, as in Louis XIV's day. Even President Mitterrand has developed a pronounced taste for pomp and circumstance. The1981 economic summit was staged at the Versailles Palace and a key ceremony consisted of Mitterrand standing at one end of a long red carpet and receiving the visiting heads of state who approached him from the other end.

If God were to test current French preferences by sending both Jesus and Louis XIV to Paris and having each of them walk down Boulevard Saint-Michel on opposite sides of the street, I am convinced that 90% of the Left Bank residents would flock to Louis XIV. Coming back to Mitterrand, whom some people are already calling *François dernier*" in counter-distinction to the great king François I, he is desperately looking for a gimmick to regain a few points of popularity. With great difficulty he is making good on his 1983 promise to reduce the tax burden by one percentage point. But to make up for the lost revenues, the government rather clumsily raised telephone charges for all calls by some 15%. Gasoline taxes were also increased. When the State has its hand in everything, it is able at times to collect revenues in forms which are not called taxes, but people are not as easy to fool nowadays.

The National Assembly, debating the 1985 Budget, pulled a couple of cheap shots to show the common man that the Socialists were still out to "soak the rich." The first was to increase the top rate of the wealth tax to two percent for the portion of net worth exceeding F. 20-million. The second, much more controversial, was to eliminate the 25% lump-sum tax on interest paid on the famous "Giscard loan." In 1973, when Giscard was Minister of Finance, he floated a loan, the principal of which was indexed to the value of gold and could not be called until 1986. Thus the State will lose a fortune when it has to be repaid. Moreover, the interest was taxed at only 25%, a real boon to persons in high tax brackets. It is the latter feature which the Socialists are eliminating in the face of charges that they are violating "the word of the State." A regime which raises taxes retroactively, as it did in 1981, is not overly disturbed at overturning the disadvantageous features of a loan floated by its predecessor.

The three principal leaders of the opposition, Giscard, Chirac and Barre, issued a joint declaration condemning the tax measure. Giscard has managed to return to the limelight in a carefully orchestrated comeback. In September, he stood for election as *Député* in his home district in the Auvergne and won handily, on the first ballot. The press played up his victory but neglected to stress that 50% of the registered voters stayed away from the polls.

Whereas Chirac and Giscard were enemies in 1981, now it appears that the two have made a temporary alliance to block Barre. As the economy weakens, Barre, a former professor of economics, seems to be gathering stature as the future Poincaré or Pinay, who will restore France's well-being. What I haven't fathomed is what kind of deal Chirac and Giscard could possibly make to prevent Barre from becoming President. Giscard acts as though he plans to run again for President in 1988. If all three of them run again, the result could be devastating. But it's too early to begin weeping; there's enough rain as it is. ✓

The Unjust Force of the Law

Vol. VI, Nº 6, December 1984

Kind Thoughts about France

Often I feel guilty after writing an unkind description of the latest Socialist debacle, and I promise myself to write a nice newsletter next time, telling all that is right and good in France. But then, the Socialists provide new entertainment, which I find it impossible to ignore, such as the New Caledonian farce, about which more later. This has been going on for three years.

However, as I write this on Christmas Day, charitable urges overwhelm me, and I am determined to start off, at least, with some upbeat things to say about France.

The first and foremost point to make is that surely the French must have astounding grit and genius to be able to survive three years of Socialist ruination. I am convinced that even if Mitterrand lasts out his full seven-year term (and he seems determined to do so even if it takes a figurative dose of embalming fluid to help him along) the French economy will soar back to acceptable heights. Partly, even largely, this will be due to the Socialists themselves. As there is no money left for Santa Claus hand-outs, which used to keep moribund companies alive, the Socialists are allowing these companies to die, whereas salvagable enterprises (even some that are state-owned) are being permitted to purge themselves of unneeded personnel. Inevitably, considerable modernization of plant will take place during the next four years, in order that French industry become competitive once again.

Accordingly, foreign investment will be a necessity, and therefore most welcome. Indeed, it is in my opinion already a good moment for foreign companies to look for investment opportunities, since this is a buyer's market. There are plenty of plants available which can be bought at a fraction of the cost of building new ones, and a chastened labor force now respects the value of a steady job. In addition, government grants are plentiful, such as those the DATAR gives for creating new jobs, and tax breaks abound. The high parity of the dollar, of course, makes any investment relatively cheap for Americans compared with the days when the dollar was worth barely four francs.

On top of this, or rather at the bottom, France has an extraordinary infrastructure of public services. Although we rightly grumble about high taxes, at least we are getting something for them. Here are some examples:

1) The trains run on time (may those who remember Mussolini forgive me!) and are fast and plentiful. The TGV zips to Lyon in two hours, and soon will serve other cities with its phenomenal top speed of nearly 200 miles per hour.

2) Postal service is infinitely better than in the United States. In Paris, we receive mail three times a day from Monday through Friday and once on Saturday. And within a seven-minute walk from our office, one can find at least four post offices.

3) Phone service has improved by leaps and bounds in the last five years. Whereas one used to wait three years to get a phone line installed, this now takes only a few days in most cities. The state-owned postal service has issued hundreds of thousands of tiny computer terminals, called Minitel, with which one can get a phone number rather than cope with the dreadful phone book. The Minitel moreover has access to dozens of data banks, ranging from the legal to the scientific. In addition, the ubiquitous PTT now distributes efficient fax machines that are becoming invaluable for rapid transmittal of documents through the phone lines.

4) In Paris garbage is collected every day, even on Sundays and holidays and, what's more, efficiently and noiselessly. A few years ago Parisians were given free plastic garbage containers, which facilitate disposal into the modern trucks that pass at a decent morning hour. If you have ever been awakened by the unbearable drone of New York garbage trucks in the middle of the night, you can appreciate how much superior the French system is.

5) Public gardens such as the Tuileries and the Jardin de Luxembourg are a joy to behold. But even small unfamiliar squares contain clusters of flower beds that devoted, unseen municipal gardeners are constantly restoring with taste and imagination.

Ultimately, France is still the world's greatest bastion of good taste, good eating and good living. When it comes to smartly decorated restaurants and stylish shops of all kinds, the free-enterprise system still flourishes. Thank God that the Socialists have not found a way to nationalize the restaurants or the fashion industries!

And let's face it, the French are an intelligent, innovative race, with a strong culture that even converts migrating Latin neighbours such as Italians and Spanish into creditable Frenchmen in less than a generation. French scientists and engineers still have not said the last word in most fields, and the French excel in software even if their computer hardware is not avant-garde.

Now if you want a clincher, can a country with so many beautiful women be far from the truth?

When you add all this up, why should one be pessimistic about the future of France? Fundamentally, it is only the political sphere and certain concomitants of it, such as the impregnable bureaucracy, and continuing centralism, that hobble the French potential.

It is commonplace to say that a country has the politicians it deserves. Perhaps it would be more apt to state that politicians occupy their rightful place in a given society. After all, Ronald Reagan is a better President than he was an actor. And shouldn't we be thankful that young Fabius is only Prime Minister of France rather than in a job where he could really injure this country's reputation, such as *saucier* at Taillevent or a *styliste* at Christian Dior?

The latest example of political farce is the New-Caledonian mess, wholly a product of Socialist wishy-washy thinking. Hardly anyone in France knows where to find New Caledonia on the map. Such was my case until 1977, when a client asked me to go there, and I hastily located it on the globe. In case you're wondering, New Caledonia is an island lying northeast of Australia in the Pacific Ocean.

The French annexed the island without a fight from the natives in the 19th century, and found it a convenient place to send convicts, just as the British had with Australia. When huge nickel deposits were discovered, the island became a precious possession, and the local economy flourished, particularly since there were no taxes, other than import duties. Then about 10 years ago, nickel prices collapsed, and the island became a less attractive place for the French government to cling to.

Before Mitterrand was elected in 1981, the French Socialists had flirted with the native independence movement. The natives are diversely called *Canaques* or *Kanaks* and the white settlers are called *Caldoches.* The latter even outnumber the natives, when civil servants are counted. To be sure, the *Caldoches* run the show. In November of this year, elections were held to create a territorial assembly. Most of the *Canaques* boycotted the elections and the *Caldoches* elected an assembly largely composed of RPR candidates (linked to Chirac's party). This obviously displeased the Socialists and the minister responsible for territorial affairs made himself immortal by contrasting the "legal country" and "the real country." ("*pays légal*" and "*pays réel*"), as though Frenchmen were not real when they are far from the mainland.

In no time, the independence movement set up its own provisional government and declared the birth of "Kanaky." A handful of *gendarmes* could have squelched this "government" but instead of doing so, they stood guard to protect the Kanaky headquarters in Noumea, capital of New Caledonia. The opposition, led by Chirac and Giscard, has protested vociferously against this strange way of defending French sovereignty. To make matters worse, President Mitterrand appeared on television and defended his government's flabbiness towards the independence movement by uttering another immortal phrase: "the unjust force of the law" ("*la force injuste de la loi*").

As an amateur philosopher, I would be the first to concede that a law can be unjust, but no one has elected me President of the Republic. Coming from someone who has sworn to uphold the Constitution, a reference to the injustice of applying the law of the land seems very quixotic.

Faced with a storm of protest, Mitterrand took the easy way out. He named a sort of high commissioner to run the show in New Caledonia and come back with a solution. This is none other than a former Gaullist Minister, Edgard Pisani, who turned his back on de Gaulle when the latter was on the ropes in May '68. Unfortunately for Pisani, de Gaulle returned triumphantly and Pisani suffered a long eclipse. Doubtless he is getting ready for another period in the back room.

It is clear that the Socialists would like to grant independence to the Kanaks. But it is probable that a majority of the local population wants to remain French, whence the idea of somehow diluting or ignoring the white vote. One of the suggestions advanced by the Socialists is to have the Kanaks vote separately. Another is to allow only those whose parents or grandparents were born on the island to vote. To some opposition leaders, the French Socialists seem to be approaching the concept of apartheid from the left side of paradise.

Legal experts keep pointing out that such wild ideas would run afoul of the Constitution. The Socialists have already inured us to the notion that one can ignore facts that conflict with ideology. Now they are adding a new twist: When a law conflicts with ideology, ignore the law.

And with this, let me wish France and all of you a Happy New Year.

A family of “black feet”

Vol. VIII, N° 1, February 1986

A Quarter Century

This is a big year not only for France – which will elect a new Parliament – but also for me, as April will mark the completion of 25 years of practice in France. I started here on April 11, 1961, having landed with my family a week earlier at Cherbourg on the now defunct liner, the "United States."

During the last few years, as the 25th milestone approached, I tended to think that it would be an exciting event in itself – bells would ring and memories spill forth. But now that 1986 is here, I am finding out that it is just another year, so far as my daily life is concerned.

Nevertheless, I do feel a duty to make something of this anniversary, and so I have done some reminiscing. The year of my departure from New York was an eventful year. John Kennedy had been inaugurated President in January. Shortly after I arrived in Paris in April, Gagarin made his historic tour in space, and during the same month, I had a terrible fright when I learned that the French generals had taken power in Algeria, and were threatening to send paratroops to Orly Airport, only a few minutes away from the house into which we had just moved at Villeneuve-Le-Roi.

General de Gaulle's firm stance soon crushed the revolt, and I breathed easier. But then the OAS (Secret Army) led by the fugitive general Raoul Salan brought terrorism to Paris. Bombings and grenade attacks were commonplace, and police carrying machine-guns became part of the landscape.

It was also in April 1961 that I met William Saroyan the great Armenian-American writer who was then living in France, and who became my client and friend. Just having known him would be reward enough for the years spent in Paris.

The '60s were marked and marred by the Vietnam war, beginning with self-deluding subtlety under Kennedy – and then mad escalation under that most devious President, Lyndon Johnson. While the French had experienced their own Vietnam war – called *la Guerre d'Indochine* – public opinion quickly turned against the United States. Although it is not usually cited as a cause of the "events of May 68," I am convinced that the general disillusionment of French youth with the United States contributed to the state of mind which led the students to revolt.

From the purely French viewpoint the "events of May 1968" were the most striking days of the past 25 years. I had never experienced anything like it: a whole country paralyzed by strikes, with no apparent cause. It all seemed so silly: a great country going on holiday at the wrong time.

I was privileged to participate in the greatest mass demonstration that Paris has known – the famous march from the Concorde to the Etoile on May 30, 1968, after General de Gaulle's stirring radio address. This was a spontaneous reaction of the "silent majority" – the party of order. The next day, when gasoline suddenly became available, I witnessed the biggest traffic jam in French history!

General de Gaulle's party won a huge majority in the legislative election that ensued in June, but a year later, de Gaulle tried to push through a fuzzy constitutional reform, which failed to capture the popular fancy. The referendum was defeated, and de Gaulle resigned without fanfare.

His successor, Georges Pompidou, died in the fifth year of his seven-year term. Probably his greatest contribution was to prove that de Gaulle's Constitution, tailor-made for him in 1958, could survive that great leader.

Pompidou's death led to a new presidential election, from which Valéry Giscard d'Estaing emerged victor in the second round, defeating François Mitterrand by a narrow margin. At first, Giscard tried to be a "different" president. He invited himself to ordinary people's homes for dinner and once he even called in the passing garbage collectors for breakfast! This sort of "slumming" behavior soon earned him ridicule, and Giscard then settled into a monarchical incumbency, surrounded by technocrats like himself. Giscard soon lost touch with reality. His first Prime Minister, Jacques Chirac, who had earned this post by sabotaging the candidacy of the Gaullist leader Chaban-Delmas, found that he could not cope with Giscard's brain-trust, and resigned after two frustrating years. He was succeeded as Prime Minister by a relatively unknown cabinet minister, Raymond Barre, whom Giscard graced with the title of "best economist in France."

Giscard's reign, which began in April 1974, followed closely the 1973 oil crisis that heightened France's financial problems and chronic inflation. The second oil crisis of 1978 made matters worse. As unemployment increased, Giscard's policies, restricting layoffs, and granting extraordinarily high unemployment benefits, worsened the plight of business entreprises by raising taxes and social charges to the highest level in French history.

Of course the more recent past, beginning with Mitterrand's election in May 1981, hardly needs recounting.

Having sketched a tableau of the past 25 years of French political history, I believe it worthwhile to cite what I consider to be the most salient "French facts" of the past quarter century. In many respects these are "non events" but they are nevertheless facts which have made the most impact on me.

1) The saving of Paris

There seems to be little public awareness, even among Parisians, of how close Paris came to being marred forever by the builders. The ugly Maine-Montparnasse skyscraper stands as stark testimony to the Paris that might have been. Few people know that the same promoter had obtained a building permit to place another skyscraper in the heart of Paris, where Les Halles used to be, and yet another permit had been issued for a high-rise building on Quai Kennedy, next to the Radio-TV building.

Ironically, during the 1981 presidential campaign, the man who saved Paris, President Giscard d'Estaing, did not claim any credit for what was his most valuable achievement.

His predecessor, Georges Pompidou, while an esthete and traditionalist, possessed nevertheless a modernist streak. He had resigned himself to what he thought was the inevitable, that is, skyscrapers. And just like Robert Moses in New York, Pompidou thought that cities must adjust to automobiles. Thus, he had authorized construction of the expressway on the left bank of the Seine.

Pompidou's otherwise untimely death saved Paris. Even though he had no official say on the question, Giscard saw to it that the building permits mentioned above were revoked, and the expressway plan scrapped. In addition, Parisian height limitations were tightened to make it impossible to plan such tall structures as Maine-Montparnasse in the future.

All those who love the architecture and skyline of Paris owe a debt of gratitude to Mr. Giscard d'Estaing. He would have been a great Mayor of Paris.

2) The return of the "Black Feet"

The single outstanding sociological fact of the past quarter century is one about which no one talks – the influx of a million French people from Algeria. It is hard to imagine what France would be like without the contribution of these dynamic, energetic and innovative men and women.

It will be recalled that de Gaulle was brought back to power in 1958 largely through the efforts of the French ruling class in Algeria. Yet in 1960 de Gaulle had the courage to turn against them and move toward the independance of Algeria. Not only did this almost cost him his life but, also, in 1962, he had to face the unparalleled problems of settling a million people in the mainland, when the *pieds noirs* (literally, "black feet") scampered pell-mell out of Algeria, leaving behind their homes, their belongings, their businesses, and, saddest of all, the graves of their ancestors.

The French had been in Algeria since 1830. They had planted crops and vineyards, built factories, and created modern cities and resorts. Overnight, these people were uprooted and inserted into a society completely unprepared to receive them.

Beginning in 1962, one felt the presence of the *pieds noirs* everywhere. Here a new doctor, there a dry-cleaner, everywhere new businessmen and professionals showed up, giving a tremendous boost to the French economy. In southern France, and even in Corsica, new vineyards cropped up in hitherto unplanted or abandoned fields. This often created resentment among the more lethargic natives.

In a generation, the *pieds noirs* have achieved eminence in every walk of life. It is one of the ironies of history that much of the economic success of the Fifth Republic is owed to its principal victims. I know many of them and, almost to a man, they have turned their backs on the past and have resolutely determined to live only in the present.

I have often wondered why it is that a people from a hot climate like Algeria should have turned out to be so dynamic and hard working. The only explanation I can muster is that the status of immigrant makes all the difference.

And while we're on the subject of immigrants, we should salute the five million aliens, mainly from Portugal, Spain, Italy and North Africa, without whom the French economy would stop dead in its tracks.

3) The Republic of Functionaries

The least commented aspect of de Gaulle's heritage, and in my mind the most nefarious, has been the conversion of France into a country dominated by functionaries. That there are five million of them is bad enough, but that they should wield such political power is the crowning blow.

De Gaulle had such contempt for the political class which dominated the Fourth Republic – the parliamentary "*notables*" – that he fostered the growth of the civil service, led by the prestigious graduates of the Ecole Nationale d'Administration (ENA).

In 1963 when de Gaulle named Valéry Giscard d'Estaing Minister of Finance, this made the headlines, for it was the first time that a professional technocrat held such a powerful post. Some 15 years later, when Giscard gave the same post to a businessman, René Monory, this again became news, for in the meantime the French people had become habituated to a succession of civil servants in cabinet posts.

The Constitution which de Gaulle imposed for the Fifth Republic contains a fatal lacuna: nothing prohibits a public servant from holding political office. All the functionary has to do is to take a leave of absence while he holds an elective position. As a result, more and more *ENArques* (as they are called) and other civil servants have become politicians, while clinging to the civil service status, which gives them security and generous retirement benefits. Giscard, for example, retired as Inspecteur Général des Finances after leaving the Presidency. Another flaw of the Constitution is that politicians can accumulate elective and governmental posts. Thus for example, Chirac is Mayor of Paris and Député in the Corrèze. Giscard was a Mayor of his home town while a Minister.

It suffices to cite the names of prominent politicians to realize what a hold this class has over the French political system: Giscard, Chirac, Barre, Simone Veil, Rocard, Chevènement, Léotard, Jospin. These are all public servants who have never worked a day of their lives in private enterprise. Yet they rule the French economy.

I have often said that French has a single party – *le Parti des Fonctionnaires* – with its left wing and its right wing. No matter which wing wins a particular election, one can be sure that the country will be ruled by a caste having the same background, habits and ideology.

The single greatest intellectual error of the French is their failure to see that the shibboleth of "Right and Left" is outmoded. Its maintenance obscures the basic truths that a self-perpetuating caste has taken power, and that the real clash of the future will be between the State and the individual.

Giscard, Chirac and Barre talk of *l'Etat* with the same tremor in their voice that we hear from Ronald Reagan when he speaks of motherhood and freedom. *L'Etat* in France has become so vast and powerful that it owns the leading advertising and travel agency, the largest automobile company, the main oil companies, the coal mines, the principal chemical enterprise, the leading electronics companies, the whole tobacco industry, the principal airline, all the railroads, the major insurance companies, virtually all the banks, the main television channels and, of course, all the universities. To begin to grasp the significance, an American would have to imagine that the federal government owned General Motors, IBM, du Pont de Nemours, Citibank, Young and Rubican, R.J. Reynolds, American Airlines, Prudential Insurance Corp. and Harvard University.

The same blindness of most French intellectuals prevents them from seeing that the great ethical principle which condemns conflicts of interest should apply most of all to the State. How can a government which manufactures cigarettes and automobiles adequately protect the public against cancer and pollution?

De Gaulle's Constitution gives the President such complete power that, like Louis XIV, a modern President can say *"L'Etat c'est moi."* Will the French people wake up in time and find a political leader who will have the courage to dismantle *l'Etat*? Frankly I doubt it.

Vol. VIII, N° 3, June 1986

John Geoffrey Laughton

1933-1986

"Do not go gentle into that good night
Rage, rage against the dying of the light."

These words of Dylan Thomas sum up our sentiments on the sudden and quiet extinction of our beloved colleague's life on June 6, 1986.

John was the gentlest soul I have ever known. He was incapable of rage; alas, not even that rage which we would have wished him to summon up to prevent his passage into the night.

If a popularity poll had been taken in our office, John Laughton would easily have won. He was particularly loved by our junior lawyers, who found him a fountain of knowledge. If you did not know how to start off with a new matter, John was always helpful.

The words "generous to a fault" took on real meaning when applied to John. He was so unsparing of his time and money that one would often feel that he was neglecting his own interests.

John had a special place in my affection, not only for his personal qualities, but also because of his long professional association with me. I met John on the very first day that I showed up for work in Paris at Coudert Frères in Paris on April 11, 1961. He had become an associate there several months earlier, and among his assignments was taking care of residence and work permits. So within a half-hour of my reporting to the senior partner, John was called in to take me to the Préfecture de Police in the Ile de la Cité. John ushered me through the formalities with the quiet efficiency which was to become his hallmark.

That same month, John earned a permanent place in my affection. In the February issue, I briefly alluded to the panic I felt when I learned that the French generals had taken power in Algeria and were planning to send paratroops to Orly Airport. I pictured them descending into the garden of the house we had just moved into only a few hundred yards from the airport! When I arrived at the office that day, I communicated my fears to John. He laughed and said: "Don't worry; that'll blow over in a few days." These words gave me instant reassurance, and when John turned out to be right, I felt tremendous respect for his judgment. Here was a 27-year-old reading a major event "on all fours," whereas the leading French newspapers of the day were predicting a prolonged confrontation between the generals in Algeria and de Gaulle's government.

In the ensuing months, I gradually learned more about John. Despite his reluctance to talk about himself, we often had occasion to travel together in the commuting train, for John then lived with his parents at Ablon-sur-Seine, the town next to mine, Villeneuve-le-Roi.

John was half English and half French. His father, an English chartered accountant, had married a gracious French lady, and decided to remain in France. John was born in France but had been sent off to English public schools. He was graduated from the University of London, with honors, after which he studied law in France, and successfully made the transition from the English to the French educational system. He obtained his Doctorate of Laws from the Sorbonne, again achieving high honors. Then John did a stint in the French Army. I was both amused and amazed when I learned the circumstances. Having an English passport only, John had assumed that he was not a French citizen despite having a French mother and being born in France. One day he went to the local gendarmerie for a residence document. After studying his basic data, a gendarme said: "Young man, you are French and the French Army is expecting you." Within days, John, the gentle Englishman, found himself a French soldier! He quickly became an officer in the tank corps, and then actually engaged in combat in Algeria where a bloody civil war was in course.

I had trouble picturing John Laughton as a French officer shooting at the *fellaghas* in the hills of Algeria. Despite my prodding, I could never get John to talk about his combat experience. It was obvious that he regarded this bellicose interlude as a mere accident. He was, above all, an Englishman doing his duty, even if it meant serving in the French Army!

Only after his death did I learn from his father that John had been twice decorated for bravery while in the French Army. Physically, he was as unlikely to be taken for a hero as for a film idol. He was of middle height and husky when I first met him, but his spectacles and pink cheeks gave him an air of innocence. At the end he was Falstaffian in girth, but not in mirth. Nevertheless even during the worst days, John could always muster a shy smile for his friends.

Professionally, I quickly came to admire John's work and eagerly sought his assistance whenever he was available. At Coudert he had been assigned to assist Lazar Focsaneanu, the erudite specialist in EEC competition rules. John had done his doctorate in private international law with the great professor Battifol and throughout his career maintained his interest in what Anglo-Saxon lawyers call "conflicts of law." If there was any problem with John, it was that he couldn't say "No" to any lawyer or client seeking assistance. I sometime kidded him about his using the LIFO method – last-in-first-out – with work assignments.

John's complete fluency in English and French made him an invaluable asset. He was the only lawyer I knew who could simultaneously draft French-English contracts in parallel columns. When he took on a drafting assignment, even with the most complicated subject, he could come up with a credible draft within hours, when other lawyers would require days.

John was also our office expert in price and premium legislation, and trade regulation in general. I take sardonic comfort in the fact that the Chirac government plans to abolish price controls and undertake a policy of deregulation. John was ever a source of surprises. One day I needed to have a German document translated and discovered that John was fluent in German. On another occasion, I learned that he also had a good knowledge of Italian. On yet another occasion, I discovered that he had a pilot's license. As John never boasted, or talked about himself, one learned these things only in a desultory fashion. I was amazed that at age 27 John had already achieved so much.

But the biggest surprise came the day in 1964 when John announced his engagement to Jacqueline Joly. She had been my shy secretary at Coudert and I never suspected that John even looked at her, let alone dated her. It was typical of John that he could carry on an intra-office courtship with the utmost discretion. I was, of course, delighted that John had found a spouse. Jacqueline was an attractive and bright young woman who soon overcame her girlish shyness, and became the activist spouse that John needed. Two daughters were born, Magali and Muriel. After a few years, Jacqueline decided to resume work, and found her niche at the Stanley Home Products French subsidiary, where she became a top sales representative and ultimately a regional manager.

But then tragedy struck. Jacqueline fell victim to breast cancer. For years, she conducted a valiant struggle against this dreadful disease, while carrying out her family and professional obligations. Those years were almost as trying for John as for Jacqueline, yet he rarely shared his distress with friends, as he simply could not bring himself to show emotion. When Jacqueline finally succumbed to the inexorable, a good part of the light had left John's life. By now, his daughters were adolescents, and John bravely tried to cope with raising them during their difficult years, when they needed a mother more than a father.

As John never complained about his fate, one could only guess at his state of mind, from seeing the progressive deterioration of his body. John kept putting on weight, giving his friends concern for his health. Stoic and taciturn, John did not readily heed advice from his friends and family.

Three weeks ago, he called in to say that he was not feeling well and was entering a hospital for examinations. On June 5th, he underwent an exploratory operation from which he never awoke.

I am glad that on April 11th of this year, I had invited him to lunch without telling him that it was to celebrate the 25th anniversary of our friendship. He seemed surprised that I would remember such a specific date, but the reader now knows why I did remember.

I am glad also that several weeks ago, I finally got John to display a bit of anger. In 25 years I had never heard him raise his voice or say an unkind word about a fellow man. I kept telling him that there were occasions when one should get angry. I finally provided him with such an occasion by goading him about a matter he was handling. To my amazement, he got aroused and shouted back at me. I was so delighted at this unique display that I embraced him and told him he should do it more often.

John had once confided to me that if he retired some day he would like nothing better than to operate a modest café in a village, somewhere in France, where he could chat with his neighbours and live a tranquil life. I would like to believe that God, by removing John from among the living, not only reunited him with his beloved Jacqueline but also handed him an assignment tending bar in heaven's best bistro.

Volume X, Nº 5, December 1988

What Every Armenian Knows

The devastating earthquake which struck Armenia at 11:38 on December 7th has been front-page news in the French newspapers. French rescue teams, with their trained dogs, were among the first to fly to Erevan, along with physicians enlisted by that remarkable humanitarian organization Médecins Sans Frontières. One of the surgeons who went – Yves Ternon – was already a hero to Armenians, because he has become the outstanding French historian of the Armenian genocide of 1915.

I spoke with Dr. Ternon on Saturday, December 17th, the day after his return from an exhausting five days in Soviet Armenia. His wife and son told me that they had never seen him so shocked. Despite his fatigue, Ternon was eager to get the message out and spoke on television before he slept.

These are the central facts that he recounts. The number of dead is far more than the official figures, which have varied from 30,000 to 55,000. Ternon says that the real figure is at least 150,000 and could reach 180,000. In Leninakan, where he spent two days, he estimates the dead at 80,000. The city had some 250,000 inhabitants, but there were present also thousands of refugees from the Karabagh region located in Azerbaijan. In Spitak, there were at least 20,000 dead; the city was entirely razed by the quake. Tens of thousands more died in other cities and villages. These figures take on meaning only when stated in relative terms. With but three million people, Armenia's loss of 150,000 children, men and women represents five percent of the population. Translate this to France, or Italy, or Germany, or the United Kingdom, and you have some three-million dead. Translate it to the United States and you have thirteen-million dead. Can Americans imagine losing thirteen-million persons in a single catastrophe?

Alas, or fortunately, in our century only the Jews and the Armenians can grasp figures like that. Just as the modern Jewish soul is reeling from the Holocaust, the Armenian soul of the 20th century has been trying to recover from the genocide of 1915, when the Turkish Army killed a host of Armenians whom they did not bother to count, but which historians, and the Armenians themselves, estimate at between one million and one-and-a-half million people, more than half the population of Turkish Armenia.

Among the victims of the 1915 genocide were my father's whole family who, with 10,000 other Armenians, lived in a town called Chunkoush. They were all massacred in April 1915, including my father's sister and two brothers, Aram and Hagop, whose names were given to me (Hagop becoming Jack in school!). My father had managed to get out in 1912, when he was 16, and came to America. In 1919, he founded an Armenian-language weekly newspaper in Philadelphia. This became his life work for 43 years.

My father was a cheerful person, always telling humorous stories with a point. But one day, while helping out in my father's printing shop, I witnessed a scene which made me understand what he left unsaid. Another refugee from Chunkoush dropped in on him. Unobtrusively I listened to their conversation. They reminisced happily about their childhood in Chunkoush. Then suddenly the visitor stopped talking. After a silence which seemed eternal, I heard him groan, "*Akh, mairig*" ("Ay, little mother.") My father was sitting at the keyboard of his Linotype, his right profile in my sight. I could sense that he was straining to keep his composure. He dared not even budge an eyelid. Staring straight ahead, while fighting the tears, he finally managed to utter one word "*Ayo*" ("yes").

Later, when I reached adolescence and became "sensitive" to all the suffering that existed in the world, I could not understand how my father could laugh so often, particularly since our life during the Great Depression was no bowl of cherries. Even in the worst times I could hear my father singing over the roar of his printing press. To be sure, they were the sad songs of Armenia, but still, I would say to myself, "How can he sing today?" It was only years later when I discovered Yeats' poem, *Lapis Lazuli*, that I found the answer:

"All things fall and are built again,

And those that build them again are gay."

A few weeks ago, I bought a rug from a Turkish merchant in Paris. When I told the charming young vendor that my father was from Chunkoush, he replied, *"Oh, Chunkoush has never been the same since the Armenians left."* I was amazed to find myself smiling at this remark, and feeling sympathy for this Turkish lad who sincerely believes that the Armenians "left" Chunkoush. I wondered why I had not become angry, and why I felt more sorry for the young Turk than for myself.

In Leninakan, Armenian survivors told Yves Ternon that they felt "abandoned by God." Their peaceful struggle to be united with their compatriots in Karabagh had already become front-page news. Now they fear that Gorbachev will use the earthquake as a pretext to disperse the Armenians. Above all they want to stay in their towns and villages. To do this they need shelter and heat during the bitter-cold Armenian winter.

So, what is it that every Armenian knows? Even if abandoned by God, he must believe in life, endure suffering with dignity, rebuild, love and laugh. And when he is deprived of liberty, his yearning for it is the next best thing.

If you are saying to yourself, "It is not only the Armenians who know this," I willingly add, "That, too, is what every Armenian knows."

Vol. XI, N° 3, August 1989

Two Men in May

According to T.S. Eliot, "April is the cruellest month," but in 1989, I would say that May surpassed it in cruelty, for in rapid succession I lost two old friends, Larry Fleisher and Franc Ricciardi. Larry died suddenly after playing squash in New York. He was only 58. Franc died of a heart attack at the age of 65. Both were dynamic men, who had made the best of their lives, but still had a lot of life in them. Months have passed but I have still not got used to the idea that they are gone.

Official obituary notices never catch the flavor of the departed. While I cannot claim to be able to "tell the whole story," I would like to set down here some recollections of these friends.

Larry Fleisher

Senator Bill Bradley eulogized Larry as having been *"one of the most effective labor leaders of the last three decades."* With all due respect to the Senator, I can no more think of Larry as a labor leader than I can think of Bill Bradley as a laborer. Larry's love of basketball drove him towards professional involvement with that game. He ended up representing star players, and founding the NBA Players Association. Larry obtained tremendous benefits for the players; his last Collective Bargaining contract, signed in October 1988, will stand as a monument to his memory. Nevertheless, Larry was basically a lawyer and a business-man.

When a person achieves prominence in a given field, it is easy to take for granted all the stepping stones and obstacles that he had to overcome to reach the top. I doubt that the famous basketball players who looked up to him (professionally, for they surely looked down, otherwise) had any inkling of the difficulties Larry had encountered.

When I entered Harvard Law School in September 1950, I discovered that my class had two distinctions: it was the first to comprise women (only twelve!) and the first to occupy the new Harkness Commons and dormitories designed by Walter Gropius, one of the old Bauhaus architects. In those Puritan days, these facts were unrelated, since only men were allowed to live in the dorms.

I was lucky to be assigned a room on the ground floor of Dane Hall. Across the hall from me were two New Yorkers, Larry Fleisher and Herb Semmel, who were friends and had been classmates at NYU. My first recollection of them is of a loud argument, which provoked me to cross the hall and enter the room, the door being open. Larry was yelling at Herb, *"Dolph Schayes is only this much better than..."* (name of another player which I have forgotten), and his right hand indicated a tiny space between his thumb and index finger. Coming from Philadelphia, not a basketball town, I was amazed to see how seriously New Yorkers took basketball, even purporting to measure minute differences.

Larry and Herb would argue for hours about the comparative merits of basketball players. This amused me, and even served to relax my tensions. The first year at Harvard Law School is a traumatic experience for most students, but this first year provided an extra source of anxiety: during the summer of 1950 the Korean War had begun, and our generation, which had been in high school when World War II ended, and had seen the United States dismantle history's most powerful armed force, suddenly found itself facing the draft.

I used to spend hours in Larry's room, which overlooked Everett Street; we even played an improvised basketball, with a ping-pong ball, using the small lampshade which Gropius had designed, as the basket. And we used to watch the pretty Lesley College girls pass by.

Of course we talked about things other than basketball. Larry was a liberal in politics, as I was, too, then. When I started this Newsletter eleven years ago he would occasionally chide me for having turned "reactionary." (Larry had remained a Democrat of the New Deal type.) I used to rejoinder that if he were living in France and paying as much taxes as I, he, too, would become a conservative.

The results of the first-year exams were a shattering experience for Larry. Whereas his room-mate Herb Semmel ended up near the top of his class, and "made" Law Review, Larry, who had seemed equally gifted to me, had a ranking nearer the bottom of our class of some 500 students. In those days, we were given numerical rankings, not just grades, so that you knew precisely where you stood in the class.

It was a very painful experience for some, to return to Harvard after the summer break, and compare their ranking with all the "buddies" of the first year. Harvard Law School was full of students who had been outstanding scholars in high school and college, many of whom would for the first time experience the humiliation of comparative failure. Some are marked for life by such failure.

I lost touch with Larry for a few years after law school, but when I returned to New York in 1958 after serving in the US Army in France, I would see Larry often. He had married Vasso, a lovely Greek-American girl from Boston, whom he had met while at Harvard, and they already had two sons. I rejoined my old Wall Street firm, but Larry was working for an accounting firm, as he had not been able to get a job with a good law firm. It must be said that, in those days, it was not easy for Jews to find employment with the major "white shoe" firms, which at best practiced tokenism. For that matter, even Catholics found it difficult to get admitted to the WASP firms. So-called "Jewish firms" thus had their pick of the "best" Jewish graduates, and Larry's record at Harvard was not enough to place him in that category.

In those days, it was not infrequent for Jews to change their name to help overcome the handicap created by the prejudices of employers and clients. During law school, I recall Larry kidding around with us about the possibility of a name change. "Fletcher" is the one he fictitiously adopted; in fact, for a time, it was his nickname.

If I mention these facts, painful as they might be to those who would like to forget that the Establishment did not welcome Jews, Catholics, and other minorities with open arms, even in the '50s, it is because Larry's achievements must be measured against the handicaps he faced. Also, I have come to realize that, for the courageous person, it is often an advantage not to have academic success, which leads to a conventional career, whereas setbacks may create opportunities that propel one further. This turned out to be Larry's case. Working in an accounting firm, he came into contact with the Wechsler Coffee Company, a family-owned firm. His agreeable personality, combined with his accounting background, and common-sense approach to business, led him to gain the confidence of the family. The long and short of it was that Larry became a business-man, ending up as Executive Vice President of Restaurant Associates, Inc., which at one time owned some of the most successful restaurants in New York, including The Four Seasons and Mama Leone's.

Not long after I moved to France in 1961, with my French wife, to take up the career of international law, Larry's path crossed mine professionally. The principals of the coffee company had started an investment company, which was involved with vending-machine companies. Larry wrote to me expressing interest in making an investment in France in this industry. Luck had it that the firm I was with had a vending-machine client. In the ensuing months, Larry's company made the investment, in the form of convertible debentures, which, I learned, did indeed exist in France.

When the relationship matured, Larry succeeded in organizing a consortium which purchased the European business of Automatic Canteen Company, providing me with some challenging legal work. In December 1966, when I started my own firm, Larry and his group were among our first clients. His encouragement, along with that of William Saroyan, the writer, was most precious to me during this difficult time.

Before we started our New York office, in December 1970 (the first, incidentally, to be opened by a Paris-based law firm) I would often use Larry's office as my base during my New York trips. Larry had had the good fortune to find a first-rate male secretary, Curt Parker, who stayed with him to the end. It was Curt who called to inform me of Larry's death.

Despite the fact that he was a lawyer, or perhaps because of it, Larry was a wonderful client: he was supportive, generous in his praise, and never nit-picked our drafts. He was an excellent drafter himself. His letters went straight to the point, avoided verbiage and repetition. As I had little sense of business at that time, I marvelled at Larry's rapid rise as a business executive. Aside from the fact that he knew how to read a balance sheet, I believe that his success was mainly due to his personality. He was likable, direct and candid as a negotiator, and a good listener.

Larry's love of basketball kept prodding him to try to combine business with sports. In 1968, Larry gave me one of my most glamorous assignments. He had started a company to do representation of athletes, hiring Marty Glickman, a former New York sports broadcaster, as the manager. Larry phoned me one day and asked me to go to Sun Valley with Glickman to negotiate with Jean-Claude Killy, who was going there with the French ski team. For the Philadelphia boy, who had been dazzled by Sonja Henie in "Sun Valley Serenade" and had never been farther west than Chester, Pa., it was incredibly exciting to fly from Paris to New York, then to Salt Lake City, then board a small plane to Sun Valley, see the famous hotels and slopes, and meet the celebrated French stars, including the Goitchel sisters who, with Killy, were gobbling up gold medals.

It turned out, incidentally, that Killy had already committed himself to Mark McCormack, the innovating sports representative who got his start promoting Arnold Palmer. Ironically, some 20 years later, Larry joined McCormack's organization, the International Management Group. When I last saw Larry in New York in March of this year, he expressed enthusiasm about his new venture. A month earlier he had visited me in Paris, on his way to the USSR, to recruit some top players there.

Larry's own break-through in sports representation had been obtaining a lucrative professional contract for Bill Bradley after his graduation from Princeton, where he was an All-American. I remember spending a weekend in Larry's house in Chappaqua during the '60s, and meeting Bradley. Larry told me then: "This guy is incredible: he's a Rhodes Scholar; he's going to be an outstanding professional basketball player, and then he'll go into politics; he's serious, intelligent and ambitious. He'll be President some day."

Later, the main beneficiaries of Larry's efforts became black athletes, who now dominate the NBA. Is it any accident that Larry Fleisher, the outsider, played such a key role in improving the lot of so many black players?

One little anecdote: About a year ago, I met a hard-nosed New York lawyer who told me that he had once been Larry's law partner. When I asked him why they had separated, he replied, *"I loved Larry, but all of sudden, in the middle of the afternoon, he would get up and say, 'Let's go to the movies.'"*

The story warmed my heart. I recognized the same Larry I had known in Dane Hall. Today the lawyer has 90 partners who never go to the movies during working hours. Perhaps he now realizes that he was lucky to have once had a partner who knew what was important in life.

Franc Ricciardi

Franc was a more recent friend: our first meeting goes back only to November 1973, in circumstances that Franc loved to recall. About a year earlier, I had received a telephone call from an unknown man, who said he had been given my name by his New York lawyer, Nat Gates. I proposed giving him an appointment, but he said he was too busy, and then proceeded to pick my brain on a French-law question, going into more detail that I am wont to on the phone. His voice sounded gruff, and he was all business, not wasting any time on small talk.

This happened a couple more times in the ensuing months, and each time I became more irritated. Finally, one Saturday morning, Ricciardi called again, and before he could get his questions started, I said:

"Look here, Mr. Ricciardi, this is the fourth time you've called me and I've never seen your face. I don't like having clients whom I've never met. Tonight we're having a housewarming for our new home; you must come over, so we can meet." There was a pause, then a laugh, and he said, *"O.K. I'll be there; give me the address."*

That evening, I had all but forgotten the invitation, and was busy showing guests the house, when on a staircase a smiling man held his hand out and said, *"I'm Franc Ricciardi."* He was not at all as I had pictured him: big, gruff, and sour. He was small, but solidly built; his face, with its trim mustache, was warm, and his bright brown eyes twinkled as he told me how surprised and delighted he had been to be talked to that way in our morning conversation. Franc was accompanied by Stan Leifer, a long-time associate. We all had a great time that evening, and when it was over, Franc and I were friends.

Franc loved telling the story of the Saturday morning phone call that led to our meeting, and he would add, *"Of course, a few days after that I got a bill from Kevorkian for all those telephone conferences!"*

We had lunch the following week, the first of many great meals we had together, for I was to learn that Franc Ricciardi was a *bon vivant*, and what we call in French *un fin gourmet*. He would always stay in the Plaza Athenée in Paris, and eat in the best restaurants. Taillevent was one of his favorites. I introduced him to Lasserre, which then had three stars in the Michelin, and got him into the Club de la Casserole.

On one of his visits to Paris, I met his lovely wife, Rose Marie, who was also of Italian origin, and whose blond beauty reminded me of a Botticelli portrait. I had taken them to lunch at the Vivarois, on avenue Victor Hugo, whose chef had made a meteoric rise in the Michelin. I got to learn that Franc was an opinionated man. As Franc did not believe me when I told him that Vivarois had three stars in the Michelin, we bet a box of Monte Cristo No. 1 (then my favorite Havana cigar). After lunch we walked to the nearest *librairie* and bought the red Michelin guide-book. Sure enough Vivarois had three stars; Franc insisted on paying off his bet right away. We hunted for a *tabac*, and I walked away with the coveted yellow box in my arms.

Franc had founded Richton International only a few years before I met him. Prior to that he had been President of Walter Kidde & Co. which he built into a $500-million company in a few years by making major acquisitions. He had learned the art of acquiring companies with Fred Sullivan at Litton Industries, the first of the major conglomerates. In starting Richton from scratch, Franc wanted to do his own thing. The conception was brilliant: set up a fashion group of companies. He first took over Corocraft, a costume-jewelry compan;, then in rapid succession he acquired Oscar de La Renta, the clothing designer; Valerian Rybar, the decorator; Aspen Sportswear, Hang Ten and other lines. The company was quoted on the American Exchange and seemed to be headed for the big time. However, despite his hands-on management, or perhaps because of it, Franc was to find that fashion people are not the easiest to manage, nor to get to live up to budgets and forecasts. Little by little Richton began to divest its components. In the early '80s Richton even went into Chapter 11, when its bankers became uncooperative. Franc Ricciardi pulled Richton through but, at the end, all that remained of Richton was its original acquisition: Corocraft.

Despite his reverses, Franc Ricciardi remained true to himself; he maintained his dignity, and continued to travel, to go hunting in exotic places, and to live the good life. The Ricciardis had an apartment on East 54th Street, and a house in Ridgewood, New Jersey. On my first visit to their spacious home, in 1975, I could observe that Franc prized his family life. His oldest daughter, April, then had two young children who were Franc's pride and joy. Franc was an excellent cook, and he possessed a fabulous wine-cellar. During that visit I made the discovery of California wines. Having foolishly spoken disparagingly of them, I was challenged to a blind test, pitting two Bordeaux against three California wines. To my credit, I placed first Haut Brion 1964, followed by the three California wines, the best of which was a Freemark Abbey Cabernet Sauvignon, Franc's first choice in the blind tasting.

Several years ago the Ricciardis suffered the most tragic of losses: their second daughter, Johanna, a lovely, vivacious young lady, succumbed to leukemia after a heroic struggle to live. Not long after that, Franc had open-heart surgery and was on the brink of death. Yet he bounced back to an active, full-time regime. I continued to see the Ricciardis often in New York and Paris, and admired Franc and Rose Marie's courage and dignity in the face of adversity.

There was a heroic quality to Franc Ricciardi, exemplified by Browning's words: *"... a man's reach should exceed his grasp, Or what's a heaven for?"*

* * *

So far as I know, Larry Fleisher and Franc Ricciardi never met each other. Probably, if they had met, they would have argued over politics, for Larry remained a liberal Democrat all his life, and Franc was as Republican as you can get. Yet my two friends had so much in common: they had married young, raised a family, and remained married to the same woman until their death. They were devoted to their children. They loved big suburban houses where they could escape the noise and bustle of New York City.

But beyond that, both men were representative of the "melting pot" and the American dream. Larry's grandparents were immigrants to the United States from Russia. Franc's father, a tailor, emigrated from Italy. Yet Franc and Larry became true Americans. They believed in American ideals, their lives demonstrated that the United States is a land of opportunity, a meritocracy, where hard work and initiative make all the difference. And the reason why these qualities make all the difference is that the overwhelming majority of Americans accept the rule of law, and have adopted fairness as the national creed.

Some European still snicker at Americans for their naïveté; they profess not to understand how a "trifle" like Watergate could have led to the undoing of an "outstanding" president like Nixon. Yet it is no accident that such a country produced men like Larry Fleisher and Franc Ricciardi, whose ancestors had their fill of cultures which accept the abuse of power.

Many Europeans also criticize America for its emphasis on money. It is true that in a classless society money tends to become the measure of success. But better that measure than to say that one man is better than another because his ancestor was "ennobled" by Henry IV. What Europeans so often fail to see is what anyone could have observed by spending a Sunday afternoon at the Ricciardi house or the Fleisher house, that American families are the propagator of values as simple and naive as decency and fair-mindedness.

That is why I would not have traded my friendship with Larry Fleisher and Franc Ricciardi for the favor of all the princes and dukes of Christendom.

Tchador and the Law

Vol. XI, N° 4, October 1989

Tchador or Not Tchador

With that pious reverence for the noble century of Louis XIV, when the French language reached, it is claimed, perfection, the powers-that-be in Paris have done their utmost to repel the invasion of foreign terms. Nevertheless, in recent weeks, two new words have been added to the vocabulary of the average Frenchman: *lambada* and *tchador.* The former is a sexy dance, suggestive of Brazil, but in fact invented by two French showbiz types, who managed to record a video clip in great secrecy, which suddenly burst on the French television scene. Sponsored by a soft-drink company, and having a catchy tune, the first *lambada* clip, featuring luscious chocolate buttocks, has proved irresistible to the average viewer, and a gold mine for its authors.

Less entertaining has been the furor over the wearing of the *tchador* (Arabic for scarf) by two Moslem schoolgirls. Not a day goes by without a news item and numerous interviews and "Letters to the Editor" in every daily. Ironically, *tchador* has become such a household word that I would not be surprised to find it immortalized in next year's edition of *Le Petit Larousse*.

What is all the fuss about? Simply that a Tunisian father, a Moslem fundamentalist, has been sending his two daughters to public school in Creil, a dull industrial town north of Paris, with instructions to keep the *tchador* on, no matter what, and the school principal has ordained that the girls can not wear a head-covering in the classroom. This conflict has become a national issue.

One might be tempted, at first blush, to suppose that this issue pits the traditional Right against the traditional Left, as so often happens. But no, what is amusing about the *tchador* problem is that even the Left is divided. Oliver Wendell Holmes, Jr., familiarly known as Justice Holmes (and one of my intellectual heroes) used to say that *"I can grant you any abstract proposition and still decide the case either way."* What he meant was that all interesting controversies arise at the intersection of at least two established principles, and the judge must decide which one takes precedence.

Traditionally, the Left in France prides itself on being anti-racist. Whenever a Moslem is attacked, the Left will mobilize, organize a parade from the Bastille to the Place de la République, headed by the remarkable founder of "S.O.S. Racisme" with the improbable name of Harlem Désir. Yet there have been no parades on the Left, because the abstract principle of anti-racism has collided against another abstract principle, dear to the heart of the socialists, *l'école laïque*, that is, public schools free of religion.

Until the mid-19th century, what public schooling there was in France was controlled by the Catholic Church. When Jules Ferry instituted truly public education, the lay nature of the schooling was the key point. Since then, *l'école laïque* has been one of the rallying cries of the Left, and it is no accident that many public school-teachers are card-carrying members of the Socialist Party.

Thus the dilemma faced by the average Socialist: If a Moslem girl were attacked on a bus because she was wearing a *tchador*, the Left would cry "racist," but if a card-carrying school principal wants to exclude a *tchador*-wearing pupil, he appears to many Socialists as the defender of one of their main articles of faith: *l'école laïque*. No less a stalwart intellectual of the Left than Elisabeth Badinter, wife of the former

Minister of Justice, came out in favor of the principal, saying that if religious symbols were permitted in public schools, what would prevent Jewish pupils from staying away on their Sabbath? (Saturday is a school-day in most parts of France.) That Mrs Badinter is Jewish herself adds punch to the remark.

Even Danièle Mitterrand, wife of the President, could not stay out of the fray, coming out the other way. Her point was that although she is a devotee of *l'école laïque*, she nevertheless sees no harm in allowing the girls to wear the *tchador,* if it is worn out of religious principle. Perhaps the most fatuous statement that I read was that of a Socialist hard-liner who stated, in effect, that the Moslem father was not justified in interfering with his daughters' right to a public education. I had to re-read that remark several times to be sure I had it straight. In other words, the girls have the right to go to public schools, but the father has no right to tell them what to wear, even if his opinion is dictated by religious conviction!

Americans will doubtless think of the parallel in the celebrated case of *Wheeling v. West Virginia,* where the child of a family of Jehovah's Witnesses had been excluded from a public school because he refused to salute the flag, out of religious conviction. In a stirring opinion written by Justice Jackson, the US Supreme Court ruled in favor of the child, reversing an earlier decision where the same Court, led by Felix Frankfurter, held for the school.

The *tchador* case, with its divisive effect on the Left, places the immigration issue in a new light. Hitherto, if conservatives like Jean-Marie Le Pen called attention to the fact that large numbers of Moslem immigrants were resisting traditional French values, they would be branded as "racists." Now, the Left is seeing that that their favorite values can be affected by immigrants who let their religion dictate dress codes in school.

I tend to sympathize with the Moslem father, who has come to France not to learn a new culture, but to earn a living, and who wants his daughters to carry a little of his dignity with them to school. Yet my wife shed yet another light on this affair by raising the specter of feminism. She believes the girls would like nothing better than to look like all the other girls. Why should an old-fashioned father interfere with their liberty?

So it is clear that the *tchador* controversy touches on some of the most intimate and difficult problems of society: family, religion, the state and the individual. When I re-read Plato's Republic some years ago, I discovered what I had failed to note the first time: in the first chapter, Socrates and his friends get into an argument, and someone asks, "what is justice?" To answer that question, Socrates ends up designing an ideal republic. The point I learned is that justice has no meaning unless we decide what the proper relationship is among all those who live in a given society.

Socrates designed his republic for Athenians. The French have to decide whether they can provide justice to those who do not want to become French.

Vol. XII Nº 1, February 1990

From Lenin to Mitterrand

As I write this, the latest news is that Gorbachev is finally going to propose the elimination of the Communist Party's unique role in governing his country. My Russian history is rusty but I seem to recall that in 1917 there were two branches in the Party, the Mensheviks, who were gradualists, and the Bolsheviks... Well, we know what they were.

For decades the Mensheviks were scorned as losers, and their brethren Socialists in the Western European countries were laughed at as ineffectual theorists, who were not realistic enough to know that one achieves power by force, and keeps it in the same way. It has taken 72 years, but if any of the old Mensheviks are around, they must be having their well-deserved last laugh.

The scene shifts to the good old USA, which was blessed with very little of either "iks." I imagine George Bush, feeling heady, because the brightly bedecked Marine Band has just struck up "Hail to the Chief." As soon as he returns to his boudoir, the President pulls back the magic curtain, and like the Queen in *"Snow White and the Seven Dwarfs,"* he asks:

"Mirror, mirror on the wall,
Who is the most powerful of us all?"

And the dutiful mirror replies:

"Georgie, you are pretty powerful,
And even pretty, considering your age,
But when it comes to power,
You are no match for that man
Accross the Atlantic, who sits
In the Elysée Palace."

Furious, the President asks:

"But what must I do to become more powerful?"

And the mirror replies:

"First you might learn some French.
Then you must figure out a way for you
To be able to name the Board of Directors
And the President of all these companies:"

These are the companies enumerated by the mirror:

A T & T and all the Bell companies
I.B.M.
General Electric Co.
Westinghouse Electric Co.
E.I. Dupont de Nemours & Co.

Alcoa Aluminum
US Steel
American Airlines
PanAmerican Airways
United Airlines
Amtrak
Texaco
Exxon
American Broadcasting Co.
Associated Press
General Motors
Reynolds Tobacco
American Tobacco
Chase Manhattan Bank
Citibank
Chemical Bank
Prudential Bache
Metropolitan Life Insurance Co.
Con Edison
Merck, Sharpe & Dohme
Pittsburgh Plate & Glass

According to my fable, George Bush did not hear the end of the list because he fainted half way through.

Yes, the French president has the final say on naming the people who run the French equivalents of all the companies named above, and many more. Can anyone imagine the sheer economic power that President Bush would possess if he could appoint not only the Chief Executive Officer but also the entire board of directors of all these companies? And with it, would there not result a pollution of the political system, considering the enormous patronage that such appointing authority implies, and the power to obtain campaign contributions?

In my book, the French president is the most powerful leader among what I will call "elective democracies." To be sure, the American president names a host of people, including cabinet ministers and Federal judges, but the French president does that also, without having to run the gauntlet of getting his nominees approved by the Senate.

I suspect that Gorbachev looks with envy at the French model. Whereas his own economy is in shambles, the French one seems to be thriving. Just as Dubchek wanted to do in Czechoslovakia, some 21 years ago, Mr Mitterrand has shown that Socialism can have "a human face." There are no political prisoners, the opposition press is not muzzled, rival political parties freely contend for power. Gorbachev must be saying to himself, *"The Mensheviks were right. Why did we have to kill so many people? With a little patience, we could have ruled the roost the way the French Socialists are doing now. Mr Mitterrand has shown us the way."*

One major consequence – perhaps indeed, the most important – of the failure of the Communist regimes will be to put the spotlight on the pernicious, if masked, threat to freedom that is presented by the slogan "Socialism with a human face."

Many years ago, it was reported that de Gaulle referred to his countrymen as "40 million calves." (An American would understand the phrase better if he had said "sheep.") Moreover, de Gaulle was not being statistically charitable; he was taking in the then population. His point was that the French are not as politically individualist as they would like to think they are, and rarely see beyond their noses.

This is certainly true today. Befuddled by television, contrived news, phony issues, insignificant political campaigns, and satiated with glorious eating and five-week vacation, the French public is blissfully unaware that it has conferred greater powers on its elected president than any other democratic nation has ever done.

"What is wrong with this?" you might ask.

Well, I am old-fashioned enough to take seriously the adage: "Power corrupts." That is a sufficient answer. But I would add an objection that has a different foundation: the French state, personified by its president, daily violates a fundamental ethical principle, quite simply because it has a conflict of interest in virtually all it does.

The French, as is so frequent, have a wonderfully pithy way of expressing this principle: *"L'on ne peut pas être juge et partie."* (My translation; "One can not be [at the same time] the judge and a party.") Yet consider a few examples of how this rule is violated:

1) When Mrs Simone Veil, the then Minister of Health, wanted to propose laws against tobacco advertisements and require strong labeling, who prevented her from carrying out her objectives? You guessed it; the French tobacco monopoly, called SEITA. What business does the government have selling cigarettes and matches? Answer: it's a great racket, and a terrific way to give jobs to people you like.

I read somewhere that it was Napoleon who nationalized the tobacco "industry," after he attended a ball and discovered that the woman wearing even bigger jewels than the Empress Josephine was the wife of a wealthy tobacco importer. At least Napoleon made no bones about what was good for his family being good for the nation.

2) Paris is one of the most polluted cities in Europe. For years the government delayed enacting legislation for anti-pollution devices on automobiles. Why? It owns the biggest automobile manufacturer, Renault, which had been nationalized by de Gaulle because its founder, Louis Renault, was alleged to have "collaborated" with the Nazis. Hence, French cars are only beginning to get equipped with catalytic converters, whereas the same cars, exported to the United States, have been so equipped for two decades. Thus the State's interest as a manufacturer takes precedence over its duty to protect its citizens' health.

3) Air France is owned by the State. For years, its privately-owned French competitor, UTA, led by its battling President, René Lapautre, had been trying to compete head-on by obtaining the right to fly to New York. When Lapautre appealed to the French Minister of Transport, who is supposed to be protecting the public interest, the latter replied, *"My main concern is Air France."* UTA filed an antitrust complaint with the EEC but the French government succeeded in stalling the proceedings. Now the government has solved the problem by buying out UTA, at an enormous premium and, to boot, obtaining control over the interior air carrier, Air Inter, in which UTA held a substantial minority interest!

Can one find a more blatant conflict of interest than placing in the same hand the regulation of transportation and the ownership of the main carriers? Suppose that Roger Smith, the much maligned Chairman of General Motors, were appointed head of the Michigan pollution-control agency while keeping his position at GM; one has no difficulty in imagining the cries of protest that would be heard. But in France, the main cry when Air France bought UTA was *cocorico*, the Gallic equivalent of "cockadoodle do," which connotes chauvinistic satisfaction.

The French experience makes clear that the more a state owns the more it behaves as an owner, and the less as a protector of the public interest. The most bitter proof of this is found in the USSR which has not only polluted its atmosphere but also destroyed lakes, forests and other natural resources in the sole interest of meeting production schedules. Who defends the public interest when the state runs the factories?

Indeed, French antitrust policy and practice is a big joke. To be sure, there have been laws on the books for decades, and the short-lived Chirac government even modernized the rules by its *ordonnance* of 1986, which set up the Conseil de la Concurrence (which I call Con-Con for short). If 12 bakers in a provincial city get together to rig the price of the *baguette,* the Con-Con will go on the warpath, but if a government-owned company obtains a monopoly, the Con-Con will charitably turn the other cheek.

French government flirtation with state ownership of business goes back centuries. Colbert, Louis XIV's clever Minister, was the first to see the advantage of getting the King involved in lucrative industries. In more recent times, the leading banks and insurance companies were nationalized before World War II, ostensibly to keep them out of foreign hands. As we have seen, de Gaulle took over Renault after the war. So-called "*libéral*" presidents like Pompidou and Giscard did nothing to return state-owned businesses to private hands. Chirac was Giscard's prime minister for two years, succeeded by Raymond Barre, who held office for five years. Although they now profess to be free-market people, they did nothing during their tenure to reduce state ownership. To be sure, when Chirac returned to power for his "cohabitation" with Mitterrand he dutifully denationalized a handful of companies, leaving the great majority in State hands.

All this is to point out that State ownership in France is not a socialist invention. The boys in office like the power that stems from nationalized companies; they appoint their buddies and allies to juicy plums, and when they are booted out by the electorate, they make deals with their adversaries to keep a few key jobs for themselves. The dream of every high-level technocrat, particularly the *ENArque*, is to "*pantoufler*," that is, get a well-paying job in state-owned or regulated companies, after some 15-20 years of government service. More often than not, these jobs happen to be in businesses which the technocrat was supposed to be regulating!

It is not surprising that the average Frenchman fails to see, let alone protest, the highly unethical aspects of this system. French children are taught that Louis XIV was the golden age, and Napoleon the greatest genius since Alexander the Great. Contemporary France has monarchical values: the King controls all the rackets, and hands out the favors. It is an irony of history that Marxism provided an intellectual excuse for the French elite to do what they always liked to do. The French socialists, even today, sing the Internationale at every official gathering, but each leader is thinking: *"Will the President invite me to his next state banquet?"*

Only against this background can you begin to understand why I hold the EEC in such scorn. The EEC is one of the biggest public-relations frauds perpetrated on the Western World; it is a profoundly undemocratic plaything of the technocrats who control the individual member States. Many Americans have a favorable attitude towards the EEC, naively assuming it is a step towards European unity along the American model. Nothing could be further from the truth.

The United States began with a Federal legislature, having real power, a strong executive, and last, but surely not least, a Federal judiciary, at both the local and appellate levels. The last thing the United States acquired was a bureaucracy, whereas this is the first thing the EEC acquired, and it still does not have a true legislature, nor a true executive, nor any Federal judiciary. Do you begin to see the difference?

Just in case you don't, let me illustrate. Suppose a bureaucrat in France comes up with some hare-brained idea, such as requiring all private automobiles to be painted yellow, for greater visibility. He knows that if he proposes the idea for legislation to be enacted in France, it will be hooted down in parliament. But if he proposes it to a fellow bureaucrat in Brussels, the idea can make the rounds, and become adopted by fiat as an EEC Directive, and then it becomes binding on the legislature of each Member State! This is one of the greatest miracles since the "Fishes and the Loaves." The people of 12 nations become bound by a law which has not been enacted by any parliament!

Isn't is wonderful what ingenious technocrats can dream up? And is it any wonder that the French *dirigistes*, like Jacques Delors, are flocking to Brussels, where they can do their bit for humanity, without humanity having a say in what they do? Is it any surprise that Jacques Delors was Mitterrand's first Minister of Finance when all the nationalizations were carried out, including those of the banks? And is it any surprise that Europe is undergoing a tremendous concentration of enterprises?

That the Common Market was meant to be a bureaucrat's paradise was signalled in Article 85 of the Treaty of Rome, which was modeled after Section 1 of the US Sherman Act, with one crucial difference. Instead of establishing standards of illegal restraints of trade which the courts would apply, as in the United States, the Treaty empowered bureaucrats to make exceptions and grant exemptions. Thus enforcement is in the hands of bureaucrats, rather than an independent judiciary. Whereas it is unethical to make *ex parte* contacts with a judge, bureaucrats just love *ex parte* visits. And of course, they are sensitive to government pressures, and enticements of all sorts, like the promise of juicy jobs.

And bureaucrats just love concentrated industries; they're much easier to control; there are fewer people to talk to. I predict that in a few years, EEC bureaucrats will work from 11 am. to 3 pm, with two hours for lunch. Most of the business will, of course, be conducted over the lunch table, with friendly discussions between the bureaucrats and their beloved cartel operators.

One need only read the newspapers to see that the EEC is becoming a vast cartel, the tacit assumption being that in each industry there will be one or two dominant companies within each of the major countries, and they will engage in friendly competition. And no one should be surprised that the EEC is becoming a cartel: it started that way, with the Coal and Steel Community, which was nothing but a multi-government organized cartel.

Until the recent events in Eastern Europe, the only resistance to the French orientation of the EEC came from Margaret Thatcher, who rightly saw that centuries of struggle to create a parliamentary democracy in Great Britain were not to be discarded in favor of bureaucratic oligarchy. It is a sad commentary on the press that this courageous lady, who is taking her government out of the conflicts of interest that result from ownership of business, thereby reducing her own power, is seen as "heartless," while François Mitterrand, who presides over an unethical government that prefers to act as a factory owner with vast economic power, rather than a protector of the public interest, is perceived as "humane." True, one prefers that the powerful be benevolent, but it is even more desirable that they shed power and pursue ethics.

Years ago, when it was almost required reading, I read Lincoln Steffen's autobiography, and was struck by his youthful quest for ethical absolutes, which he did not find. For years I assumed that ethical values were relative, but I have come to the belief that certain principles are made in heaven or, if you prefer, in our genes. My theory is that the seeds of universal values are found in what children intuitively perceive as unfair. This insight came to me one day when I tried to give two lollipops to one daughter and only one to her sister. The latter was hardly old enough to speak, but she pointed to her sister and shouted "two!" This is the birth of the concept of "equal protection under the law." Even a child knows that there is something wrong in being punished for violating a rule that his mother had not promulgated before the offense. And a child knows that when he plays "cops and robbers," the boy playing the robber cannot also be the judge.

Thus, to my mind, a government which permits itself to take on conflicts of interest violates a fundamental rule of justice, fairness or ethics, call it what you will. To be sure, the members of the present French government would be offended at the idea that their ethics might be questioned. They are all honorable men, and are convinced that their high-mindedness is a sufficient antidote to any potential conflict of interest. But the adage: *"One can not be both judge and party"* suffers no exceptions, particularly since even the appearance of evil is an evil.

In this context, it is dismaying to observe the total absence of any discussion in France of the ethical aspects of state ownership of business. On the contrary, the French have been brainwashed into assuming that the socialist state is inherently more ethical than the capitalist system. To some extent this is a byproduct of French Catholicism.

As some readers may be tempted to commit the fallacy of the "undistributed middle," let me interject here that I am not going to the other extreme of asserting that capitalism is free of unethical conduct. Taking my cue from P.T. Barnum's immortal remark: *"A sucker is born every minute,"* I believe that we must accept the corollary that *"A crook is born every hour."* This is turn leads to the hope that a policeman or judge be born every day. We need government to regulate, police and adjudge, not to own businesses.

André Malraux supposedly stated that: *"The 21st century will be religious, or it will not be."* Having seen what Ayatollah Khomeini accomplished, I am afraid that Malraux may be right, even if not in the way he intended. But, I would prefer a safer prediction: *"The 21st century will be ethical, or will be very hot."*

Vol. XII, Nº 2, May 1990

More (and less) on Ethics

The last issue aroused a great deal of favorable comment from readers. I try to answer all letters individually, but just in case I have forgotten anyone, let me thank all those who took the trouble to write to me.

My emphasis had been on the conflict of interest prevalent at the highest spheres of the French state, where the people who are supposed to regulate an industry are at the same time responsible for the operations of state-owned businesses, such as Air France or the nationalized banks. These people would consider themselves honest, in the sense that they would not steal a loaf of bread, but they simply fail to see that they are violating a fundamental rule of ethics by wearing two hats.

In trying to understand the reasons for this blindness to conflicts of interest, the main explanation that I come up with is tied to the Catholic and monarchic traditions in France. As for the Church, ethics descend from on high. The King, as defender of the faith and source of all rights, could, in his day, do no wrong. By hypothesis, he could have no conflict of interest. The King has gone, but the state which he left remains, and those who embody it still think they have the same prerogatives as the sovereign who could do no wrong. The Catholic tradition contributes to this situation by tying morality to authority, rather than deducing rules of ethics, as in the Platonic tradition, from the rational and harmonious organization of human beings in society.

Well, perhaps I am getting too deeply philosophical but, from time to time, when I inquire as to first causes for French phenomena, I end up with the Catholic Church and the monarchy. Which leads me to another example that has been much in the news lately: amnesty for criminal offenses connected to political campaigns. The very notion of periodic amnesties – there is one after each presidential election – seems to me a Catholic phenomenon; countries which are predominantly Protestant do not appear to practice it. When a new president is elected, hardly anyone complains about the amnesty law which is invariably enacted by the Parliament; the reason: traffic tickets do not have to be paid! (Some people accumulated hundreds of tickets called contraventions in anticipation of the 1988 elections. No one seems to pity the poor citizen who dutifully paid for his violations!)

However, the most recent amnesty law has raised a furor, because its main beneficiaries are French politicians. It has been common knowledge for years that all the political parties use illegal means to raise money, because politicians do not have the courage to admit how much money is actually needed to finance their parties and their campaigns. Perhaps the most prevalent method involves having the printer's invoice for campaign posters and "literature" paid for by a business enterprise, which deducts the cost on its tax return. This is called a *fausse facture*, or phony invoice, since the printer typically itemizes non-existant work on the invoice. There have been dozens of cases pending against politicians of all parties, their printers and contributors. As a number of the culprits are Socialists, the government, headed by Michel Rocard, pushed through a law last year amnestying most offenses connected with campaign financing. Most of the opposition either voted against it or abstained, but this was largely hypocritical, as each party saw to it that enough members voted for the law to ensure passage. Even Raymond Barre voted for the amnesty.

As so often happens in France, the furor began not when the law passed, but only later, when its effects became visible, that is, when charges were dismissed and people released from jail. The most notorious beneficiary of the amnesty (actually, under an earlier law) was Christian Nucci, a former Socialist minister, whose main assistant admitted siphoning millions of francs from the budget of an African summit meeting. And the most vehement critics of the amnesty were the very judges who had to implement the law. This in turn created what the press called *le malaise de la justice*. As judges are civil servants in France, and subject to the authority of the Minister of Justice, the lack of true independence of the judiciary has long been a festering sore in this country. But when judges are prevented from applying the law equally because a privileged class votes itself an exemption, the embarrassment becomes acute. Hence many judges took the rare step of publicly criticizing the amnesty; in some cities, judges gave nominal sentences to other offenders as a sign of protest.

This *malaise* was front-page news in all the papers in March and April, and the main heat was on the Socialist Party, sponsor of the amnesty. The embarrassment of Messrs Mitterrand and Rocard was acute, particularly as, for the first time since 1988, they began to take a nose-dive in opinion polls. To make matters worse, the Socialist Party held a disastrous convention in March, in which the contending factions were unable to make even a show of harmony. The immediate issue was the effort of Laurent Fabius, Mitterrand's fair-haired boy, to unseat Pierre Mauroy as head of the party. Determined to block him was not only Mauroy, but a Fabius-hater of the first rank, Lionel Jospin, the former party head, and now Minister of Education. Prime Minister Rocard benignly claimed to be above the fray, while doing his best behind the scenes to neutralize Fabius. The convention ended at an impasse, which meant a practical defeat for Fabius as Mauroy was renamed Secretary-General of the party, although a Fabius stalwart was named his assistant as a gesture of compromise.

Much of the embarrassment rubbed off on Mitterrand, who thereafter appeared on a well-known TV interview show, and worsened his case by devoting an inordinate amount of time to these petty squabbles, to the detriment of more important issues. For reasons best known only to himself, Mitterrand's favorite candidate to succeed him is young Fabius, whom he named Prime Minister during his first term, to succeed Mauroy. Fabius' performance was undistinguished; he spent a good deal of energy trying to dissociate himself from the Rainbow Warrior scandal, and in doing so forced Defense Minister Charles Hernu to resign. Fabius' own efforts to avoid appearing responsible for anything controversial were so blatant that the great *Figaro* cartoonist, Faizant, pictured him with an open umbrella eternally over his head. Once, when a journalist asked Fabius how he differed from Mitterrand, his now celebrated answer was *"Lui c'est lui et moi c'est moi" ("He is he and I am I.")* In a country that produced Louis XIV, Napoleon, Clemenceau and de Gaulle, one might have expected better phraseology.

After Mitterrand's re-election he tried to get Fabius named head of the Socialist Party. When this failed, Fabius got the consolation prize of president of the National Assembly. As Fabius is clearly unpopular in his own party, and has shown himself to be undistinguished in ideas or accomplishments, it is not unreasonable to ask what Mitterrand sees in him. My guess is that the President appreciates Fabius because he is no more socialist than Mitterrand himself! This opportunism doubtless has appeal for the old master, who is keenly aware that a politician who wants to survive must know which way the wind is blowing. But the comparison ends there, for Mitterrand reached the top without presidential sponsor whereas, absent Mitterrand's support, Fabius would be a minor functionary in the Ministry of Finance.

As indicated above, the President's popularity was at its lowest ebb since his re-election, and the Socialist Party was consequently on the defensive, when a shocking event occurred on May 10th: the Jewish cemetery at Carpentras, an agricultural town which was once under the papal authority of Avignon, was the scene of horrible vandalism. Some thirty graves were desecrated, and the body of a recent deceased was removed from his grave and, according to Fabius, impaled by a parasol stick. It is said that the local Jewish authorities did not want to publicize this evil event but the Socialist Minister of the Interior, Pierre Joxe, saw to it that Carpentras become the number-one topic of conversation, doing his best to associate this desecration with Le Pen's National Front, which has often been accused of anti-Semitism.

Le Pen wasted no time in denouncing both the cemetery desecration and those who wanted to blame him for it. He made the obvious point that his party had nothing to gain from committing such an odious act, which no civilized person could condone, and he suggested that it would be wiser to seek culprits elsewhere, perhaps among Moslem terrorist groups. As the month ends, the police have not been able to apprehend a single suspect, despite the sending of 60 special investigators from Paris at the behest of the Prime Minister. Much attention has been paid to the possibility that the desecration could be the deed of one of the "skinhead" gangs that have been proliferating all over France.

Politicians were quick to capitalize on the horrible deed, thankful as they were that it turned attention away from the amnesty law. A major demonstration was held in Paris, the itinerary being the favorite one of the Left, from the Bastille to the Place de la République. Of course, politicians of the Center and the Right, except for Le Pen, participated, and Mitterrand himself joined the crowd. All the newspapers and magazines featured articles on the theme: *"Is France anti-Semitic?"* and most replied *"No, only a small minority is anti-Semitic,"* an opinion which I happen to share.

The more time that passes without identifying the authors of the Carpentras desecration the more you hear (in private) remarks to the effect that it was a "provocation." When you ask what that means, you are asked, in turn, *"Well, who benefited most from the event?"* The idea you are supposed to grasp is that maybe it was the "powers that be" who organized the vandalism to detract attention from their own problems, or perhaps it was even Israel. The fact that a few days after the Carpentras incident an Israeli was arrested for vandalizing a Jewish cemetery in Israel, to lay the blame on Arabs, tends to comfort those who adhere to this theory. I find the very idea abhorrent, but I am merely reporting what I have heard said. So long as the real culprits are not found, these ugly suggestions will be bruited.

My best guess is that the vandalism was the work of local teenagers who have seen too many horror films on French TV. Perhaps I am showing my age, but I hate horror films; a recurrent theme seems to be the dead rising from their tombs; thus cemeteries are a typical situs. How can some teenagers not be tempted to imitate the gruesome rites they witness on TV?

After the cemetery incident, the main news has been the "round table" that Rocard organized to seek a political consensus on the immigration issue, which is a real hot potato. Even the Socialists now admit that there are too many unassimilated immigrants in France, this being a polite way of saying that there are too many Moslems. Le Pen's solution to this problem is to send them all packing unless they have steady jobs, whereas the Socialists' utopic solution is to "assimilate" them, that is, turn every Moslem into a certified Frenchman. Obviously both solutions are extreme and unrealistic. Chirac's party – the RPR – announced that it would not attend the "round table" unless Rocard renounced the Socialist platform promise to permit immigrants to vote in municipal elections. Finally, Rocard stated that this issue was put off, whereupon Chirac and his henchmen attended, while denouncing the government for not having a solution to the immigration problem. Need it be said that Chirac has no solution either?

The petty squabbling of French politicians is alienating more and more voters, who seek comfort in abstention or in Le Pen. In the last elections near my country home, National Front candidates garnered as much as 40 percent of the votes in villages where there is not a single Arab or Jew. These voters are not haters, they are protesters.

It should not be forgotten that Le Pen was a marginal figure, never having won an election until 1986, at which time the Socialists introduced proportional representation for the parliamentary elections, whereupon Le Pen became a *député,* and his party garnered 30 seats in the National Assembly. In 1988, he lost his seat, and his party returned to nothingness in parliament after Chirac abolished proportional representation.

The present government is foolishly doing its best to make a martyr of Le Pen. In May, he was convicted of a criminal offense for stating that the extermination of the Jews was a "point of detail" in the history of World War II. Those who believe in freedom of speech must surely be outraged that a person can be prosecuted and convicted for such a remark. Some years ago, in the United States, Jewish lawyers working for the American Civil Liberties Union defended the right of neo-Nazis to march in Skokie, Illinois. I have not heard or read a single public statement by a French leader, even a leader of the Bar, defending Le Pen's constitutional right to make irresponsible statements. Just as France has forgotten Montesquieu, it has forgotten Voltaire, who uttered these immortal words two centuries ago: *"I disapprove of what you say, but I will defend to the death your right to say it."*

Weep, weep for a France that can produce the likes of Le Pen but not know how to deal with him.

Vol. XII, N° 4, November 1990

Confessions of a Francophile

For years now, I am used to hearing, after a caustic Newsletter about French politicians, at least one kind friend ask me: *"Aren't you worried that they may throw you out of the country?"* The answer has invariably been "No."

In the first place, this is a free country. And in the second, the French are quite tolerant of criticism from those who love them. My credentials as a Francophile can hardly be suspected: with a French wife, seven French children and seven French grandchildren, I am the head of a growing French family even if I am a foreigner. Having been born and raised in the United States, I first came to France at the age of 24, too late to become a credible Frenchman, but not too late to become a Francophile. Therein lies a story.

As a Fulbright "scholar," to use the official term, I was exposed to an indoctrination session, shortly after my arrival at the University of Strasbourg. One of the speakers made a passionate speech, the gist of which was *"we do not ask you to admire us, but to love us."* Fresh from the analytical rigors of Harvard Law School, I found the speech silly and irrational: how can you love a people if you don't admire them?

Yet a year later, I realized what the speaker meant, for I had come to love France and the French, and that love had not proceeded from admiration but from familiarity. After all, when it comes to the people one is closest to, to wit, family, love is independant of admiration. And that was what the passionate speaker was trying to convey: get to know us, foibles, faults and all, and perhaps you will find us worthy of your affection.

Occasionally, one meets foreigners who profess to like France but not the French. I find such an attitude incomprehensible, for France is the French; they made the country, they are the country. The beauty of France is not an accident; it is the result of dozens of generations of conscious effort to make and preserve beauty. Inded, if there is a single French quality which I would rate as foremost, it is the esthetic sense. This is what struck me the most during my first months here: the general level of taste was so much higher that that which prevailed in America, whether in the décor of shops and restaurants, even the most modest, the way women dressed, even those without means, and even in the literal sense, the fact that tomatoes still tasted good, whereas in the United States, they had long since given up any pretension to having an olfactory purpose.

Paris alone was a revelation: this was man-made beauty. The beautiful perspectives from the Place de la Concorde did not happen by chance. The banks of the Seine were not always that way. Once, I found a book of engravings of Paris in earlier centuries; the Seine had been disfigured by factories, and ugly constructions. Beautification had thus been adopted as a conscious and no doubt costly project. By comparison I though of the ugliness of most inner-city rivers in America, such as the Schuylkill in my native Philadelphia.

Yet the Paris of the '50s was a relatively dingy city, most buildings being covered by grime. On de Gaulle's return to power in 1958, his Minister of Culture André Malraux revived an old law requiring periodic cleaning of the facades of buildings, producing a lighter and lovelier Paris. These cleaning jobs, called *ravalements*, are costly; yet most building owners pay for them cheerfully knowing that they are enhancing the esthetics of their city and the value of their property.

Paradoxically, the French take for granted their esthetic preeminence. They are rather embarrassed if you place cuisine, wine, perfumes and fashion as their main current contributions to civilization, as though these were minor arts, suffering in contrast with the productions of their stolid German neighbor: heavy chemicals, machine tools, Mercedes and BMW cars. But considering the millions of years that man and his predecessor have been on this earth, I believe that refinement of taste and devotion to beauty are the principal distinctions of our race, and no people have contributed more than the French to the sheer pleasure of living.

Well, the reader must be saying: *"So you do admire them, after all!"* Yes, of course. But love preceeded admiration, and moreover, there is much that one can not admire. I find the French endearing, despite there faults, perhaps even because of them. Doubtless the fault that gives the most irritation to foreigners is their chauvinism, which seems to accompany every profession and calling. When my eldest son was in the *lycée*, we were talking one day about science, and he told me: *"The French are the best scientists."* Astounded, I asked, *"Where did you learn that?"* He replied, *"From my physics teacher."* I told him, *"The fool, instead of teaching you physics, he's teaching you chauvinism!"*

Another illustration: several years ago, when the new Code of Civil Procedure went into effect, the *Figaro* carried a front-page article about it, written by one of the authors of the code, which described it as "already one of the best in the world." This need to puff about the pre-eminence of French accomplishments is often inversely proportional to the realities, as these exemples demonstrate, for French science and French law are hardly in the forefront of progress. It is as though chauvinism makes up for backwardness.

Indeed, one of my problems with the French is that the élite are so often among the backward, and the most modest those who deserve the most praise. As the post-World War II era closes, with the debacle of Marxism, hardly anyone would deny that French intellectuals (essentially Parisian) were the most fatuous band of glib baloney artists, flirting with Stalin, Mao and Castro, and closing their eyes to the most crying facts of life. The people I like best in France are the modest doers, the artisans, whether in the kitchen or the woodshop, the antique dealers, the farmers, the taxi drivers, the shop-keepers, the garage mechanics, the *boulangers*. My neighbor in the country tills 125 acres of land all alone, uncomplaining and in good humor; he speaks eloquently about farm problems. France is full of modest, hard-working people like him.

Indeed, one of the most charming and redeeming features of France is that it has some 36,000 communes, mainly small villages and towns, each with its mayor and municipal council. Here, democracy is at its best. You can fool a lot of people in a national campaign on television, but you can not fool your neighbors in a village of 200 souls. If you promise a new water tower, you had better deliver! And every one of these communes has its *Monument aux Morts*, a somber reminder that the first World War spared not a single village in all of France.

What saves France is that its heart and lungs are rural. It is in some village that virtually every family has real or adopted roots, whether in the Ile de France, the Auvergne, the Dordogne, Normandy or Brittany, or the Midi. Foreigners often mistakenly judge the French by visiting Paris alone; this is as silly as judging Americans by visiting New York. Most of the French live away from Paris; indeed many French have never even visited Paris. And Parisians are not popular in the provinces. So if you want to know the French you should visit the countryside, and provincial cities.

Now for some interesting statistics. Some 15 years ago, when one of my daughters was applying for admission to an American university after finishing her *lycée* studies, I decided to seek statistics from the French Ministry of Education which might help evaluate the worth of the baccalaureat degree. To my amazement I learned that at that time only some 25 percent of an age group ever obtained the coveted degree, and at an average age of 19. This meant that for 100 students born in 1957, nineteen years later 75 of them had either been eliminated from the school system or failed the baccalaureat exam. It meant also that the average student who passed the exam had repeated at least one year of schooling. As roughly two thirds of those who took the exam at that time were successful, my estimate is that more than 60 percent of the given age group had been eliminated before reaching the age to take the exam.

Once I thought about them, these statistics confirmed my own observation of the French school system as a parent who suffered through the schooling of seven French children. The emphasis, from the earliest age, was learning things by heart, rather than learning to understand. And, in later years, mathematics was taught in the most abstract manner, the emphasis again being on learning rules by heart, rather than solving problems. It is notorious that mathematics is used as the supreme eliminator in all French schools. If your child loved animals and hoped to become a veterinarian, there was not the slightest chance for him if he was not good at math. And in the last year of *lycée*, students are required to take "philosophy" which involves exposure to the great God of the French mind, Descartes and his *Discours de la Méthode*, whose first principle is that "The things that one sees very clearly and very distinctly are all true."

In an early Newsletter, called "A Word about the French Spirit," I describe the French emphasis on form and on *a priori* reasoning, as exemplified by Descartes, who thought that he could stay in bed and reason himself through all problems faced by human kind. Among other things, I explained that in a French exam the student is judged as much (if not more) on the *plan* which he must set forth at the outset as on the content of his answer of essay. I would add that in the *lycée*, as later in the competitive exams which bar the entry to the French *grandes écoles*, heavy weight is given to oral exams, even in mathematics! This benefits youngsters who have the gift of gab, and who are never at a loss for words. One such bright young man explained to me, years ago, why he did so well in school despite a lack of serious study. Suppose the professor asks *"what was the foreign policy of Louis XIV?"* An honest student might reply, *"Sorry, I did not read that chapter"* and get a zero, but the bright lad (who also skipped that chapter) would reply, *"One can not understand the foreign policy of Louis XIV without first examining that of his predecessors,"* and then would expound sufficiently on the wrong subject until the professor gave him a passing grade, recognizing one of the future élite of France.

Just recently, I obtained statistics as to the number of persons holding a university degree in France: only 1.6-million out of a population of more than 50-million; that makes some three percent of the total. For, you see, even though the baccalaureat degree entitles the possessor to a free university education, the universities do their best to eliminate as many as possible in the first year. In Paris, for example, some two thirds fail the first-year exams, or drop out earlier. In medical schools the failure rate is 90 percent! Thus, only a small fraction of the entering class ever is ever graduated from the university.

By this time, the reader may be wondering what my point is. Well, to start with, the point is that the great majority of the present French population are rejects of the educational system. A corollary is that the Ministry of Education should better be called the Ministry of Elimination, because its main purpose until now has been to eliminate and reject the overwhelming majority of those who have come within its grips.

Putting the two parts of this essay together, let me say that it is only recently that I realized that as a Francophile, the people I liked best in France were, on the whole, the rejects just identified, and those I tend to like the least are the prized élite. The reader not familiar with France should ponder this fact: most of the people he will meet during a visit to France – the cab drivers, the restaurateurs, the antique dealers, the shop owners, yes, even the grands couturiers – are rejects of the educational system. At some point they have been eliminated, because they were not good at mathematics, abstract language and *a priori* reasoning. Yet these are the people who keep the country going. They are the pragmatists, the empiricists and the realists.

And is it any wonder that French intellectuals are the class the most despised by the rest of the world? They are the survivors of a ruthless, élitist educational system that has deliberately put a premium on those who have facility in wielding words and abstractions and are indifferent to the concrete, the real. For some 40 years since the end of World War II, while the French educational system has rejected the great majority of the French people, the élite that it produced continued to flirt with Marxism, and was oblivious to the realities of the world behind the Iron Curtain.

Although I started to write this Newsletter months ago, it has turned out to be most timely, because France is presently in turmoil with the demonstrations and strikes of the *lycée* students. By reason of its extreme centralization, the French Ministry of Education has the most employees and the biggest budget of all government agencies. Yet its productions, whether at the *lycée* or university level, are a crying failure. The current government has adopted as its objective gradually to bring the baccalaureat earners to 80 percent of an age group. This will be as herculean a task as converting collective farms in the USSR to private landownings! The ministry is dominated by strong unions, and most card-carrying Socialists are teachers. How can one change the educational system without changing the teachers? And who is going to educate new teachers not to think that *"The things that one sees very clearly and very distinctly are all true."*?

Obviously this subject is much too vast to be dealt with in this Newsletter, but I did want the reader to know that I finally understood why I am a Francophile: I love losers.

Vol. XIII, Nº 2, March 1991

The "Machin" Strikes... Out

As I write this, the 100-hour ground war has ended in Iraq, but Saddam Hussein is in place, proclaiming victory, a phenomenon which reminds me of the night following French elections, when every party claims a victory of sorts, no matter how few votes it received. As an American living in France I am, of course, pleased that the armed forces of my two favorite countries fought so effectively side by side. When I left off my last Newsletter, the bizarre French Minister of Defense, Jean-Pierre Chevènement, had just been replaced by Pierre Joxe, who seems to have done a superb job in carrying out his mission on short order, without the *états d'âme*, to use the allusive French expression, that characterized his predecessor.

Newspapers, at least in non-Arab countries, are singing the praise of President Bush and the high military command that accomplished the rout of the Iraqi army while suffering so few "coalition" (the word that replaced "allied") casualties. This is being proclaimed a victory for the United Nations. No less a non-party-liner than Anthony Lewis writes: *"The UN system can work; we know that now."* At the same time, the UN Secretary-General, Perez de Cuellar, states on French television that it is not the business of the UN to get rid of Saddam Hussein, the chief of state of a member nation, and sovereign at that.

With my readers' indulgence, I beg to differ with all that rejoicing. One cannot blame de Cuellar for his fatuous remark, for fatuousness is built into the job description of every UN Secretary-General. But Anthony Lewis' lack of perspicacity is disturbing. To me, the lesson to be learned is just the opposite: the Gulf War was the limiting case which proves the utter worthlessness of the United Nations, which de Gaulle scornfully used to call, in private, "*le machin*" (slang equivalent to "the thingamabob" or, for short, "the thing").

Need one recall that it was nothing short of a miracle for President Bush to get 12 resolutions enacted by the Security Council, two of whose veto-wielding permanent members are those stalwart defenders of freedom known as the USSR and the "People's Republic of China," and whose present membership includes such other lovers of free elections as Cuba and the Yemen? It is now clear why Gorbachev did not veto American intervention in Iraq. While the United States was busy helping to restore the Emir of Kuwait to his throne, Gorbachev took advantage of the distraction to try to crush freely-elected regimes in the Baltic Republics whose annexation by Stalin had been sheer aggression and, to boot, never recognized by the United States. China did not vote in favor of the key resolution; it merely abstained. Aside from the Chinese leaders, only God and President Bush know the price of that abstention. But one can guess that the price is payable in US dollars!

As de Cuellar's remark demonstrates, the whole premise of the United Nations is cockeyed: to wit, that sovereign nations are all equal before international law, and must be treated with equal respect. Thus the invasion by one undemocratic country of another undemocratic country is deserving of UN intervention, provided the latter is a member of the United Nations. But even if the former is a member, as is Iraq, perish the thought that it should be excluded from the UN, or its leaders punished, for that would be interfering with the sovereignty of a member nation!

To make matters worse, a news story in the *International Herald Tribune* describes the "gruesome remnant of an Iraqi convoy" of more than 1,000 vehicles fleeing Kuwait City which *"US fighter-bombers relentlessly bombed and rocketed,"* doubtless killing thousands of Iraqis, whose number will never be known because it is now US Army policy not to count the enemy dead, to make up for the over-counting during the Vietnam War.

I confess to being troubled by this new Pentagon policy of ignoring the Iraqi dead. They count the tanks, the artillery pieces destroyed and the aircraft, but not human beings. In Sophocles' *Antigone*, we observe the victorious king's desire to punish his dead enemy by denying him burial. The Pentagon adds a new dimension of indignity: the enemy dead need not be counted. General Schwarzkopf states: *"We are not in the business of body-counting."* Perhaps not bodies, General, but isn't there a laser machine that can detect dead souls?

Another article in the same paper quotes President Bush as saying that his policy is not to "hunt down" Saddam Hussein to stand trial for war crimes. Thus, it is permissible to kill a hundred-thousand Iraqi soldiers, most of whom have been pressed into the army against their will, but it would be a terrible offense against humanity to arrest the irresponsible and amoral leader whose worst crimes have been committed against his own people.

The absurdity of this posture can be illustrated as follows: suppose a gang of thugs breaks into your house at night, rapes your wife and daughter, steals your appliances and occupies your bedroom. What would one think of the local police chief who limited his intervention to evicting and shooting the thugs but took no action against their known gang leader?

Such is the morality of 20th-century international law, which is even embodied in an Act of Congress forbidding the assassination of foreign heads of state: to respect sovereignty, one must not harm the most vicious, self-appointed dictator, who gassed his own citizens, but it is legal, with UN blessing, to shoot thousands of fleeing soldiers in the back! While I am not sure I will ever see the 21st century, I do hope that men of that century will say, as the most famous man of the first century might have: *"Those fleeing soldiers were as much my brothers as those who shot them in the back."*

A third article in the same paper caught my attention: a Marine is quoted as saying: *"It would have been very difficult for me to have to kill Iraqis. They are not really my enemies, and I have nothing against them. It is their leader who is a problem."* Thank God for that Marine: he could give a few lessons in morality to his superiors in the Pentagon. Is it not curious to find an "objective alliance" (to use the Communists' expression) between Saddam Hussein and the Pentagon to conceal the number of Iraqi dead? Saddam's motivation is obvious, but I would expect more from the United States. How can I believe in my own dignity if I do not grant dignity to those whom my countrymen left dead in the desert sands? My values hold that we owe it to History and to the dead soldiers of all nations to count them and remember them.

During the reign of terror of the French Revolution, Madame Roland, put to the guillotine, achieved immortality by exclaiming, *"Oh Liberty! What crimes are committed in thy name."* As the 20th century ends, we can say, looking Perez de Cuellar straight in the eye, *"Oh Sovereignty! What crimes are committed in thy name."* The grotesqueness of the official position of international law, as interpreted by the US State Department and the UN, is worth stressing simply by recounting what has happened: it is better that one-hundred-thousand Iraqi soldiers, herded to the front by a tyrannical government that was never elected, should die under bombardment of forces operating under UN authorization, than to disturb the "sovereignty" of that very government! If international law says this, then I say, along with Dickens: *"the law is a ass, a idiot."*

To my mind, the main victims of Saddam Hussein are not the Kuwaitis, but rather the people of Iraq, who, as one Iraqi friend told me recently, have been held hostage by their brutal leader for more than a dozen years. Yet the UN has done nothing to help them, as that would be offending the notion of sovereignty.

Is it any wonder that there is such sadness and resentment in the Arab world, particularly among the common people, whom the American press continually caricatures as the "Arab masses." (Why is it that America has "people" but Arabs only have "masses"? (When alive, the Arab is not an individual; when killed he is not even a statistic.) Are Arabs supposed to forget that the US, France, Britain and Germany provided vast amounts of arms to Saddam Hussein? Does one have to be guided by herd instincts to ask why the UN did nothing when the USSR invaded Afghanistan, or more recently sent in troops to crush the Baltic freedom movement, or when Iraq used poison gas against Iran, or against the Kurds? To apply law arbitrarily or in a discriminatory manner is to violate the basic principle of justice embodied in the concept of "equal protection of the laws."

This brings me back to the fundamental and irremedial flaw of the United Nations: it is premised on sovereignty, so that a non-democratic country is entitled to the same treatment as a democratic one. To make matters worse, two totalitarian governments have veto power in the Security Council which is supposed to preserve peace. It is time to put an end to this farce. Thus, I am ready to propose a radical change in US policy: to wit, withdrawal from the United Nations and formation of a new organization composed of only democratic nations, and committed to promoting democracy throughout the world. Its basic premise would be that sovereignty belongs only to peoples, not governments, and that any people governed undemocratically should be directly assisted to obtain democracy, by whatever means appear suitable.

Of course, the objection will be made: *"How do you define democracy?"* My first reply is to cite Dr. Johnson's remark: *"We all know what light is, even if we cannot define it."* It is not difficult to distinguish democratic regimes from those that are not. The three tests that suit me are: (a) a freely elected legislature, with an executive responsible to it or directly to the people; (b) the rule of law, enforced by an independent judiciary; (c) minority rights, *i.e.,* individual liberties.

It is clear to anyone who stops to count that a majority of the members of the *machin* would not pass this test. Africa is full of one-party, corrupt regimes; the Arab world knows no democracy; South and Central America struggle to avoid military *coups d'état;* much of Asia is dominated by one-party or military regimes.

The true democracies should cease giving respectability to those regimes by treating them as equals within the forum of the United Nations, under the flag of "sovereignty." By banding together, the democracies can speak the same language and serve as an example for dissenters everywhere who aspire to bring democracy to their homelands. Once the shibboleth of sovereignty is abandoned, the excluded nations would find it tempting indeed to achieve membership in the democratic club. And the club could, in appropriate cases, use force to do away with oppressive regimes.

To get a glimmer of how things would be different if this idea were adopted, let us suppose that the League of Democratic Peoples had been in existence in 1990; it need not have intervened to prevent one non-member (Iraq) from attacking another one (Kuwait). Rather its efforts could have been devoted to aiding dissidents in both countries to take power and install democratic government. What a difference in perspective!

I am well aware how far out these ideas may appear at the present time. Mr Bush is too preoccupied with planning his re-election next year, along with his secretary of state, who doubles as campaign manager, to be concerned with "the vision thing" of what American policy should be for the next century. But perhaps people can be found to subscribe to the view that on the eve of a new century it is not too early to formulate a program, not to say an ideal, that could well take the whole century to achieve.

The West is often accused of lacking a faith. Well, here is one that I think is worth taking up, and achievable. Communism has been discredited. Modern communications have made it possible to reach the most remote hamlets of the planet. The conventional wisdom that *"some peoples are not ready for democracy"* is in my opinion highly questionable; even India with its huge population and immense social problems has been able to absorb democratic structures. And those once totalitarian powers, Germany and Japan, have been practicing for 45 years the democracy that was thrust upon them by their Allied occupiers. But even if it turns out to be true in some cases that democracy is unachievable in a given territory, this would not discourage me from trying. That's what faith is all about. We've tried sovereignty and it has failed. There are enough peoples desperately craving for democracy that it should be the primary goal of existing democracies to encourage and assist them, rather than squandering resources and outmoded rhetoric on the preposterously-premised United Nations.

That is why I say the *machin* has struck out. The credo of the future should be that a government which sins against its own people sins against all humanity. Long live the League of Democratic Peoples!

Vol. XIII, N° 3, May 1991

That Was the Month

During most of last year, our firm was involved in a major transaction for an American corporate client. Because of the novelty of many of the issues presented, I often found myself saying to the in-house counsel for our client *"In 29 years of practice here, I have never seen"* such and such. After several months of this, the lawyer asked me, trying to hide his exasperation behind a diplomatic smile: *"For months now you've been talking of your 29 years of practice in Paris; when in heaven will it be 30?"*

Well, on April 11th, last I sent this kind inquirer a fax informing him that the 30th anniversary had finally arrived. Yes, on Tuesday, April 11, 1961, I showed up for my first day of work at Coudert Frères in Paris. My family (including my French wife whose displeasure with New York was the cause of our move) and I had left that city on March 30th, sailing on the now-departed SS United States, then the fastest steamer afloat. We landed in Cherbourg on April 4th and I took a week off to look for a place to live.

At Coudert, Charlie Torem, the senior partner, installed me in a handsome wood-panelled office next to his, and announced that I was to be his "personal assistant." I am pleased to say that Charlie is still going strong. He is one of a handful of lawyers who taught me the most, the others being three partners at Dewey, Ballantine, Bushby, Palmer & Wood, namely, the late Phil Scott, Everett Willis and Charlie MacLean.

Charlie Torem wasted no time in getting me involved in French legal work. Without any preparation I attended a meeting the first afternoon, the subject of which was the construction of a factory in Besançon. During the discussion one of the participants mentioned "TVA" and for a split-second my mind was wondering what the Tennessee Valley Authority had to do with Besançon. Observing my puzzled look, Jacques Knight, the architect responsible for the plans, smiled the kindest smile one can imagine and said, pausing after each word: "*Taxe sur la Valeur Ajoutée*."

As the reader has now surmised, I was totally ignorant of French tax and commercial law, despite a Fulbright year at the law faculty of the University of Strasbourg, and two-and-a-half years in France serving as a US Army Judge Advocate, where my involvement was in criminal and public law. However, with Charlie Torem's sink-or-swim methods I learned a lot of things quickly, being of an age at which I had at least enough experience to ask the right questions.

Dean Griswold of Harvard Law School used to tell his students in the Federal Taxation course, *"Don't think great thoughts, read the Code."* What he meant was that all your beautiful thinking about what the answer ought to be is of no avail if the Internal Revenue Code says otherwise. So the place to start is the Code. Curiously I found myself quoting Griswold often during my early days at Coudert, for when I would ask a French lawyer what the law was on a particular subject, I would frequently get generalities, rather than a reference to the Civil Code. Once, when I asked a young lawyer what his authority was for the answer he had just given me, he replied (so help me God): *"Sir, I am a doctor of laws!"*

April 1961 was a fateful month in other respects. A day after I started working, Yuri Gagarin made history by becoming the first man in space. John Kennedy, who had been inaugurated only a few months earlier, responded to this challenge by promising an American on the moon before the end of the decade.

And later in the month, dramatic events occurred in Algeria, where the French generals took power and threatened de Gaulle's régime. My family had just moved into a rented house in the southern suburb of

Villeneuve-le-Roi, close to Orly Airport. During our first weekend there, the Algerian *coup d'état* took place and I read in the newspapers on Monday morning not only that the generals were planning to send paratroops to occupy Paris, but also that Prime Minister Michel Debré, was urging citizens to go to Orly to head off the paratroops! For a brief moment I was panic-stricken; here I had taken my family from the safe precincts of Hartsdale, NY and now paratroopers might land in my garden! As soon as I got to the office that day I expressed my concerns to a young French lawyer, who laughed and said *"Don't worry, it will all be over in a few days."* I was so relieved, I could have kissed him on both cheeks.

That lawyer was right: the generals conceded defeat before the week ended, thanks to the refusal of the French conscripts to support them. To this day, I remain amazed at how sure the lawyer had been of the failure of the generals. His name was John Laughton, and he later became a beloved colleague when I started my own firm. His untimely death five years ago was the subject of my Newsletter of June 1986. For those interested in French history, let me recall that some of the rebellious officers, led by General Salan, refused to give up and started a subversive organization known as OAS which made several attempts to assassinate de Gaulle, and was responsible for numerous bombings in Paris.

Another memorable personal event of April 1961 was my meeting William Saroyan, the Armenian-American writer from Fresno, California. On my first day, I learned from Gil Carter, a young partner, that Saroyan was a client of the firm, and I made him promise to introduce me to the man whose stories, plays and novels made him the "enfant terrible" of the '30s Two days later, Gil phoned me and said, *"There's someone here you want to meet."* I rushed to Gil's office and as soon as I opened the door, there was Bill Saroyan. I blurted out *"My name is Aram, and what's more, my son's name is Aram."* (Just in case you have forgotten, *"My Name is Aram"* was a best-selling collection of short stories about his boyhood in Fresno.) Saroyan's laughter marked the beginning of our friendship, which ended 20 years later when Bill died, at the age of 72. I hope to write some day about my experiences with Saroyan in Paris. When I first met him, he was in the throws of a terrifying gambling streak, having lost at the baccarat tables of The Aviation Club and other private gambling joints in Paris all the money he had come to Paris to earn to pay off his back taxes.

Well, enough reminiscing. I must confess that the approaching 30th anniversary loomed very large in expectancy, but when the day came it seemed just like any other day. The above title, incidentally, is what is left of my plan, had I written this last month, to call the piece *"This is the Month."* And that by way of tribute to my favorite short poem of Milton (John, that is, not Berle) whose first line of iambic pentameter is: *"This is the month, and this the happy morn..."*

Sequel to "le Machin"

I was very touched, and not a little surprised, by the highly favorable reader response to my last Newsletter, which was critical of the accepted standards of international law whose effect is to allow Saddam Hussein to remain in power while his countrymen are slaughtered by the thousands, with United Nations blessings. The only reason for the surprise is that wartime brings out jingoistic juices and does not favor dissenting thoughts. I am pleased to state that the most favorable reactions came from my fellow Americans, which seems to indicate that I have chosen my readers well.

Of course, when I wrote that piece, the Kurdish fiasco had not yet taken place, which merely heightens the grotesque posture of the United Nations and its leading warrior-members who respect the "sovereignty" of Iraq, led by a blood-thirsty dictator and supported by a minority of the population, while the majority are deprived of their right to self-determination, not to mention other fundamental liberties. I am pleased to note that many journalists have now taken up my theme, but not one of them has been willing to state the obvious: that the United Nations cannot represent the hopes of humanity when it places sovereignty over democracy. It is as simple as that. Down with *le Machin*.

First Woman Prime Minister

Enough of this serious stuff. Let's return to the entertaining world of French politics. As everyone knows by now, France has just acquired its first woman Prime Minister, Edith Cresson, one of President

Mitterrand's favorites. She burst onto the political scene in 1975 when, with Mitterrand's help (he had lost the presidential election to Giscard a year earlier), she tried to storm the bastion of Chatellerault, a small town near Poitiers, which was the fief of the centrist Abelin family. She lost the legislative election that time around but came back in 1981 to win the *député* post when her mentor was in the midst of obtaining the presidency.

Cresson (this is her husband's name – she was born Campion) has held various ministerial portfolios over the years, and most recently resigned from Rocard's government last year to "go private," doing public-relations work for the Schneider group (which just made big news by taking over Square D in the United States). To name her Prime Minister, Mitterrand had to evict Michel Rocard from his Matignon residence, and evict he did. Rocard made no bones about the fact that he had not volunteered his resignation.

Contrary to some reports in the American press, the French President does not have the constitutional power to fire the Prime Minister, who may be removed only by the National Assembly. Although de Gaulle, the author of the Constitution, originally planned it this way, he soon changed his mind and initiated the custom of asking his Prime Minister to depart. All succeeding Presidents have followed suit when their party is in power, the only exception being during the "cohabitation" period when the opposition won the legislative election of 1986 and Mitterrand had to name Chirac Prime Minister, someone who obviously would not have resigned at the President's request.

It is common knowledge that Mitterrand and Rocard have cordially detested each other ever since Rocard posed himself as a presidential candidate against the leader of the Socialist Party. I am convinced that a deal was made in 1988, before the presidential elections, whereby Mitterrand agreed to name Rocard Prime Minister in exchange for the latter's withdrawal from the race. Mitterrand lived up to the deal, but that did not oblige him to keep Rocard in place for his full seven-year term.

Rocard is now the leading contender to succeed Mitterrand, but the latter's fair-haired (albeit balding) boy is Laurent Fabius, who is unloved by most of the other leading Socialists, including Pierre Mauroy, head of the party, and Lionel Jospin, the former head, and now Minister of Education.

The "wise men" of the French press, who are always eager to pass judgment on future events, say that Mitterrand chose Mme Cresson precisely because she is not of presidential timber, which permits him to run the show. I am skeptical of such premature judgments. The Prime Minister's office is one that permits any ambitious person to gain wide exposure and build up a power base. I doubt very much that Rocard, for one, will be discounting her threat for the next presidential election, slated for 1995, or earlier if Mitterrand resigns or dies.

Prior to the change in Prime Minister, the main news in France concerned the continuing scandals of political financing. In April, the most famous new face (and a very boyish one at that, capped with curly blond hair) was that of "*le juge Jean-Pierre*" (this being his last name) who burst into the limelight by conducting a Sunday search at the Paris headquarters of a front organization of the Socialist Party, known as "URBA-Technic."

For years, beginning with the Communists, all political parties have used various "consulting" firms as a means of collecting rake-offs when municipal contracts are awarded. The Socialists got into this in a big way some years ago, with URBA and another company called Gracco. Ultimately, the secret got out and various cases have been pending in the courts involving accusations of corruption. To make things more embarrassing for Mitterrand, his campaign treasurer in 1988 was none other than the present Minister of Justice, Henry Nallet, whose name has come up in one of the court cases.

Last year, it will be recalled, political financing was a big issue, particularly since the Socialists had enacted an amnesty law of which most French judges were extremely critical because it removed many cases from their jurisdiction. As recounted in our Newsletter of May1990, the stink over the amnesty law disappeared conveniently when the Carpentras Jewish Cemetery was desecrated, giving the Socialists an excuse to point the finger at the right-winger Jean-Marie Le Pen. A year has gone by and the police investigation into the desecration has led nowhere, a situation which lends credance to Le Pen's accusation that the desecration was organized by those in power, to distract attention from the amnesty law.

Against this background, let us return to the young Judge Thierry Jean-Pierre. He is a *Juge d'Instruction* (generally translated as "examining magistrate"), the French one-man equivalent to a Grand Jury, based in Le Mans. While handling a case, he began to suspect the involvement of URBA, so he decided to go to Paris and search URBA's premises for incriminating documents. Feeling that this politically-sensitive case might lead to obstacles, he decided to conduct the search on a Sunday afternoon, an action which is highly unusual, but not *per se* illegal. Before he could cart off his five boxes of documents, word reached him that the case had been taken out of his hands by his superiors, with the approval of the Minister of Justice.

As a result, the case became front-page news. The Minister of Justice and his delegate Georges Kiejman, a former barrister who is very close to the Mitterrand family, issued statements attacking the judge for alleged violation of accepted procedures. Kiejman went so far as to call Jean-Pierre's deed a "judicial burglary." Unfortunately for the two Ministers, the Court of Appeal of Angers sustained the validity of Jean-Pierre's actions, even though it could do nothing to prevent the case from being turned over to another judge. The latest word is that the new judge has accomplished nothing since he received the case, as he is waiting for various police reports.

All this was front-page news for weeks, with many opposition politicians calling for the resignation of Henri Nallet, the Justice Minister. Others brought up for the hundredth time the common criticism that the French judiciary is not really independent, and something must be done about it. It is true, as I have often written, that in the homeland of Montesquieu, the notion of separation of powers is honored more in history courses than in current practice. The legislative function is essentially subservient to the executive, and as no law prevents civil servants from running for office, while maintaining their status even if elected, a great number of *députés* to the National Assembly are *fonctionnaires.*

As to the judiciary, they are also civil servants, rated and promoted by the Ministry of Justice. To become a judge in France one goes to a special school in Bordeaux called Ecole Nationale de la Magistrature. Thus, at age 26 or so, one can become a sitting judge or a *Juge d'Instruction,* in a small provincial city without any prior legal experience! What I find particularly appalling is that the so-called *magistrature* includes the prosecutorial function. Yes, the prosecutors, known as *procureurs*, are also considered magistrates; thus the career of a graduate of the Bordeaux school can include alternating periods of serving as judge or prosecutor.

If this isn't bad enough, the young judge or prosecutor is rated like any civil servant and if he makes too many waves he is likely to be buried forever in that provincial city. The *magistrats* who get good ratings ultimately work themselves up to Paris, where they get appointed either to the Ministry of Justice or to high judicial or prosecutorial functions. As a foreign observer, I consider that the melding of judicial and prosecutorial careers under the tutelage of the Ministry of Justice is a terrible system, but who am I to know better than Napoleon?

When I was an officer in the US Army Judge Advocate General's Corps one of my missions was to observe French criminal trials of American soldiers under the NATO Status of Forces Agreement. At my first trial, I was shocked to discover that the prosecutor sat high on a bench next to the judges, while the accused and his lawyer sat below with the ordinary people. Some 35 years later I still find it shocking that in a country which asserts that the accused is presumed innocent, the prosecutor is invested with the trappings of a judge.

While I am at it, let me recount another custom which shocked me 35 years ago: when the criminal trial starts, the first thing the presiding judge does is call the accused and ask him? *"Do you acknowledge the facts?" ("Est-ce que vous reconnaissez les faits?")* I never could understand how, if the accused is presumed innocent, the accusations against him become facts before the trial starts. In 35 years no French lawyer has ever given me a satisfactory answer, assuming that you exclude the response that it was that way under Louis XIV as such an answer!

To return to the Judge whose last name is Jean-Pierre, it is a safe guess that as long as the Socialists are in power he will remain in Le Mans unless he prefers a nice harmless city like Tarascon in which to vegetate. Now, guess what has taken Mr. Jean-Pierre off the front pages? Yes, it is the naming of a new Prime Minister. And guess who is still Justice Minister. You're right. It is Henri Nallet.

Ah, la belle France. Plus ça change, plus c'est la même chose.

Vol. XIII, N° 4, August, 1991

Report on Armenia

Earlier this year, I was invited to visit what we can still call Soviet Armenia, in order to give advice on the new constitution which is being prepared. Thus, for the first time in my life I touched Armenian soil in March 1991, flying on the only direct flight to Erevan available outside the USSR, that which leaves Paris every Thursday evening and returns the following Thursday.

As a preamble, let me admit that while I have always held objectivity to be an illusion – were I to write about Hamlet, the reader would learn more about Kevorkian than about that unhappy Prince, or his author – this becomes much more apparent when the subject is the country of my ancestors. Although I was born in Philadelphia my childhood was seeped in Armenia, as my father was the publisher of an Armenian weekly newspaper, which was his whole life. It was like being the son of a rabbi. It becomes important to add that my father's whole family – along with the entire Armenian population of Chunkoush, an Anatolian mountain town lying near the source of the Euphrates – was massacred by the Turkish army in April 1915. Were it not for the fact that Karnig Kevorkian, aged 16, escaped from Turkey in 1912 and made his way to Ellis Island, a saga not unlike that described in Kazan's memorable film, "*America, America*," there would be no Kevorkians from Chunkoush alive today. My mother's family was more fortunate; living in the coastal city of Smyrna, they were able to escape to Marseilles before the Turks eliminated the Greek and Armenian populations of that city in 1922.

If I give these details, it is to explain that Soviet Armenia is not exactly the homeland of my ancestors, since they came from the part of Armenia which had been conquered centuries ago by the Turks, and in which virtually no Armenians have survived. Indeed it is ironic that the recent Kurdish refugees have been treading in reverse direction those very mountains which were once the homeland of the Armenians. I call them "the reusable mountains," for the snow and the rain remove the bloodstains of prior generations, and when flight is necessary, the mountains come in handy, even if only the strong and sturdy survive.

Thus, the only present territory which can be called Armenia is that which had been occupied by Tsarist Russia and which, after a brief period of independence from 1918 to 1920, became one of the 15 so-called republics of the USSR. It is the smallest of the Soviet republics, occupying a space comparable with that of Belgium, most of which is mountainous, and having a population of some 3.5-million, virtually all of whom are Armenians. Thus, unlike its neighbor Georgia, or the Baltic countries, Armenia has no significant minority to contend with. This advantage is offset by the fact that Armenia is landlocked, with no direct access to any sea. To the north, Georgia fronts the Black Sea, to the east, Azerbaijan lies on the Caspian, to the west there is Turkey, and to the south, Iran.

This geographic situation is hardly enviable, when one considers that the Armenians have the dubious distinction of being the first Christian nation (the Armenian king Drtad adopted that religion in the year 301), and their neighbors are mainly Moslems, a situation which accounted for countless pogroms and massacres in the past. Indeed, for some 70 years the Armenian Diaspora, concentrated in a handful of countries – the United States, France, Argentina, Lebanon and Iran – has been schizophrenic over Soviet Armenia. While the slogan "Better Dead than Red" makes for good rhetoric on the bumper sticker of a middle-western farmer who never has had to make the choice, it was difficult for most Armenians in the West not to feel that their compatriots were better off alive under communism than dead in Turkey. Of course, Armenians, like

everyone else in the West, were targets for Soviet propaganda about the "workers' paradise." But as the facts on Stalinism emerged, few of us had any illusions that Soviet Armenia was spared the tribulations of its sister republics. Nevertheless, one has to see the system first-hand to grasp its dreadful significance. When my father first visited Erevan in 1965, he was so embarrassed by what he experienced that he was reluctant to talk about it, even with me. His fellow Armenians had become hustlers; everyone was proposing a deal of some kind; the "workers' paradise" had become a vast black market where no one worked except on his own hustle. Later, when I read Hendrik Smith's *"The Russians"* I understood why the Soviet people did not revolt. They were too busy standing in line to buy goods or evading the ridiculous laws which made normal economic activity, such as buying a used car, a crime.

Economically, this is basically the Armenia I found in March 1991 for, despite the election, the prior year, of a Parliament which is not dominated by the Communist Party, Armenia is still part of the Soviet Union, and the local government is not master of the situation. To get a visa, one has to apply to the Soviet Consulate; the airplane belongs to Aeroflot, the customs officials are under Soviet control, the Red Army stamps the passports, and of course, has bases in the country. Worse, Armenian factories are dependent on the Soviets for raw materials, for fuel, and for orders, since the central-planning system gave no responsibility to the plant manager for getting supplies or finding customers. Let me add that Erevan (sometimes spelled Yerevan) was one of the most polluted cities in the world, until the new government closed a tire factory (with dire economic consequences) that spewed untreated chemical waste into the air and helped obscure the view of Mount Ararat, the biblical mountain where Noah's Ark landed, now "owned" by Turkey.

Outside Armenia, little is understood about its quest for independence, and this small nation is often brushed off by inhabitants of the greater powers as being on a "nationalistic" binge. A Frenchman or an Englishman finds it only natural that his country be sovereign and independent. He does not consider himself a nationalist merely because his country is free of another's yoke. But if an Armenian, a Georgian, an Estonian or, now, a Croatian, wants independence for his people, he becomes a narrow-minded "nationalist." This is part of the double standard which the more fortunate nations have adopted, akin to that which I commented on recently with regard to the Arabs, who have "masses" while other countries have "people." So too, Croatia has "nationalists" while the United States has "citizens."

However, I must confess that until I visited Armenia I unthinkingly held the view that the country had to remain federated with Russia. But it took only a few conversations with the leaders of the country, including President Levon ter Petrossian, to become converted to the cause of independence. I invoke this analogy: Armenia is like a mouse clinging to the back of a drowning elephant; if it keeps clinging it is sure to drown but if it tries to swim for itself the mouse has some hope of survival. Inevitably, then, understanding Armenia's options requires comprehension of the complete mess in which the Soviet economic and political system finds itself. For many people in the West, this mess is obscured by the glamour surrounding President Gorbachev, the progress made in disarmament treaties and the liberation of the Eastern-bloc countries. But anyone observing the Soviet Union in depth becomes quickly aware of the quasi-total bankruptcy of the economic system, the abysmal absence of legal institutions which could furnish a framework for effective reform, and the infection of people's minds with what I call the "non-work ethic."

It is meager consolation for anyone who suffers under this system to know that East Germany is now consolidated with West Germany. The present Soviet leaders, as distinguished from Russian leaders like Yeltsin, have steadfastly resisted fundamental reforms. While giving lip-service to "market economy," Gorbachev has yet to come out for private property and free enterprise; he has squelched ambitious reforms like the 500-day plan of Shatalin, proposed last year. The Armenian leaders, who get their information first-hand, are well aware that Gorbachev represents centralism not reform. That is why the Armenian mouse cannot cling to the Soviet elephant.

Having declared its intention to seek independence for Armenia, the non-Communist parliament elected last year has scheduled a referendum on this subject for September 21st. The Soviet Constitution permits secession in accordance with a time-table that could take five years. Unlike the other republics (Georgia, Moldavia and the Baltics) which have claimed the right to immediate independence, the Armenians are saying *"We'll do it by the book."* Instead of appreciating this adherence to legality, Gorbachev has been putting pressure on Armenia, in particular by siding with Azerbaijan on the issue of Karabagh, the enclave of

Armenians which Stalin placed within the Azeri borders. In addition, basic commodities controlled by the Soviets, such as milk and gasoline, are quite scarce, although it is hard to determine whether this is punishment (as many Armenians claim) or simply due to the breakdown of the Soviet economy.

The government named last year, led by Vasken Manoogian, Prime Minister, and Hrant Bagratian, Deputy Prime Minister and Minister of Economy, wasted little time in attempting to institute basic economic reforms. While Gorbachev continues toying with his economists, the Armenians in March of this year actually privatized farmlands, selling (on favorable terms) to each peasant who wanted it a basic plot of about one hectare. This plan happened to go into effect during the week of my first visit and, when I returned in June, I was elated to learn that it had been highly successful. Whereas in March some officials expressed concern that the peasants had been demotivated by 70 years of receiving a salary without any obligation to produce anything, it turned out that most families were delighted to own their own plot and were working night and day to make their soil productive.

Following this success, Bagratian's team of young reformers started selling off state-owned shops. The first auction was hugely successful, the prices exceeding everyone's expectations. Bagratian told me in June that the second auction was less successful, because the bidders had become "wise" and had got together to rig the bids. I laughed and told Bagratian that this is what one has to expect in a free economy; that is why we have antitrust laws in most western countries!

This illustration points out the difficulty of converting from a communist system to a "free" one. As President ter Petrossian pointed out to me, the Soviet system had a facade of political institutions and legalism, but behind it the reality was that the Communist Party ran everything: factories, shops, courts, whatever. When I stressed to him the importance of a strong judiciary, ter Petrossian smiled wanly and said: *"Mr. Kevorkian, do you realize that we do not have a single honest judge in this country?"* *"What about lawyers?"* I asked. Same answer. Under the old system, "students" could buy their entrance into the law faculty (and some others). As getting in meant getting out with a degree, and then playing the system's game, there was obviously no independent bar. (Those who complain about lawyers in the western world would complain even more – were it allowed – if they lived in a system where lawyers serve the Party rather than the individual.) I discussed with the President the possibility of starting a law school from scratch, one of the many urgent tasks facing the country.

Much of my discussion with ministers and officials involved what I call good-natured preaching by me. Expectations are so high with respect to the move to a free economy that I felt obliged to repeat often that crooks abound in a free society. Indeed, I believe that my only contribution to political thought is the remark that if, as P.T. Barnum is credited with saying, *"A sucker is born every minute,"* then a crook is born every hour. In my preaching, I stressed that a principal role of the state in a free economy is to be the policeman and the judge, that is, to protect the suckers from the crooks. It is not easy to look eager drafters of new liberal legislation in the eye and say: *"You have set forth rules for new enterprises; now you have to deal with all the ways people will try to cheat and to beat the system."* Just as the principal art of computer programming is to anticipate all the errors that the utilizer will make, so the art of legislating must deal with dishonesty and failure. For example, what is the use of encouraging people to set up businesses if you do not anticipate bankruptcy, fraudulent and otherwise, particularly in a country where capital is so scarce? And where are the bankruptcy judges and lawyers to come from?

To the person who was drafting legislation for stock and commodity exchanges, I pointed out the long history of manipulation and swindling which preceded securities legislation in the USA, during the '30s, and the fact that the French waited thirty more years before instituting their SEC in 1967. I did not have the heart to say that despite relatively sophisticated regulation, people like Boesky and Milken still tried to beat the system in the '80s. (Nor was I aware of Salomon Brothers' greedy plan to control the US government bond market). Just as every generation has to discover for itself the basic rules of good and evil, Armenia and the other newly-liberated nations will have to learn that democracy and free enterprise are not miraculous self-healing systems, but rather require "eternal vigilance" if they are to remain viable.

Despite my contacts with high officials, the most illuminating conversation I had in Armenia was with a humble waiter in the restaurant of my hotel, on the eve of my departure in March. The waiter, whom I'll call Mesrop, had been ignoring me during the week, but after I gave him a pack of Marlboros he sat meekly at my table and apologized for the poor service. With a plaintive look, he said (in Armenian): "I'd like you to know my situation. My official salary is only 80 rubles [less than $3 at the black-market rate] a month. As I do not have a car, and live far from the hotel, I have to pay 10 rubles every day for someone to drive me back and forth. As I work 14 days a month, my transportation cost exceeds my salary."

I asked Mesrop how much he needed to live on and to support his family (wife and two sons). He replied: 2000 rubles a month. His wife worked in a shop and earned, officially, 100 rubles, but the manager gave her 200 more on the side. (One can guess that the manager had some deals going!) This added up to 380 rubles, by my count, so I asked Mesrop how he managed to make up the extra 1620 rubles. He rolled his eyes and said, *"I have to lie and cheat."* He went on to explain that he overcharges the customers in the restaurant. He did not have to explain the rest, for just then I saw one of the waitresses leaving for the day, carrying two bulging shopping bags. That week, for example, there had been a delivery of eggs, but none were served to the customers! It was obvious that Mesrop, thin and emaciated, was not eating his share of the merchandise, but selling it on the thriving black market. Mesrop told me how disgusted he was with the system that forced him to lie and cheat. *"I'd like to be able to live honestly,"* he said, *"and I'm willing to work hard."* He had been trying to get permission to emigrate to France where he has a cousin.

The next day, in the airplane carrying me to Paris, I was haunted by this conversation with Mesrop. Here I had spent a week hob-nobbing with the President and other dignitaries, yet the conversation which affected me the most was the one with a waiter who explained his personal economy, revelations which damned the system. In June, I again spoke with Mesrop, still serving, still looking emaciated. He said that his wife no longer worked; she stays home to watch over the sons, who are adolescents. He did not have to spell it out. Having visited the miserable slums which go for public housing in Erevan (one is even called "Bangladesh" by the residents) I could guess at the despair that Mesrop felt at his kids running around with gangs while their parents worked. And he told me that he had a second job, selling shoes. God knows what "deal" is involved there.

If I have dwelled on the case of Mesrop, this is because it brought home all that is despicable in the Soviet system and made me feel sorry not only for the Armenians but also for all the decent people who aspire to honest lives in the Soviet Union. The Turks often destroyed the bodies of Armenians, but when Armenians managed to stay alive, their basic values – religion, family, integrity and hard work – were left intact. Both my parents came to America honest and remained honest all their lives. The Soviet system attacks the mind and soul of individuals by its absurd pretense of improving human nature; its failure to face reality made liars and tyrants of its leaders, and forced ordinary, honest people to become thieves and crooks. This is the unpardonable crime of Communism.

Those of you who persist in considering Armenians, Estonians and Croatians as "nationalists" bent on destroying the "stability" of sovereign nations, would do well to reflect on the case of Mesrop. He is no nationalist, no tribalist. He merely wants to live an honest life and raise his family honorably. Democracy can not guarantee that every man will be honest, but any government worthy of respect can and should guarantee that an honest person can live honestly within its jurisdiction. I can think of no higher function of government than that.

Against this backdrop, I despair when I read some of the "anti-nationalist" statements of Western leaders, such as the obtuse speech of President Bush before the Ukrainian parliament, which doubtless was written or inspired by a State Department flunky. I respect George Bush, whatever his merit as President, because he is a family man who has raised five children. If only he would forget pseudo geopolitics, and remember that hard-working family men like Mesrop represent the hope of this world, he would get on the right track in dealing with the aspirations of small nations which are seeking independence from Communist regimes. Some may find it paradoxical that these peoples want independence at a time when EEC countries have been moving towards federation and have already given up a measure of sovereignty. But the paradox is only superficial, for these countries were democratic already, and their people freely chose whatever degree of union they now have. The Armenians, the Georgians, the Baltic peoples were never given a choice by Lenin and Stalin. Once independent, these peoples might then freely choose to federate or to unite.

First things first; freedom is the right to choose, not to be told what "wiser" heads have chosen for you.

Vol. XIV, N° 2, February 1992

Dr. Habash and Mr. Einstein

L'affaire Habache, as the French call it, brings to mind that perhaps the greatest new insight of the 20th century was the notion of relativity, initiated by Albert Einstein in 1905. I would be at a loss to try to describe the scientific theory accurately and succinctly but the general idea is that events look different depending on where you are when you do the looking. Of course, this insight had occurred to others well before the current century; certainly Montaigne, to name one of my favorites, made the point somewhere in his essays.

All this by way of introduction to the fact that the Habash affair cannot be understood without the realization that one man's terrorist is another man's hero. To drive the point home, can there be any doubt that George Washington looked different in 1777, depending on whether you were looking from Valley Forge or from Windsor Castle? To take another example, French resistance fighters were branded as "terrorists" by the occupying German authorities but given medals by de Gaulle after the war. There would have been no "affair" had not Dr. Habash been perceived differently in Tel-Aviv from Tunis.

While all the papers that I read take it as fact that Habash was (and therefore is) a terrorist, as a lawyer I find it strange that no one points out that he has never been tried, and thus never convicted, of such an offense. The presumption of innocence does not seem to attach to alleged terrorists. Even the French officials who were responsible for allowing him hospitality do not appear to have defended their action on that ground, but rather put forth the humanitarian duty to help a sick person. Thus, Georgina Dufoix, head of the French Red Cross, who lost both that job and the post of adviser to President Mitterrand, defended her action of providing transportation and hospitalization to Habash on the ground that he was gravely ill. It did not help her case that Mrs Habash was later quoted as saying that her husband had merely come to Paris for a check-up!

It was this same Georgina Dufoix who was Minister of Health when the decision was made to let the French government agency which has a monopoly on blood to keep selling the same, even after it learned that the blood was contaminated by the AIDS and hepatitis viruses. When the blood scandal broke out, Mrs Dufoix was interviewed on television and made the gem of a statement that she felt "responsible but not guilty"! Many of us have been pondering that distinction ever since, and the French press has brandished the phrase "*responsable mais non coupable*" as an illustration of the strange mores of the Mitterrand régime.

Of course, the big issue in France has been why lower-ranking officials in the Ministries of Foreign Affairs and the Interior, were made the scapegoats rather than the Ministers themselves. The truth seems to be that Habash and other Palestinian leaders have been secretly receiving health care (some even say "rest and recreation leaves") in France for years. The only thing new is that this visit was not kept secret: someone leaked it to a French television channel, which actually filmed Habash's arrival at Le Bourget airport. One minor official told me that apparently such visits have been occurring "since de Gaulle" and that it may have been the Israelis who leaked the news.

At any rate, when the story hit the front pages, Mr Mitterrand, who had been enjoying an official visit to Oman, professed outrage and forced the resignations not only of Georgina Dufoix, but also of the directors of the cabinets of the Ministers mentioned above, who were identified as having given the clearance for

Habash's arrival. Both Roland Dumas and Philippe Marchand, the respective Ministers, disclaimed actual knowledge of the event, as did Prime Minister Edith Cresson and Mr Mitterrand himself. With impeccable logic, disgruntled former Prime Minister Michel Rocard made the cruel point that if these persons had known of the decision they were now guilty of lying, and if they had not known, this was even worse!

The opposition press stressed the contrast between the French reaction and the British manner of handling such scandals, to wit, the minister accepts responsibility for his subordinate's actions and resigns. Indeed, it now seems clear that the very fact that these visits had become routine explains why the cabinet directors did not bother to inform their bosses of this particular visit. Thus, one can enjoy the relativity of truth: Mr Dumas can honestly swear before a parliamentary committee that he was not aware of this visit. Apparently no one bothered to ask him whether he was aware of prior authorized visits of the same type!

Once the news broke out, the real dilemma for the French government was what to do with Georges Habash, still quietly occupying a room in a Parisian hospital operated by the Red Cross. The *juge d'instruction* (examining magistrate), Jean-Louis Bruguière, who specializes in terrorist cases, felt obliged to place the Palestinian under police custody, which meant simply that a policeman sat outside his room. When the judge tried to question Habash, he was met with a refusal. Then the judge appointed four physicians to examine Habash, but they, too, were denied access. Frustrated but obviously relieved to get rid of a hot potato, the judge quickly came to the conclusion that he had no evidence against the Palestinian and ordered his release from the token custody just described, whereupon the government hustled Habash out of the country. It seems obvious that the haste was due to the concern that the Israelis or another government might request extradition! This would surely have created a major problem for Mr Mitterrand: the Arab world would have been furious if a person given express or implied sanctuary were handed over to a hostile state.

This, of course, is why it was a dangerous game to play in the first place. It is one thing for the Israelis and the Arabs to have divergent views on the virtues of Mr. Habash. It is quite another for one part of the French government to treat him as a deserving guest while another has him on the wanted list of terrorists. France, as I was often told when I first came here in 1953, is a country of nuances. Thus the government feels capable of bifocal vision; the judicial branch can take the view that a given person may be a terrorist, while the diplomatic branch can look on him as a leader of a friendly future state.

Such double vision, or relativity, is feasible when secrecy is maintained. One can safely guess that Mr Mitterrand's anger was not at Habash's visit itself, but at the fact that the news leaked out. Double-dealing is as old as government; the whole trick is not to get caught.

Vol. XIV, N° 4, May 1992

Bad Vichyssoise; Maastricht Rhymes with Ostrich

The French are proud of the cock (should we say the rooster?) as their national mascot, but judging by recent events one might suppose that the ostrich enjoys the favor of a goodly portion of the population. I have in mind two issues which have aroused deep passions – the Touvier case and the Maastricht Treaty – while reminding us that many people have chosen to bury their heads in the sand.

L'affaire Touvier has been lurking beneath the surface for decades but recently emerged on the front pages when a Paris Court of Appeals decided that this Vichy collaborator could not be charged with "crimes against humanity." During the German occupation of France, Touvier was one of the chiefs of the Milice, a dreaded corps of militia who did the Nazis' bidding, often more cruelly than the Germans themselves. After the war, Touvier went into hiding, was tried in absentia and sentenced to death. Captured in 1947 he managed to escape in mysterious circumstances. In more recent times, rumors abounded that Touvier was being hidden by the Church and, sure enough, when he was arrested in 1989, the police found him in a monastery in Nice. By this time the statute of limitations had run out on all common-law crimes and war crimes, and even on the enforcement of his conviction *in absentia*.

Let me comment here that in the United States there is no statute of limitations on murder, and being a fugitive from justice tolls whatever statute there is. Instead of adopting such simple rules, which would have obviated the present problem, the French found a more complicated solution to the problem of time running out on unpunished wartime murderers. The Parliament in 1964 enacted a law declaring that "crimes against humanity," as defined for the Nuremberg trials, could never be barred by the statute of limitations. However, the allied protocol which defined such crimes was not very precise and, of course, in 1945 the problem was not the statute of limitations but rather finding a jurisdictional basis for subjecting war criminals to trial for offenses which were not defined when they committed them.

An examining magistrate brought seven serious charges against Touvier, under the heading of crimes against humanity but the appeals court (called *Chambre d'Accusation*) which reviewed the charges before trial, decided that there was insufficient evidence on six of them, while holding that the seventh – participating in the execution of seven French Jews, where the facts were undeniable – did not constitute a crime against humanity and was thus barred by the statute of limitations.

The outcry against this decision is still going on as I write this Newsletter. Where the ostrich comes to mind is that on reading the decision one discovers that the court has rewritten history. In effect, it whitewashes the Vichy regime, headed by Marshal Pétain and Pierre Laval, by holding that only crimes committed on behalf of a totalitarian regime practising "ideological hegemony" can be considered as being against humanity, and Vichy was not one of those. This strange reasoning would not have held up in the first year of Harvard Law School, at least not in my day.

One of the best and most useful courses I ever took was Agency, taught by the incomparable Warren Seavey. (It seems that Agency is not taught any longer, its principles being thought too easy. I find this regrettable, since there is hardly any subject more important for lawyers than fiduciary duties.) It should have been an easy matter to find that the Milice was really working for the German occupants, acting as their agents, in effect, thus avoiding the tortured analysis of what the Vichy regime stood for.

As one of the few people who have actually read the court's lengthy decision, I have no hesitation in stating that it is appalling. The judges were clearly influenced by Touvier's long *apologia*, in which he defended his participation in the execution of the seven Jews by proudly asserting that the Gestapo wanted to execute 100 Jews in retaliation for the assassination of a French collaborator in Paris, but he managed to convince them to reduce the number to 30, then to seven. In other words: *"I did a good deed: I saved 93 lives."* By this twisted reasoning, one could argue that it was the humanitarian duty of every able-bodied French thug to join the Milice so as to save more Jews from extermination!

Merely to recite Touvier's crime – collaborating with a brutal occupying power and selecting victims for execution solely on the basis of their religion – is to describe an abominable crime against humanity. To reach its decision the eminent judges borrowed from the only French court precedent available: the ruling of the *Cour de Cassation* in the case against Klaus Barbie, the German Gestapo chief in Lyon. Here, the lower court had been faced with the same statute of limitations problem. The highest court, in overruling the dismissal of the charges, held that acts constituting war crimes can also be crimes against humanity if performed *"in the name of a State practising a policy of ideological hegemony."* Applying this phraseology religiously, as though it were the only possible formulation, and as though it could only apply to Vichy since the Milice was formally part of that regime, the Touvier court decided that Vichy had no clear ideology. Thus the Barbie test was not met.

Amazingly, the court devoted less than a full page to the agency issue. Its reasoning is hard to follow, since it seems to say that there was no proof that the Germans ordered the execution, despite Touvier's claim that the Germans wanted to execute 100, then 30, Jews. The court did not even deal with the broader point that the very *raison d'être* of the Milice was to help the Nazis do their dirty work. By the court's reasoning, if the executions had been a "joint venture" between the Germans and the Milice, the Germans would have been guilty of a crime against humanity because they worked for a totalitarian regime having a clear ideology, whereas the French executioners would not be so guilty, since Vichy's ideology was not so clear! But if Touvier was really acting on his own, how is it that he had the power of life and death over human beings whose only crime was to be Jews?

This case presents an interesting question: if to decide whether a crime has been committed, a court has to interpret history, where does the court get its history? No historians testified, and the court cited very few sources. While I have not read the briefs, I doubt very much that the lawyers dealt extensively with the history of Vichy; the practice of presenting what used to be known in the United States as a "Brandeis brief" (that is, providing extensive background facts that illuminate the legal issues) is light years away from France. Nor did the Court mention the fact that the Vichy regime enacted a special law on the "status of Jews" and set up commissions which revoked thousands of naturalizations of Jews. Many historians have protested the decision, stressing the absurdity of three judges, who were too young even to remember the war, deciding what the official history of Vichy is on such a flimsy basis. However, no one has pointed out the absurdity of having a statute of limitations of 10 years for serious capital crimes, and allowing fugitives to wait out whatever statute there is. Without this prescription there would have been no necessity to interpret history; after all, murder is murder.

Fortunately this ruling is subject to review by the highest court, the *Cour de Cassation.* I am confident that the decision will be reversed, provided that Touvier's untimely death does not render the matter moot.

I cannot recall any French court case which has aroused such a level of protest: even President Mitterrand issued a statement to indicate his surprise, and Prime Minister Bérégovoy expressed sympathy with victims of the war, the point being that it is not considered cricket to criticize a court. Two French *avocats* refused to argue a case before the same panel. There have been hundreds of "letters to the editor" on this subject. Of course, some people criticize the criticizers on the ground that 50 years after the war, it is time to heal wounds and "reunify" the nation. While there may be something to be said for this position, I do not buy it. No one really objected to the dismissal of the six counts on the basis of lack of evidence. This is the work of judges. But when judges rewrite history to whitewash an odious regime that was Hitler's accomplice and the perpetrator of unforgivable crimes, this is going too far.

Justice Holmes once stated, *"Hard cases make bad law."* He might have said, "Bad history makes bad law."

In conclusion, let me pay tribute to Touvier's victims by citing their names: L. Glaeser, L. Krzyzkowski, Schlusselman, C. Ben Zimra, S. Prock and E. Zeizig. The seventh was not identified. Let us call him the Unknown Jew. May God rest their souls.

The Maastricht Treaty.

Another raging controversy pits against each other proponents and opponents of the Maastricht Treaty, which is supposed to turn the European Community into a real entity having, among other things, a single currency and real citizens, since nationals of member states will also be considered citizens of the whole. Again, a court decision set off the fireworks: this time it was rendered by the Constitutional Court, presided over by Robert Badinter, the distinguished jurist who was Mitterrand's most effective Minister of Justice. Asked by President Mitterrand to opine, the Court held that the Maastricht Treaty, negotiated last year by the various EC heads of government, could not be ratified without modifying the French Constitution, which it would otherwise violate. Among the infringing provisions the most sensitive one is that which would allow non-French EC citizens to vote in municipal elections, closely followed by that which turns over immigration policy to Brussels.

Where the ostrich comes in is that this decision was so predictable that no one should have been surprised by it. Yet, judging by the reaction of French politicians and the population at large, it is clear that they have all been hiding their heads in the sand for months, just wishing the ratification issue would never come to light. All of a sudden, the decision provoked turmoil in the "political class," as the French call it, with both the Left and Right sharply divided among themselves, not only on the merits of the treaty but also on how the Constitution should be amended.

As to the latter, the problem is that there are two ways: the first by passage of an identical bill by both legislative chambers followed by a three-fifths vote of the members of the chambers united in Congress; the second by referendum. Mitterrand chose the former method, whereupon many politicians and scholars are saying that he should have chosen the latter. The second school has a rather easy time in pointing out that the EC transformation and corresponding loss of French sovereignty are such fundamental issues that only the people can validly decide, considering also that the National Assembly's Socialist majority is hardly representative of current public opinion. While few Socialists are taking that position, some of them are coming out against the Treaty itself, particularly the maverick Jean-Pierre Chevènement, the former Minister of Defense who resigned that position during the Gulf War. The Communists are also opposed on the merits as are the members of the *Front National,* the party of Jean-Marie Le Pen.

More disturbing to many citizens is the fact that the so-called moderate Right is also divided, not only on the methodology of constitutional change but also on the issue of ratification. Members of the leading party, Jacques Chirac's RPR, were quarreling with each other publicly on both issues, the majority being in favor of a referendum and the treaty itself. However, their ally, former President Giscard d'Estaing, who heads the UDF, came out quickly in favor of Mitterrand's proposed parliamentary ratification method. Giscard is eager, almost desperate, to get on with European unity, as he aspires to be the first President of the Community. The mere thought of it is enough to want me to see the whole thing dissolved forthwith!

It seems silly that these supposedly intelligent and experienced politicians should be engaged in public debate on these issues, when they had several months to deliberate among themselves and reach a consensus. After all, a crucial parliamentary election is slated for next year and the two parties have been preaching unity. Instead, their dissensions have been providing glee to Mr Mitterrand, who only a few weeks ago was depressed and jolted by poor election returns and negative opinion polls.

To make matters worse, hardly anyone has read the Treaty itself, whose actual text is as difficult to find as the unexpurgated version of "*Lady Chatterly's Lover*" was in my youth. Not that reading it would add much to the average citizen's understanding, since it is about as far removed from the elegant prose of the *Code Civil* as George Bush's typical speech is from the Gettysburg Address.

The shocking point about the Maastrich Treaty is that fundamental changes are being urged on a French nation which is hardly aware of the contents of the voluminous document.

My own reservations about the European Community were expressed in the Newsletter of February 1990; essentially it is a bureaucratic structure in which major decisions are made without the participation of national legislatures, the European Parliament itself being basically a powerless institution. Even pro-EC politicians acknowledge, euphemistically, that it suffers from a "democratic deficit." The analogy to the United States is completely skewed: the last thing the USA acquired was a bureaucracy, whereas the EC started with bureaucrats and is saving representative government for last!

To illustrate how the system works, let us suppose that a French functionary wants to promote the rule that corporations should have worker representation on the board of directors. Only the French Parliament can enact such a rule. However, if the functionary proposes it to a colleague in Brussels, who persuades the EC Commission to propose it to the Council of Ministers, the latter can adopt a Directive which then becomes binding on the French Parliament! Thus two layers of executive action are sufficient to usurp legislative authority. Put another way, what President Mitterrand cannot impose on France directly, he can do indirectly by sitting in a room with other heads of government. This is worth repeating: at the present time, even before the Maastricht treaty goes into effect, 12 heads of government, all elected to execute laws in their own country, not to make them, become a super legislature which can make laws binding 300-million people! To me this is mind boggling. If one person alone had this power, he would be called a dictator; when 12 have it, they are called a Council of Ministers. A better term would be the "12 Consuls."

If you ask why the French put up with this, you would be requiring me to write a short history of France. Sufficient it is to say that the average citizen has only the vaguest idea how the EC is organized, and until now it has suited most French politicians to keep quiet on this extraordinary usurpation of the legislative function. (I have coined a word for the euphoric ignorance of the average Frenchman on EC matters: Europhoria.) Let me remind my readers that France is governed by functionaries who have managed to efface any semblance of separation of powers. They are so used to this that it was only a matter of time before they decided to run Europe the same way they run France. It is no wonder that men like Chirac, Giscard d'Estaing and Barre, who have spent all their lives on the public payroll, are now joining the Maastricht bandwagon. And it is no accident that a French technocrat, Jacques Delors, is now running the EC Commission. Delors was one of the worst Ministers of Finance that France has produced in 50 years. His tenure, beginning in 1981, was marked by nationalization of leading industrial companies and virtually all banks, and was marred by heavy inflation. This bad record obviously qualified him to head the bureacrats in Brussels, and the fact that he is now leading opinion polls in France as a man worthy of becoming President of France suggests how short are French memories.

The notion that European unity is a desirable end in itself, regardless of the extent to which democracy is ignored, is an outlandish one that would have been music to the ears of Lenin and Stalin. As I pointed out in my Newsletter called "From Lenin to Mitterrand" the latter is the world's leading proof of the notion that you can get away with stupendous concentration of economic power, so long as you do not suppress civil liberties.

The urge of bureaucrats to enhance their own power, and to promote uniformity, is virtually uncontrollable. One opponent of the Maastricht treaty, Philippe de Villiers, a conservative from the Vendée, points out that Brussels wants to regulate the size of eggs that farmers can sell! And they want uniform company laws in all member countries. The United States has survived two hundred years with each state having its own corporate laws. What's wrong with diversity? Everyone knows the famous definition of a camel: a horse designed by a committee. Well, I have a new definition of an octopus: a sardine designed by EC bureaucrats.

If I were a French citizen, I would vote against the Maastricht Treaty. Let me make it clear that I am not opposed to European unity, but I much prefer to the Maastricht monster a true federation, based on the separation of powers, with true legislative powers in a bicameral legislature based on the American model. It matters greatly to me that laws be enacted by elected representatives and not by the executive branch, goaded by a permanent bureaucracy! Short of that I see no reason why the EC can not simply be a free-trade zone.

Some opponents to the treaty stress that instead of seeking to strengthen the present community, priority should be given to enlarging it, in particular by admitting newly-liberated Eastern European nations such as Poland, Czechoslovakia and Hungary. The EC has made a deal with the European Free Trade countries; soon Sweden and Switzerland are likely to become members.

Of course, very few people are facing up to the fundamental obstacle to European unity: to wit, language and culture. Instead of resisting a single currency, Mr Major would have been wise to insist that it be accompanied by a single language; and thus demand adoption of English as the official language of the European Community. That would have been enough to get Monsieur Mitterrand to use the three English words that he probably knows best: wait and see.

At any rate, I propose a new word to describe the future citizens of the European Community: Eurosheep.

Vol. XIV, N° 5, July 1992

Kidnapping Catches the French Eye

Two types of reader reaction to my criticisms of French foibles in these Newsletters recur frequently: the first being *"When are they going to deport you?"* (short answer: my French wife won't let them), the second being *"Are things any better in the United States?"* The latter objection reminds me of the hoary joke about the Soviet Union that was current some 40 years ago: When an American tells a Russian that he likes the Moscow subway except that the trains do not run on time, the Moscovite replies: *"And what about the lynchings in Georgia?"*

This *non sequitur* illustrates my point that if I criticize something in France, that does not mean I am claiming superiority for any other place, including the USA, of which I am proud to be a native-born citizen. Rest assured, dear Reader, that if I were to write a *"Legal Newsletter from New York"* it would be replete with barbs about the things I find objectionable, not the least of which is the political system that produces incredible mediocrities as presidential candidates. When one considers that the original 13 states, with only a few million citizens, generated such giants as Washington, Jefferson, Hamilton and Madison, one wonders why a country of 250 million cannot find leaders capable of writing an English sentence without a battery of speech writers, let alone having some ideas that project more than six days into the future. Is there an American politician capable of reading, let alone writing, the "Federalist Papers," that masterpiece of political thinking that was largely the work of Hamilton and Madison? At one extreme there is a president who cannot keep track of his hyperboles, saying that Saddam Hussein is "worse than Hitler," yet keeping him in power. At another, a candidate who feels it necessary to confess that he once "smoked marijuana but did not inhale." It is only a matter of time when the press will force a candidate to admit that he fooled around with Daisy Dumpling in the back seat but did not penetrate!

Thus, I do not write about the United States only because my subject is France, where I live and work. This being said, I do have an excuse to make an exception to the rule, because a recent decision of the United States Supreme Court got a lot of attention here. I am referring to *United States v. Alvarez*, which held that it was permissible for a Federal court to try a Mexican drug dealer who had been kidnapped in Mexico by United States law-enforcement officials and brought to the United States. This decision was given wide attention in the French press and – rarity that it is – was even mentioned on TV newscasts. The Supreme Court's condonation of lawlessness by a great power which professes to abide by the rule of law is certainly difficult to justify before world opinion, even if other civilized countries have performed similar acts.

This decision rang a particular bell for me. Forty years ago, when I was a student editor of the *Harvard Law Review*, I wrote a section of the annual Note which summarizes the key Supreme Court decisions of the prior term. My part dealt with constitutional law in the criminal area, a subject which then did not much appeal to me, but fortunately my fellow student editor who reviewed (and improved) my draft was none other than my dear friend Gerry Gunther, who was already a learned constitutional scholar and who went on to become a pre-eminent authority on constitutional law, teaching first at Columbia and now at Stanford Law School.

One of the cases I discussed involved a defendant who had been kidnapped in another state by Michigan police and brought to trial in Michigan. A unanimous court held that the State could legally try him despite the illegal manner by which he was brought within its jurisdiction (*Frisbie v. Collins,* 342 US 519

(1952)). I found this decision strange in light of another case decided the same year, in which the court threw out the conviction of a defendant against whom evidence had been forcibly obtained by means of a stomach pump (*Rochin v. California*, 342 US 165 (1952))

This is what I had to say:

"Yet in other situations, uncivilized methods outside the courtroom have vitiated convictions; it is arguable that there should be no constitutional difference between a trial using reliable evidence brutally obtained and a proceeding against a defendant brutally obtained."(66 Harv. L. Rev. 127 [1952]).

It is distressing to note that 40 years later, the Supreme Court has clung to the "old law" that it does not matter how a defendant comes within a court's jurisdiction; once he's there he can be tried. I find it shocking that the Supreme Court, which offers considerable protection to an accused within a given state, can be so indifferent to brutality and illegality committed without the state in order to bring an accused to trial.

This line of decisions stems from the old shibboleth that "jurisdiction is power," *i.e.*, if you have power over a person you have jurisdiction. But, really, is that not another way of saying that "might makes right"? The United States invaded Panama – spending hundreds of million of dollars – to arrest General Noriega and then spent tens of millions of dollars giving him a "fair trial" in Florida. Just as I did 40 years ago, I find it incongruous that a government uses violence against a person in another state in order to give him a fair trial at home.

One of my favorite quotations from Holmes is this: *"We have to choose, and for my part I think it a lesser evil that some criminals should escape than that the government should play an ignoble part."* When we urge such a rule in the international context it is not to do favors to the Mexicans or the Canadians; it is to protect our own liberties. The government should not be above the law. I hope that the Justices of the United States Supreme Court will come to realize that their decision did a great deal of harm to the standing of their country in the world community, not to speak of the injury done to the rule of law.

Blood, Crimes, Socialism

In an earlier issue I referred to the scandal of contaminated blood, which is surely one of the most heinous episodes, not only of the past eleven years of Socialist rule, but also of the 20th century. I refer to it again because the misdemeanor trial of four medical doctors opened in June in Paris. The facts are unbelievable: in 1985 the state-owned blood-transfusion monopoly (yes, blood is too sacred to be peddled by capitalists for profit!) sold its inventory knowing that all the blood was contaminated with the AIDS virus and knowing that the hemophiliacs who were its main customers would die from that disease. Thus far, 256 have succumbed to AIDS and many hundreds more are dying. The only reason for continuing the sale was to get rid of two-million-dollars worth of inventory and thus avoid a financial loss! Various government officials, including the then Minister of Health, Georgina Dufoix, and the then Prime Minister, Laurent Fabius were aware of, and condoned, the commercial decision. I have already referred to Mrs Dufoix's famous phrase: *"I feel responsible but not guilty."*

The physician who headed the agency, Michel Garretta, was given a "golden handshake" last year when he was finally hounded by the press into resigning. He received three million francs (some $ 600,000) plus a Legion of Honor. Unbelievable! His only defense is that the politicians above him "covered" his crime. The whole scandal would have been hushed up but for the alertness of a few victims and their lawyers who discovered the guilty knowledge of the responsible officials. When a criminal complaint was brought, the examining magistrate never called any of the government officials to testify! Moreover she decided that this unforgivable crime constituted only the misdemeanor of selling mislabled goods, not the felony of poisoning, as the victims had alleged. Thus the four defendants face a maximum of only five years in jail for killing 256 innocent victims and condemning many others to a horrendous end.

The French press, as usual, misses a vital point: this case highlights once again the enormous ethical flaw of Socialism, which I demonstrated in my Newsletter called "From Lenin to Mitterrand." When the State owns a business, while at the same time professing to look out for the public interest, it has a conflict of interest. As a result, it acts like the worst of businessmen and neglects its governmental function. This has been proven time and time again during the past years not only in France, but also in monumental fashion in the ex-Soviet Union, which polluted and poisoned millions of human beings in order to maintain industrial production.

To revert to the blood case, had the seller been a private company, its president would have been thrown in jail immediately and the government officials (and the Leftist press) would have waxed eloquently on the evils of capitalism and the profit motive. But here was a government agency which acted like the worst of greedy capitalists: it knowingly sold poisoned blood just to get rid of its inventory.

Another aspect of the case is worth mentioning as it bears on another French flaw: chauvinism. One of the reasons for delaying decisive action in halting the sale of bad blood was that an American company had discovered a method for killing the virus by heating the blood, whereas the Institut Pasteur, the pride of French medical research, was still months away from perfecting such a method. Thus, rather than have recourse to an American manufacturer, the French officials delayed action, fully cognizant that every day that passed would condemn hemophiliacs to a deadly disease. Oh Socialism, oh Chauvinism, what crimes are committed in your names!

In all fairness, I want to say that this type of socialism is not an invention of Mr Mitterrand and the present Socialist Party. They are inheritors of a long tradition of state involvement in business, beginning with Colbert in the 17th century, who got Louis XIV to create royal monopolies in industries which are elsewhere private. De Gaulle was equally guilty of the practice, since he nationalized Renault and various insurance companies after World War II and did nothing to privatize them when he returned to power. Thus France remains devoted to monarchical monopolies, and the average citizen, just like the press and the intellectual elite, are so inured to the notion, that there is no significant movement to reverse the tradition. I have not seen a single article in the press suggesting that selling blood is not the business of the State.

Something's Great in the State of Denmark

I must confess to having experienced great delight when the Danish people, despite the unanimity of their politicians in favor, rejected the Maastricht treaty. In my book, God rewarded the Danish by granting them a most unexpected victory in the European Soccer Cup. Mr Mitterrand took advantage of the Danish vote to call for a referendum in September on the ratification issue. In doing so he again demonstrated that the opposition politicians are babes in the woods. When Mitterrand first raised the issue, he announced that he was electing to resort to parliamentary ratification, as the Constitutions allows, while alluding to the possibility of ultimate recourse to a referendum. He thus laid a visible trap for Messers Giscard d'Estaing, Chirac and cohort, who fell right into it. They could have adopted the stance that only the people can decide and thus abstain from taking a position on the merits of the treaty until Mitterrand agreed to hold a referendum.

Instead, Giscard, Chirac and many of their allies came out in favor of Maastricht when the issue was before the Parliament. Having seen that a majority of politicians on the Right were in favor, Mitterrand then cleverly called for a referendum, hoping that a "yes" majority would enhance his domestic stature which has fallen dramatically in recent months.

Mr Chirac, as usual, realized too late that he had been had. Clearly he wanted to avoid giving Mitterrand an electoral victory; yet how could he reverse himself? After an embarrassed silence he finally announced at a party meeting that he would vote "oui" but allow his supporters to decide according to their conscience. This earned him many catcalls and opened the way for his fellow RPR moguls, Charles Pasqua and Philippe Seguin to initiate a vigorous campaign against the treaty.

While the polls claim that the majority of people are in favor, my hunch is that the "no" vote will be much higher than expected, particularly in light of the large number of discontented citizens, including the farmers, the truckers (who are rebelling against the new point system under which drivers' licenses can be revoked) and the three-million unemployed. If I were Mr Mitterrand, I would be praying that it does not rain in August, for the French will forgive their leaders everything, except bad weather during their vacation!

Vol. XIV, N° 6, September 1992

The Maastricht Elephant

Having been fortunate to attend public school in Philadelphia at a time when children still learned about Aesop's fables (no one in France seems to have heard of him, doubtless because they were taught that La Fontaine invented that literary form), I often think of the one about the seven blind men who each feel a different part of an elephant: the one who touches the tail says it's a snake, the leg-toucher identifies it as a tree trunk, and so on.

The average French citizen is approaching the Maastricht treaty in the same way. In the first place, hardly anyone has read the treaty. In the second, those who have find it incomprehensible: as it consists mainly of amendments to the Rome treaty and other documents, without restating the whole. (It is like reading an Internal Revenue Code Technical Amendments Act.) In the third place, the Maastricht treaty is itself an elephant, containing a number of major innovations each of which should be the subject of informed debate, such as:

- European citizenship for all citizens of member nations;
- the right of such citizens to vote in municipal elections where they reside;
- creation of a single currency, managed by a central bank;
- enlargement of the community's powers to such areas as foreign policy, education, immigration and the environment, so that it is no longer merely an economic community;
- the principle called "subsidiarity" under which the community can deprive member states of the power to legislate in areas of shared jurisdiction.

What I find shameful is the fact that the sponsors of the treaty have sought to shove these tremendous innovations down the throats of 340-million people without having consulted them first or later explaining what they drafted, relying instead on slogans and intimidation to get the treaty ratified. The French government has used taxpayers' money to print posters suggesting that the treaty will save them from Uncle Sam and a future Hitler! The basic position of the government is *"Trust us, we have drafted what is good for you."* And the "opposition" politicians who support the treaty, like Giscard d'Estaing, who would sell his soul to the devil to be elected the first President of Europe, state that rejecting the treaty will "break Europe." No one has explained how not amending the Rome Treaty prevents it from remaining in force! And no one explains why, on the eve of the entry into effect of the single market, it was so urgent to expand the community's jurisdiction without even seeing how that measure works.

As the August break ended, the opinion polls showed that the "No" leaners were actually a majority, with a substantial number of undecided. Then Mr Mitterrand entered the fray by appearing on a three-hour television show, and turning in a remarkable performance in favor of the treaty. Philippe Seguin, the Gaullist *député*, who has been one of the most outspoken opponents of the treaty, debated with the President during the program but unfortunately was too deferential and ineffective. Polls taken after the show indicate that the "yes" vote is again in a majority. Virtually all the so-called "opposition" leaders are in favor of ratification. Many people with whom I have spoken are confused and undecided, but of those who have decided, the majority say they will vote against the treaty.

Based on my discussions and newspaper readings, I would list the reasons why people will vote no as follows:

1) Opposition to Mitterrand and the Socialists. This needs no explanation.

2) Foreigners voting: the idea that non-French citizens can vote in municipal elections appalls many people, the fear being expressed that sooner or later even non-EC citizens, such as Algerians, will be allowed to vote, as has often been urged by Mitterrand.

3) Loss of sovereignty: the transfer of much of France's powers to the community is itself considered a fundamental diminution of the nation's identity.

4) Aversion to bureaucracy: greater numbers of French citizens are becoming aware that the Europe being put forward is a technocratic one, dominated by a permanent and faceless bureaucracy, not subject to any meaningful controls.

5) Undemocratic institutions: similarly, increasing numbers of the French are waking up to the fact that the community violates the basic principles of the separation of powers by concentrating executive and legislative powers in the Commission and Council of Ministers, who can enact laws (called "Directives") binding on each country, whereas the so-called European Parliament has no legislative powers.

Maurice Allais, the French economist and Nobel Prize winner, wrote a series of articles criticizing the treaty, one of the grounds being the lack of separation of powers, which he considers a violation of the French constitution. But in a footnote, he admitted, somewhat sheepishly, that this is not an innovation of the Maastricht treaty but a pre-existing feature of the Rome Treaty, to which few persons paid any attention until recently.

Proponents of the treaty tend to resort to slogans such as *"Europe must be strong in order to stand up to America and Japan," "Maastricht to ensure peace"* or *"We must make progress."* If you ask how a technocratic, centralized Europe will be stronger, whereas a technocratic, centralized Soviet Union has just collapsed, all you get is a blank stare. If you ask, *"Why is centralism progress?"* the answer is again silence or another slogan, like *"We must move ahead."* And if you ask, *"Where was the danger to peace in the Rome Treaty?"* you are suspected of irreverance to irrelevancy.

The slaughter going on in ex-Yugoslavia is often given as another reason for approving the treaty, the idea being that if the community had foreign-policy powers, it somehow might be more effective. But no one has explained to me how uniting 12 cowards in a room will make the assembly less cowardly. After all, the United States have had a "united" foreign-policy for 200 years, but the reaction of President Bush and the State Department to murder in Boznia-Herzegovina is just as cowardly as the separate policies of France, Great Britain and the other spineless states of Europe.

In one discussion I had with an intelligent advocate of the treaty the point was made that Maastricht will help keep Germany in tow, and discourage it from doing its thing in "*Mittel Europa*". A single currency, administered by a central bank, like the Federal Reserve, will, it is thought, prevent the Bundesbank from calling the tune on interest rates and exchange parities, as it is doing now.

It is true that leading French politicians fear, but are reluctant to say too openly, that a rejection of the treaty will encourage Germany to become a lone wolf in Eastern Europe, whereas they think that the technocratic chains that they are so expert in forging will somehow keep Germany in line. While it is impossible to evaluate an argument so imbedded in the future, I am skeptical about the capacity and competence of Brussels bureaucrats in containing German hegemony. It is German industry and a disciplined labor force that have made that country dominant economically.

When the Berlin wall fell so suddenly, Mitterrand deluded himself into thinking that he could put off German unification for decades. Instead Chancellor Kohl accomplished it in months. For years, French policy has been to seek to impose its social and fiscal policies on the rest of Europe, so as to prevent French industry from being at a competitive disadvantage. But this has not stemmed the advance of the Germans. In the next century, I predict that France's main export will be functionaries for Brussels, just as Portugal has been exporting *concierges* and *femmes de ménage*, while the Germans will continue to export chemicals and heavy machinery. Moreover, no one has explained to me how Europe will be able to compete with Asian powerhouses such as Japan, Korea, Taiwan, and someday "Red China," when the French convince the rest of Europe to adopt five weeks of vacation and to close down factories in the month of August, as they do now. If France wants to survive industrially, the best thing it could do is lend Jacques Delors to Asia for five years and promise him a Nobel Prize in Economics if he convinces the Asians to work less, take more vacation and commit 48 percent of their Gross National Product to taxation and social charges. A friend of mind disclosed that he favors the treaty for "none of the above" reasons but rather because of the coming Islamic threat. Only a strong Europe can stem the tide, he feels. To my mind this is wishful thinking, as it confuses centralism with strength.

The principle of "subsidiarity" in the treaty has been cleverly drafted so as to give the impression that what we call in the USA "states' rights" are being preserved: the community will get involved in areas of joint jurisdiction only where it can do a better job than the individual states. But who will decide that? You guessed it: the Commission and ultimately the European Court. When will they ever say that the Commission cannot regulate better than the individual states, particularly when uniformity is seen as an objective? This is like a man holding you up and saying *"You can keep all your money except for the amount I can spend better than you."* And when you have the temerity to ask, *"Who will decide whether you can spend it better?"* the answer is, *"The fellow holding the gun."*

What I find most distressing in the argumentation of those who favor the treaty is their indifference to the undemocratic nature of community institutions. Ultimately they believe that the end – European unity – justifies the means. But Hitler, and Napoleon before him, tried to unify Europe. What democracy is all about is that the means are more important than the end. Democracy is not about ends but about process. In one discussion I had, a proponent of Maastricht admitted to me that he scorned democracy: what do the hoi polloi know about running a state? Philosophically, of course, this is a respectable opinion; Plato held it 2500 years ago when he advocated that philosophers rule the Republic. But in the intervening years we have discovered not a single philosopher capable of ruling the roost without the power going to his head, usually followed by other people losing theirs.

When I asked this person if he favored a single person making laws for 340 million people, he replied, "But they are 12." It gives me small consolation to know that instead of a single *capo*, the Mafia is ruled by a *consiglio* of 12. The eagerness of French presidential hopefuls, like Giscard, Chirac, Balladur, Rocard and Fabius, who are all professional civil servants, to support Maastricht is explained, to my mind, by their aspiration to join this *consiglio.*

How the EC allowed itself to get that way is a fascinating question. In the early days, de Gaulle was opposed to a federation, which would necessarily require a true parliament; he favored l'*Europe des Patries.* The British, too, were opposed to supranationality. As a result, the anti-federalists tolerated the growth of a central bureaucracy in Brussels, led by a Commission made up of appointees, responsible only to a Council of Ministers representing the executive power in each state. Thus, to avoid a democratic federation we got a bureaucracy, just as de Gaulle, to avoid the hegemony of parliament, created the Fifth Republic, dominated by the executive branch. Much as I admired de Gaulle, I believe his aversion to political parties and parliaments has led to nefarious consequences, both in France and in the community.

A true federation like the United States would be based on the separation of powers, with a real legislature and an independent judiciary, while the member states retain significant powers, thus fostering local responsibility. Instead, the monster created in its place has featured a bureaucracy seeking to impose uniformity throughout the community while enhancing its own powers. The irony is that to avoid a democratic federation we have moved closer to a unitary government running the community, and welding executive and legislative powers in the same people. The French model dominates: just as France has become *la République des fonctionnaires* so the European Community is becoming *l'Europe des technocrates.*

Even those proponents who profess to believe in democracy say that we must first put up with technocratic domination and trust them to democratize once unity is achieved. Such a thing is conceivable in theory, but experience teaches us that it is highly unlikely in practice. When did a ruling caste ever voluntarily give up its power? And why should we take the chance? The drafters of the treaty preferred enhancing the already large powers of Brussels bureaucrats to enhancing democracy. In my opinion, Mr Major (I find it increasingly difficult not to call him Mr Minor) played a nefarious role in the process; in exchange for not being bound to participate in the single currency or other features, he subscribed to a treaty which favors centralism over democracy.

One question the French government has not answered is how the Maastricht treaty has managed to stay alive despite the Danish rejection. Under its very terms, it can go into effect only if ratified by all the signatories. As the Danes have already rejected it, why does that not dispose of the matter?

Despite the all-out efforts of the French government and their technocratic henchmen in the so-called opposition, it is still possible that the "No" will prevail in the referendum. And even if a majority vote "Yes", this may be a Pyrrhic victory, for the strength of the criticism directed against the treaty indicates already that there is no consensus of the French population in favor of concentrating more power in Brussels.

The best short argument against the treaty was supplied by a Parisian cab driver to André Frossard, the incisive columnist of *Le Figaro: "They should have asked my opinion before signing the treaty."*

Vol. XIV, N° 7, November 1992

Citizen Arletty

Most of my readers will doubtless be surprised by this title, for the recent passing of the great French actress Arletty, at age 94, is hardly a topic one would expect to find in this Newsletter. Yet it was my good fortune to stumble into the life of Arletty some 22 years ago and, with my wife Eve, to become close to her. Aside from my parents, only one other person can rival her as the most unforgettable character I have ever known – William Saroyan – whom I also met in Paris, in April 1961.

Film buffs need no reminding as to who Arletty was. She starred in several French films which have been recognized as classics, chief among them being *Les Enfants du Paradis*, directed by Marcel Carné, in which she portrayed (the French word *incarnée* is so much more expressive) Garance. Several years ago a French poll placed this film at the top of the 10 best motion pictures of all time. Among her other classics are *Le jour se lève*, with Jean Gabin, another immortal; *Les Visiteurs du Soir*, a haunting film set in a medieval setting (shot in St Paul de Vence); and *Hôtel du Nord*, where her co-star was Louis Jouvet. It is in the last named film that Arletty spoke what is probably the most famous single line in French motion picture history: *"Atmosphère, atmosphère, est-ce que j'ai une gueule d'atmosphère?"* (Atmosphere, do I look like atmosphere?).

Of these pictures the only one I had seen before I met Arletty in 1970 was *Les Enfants du Paradis* and I knew nothing about her life. She was then 72 and virtually blind, having accidentally injured her eyes by placing in them a medicine she mistook for eye drops. She could no longer perform. Her last role had been a minor one in Zanuck's *The Longest Day* (recounting D-Day in Normandy) and prior to that she had appeared in *Le Voyage à Biarritz* with Fernandel.

Our meeting came about by chance. I had become friendly with a French sculptor – Saint-Maur, a pioneer in plastic sculpture, who lived on a boat docked in the Seine at Louveciennes. Visiting him one Sunday morning, I met another visitor, Danielle Bigata, who was earning her living doing instant portraits in oil. Bigata did some portraits of my family and became friendly with my wife. One day she asked Eve to tag along on an afternoon visit to Arletty, to whom she had wangled an introduction, in the hopes of doing a portrait. Arletty took a liking to Eve, and when she revealed that she was trying to get a book of memoirs published but was running into legal complications, my wife told Arletty that her husband was a lawyer and could help. Arletty invited her to come back soon with me. Thus, I visited her apartment located on the third floor of 14 rue Rémusat, in the 16th *arrondissement*, and soon joined *le cercle d'Arletty*. Despite our differences in age and background, we hit it off well and soon we were seeing each other virtually every week for lunch or dinner.

Although Arletty was pessimistic about her chances of getting out of her entanglement with a literary agent who was taking her book nowhere, I managed to free her of the contract and negotiated with the publisher, *La Table Ronde*, who agreed to publish *La Défense*, paying more of an advance than they would have liked. Arletty insisted on my billing her for my services, so I sent her a mock invoice, requesting "One box of Montecristo Number 1," my favorite Havana cigars at the time. (I have, alas, since given up smoking, but still have fond memories of these wonderful stogies.) Arletty sent me not only the cigars but also a handsome wooden cigar case from the best shop in town. When the book came out she dedicated a copy to me with the words, *"Jacky, qui m'a protégée dans la jungle des éditeurs." (Jacky, who protected me in the jungle of publishers.)* In another copy, she called me *le défenseur de la Défense (*"the defender of the Defense"*). La Défense* was an ambiguous title. One might have thought it was an *apologia* for her wartime record (her career was at its height during the German occupation, but she was incarcerated upon the "liberation" because she had had an affair with a German officer) but in reality it referred to her place of birth, in Courbevoie, a suburb west of Paris, where a monument was built to commemorate the defense of Paris during the Franco-Prussian war, and now houses a hideous collection of skyscrapers. Arletty was proud of her modest working-class background and her origins in the Auvergne. Her father died accidentally at an early age, and Arletty, whose real name was Léonie Bathiat, worked as a secretary, then went into modeling, which led her to vaudeville, called *music-hall* in France. Achieving fame during the '20s, she got into movies only during the '30s, and was in her 40s when she appeared in the famous films mentioned above, but her beauty and physique were such that she looked much younger.

In fact, my wife and I marveled at how well preserved she was, even in her 70s and 80s. Her skin was smooth and wrinkle free, despite the fact that she never had a facelift, and her body was still lanky and slim. However, her most extraordinary feature was her mind. I do not have the art to put into words what it was like to be with her. Like Bill Saroyan at his best, she was totally alive all the time. Unlike many celebrities, she could listen as intensely as she could sparkle when she talked. Even though she could hardly see, she gazed intently at the person who was speaking to her. She had a phenomenal memory. I was constantly amazed that she could remember the names of all our seven children and each time we met, demonstrate that she recalled their individual histories. Above all, Arletty loved to laugh, even at herself. During her incarceration, one of her jailers asked her how she felt, and she replied, *"Pas très résistante!" (*"Not very resistant!"*).* Her most famous justification of her wartime romance was *"Mon coeur est français, mais mon cul est international." (*My heart is French but my a.. is international.)

Arletty was constantly inventing *bon mots* and she delighted in those of others, thus bringing out the best in people who were with her. Once, Eve and I accompanied her to the Opera, for the première of "Sud," based on the novel by Julian Green. We had been invited because the décors were designed by André Beaurepaire, a painter whom Arletty had met 30 years earlier, when he was quite young, and who remained a friend to the end. As the music in the first act was mediocre, I whispered in Arletty's ear during the intermission, in French, "It seems that the music will come in the second act!" She giggled with glee and repeated this remark several times.

A lunch or dinner with her was a treat of the first order. As she slept very little, she listened to the radio frequently during the night, and thus was aware of the day's events, big and small, which then became a source of witty, often acerbic remarks, frequently at the expense of politicians.

Arletty often regaled us with anecdotes about her numerous friends, including Sacha Guitry, the actor-playwright, and his father, Lucien Guitry. She related that when Sacha suggested marriage, she said "OK, provided that the Pope presides at the ceremony," a most improbable event in view of his four previous marriages. As to Lucien Guitry, the two stories we never tired of hearing were these: Guitry is among a dozen people invited to lunch by a *nouveau riche*. The table is set with expensive silver and porcelain, and attended by waiters in livery, but all there is to eat is a miserable chicken. Guitry stares at the fowl in disbelief and, when the host asks why he is doing so, he replies, *"I am looking at this chicken and it seems to be saying, 'My God, what a crowd.'" (Mon Dieu, que de monde!).* And when Arletty recounted the story, she moved her arms to imitate beating wings and giggled like a school girl. The other story is the continuation of the first, so to speak: When the host bids the famished Guitry farewell with a polite, *"Mr Guitry, you must come for dinner one day,"* Guitry replies, *"Right away, if you wish!."*

Often, while we were dining and having fun, Arletty, in her inimitable high-pitched voice, would sing some of her old vaudeville hits, including *La Tonkinoise*. She did not eat much, but did enjoy good food. Often she would let Eve choose for her. We always started with champagne, but during the meal Arletty enjoyed a red Bordeaux, preferably a young one. Through Arletty we discovered several restaurants in her *quartier*. Her favorite was *Le George Sand*, located at the corner of that street and rue La Fontaine, and owned by Robert Dorin, who died about 10 years after we first met him. Another restaurant we frequented was the nearby *Le Petit Marguery*, also on rue la Fontaine, then operated by Robert Rayon, who became a friend. In the early days, we dined often at an Italian restaurant, called San Francisco, which is still located on

Avenue de Versailles, but with a different owner. In more recent years, we went almost always to Le Hameau, on the Place de Barcelone, at the foot of rue Rémusat.

By this time, the reader will have understood that Arletty was not one of those fading actresses basking in her former glory or in Shakespeare's words, *"wearing her brave state out of memory."* She had short shrift for those who fawned over her. If someone referred to her famous "*Atmosphère*" line, she would cooly say, *"That was a great line of Henry Jeanson."* If one recalled her Garance, she would say *"Jacques Prévert was a genius."* She constantly gave credit to her directors, *scénaristes* and fellow actors.

During one conversation which turned on nobility, I mentioned to Arletty that I was a Baron, since that is the word for "Mister" in Armenian. Arletty got a big kick out of that, and called me thereafter *Le Baron.* She told me that the only title she coveted was *Citoyenne* (Citizen) so I then started calling her *Citoyenne Arletty.* Whenever I traveled outside France I used to send her a post card, addressing her by that name, and signing *Le Baron.* After Arletty's death, I was very touched to be told by Alain Bourla, a friend who had looked through her affairs, that although she had thrown away countless cards and letters, she had kept my post cards.

Arletty knew very little English, and had not travelled extensively in English-speaking places. She was a true product of French culture. And as she did not have many contacts with Americans, I was an atypical friend for her. But she was very open to learning new expressions in English. I once taught her "Keep Smiling." She loved that, and for many years it was the sign-off whenever we spoke on the phone. I was delighted to note that she used this expression in one of her last published interviews. In return for the little I taught her, Arletty taught me a lot. She was a voracious "reader," in the sense that she imbibed the contents of many books that were read to her by devoted friends. Arletty would often give me books that she had just "read." Thus, I first discovered Jean Orieux's marvelous biography of Voltaire, and later that of Talleyrand, as well as Frederick Grendel's life of Beaumarchais, all of which I would heartily recommend to my readers. Arletty was truly proud of French culture and enamored of the French language.

Through her, more than any other person, I came to appreciate the extraordinary versatility of that language, for she could say the crudest words in one breath, the most expressive in the next, and still be the same person. Her mind was like a kaleidoscope through which the most ordinary objects became beautiful.

My wife and I were among the few friends to be invited to visit Arletty in Belle-Ile, the aptly-named "beautiful island" off Quiberon on the Brittany coast, where she had built a small fisherman's cottage. Despite her poor vision, Arletty insisted on touring the island with us and "showing" us all the sights, indicating places out of memory. When it became difficult for her to travel, she sold the house in 1974 and remained permanently in Paris.

Eve and I were privileged on several occasions to lunch alone with Arletty on her birthday, May 15th. She came also to several firm functions, including our traditional Thanksgiving lunches. On one such occasion, she entertained us by recounting what women of various nationalities say after making love to a stranger:

The German woman*: Now you will scorn me!*
The Russian woman*: You had my body but not my soul.*
The American woman*: What's your name again?*
The French woman*: Where shall we have lunch?*

After a few months of exposure to Arletty I became convinced that she was one of the great treasures of France, an incomparable combination of the ordinary and the sublime. She could speak small talk with my wife one minute and then wax eloquent about Jean de la Fontaine or Guy de Maupassant the next. Wit and humor were her constant companions, despite the dark nights of the soul brought on by her blindness. As we would walk her home after a lovely dinner, she would exclaim, *"On a bien ri!"* (We had good laughs). Because of her I coined the word *rirathérapie* (laugh therapy) and became convinced that her ability to laugh was what kept her alive, despite the hard knocks she had experienced. Arletty never married. She would get irritated when a waiter called her Madame Arletty and would reply firmly but not unkindly, *"Je suis Mademoiselle Arletty."*

I think that it was in 1974 or thereabouts that I was finally able to bring together my two favorite people, Bill Saroyan and Arletty. I did not know what to expect, since neither spoke the other's language, and I had to do the translating. Bill came to 14 rue Rémusat one evening for a drink, but the encounter was not scintillating; each seemed to be intimidated by the other. Bill in particular remained untypically subdued, as if in awe. When he left her apartment, Saroyan told me, *"Aram, did you notice her ankles? They're swollen."* This observation irritated me, because it seemed so trivial, but on reflection I understood that it stemmed from Bill's concern for her health, as swollen ankles were once identified with heart disease. The irony is that Saroyan died well before Arletty, in 1981, at the age of 72, while the great Mademoiselle survived until the age of 94, swollen ankles and all.

To make up for his lack of scintillation at that meeting, it is fitting that I cite one of Saroyan's short plays called *"The People with Light Coming Out of Them."* Arletty was one of those people who exuded light. And for those who knew and loved Arletty, what better epitaph than to recall Nehru's words on the death of Gandhi, *"A light has gone out of our lives."*

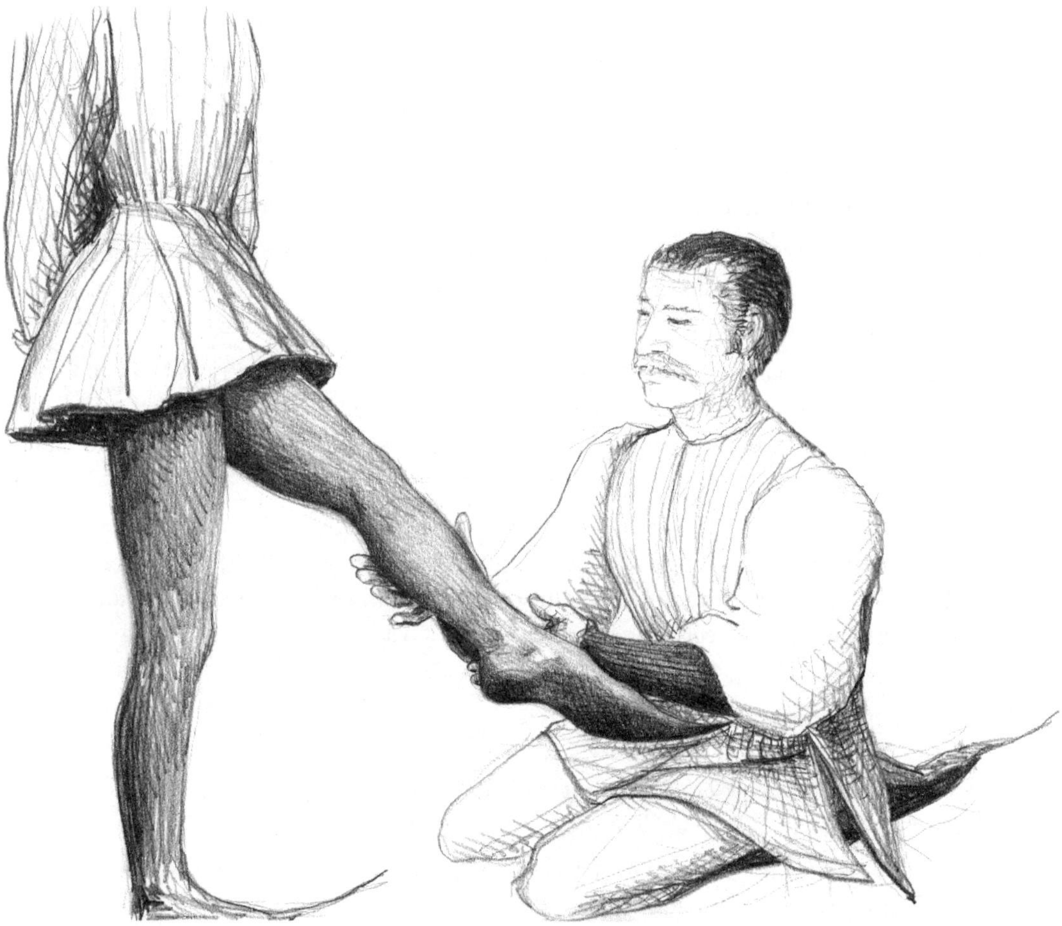

Citizen Arletty meets Saroyan

Vol. XIV, N° 8, December 1992

Yes, Gay, There is a Christmas Issue

This issue would not have been written but for a surprise visit to the office from one of my favorite young couples, Gay and Ulrich Gassmann, who brought me a bottle of Champagne as a Christmas offering. Telling me that she enjoys the Newsletter and saves every issue, Gay then asked me, her face lighting up as though she were asking Santa Claus for a special present, *"Will there be a Christmas issue?"* I was so touched at the expectations contained in her look that I did not have the heart to say "No." I am actually writing this on December 25th, so it is in some sense a Christmas issue, but at any rate, you should be receiving it in time for the Armenian Christmas, which comes on January 6th!

The notion that Christmas still represents hope for some people is itself one that has me pondering, so long it has been since I thought of it that way. This year-end seems a particularly sombre one for the world at large: a distressing economic situation in most of the highly industrialized nations, the EEC in a quandary, the ex-USSR in a mess, Somalia starving, and, worst of all, a horrible blood-bath in Bosnia-Herzegovina while the democracies look the other way. As I am old enough to remember Munich, and a gentleman with an umbrella proclaiming "peace in our time," I have a sickening feeling of *déja vu*. Cowardly incompetent governments seem everywhere ensconced. At least in 1938, there was a Roosevelt in place, a Churchill in the wings, and a de Gaulle on the horizon. Perhaps destiny is preparing comparable leaders for us, but in saying that I am afraid that I cannot muster that hopeful smile that Gay Gassmann flashed at me.

When one witnesses, with the help of daily television, the "ethnic cleansing" perpetrated by the Serbs, I cannot help thinking that in 1915 the world stood by and let the Turkish government cleanse Anatolia (and what is now Syria) of a million-and-a-half Armenians, and in the 1940s let the Nazis do the same to six-million Jews. In 1915, the courageous American ambassador to Turkey, Henry Morgenthau, a Jew himself whose father Lazarus was an immigrant from Germany, did his best to call attention to what was happening, but all he could do was organize relief for the relatively few survivors. I recommend to my readers "Mostly Morgenthaus" a history of the family written by the third Henry, the second being F.D. Roosevelt's outstanding Secretary of the Treasury. A younger brother of the author is Robert Morgenthau, the hard-hitting District Attorney of Manhattan. It is a pleasure to pay tribute to the Morgenthau family which has produced so many working idealists.

I was disgusted to read recently a sophistic argument by a journalist to the effect that what is happening to the Bosnians is not genocide. One should laugh, to avoid weeping, at the realization that semantics is coming to the aid of cowardice in the western world. If we quibble long enough about what constitutes genocide, the Serbs will have gotten rid of all the Moslems in Bosnia. The term "genocide" was not yet coined in 1915. In my youth we referred to the Turkish crimes by the old-fashioned term "the Armenian massacres." "Genocide" came into style only after World War II, and learned scholars have been arguing about what it means ever since. The Turkish government, aided by powerful public-relations firms, claims that what happened to the Armenians (including my paternal grandparents and their three children who stayed in Chunkoush, my father having escaped in 1912) was not only not genocide but, also, in fact never happened. A million-and-a-half Armenians disappeared from hundreds of towns and villages in the Ottoman Empire and now they are being asked to disappear from history.

Some American and British newspapers now refer to the historical facts, which were chronicled by such contemporary figures as Arnold Toynbee and Lord Bryce, as mere "allegations." I would have no objection if only these journalists would tell me what happened to my grandparents' family and the ten thousand other Armenians in their town who left the face of the earth. Were they the first astronauts in history? Did they take off for the moon? I have no desire for vengeance, nor any territorial or monetary claims against Turkey, but to deny what happened to my family is to deny a part of my own identity. Man is memory.

An extraordinary book has just been published in France, called *"The Armenians in the Ottoman Empire on the Eve of the Genocide."* Written by Raymond Kevorkian (no relation), with pictures assembled by Paul Paboudjian, it describes, with a multitude of facts, figures and photographs, the Armenian communities in hundreds of towns and villages throughout Turkey, listing their churches, schools, trades and occupations, as they were in 1915 just before the non-event that led to their slaughter. Fortunately, the authors found thousands of documents, pictures and statistics attesting to the Armenian presence in what was, after all, their homeland for some three-thousand years, starting well before the Turks arrived from Asia.

If I write about the Armenians – a Christian people – it is because my heart now bleeds for the Moslems in Bosnia, who, too, are being asked to die with a minimum of noise and fuss, and will soon be forgotten. In the year 2025, the Serbian government will hire PR firms to convince us that the few Moslems who once were in Yugoslavia actually left of their own free will, after finding the climate too rigorous. My advice to the Moslems is to take a lot of pictures of what remains of their homes, schools, mosques and hospitals. They will need a lot of evidence in the year 2025 to prove that they once existed.

Sooner or later, we realize that all themes are interrelated. A few issues back, I described the Touvier case and the effort of the Paris Court of Appeals to whitewash the Vichy regime by holding that this dreadful Milice official, who participated in the execution of seven Jews, had not committed a "crime against humanity" because, in sum, Vichy lacked a totalitarian credo. Fortunately, as I predicted, the highest French court, the *Cour de Cassation*, reversed this decision but managed to avoid characterizing the Vichy regime, by holding that Touvier had acted for the Nazis. Why the eminent judges in Paris had not seen the agency point that any first-year law student could recognize is a puzzle. Despite their satisfaction with the result, many commentators were disappointed that the *Cour de Cassation* skirted the issue of the Vichy régime's own guilt. Is there not a tendency of all nations to whitewash their past crimes?

Speaking of crimes, let me update another case that I had commented on, *United States v. Alvarez*, where the US Supreme Court upheld the right of American officials to kidnap a Mexican in his own country and bring him to the USA to stand trial for allegedly participating in the murder of an American narcotics agent. I am pleased to report that my criticism of the Supreme Court decision prompted two distinguished constitutional scholars, who happen also to be law-school classmates and dear friends, Norman Dorsen and Gerald Gunther (in alphabetical order), to send me approving letters.

Gerry Gunther, who teaches law at Stanford, is the author of the leading American constitutional-law casebook, and a former law clerk to the illustrious Judge Learned Hand and to Chief Justice Earl Warren. His commitment to constitutional law finds its source in his childhood in Usingen, Germany, when he experienced first-hand what Nazism is all about. He was called a "Jewish swine" by his elementary school teacher, who was incensed that Gerry commanded a better knowledge of the early Teutonic kings than did his "aryan" classmates. Despite this slur, Gerry's father, who thought of himself as a German, decided to leave the country only when the Nazis attacked the local synagogue.

Norman Dorsen is a professor at New York University Law School and recently retired after 20 years of valiant service as Chairman of the American Civil Liberties Union. His tireless efforts to defend and expand civil rights are chronicled in numerous articles and books, as well as in several Supreme Court cases that he has argued. Early in his career, he helped hasten the downfall of Senator Joe McCarthy by representing the Army in the famed hearings which led to the censure of that notorious rabble-rouser. It is a pleasure to salute the accomplishments of these two outstanding scholars and proponents of civil liberties. Each of them is worthy of being named to the United States Supreme Court.

To return to the *Alvarez* case, it is noteworthy that the trial court just acquitted him on the ground that the government had not proved its case. While this indicates that justice works at the trial level, the result still does not excuse the American government's violation of the laws of another country by organizing a kidnapping on Mexican soil. It would appear that in the Supreme Court Alvarez's counsel based his position entirely on the extradition treaty with Mexico, rather than challenging the kidnapping on due process grounds, doubtless because of established precedents that a court has jurisdiction over anyone physically before it, no matter how he got there. I hope that in a future case, these precedents will be squarely challenged and overturned.

Not everyone agrees with my comments on the *Alvarez* case. A younger friend, John Hummer, who is now a leading citizen of Silicon Valley, having retired as a professional basketball player and then obtaining an MBA from Stanford, writes me that the American government should defend its officials abroad by demonstrating to terrorists and criminals everywhere that they are not immune from direct action. This recalls the eternal debate as to whether the end justifies the means. It also, to my mind, raises the question whether the Golden Rule should not apply in international relations. For if Americans assert that they can kidnap Mexicans for trial in the United States, how would they like it if Mexicans kidnapped Americans for trial in Mexico? Or is this too simple a question?

We are not through with trials, for I shall conclude with the contaminated-blood case, which I discussed in the July issue. Dr Garetta, the former head of the government blood-transfusion agency, who issued the order to keep selling blood in inventory containing the AIDS virus, was sentenced to four years in jail. His lawyer then initiated a press campaign claiming that this punishment was unjust, because it was not proved that his client had actually killed anyone, the idea being that the hemophiliacs were already contaminated (with blood sold before the agency knew of the danger) and would have died anyway! In other words, if a man is already dying of arsenic poison why not keep selling him arsenic if he likes the taste? This reminds me of Touvier's argument that he really did a good deed by talking the Nazis into killing only seven Jews rather than the 100 originally slated for execution.

Surprisingly, the jailing of Garetta earned him some sympathy, on the ground that he was taking the rap for higher-ups. This led to an outcry to bring charges against two former Socialist Ministers of Health, including the hapless Georgina Dufoix, who achieved immortality with the now infamous remark: *"I am responsible but not guilty,"* and the then Prime Minister, Laurent Fabius, now head of the Socialist Party. Under a never-used provision of the constitution, these ex-ministers can be tried only by an unwieldy parliamentary process called the "High Court." As the Socialists control the National Assembly, it looked impossible that they be tried, but to everyone's surprise, and to the ex-ministers' dismay, President Mitterrand appeared on television and opined that the High Court should be convened. There has ensued a multi-episode farce within the parliament which it would take pages to describe but which could be entitled *"On Again Off Again On Again."* When both the Senate and the National Assembly voted not to bring charges against Fabius, the Elysée Palace, that is, Mitterrand, intervened behind the scene, and Fabius was forced to put himself in the ridiculous position of pleading with his colleagues to charge him so that he could be cleared of the charges. In other words, his argument was "I am innocent, but please bring baseless charges against me so that I can be properly acquitted!" This is Cartesian logic in its quintessence, and if you do not understand it, that is simply because you have not read enough of the *Discours de la Méthode*. But just to prove that you do not have to be French to be Cartesian, let me recall my favorite episode from the old "Amos and Andy" radio show, which was the hit of the '30s. Andy has rented an office and hired a secretary named Miss Blue. Unfortunately, when he installed a buzzer system, the electrician made a mistake and put the button on Miss Blue's desk and the buzzer on Andy's. The hilarious part came when Andy explained to Amos how the system worked. He would yell out, *"Miss Blue, please buzz me."* And when she buzzed him, Andy would yell again, *"Now will you come in please."*

To return to Fabius, the Parliament obediently complied with his plea, charging him with *"non-assistance to persons in danger,"* a misdemeanor which some lawyers think is already barred by the three-year statute of limitations, since the events occurred in 1985! This farce will continue in 1993, so please do not cancel your subscription to this Newsletter.

As you can see, Gay, there was a Christmas issue after all, thanks to you, even if there is no Santa Claus.

Vol. XV, N° 1, February 1993

Poor and Burning Armenia

During my first dinner with William Saroyan, in April of 1961, which took place in a small restaurant near Pigalle, I discovered what separates a creative genius from an ordinary intelligent being (to wit, me). I told Bill, whom I had met just the week before, how thrilled I had been, as a child in Philadelphia, to read *"My Name is Aram,"* his collection of short stories about his boyhood in Fresno. I mentioned *"The Poor and Burning Arab"* as one of my favorites: a simple but haunting story about an Arab who comes to visit the Armenian family and remains silent for hours at a time. Saroyan looked at me and said in Armenian, *kheghjou-grag*. I couldn't have been more puzzled if he had shouted "Kaiser Wilhelm." He repeated the word. And then, suddenly, it dawned on me. I had heard this word *kheghjou-grag* often as a child; my mother, in particular, used it to describe occasional visitors to our house. From the context, I had deduced that it was somewhat pejorative: applied to a man, it signified a wretch, a loser; in French, one would say, *un pauvre type*. Yet, in all those years, it had never occurred to me to break the word down into its component parts: *kheghj* means "poor" and *grag* means "fire." How obvious! That was Saroyan's genius; he had unleashed the components and turned what was a derogatory word into a haunting description of a suffering man: the poor and burning Arab.

Without doubt, many Armenians would be offended if I used the Armenian word *kheghjou-grag* to describe the present state of the Armenian republic, but Saroyan's transliteration – "poor and burning" – does confer more dignity to the description, while conveying the despair that I feel. Of course, "burning" must be understood figuratively, *i.e.*, wasting away, since the problem is not fire, but, as Robert Frost might have said, ice. As I write this, Armenians are freezing in their unheated homes, subjected to temperatures below zero centigrade. New-born infants, and the elderly, are dying of cold in hospitals. Armenia has no oil, no coal; the once handsome trees of Erevan are denuded of branches. The Azeri blockade, brought on by the conflict over Karabagh, prevents all supplies from Russia from reaching Armenia. Georgia is in a state of anarchy: supplies coming through that country are pilfered or destroyed. Turkey, Armenia's neighbor to the west, has sealed its border, in solidarity with its cousins, the Azeris. Armenia has a border with Iran to the south, represented by a river, without a bridge to speak of. In short, Armenia is an enclave, whose only significant natural resource is its freezing and starving people, three-and-a-half million losers.

How did this happen? That's a good question, but an even better question is, why is the civilized world letting it continue? The Armenians of the Caucasus are an endangered species. If they were seals, bears or whales, thousands of do-gooders, ecologists and conservationists would come to their rescue. Brigitte Bardot would go on television and hold a press conference. And the US Congress would pass a law. But as Armenians are only human beings, they do not benefit from the same consideration given to endangered species of the animal kind.

One would think that the United States might pressure its ally – Turkey – to provide needed heating oil to keep Armenians from freezing. But Mr Clinton has other priorities: he is busy deciding which of his campaign promises to keep. He has already discarded "unimportant" promises – they were not meant to be taken seriously. Now he is choosing among the "important" ones. The Armenian diaspora, located principally in the United States and France, and scattered elsewhere, make up only another three-million people. They are not mobilized because they are neither united nor well-informed. Unlike the Jews, who have two-

noah's ark.

thousand years of diaspora experience, the Armenians have less than a century. They have not established the structures necessary to aid their Caucasian compatriots effectively, whether through lobbying or direct aid. And worst of all, the Armenians in Armenia have a total lack of know-how in communication. It is almost maddening to realize how little they know about subjects we take for granted in the West: letter writing, press releases, public relations, policy statements; basic communication skills are lacking. And they do not know enough to know what questions to ask.

On top of this, Armenians there have a touching quality which is best described by the French word *pudeur*, a kind of modesty and resignation about their suffering which prevents them from screaming for help. Armenians do not like to beg; they do not wear their heart on their sleeve. They die with dignity. I am reminded of my own parents who, in the thick of the depression in America, would rather have died than accept handouts. I can recall my mother speaking in a whisper of a woman who was reputed to have accepted "relief" (that was the word for welfare). My mother uttered the word "relief" as though she were speaking of syphilis. A phrase comes to mind, which I first discovered in Karen and John Hess's remarkable book, *The Taste of America:* "Only the innocent feel guilty." It is a strange phenomenon that Armenians, like victims everywhere, tend to convert their own vulnerability into guilt. Psychologists can perhaps provide an explanation.

A year and half ago, in my "Report on Armenia," I wrote that the Armenian leaders planned a legal secession from the Soviet Union, a process which could have taken five years. But the August 1991 putsch precipitated events: in a matter of weeks the Soviet Union broke up, and Armenia found itself independent. Its leaders, particularly President Levon der Petrossian, who is a philologist by training, were intellectuals with no practical experience in government, and even less in economics.

Like all the republics of the USSR, Armenia was merely a cog in a central machine. To illustrate: a tire factory was located there, but the plant manager did not have to worry about getting raw materials or customers. Moscow sent him rubber and when the tires were manufactured, Moscow told him where to ship them. Now with Russia in chaos, the factory exists, but there is no rubber, no fuel and no customers. Another example: in June 1991, I visited a brand-new semiconductor factory that Moscow had established near Erevan; it cost hundreds of millions of dollars, but the plant is inoperative. Without Moscow, the plant manager can get neither the raw materials nor the customers for the products he is supposed to manufacture. The total dependence of Armenia on what they called "the center" became clear to me when, in all innocence, I asked officials of the Ministry of Economy how workers were paid. The answer: every month a truck would come from Moscow, filled with rubles, and everyone received his salary in cash! I made them repeat this answer twice before I could believe it! Now, the trucks come no more.

As a result of its premature independence, Armenia's economy is a shambles. Central planning meant that all of Armenia's needs were provided for by Moscow and by the local agents of the "center," all beholden to the Communist Party. With the "center" gone, the Party dissolved, and the Russians preoccupied with their own survival, Armenian has been left to fend for itself. There was simply no way that a naturally poor country could go from total dependence to economic viability in so short a time, particularly since it lacked all the other concomitants of a free economy, such as a legal system, a judiciary, lawyers, accountants, banks and the paraphernalia that we take for granted in the Western World.

In retrospect, it is easy to say that this should have been obvious to Armenia's leaders, except that I am tempted to recall the famous phrase: "We need lessons in the obvious." I do tend to fault President der Petrossian for being completely engrossed in political issues, to the detriment of the economy, even while reminding myself that George Bush lost his job because of the same failing! But for Armenia to neglect the economy is a matter of life or death. Politics, one hears, is the art of the possible, and nothing is possible politically if your people are freezing to death.

The process which led to this sorry state began during the communist regime, when der Petrossian and others created the "Karabagh committee" to agitate for return of the enclave to Armenian rule, thus correcting the cynical decision of Stalin, during the '20s, to place the heavily Armenian region under Azeri rule. At a time when the USSR was still a dictatorship, albeit a benign one, the committee reasoned that what Stalin had done could be undone by Gorbachev. While Gorbachev dragged his feet, the Karabagh committee came to power in Armenia in 1990, by winning the first parliamentary election in which the Communists were not the sole candidates. But the August 1991 coup against Gorbachev precipitated, as we have seen, the downfall of the Communist Party, the disintegration of the Soviet Union, and the independence of Armenia, among other republics. Thus, there was no longer a dictator who could, with a stroke of the pen, make Karabagh a part of Armenia.

At this point the story becomes murky: the Armenians in Karabagh declared their independence; the Azeri government refused to recognize this, and the end result was that Karabagh became the scene of murderous fighting between Armenians and Azeris, each village of once peaceful mountaineers witnessing death and destruction. As the Azeris lost terrain, their government instituted a ground blockade which has cut Armenia's principal supply line from Russia and the other once-Soviet republics.

While the official stance of der Petrossian is that Armenia is not involved in the Karabagh war, there is little doubt that he has been giving aid and comfort to the Armenian combattants there. This has not only consumed scarce resources but also rendered impossible the pursuit of the government's principal duty: looking after the interests of a population which, in the best of circumstances, would have had a hard time establishing a free and healthy economy. I believe that it was a terrible mistake for Armenia's government to give priority to the Karabagh issue when it lacked the means to feed and heat its people. One does not sacrifice three-and-a-half million people to fight for political independence of an enclave of two-hundred-thousand compatriots, no matter how bad their state or just their cause.

To make an analogy: de Gaulle, in 1961, had the courage and the vision to end the Algerian civil war, even at the cost of causing a million French people to abandon their homes, shops and farms and return to a homeland that most had never known. I am not saying that Armenians should leave the Karabagh mountains which have been their home for three-thousand years, but I am saying that a nation can fight only the wars that it can afford. If Armenia wants independence it must live in peace with its neighbors.

Few people are aware, not even Armenians, that after World War I, the League of Nations, with President Wilson's blessing, offered to the United States a mandate over the then newly-formed Armenian republic. (I wrote my senior thesis on this subject at the University of Pennsylvania.) However the Senate rejected the mandate in 1919 just as it refused to ratify the Treaty of Versailles. Had the Senate decided otherwise, Armenia might have been spared 70 years of communism, and been trained in the art of self-government. Now the country, nominally independent, is in desperate straits, and so obviously in need of one or more protectors. Israel, with an equal number of inhabitants, receives annually three-billion dollars a year from the United States, as well as a guaranty of security. I don't begrudge Israel that aid, but with one-tenth that amount of money, Armenia could go a long way. Armenia became the first Christian nation in 301 A.D., and now shares with Israel the dubious honor of being a democracy surrounded by hostile Moslem nations.

In the last year of his life, my father astounded me one day, over a lunch table, by musing, "I wonder if we did the right thing to convert to Christianity." When I got over my astonishment I asked, "But what would have been our religion?" He replied, in Armenian, *luys*, that is, "light." Our then-dominant neighbors, the Persians, practiced Zoroastrism and tried hard to force the Armenians to do so as well. If they had succumbed, perhaps the Armenians, like the Persians, would have later become Moslems, and avoided much persecution. But Christianity is not an easy religion to give up, particularly when it promises eternal life.

For having rejected light as a religion some 17 centuries ago, the Armenians of the Caucacus are now living in darkness and dying of the cold. It is a tragic fact of history that the common people everywhere are as much victims of their own improvident leaders as of their enemies. No one expects the whales and the seals to have competent leaders; kind-hearted souls of the human species come to their rescue. Noah's ark landed on Mount Ararat, in the heart of historic Armenia, letting loose a number of animals and a handful of humans.

Is there anyone out there willing to save the endangered species that survived the Flood?

Vol. XV, N° 3, May 1993

A French Tragedy

The May Day suicide of former Prime Minister Pierre Bérégovoy, at the age of 67, created a trauma which brought politics to a standstill for a few days, while temporarily uniting Socialists and the current government in contemplation and mourning. President Mitterrand, however, quickly broke the spell, when in his funeral oration, he blurted out that the "honor of a man had been thrown to the dogs." This accusation, delivered on the steps of the Nevers cathedral, seemed to many to be out of place, and inevitably had the consequence of converting a personal tragedy into a political controversy.

Leaving aside the fact that dog-lovers, more numerous today than Socialists, did not appreciate Mitterrand's metaphor, critics such as Jean d'Ormesson, of *Le Figaro*, wasted no time to point out that a man is more likely to kill himself because of the friends who deserted him than because of his enemies. Indeed, my best reading of the published accounts of Bérégovoy's behavior since he left office as Prime Minister early in April confirms that interpretation.

There can be no doubt that Bérégovoy was stung by the humiliating defeat suffered by his party in the March parliamentary elections, which gave a huge majority to the RPR-UDF coalition, and led to the predictable appointment of Edouard Balladur as Prime Minister. To make matters worse, Bérégovoy was obsessed by the idea that the scandal over the loan he had received in 1986 from the Mitterrand crony, Roger-Patrice Pelat, would continue to pursue him. He feared also that he might be called to testify in the June trial of persons accused of having benefited from inside information in state-owned Pechiney's purchase of Triangle stock in 1988. It will be recalled that Bérégovoy, as the Minister of the Economy, had to approve the transaction and that his chief-of-staff, Alain Boublil, resigned when the scandal broke out and is now one of those facing prosecution. Thus, to explain the suicide, it is not enough to relate what Bérégovoy was obsessed with, any more than to explain a man's death does it suffice to say that he had pneumonia. People with pneumonia generally get cured, just as most defeated and scandal-haunted politicians manage to stay alive. Bérégovoy left no message, no "suicide note," but various newspaper and magazine articles have been piecing together incidents that shed light on his state of mind since he left office. As Bérégovoy was one of the few Socialists "bigwigs" who managed to keep his parliamentary seat, he was often seen at the National Assembly during April, and as he remained Mayor of Nevers – the fiefdom left to him by Mitterrand – he continued to perform official functions in that town situated some 140 miles south-east of Paris. Indeed, on his last day alive, Saturday, May 1st, he presided at various ceremonies in Nevers, including a meeting with union representatives and attendance at a canoe-kayak race on the Loire, the latter barely an hour before he shot himself on the banks of a canal where he liked to stroll. The choice of May 1st to end his life seems quite deliberate, for that is the French Labor Day – chosen in commemoration of the celebrated 1886 Haymarket riots of Chicago – and Bérégovoy was identified with the labor movement throughout his life. Morever, in an interview that he gave not long ago, Bérégovoy proudly noted that all the important events in his life had occurred in May, including the elections of François Mitterrand as President of France in 1981 and 1988.

It appears that Bérégovoy felt distressed over the fact that he had absolutely no contact with Mitterrand since ceasing to be Prime Minister. Not only did the President not invite him for lunch or dinner but also he did not even take his telephone calls! When on Thursday, April 29th, Mitterrand finally spoke with Bérégovoy on the phone, that was because he had been alerted to the depressive state of mind of his former

Prime Minister. Apparently, the two men agreed that they would meet early in May, but I would guess that the tone of the conversation did not assuage Bérégovoy. Various politicians who saw Bérégovoy at the National Assembly noted that he seemed aloof, lonely and distraught. The Pelat loan and concern that he would be blamed by the new government for France's deplorable economic situation were recurrent themes. It now seems obvious that the poor man needed help and therapy. To me, the most poignant incident reported in the press is that of Bérégovoy standing alone and sipping a beer at a bar near the National Assembly. An old Socialist crony, Jean Poperen, passes by and Bérégovoy suggests having a drink together. The crony replies that he has no time; he is to join some friends for a political lunch. Bérégovoy must have told himself: *"A month ago when I was still Prime Minister, no one would have refused to have a drink with me, no matter who was waiting."*

To my mind, the tragedy of Pierre Bérégovoy has its source in sociology rather than politics. He was the son of a Ukrainian immigrant and a poor one at that – what we call "working class." Bérégovoy left school at 16 and became a laborer himself. World War II and the German occupation gave him the opportunity to join the Resistance and acquire some dignity and self-assurance. After the war, he became a white-collar worker in the state-owned gas company, and rose through the ranks to a high administrative position. Early on, he became a union "militant," an activity which led him to politics and to Pierre Mendès-France, who during the '50s and '60s was the darling of the Left, perhaps because he was too principled to obtain office. When Mitterrand, who never let principles get in the way of personal ambition, wrested control of the Socialist Party in the '70s, Bérégovoy joined his bandwagon and, being virtually the only genuine "laborer" in the Party, acceded to responsible positions upon Mitterrand's election as President in 1981. However, it appears that Bérégovoy suffered from never being admitted to Mitterrand's inner circle. Not once was he invited to the President's apartment in rue de Bièvre, or to his country estate at Latché, south of Bordeaux, or to the annual hill-climbing pilgrimage at Solutré. It is said that Mitterrand could not forgive Bérégovoy for having preferred Mendes-France to himself for so long. On top of that, the fact that Bérégovoy was not a brilliant conversationalist made him a unsuitable guest for Mitterrand's frequent forays into Parisian restaurants.

Consequently, I have little doubt that Bérégovoy's fall from office brought home to him that he was, after all, a social misfit in the halls of power. To be an authentic Socialist, you must have either a rich father or a university degree; it helps to have both, like Laurent Fabius, long the fair-haired boy of Mitterrand, because then you wear the right suits and quote the right poets.

A few years ago, when corruption scandals were rocking the Socialist boat, Pierre Joxe, then Minister of the Interior, and one born into the Establishment (his father, Louis Joxe, had been a Gaullist "Baron") came to the defense of his colleague Pierre Bérégovoy, then Minister of the Economy, asserting in parliament: *"Look into his closet, look at his suits, his shirts, his socks."* The implication was that if he were corrupt he would wear fancier clothes! These patronizing words, which were probably "the most unkindest cut of all," must have haunted Bérégovoy in his final month.

I have heard unsympathetic comments to the effect that Bérégovoy, as an experienced politician, should have been made of "sterner stuff," but I feel truly sorry for the man. My faithful readers know of my fondness for the expression: *"Only the innocent feel guilty."* A corollary, which I have expounded, is that *"Only the guilty feel innocent."* I have never heard of a Mafioso committing suicide. So far as I can make out, Bérégovoy was a fundamentally honorable man. For such a person, one blot on the escutcheon does more damage to the psysche than a thousand trangressions to a hardened culprit.

The point of *An American Tragedy* by Theodore Dreiser (who does not seem to be read any more), was that it is very difficult to rise beyond one's original station in life. Pierre Bérégovoy must have seen his own story in such terms: living for many years in a rented apartment in the working class suburb of Clichy, he, finally, at the age of 60, is able to buy a 100-square-meters apartment in the fashionable 16th arrondissement of Paris, but even then must borrow to do so, both from a bank and a crony of his boss. This modest acquisition costs him his reputation and makes him the butt of jokes, because of his implausible claim to have reimbursed part of the loan with rare books and antiquities. Out of power, he finds that he has few friends; the President he served so loyally has no time for him, and to the Socialist Party, he is a superannuated leader. Significantly, after Bérégovoy's burial, his old neighbors in Clichy improvised a memorial service for him, but his new neighbors on rue des Belles-Feuilles ignored his passing.

It is natural to wonder why Pierre Bérégovoy could not have gleaned sufficient comfort from his wife, children and grand-children to avoid total despair. I suspect that he felt that he had failed them; that by bungling the last stage of his career he had lost the right to their sympathy. Thus, far from being a solution to his depression, his family became part of the problem. It is a terrible thing when a man comes to dread life more than he fears death, and when the sight of his loved ones inspires pain rather than joy.

And so, Pierre Bérégovoy chose the day that honors the working man to remind his fellow Socialists that he had not forgotten his place. In the April issue of *L'Idiot International,* I found this striking sentence by Jean-Edern Hallier, a brilliant and controversial French writer: *"La vie ne vaut rien quand on oublie que rien ne vaut la vie." (*"Life is worth nothing when one forgets that nothing is worth more than life.*")* We might compare that to the immortal words that Plato places in Socrates's mouth: "The unexamined life is not worth living."

Perhaps Bérégovoy's final thought was that "The overexamined life is not worth living, either."

Dr Soft and Mr Hard

Those who want to understand what the new government of Edouard Balladur is all about would do well to take note that the only thing that counts in French politics, currently, is the presidential election, slated for May 1995, if Mr Mitterrand lives until then, despite his prostate cancer.

As indicated in my prior Newsletter, Jacques Chirac, who heads the RPR party, identified with Gaullism, clearly has a deal going with Balladur, whereby the latter serves as Prime Minister and does everything to favor the election of the former in 1995. Obviously such a deal has to be based on trust, as well as Chirac's ability to control his party. Cynics are already wagering on the date when Balladur will decide that, after all, the French people need him more than Chirac, but I would not bet against the deal holding up.

The reason is that the two men have been close ever since they served, as young technocrats and fellow *ENArques*, under Georges Pompidou, when he was Prime Minister during the '60s and later President from 1969 to 1974. Pompidou fondly referred to Chirac as "*mon bulldozer*," because he lacked neither energy nor ruthlessness in carrying out the slightest command of his boss. Balladur displayed far different qualities: discretion and self-effacement. Another Pompidou intimate, Marie-France Garaud, is said to have referred to him as "Ballamou," a play on words based on the fact that *dur* means "hard" while *mou* means soft.

When Pompidou died suddenly in April 1974 (after a long illness that had been kept secret) the two close aides took radically different paths: Chirac quickly bolted his party's candidate, Jacques Chaban-Delmas, who had been Pompidou's first Prime Minister, and instead vigorously supported Valéry Giscard d'Estaing, who won the presidency and rewarded Chirac with the prime-ministership. Balladur quietly retired from government and accepted a plush executive position with a private company. It was only in 1986, when the Right gained control of parliament, that the two men reunited officially, Chirac, as Prime Minister, naming Balladur Minister of the Economy. Their "cohabitation" with a hostile President Mitterrand did not operate in Chirac's favor, since Mitterrand defeated him for the presidency in 1988. Hence Chirac's desire to maintain a laid-back posture and put Balladur in the front line, the idea being that the French tend to reward politicians who stay out of the limelight.

Thus far, Balladur has managed to remain very popular, despite his proposal to raise taxes, contrary to his campaign promise, wherein he borrowed a leaf from Bill Clinton's book, to wit, *"Gee whiz, the deficit was worse than I had imagined!"* (It sounds better in Balladur's elegant, if circumlocutious, French.) Considering that unemployment mounts dramatically every month and that the economy is experiencing zero growth, one wonders how raising taxes will solve these problems. Interior Minister Pasqua's get-tough policy on immigration and crime has doubtless enhanced the new government's popularity. Balladur has also disclosed a massive privatization program, which will surely be beneficial to the country, if he can carry it out.

Other than that, do not expect major reforms until 1995, since the game plan is to await Chirac's election before the Right carries out the "massive structural changes" which are being studied by various think-tanks. I repeat this party line with considerable skepticism, and close with two of my favorite quotes: *"Plus ça change plus c'est la même chose" (*"The more it changes the more it's the same thing.*")* and this from Robert Burns: "The best laid schemes o'mice an' men gang aft a-gley."

Vol. XV, N° 4, July 1993

1992 Losses: Vittorio Cassoni and Georges Bret

The contents of this issue were written in January, not long after I learned of the death of Georges Bret, and should have been sent out in February. However, the dramatic situation in Armenia caused me to give preference to "Poor and Burning Armenia." Then in March, the French legislative elections seemed more urgent. Finally, in May the suicide of Pierre Bérégovoy appeared more newsworthy. By this time, I felt somewhat like the farmer in Erskine Caldwell's *God's Little Acre*, who kept shifting the acre on his property that he was going to devote to God. The truth is that the dead can wait to hear their praises sung, *n'est-ce pas*? To others, however, these tributes may seem stale. Our age lives intensely; famous men die, their death is news, and six months later they are forgotten. I am amazed at how few people will take the trouble to put pencil to paper and memorialize those who have marked their lives, even their own parents. Probably the sublimest utilitarian thought ever uttered was that of Jesus of Nazareth: "Judge not, that you be not judged." My own, more modest contribution, is "Forget not, that you be not forgotten."

Some years ago, in an essay written for my own edification, I formulated what I called "the qualitative equation." Taking my cue from two great poets (a category of men possessing the keenest insights – even more than lawyers!), I put together "death is the mother of beauty" (Wallace Stevens) and "beauty is truth" (John Keats), to get "death is the mother of truth." One of these truths, which it took me years of both to realize, is that living is dying, just as dying is living, and a curious paradox of language and existence is that the same event puts an end to both living and dying.

These sardonic thoughts were prompted by the sad news which reached me just after Christmas of the death, due to a brain tumor, of Georges Bret, a client who had become a friend. As it is painful to think about such an untimely end – at age 58 – to a man whom I had last seen vigorous, I might not have written about it, had it not recalled the tragic death, last summer, of another client become friend, also from a brain tumor, Vittorio Cassoni. The death of Vittorio came as such a blow that I did not have the heart to write about it. But, strangely enough, a second blow within the year aroused my determination to memorialize these two outstanding men whose lives were snuffed out prematurely. A similar burden befell me several years ago when I lost two friends within a matter of days: Larry Fleisher and Franc Ricciardi, both Americans, products of the "melting pot," who "made it" in the business world. Vittorio Cassoni and Georges Bret were both Europeans, born in Italy and France, respectively, but who also achieved success in American business.

There seems something particularly cruel in the fact that these men, who were among the most brilliant that I ever encountered, should have proved vulnerable in the very organ that was their distinction. After all, if God should choose to attack me in the liver, an organ which I have sinned against time and again, that would seem only fair, but to vitiate the brain with which I am seeking to find Him would strike me as divinely unjust.

So far as I know, Vittorio and Georges never met each other. Their careers followed different paths but both involved high technology: Vittorio made his mark as an executive at IBM, Olivetti and AT&T, while Georges was, for a Frenchman, a rare entrepreneur who succeeded in a new venture in the United States, having founded Quantel International (now Continuum), manufacturer of laser equipment. But to speak of their achievements in the business world does not convey the qualities and flavors that endeared these men to me. I should like to describe what I know of them.

But first, a slight digression to speak of friendship. This word is too often profaned in the business world, particularly in the United States. It was from the lips of Ike Eisenhower, while President, that I first heard the words "personal friend," a term that made me shudder. Was "personal friend" supposed to distinguish the person from an "impersonal friend?" After a while, I got the point that people were now separating their business "friends" from their real ones. As to the former, anyone you know in the business world who is not an enemy is a friend. I once knew a man who told me that he had squealed about another person to the Internal Revenue Service. When I asked him what the man had done to him to earn this enmity, he said, "He's not an enemy, he's a friend!" As someone once said, "With friends like that, who needs enemies?"

Over the years every lawyer comes to realize (and my wife keeps reminding me!) that being friendly with a client is not the same thing as having a friend. My definition of a friend is that he is, as a first criterion, someone you want to be with, absent any thought of profit or self-interest, and when you are with him, you want to talk about everything but business. The second criterion, much rarer to find, is that he will help you in time of need. I did not have occasion to test the second factor with either Vittorio Cassoni or Georges Bret, but they certainly satisfied the first. The last time I saw Vittorio, in Milano over a delightful lunch, I twitted him gently over the fact that I had not gotten any business from Olivetti. He replied, "Wouldn't you rather have me as a friend than a client?" He was right, of course, and I felt honored by that rhetorical question.

Vittorio Cassoni

I first met Vittorio Cassoni in November 1979, when he made an appointment for a consultation. He came in with another Italian executive of IBM (let's call him "V") based in Paris. They said that an American banker had given them my name, but he had asked to remain anonymous, as he did not want IBM to learn that he had recommended me. Both men, natives of the Emilia-Romagna region of North-Central Italy, had made their entire careers at IBM, rising rapidly to responsible positions while still in their 30s. V was in manufacturing, while Cassoni was assistant to the area manager of Northern Europe. Their careers had been stainless until they were interviewed in Paris by an IBM security official, who was investigating a leak about a new mainframe that had been mentioned in the press by a securities analyst, noted for being an "IBM watcher." The investigator had gotten to V first by checking IBM phone logs and finding the executive had made calls to the Paris brokerage house for which the analyst worked.

The calls were perfectly normal, since V had an account with the brokerage firm, but in the course of his interview V acknowledged knowing the securities analyst, and revealed that Vittorio knew him as well. It turned out that both Italians, who were living bachelor lives in Paris, played tennis with the analyst and occasionally had dinner with him. While both vehemently denied leaking any confidential information, they were called in a few days later by a top executive at IBM Europe and told that as punishment for their association with the analyst, they would be transferred to IBM Italia. It was at this point that the two executives came to see me.

It did not take me long to realize how traumatic this event was for Vittorio and his Italian colleague. Both had reached enviable positions with IBM, a company whose "culture" had become part of their lives – to the point of wearing only white shirts at work – and they knew that accepting a demotion to Italy would leave them permanently under a cloud. The procedure by which they were punished seemed to violate what I later came to call "corporate due process," since they were given no hearing, other than the interview with the investigator, and had no access to the file. Yet their loyalty to IBM was so strong that they could not believe that this punishment could stick. It must be recalled that at this time, when PCs were undreamed of at "Big Blue," IBM was king of the hill in computers. Its hold over mainframes was such that IBM's only paranoia was that word of enhancements and new products might reach competitors, *i.e.,* clone manufacturers who had only a miniscule share of the market. Considering the present troubles of IBM, these were golden days for its management!

After that first meeting, "V & C," as they came to be known in our firm (after a brief period of "Sacco and Vanzetti") became almost daily visitors. They were very popular with our staff as they were congenial and considerate. It was not long before I realized that Cassoni was a potential superstar. He spoke French and English fluently, was smooth, responsive, analytical, decisive and dedicated to his company. He had had a meteoric rise with IBM, having been placed in a special career program for those with outstanding skills. He was such a believer in IBM that he insisted on availing himself of the "open door" policy of that company, by which any employee can appeal any decision to any executive. The two men, with my help, drafted an eloquent petition to the Chairman and CEO of IBM, who delegated an executive in the personnel department (doubtless called Human Resources) to make an investigation. As true believers, V & C entertained the hope that this executive would find in their favor, despite my suspicion that a whitewash was more probable. I turned out to be right. The Chairman sustained the decision, basically on the ground that the two men had no right to have a security analyst as a friend!

This struck me as "guilt by association" and I advised V & C that if they refused the banishment to Italy, this would not be considered a resignation but that IBM would have to terminate them, whereupon they could sue for wrongful termination. It was a dramatic decision for V & C to leave a company to which they were so devoted but, ultimately, upholding their dignity required them to fight IBM. This is what ensued. We brought suit in the French labor court, and even carried the battle to Armonk, taking advantage of a little-known provision of the Federal Rules of Procedure, which allows discovery in connection with a foreign law suit. The case was finally settled, with both men receiving significant indemnities.

In the meantime, Cassoni had written to Carlo di Benedetti, the Chairman of Olivetti, who wasted no time in recognizing a good catch. I was sorry to see Vittorio leave Paris, because we had become very friendly, but I was sure that he would soon rise to the top at Olivetti. Paradoxically, it was somewhat of a cultural shock for this Italian to join Olivetti in Ivrea. Compared with the structured, disciplined environment at IBM, replete with several layers of management, Olivetti represented improvisation and flair, but Vittorio quickly made the adjustment. Before long, he was assigned to New York to head operations in North America. Then de Benedetti "loaned" him to AT&T, with which Olivetti had negotiated an alliance. Cassoni was put in charge of all computer operations at AT&T, the first foreigner ever to hold a position of Senior Vice President at that sacrosanct American institution. He had a palatial office in the fancy tower put up at 56th and Madison, God knows why, since the real head office remained in New Jersey, to which a chauffeur-driven limousine carried him every morning.

After moving to Italy, Vittorio had met and married a lovely Italian woman, Giovanna, who was a gifted research biologist but who given up her career to bear him a son and then follow Vittorio to New York. I visited them once in their elegant rented townhouse in the East 70s. Vittorio seemed at the height of bliss, holding one of the most challenging jobs in all computerdom and living the life of the successful in Manhattan. By this time, the computer world was in the throes of a major evolution whose implications no one in high place seemed to realize. IBM was still king of the hill, having let loose the Personal Computer, which was wildly successful, while apparently not disturbing the mainframe market. Cassoni struggled valiantly to make AT&T a factor in a market which its telephone executives were not equipped to understand.

Before he could complete his assignment, di Benedetti – who was busy pursuing European diversification – called Cassoni back to Italy to head Italian operations. Soon he became Managing Director, the top man at Olivetti. It was then that Vittorio confronted the inexorable forces which wreaked havoc with every major computer manufacturer: the lowly PC, becoming more and more powerful and cheap, thanks to clones made in the Far East, was dethroning minicomputers in the office, with the help of networking. Companies that once seemed solidly entrenched in the office market, such as Wang, DEC and Olivetti, were not able to meet their forecasts. Today we see that IBM itself is on the ropes. All of Cassoni's skills and diligence were to no avail. After two successive loss years at Olivetti, di Benedetti took back the helm, surely a tremendous blow to the pride of a man who had never known failure. In 1992, he accepted the position of Executive Vice President at XEROX Corporation, to head their non-copier operations. He was on the job only a month when he had to return to Milano to be operated on. While I do not know the details, I understand that a fatal brain tumor was discovered and Vittorio died shortly after the operation, having lived only 48 years.

This dry narration of the business career of Vittorio Cassoni simply fails to convey the way he was. He exuded intelligence, warmth, charm, decency, and a love of life, of work, of friendship and of family. To the extent that cancer can be caused by non-physical phenomena, I cannot help but feel that the dramatic downturn in the computer industry hastened his death. Vittorio was not a man to blame others for his troubles but inwardly he must have suffered intensely.

When a life seems so unfinished and death so unjust, I can do no better than to close with these dying words attributed to Sir Walter Raleigh:

Even such is time that takes in trust,
Our youth, our joys, our all we have,

And leaves us but with earth and dust.
But from this grave, this earth, this dust,
My God will raise me up, I trust.

Georges Bret

I first learned of the existence of Georges Bret on reading François de Closet's 1982 best-seller *"Toujours Plus,"* a criticism of the rigidity of French society and, in particular, the corporatism which characterizes so much of economic activity. After citing dozens of illustrations of what is wrong in France, the author showered extraordinary praise on Bret for having bucked the tide of mandarinism by moving from an academic career to entrepeneur status. Indeed, Bret, who studied physics at Harvard and was graduated at the top of his class from the prestigious Ecole Supérieure d'Electricité in Paris, had been the youngest person in French history, at age 30, to hold a professorship of physics, at the University of Paris, but he left that sheltered world to found Quantel S.A., the first French manufacturer of lasers.

I do not recall how he got my name, but Georges consulted me on several occasions when his business began to expand internationally. Then I lost sight of him for a few years, but he came in again in 1988, after having shifted his terrain to Silicon Valley, where he had set up a subsidiary of his French company. He had sold control of the parent company to a French nationalized company, but he ended up forming a consortium to buy its US subsidiary, Quantel International. As one might expect, the former subsidiary, berthed in the heart of high-tech, soon proved more dynamic than its former parent, a situation which ultimately led to litigation when the US company began to compete in the European market.

It was during this period that I got to know Bret better. What struck me the most about him is what Saroyan once described in someone else as "smiling intelligence." Georges was not one of those grim intellectuals who carry their intelligence as a burden. He smiled naturally and found amusement in most situations which involved human foibles. Of course, for me his rarest quality was that he was a Frenchman who had become an entrepreneur and enjoyed it, while losing nothing of his intellectual curiosity. Anyone who knows France is familiar with the type of pseudo businessmen who have moved from the *grandes écoles*, such as Polytechnique and ENA, to high positions in state-owned companies, without ever having to take a risk. These people play with what Brandeis called "other peoples' money." Bret put up his own money, and also borrowed, to found Quantel S.A. Having sold that company, he later sold the American entity, whose name was changed to Continuum, and was involved in another capital-risk venture, called Chromex, in New Mexico when he died.

Unfortunately, distance kept us from seeing each other often. I will cherish the memory of two exquisite evenings with him. Once he came over to my house for a drink, but our conversation was so enjoyable, and he was so gracious, that my French wife conferred on him the extremely rare honor of improvising a dinner. Georges was equally at home with small talk and "big talk." On another occasion, in 1991, I had dinner at his home in Sunnyvale, California, and met his wife Françoise, who is an accomplished pianist. I dabbled with some Bach on the piano and Françoise played some more romantic pieces, with Georges beaming happily. Over dinner we indulged in our favorite subject: why do the French élite insist on remaining Cartesian?

Early in our relationship I had given Georges my essay written in French, "Montaigne et Descartes," where I blast away at the latter's *"Discours de la Méthode,"* and advance the thesis that the former's *"Apologie de Raymond Sebond"* provides a better guide to today's world. The essay was inspired by my discovery that Montaigne was taught as literature in French lycées while Descartes is treated as a philosopher. My conclusion was that these roles should be reversed. Georges got a kick out of the essay, which became a leitmotif for many of our discussions. For me, he exemplified what I call Montaignism: the absence of *a priori* reasoning, a willingness to examine facts, skepticism about dogmas, and above all, humanism. It is no wonder that Georges Bret exiled himself to the United States, for it is very difficult to be an entrepeneur in the field of high technology in France, where so much of industry is controlled by state-owned enterprises, themselves operated by graduates of the *grandes écoles*, steeped in Cartesianism and Colbertism.

Georges Bret demonstrated that true intellect needs no passport and that a keen spirit can travel freely not only from country to country, but also from *academe* to the world of practicalities.

Sadly, France's loss has now become that of the United States. As a Montaignian, I shall miss Georges Bret immensely.

Vol. XV, N° 5, August 1993

Say It Ain't So, Bernard

Baseball lovers, who are, by hypothesis, lovers of history, will identify the source of this title. For the unfortunate others, let me recall that when a beloved baseball star, known as "Shoeless" Joe Jackson, was accused with several other members of the Chicago White Sox of taking bribes to lose the 1919 World Series, a heartbroken young boy accosted him, tears in his eyes, and uttered the immortal plea: *"Say it ain't so, Joe."*

This incident came to mind recently when the most momentous sports scandal in French history erupted over the allegation that an official of the Marseille soccer (*football* in France and most parts of the world) team was accused of bribing three players on the Valenciennes team, just prior to their game of May 20th. The tragic nature of the accusation to French soccer fans stems from the fact that in late May the Marseille team, known as the Olympique, brought ecstasy to France by winning the European Cup in the final against Milan. Not only was this the first time a French soccer team had won the European championship, but also the first time that a French sports club had won any European championship! Having brought "joy to Mudville" (baseball-poetry lovers will get the allusion), the Marseille team became national heroes in a country accustomed to seeing their soccer teams chicken out in finals and semi-finals (*cf.* World Cup, 1986).

Now, to make the scandal juicier, we must introduce the near-mythical character of Bernard Tapie, who heads the Marseille team, while also serving as a member of Parliament (representing a Marseille suburb, of course), and controlling a rapidly-crumbling business empire which briefly encompassed the Adidas company. Tapie has a shady reputation as a businessman; last year he barely squeaked out of criminal charges of cheating a former partner, paying off handsomely for the latter to drop charges. A self-made man, he had a short-lived career as a pop singer, but stumbled on to business, making his mark buying up bankrupt companies during the Socialist era. Good-looking, with a gift of gab, Tapie quickly learned the art of self-promotion via television. But, most of all, he had the flair to realize that when most businessmen are on the Right, there was money to be made by becoming a mascot of the Socialists.

With the French Socialists, who nationalized all the major banks, Tapie found it easy to get loans, particularly from the Crédit Lyonnais, which seems to be the easiest touch in town, judging, among other things, by the billion dollars it inexplicably loaned to Gian-Carlo Paretti to buy MGM. Capitalizing on his public image and the popularity he captured by taking over the Marseille team (and buying up expensive players), Tapie scored big by taking his holding company public, under the modest name of "Bernard Tapie Finance." Virtually all the businesses acquired by Tapie became (or never stopped being) money-losers, including Adidas, but that did not prevent Tapie from remaining the fair-haired boy of President Mitterrand and Prime Minister Bérégovoy, who had the temerity to name him *Ministre de la Ville*. As the French have no sense of conflicts of interest, Tapie kept running his companies and the Marseille team, while holding office as Minister and, since the Socialist defeat, he continues to manage his businesses while a member of Parliament!

With this long introduction of Tapie, let me return to the bribery scandal. When the news broke that three Valenciennes players claimed to have been bribed through a former teammate, Jean-Claude Eydelie, now with Marseille, the latter first denied it. But after the examining magistrate slapped him in jail, his wife went to the judge and confessed her husband's role, whereupon Eydelie acknowledged having done the dirty work at the behest of the general manager of the Marseille club, Jean-Pierre Bernès. Tapie took the initiative to distance himself from the accusation, even though Bernès – his right-hand man – was identified by Eydelie as having provided FF 250,000 in bribe money and promised FF 350,000 more after the game. Bernès steadfastly denied the charges despite being placed in confinement for a couple of weeks.

The daily developments in the case brought into the spotlight the public prosecutor of Valenciennes, who bears the unforgettable name of Montgolfier (the same as that of the two brothers who invented the hot-air balloon in the 18th century). In a country where a Procureur de la République is rarely seen and even more rarely heard, Montgolfier's daily briefings of the press seemed extraordinary, not only because they happened but also by the extreme frankness of his personal comments. Doubtless many lawyers were aghast when Montgolfier blurted out that Eydelie, the Marseille player, had been kept in jail as a form of pressure for him to confess. The Minister of Justice, Pierre Méhaignherie, summoned Montgolfier for a dressing-down, and the prosecutor promised to make future announcements only in writing. Another exceptional twist to the case emerged when President Mitterrand used his Bastille Day television interview to express support for Tapie.

Indeed, the heat was now concentrating on Tapie. If the accusation were true, everyone wondered how Tapie could escape incrimination, since it is well-known that he runs the team with an iron hand, and could hardly have been unaware that FF 250,000 of the team's cash had been expended. But while the examining magistrate steered clear of Tapie on the bribery itself, the businessman became a suspect himself when a soccer coach, named Boro Primorac, alleged that Tapie had asked him to take the rap on the bribery charge in exchange for favors. Primorac told the judge that he had lunched on June 17th at Fouquet's with an emissary of Tapie, who then took him to Tapie's nearby office on avenue de Friedland, where Tapie briefly spoke with him. In what may turn out to be the biggest tactical blunder of his career, Tapie chose to deny even having seen Primorac that day. It thus became a matter of one man's word against another's.

After a few weeks of this standoff, a dramatic alibi witness was produced by Tapie: none other than Jacques Mellick, a fellow-member of Parliament, former Minister and now assistant mayor of Béthune, a city north of Paris, where one of Tapie's companies is located. Mellick asserted on July 31st that he had visited Tapie's office at 2:30 PM on June 17th, about the same time that Primorac alleged to have been with Tapie. But Mellick's account did not ring particularly true to the examining magistrate, who dispatched several police investigators to Béthune to check with municipal employees as to Mellick's schedule. Mellick's story seemed to be shattered when the judge unearthed a photo of the politician, surrounded by Béthune employees, published in the municipal bulletin, with a caption saying that the picture was taken at 2 PM! As it is impossible to drive the 213 kilometers from Béthune to Paris in less than 90 minutes, Mellick had some explaining to do, but the glib politician asserted that the caption was wrong and that the photo had been taken around 5 PM. The judge, not to be outdone, then discovered a gas station in Béthune which had filled the tank of Mellick's car at 1:20 PM, thus again exploding Mellick's version. The judge also checked with the toll booth on the super highway and ascertained that Mellick's payment card had not been used on June 17th, whereas it had been on the 16th and the 18th!

As I write this, the investigation is continuing, and Mellick is visibly on the defensive, and Tapie with him. All of this detective work may seem overdone on a relatively minor crime, but Tapie is a target larger than life. While most people I speak with consider him despicable, Tapie does have a following in France among the young and has managed to be elected to Parliament twice. After flirting with the Socialists, he took over a minor party last year, known as the *Radicaux de Gauche,* and some commentators expected him to make a try at the mayoralty of Marseille and, why not, the presidency in 1995. His motto seems to be: *de l'audace, toujours de l'audace*. There have been suggestions in the press that the Valenciennes bribery case is but the tip of an iceberg of corruption in the soccer world. The most puzzling aspect is why a team as strong as Marseille, already the league leader, needed to bribe the weakest team in France? The answer may be that bribery is how they got to be league leader in the first place, and the Marseille club management did not want to take any chances about staying in the lead.

But, aside from the sports interest, this case focuses on some of the flaws in the French penal system, to which I will now turn. For scholars, the standard one-word description of the French system is to call it "inquisitorial" as distinguished from the American and British system which is called "adversarial." Curiously though, in more than three decades, I have never heard a French jurist call his own system "inquisitorial," whereas American lawyers commonly refer to their own as "adversarial." Doubtless, the explanation for the French silence is that *le grand Inquisiteur* left an unsavory reputation which centuries have not effaced.

I had a wonderful exposure to comparative criminal law, while privileged to serve in France as an officer in the US Army's Judge Advocate General's Corps, from 1955 to 1957. The United States Senate, in ratifying the NATO Status of Forces Agreement, which permits host countries to try American military for off-duty crimes, had required the attendance of an American officer to report on the fairness of the trial. Thus, one day I might defend a soldier charged with rape before an American general court-martial and the next day attend, as an official observer, a French trial of a soldier charged with a similar offense. After 30 months of this, I came to the conclusion that the French system is essentially Catholic justice while the American system is essentially Protestant. French courts judge the criminal more than the crime, whereas American courts do the reverse. To the French, then, the confession is the prime focus of the whole process; if the accused confesses, expresses remorse and promises to behave in the future, the court gives him a light sentence; if he denies guilt, the court accuses him of bad faith and "racks him up," as we used to say.

The inquisitorial label stems from the fact that in France it is the role of judges to ascertain and develop facts. In the investigation stage, this function is performed by the *juge d'instruction*; in the actual trial, it is the presiding judge who asks the questions and conducts the entire trial. At the outset, he has before him the entire file of the case, resulting from the investigation. In the American system, the judge and jury start with a *tabula rasa*; they know nothing about the case at the outset and all the evidence is produced before them by the prosecuting and defense attorneys; hence the term "adversarial." In the French system, the judge begins by interrogating the accused, whereas in the American system, neither the judge nor the prosecutor can call the accused to the stand. Theoretically, a French defendant may remain silent but the court can consider this as evidence of guilt. Curiously, the accused is not allowed to take an oath, presumably because he is expected to lie in his own defense. How this squares with his duty to confess, I have never understood. (Logically, the two propositions can be reconciled if the accused confesses to a crime he did not commit; at least he is not a perjurer!) As a trial observer in French courts, I used to be driven up the wall when the judge began by asking the accused: *"Reconnaissez-vous les faits?"* (literally, "Do you acknowledge the facts*?"*). "How could they be facts at the beginning of the trial?*,"* I would ask, "it's only an accusation*."* No French lawyer could ever give me a satisfactory explanation in fact, they did not even understand my question, so natural did it seem to them that the judge had the "facts" in his possession, despite the presumption of innocence which the law professes.

This system helps explain the events in the Tapie case, still unfolding. No matter how much hard evidence the judge may have, the accused's failure to confess is a disturbing element in a Catholic country. The fact that Bernès, the alleged briber, and Tapie, the alleged suborner, refuse to "acknowledge the facts" is not only deemed a thwarting of justice but also an offense to religion. And just as the Grand Inquisitor thought it normal to torture the accused to get him to confess, so is it that examining magistrates routinely use incarceration of even harmless suspects as a means of exacting confessions. It should be noted that in Italy – a Catholic country par excellence – the same methods have been used with notorious results: cramming a suspect into a prison cell with 20 hardened and smelly criminals does wonders for a man's memory; occasionally, also, it incites him to meet his Maker.

To make matters worse, French police have the power to detain anyone for 24 hours without bringing charges and, with the permission of the Public Prosecutor, can prolong the detention another 24 hours. Until this year, the suspect had no right to counsel during his detention and could not even make a phone call to his family! A 1993 "reform" allowed the detainee to see a lawyer for a half-hour after the 20th hour of detention, but the lawyer did not have the right to be present during questioning. This law has been reworked again by the new Parliament but with no significant improvement in the rights of the accused. As one might infer, there is no writ of *habeas corpus* in France.

I hold no brief for the alleged bribers of Marseille, but as a believer in civil liberties I am incensed at the abuses permitted by the French system of pre-trial detention. In a country that prides itself on having invented "the rights of man" it is a disgrace that these practices continue, and meet with such little protest on the part of the majority of the bar and the citizenry. To me, deprivation of liberty merely to exact a confession, particularly in degrading and uncomfortable circumstances, is a form of torture. While France is a signatory of the European Convention of Human Rights, most French lawyers are so little aware of the real meaning of civil liberties that they take very few cases to the Commission created by the Convention. Ironically, Tapie is now protesting the abuses of the French penal law, whereas he did nothing as a member of the government and the Parliament to remedy these defects.

Some years ago, I considered forming a branch of the American Civil Liberties Union in France, but was discouraged by the Left-Right cleavage, which causes people to consider the politics of the person concerned before they will defend him. Thus, Leftists cheered when Jean-Marie Le Pen was convicted of a criminal offense for saying that the Holocaust was a "detail" of World War II. I detest anti-Semitism, and am incensed when Turks deny the Armenian Genocide, but I would defend any man's right to say that the latter was a detail of World War I.

In earlier days, I used to quote to my French friends Voltaire's famous phrase about "defending to the death" but stopped long ago: it earned only smirks.

Vol. XV, N° 6, October 1993

Montaigne and Descartes

The main satisfaction I get from doing these Newsletters is to hear from readers. My tributes to Georges Bret and Vittorio Cassoni, for example, stimulated quite a few people to comment favorably, both orally or in writing. One woman told me that she wished that she had known these men, and others wrote that the men had come alive for them. These remarks are flattering, despite my awareness of how far I fell short of translating the reality of such complex and genial beings.

Another reader, from Haifa, was intrigued by the mention of my essay "Montaigne et Descartes" and asked whether an English translation was available. I thought about doing one for him, but as I had written that piece directly in French for a French audience, it seemed to me a better idea to do up a fresh piece on the subject for my English-language readers.

It Began with T.S. Eliot

Many years ago when I was still in Philadelphia, I went through a T.S. Eliot period, reading virtually all his poems and essays. In one of the latter, he commented that the strongest exposition of religious skepticism was Montaigne's essay, *Apology of Raymond Sebond.* (For younger readers, it may be worth mentioning that Eliot was born in, of all places, St. Louis, Missouri, but converted to Anglo-Catholicism and ended up living most of his adult life in England, where he worked at the publishing house, Faber & Faber.) Long after I stopped reading Eliot, his remark on Montaigne lingered in my memory.

In the late 1960s now living in Paris, I stumbled upon Montaigne's essays and read *Apologie de Raymond Sebond.* It turns out that Sebond was a Spanish theologian much in vogue in Montaigne's time, which was the 16th century. The essence of this long essay is that the existence of God cannot be proved by reason, but how lucky we are that we have the faith. Without the latter part of the message, Montaigne risked being burned at the stake, but even the first part was audacious after centuries of scholastic proofs of the existence of God. What interested me most was the way he went about demonstrating his thesis: he revealed himself as a relativist and empiricist. Eschewing the scholasticism that dominated learned writing, he looked at the world as it is, marshaled facts and reasoned by induction. Among other things, Montaigne anticipated Darwin in a long passage devoted to demonstrating the resemblance of men to animals, not only physically but also in behavior patterns. And he endeared himself to me permanently when he explained his mistrust of reason by pointing out there is a tribe of cannibals who justify eating their own parents as a sacred duty!

Excited by my discovery of Montaigne, I asked my oldest son, who was then in his last year in a French *lycée*, whether he studied that author in his philosophy class. His reply jolted me: "Philosophy? Why, no, Montaigne is literature!" In other words, he read some essays of Montaigne at an earlier age, in French class. I asked then, "But what do you study in Philosophy?" The answer: Descartes. And so, I embarked on a reading of the *Discours de la Méthode*, Descartes' most famous essay, written in 1632, which contains his celebrated remark, "I think, therefore I am."

The more I read and re-read this essay the more I became convinced that it was written to rebut Montaigne's *Apologie,* even though neither Montaigne nor his essay is mentioned. For example, Descartes asserted that animals have no soul, whereas Montaigne had stressed the similarity of the human race to the animal kingdom. But the main point of the *Discours* is to give logical proofs of the existence of God, something Montaigne, in the prior century, had said could not be done. Descartes' proofs would embarrass a sophomore in college today, but he seemed very proud of such arguments as: "Since I know imperfection, that means perfection exists, and only God can be perfect; therefore He exists" (my paraphrase).

What intrigued me the most, however, is that Descartes starts off by saying that he has invented a method of reasoning, the first principle of which is that "the things that we conceive very clearly and very distinctly are all true." (I just love the "very" in that sentence: if one sees only "clearly and distinctly" it's not true, but add the "very" and it becomes true!)

Using this method, Descartes first tries it out on anatomy: he "demonstrates" that the circulation of the blood is what makes the heart beat, contrary to the discovery of Harvey. In other words, Descartes got the thing "ass backwards" as we used to say in Philadelphia. Then, convinced that his method is the right tool for discovering truth, he goes on to prove the existence of God, and having done so, he concludes that it is God who allows him to know that what he sees "very clearly and very distinctly" is true! God, in other words, has shown him the light.

In my naïveté, it seemed obvious that of the two, Montaigne was the more modern philosopher, and had more relevance to today's youth. And so I wrote my essay, *Montaigne et Descartes,* the central theme of which was that it is Descartes who should be relegated to the literature class and Montaigne taught as philosophy. As the legal journal, *La Gazette du Palais,* had published a few of my pieces, I sent the new essay to its co-editor, André Toulemon, an exquisite old man, who was born in the wonderful medieval city of Sarlat, and who was then approaching 90. A couple of weeks later, I ran into Toulemon in a restaurant near the Palace of Justice, and I asked him what he thought of my essay. He hesitated a moment and then replied, almost plaintively, "When you speak well of Montaigne that pleases me, but when you speak ill of Descartes, that pains me, for it is, after all, Descartes who formed our minds." *("C'est, tout de même, Descartes qui a formé nos esprits.")*

On hearing this comment and seeing the pained expression on the face of this frail old man, I blushed and felt like a heel. I realized that in attacking Descartes, I had injured one of the tenets of Toulemon's faith. It was as though I had told a village priest that the mother of Jesus was not a virgin. And so, I asked Toulemon not to publish the article. *Montaigne et Descartes* languished in my desk drawer for many years. Occasionally, I would muster the temerity to give a typed copy to a French visitor if, after a long conversation with him, I felt that he would not be offended. (It was almost like giving out a pornographic novel during Victorian times.) Unbeknownst to me, one such visitor sent a copy to a law professor in Toulouse, who sent it to another legal journal, *Les Petites Affiches,* whose editor asked my permission to publish it. Thus, it finally reached print, some 15 years after it was written.

Cartesian Hegemony

I would not have bored my readers with these details, except that they serve to demonstrate the incredible hold that Descartes still has on the French mind. Any foreigner who wants to understand France and the French cannot ignore Descartes and Cartesianism, as his method is known. I might add that when my youngest son, some 10 years after the first, studied philosophy in a French *lycée,* Descartes was still required reading, and Montaigne taught as literature. To add insult to injury, my son told me that his philosophy instructor had referred to Montaigne as a "*cuistre*," the French equivalent of a silly pedant!

Because of an incredibly centralized system under which the Ministry of Education determines the curriculum throughout France, generation after generation of French pupils have had their minds "formed" by the Cartesian "method," which is a hodgepodge of *a priori* reasoning, formalism, deduction from unproved premises and verbal symmetry. The sign of a Cartesian is that he's always saying "*c'est logique*" and doesn't want to be bothered by ugly facts that would destroy his beautiful theory. As pointed out in an incisive essay called *Descartes – Inutile et Incertain*, by Jean-François Revel (the title is borrowed from Pascal), one of the few French contemporary heretics who knocks the great god, Descartes himself refused to engage in debate or show his drafts to others, for fear that his argumentation and "proofs" might be demolished.

Ever since I started practicing in France, I have encountered Cartesians galore. Not long ago, a brilliant young French lawyer worked for me; his only failing was that he was reluctant to have his opinions reviewed by another lawyer. When I asked him if he did not fear making mistakes, his answer was "Yes, that's why I carefully review my work to be sure there are none!" Recently, an outside accountant told me the same thing. This is quintessential Descartes.

By contrast, the essence of Montaigne can be summarized as "I have no choice but to use my brain; however, its first lesson is to warn me to beware of itself and to seek corroboration from other minds, because pride, passion, pain and prejudice can lead it astray." Against this, Descartes boasts: "When I see the light, man, I know I am right; no need to corroborate!"

For years I have been pondering the question, why is it that Cartesianism has persisted so long in France? As I point out to French friends, outside of France one rarely meets an avowed Cartesian. Another Frenchman – Pasteur – is universally revered, but not even French-speaking Belgians, Swiss or Canadians profess to be disciples of Descartes. Another way of stating the question is, why does the educational system continue to teach Cartesianism as the established quasi-religion of the French mind?

It was only recently that I began to formulate an answer to that question, in connection with my slow-dawning realization that the Catholic-monarchical tradition still dominates all French institutions. In the 17th century, science was beginning to intrude on faith by penetrating the secrets of the universe, while the Church continued its ideological grip over civil society. Thus, an intelligent man like Descartes – a brilliant mathematician (his invention of analytical geometry assures his immortality) – could not content himself with "God exists, the Bishop told me so." But he could get away with "God exists, because He allowed me to see the light."

By reconciling the indulgence of his own intelligence with faith, Descartes opened the way for generations of French intellectuals to become "modern" while remaining true to their Catholic tradition. There is indeed something very touching about the French faith in reason. I have long considered the French spirit to be one of the fine arts. It is no accident that in the most fanatic period of the French Revolution, the Christian deity was replaced by the Goddess of Reason. One cannot imagine a more blatant rejection of Montaigne, whose suspicion of reason dominated all his writing.

The "down side" (to use contemporary jargon) to this faith in one's own reason is that it can lead to arrogance. And by combining a pseudo-rigorous method with a subjective definition of truth ("whatever I see very clearly is true") Descartes made it easy for the lazy to be "truth-seekers" without dirtying their hands, digging for facts and subjecting their theories to outside corroboration.

Cartesian Ethics

But this is not all. Just recently, it occurred to me that Cartesianism is also linked to another phenomenon which has caught my attention: the absence of ethics in contemporary France. This, too, is a product of the Catholic-monarchical tradition. Coming from the horizontal society of the United States, it took me a long time to realize that France remained a vertical society. In a horizontal society, ethics are basically the product of a consensus. In a vertical society, rules come from on high: the king and the bishop. Citizens are not trained in ethics but rather in obedience to authority. Despite its espousal of democratic jargon ("*Liberté, Egalité, Fraternité*") France adheres to values based on authority.

In all walks of French life, ethics plays second fiddle to kow-towing to authority. But nowhere is the absence of ethics more apparent than in the political system. I am not referring to bribery or thievery, such as the recent Italian scandals have exposed, but to the institutionalization of conflicts of interest throughout the system. France, today, is in the hands of a caste of functionaries who have legalized their own conflicts of interest in three spheres: the first being the effacement of the separation of powers between the executive and the legislative branches; the second, the combining of national and local offices; and the third, the joinder of the regulatory function with ownership of business. I could write a book about this, but just a few examples will illustrate the points:

1. No law or constitutional provision prevents civil servants from running for Parliament (or other elected office). If they win, they simply take a leave of absence from their administrative corps, to which they return when they cease their elective tenure. Thus, their ultimate loyalty is to the executive branch. During the early Mitterrand years, a majority of the National Assembly was made up of civil servants and even the current Parliament is heavily dominated by that category. Judges are also civil servants, dependent on the Ministry of Justice for their promotions and appointments. Thus, the separation of powers is non-existent in the country of Montesquieu!

2. Similarly, nothing prevents a national office-holder from being a local official at the same time. Thus, several prime ministers of the Fifth Republic, such as Chaban-Delmas, Mauroy, Fabius, Chirac and Rocard, have been simultaneously mayors of large cities. The feudal system has returned to France; just as, in olden days, the noble did his duty at the Court in Versailles while ruling the roost in his local fiefdom so, today, numerous national figures have built up local bastions, holding offices at the municipal, the departmental and the regional levels.

3. Finally, officials in regulatory functions also are responsible for the operations of nationalized businesses, such as the Minister of Transport who looks after Air France. As the French government controls most of the banks, insurance companies, transportation facilities, coal mines, and much of basic industry, officials charged with regulating these industries hold directorships in state-owned companies and generally end up with plush jobs in the companies they once regulated.

What is so extraordinary about all this is that nobody in France sees these phenomena as posing ethical problems. Of late, there have been movements to limit the *cumul des fonctions,* that is, the accumulation of offices, but this is seen merely as a way of spreading the honors, not as a problem of conflict of interest. A French population inured to this situation simply fails to see an ethical problem. That is why I describe the French scene as one of absence of ethics rather than breach of ethics.

What has this to do with Descartes? The insight which came to me recently is this: if, for example, you asked a man like Mauroy, "Didn't you have an ethical problem in being prime minister and mayor of Lille at the same time?," he would surely reply "No." His explanation? "When I'm in the prime minister's mansion I think only of the national interest, and when I'm in the Lille city hall, I think only of Lille." Just as Descartes saw truth as a subjective perception, so French political figures believe that ethics are subjective. Their own mind suffices to judge whether they can handle two jobs with conflicting interests. If they see "very clearly and very distinctly" that there is no problem, then there is none.

This explanation may seem simplistic but I believe that there is a lot to it. It may seem strange to attribute an entire intellectual and political tradition to a self-satisfied propensity for subjectivity but, judging by what we know of human vanity, is the idea so outlandish?

To me, the avoidance of conflict of interest is the most fundamental rule of civil society, for it is the underpinning of confidence and trust. By hypothesis, the test of conflict of interest is not subjective but objective. For example, a judge might well be capable of sentencing his own brother to jail, but the mere fact of the relationship is enough to disqualify the judge. By using a subjective standard of ethics, the caste of functionaries which rules France is using the Cartesian method to serve its own class interests. Of course, they profess to be unselfishly devoted to the public interest, while holding lifetime jobs in a country racked with unemployment. If you ask them individually, each would say, "I see very clearly and very distinctly that whatever power I wield is for the good of France." It is as though this caste of functionaries sees itself as the high priests of the Goddess of Reason.

The notion that self-interest is far from their minds is one of the prime fictions with which this ruling class deludes itself and the French public. According to this credo, corruption is not so bad if it is done for the good of the party, and thus of France. Recent amnesty laws have established the standard that violations of penal laws governing political contributions can be forgiven if the culprit did not act for "personal enrichment."

Cartesian Elite

The influence of Descartes is highly visible in the graduates of the two principal schools (state-owned, to be sure) which breed the top civil servants: the Ecole Nationale d'Administration (ENA) and the Ecole Polytechnique, known commonly as "X." The latter, indeed, used to be located on rue Descartes. It selects students exclusively on mathematical ability. The former uses the famous Institut des Sciences Politiques (familiarly known as "*Sciences Po*") as its preparatory school. *Sciences Po* practices what I call "verbal Cartesianism:" all writing must have a "*plan*," which involves breaking down all subjects into two parts. If Moses had attended *Sciences Po* he would have had to divide his ten commandments into two main categories. As for Jesus, he would have had to work all night to put Cartesian order into the Sermon on the Mount. Obviously, Plato could not have been admitted to *Sciences Po,* without forewearing the Socratic method of dialogue. And, of course, the worst sinner of all was Montaigne, whose diffuse and anecdotal essays were always bereft of a "*plan.*"

Many graduates of each school have told me that the educational contents of "X" and ENA are mediocre. What counts is that they got in. Nobody flunks out, and any graduate has a job for life, no matter how incompetent he turns out to be. It was in thinking of the latter that I coined the word "*Cartésocon*," my only contribution to French culture, thus far. Occasionally, a particularly bright and ambitious lad competes for, and is graduated from, both schools. Two of the more notorious illustrations are Valéry Giscard d'Estaing and Jacques Attali, who would qualify as eggheads in the USA.

The restoration of feudal values is exemplified by an emerging political figure, Philippe Séguin, who is, of course, an ENA graduate and civil servant, doubling as mayor of Epinal while serving as President of the National Assembly. He distinguished himself last year by opposing the Maastricht treaty but at the same time, in my opinion, he helped the "Yes" vote by his totally obsequious behavior in a key television debate with President Mitterrand. Each time Séguin addressed Mitterrand, he excused himself and called him "*Monsieur le Président de la République*." (Can you imagine Senator Dole debating Clinton and calling him each time "Mr. President of the United States?") Not long ago I read a remark by Séguin to the effect that far from abolishing the *cumul de fonctions* of national and local office, it should be made compulsory, since it is good that a national official hold local responsibilities. That's what feudalism was about.

Another reason why Cartesianism has persisted so long in France is simply that it is a French invention. Chauvinism is so strong here that a French falsehood is preferred to a foreign truth. As indicated in an earlier Newsletter, Voltaire struggled for 20 years to introduce Newtonian physics to a country which wanted to believe that one of theirs, Descartes, had said the last word on the subject. I read somewhere that even in the 19th century, the French Academy of Sciences was loath to abandon Cartesian physics.

A little anecdote will illustrate the depths of chauvinism in the educational process: the same son whose failure to read Montaigne in philosophy class led to my essay once told me that "the French have the best scientists in the world." I asked him where he had got that notion. From his physics professor, he replied. After catching my breath, I said, "That fool, instead of teaching you physics he's teaching you chauvinism." Indeed, judging by my son's close-to-zero grade, he had learned virtually no physics from that *lycée* professor.

A more recent illustration of French chauvinism came in the aftermath of the decision of the International Soccer Federation to ban the Marseille team from European Cup play for one year. The same press that featured for weeks news of Marseilles's bribery of rival players treated this banishment as a national catastrophe, a rank injustice. Jacques Chirac said that he was "very sad," and Prime Minister Balladur opined that it was "too bad" (*très dommage*). Not a word was said that this might be a fitting punishment for dirty tricks, nor that it was good for sports. The implication is now that if Mr Tapie's team bribed its way to the championship this was done for patriotic motives, for the good of France!

Without getting too far afield, I would merely like to mention that the French functionary caste is doing its best to introduce its rules of civil society at the European level. Jacques Delors is an arch-type of French functionary who sees "very clearly and very distinctly" what is good for the European citizenry. It is no accident that most French functionaries support a bureaucratic Europe with a powerless so-called "Parliament."

The Cartesian Ultimate: L'Etat

I learned from Conyers Reid at the University of Pennsylvania that there is no fun in studying history if one cannot generalize. Thus, I would summarize five centuries of French history as follows: In the 16th and 17th centuries, Montaigne (although a Catholic) and the Huguenots lost their battle to free men's minds from the dominance of the Church and King. Along came Descartes in the 17th century and his kind of rationalism co-existed well with authority. The turbulent 18th and 19th centuries finally did away with Church and King, but Cartesian rationalism, which threatened no one, subsisted, along with the bureaucracy which the centralism of both the Monarchy and the Church had fostered. In the 20th century, gradually but inexorably, the power vacuum at the top was filled by a new breed of elite, whose power stemmed neither from wealth nor birth, but from its mastery of the Cartesian formalism which an elitist educational system uses as the chief criterion of selection. Ironically, what was once a two-headed monster – Church and Monarchy – is now replaced by a single concept, *l'Etat*, an abstraction which the elite put forward to mask their own tremendous power, both political and economic. And the beauty of it is that the common people put up with this system because of the Pavlovian obedience that centuries of submission to authority have thrust upon them!

When I consider how little knowledge, how little imagination, how little common sense is required for a student to be admitted to ENA and X, and how little these ingredients are present once they are graduated, I wonder what the future holds for a country relying for leadership on such an elite. Fortunately for France, there is imagination in the kitchen and the couture houses. Had Descartes written "I think therefore I cook," France might have had the worst cuisine in the world.

Well, dear reader, I would wager that when you saw the title "Montaigne and Descartes," you did not expect that these classic authors would have such relevance to contemporary France. While I am glad to be living in a country where philosophy does matter, even if it's the wrong philosophy, I do worry when a monolithic caste has too much power. At the present time, I do not see how their grip on France can be loosened, but only a few years ago I thought the same of the hold that the Communist Party had on the Soviet Union. However, in the case of France and Europe, I fear that things will get worse before they get better.

Lest some readers be tempted to make the silly inference that because I criticize the Cartesian canon I am advocating an American one, let me add that I deplore the American system of selecting its educational elite through multiple-choice tests, such as the SAT and the LSAT. These tests favor glibness and superficiality to the detriment of originality and profundity. At least French leaders learn to speak and write clearly! But why choose an elite through a single method? Moreover, in America, the educated elite have to prove themselves in real life and self-made men can still rise to the top. In France, the elite gravitate in a closed system, where the Cartesian canon prevails, and the rigidities of the business and tax laws – written by the Cartesian functionaries – make it extremely difficult for entrepreneurs to exist.

As a foreigner in France, I feel somewhat like a missionary, but unlike the typical one who introduces an alien faith, I am trying to persuade my French friends that one of theirs – Montaigne – is a better role model than Descartes for the 21st century. My preference for Montaigne over Descartes implies a radically different vision of how the French should be educated and led. I dream of France becoming Montaignian, with the help of my other French heroes – Voltaire, Montesquieu and Molière. These men are the true glory of France.

Alas, when I get discouraged, I remind myself that Montaigne is dead, Voltaire is dead, Montesquieu is dead, Molière is dead… and I'm not feeling so well, myself.

Vol. XV, N° 7, December 1993

The Christmas Issue: The Blockhead and Other Subjects

Last year, spurred by a young-lady who asked, almost imploringly, whether there would be a "Christmas Issue" of this Newsletter, I wrote one for the occasion. That is enough, for the likes of me, to create a tradition. And so this is the second Christmas Issue, for what it is worth. Let me start by mentioning that I am well aware that by not charging any money for this Newsletter I am deserving of Dr Johnson's posthumous anathema, since he told Boswell: "No man but a blockhead ever wrote except for money." I enjoy being considered a blockhead, just as I get a kick out of producing something that money cannot buy.

I am also aware that the sub-heading "Legal Newsletter from France" seems more and more inappropriate as I write less and less on legal subjects. One reason for this is that I get much more fan mail when I treat non-legal subjects. Another is that expounding on French politics and sociology is a way of educating my clients and correspondents on the realities of the society with which they are dealing. In this connection, the reaction to the last issue, "Montaigne and Descartes," was most gratifying.

A third reason is that reporting on new French laws is a disillusioning experience. So many laws are unenforced or rewritten that it is hard to take seriously newly-enacted French statutes. The last French law on which I reported extensively was the one that supposedly legalized comparative advertisement, in reaction to established case-law that prohibited one competitor from comparing his wares with another's. But the statute was so restrictive, including a ridiculous Cartesian requirement that an advertiser submit his copy in advance to a competitor named in it, that it was not difficult to predict that it would be rarely utilized. Indeed, in the almost two years that the law has been on the books I have not seen a single comparative advertisement. Recently I read an article reporting that only 10 such advertisements had been published in a year!

Another illustration of the vagaries of French legislation is the law "reforming" penal procedures, mentioned in the issue devoted to Bernard Tapie. The original statute, enacted early in January 1993, contained a chapter, effective as of January 1, 1994, that would have radically curtailed the inquisitorial nature of criminal trials, both in the Cour d'Assises and the Tribunal Correctionnel. Instead of the judge interrogating the accused and witnesses, the examination would have been conducted by the prosecutor and the defense attorney, as in common-law jurisdictions. Yet, before this new procedure could go into effect, the whole chapter was repealed in July! Why? For one reason, there was a conservative parliamentary majority elected in March, but I suspect that the main reason was that the judges revolted at the notion of losing their inquisitorial power.

What is typical, however, is that affected categories do not get much opportunity to lobby in advance of enactment of legislation and then, when they wake up to what has happened, begin to protest, saying, in effect, "Gee whiz, you didn't really mean to do that, did you?" And, more often than not, the Parliament (meaning the government, which controls the agenda) replies, "Well, perhaps not." The same applies to decrees and regulations issued by government edict. Unlike in the United States, where prospective regulations must be published in the Federal Register, to give affected persons the opportunity to comment, French bureaucrats like to concoct regulations in secret, letting only a selected few get a peek at the draft. As readers of my last Newsletter know by now, this is Cartesianism par excellence.

This being said, I do hope in 1994 to report on new legal developments, and will review the 1993 crop for items worth mentioning.

Vol. XVI, N° 1, February 1994

L'Affaire Gregory: "Écrasez l'Infâme"

Just as my essay "Montaigne and Descartes" was prompted by an inquiry from a reader in Haifa, so this issue results from the urging of a faithful reader, an American in Paris. Like him, I had been exposed, *ad nauseum*, to countless newspaper and magazine articles, following the mysterious murder in October 1984 of four-year-old Gregory Villemin, whose body was found floating in the Valogne river several hours after his disappearance from his parents' home in Lépanges, a small town in the Vosges area of eastern France.

What made this a *cause célèbre* was a number of dramatic *rebondissements*, as the French call unexpected events: first, Bernard Laroche, a cousin of the victim's father was arrested for the murder, then he was released when his 15-year-old sister-in-law retracted testimony against him, after which suspicion was cast on the mother, Christine, which did not prevent the boy's father, Jean-Marie, from murdering Laroche. The mother was eventually charged with killing her own son but ultimately cleared and, only last year, Jean-Marie Villemin was tried and convicted for Laroche's murder, but the person responsible for the child's death remains an official mystery.

Stated this way, *l'affaire Grégory*, as it came to be called, sounds like soap opera; indeed, the French media often compared it with *Dallas* and *Dynasty*. Recently, I took advantage of a week's respite in the French Alps to read a thick book about the case, written by Laurence Lacour, a young radio-journalist who has devoted most of her waking hours for the past nine years to the saga. Called *Le Bûcher des Innocents* (which might be translated, *"The Bonfire of the Innocents"*), the book taught me enough about the tragic events to make me realize that some of my favorite themes about France are exemplified.

Central among these themes is the relative indifference of educated French people to facts, just plain facts. This failing is concomitant to a trait which is the touchstone of the selection process used in French schools: the capacity for abstract thought. Add to that the Cartesian penchant for *a priori* reasoning and the result is an educated elite who, with rare exceptions, consider facts to be beneath their dignity. If you read French newspapers, as I have been doing for more than 30 years, the hardest problem is to learn the facts of any story. Journalists start editorializing in the first sentence. A few years ago, the retirement of Edmond Maire as head of the influential CFDT labor union was front-page news. I read and re-read the entire article in *Le Figaro* but nowhere could I find out Maire's age. I read at least three other journals, and listened to radio and TV accounts, but not one mentioned Maire's age. An important person retires but his age is not relevant!

In my law practice, I constantly run up against the lack of fact-consciousness of French lawyers. About 20 years ago, I hired a young lawyer, who seemed promising because of his mixed Anglo-French background, although his legal education was French. For his first assignment, I sent him a matter which had just arrived, asking him to prepare a memo on the issues. The next day, on receiving his memo, I called him in to discuss it. While reading his memo, I asked him, "Who is our client in this matter?" His answer, "I don't know." When I expressed amazement that he could study a file and not know who our client was, he replied, "What importance? You asked for a memo on the law; the law is the same for everybody." A few days later, this lawyer came in and resigned, saying, rather belligerently, that he had checked with his buddies in other firms and their bosses gave them much more leeway than I did in handling cases!

Some years ago, in my Newsletter entitled, "The French Court System or Miracles Will Happen," I pointed out that after 20 years of practice here, a mystery that still remained is how one proves facts in a French court. More recently, I was brought into a case by a worried client who had been sued by a customer to whom he had provided advice on the choice of computer hardware and software for servicing insurance claims. The court had appointed an official expert who had held several hearings with the parties and their lawyers, including my client's barrister who was a self-proclaimed specialist in computer law. On short notice, I attended one such meeting and discovered that the expert had never examined the hardware and software, although its functioning was the only issue in the case! The lawyers and expert were content, meeting after meeting, to sit around a table and talk about the system, but no one had suggested testing it to see if it worked. It took me weeks to get the expert to visit the plaintiff's office to look at the computer and software and, even then, he limited his inquiry to letting the dissatisfied customer show him what did not work, rather than examining the system as a whole. We finally won the case by showing, through extrinsic evidence, that the customer had been using the system commercially on a daily basis for over a year, yet neither the expert nor the lawyer whom I replaced had ever asked this simple question, "Are you using the system?"

I thought of all this in reading Lacour's book, because the basic failure in the Gregory case was the botching of the investigation by an incompetent, 30-year-old *Juge d'Instruction*, Jean-Michel Lambert, based in Epinal, who became famous, even notorious, because of this assignment. The *Juge d'Instruction* is a peculiar French institution. We generally translate the title as "Examining Magistrate," the idea being that in an inquisitorial system, an impartial judge, rather than a prosecutor, is supposed to ascertain whether a crime has been committed and by whom. Where do these judges come from and how do they learn their trade? That's the rub. At the age when other law-school graduates prepare for bar exams and clerkships, young men and women, like Jean-Michel Lambert, go to school in Bordeaux, to the Ecole Nationale de la Magistrature, and after three years of study they become judges. You see, judges in France are civil servants who start at the bottom of the ladder and gradually move to the top. As prosecutors are also considered *magistrats,* these graduates have careers which can include prosecuting as *Procureur de la République* (or *Substitut* as deputies are called), investigating as *Juge d'Instruction*, sitting in judgment in the civil or criminal courts or even serving as administrators in the Ministry of Justice (a good way to get juicy judicial appointments).

I find it striking, yet not surprising, that in a volume of 650 pages, author Lacour devotes no space to the very role of *Juges d'Instruction* or to the background of Jean-Michel Lambert. The failure to question basic institutions is symptomatic of French intellectuals, who are the most sophisticated provincials that the Western world has produced. By "provincial" I mean someone who cannot see beyond the cultural framework of his geographical origins. (Bill Clinton is a whale of a provincial, despite a year at Oxford studying how to beat the Vietnam draft, but he is not sophisticated.) Lacour waxes very eloquent in treating the tree – Lambert's handling of the judicial investigation – but completely fails to see the forest, *i.e.,* the flawed system which put him in charge of the case.

Similarly, she does not question another peculiarity of the French system of justice: the sharing of police authority between the *Gendarmerie* and the police. Many, if not most, foreigners tend to equate *gendarmes* with police. In fact, the former are part of the French army, they are military people, subject to the authority of the Minister of Defense, whereas the police are civil servants who are subject to the administrative authority of the Minister of the Interior, but when they participate in judicial investigations, they are responsible to the Ministry of Justice. Yet both services have the power to enforce the penal laws against the general population; the *gendarmes* can issue speeding tickets and investigate murders. While I suspect that the role of the *gendarmerie* dates to the monarchy, Napoleon, who was, of course, a military man, gets the credit for instituting the present system, to make sure that he could control the civil population. Why, at the end of the 20th century, military police should continue to have authority in civil matters is a question that the people who pride themselves on being the most intelligent on earth never ask.

At any rate, this concurrent jurisdiction, which over the years has generated intense and hateful rivalries, turns out to have been a major factor in the Gregory case. The *gendarmes* of Epinal were the ones who first investigated the murder of little Gregory, and so, Judge Lambert, as was his right, continued to use them for several months.

One of the most fascinating, and dreadful, aspects of the case, is that over a period of three years preceding the murder, an anonymous person, identifying himself as the "Crow" (*le Corbeau*), made nasty telephone calls and sent hate letters to the Villemins and other members of the large family, which included two parents and several brothers and sisters. The *gendarmes*, frequently called in, had failed to identify the person, whom everyone assumed to be a man close to the family, since he frequently alluded to intimate details, and seemed particularly hateful of Jean-Marie Villemin, Gregory's father. Both Jean-Marie (26 at the time of the murder) and his wife Christine (24 then) were of modest origin, and might be called by their patronizing betters, "deserving working class" people. They had built an attractive house on a hill overlooking Lépanges; each worked in local factories, and each had a modest automobile. Jean-Marie seemed to incur the Crow's wrath when he was promoted to foreman (*contre-maître*) in his factory.

The kidnapping of Gregory occurred within a very tight time-span, which became crucial. Leaving work shortly before 5 pm on October 16, 1984, Christine picked up Gregory at his baby-sitter's place. She arrived home at 5 pm and told Gregory that he could play outside while she did some ironing. A few minutes later when she looked for Gregory, he was nowhere to be seen. Thinking that he had wandered into the nearby village, Christine took her car and went looking for Gregory in Lépanges. Not finding him, she returned home and was seen at 5:32 pm by a bus driver who had been blocked because of sheep crossing the road. At the same moment, Michel Villemin, one of Jean-Marie's brothers, received a call (he so testified) from the Crow claiming credit for the crime.

Family and friends began looking for the boy in the Valogne river which flows through Lépanges on its way to Epinal. Finally at 9:15 p.m., the body was found in the river six kilometers away, where the Valogne passes through the town of Docelles. Gregory was fully dressed, his bonnet covering his eyes, which were open, and his hands and feet tied with a white cord around his neck. The body bore no signs of violence and rigor mortis had not set in.

In the ensuing days, those who witnessed the reactions of the parents could not help but be impressed by the depth of their grief. By all accounts, Gregory was an adorable boy, intelligent and affectionate, the apple of his parents' eyes. Yet despite this, an incredible event took place which would have fateful consequences for the parents. A journalist, Jean-Michel Bezzina, visited the Villemin house in search of an interview. Seeing the mother, who had been placed under sedatives, emotionless and dazed, Bezzina told himself: "She's the one who did it." This would be laughable if it were a laughing matter but, incredible as it must seem to any normal person, the journalist, on the basis of this single "insight," spared no effort in the ensuing months and years to pin the crime on the last person in the whole world whom a decent person would suspect. And Bezzina almost succeeded in his despicable endeavor, inflicting enormous suffering on this unfortunate woman. Most of Lacour's book is devoted to the efforts of Bezzina, his wife and the hound-pack of pseudo-journalists who followed his lead, to mount an unbelievably effective media attack on Christine Villemin, making a mockery of the French judicial system in the course of it. Even the author, at certain moments, succumbed to their insidious and fraudulent campaign, based on innuendoes and outright falsehoods, and admits to having doubted Christine's innocence at moments.

Of course, Bezzina's intuition of Christine's guilt reminded me of Descartes' first principle: "the things we conceive very clearly and very distinctly are all true." When one reads this book, one understands, also, how the Dreyfus affair reached the proportions that it did. Facts ceased to count, people took sides for or against Dreyfus, based on Cartesian perceptions of truth, on ideology and on institutions; the individual, wasting away on Devil's Island after a conviction based on forged evidence, ceased to count.

But let us return to the investigation. The *gendarmes*, led by a remarkably honest and devoted officer, a graduate of the St-Cyr military academy, Captain Etienne Sesmat, quickly latched on to a prime suspect, Bernard Laroche, cousin of Jean-Marie. Voice and hand-writing samples, required of all family members, led two experts to identify Laroche as the *Corbeau*. On top of that he had no good alibi for the time of the abduction. Then, his 15-year old sister-in-law, Muriel Bolle, who lived with the Laroches to care for their handicapped son, of Gregory's age, was interrogated by the *gendarmes*. At first, she denied knowledge of the crime, claiming to have taken a school-bus home, right after school. But, asked to identify the bus-driver, she described the regular one, whereas on that day another driver had replaced him. Moreover, two school mates told the *gendarmes* that Muriel was not on the bus. Confronted with these discrepancies, Muriel admitted that

Bernard had picked her up after school, that they drove to the Villemin house, where they stopped. Laroche left and returned a few minutes later, leading Gregory by the hand. They then drove to Docelles, where Laroche stopped the car and took Gregory with him, returning alone some minutes later.

Muriel Bolle confirmed this story several times to the *gendarmes* and signed two statements to this effect on Friday, November 2, 1984. Significantly, Judge Lambert, who was called by the *gendarmes* around 6:15 pm did not bother to interrogate the youngster that day. According to the author, Lambert was a nine-to-five man; he never worked evenings or week-ends, whatever the urgency! Bolle was held overnight by the *gendarmes* and repeated the story the next morning, whereupon she was examined by her own family physician, who found her in good health and spirits. Muriel returned home over the weekend, and repeated her story the following Monday to the Judge, following which he ordered the arrest and incarceration of Laroche.

At this point, one might think that the case is over but, incredibly, it is only beginning. A few days later, Muriel Bolle retracted her story, claiming that the *gendarmes* had threatened her. Thereafter, Judge Lambert never interrogated Bernard Laroche or ordered further investigations about him, including the customary psychological examinations. Laroche hired two lawyers, one of whom was a member of the same Masonic lodge as were Bezzina and an officer, Jacques Corazzi, from the judicial police of Nancy, who was itching to take over the case from the *gendarmes*, and to prove, with Bezzina's help, that the real culprit was Christine.

One mistake made by the Villemins, understandable because they had no experience with lawyers, was to hire a celebrated *avocat*, Henri-René Garaud, to represent their interests as civil complainants (*parties civiles*) in the criminal proceeding. This turned out to be a doubtful choice, as Garaud was identified with the far Right politically, in particular, as the advocate of persons who claim the right to kill burglars and the like in self-defense, a heated issue at the time. One of Laroche's lawyers was on the far Left, close to the Communist party. As a result, he saw everything in ideological terms; to wit, accusing Laroche is a plot of the far Right to humiliate the working class. Moreover, Garaud was too much of a traditionalist as a barrister to get involved with the facts. Remember, that under French rules, it is considered unethical for a lawyer to interview witnesses! What a convenient system – placing ethics on the side of ignorance and leaving it to a lazy and inexperienced 30-year-old judge to get the facts on the murder of a child!

To understand the incredible turnabout of this incompetent judge, one must recall that French justice is Catholic justice, founded on the confession. If Muriel Laroche retracted her story and Laroche refused to confess, then that's the end of that line; now Lambert must find another suspect who will confess. Laroche's lawyer, Wetzel, aided by his lodge brother, Bezzina, who built a business selling articles to the press and radio, using two pseudonyms in addition to his real name, planted the idea in Judge Lambert's head that the guilty party was Christine Villemin. On top of that, he used a subtle pressure tactic against Lambert: to wit, he has made so many errors of procedure, in a country where form counts more than substance, that he can be challenged and removed from the case; on the other hand, if he brings charges against Christine, these errors might be overlooked. The judge, weak and vain, went along with this ploy. He desperately sought every shred of evidence that might implicate the mother. He got some help from three co-workers in Christine's factory, who, several weeks after the event, claimed that they had seen her posting a letter at 5 pm the day of her son's abduction. This could be relevant because the murderer had mailed a letter in Lépanges to Jean-Marie announcing his crime. Christine replied that she mailed a letter the prior afternoon, to a mail-order house. This was later confirmed by the *gendarmes* who located the letter.

The only really damaging evidence against Christine were new reports of handwriting experts who apparently claimed that there was some resemblance between the Crow's scribbling and Christine's writing. The reports of the first handwriting experts, implicating Laroche, were simply ignored by the judge. Why Christine would have written such letters was never explained and she, of course, denied writing them.

In 1988, Christine became pregnant, a fact for she was criticized; how dare she make love to her husband only three months after Gregory's death? Laroche was released from prison, with charges still pending against him, although the judge was doing nothing to develop evidence against him. Rather, he was succumbing to the blandishments of the Bezzina-Wetzel-Corazzi axis, who were doing their best to get the *gendarmes* removed from the case in favor of the Nancy police, waiting in the wings to do their thing against

Christine. Soon they got their way. Incredibly, the judicial police now assigned to the case did not even bother to interrogate the *gendarmes* to get leads and guidance. Their chief boasted that in 10 days, the case would be solved. They grilled Christine during nine straight hours. Realizing that it was physically impossible, in the short time-span, for her to assassinate her own son and throw him in the river several kilometers distant, they suggest that she must have had an accomplice, who obviously is her lover. Was it Laroche, they ask? Christine replies calmly that she never had a lover. The police find not the slightest evidence to contradict her.

This does not stop the police and Judge Lambert. If she did not kill her son because of a lover, and there was no prior history of mistreatment of the child, she must have done it in a moment of madness. Only a mad mother, like Medea, would kill her child. Lambert has Christine examined by 11, repeat 11, psychiatrists, in a desperate effort to prove that she had a mad streak that led her to kill Gregory. But the doctors all find Christine eminently sane and normal, if a little belligerent on occasion. In the meantime, the irreparable occurs. In April 1985, Jean-Marie, Gregory's father, disgusted that justice is not being done, takes his shotgun and shoots Laroche dead in front of his house. He is, of course, incarcerated, leaving his pregnant wife to endure alone the onslaughts of the police and judge. The press campaign led by the "Bezzina pool" of journalists is blackening Christine every day. The weak judge, realizing that he must do something, or be recused by the Laroche camp, orders the arrest and jailing of Christine in July, 1985, despite her advanced pregnancy. Thus the two young parents, who have lost a beloved child, find themselves in jail. Fortunately, within ten days the court of appeals orders the release of Christine, indicating that incarceration is unjustified as she has always cooperated with the investigation, and the charges against her are weak.

A few weeks later, Julien, the second son, is born, a source of consolation, if not joy, to the unfortunate parents. But the "little judge," as he is now being called, continues to seek ways to charge Christine with the murder of her son, egged on by an indecent press and the police of Nancy who leak items to their buddy Bezzina. The judge himself has committed countless violations of the rule against divulging *le secret de l'instruction*, a criminal offense, which the Ministry of Justice is afraid to prosecute, for fear of offending public opinion, now convinced that Christine is a horrible Medea, who has produced a second son only to gain sympathy. To add to the pain of Christine and Jean-Marie, his parents hire a famous lawyer, Paul Lombard, to file a complaint in the criminal case, thus indicating that they believe her guilty, also.

Months later, in December 1986, Judge Lambert, eager to embark on a sabbatical year, finally brings charges against Christine, although no serious evidence exists against her and no motive is shown. All he needs to support the charge is his *intime conviction*, literally, "intimate conviction," the only standard that French criminal justice has found to support a finding of guilt, as compared with the "beyond a reasonable doubt" of the common-law system. This time, the Court of Appeals allows the charges to stand, hoping to pass the buck to the *Cour d'Assises,* consisting of three judges and nine jurors who have the final word. Revolted by this horrible accusation, Christine's iron strength finally fails and she attempts suicide by swallowing two tubes of medicine on December 14, 1986. Fortunately, her grand-mother finds her and doctors are able to save her.

Then sanity returns to France when, in March 1987, some 30 months after the crime, the highest court, the *Cour de Cassation*, reverses the decision to charge Christine, and sends the case to another court of appeals, that of Dijon, for a fresh start. The Dijon court, encouraged by the Ministry, takes a highly unusual step. Instead of sending the case to another *Juge d'Instruction*, the President of the Court, Maurice Simon, age 64, decides to handle the investigation himself. Starting in June, operating with secrecy, never talking to reporters, Simon conducts a remarkable inquest, verifying every detail and taking nothing for granted. To everyone's surprise, he uncovers witnesses who have never been questioned. He discovers that the child had been placed in the river much closer to the time that he was found than had previously been assumed. Clearly Christine could not have done it.

Just before Christmas 1987, Jean-Marie is released from prison, because the decision has been made to defer his trial for killing Laroche until Judge Simon's report on Gregory's murder is completed. A crucial witness to be heard again is Muriel Bolle, but Laroche's lawyers use every trick to prevent Simon from interrogating her. An important new witness is found, the nurse who cared for Muriel's diabetic mother until her death. An insulin vial and a syringe had been found hidden in the bushes near the river where Gregory was immersed. Judge Lambert had neglected this evidence. The nurse revealed that she had taught Muriel

Bolle how to give injections to her mother; to boot, the packaging found had been opened the way she had taught Muriel to do it. Taking advantage of a phony interview of Judge Simon published in Détective magazine, Laroche's lawyer files a complaint against Simon. This honest and competent juge, already in poor health, suffers a stroke, and after a coma lasting 48 hours, becomes amnesiac.

We are now in January 1990, five years and three months after the crime. Several months later, his health not improved, Judge Simon withdraws from the case, and another Judge from Dijon is named, Jean-Paul Martin. By this time, everyone is convinced that Christine is innocent. A new witness is found, who was told by a farmer neighbor of the Villemins that at the hour of the abduction they had seen a green car driven by a man resembling Laroche, accompanied by a red-haired girl. Confronted with this evidence, Muriel Bolle, who has red hair, stonewalls. Finally, on February 3, 1993, more than eight years after the crime of October 1984, Judge Martin delivers his report clearing Christine of any involvement in her son's death. In December 1993, Jean-Marie is sentenced to five years imprisonment, but his time in pre-trial confinement and good behavior lead to his release by Christmas day.

In the 18th century, Voltaire, revolted by the horrible injustice committed by the Parliament of Toulouse which ordered an innocent man, the Huguenot Calas, to be tortured on the rack, strangled to death and burned at the stake, for a crime he did not commit – the alleged murder of his son for converting to Catholicism – aroused the conscience of France with the words *"Ecrasez l'Infâme."* Two centuries later, the French legal system, aided by an unconscionable press campaign that it did nothing to stop, inflicted emotional torture on an innocent woman who deserved every sympathy over the loss of her child. I find it painfully striking that the Cartesian canon – premised on the subjective nature of truth – which I criticized in "Montaigne and Descartes," is also at the heart of this injustice, personified by an unscrupulous journalist who, in a glance, "sees the truth" of a mother's guilt and an inept judge who, failing to extract a confession from an innocent person, allows his *intime conviction* to replace hard evidence. Together they violated every rule of fairness and due process. Alas, I do not see the slightest evidence of remorse or guilt in either the journalistic or the legal spheres about the miscarriage of justice in this case. Nor do I see any movement to reform this infamous system, by which the press can prejudge the guilt of those the law presumes innocent.

In closing, let me pre-empt a reaction that some readers are bound to have; in criticizing the French system of justice, I am not defending the American one. At least, when the French seek a confession they yearn for contrition; American justice seems to be heading toward a system by which confession leads to acquittal based on the previous nastiness of the victim: *viz,* Menendez and Bobbit. Jean-Marie Villemin, a father who killed the man he thought murdered his son, was convicted of murder and spent three-and-a-half years in prison. He paid the price!

Through this tragic case I learned of the existence of an extraordinary couple, Christine and Jean-Marie Villemin, who deserve to be remembered and honored wherever love, fidelity and decency are valued. Their letters to each other in prison are beautiful expressions of love and support. The Villemins illustrate the point I made in "Confessions of a Francophile" (November 1990): on the whole, the best people in France are those whom the elitist educational system has rejected. In reading the touching letters of this distraught couple, I thought of Matthew Arnold's lines in Dover Beach:

"Ah, love, let us be true
To one another! For the world...
Hath really neither joy, nor love, nor light
Nor certitude, nor peace, nor help for pain."

I wish I could have cited a French poem on this theme, but that's the price I pay for having been born and raised in Philadelphia.

Vol. XVI, N° 2, April 1994

"Jacques le Bouteur" and "Edouard the Killer"

After the heavy subject treated in the February Newsletter, I feel that my faithful readers deserve some lighter entertainment. Yet, be forewarned, I find it impossible to avoid recurring themes such as French justice, *dirigisme* and language follies.

Spring has come to France and, with it, daylight saving time, which the French call, in hopeful anticipation, "summer time" (*heure d'été*). The end of March marks also the first anniversary of the accession of Edouard Balladur to the prime-ministership. A year ago, I reported that the game plan of Jacques Chirac – the perennial Mayor of Paris and head of the leading political party, the RPR, a relic of Gaullism – was to be elected President of France in May 1995, when Mitterrand's second term expires, by eschewing the active leadership of the government in favor of his henchman Edouard Balladur. The theory was that the colorless Balladur would do the day-to-day work of governing while Chirac stayed "in reserve" and thus avoided the erosion of popularity that the Prime Minister was bound to suffer. It was assumed that both men had agreed on this scenario but, skeptically, in one of my Newsletters, I cited Robert Burns' famous phrase about the best-laid plans of mice and men. Indeed, until a month ago, my skepticism seemed right on point, for Balladur was amazing all political observers, and dismaying Chirac, by maintaining incredible popularity ratings in the polls, consistently more than 60 percent of "satisfied" people.

This feat was all the more puzzling because Balladur began his reign by increasing taxes and social-security charges while doing nothing significant to stem unemployment. Although official statistics place the level of job-seekers at close to 13 percent of the work force, in reality the percentage of the unemployed in the private sector is much higher, when one eliminates from the denominator the millions of civil servants who are never laid off, and those that the statistics ignore, such as persons in job-training programs and those receiving pre-retirement benefits.

But French realities caught up with Balladur in early March when his government botched-up a well-meaning measure to encourage first-time employment of young people. In typical Cartesian, technocratic fashion, the Minister of Labor concocted a decree calling for a "work-insertion contract" (*contrat d'insertion professionnelle* – shortened by the press to CIP) by which employers could hire young unemployed at less than the minimum wage, in exchange for devoting 20 percent of their time to on-the-job training dispensed by an old-timer slated for retirement. It sounds good in theory, but the decree went over like a lead balloon. The employers association (commonly called the *patronat*) let it be known that it had not asked for this measure; the unions opposed it, as they object to any erosion of the minimum wage, but, more significantly, most of the youth, including high-school, vocational school and university students, rose up in arms against the decree. All it took were a few mass demonstrations for the government to beat a hasty retreat, by modifying the decree to provide that the minimum wage (called the "SMIG") must be paid. But the young, having tasted blood, continued to demonstrate all over France, demanding outright repeal of the decree and its interpretative measures, with which the government had continued to tinker, in an effort to propitiate the demonstrators. But it was soon apparent that the young were not so much protesting this decree as the general bleak future that they see for themselves, not without justification.

For weeks, scenes of violence were commonplace on television, as the students were constantly joined by *casseurs* (literally "breakers") who took advantage of the demonstrations to throw rocks, break store

Mr. Dupont tries a new pair of *"paniers"*

windows and pilfer goods. The press was quick to evoke the celebrated events of May '68, which are now part of French mythology. The temptation to speak of May '68 was all the greater because Edouard Balladur played a prominent, if unheralded, role in those events, as one of the chief advisers to Georges Pompidou, then Prime Minister under de Gaulle. Jacques Chirac was also in Pompidou's cabinet then, and participated in secret negotiations with union chieftains in an effort to get strikers back to work. The entire history of this tandem is recounted in a recent book, *De Si Bons Amis* ("Such Good Friends"), written by two French journalists.

Balladur, it is said, is haunted by memories of May '68. Facing the cruel dilemma of either caving in to the students, and risk damaging his reputation with the rest of the population, or sticking with his decree and exposing France to a generalized "explosion" (as the press calls it), he chose the former. The CIP decree was cancelled and in its place a subsidy was granted to employers who hire young unemployed. Balladur's popularity has fallen to a low of 40 percent, a descent which is giving Chirac some grim satisfaction, even though commentators do not see how a collapse of Balladur could ultimately bring about Chirac's election to the Presidency next year. Balladur, of course, having tasted power and popularity, now covets the Presidency as much as Chirac does.

Against this background, so-called "cantonal" elections were held during the last two Sundays of March, to select members of the departmental legislatures, called *Conseil Généraux*. A *canton* can be compared with a county in American jargon, often comprising several towns in rural areas, but it is merely an electoral district having no government of its own. Because of the decentralization program initiated by the Socialists after 1981 the *Conseil Général* has considerable power over local matters, even though the central government, represented by a *Préfet,* still has the upper hand in each department. The first round led to the typical television pronouncements, which never fail to amuse me: each party claimed complete satisfaction with the results. The leaders of the RPR and UDF, the coalition controlling Parliament, crowed because they had the most votes (about 41 percent). The Socialists beamed because they got 30 percent, much more than last year. The Communists were happy because they exceeded ten percent. Le Pen's National Front was elated because it held its own despite a media blackout. Even the Ecologists, who got only three-and-a-half percent of the total vote, professed satisfaction because, as their spokesman, Brice Lalonde explained: "As we ran in only half the cantons this means our total score was twice as much." (By this reasoning, if the Ecologists had run in only a tenth of the cantons, their total score would have been 33.5 percent!) Isn't it wonderful to have elections where everyone wins and there are no losers?

Further entertainment and diversion have been supplied recently by the prominence given to reports that the Minister of Culture Jacques Toubon is preparing to tighten laws forbidding the use of foreign words in advertisements and in the workplace. This recurring theme has been met with mirth by many French journalists and business people, who are conscious that governmental decrees cannot keep a language "pure" at a time when communications, commerce and travel are bringing all nations closer together. It should be obvious that only a dead language like Latin can be kept pure. Yet despite the flaws in the technocratic approach, the defenders of the French language manage, from time to time, to put through regulations which purport to abolish foreign terms and substitute for them new French expressions. The government has just published a *Dictionary of Official Terms* which provides amusing reading and has inspired the first part of the title of this Newsletter. When Jacques Chirac worked for Pompidou, the latter was fond of referring to him as "*mon bulldozer*," so effective was the young *ENArque* in running over people who got in his way when carrying out his boss's instructions. Well, I have just learned that "bulldozer" is one of the terms banished from the French language by official fiat; the correct French word is now *bouteur,* invented in 1986 by a government agency. Thus Chirac becomes *Jacques le Bouteur*. Another such term, invented in 1986, is *restovite* for "fast food restaurant." Perhaps in time "Burger King" will become *Roi Bourgeois*. Significantly the new dictionary has quietly dropped the French term *marge brute d'autofinancement*, invented some years ago to replace "cash flow." Perhaps the fact that "M.B.A." represents the favorite foreign degree of French businessmen contributed to the banishment of the intended replacement.

The other half of my title is explained by another recent incident which provided entertainment just before the student demonstrations: the ousting of André Rousselet as head of the French private TV channel Canal Plus. To understand the incident, one must first harken back to a murder case which attracted national attention earlier this year when a Moroccan gardener, whose name is Omar Raddad, was tried for killing a

French woman for whom he worked in southern France. The victim had been stabbed in the basement of her house but before dying she had managed to find the strength to bolt the door and write on it in her own blood, *"Omar m'a tuer"* ("Omar killed me"). As this was the only evidence linking the gardener to the murder, the case aroused intense interest, including allegations of racism by the controversial defense counsel, Jacques Vergès. But the most fascinating aspect of the case was the emphasis given to the grammatical error made by the dying woman, since she used the infinitive *tuer* instead of the past tense *tuée* (the second "e" because the feminine object precedes the transitive verb). In a country where even dying people are expected to avoid grammatical errors, this lapse was advanced as a ground of the gardener's innocence, particularly since the victim was well educated. I must confess that I sympathized with the poor woman because I have often made the same type of error in writing French hurriedly, where the infinitive and the past tense have the same pronunciation. At any rate, Omar was convicted but the phrase lingered on.

To return to André Rousselet, he is a close henchman of President Mitterrand, who rewarded his fidelity several years ago by naming him first to head the nationalized advertising giant, Havas, and then allowing him to set up Canal Plus, which has been hugely successful as a pay-TV channel, using home decoders rather than cable. Of course, the advent of the rightist parties in 1993 made Canal Plus a choice plum for a power play. In February, the two leading shareholders of the publicly-traded company, including Havas, made a pact which assured their control of Canal Plus. Rousselet resigned in protest, and then published an article in *Le Monde*, entitled, *"Edouard m'a Tuer,"* deliberately imitating the same error, and pointing a finger at Edouard Balladur as the instigator of the power play. Only a day earlier, Balladur had proclaimed on television that he had learned about the Canal Plus moves only by reading the newspapers, an explanation which hardly anyone believed since his close friend and appointee, Jacques Friedman, who had been ousted as head of Air France years earlier by the Socialists, was behind the maneuverings concerning Canal Plus.

The bold use of the phrase "*Edouard m'a tuer*" was considered a stroke of genius, and constituted the first serious accusation against the bona fides and credibility of Balladur, who had managed to portray a public image of "Mr Clean," above the fray of partisan politics. Already, in December, Balladur had lost points over the controversy surrounding the repeal of the 19th-century statute, known as the *loi Falloux*, which limits the financial aid that municipalities can give for the physical maintenance of private schools, most of whom are Church-operated in France. The repeal was rammed through Parliament in November, and led to nation-wide protests by advocates of the public-school system, carrying the banner of *l'école laïque*. Stunned by the scope of the protests, Balladur was forced to pledge substantial aid to renovate public schools, and then was humiliated further when the Constitutional Court held the key provision of the new law to be unconstitutional.

This embarrassment and the Rousselet incident, coming on the heels of Balladur's retreat last October from the reorganization of Air France, necessitated by its huge losses, and his botched handling of the Brittany fishermen's strike, were preludes to the debacle over the CIP, which finally caused Balladur to lose his amazing standing in the opinion polls. Of course, many people are reminding themselves of the epithet that Marie-France Garaud pinned on Balladur during the Pompidou era – Ballamou, playing on the fact that his name ends with *dur* which means "hard" whereas *mou* means "soft."

Beyond the immediate fun of all this, many people, including myself, have been calling to mind the title of Michel Crozier's book, published more than 20 years ago, *La Société Bloquée*. I must confess that I never read the book because the title itself told it all. France remains a blocked society, where reforms are thwarted, repealed or cosmetic. If you have been reading my Newsletters you are aware of the causes of this situation: a Catholic, monarchical tradition favoring authority and the maintaining of privileges, led by a dominant caste of functionaries, coupled with an educational system which foists taboos and myths on each generation coming of age. It is not Edouard Balladur or Jacques Chirac who will unblock French society. Their only concern is to be the next elected king of France, and their rivals, such as Michel Rocard, Jacques Delors, Raymond Barre and Valéry Giscard d'Estaing – *fonctionnaires* all – have no different aim.

There is one, and only one, significant reform which could change France radically, but not one of these would-be kings is proposing it, for obvious reasons: a constitutional amendment requiring civil servants to resign before running for or holding elective office. One paragraph can do it, but a thousand years of history provide a thousand reasons why it will never happen.

Vol. XVI, N°s 3-4, May-June 1994

L'Affaire Dreyfus, a Century Later

In my report on the Gregory case, I made reference to the celebrated Dreyfus Affair. A distinguished reader from Tel Aviv seized on this remark to request that I devote an issue to the trials and tribulations of Alfred Dreyfus, an obscure French Army captain who was court-martialed 100 years ago on a charge of espionage for Germany. The fact that Dreyfus was Jewish became central to the affair which shook and divided France for more than a decade. Amazingly, controversy broke out recently about this case when a French Army archivist was sanctioned for describing the case in an ambiguous manner, suggesting that Dreyfus might have been guilty.

I first learned of Dreyfus while still a child in Philadelphia, on seeing the moving picture called *The Life of Emile Zola,* which starred Paul Muni in the role of the great novelist who took up the cause. Later, I read more than one book in English on the affair but that was a long time ago. To refresh my memory and obtain the benefit of more recent research, I have just finished reading Jean-Denis Bredin's well-documented opus, aptly called *L'Affaire,* a revised edition of which was published in 1993. Not the least virtue of this monumental work is that it devotes several chapters to placing the Dreyfus case in its historical and social context of France in the last decade of the 19th century.

The key insight is to recall that in 1894, France was still smarting from the humiliating defeat its army suffered in 1871 in the Franco-Prussian war, which resulted not only in the downfall of Napoleon III but also, more significantly, in the annexation by Germany of the Alsace and the Lorraine. The return of these provinces was at the top of the agenda of French politicians, just as the French army placed as its first priority revenging its 1871 defeat. Military preparedness was building up and espionage and counter-espionage were sensitive subjects. The Germans were, of course, keen on learning what the French army was developing in the way of weapons and, so, a military attaché, Colonel Maximillien von Schwartzkoppen, at the embassy in Paris, was placed in charge of obtaining information. Fortune smiled on him when a French army officer visited the embassy and proposed information for money. This traitor, Major Charles-Ferdinand Walsin Esterhazy, was an utter rogue: a gambler, seducer of women and a con-man of the first order, who was always in need of money.

The French army's counter-espionage unit, called the "statistical service," had placed a cleaning woman of the German embassy on its payroll. Incredible as it seems, Schwartzkoppen was as sloppy then as the CIA is today, with much less technology. He was wont to discard sensitive documents in his waste-basket, often simply crumbling them instead of shredding them. As a result, the cleaning woman, Marie Bastian, would make daily deliveries of discarded papers to the intelligence unit; this channel was known euphemistically as the "ordinary route" (*la voie ordinaire*). One such delivery in September 1894 produced a paper which was to seal Dreyfus's fate: it was simply a hand-written cover-letter by which Esterhazy transmitted secret documents about French artillery pieces and plans. This document came to be immortalized as the *bordereau.*

Let us examine the process by which Dreyfus was accused, and thereby learn the names of some of the villains of the affair. General Auguste Mercier was the Minister of War. He told the chief-of-staff of the Army, General Charles de Boisdeffre and his next-in-line General Charles Gonse, to find the guilty officer. Photographs of the *bordereau* were distributed to various bureaux, including the artillery section of the general staff. At first no one recognized the handwriting, but then an officer suggested to Colonel Pierre Fabre, an underling of the two generals, to look among officer trainees who had rotated among the various offices of the general staff, thus having access to the artillery information transmitted to the Germans. As Captain Dreyfus had recently been one such *stagiaire*, suspicion fastened on him; he was the most likely spy simply because he was Jewish. Anti-Semitism was rampant in France at the time; it was barely a century earlier that Jews were "emancipated" by the French Revolutionary Assembly, that is, given the rights of citizenship. (I recommend to readers Robert Badinter's illuminating book on this subject called *Libres et Egaux*). Alfred Dreyfus was the most innocuous person one could imagine. Member of a wealthy family who, like most Jews, left Alsace rather than become German subjects, he was intensely patriotic and devoted to the Army. He was blond and blue-eyed and had just turned 35 when misfortune struck.

Colonel Fabre was all the more inclined to believe Dreyfus guilty because he had given him an unfavorable rating the prior year. A superficial comparison of handwriting convinced Fabre and other officers that Dreyfus had written the *bordereau.* Fabre reported to General Gonse, who reported to General de Boisdeffre, who reported to General Mercier, that the guilty officer had been found. Mercier, however, pointed out that the accusing officers were not professional graphologists, and so he assigned as investigator an officer who fancied himself a handwriting expert, Major Ferdinand du Paty du Clam. Du Paty quickly compared the handwriting of Dreyfus with that of the *bordereau* and declared them identical. Dreyfus, like the dutiful student he had been, had learned penmanship in the standard way, as did Esterhazy; thus there was a superficial resemblance between the two scripts. General Mercier then discussed the matter with the President of the Republic, the Prime Minister and several key ministers.

Despite their concern about creating a diplomatic incident with Germany, Mercier decided to arrest Dreyfus, but first he tried to bolster the case by consulting an independent handwriting expert, Alfred Gobert, who expressed doubt that Dreyfus was the author of the *bordereau.* Mercier turned to another "expert," Alphonse Bertillon, who quickly took the opposite view. De Paty then conceived a marvelously Cartesian plan to confound the suspect: Dreyfus would be summoned to the ministry on a pretext and asked to write a dictated text reminiscent of the *bordereau:* if he trembles, he is guilty; if he doesn't tremble, he is even more guilty, since only a hardened criminal would keep his composure in such circumstances! On the basis of such ridiculous logic was an innocent man's life ruined!

Thus, on Saturday, October 13, 1894, Dreyfus received a notice to appear the following Monday morning for a routine inspection. Unsuspecting, Dreyfus spent a tranquil Sunday with his wife Lucie and their two young children, Pierre and Jeanne. When he showed up for the appointment, Dreyfus was received by Major Georges Picquart, who was later to become a hero of the case. Picquart led Dreyfus to a room where Major du Paty was waiting along with three unidentified civilians, and behind a screen there was hidden an observer, Major Hubert Charles Henry (who was to become the worst villain of the affair). Du Paty, claiming that he had injured his right hand, asked Dreyfus to write a letter for General de Boisdeffre based on his dictation. Sure enough, Dreyfus's hand trembled a bit and du Paty questioned him on this. Dreyfus replied that his hand was stiff because the outside temperature was cold; doubtless, also, he was nervous since the dictation ploy was decidedly strange. Major du Paty then laid his hand on Dreyfus's shoulder and solemnly bellowed: "In the name of the law I arrest you. You are accused of high treason." The dumbfounded Dreyfus protested his innocence, but du Paty read him the applicable Penal Code section while opening a desk drawer to show Dreyfus a revolver with which the guilty man was supposed to do the "honorable thing." Dreyfus cried out: "I am innocent; kill me if you wish." He was then searched and carried off by Major Henry to the prison on Rue du Cherche-Midi, where he was kept incommunicado for three weeks before he could see a lawyer or his wife. Thus, Dreyfus's nightmare had begun.

Before I resume the chronology, I want to make some remarks about military justice which, as Clemenceau said, is to justice what military music is to music. (Such a comparison is unfair to John Philip Sousa, the composer of some sublime marches, including *The Stars and Stripes Forever.*) During the 1950s, I was privileged to serve for three years in the Judge Advocate General's Corps of the United States Army. As a defense counsel in general courts-martial, I learned first-hand the meaning of the term "command influence." After one hard-fought case where my client was convicted of statutory rape, an officer-member of the court came to see me and said, "I'll deny this if you use my name but I had to vote to convict your client; the presiding officer told us that he would not let us out of the room until we found the accused guilty." I was later to learn that many officers held the view that if the commanding general ordered a soldier to be tried by general court-martial, he had to be guilty. Therefore they so voted, and meted out the maximum sentence, leaving clemency to the commanding general. If this was prevalent in the US Army only 40 years ago, you can imagine what the attitude of French officers was a century ago in the rigid hierarchical framework of the French Army.

My point is that in the best of circumstances Dreyfus did not have a chance to be acquitted once he was brought to trial in a military court. (Bredin does not discuss the question why the civil courts did not have jurisdiction; it took almost a century for the French parliament to abolish courts-martial for peace-time offenses, at the instigation of his former law partner, Robert Badinter, who became Minister of Justice in 1981.) But Dreyfus was in the worst of circumstances, not only because he was a Jew but also because his superiors made up for the lack of hard evidence by using every trick of the trade to have him convicted. When a new expert expressed doubt that Dreyfus was the author of the *bordereau,* Bertillon concocted an incredible theory to explain away the dissimilarity of the handwriting: Dreyfus had deliberately disguised his own writing. In other words, the less the *bordereau* resembled Dreyfus' writing the more this proved Dreyfus's guilt! Bertillon then developed an elaborate theory to the effect that Dreyfus had imitated his own writing and that of his brother and wife. On two successive days he expounded this concept of "auto-forgery" to the French president Jean Casimir-Perier and the latter concluded that Bertillon was a madman. Yet Bertillon became the star witness in the trial of Captain Dreyfus!

And in a court system which has no rule against hearsay evidence and no cross-examination, Major Henry had the effrontery to testify that an unidentified source had revealed that Dreyfus was a traitor. Then to button up the case, Major du Paty passed to the court a secret file containing old documents which Major Henry had trumped-up to incriminate Dreyfus; one of them was an old letter recovered from Schwartzkoppen's office which referred to "*ce canaille de D*" ("that rascal D"). Obviously, the court was supposed to understand that D referred to Dreyfus. The existence of this secret file came to light only years later.

On December 22, 1894, the court-martial found Dreyfus guilty of espionage and sentenced him to be publicly stripped of his rank as officer, and to be deported to Devil's Island for the rest of his life. Why wasn't Dreyfus sentenced to death? Simply because the law at the time did not provide for this penalty in time of peace, an omission which the Parliament was soon to remedy. But in any event, no one was expected to survive even a few years on Devil's Island!

On Saturday, January 5, 1895, an atrocious ceremony was held on the parade ground of the Ecole Militaire in Paris. While the crowd shouted "Death to the Jews – Death to Judas," Dreyfus was marched in and stood at attention facing a general who said: "Alfred Dreyfus, you are no longer worthy of bearing arms. In the name of the French people, we degrade you." Then an officer broke Dreyfus's saber and stripped him of all his insignia. His uniform in tatters, Dreyfus cried out, his voice breaking: "Soldiers, an innocent man is being degraded. Soldiers, an innocent man is being dishonored. Long live France. Long live the Army." To complete the humiliation, Dreyfus was marched up and down the parade ground, while the crowd jeered and insulted him.

On April 13, 1895, Dreyfus arrived in Devil's Island (a tiny French possession off the northeast coast of South America). His life there was a living death: in 110-degree heat, almost devoured by insects, racked with fever, seeing no one but his jailers, to whom he was forbidden to speak, eating miserable food, receiving sparse mail from his wife, whose censored letters were not allowed to allude to the efforts of his family and friends to overturn his conviction, this innocent man had despair as his constant companion. Several months later, in a desperate attempt to call attention to his case, his brother Mathieu allowed an English newspaper to report that Dreyfus had escaped from Devil's Island. Although this was obviously false, the prison authorities stupidly put Dreyfus in chains and erected palisades around his small hut, cutting off the only consolation he had – a view of the ocean.

In a short time, this young man of 35 aged beyond description, his hair turned white, his teeth fell out, his body was emaciated by disease and malnutrition. At one point, the prison authorities began preparations for returning his body to France, so sure they were of his imminent death. But Dreyfus managed to survive, in what was surely a triumph of will and faith that justice would be done.

While Dreyfus was suffering this ignominious fate, unaware of developments in his cause, the tide slowly began to turn in Paris. On July 1, 1895, Major Picquart, an anti-Semite himself, who had never doubted Dreyfus's guilt, was named to head the "statistical service" whose efforts had led to Dreyfus's conviction. Several months later, in March 1896, Picquart came into possession, through the *voie ordinaire*, of a document (later known as *le petit bleu*) which was to cause him to doubt Dreyfus's guilt. Madame Bastian had recovered torn-up bits of a telegram form which Colonel Schwartzkoppen had drafted but not sent. When the bits were pieced together, the addressee's name and address were visible; "Major Esterhazy, 27 rue de la Bienfaisance." It thus appeared that a second traitor existed in the French Army. Picquart, a conscientious and honest officer, began a discreet investigation of Esterhazy. A month later, he obtained samples of Esterhazy's writing. The hand looked familiar; Picquart took out his copy of the *bordereau* and compared it with the Esterhazy samples. The handwriting was identical!

At this point, the case takes on a grotesque turn and Picquart will become the second victim of the Dreyfus affair. Naively thinking that his superiors will be eager to learn the guilt of Esterhazy and the innocence of Dreyfus, Picquart prepares a report on the new-found facts for General de Boisdeffre. Meeting with Picquart, the general seems less than enthusiastic about the report and tells Picquart to see his deputy, General Gonse. Again, the reaction is unenthusiastic; Picquart is amazed to hear Gonse tell him, "Separate the two cases." "How is this possible?," Picquart wonders. The guilt of Esterhazy means the innocence of Dreyfus. This was not the way it was to be; the worst is yet to come. In the ensuing months, Major Henry, with full knowledge of his superiors, concocts what was to become the most notorious document of the affair, known as the "Henry forgery" (*le faux Henry*). This forgery, which specifically names Dreyfus for the first time, was accomplished by pasting together two pieces of paper. It was a crude job (as I will explain later), but Henry expected to get away with it by leaving the original in a closed file and making a handwritten "true copy" of it for his evidence file. This copy was "authenticated" by Major Henry, General Gonse and two other officers, who actually signed the copy, giving their name and rank! It is now November 1896, more than two years since Dreyfus has been falsely accused.

Knowing that (now) Colonel Picquart could not be corrupted into silence while serving in the intelligence section, the general staff got him out of there by "promoting" him to an assignment in Tunisia. Not content with this banishment, the generals decided to "get" Picquart by fabricating a case against him. In the ensuing months, a cover-up was planned and executed that makes Watergate look like a Sunday-School outing. As too many people knew about Esterhazy's guilt, the generals decided that the best way to keep Dreyfus on Devil's Island was to bring a collusive case against Esterhazy and acquit him. Thus, Generals de Boisdeffre and Gonse initiated half-hearted charges against Esterhazy while secretly cooperating with him to defeat the accusation!

One cannot over-stress the utter depravity of these French generals: they knew that Esterhazy was a spy, they knew that Dreyfus was innocent, yet they deliberately compounded the felony by conspiring to run a phony trial of the real spy, following the military version of Cartesian logic: if the guilty man is acquitted this will reinforce the proof that the innocent man is guilty!

Yes, Esterhazy was tried by a rigged court-martial in January 1898 and acquitted, while Colonel Picquart looked on in disgust. It is at this point that Picquart becomes one of the heroes of the story. His stony integrity, his courage in bucking his superior officers, his determination to bring out the truth of Dreyfus's innocence, are the only counters to the dishonor of the rest of the military involved in this case. And yet, the more the French generals dishonored their uniform the more they blathered on about the "honor of the Army." Was ever a better demonstration given of the truth of Dr Johnson's famous observation: "Patriotism is the last refuge of a scoundrel! "

It is also at this point that another authentic hero of the case takes his place in history: Emile Zola. The great novelist, whose realistic works such as "*Germinal*" describing the plight of the proletariat, had offended the establishment, had not followed the Dreyfus case at the start, because he was then living in Rome. Late in 1897, he got deeply involved with the facts and became thoroughly convinced not only of the innocence of Dreyfus but also of the impossibility of obtaining a retrial for him without a dramatic appeal to public opinion. Convinced that Esterhazy would be white-washed by the military tribunal, Zola began writing his celebrated "Letter to Mr. Felix Faure, President of the Republic" while the trial was going on. The newspaper *l'Aurore* had been founded only a few months earlier, and Georges Clemenceau was its first editor-in-chief. When Zola brought him his letter, Clemenceau conceived the brilliant idea of entitling it: *"J'Accuse."* Thus on January 13, 1897 – two days after the acquittal of Esterhazy, when the Dreyfusards were at their nadir of discouragement – Zola's open letter electrified Paris and the world by publicly accusing various French Army officers, including du Paty, Mercier, de Boisdeffre and Gonse, of the crime of covering up Dreyfus's innocence and ordering the acquittal of Esterhazy. It is fascinating to note that Zola described the crime against Dreyfus as one of *lèse-humanité* and *lèse-justice*, that is, literally, "harm to humanity" and "harm to justice." Thus, Zola was perhaps the first to assert the existence of crimes against humanity.

Emile Zola fully expected that his *"J'accuse"* would lead to his own indictment for defamation. Indeed, the government wasted no time in bringing charges. On January 18, 1897, the Council of Ministers decided that the Minister of War would bring a felony charge against Zola, but seeking to prevent the airing of Dreyfus's innocence, they limited the case to a single count, that of falsely accusing the Army of having ordered Esterhazy's acquittal. Knowing that Zola would call Picquart as a witness, the generals resolved to discredit this honest officer and so, on February 1st , he was brought before an Army board of inquiry on the charge of leaking classified information. The board dutifully recommended his dishonorable discharge!

On February 7, 1898, Zola's trial began in the Cour d'Assises of Paris, a felony court, the only one with jurors in France. Space does not allow me to describe this trial here: it was a free-for-all, as only French felony trials can be, with no rules of evidence. All the principal officers testified, including Colonel Picquart. (It is important to note that he was not aware at that time of the *faux Henry*.) The generals made emotional appeals to defend the "honor of the Army and the Nation." The presiding judge did his best to prevent evidence from being presented as to the innocence of Dreyfus, invoking the constant theme of *la chose jugée* (*res judicata, i.e.,* thing decided). Yet the madman Bertillon was allowed to testify, provoking even the anti-Dreyfusards to laughter by his ridiculous theories. To my mind, the most memorable moment of the trial occurred when Clemenceau (who was given special permission to join Zola's defense team, although not a barrister) pointed to the picture of Christ on the Cross, above the Judge's head (note that Church and State were not yet separated in France!) and shouted *"Voilà la chose jugée."*

It took the jury only 35 minutes to find Zola guilty and to sentence him to the maximum penalty: one year in prison. Zola remained free pending his appeal to the highest court of France, the Cour de Cassation, which fortunately reversed the conviction and ordered another trial, this time at Versailles.

But Zola's *"J'accuse"* and the publicity given to his trial had helped increase the ranks of the supporters of Dreyfus. At the same time, the anti-Dreyfusards continued their passionate campaign; anti-Jewish demonstrations took place all over France. There can be little doubt that the majority of the population was convinced of Dreyfus's guilt. Those favorable to the captain came mainly from the ranks of non-establishment intellectuals, whereas the *bourgeoisie* and the Catholic Church were predominantly hostile to his cause, as was most of the press. Even the Socialists were not initially sympathetic to Dreyfus: he was a rich Jew, far removed from the working class. However, starting in 1898, the great Socialist leader, Jean Jaurès, placed his eloquent weight behind Dreyfus.

Dreyfus's wife Lucie and his brother Mathieu worked indefatigably toward the objective of obtaining a new trial for him, which only the Cour de Cassation could order, on the basis of new evidence. By a strange quirk of fate, the desire of the Army to put forward its best case would involuntarily lead to the opposite result. The Minister of War ordered his underlings, including General Gonse and (now) Lietenant-Colonel Henry, to put their files in order and to assemble all the documents of the Army's secret file (which included the Henry forgery). When a new minister, Jacques Godefroy Cavaignac, was named Minister of War after the general elections of 1898, this determined anti-Dreyfusard decided to study the file personally in order to present to the Chamber of Deputies a definitive refutation of the thesis of Dreyfus's innocence. He did, indeed, present a devastating case on July 7, 1898, including a wholly baseless allegation that Dreyfus had confessed his guilt to a fellow officer after his trial and, in particular, Cavaignac read the forged Henry letter and other documents implicating Dreyfus, without realizing that by referring to secret evidence never presented in open court he was providing a "smoking gun" to the Dreyfus cause. Jean Jaurès seized the opportunity to publish an open letter to the Minister pointing out that his speech in parliament constituted proof that the military court had convicted Dreyfus on the basis of secret evidence.

The most dramatic development since Dreyfus's conviction was to occur a month later. On August 13, 1898, an Army archivist, Captain Louis Cuignet, was examining the secret file and, while looking closely at the *faux Henry* under artificial light, noticed that the lines on the paper were of two different colors. Curiously, this flaw was not visible in natural light! Thus, Cuignet realized that the letter which Henry claimed to have recovered from the German Embassy in 1896, implicating Dreyfus, was a collage of two different documents. It is to the credit of this out-and-out anti-Dreyfusard that he never considered concealing his discovery. The next morning he informed his superior, General Gauderique Roget, of his discovery, and together they went to see the minister, Cavaignac, to demonstrate the forgery. Again, while remaining convinced of Dreyfus's guilt, Cavaignac did the honorable thing; he confronted Colonel Henry with the evidence, grilling him firmly, until Henry finally confessed his crime. He was arrested and imprisoned on August 30, 1898, and Cavaignac issued a public statement announcing the forgery and Henry's guilt. The next day Henry was found dead in his cell, his throat slit, a razor in his hand.

One might have thought that these dramatic events would have led to Dreyfus's immediate release from Devil's Island. But no! It took almost a year for the Cour de Cassation, after incredible complications and internal struggles, to order a new trial for Dreyfus. This historic decision was rendered on June 3, 1899. The same day a Parisian newspaper published an interview of Major Esterhazy acknowledging that he was the author of the *bordereau.* Two days later, Alfred Dreyfus was given a message informing him of the court's decision, which restored to him his rank: he was once again Captain Dreyfus, entitled to wear his uniform, but he remained charged with espionage. The cruiser *Sfax* was dispatched to pick him up and return him to France for a new trial. On June 8, 1899, he boarded the *Sfax*; he had spent four years and two months – 1,516 horrible days and nights – on Devil's Island.

On July 1, 1899, Dreyfus set foot on French soil once again, on the Brittany coast, near Quiberon, where a special train took him to Rennes and prison once more. The same day, he was allowed to see Lucie in an adjoining cell. She could hardly recognize him: her husband, not yet 40, was now an old man, his hair white, his body emaciated.

Is this the happy ending? Incredibly, no! In August 1899, Dreyfus's new trial began in Rennes and on September 7th the military court found Dreyfus guilty by a vote of five to two, and sentenced him to 10 years in prison! I will not even bother to comment on this grotesque decision; by this time the whole French government, headed by Pierre Waldeck-Rousseau, was convinced of Dreyfus's innocence, but French Army officers, they are something else!

The government was determined not to send Dreyfus back to prison, which everyone knew would mean his death. The decision was made to have him pardoned by the President of the Republic, but this created a horrible dilemma for Dreyfus and his supporters. He could be pardoned only if he requested it in writing, in which case he could not appeal the verdict. By letting the verdict stand, he was implicitly admitting guilt. The Dreyfus family agonized over the decision, but there was really no choice; the poor man could not endure another public ceremony of degradation and a return to Devil's Island. Entreated by his family, Dreyfus signed the petition for pardon; on September 17, 1899, President Emile Loubet signed the pardon decree. The next day Alfred Dreyfus was a free man. He went south with his brother to his sister's home in Carpentras, where he found Lucie and their children Pierre and Jeanne. Slowly, he nursed back what remained of his health. To spoil things, let me add that, despite the protests of Dreyfus, Picquart and Zola, who wanted their own court actions to proceed, the Parliament in 1900 granted an amnesty to all persons involved in the Dreyfus affair, including the officers who had acted so dishonorably!

But the case was not over. The ignoble verdict of guilt could not be allowed to stand. A petition was again made to the Cour de Cassation to reverse the verdict. It took six years to get the court to accept the case. When it did so, the supreme court of France acted like a trial court; it undertook a laborious examination of all the evidence and heard witnesses, including mad Bertillon. By this time, no one doubted the innocence of Dreyfus. The only serious issue was how to avoid the normal effect of a reversal, that is, a new trial by a military court that was likely to convict Dreyfus again, despite the lack of evidence. Only in exceptional circumstances can the court reverse the decision without retrial – when there is simply no case against the accused. The Court finally made this decision on July 12, 1906. The case was over: it had taken almost 12 years for French justice to hold that an innocent man was innocent.

The next day, the French Parliament voted to promote Dreyfus to the rank of major and to grant him the Legion of Honor. It also voted to rehabilitate Picquart, who had been drummed out of the Army and jailed for over a year; he was given the rank of brigadier general. Thus was justice rendered to a courageous officer who risked his life and career to serve the cause of truth. Virtually alone among French army officers, he applied the precept that to honor one's nation one must first honor truth.

Despite his sorry physical state, Dreyfus served on active duty during World War I. Picquart, whom Clemenceau named Minister of War in 1909, died accidentally in January 1914. Esterhazy died peacefully in 1923 in England where he lived under a false identity. Dreyfus lived until 1935, long enough to see the rise of Hitler to power in Germany.

For a century, commentators have focussed on the aspect of anti-Semitism as the chief, if not only cause, of the injustice wrought on Dreyfus. It is time to make the point that Dreyfus was a victim not only of anti-Semitism but also of two other blights which the reader will not be surprised to see me raise, remembering that what led me to this subject was my paper on the Gregory case. There the victim of a false accusation was not a Jew but the very mother whose child had been murdered. I pointed to the chronic failure of the French educational system to train people to deal with facts, as well as a court system founded on the Catholic tradition of the Inquisition, with its focus on getting a confession from the suspect.

Incongruous as it might seem at first blush, consider the parallels: A journalist "sees" in a flash that the mother is guilty, and then spends years trying to get her convicted. The judge discards the prime suspect when he does not confess and the key witness retracts her testimony. Ergo, it can only be the mother, even though she is the last person in the world to have a motive for the crime. The more she denies it the more the judge seeks wholly baseless explanations, including adultery and insanity, to explain why she must be guilty.

In Dreyfus, the military "see" in a flash that only a Jewish officer can be a spy, ignoring the fact that he has not the slightest motivation for such a heinous crime: the patriotism of Alsatian Jews was well-established and, being rich, Dreyfus, unlike the real culprit, had no monetary motivation to sell secrets to the Germans. Then, what I call "military Cartesianism" sets in: Major du Paty, having conceived "very clearly and very distinctly" the guilt of Dreyfus, stages his stupid session of *dictée*, with a "heads I win tails you lose" logic: if Dreyfus trembles he is guilty, if he does not tremble he is even more guilty. Bertillon, the handwriting "expert," whom later judges considered stark, raving mad, employs the same logic: if Dreyfus's handwriting is different from that of the *bordereau*, this means that he took great pains to disguise it. Not one officer had the common sense to point out that if Dreyfus spent so much time disguising a simple cover letter, he would have had no time for spying! (In the Villemin case, also, handwriting "experts," influenced by the police, tried to identify the mother as the "crow.") Later, when it became clear that Esterhazy wrote the *bordereau,* this proved to some generals that Dreyfus and Esterhazy were accomplices! The most amazing case of nutty Cartesianism is that of Captain Cugniet, who discovered Henry's forgery, but became an even more rabid devotee of Dreyfus's guilt. Doubtless he reasoned that if poor Henry went to such lengths he must have had good reason to believe Dreyfus guilty!

My point is that anti-Semitism is almost too kind an explanation for the aberrations committed against Dreyfus: the role of stupidity should not be overlooked. Nor has enough attention been paid to the flaws in the French court system, where there are no rules of evidence and no objective standard for linking guilt to the weight of evidence. Years ago, as an official observer for the US Army, I attended a French trial of an American soldier accused of negligent homicide. A woman testified that she was in her kitchen when she heard a collision and then went to the scene of the accident. The judge asked her "How did the accident happen?" The witness replied, "I don't know, I didn't see it." But the judge went on, "But how did it seem to you that it happened?" In other words, he was inviting the witness to conjecture on the circumstances of the accident! It is to the woman's credit that she refused to answer this silly question.

In this respect, Bredin's book is another example of what I referred to in the Gregory newsletter as a common failing of French intellectuals, their sophisticated provincialism. Bredin, who has had a distinguished but traditional career at the bar, does not question at all a system where "witnesses" can "testify" about matters on which they have no direct knowledge, giving hearsay and opinion "evidence." Most French lawyers with whom I discuss such matters, are startled to hear me describe their court system as one based on Catholic methodology, despite the fact that a century ago the crucifix adorned every courtroom. A system in which it suffices to cultivate an *intime conviction* of someone's guilt without hard facts is bound to produce a Dreyfus case and a Villemin case now and then. To make matters worse, there is no significant review of convictions in the Cour d'Assises: the reviewing court, the Cour de Cassation, can only reverse for errors of form and procedure. It once overturned a conviction because the minutes of the trial court did not state that the door was open to the public when the sentence was handed out! But it cannot reverse on the basis of insufficient evidence or tainted evidence.

To be fair to the French, I must point out that every country produces examples of wrongful convictions based on tampered evidence. To take a recent example, English police rigged a case against several Irishmen who were convicted of terrorism. One can never banish lying and forging from the panoply of police techniques, but a court system can establish rules of evidence that would, say, prevent a Major Henry from testifying that Dreyfus is guilty because an unknown person told him so! And it can establish proper review of convictions.

Another point I want to make, ever so briefly, is that beside Alfred Dreyfus, the main victims of the Dreyfus affair were the French people themselves; they were lied to and manipulated by some of the most unworthy military and political leaders who ever lived. It is hard not to see a connection between this fact and the war of 1914-18 in which 1.4-million French soldiers were slaughtered and another four-million wounded.

To return to Alfred Dreyfus, it became fashionable among Dreyfusards and historians of the affair to consider him an anti-hero, as someone who was not worthy of the exalted cause that so many great men, like Zola, Jaurès and Clemenceau, had served. This was because Dreyfus was a taciturn, aloof man, without flights of eloquence, who liked the Army too much to be an authentic servant of a great cause. I once was taken in by this view, but I now strongly disagree with it. To me, Dreyfus was the noblest figure of them all. By staying alive on Devil's Island, and keeping his sanity, Dreyfus displayed an indomitable will that honored the human spirit. In all his letters to his wife, never once did Dreyfus complain that he was persecuted as a Jew. His true *grandeur* was to ask justice not for a Jew but for a Frenchman who was innocent of wrongdoing. Doubtless even today some French people cannot forgive Dreyfus for taking French ideals so seriously. On this 100th anniversary of his arrest, the French government would do well to enshrine his remains in the Pantheon in Paris, the temple built to honor the great men of France. His epitaph could simply be: "He believed in France."

Of course, the Dreyfus case highlighted the tragic dilemma of the Diaspora Jews: if they did not assimilate, they were blamed for being "different" but if they did assimilate, they were still the first to be blamed whenever a problem arose. (It was by reflecting on the Dreyfus case that Theodor Herzl – who witnessed the ceremony of degrading – conceived the necessity of a Jewish homeland.) The Jews of Germany, the most assimilated of all the Diaspora, were to discover this horrible truth during the Third Reich. And during the occupation of France, zealous French police rounded up Jews in Paris and other cities, sending them off to German concentration camps from which most never returned. The Vichy law on "the Status of Jews" is a momument to indecency. French "patriots" like Paul Touvier (just convicted of a crime against humanity for having seven Jews executed) volunteered for the Milice, to help cleanse France of Jews and other unwanted elements. Had Alfred Dreyfus been alive in 1942 he would doubtless have been the first to go.

From time to time, I ask French Jews why their family returned to France after World War II, considering the ignoble conduct of French officialdom. The answer is invariably a wan smile and a far-away look in their eyes. After reflecting on the lonely ordeal of Alfred Dreyfus on Devil's Island, I believe I can answer my own question: "We Jews have always lived on the hope of finding justice. Read our Bible and you'll see that we are used to societies where the worst cohabits with the best. So we love France, despite the worst, because we know that the best is also there."

Just as I concluded my paper on the Villemins with a quote from an English poet, so I think it appropriate to cite William Wordsworth's stirring sonnet written in honor of Toussaint l'Ouverture, the Haitian revolutionary leader who was tricked by Napoleon I into coming to France to negotiate independence for his people, and was cast into a dungeon where he died. After starting with "Toussaint, the most unhappy man of men" Wordsworth concludes:

"Thou hast left behind
Powers that will work for thee; air, earth, and skies.
There's not a breathing of the common wind
That will forget thee; Thou hast great allies:
Thy friends are exultations, agonies,
And love, and man's unconquerable mind."

Man's unconquerable mind: Alfred Dreyfus on Devil's Island.

Vol. XVI, N° 5, September 1994

Three Cheers for Robert Badinter

Readers of my recent Newsletter entitled "Jacques le Bouteur and Edouard the Killer" will recall that I poked fun at the efforts of the French *dirigistes*, currently led by the well-meaning Minister of Culture, Jacques Toubon, to keep the French language pure by inventing French words to replace offending English terms such as "bulldozer." Well, the *Loi Toubon,* intended to reinforce the legal barriers against the invasion of Americanisms, was enacted by Parliament in July but, in a landmark decision, the Constitutional Council, led by Robert Badinter, emasculated the law by invalidating key provisions that in effect would have allowed bureaucrats to decide what constitutes acceptable French.

This decision is a major blow in favor of freedom of expression, since it returns the French language to the French people. That is why I want to salute Robert Badinter, who happens to be the living Frenchman that I admire the most, independently of the fact that he has been a friend for 30 years.

What remains of the *Loi Toubon* is this: the French language must be used in employment agreements, commercial documents such as advertisements, warranties, instructions for use, invoices; billboards; and radio-television but, except for government agencies, no one can be required to use official terminology instead of foreign words. Basically this means that the French people are free to decide what constitutes the French language.

The decision was by no means an easy one to reach. Justice Holmes was fond of saying that "I can grant you any abstract principle and still decide the case either way." What he meant was that in all difficult cases there are at least two broad principles in contention, two roads that intersect, if you will, and the role of a court is to determine which principle has the right of way. In the present case, the Constitutional Court had to contend with a recent amendment to Article 2 of the French Constitution which specifies that the French language is the language of the republic. The other broad principle was derived from the preamble to the Constitution, which incorporates by reference the famous "Declaration of the Rights of Man" adopted in 1789 in the better days of the French Revolution, and in particular the stirring language of Article 11 (my translation): "The free communication of thoughts and opinions is one of man's most precious rights; any citizen may therefore speak, write and print freely, subject to liability for abusing this liberty in cases determined by the law."

The court did a neat job of reconciling these two principles. It upheld the parts of the law that require the use of the French language in certain circumstances, but it nullified other parts that prohibited the use of foreign expressions when a corresponding French term has been edicted by the government (as *bouteur* for bulldozer). The inference is thus clear that in writing and speaking French, private parties are free to incorporate foreign terms. In other words, it's still French if an employment agreement states: *"Votre titre sera 'Fast-food Marketing Manager'."* In theory, nothing prevents a zealous prosecutor from contending that a particular writing is not really French, but I suspect that the French courts will be loath to become censors of the language, particularly since the Constitutional Council stated that: "... the French language evolves, like any living language, by incorporating into its customary vocabulary terms of various sources, whether it be expressions stemming from regional languages, so-called popular terms, or foreign words."

Doubtless some civil libertarians (who are few and far between in France) would say that this decision does not go far enough. If a French company hires an American executive, why should his employment agreement be in French? To be sure, the law says that he is entitled to a translation in his native language, but what is the justification of requiring a French version, under pain of criminal sanctions?

In the same vein, why is it necessary to legislate the exclusive use of the French language on radio and television? It is obvious that the self-interest of any broadcaster is to use the French language when a French audience is involved. But if TF1 wants to broadcast a live show in English why shouldn't this be constitutionally protected?

Judging by the agonized response of the defenders of the *Loi Toubon*, including Prime Minister Balladur, one can understand how politically dangerous it would have been for the Conseil Constitutionnel to nullify the entire law. Both Balladur and Toubon, in their initial public reactions to the decision, harkened back to the decree of François I, in the 16th century, which required the use of French (rather than Latin) in court proceedings. Their point was that without authoritarian protection of the French language, the country would be in sorry state. I find it amusing that Balladur, who looks more and more like Louis XIV every day, should gloss over 400 years of history which gradually saw the decline of absolute monarchy and the rise of civil liberties. Someone should remind Balladur and Toubon that François I was not bound by the Declaration of the Rights of Man!

Even Jack Lang, the former Minister of Culture, albeit a Socialist, joined in the chorus criticizing the ruling of the Conseil Constitutionnel. Once a colleague of Robert Badinter, when the latter was Minister of Justice, Lang is now his bitter enemy, because the Conseil invalidated Lang's re-election as *Député* in 1993 by reason of excessive campaign expenditures.

Every time that the Council issues a major decision, as when it invalidated the law that allowed municipalities to grant higher subsidies to parochial schools, its role is called into question by traditionalists, who yearn for the good old days when no court could invalidate an act of Parliament. It was de Gaulle's 1958 constitution of the Fifth Republic which instituted the Constitutional Council. Ironically, de Gaulle's purpose was not in the least to offer greater protection for civil liberties but rather to curb the power of Parliament. You see, his Constitution granted broad powers to the executive branch, *i.e.*, the government, to legislate by decree in various domains. As these domains were off limits to Parliament, de Gaulle felt it necessary to police the line of demarcation by giving power to a court to declare parliamentary laws invalid, before they went into effect. To make it clear that the Constitutional Council was not there to benefit the ordinary citizen, de Gaulle's original version allowed only a handful of people, including himself, to refer a new law to the Council. A later amendment extended this right to 60 members of either house of Parliament. It was indeed a group of Socialist parliamentarians who challenged the Toubon statute.

Fortunately, the Constitution did not state that only laws which encroached on the government's exclusive jurisdiction could be invalidated. Thus, over the years, the Council developed a jurisprudence which invalidated acts of Parliament found to violate fundamental civil rights. This was all the more remarkable in that the Constitution contains no Bill of Rights. The Council decided that, as indicated above, the reference in the preamble to the Declaration of the Rights of Man was tantamount to a constitutional rule that was superior to legislative pronouncements. It has since gone further, in declaring that "fundamental legal principles" have constitutional status despite their specific absence from the Constitution. The Council has thus introduced a kind of "due process clause" into the French Constitution. One basic protection of the citizen that is still sadly lacking is the right to challenge constitutionality of laws and decrees in the ordinary courts. Encouraged in this direction by Badinter, President Mitterrand proposed such an amendment to the Constitution some years ago, but was not able to push it through because of the opposition of the Gaullists, who remain an authoritarian party. American jurists will find it strange that the constitutionality of a law can be determined without the benefit of "actual cases and controversies," as required by the American Constitution. But let us not forget that we are in the land of Descartes, where educated people do not need facts to know the right answers.

While I have often been critical of Socialist policies, particularly in the economic sphere (including nationalization of banks and industrial companies) since May 1981, when Mitterrand was first elected, this is the time to make the point that the Socialists have done more to promote freedom of expression and pluralism than the conservative parties that led France since 1958 under Presidents de Gaulle, Pompidou and Giscard d'Estaing. Let me give you some examples:

1. **Audiovisual.** Throughout the Fourth Republic and the Fifth, until the advent of Mitterrand, the government controlled radio and television. Not only were the official radio stations owned by the state, but also even the allegedly private radio stations, Europe 1 and RTL, were indirectly controlled by state-owned companies. As television became popular, governments took care to appoint loyal managers of the ORTF (Office de Radio-diffusion Television Française) who would do their bidding, which meant controlling the news that was broadcast and limiting access to the opposition. After Arthur Conte resigned as head of the ORTF, purportedly to protest government interference, he nevertheless disclosed in his memoirs that he would have breakfast every Friday morning with President Pompidou to get his briefings. It struck me as amusing proof of Conte's servility that in a country where no one important does business over breakfast, he did not even rate a *déjeuner* with the President. It is to the credit of Mitterrand and other Socialist leaders that shortly after his election, a host of private radio stations were given access to the airwaves. Moreover, control over television has been placed in an independent authority which appoints the president of the state-owned channels and regulates the other channels. The most popular channel – TF1 – was privatized several years ago and has remained independant.

2. **Tax deductions for private associations**. One of the key characteristics of the *dirigisme* of French governments was the refusal to allow taxpayers to deduct contributions to private associations unless they were granted the status of "public utility" by the government, a long and cumbersome process. The corollary of this is that functionaries decided what were the proper utilization of the people's money. This system explains the lack of diversity and pluralism in France, as there are hardly any institutions at university level that are not owned by the state and virtually no think-tanks financed by private funds. The Socialists made an inroad in this system by allowing deduction by individuals and enterprises of contributions to non-profit associations with charitable, educational, cultural and sports purposes. While the deductions are limited, they still have contributed greatly to the proliferation of non-profit associations which are not controlled by the state.

3. **European Convention on Human Rights**. Although the European Convention on Human Rights had been ratified by the Gaullist régime, it had refused to accept the jurisdiction of the Commission and Court created by the treaty, on the utterly fatuous ground that France never violated human rights: thus it needed no outside enforcement agencies! One of the first things that Robert Badinter did when named Minister of Justice in 1981 was to reverse this decision. Thus France now allows litigants to appeal to the European Commission on Human Rights, which in turn can refer cases to the Court of the same name when fundamental civil rights are violated by a member state.

Much of this progress in personal freedom has been due to the action of Robert Badinter, who has been a close friend and adviser to François Mitterrand for many years. While Badinter, so far as I know, has never been a card-carrying Socialist or run for elective office, his ability and reputation earned him the respect not only of Socialist stalwarts but also of most political parties in the opposition. Another of Badinter's innovations was to push for the abolition of the death penalty in France, which was voted out of existence by the Parliament in 1982, despite the fact that polls showed a heavy majority of French people in favor of it.

I met Robert Badinter in the early 1960s when we were on opposite sides of a business deal, from which we emerged friends and, as he later put it, charter members of a mutual-admiration society. I liked Robert because, despite his brilliance, he did not take himself too seriously, had a good sense of humor, and tolerated disagreement. Robert was then a private practitioner, a rare *avocat* who not only handled litigation, including criminal cases, but also negotiated business deals. While a generalist, Robert had an active practice in entertainment and media matters. Not long after I met him, Robert surprised me by telling me that he was working on his *aggrégation,* the coveted degree which involves a series of grueling competitive written and oral exams. This is hard enough to do on a full-time basis, but is a feat basically unheard-of for a practicing lawyer. I was not surprised when I learned that Robert succeeded in obtaining the title of *professeur agrégé*, and began giving courses at the University of Amiens. At about the same time, he formed a law partnership with another *professeur agrégé* Jean-Denis Bredin, who was later elected to the Académie Française.

Lest readers conclude that writing about a friend makes me lose my critical sense, let me add that I am no admirer of French universities, including law faculties, which exist more for the glory of professors than for the good of the students. A typical professor does not even have an office at the university, and merely shows up to read his lecture, leaving immediately thereafter, before a student can even ask him a question. This system of *cours magistral*, as the French call it, is an abomination, particularly since the students are expected to regurgitate word-for-word the pontifications of the professor. When one considers that Langdell introduced the case method at Harvard Law School in the 1870s, and encouraged students to think for themselves, it is not difficult to calculate that French legal education is more than a century behind that of the United States. As establishment figures, Badinter and Bredin have done nothing to change this system, but they can hardly be blamed for not attacking the impregnable fortress of inertia and self-interest that constitutes the French educational racket. It is easier to abolish the guillotine than the *aggrégation* and the *cours magistral*.

Speaking of the guillotine, it was a very bitter experience for Robert Badinter to become one of a handful of French *avocats* who in this generation had to witness the beheading of a client. In 1972, he had agreed to defend the first-named of two convicts, Bontems and Buffet, who had escaped from the Clairvaux prison by taking a guard and a nurse as hostages, both of whom were brutally murdered in the course of the aborted escape. Buffet had admitted cutting the guard's throat, but accused his accomplice of the fatal blow to the nurse. Badinter had hoped to save Bontems's life by showing that he had not wielded the murder weapon, but the jury in Troyes, while acquitting Bontems of the murder, nevertheless convicted him as an accomplice of Buffet and sentenced them both to the guillotine. President Pompidou refused to commute Bontems's sentence, and so Badinter had to undergo the gruesome experience of being called one evening to show up at the prison during the night and watch a man who had not actually killed anyone have his head severed from his body. From this experience there emerged a beautifully written and moving book, called *l'Exécution*, published in 1973, and a fierce determination to eliminate the guillotine.

One balmy afternoon, several years later, as I was walking down the Champs-Elysées, I bumped into Robert Badinter, who was heading towards me. After a warm greeting, he told me that he had just agreed to defend Patrick Henry, a young man who had confessed to the atrocious crime of kidnapping a child and murdering him despite payment of the ransom. All the *avocats* in the city of Troyes, where the crime occurred, had refused to defend Henry, in the face of an outraged public opinion. Robert told me that he had no illusions that Henry would be sentenced to death, but he felt that it was his duty to defend him. I felt pain for Robert because I knew how awful the Bontemps execution had been for him. Moreover, as a defense counsel in my Army days, I recalled the acute sense of compassion that I would feel even for a guilty man for whom I represented the only strand of hope.

Well, the "miracle" occurred. In the same court-room where he had heard the death-sentence of Bontems, Robert Badinter summoned up from the depths of his soul the right words and the right intonations and convinced the jury not to impose the death penalty. Apparently the jury was itself stirred by this admonition: *"Vous allez faire couper un homme en deux." (*"You are going to have a man cut in two.*")* After this incredible victory, Robert was called to defend every capital case, and succeeded each time, with the result that the guillotine had become *de facto* obsolete when the Parliament voted it out of existence.

I might add that I am not opposed to capital punishment in appropriate cases, such as for serial murderers. When society's needs are so great, I see no reason why taxpayers should feed, cloth and shelter human beasts for decades. Even Israël hanged Eichmann, one of the perpetrators of the Holocaust. Societies kill all the time; the French tobacco monopoly, the ignominious SEITA, has killed more people in a decade than the guillotine in two centuries. And another government monopoly in France, the blood agency, deliberately sold to thousands of hemophiliacs blood contaminated with the AIDS virus, killing thus far hundreds of innocent children and adults. Strangely, France which harbors people who pride themselves on being the most intelligent in the world, looked on capital punishment as an "either-or" proposition: either you were opposed to it, or you were for the guillotine. No one ever suggested that in the 20th century there are more humane ways of putting murderers to death than severing their head from the rest of their body.

While Minister of Justice, Badinter worked mightily on a major revision of the penal code, begun by his predecessors, and which was finally enacted only in 1993. In 1986, President Mitterrand appointed him to a nine-year term as president of the Conseil Constitutionnel. He has added luster to this institution, which has courageously expanded the domain of civil liberties, despite the "original intent" of its authors. Alas, his term expires in 1995, and it is to be feared that if a conservative president is elected next year, his successor is less likely to be as bold as Badinter.

Ever since the demolition of the Iron Curtain, Robert has been solicited by virtually all the former Soviet-dominated countries to advise about their new constitutions. In 1991, I took President Levon der Petrossian of Armenia to see Robert and he gave very useful advice that the Armenian leader took to heart. Most recently, Badinter has been working to organize a compulsory arbitration system for the member states of the Conference on Security and Cooperation in Europe. If he succeeds in this, we may avoid future Balkan wars.

With his wife, Elizabeth, an *agrégée* in Philosophy, author of two best-selling works on provocative subjects, and daughter of the advertising magnate, Marcel Bleustein-Blanchet, Robert has led an active literary life. Together they wrote a remarkable biography of Condorcet, the mathematician who became one of the most far-seeing reformers during the French Revolution. Robert also wrote an illuminating book on the emancipation of the Jews by the French Revolution and, more recently, a history of French prison reform.

Even the greatest of men have limited agendas (*cf.* Einstein suggesting to President Roosevelt the atomic bomb). In his desire to enact his own agenda – basically that of tolerance and liberty – Robert Badinter has had to cohabit with socialist-statists and, I fear, has failed to see the menace to freedom and decency that lies in the current power structure in France. As I pointed out in "Montaigne and Descartes," the greatest flaw in French society is the absence of ethics at the highest level, exemplified by the conflicts of interest which prevail in the caste of functionaries who rule the country. The contaminated-blood scandal exemplified this: functionaries sold the deadly blood purely for economic reasons, to get rid of a costly inventory, and other functionaries and ministers – charged with protecting public health – condoned this and the concomitant failure to import safe American blood. The Cartesian blindness which prevails in this country leads even intelligent people not to see that regulators of an industry cannot at the same time manage all or part of that industry. It is ironic that my friend Robert does not yet realize that an ethical society requires eliminating not only Louis XIV but also Colbert.

As a Jew, whose family emigrated from Russia, and whose father perished at the hands of the Nazis, Robert Badinter is living proof that France, too, is a melting pot, whose strong culture, language and ideals convert the children of immigrants into authentic French men and women (albeit sometimes too Cartesian for my taste). In our time, no one more than Robert Badinter has served the cause of justice, tolerance and enlightenment in France. I consider Robert still a young man, doubtless because we are the same age. And so, having hopes that he will put his enormous talents to new causes, I conclude with this quote from one of my favorite poets, Robert Browning: "Grow old along with me, the best is yet to be!"

Vol. XVI, N° 6, November 1994

From Dreyfus to Mitterrand

My treatment of the Dreyfus Affair brought in more mail than any other of my essays of recent memory. Naturally, this gave me no little satisfaction. Several readers claimed that my narration was the best digest of the affair that they had ever read. Reducing complicated facts to their essential ingredients is a key part of the lawyer's art, which I began to learn at Harvard Law School. My favorite professor, Warren Abner Seavey, summed it all up for us once when he said, "You must learn to suck the guts out of a case."

I take some pride in having done that to Bredin's book, which comprises more than 700 pages, not counting notes and indexes. One type of detail that I did not want to overlook was to give full names of each of the main villains in the case. Strangely lacking from Bredin's book were the given names of some of the principal players, including Generals Gonse and Roger and Colonel Fabre. The French tend to be indifferent to first names. Often, I receive letters addressed simply to "Mr. Kevorkian." I teach all my staff to look up first names before sending any letter, something that should be obvious. In the cases mentioned above, I had to send the firm librarian to do some legwork, since standard works did not deign to identify these nefarious officers. She came up with all missing names except for that of Colonel Fabre. Even the French Army archives could not supply his given name! It was only after the mailing of the second Newsletter that I discovered that his name was Pierre, and this thanks to an informative book which a reader sent me, called *Dreyfus: A Family Affair*, written by Michael Burns, a professor at Mount Holyoke College, who has taken the trouble to give the history of both the ancestors and the descendants of the generation of Alfred and Mathieu Dreyfus.

To me, perhaps the most remarkable thing about my Dreyfus Newsletters is that they were written at a time when I was engrossed in the biggest corporate acquisition of my career, the purchase of a major French pharmaceutical company by one of our American clients. Readers who know me as a full-time lawyer keep asking "Where do you find the time to write these Newsletters?" When I first met William Saroyan, I asked him a similar question, and his answer was, "There is plenty of time, Aram; most people don't know the usage of time." Indeed, I later discovered that what is lacking is not time but the will to use our time well. Enough said.

The Dreyfus Family

In my second Newsletter on Dreyfus, I had made a connection between the affair and World War I. Little did I realize how greatly the Dreyfus family suffered during the war. Mathieu lost his only son, Emile, and his son-in-law, Ado Reinach. Another brother, Jacques Dreyfus, lost two sons, Maurice and Charles, in the early months of the war. A third son, Pierre, fought heroically during the war, getting a battlefield promotion to Lieutenant, and earning several medals. Amazingly, he survived, despite having participated in some of the fiercest battles of that horrible trench war, including Verdun and the Somme. Alfred, himself, although 55 when the war started, volunteered for active duty and even served at the front.

It is particularly ironic that this family, which had been so vilified as "traitors" by the anti-Dreyfusards, should have thrown itself so whole-heartedly into this "patriotic war" whose main purpose, so far as they were concerned, was the restoration of their beloved Alsace to France. Reading Burns' book, I was struck again by the incredible stupidity of the French generals who planned military strategy in the early days of the war. They started out committing several-hundred-thousand men to retaking the Alsace, only to have the Germans invade France through Belgium and come close to the gates of Paris. A quarter-century later, the French generals relied on the Maginot Line, a pure product of Cartesian asininity, and the Germans once again outflanked the French by attacking through the Ardennes.

In World War II, the Dreyfus family was again not spared. Madeleine Lévy, the daughter of Alfred's daughter, Jeanne, who had married Pierre-Paul Lévy, a physician who had himself fought bravely in World War I, served in the Resistance in Toulouse, the home town of the Lévys. She was arrested and died in Auschwitz. René Dreyfus, mentioned above, also died in Auschwitz, as did Alice Dreyfus, wife of Léon, another brother of Alfred. As did Julien Schill, son of Rachel Dreyfus, Alfred's sister. Madeleine's surviving brother, Etienne Lévy, helped liberate the Alsace with the Free French forces and was wounded by machine-gun fire. He went on to become an outstanding research physician and is credited with inventing one of the most important advances in the realm of surgical care: feeding patients through the digestive system instead of intravenously. It doesn't sound like much to a layman, but one surgeon recently called it the most important development in surgery since the discovery of antibiotics!

Years ago, my friend John Hess, one of America's best (and unsung) journalists, while Food Editor of the New York Times (having been banished to this post for being too outspoken in his exposés of the nursing-home scandal) wrote a bold article entitled, *"The Best American Food is Chinese."* By analogy, I am tempted to write that "The best French family is Jewish," for I do not know of any family in this country which is more deserving of the admiration of those who respect courage, fidelity, true patriotism and devotion to family.

Mitterrand and Vichy

One forgets, to the detriment of understanding, that the past is ever present in the present. France, for example, can never escape its past. The Dreyfus case would not have occurred without the disastrous defeat of France in 1871. That defeat would not have happened without the foolishness of Emperor Napoleon III and his pretentious wife, Eugenie. Napoleon III would never have been elected if he had not been related to Napoleon I, and the latter, a lowly Corsican, would never have seized power without the disruption caused by the French Revolution. And so, from cause and effect, we can return to the Roman Empire! Looking forward from the Dreyfus case, the Franco-Prussian War surely led to the senseless World War I, because of France's desire to avenge its defeat and to recover Alsace and Lorraine. But the Treaty of Versailles and the horrendous reparations imposed on Germany led to inflation and ruination of the middle class, the rise of Hitler and World War II. Which brings us to the ignominious defeat of France in June 1940, and the creation of the Vichy government led by the senile Marchal Pétain, a hero, *faute de mieux,* of World War I.

In September of this year, a then-unknown French journalist, Pierre Péan, cast a bombshell on the French scene with a book called *"Une Jeunesse Française,"* which basically deals with the war years of François Mitterrand, including his time as a prisoner of war, as a civil servant of the Vichy government, and his purported service in the French Resistance.

While several books have recently sought to discredit President Mitterrand, including one called *"Mitterrand and the Forty Thieves,"* the Péan opus had an infinitely greater impact, for two reasons: the first, Mitterrand himself granted five interviews to the author and later praised his objectivity and professionalism; the second, Mitterrand's traditionally strong following among French Jews was seriously undermined by the revelation that he remained friendly until the end with two of the Vichy officials who organized the deportation of French Jews in 1942.

Mitterrand was so taken aback by the public outcry that he agreed to an hour-long interview on television with Jean-Pierre Elkabbach, a television journalist who is now president of the company operating the two government-owned channels. The interview started on a grisly note, as Mitterrand, who has prostate cancer, looked deathly ill and gave credence to rumors that he may die before his term ends next May. But Mitterrand reverted to his combative self when the subject turned to Vichy. He had the effrontery to claim that as a Vichy functionary he was not familiar with the ignoble laws which victimized French Jews! Starting in October 1940, various measures stripped Jews of the right to teach, to practice law, medicine, and other professions, and to hold public office. They were required to appear in public wearing a yellow Star of David. In July 1942, French police, headed by René Bousquet, rounded-up Parisian Jews and carted them off to a concentration camp, from which the Germans led them to their death in various gas chambers.

Mitterrand used as an excuse for his ignorance the fact that he was a prisoner in German camps when the Vichy laws were enacted. But, it is clear from Péan's book that the prisoners had plenty of letters and news while they were detained. Thus, I think it highly probable that Mitterrand knew even then about the Vichy persecution of the Jews. But, certainly on his return to France, at the end of 1941, he must have learned of these laws, as he spent a week with a Jewish family named Lévy-Despas, in Saint-Tropez. What did these French Jews talk about? The imminence of Christmas? And, as a functionary in the city of Vichy, how could Mitterrand not know about the régime's laws against the Jews, particularly since a key agency of the government was the Commission on Jewish Affairs? The clincher: late in 1942, Mitterrand was even offered a job with this agency! What did he think the Commission on Jewish Affairs did? Help Jews improve their elocution? Keep in mind that Mitterrand was a lawyer and was even admitted to the Bar in 1943, at a time when French Jews were being expelled from the Bar.

The fact is that Mitterrand knew, but Mitterrand did not care. The Péan book gives ample evidence that Mitterrand came from and frequented a Catholic, right-wing milieu, the same type of people who branded Dreyfus and other Jews as traitors. This explains why he was friendly with Bousquet and Jean-Paul Martin, another Vichy official involved in the round-up of French Jews, with whom he remained friendly even while he was President of France in the 1980s. Mitterrand cried at Martin's funeral. Of course, he has shed tears at Jewish memorial services as well. A politician must learn to weep easily.

Strangely enough, I do not believe that Mitterrand was anti-Semitic. He just did not care. Hate kills; indifference lets kill. The Péan book makes clear that even in the prison camp, when Mitterrand was in his early 20s, he had the makings of a politician and was called a "Janus" by one of the prisoners. Very early in his life, Mitterrand had inordinate ambitions and must have realized that an unprincipled man with a gift of gab and deception could go a long way by remaining entirely devoted to each. All his life, he has had Jewish friends, just as he has had anti-Semitic friends. The fact that the latter wanted to get rid of the former did not concern him so long as his career could be advanced.

Mitterrand's wife's sister is married to Roger Hanin, a Jewish movie actor from Algeria, who has been a bosom buddy of the President. Mitterrand has managed to fool a lot of people, including some of the smartest French Jews that the 20th century has produced. One of them told me recently that Mitterrand had convinced him that he had joined Vichy as a cover for his Resistance work, but the Péan books makes it crystal clear, and Mitterrand does not now deny, that he never came close to the Resistance until the summer of 1943, after serving a year-and-a-half as a dutiful Vichy official. Moreover, in the spring of that year, Mitterrand received directly from the hands of Pétain the highest Vichy decoration, the *Francisque.* I infer that Mitterrand distanced himself from Vichy only because the Americans had invaded North Africa in November 1942 and the Soviets had defeated the Nazis at Stalingrad at the end of January 1943. Until then, he was betting, like Pierre Laval, that the Germans were going to win the war. When he became convinced otherwise, he tried to build a record in the Resistance.

Even this Resistance record seems spurious to me. Where Péan falls short as a penetrating reporter is in failing to stress that Mitterrand's so-called *résistance* merely consisted of going from meeting to meeting, using assumed names, such as Captain Morland, and building up a constituency as a spokesman for the 1.8-million French soldiers who remained prisoners of war. The book does not relate a single act of real resistance, such as blowing up a depot or a train or giving military information to the Allies. Mitterrand never fired a shot; indeed, he did not even carry a gun. If using assumed names and establishing contacts constitutes "resistance," then there are a lot of heroes in the New York cocktail circuit!

Indeed, throughout the occupation, Mitterrand was hostile to de Gaulle and did not accept his leadership. De Gaulle's nephew, who was a real *résistant*, had contacts with Mitterrand and was very suspicious of him. When, finally, Mitterrand went to London and met de Gaulle, the latter did his best to keep him from returning to France. Why then did de Gaulle finally include Mitterrand among the leaders that he recognized in his return to France?

I believe that the answer is easy. De Gaulle's principal objective in establishing the Free French in London was to gain power after the war by demonstrating to the Allies that he was the most representative French leader. To achieve this end, in which he almost failed, de Gaulle had to cast a wide net and include among his followers even unsavory Vichyites like Mitterrand. Indeed, on his return to France, de Gaulle deliberately fostered the extravagant myth that most French people were *résistants* and had liberated Paris. This was clearly politics and the myth has persisted to this day, although on the 50th anniversary of the liberation of Paris, some honest journalists have had the courage to tell the truth about the subject, which is that most of the French were dutiful followers of Pétain and Laval, right up until D-Day.

And so, the paradox was that de Gaulle's strategy fitted in perfectly with Mitterrand's ambitions. The latter, as indicated above, had managed to appear as a key figure representing the prisoners of war, whose return and re-incorporation in French society loomed large as a post-war problem. What I am saying is that Mitterrand was a clever politician even during the war and has remained such until now. But *résistant* he was not.

As a politician, Mitterrand deserves high marks and stands tall in the Pantheon of French leaders who preferred power to principle. Henry IV became King by converting to Catholicism. Every school-boy knows his famous boutade: *"Paris vaut bien une messe" (*"Paris is well worth a Mass!"*)*. Mitterrand probably has told himself many times: "The Elysée Palace is well worth a Jewish brother-in-law."

The most interesting question in all this is why Mitterrand cooperated with Péan in the writing of the book. The answer seems to be that Péan had uncovered so much new information independently of Mitterrand that the latter must have felt that he could limit the damage by putting his own gloss on Pean's narrative. Certainly, Pean's book is never openly hostile to Mitterrand and, as indicated above, is particularly uncritical in examining his alleged resistance activities.

Another interpretation, which I would not discard, is that Mitterrand, in the last months of his life, has gotten a big kick out of the idea that he had fooled enough people to be twice elected President of France. Most French Jews voted for Mitterrand, since much of the Right, after de Gaulle's death, was still closely identified in their minds with the anti-Dreyfusards and the Vichy crowd. Mitterrand had wrapped himself in the mantle of Jean Jaurès, the great Socialist leader who defended Dreyfus and who was assassinated on the eve of World War I, because he opposed the war. But, Jaurès he is not!

To be sure, a lot of people had known that Mitterrand was on the Right until well into the Fouth Republic. Mitterrand was one of the few members of Parliament not to vote in favor of de Gaulle's return to power in 1958. His constant opposition to de Gaulle was what allowed him to gain respectability on the Left and led to his becoming a candidate in the presidential election of 1965.

Only in a Catholic country like France could Mitterrand have survived the disgrace of the notorious incident in 1959, known as the *l'affaire de l'Observatoire*, when he paid a man to stage a phony machine-gun attack on him, so as to attract attention and sympathy. Mitterrand was actually charged with the criminal of offence "giving false testimony" on this occasion but managed to squirm out of the affair, as most politicians do when accused of criminal offences in France. Most tellingly, the man who admitted the shooting was never charged!

One interesting titbit of Mitterrand's personal life touched on by Péan is his early love affair with young Marie-Louise Terrasse, who later became famous as a television announcer (called *speakerine* in French) under the name of Catherine Langeais. Mitterrand was almost robbing the cradle when he fell madly in love with the then 15-year-old girl. Later, as a prisoner of war, he was jilted by her in favor of another man, but not before he wrote her an incredible number of love letters, 2,400 in all, according to one newspaper article I read recently. He must have written several letters a day, because the romance was short-lived.

Young Mitterrand was also remarkably introspective and articulate. In one letter discovered by Péan, written in March 1942, when our hero was only 26, Mitterrand makes these self-revelatory observations (my translation):

"When I think of my destiny, I discover only uncertainties. I know but one thing: to live outside of habit and push to the maximum the intensity of living. I will flee to countries which will afford me the illusion of discovery, where in the will and the exercise of power I will find the taste for risk, but I would not like to be useless or vain."

Early in November of this year, *Paris-Match,* the picture magazine, broke a taboo by publishing a photo of Mitterrand with his 20-year-old daughter, Mazarine, whose mother is not Mitterrand's wife. (I do not like the term "illegitimate child," since it is the parents who are illegitimate!) While many people knew of this long-standing liaison, *Paris Match*, which is not known for its journalistic ethics, awaited Mitterrand's decline and virtual extinction to write about it openly. The magazine was roundly criticized for violating the President's "private life" but, undeterred, *Paris Match* pointed out in its next issue that Mazarine and her boyfriend were part of an official delegation that visited South Africa with Mitterrand earlier this year.

I suspect that Mitterrand's final satisfaction is to let the world know that he lived by his own rules and got away with it. Until recently, I assumed that Mitterrand's parting logo would be a gentle hand holding a rose; now I'm convinced it will be the left hand clasping the outstretched right forearm, in the noble gesture which the French, appropriately enough, call the *bras d'honneur*.

Vol. XVI, N° 7, December 1994

The Christmas Issue: The Light and the Keys; Six Characters in Search of a Throne

On a cold 25th day of December, I am taking up my laptop computer at home to pursue the recent tradition of a Christmas issue. The year is ending in France on the perennial note of scandals tying political financing and criminal justice, all against the backdrop of the looming election of the new King of France, otherwise known as the *Président de la République*. But, before I get to that, allow me to tell a tale which explains the title.

If I were compelled to explain to Higher Authority on Judgment Day what contribution I made to world culture, I would have to reply feebly: "Sir, I undertook to explain to a few thousand people in my lifetime what Cartesianism signifies in France." Having only this small claim to a place in Paradise, I feel obliged to add one small lesson which might, at least, make my case more convincing.

Early in the year, a French client came to see me about reorganizing his business operations. He was quite excited, as he claimed to have come up with a magic solution, which he set forth at once. When I asked him to explain his solution, he merely repeated it, adding nothing new. Pressed for details, his only reply was to reiterate the broad principle he had discovered. While observing him, I realized that I was seeing the Cartesian mind in action, on his way to Nirvana, when "the things that we conceive very clearly and very distinctly are all true." Indeed, his method consisted simply in repeating the idea over and over again until it became so clear to him that it had to be true. Finally, I looked at the organization chart that he had laid on the table and, in a short time, found a situation that did not jibe with this theory. He was crestfallen and went away unhappy.

This incident suddenly called to mind the cute story which I had heard many years ago in Philadelphia. A policeman sees a drunk looking for something under a street-light late at night. On inquiring, the policeman is told by the man that he has lost his keys, whereupon the officer starts looking as well. Not finding anything, the policeman asks, "Are you sure you lost your keys here?" and the man replies, "No, I lost them down the street but there is more light here."

This story neatly illustrates the way the Cartesian mind works: it basks in its own light, disregarding facts that spoil the fun of the process. Not long after this incident with the client, I recounted the story to some American executives who were about to negotiate a deal with a French company. They related afterwards that they had come upon several occasions when their French counterparts were separating the light from the keys. Indeed, they soon came up with a buzz-phrase to describe someone whose theories did not meet the facts: "He has the light but not the keys."

As I asserted in "Montaigne and Descartes," the worst vice of Cartesianism is the notion that truth is subjective: if you see it very clearly and distinctly it is true, so who cares what anyone else thinks about it? Today's disciples of Descartes would like to forget that in his *Discours de la Méthode,* he applied this precept even to scientific matters; he "proved" that the blood's circulation makes the heart beat! Never did he bother to check with anatomists as to whether they agreed with his theory. In my essay, I tied the success of Descartes's silly "method" in France to the fact that it was acceptable to the Church since he also "proved" the existence of God with it.

It would be difficult to exaggerate the influence of Catholic doctrine in France even among those who are not believers. One of my favorite *bons mots* is that "in France even the Jews become Catholic." By that I mean that the educated élite inevitably succumb to the brainwashing of the educational system and the cultural ambiance that is based on Catholic values, of which Cartesianism is an offshoot. Nowhere is French-Catholic teaching more striking than in the attitude toward money and profit. At least once a week I hear a business man say *"Je ne suis pas un homme d'argent"* which, translated freely, means "Money means nothing to me." Thus, when he seeks a price of fifteen-times earnings for his shares, it is not because he likes money; he is merely upholding the dignity of his shares. Just as the Church wants to make believe that people have sex only to procreate, so they are supposed to work for the good of mankind, not to improve their own lot by making money. I have already related, but it is worth repeating, that several years ago, when the leading television quiz show held its nation-wide championship, the winner was given a sealed envelope containing the prize money but the amount of his winnings was not disclosed, *par pudeur* (out of modesty)!

So what has this to do with politics and justice? The answer is what a person in the know told me several years ago, sighing heavily, "If only we could admit to the French people what political campaigns really cost!" Because politicians, emulating the hypocrisy of the Church, are not willing to admit the truth about the importance of money, and the legal system necessarily reflects this hypocrisy, all the political parties violate the law in an ingenious variety of ways. In the old days, French judges closed their eyes to these violations because they were part of the value system but, in recent years, political life has been poisoned by revelations of illicit campaign contributions. It all started with the Luchaire affair, when word leaked that the French company had made a big contribution to the Socialist Party in order to get permission to sell arms to Iran. Mitterrand was clever enough to bury this scandal but, in ensuing years, there emerged the even bigger scandal of systematic kickbacks given by contractors to Socialist-run municipalities, through front organizations such as Urba which invoiced phony consulting services. Since then, innumerable cases have reached the front pages, so much so that no one cares any more about who did what.

Now that the so-called Right is in power, the *Juges d'Instruction* have been working on prominent politicians in Balladur's government. Gérard Longuet, Minister of Industry, was forced to resign a few months ago because of charges that a contractor built a house for him at St-Tropez at a favorable price. A worse fate befell Alain Carignon, Minister of Communications and Mayor of Grenoble, who not only had to resign his ministerial job, but also was incarcerated on charges that he awarded the municipal water monopoly to the powerful Compagnie Lyonnaise des Eaux in exchange for valuable favors, including the use of an apartment in Paris. A 78-year-old Senator in southern France, Maurice Arreckx, has also been languishing in prison for several months, despite prostate cancer, while a zealous *Juge d'Instruction* is wringing evidence from him about payments made to his Swiss bank account. These cases of incarceration pending investigation display another attribute of Catholicism: the use of the Inquisition to obtain confessions from the accused. For the first time, I have seen in print this year assertions that these judges practice a form of torture, an allegation with which I agree whole-heartedly. To put a man in prison just to make him confess is indeed torture, and in my mind it is the judges who should be prosecuted for this practice. But who is going to bring charges against a *Juge d'Instruction* in a country where even the Jews become Catholic?

The most recent scandal involves a *Juge d'Instruction* named Eric Halphen, who has been investigating financing irregularities involving Chirac's party, the RPR. Let me say first that I have been listening closely ever since the Luchaire affair and I have never heard Chirac criticize the Socialists over financing issues. For good cause: he has been applying the precept that "people living in glass houses should not throw stones." What makes the Halphen matter juicy is that his father-in-law, a psychiatrist called Jean-Pierre Maréchal, is charged with having solicited from an RPR politician a million-franc payment in exchange for influencing his son-in-law. As is typical with such matters, no one knows the facts, but everyone is taking sides. The Socialists, led by the wily François Mitterrand, whom even a terminal cancer cannot prevent from seizing a political opportunity, are screaming that Maréchal was set up to find an excuse to remove a judge who was breathing too heavily down the neck of the RPR. Prime Minister Edouard Balladur, while nominally of the same party, is not unhappy to see his arch-rival Chirac embarrassed, so his minions opine that justice should follow its course. The RPR would, of course, like the judge to be removed from the case, so as to gain time and let the Presidential election take place without embarrassment to Chirac. This has the makings of a true imbroglio, and I predict that Dr Maréchal will beat the rap: his confession was not "very clear and very distinct" so it cannot be true even if he did accept marked bank-notes.

The other ancient heritage of France – the monarchy – is much in play now. The only way to begin to understand the institutions of the Fourth Republic is to realize that the President is an elected King. Unlike the British monarch, the French King is not merely ceremonial. He wields enormous powers, particularly while his party controls the National Assembly. When Mitterrand was in the opposition to de Gaulle, he violently criticized the Constitution and the powers of the President, but once elected he did nothing to change the system, despite his having a huge Socialist majority in the National Assembly. He loved his monarchical power so much so that he ran for re-election. Now waiting in the wings are at least six pretenders who would love to be King for seven years: Edouard Balladur, Jacques Chirac, Raymond Barre, Valéry Giscard d'Estaing, Lionel Jospin and Jean-Marie le Pen.

The Presidency in the Fourth Republic is thus a euphemism for a monarchy which wields more power than any other chief executive in the so-called "democracies." This system, designed by de Gaulle for himself, could have worked only if the Prime Minister took seriously his constitutional mandate to govern. But the first Prime Minister, Michel Debré, a minion of de Gaulle, set a disastrous precedent by resigning when the President requested it, whereas under the Constitution only the National Assembly could overturn him. Ever since then, all Prime Ministers of the same party as the President have resigned upon request, with the result that the President really runs the country.

The closest that any Prime Minister came to carrying out the constitutional mandate to "determine and conduct the policy of the Nation" was when Chaban-Delmas, under Pompidou, established his *Nouvelle Société* theme, with the help of Jacques Delors, his principal advisor. This independant policy irritated Pompidou's advisers and, despite the fact that Chaban-Delmas had just obtained a vote of confidence from the National Assembly, he meekly resigned when Pompidou requested it. Chirac was one of Pompidou's men who developed a dislike for Chaban. Had Chirac supported him in the 1974 elections, the history of the Fifth Republic might have been different, because Chirac's actions led to the election of Giscard, whose arrogant monarchical reign brought us Mitterrand. In Chirac's defense, it must be recalled that Chaban had become the butt of a scandal when the irrepressible *Canard Enchaîné* disclosed that he had not been paying taxes for years. But I doubt that this was the main reason why Chirac bolted his party.

This monarchy is sustained by a corps of high priests, mainly graduates of the secular seminary known as the Ecole Nationale d'Administration, chosen among the élite of the educational system, those who have mastered what I call "the Cartesian canon," which means that they see the light but not the keys. They are the new aristocracy, enjoying the privileges of lifetime jobs, with the opportunity of keeping their functionary status while dabbling in politics and business. Balladur who, like Chirac, Giscard and Jospin, is a graduate of the ENA, is a master of manipulating the high priests and has already placed many of his faithful followers in key positions in state-owned or state-dominated companies, such as banks and insurance companies. One can be sure that his coming campaign will not lack for money.

The fact that grown men in responsible positions, to wit, all the Prime Ministers of the Fifth Republic who resigned on request of the President, do not carry out the terms of the Constitution can be explained only by the obsequiousness which is part of the monarchical and Catholic tradition in France. No amount of lip service to the Revolution and to the Republic can convert France from a vertical society, in which subservience to the man on top (call it "authority," if you will) is instinctive, to a horizontal society based on the principle that "this is a government of laws and not of men."

Sad to say, the French caste of functionaries is doing its best to export the French model of government to the European Union. Delors was, of course, a life-long civil servant and already the ENA is training future functionaries from other European countries. As I've related in the past, the education at this school is devoid of substance: what counts is the recruitment process and the creation of an esprit de corps. While I admired de Gaulle immensely, I must point out that his reign was largely responsible for permitting the hegemony of the *ENArques*, as the graduates are called. He so despised the politicians of the Fourth Republic, who dominated the parliamentary system then in force, that his Constitution turned the legislature into a rubber stamp for measures decreed by the executive branch, which in turn came under the control of civil servants, who often achieved ministerial rank.

A fundamental aspect of de Gaulle's character also made the Fifth Republic palatable when he was President: he had the "class" to resign when the people rejected his proposed referendum in 1969. Mitterrand, as unprincipled a man as any who ruled France, called the Fifth Republic a "permanent coup d'Etat" when he was in the opposition, but once elected he clung to the purple robes of power as though he was born in them. Indeed, on the first occasion to show his monarchical dignity, Mitterrand staged the G7 summit meeting at the palace of Versailles and greeted visiting heads of government on a red carpet a mile long. And, by refusing to resign when his party was defeated in 1986 and 1993, he demonstrated that he was indeed a monarch who does not give up his throne just because his ministers are unpopular. After all, did Louis XIV resign?

As I see no de Gaulle on the horizon, I hope to live long enough to be able to shout one day: *"Vive la Sixième République!"*

Vol. XVII, N° 1, March 1995

The Incorrigible Francophile

Well, as I predicted, Dr Maréchal did beat the rap. It will be recalled that this fashionable psychiatrist was accused of extortion in promising to influence his son-in-law, Judge Halphen, to cool the investigation of political payoffs in a Paris suburb whose dominant figure is Charles Pasqua, the powerful Minister of the Interior. The indictment was thrown out by the Court of Appeals of Paris on the ground that evidence was obtained through illegal recordings of phone conversations by the French police. This was not exactly a wire-tap since the police made the recording with the consent of the receiver of the phone calls, a politician named Didier Schuller, who is close to Pasqua. The Minister protested the decision saying that the accepted practice was to allow such recordings with the consent of persons receiving blackmail or threatening calls. The Court held that even in such cases a recording can be made only with the authorization of a judge, as required by statute.

More embarrassing for Pasqua was the intimation by the Court that Maréchal had been a victim of entrapment, that is, he had been provoked by Schuller to commit an offense which he would not have otherwise committed. But that was only the beginning of the embarrassment. A news magazine revealed that for a week prior to his arrest Maréchal's phone line had been tapped by the police without court order. It turned out that the Prime Minister's office had authorized the tap under a provision of the law which applies to organized crime, terrorism or national defense. The ensuing publicity given to this accusation led Prime Minister Balladur to make a *gaffe* which has cost him dearly as a candidate for the presidency. On a Sunday evening, Balladur proclaimed indignantly on television that he defied anyone to demonstrate that the taps were illegal. The next day, his subordinates sheepishly let out word that the police had misled the Prime Minister's office into believing that the case involved organized crime, whereas it was now clear that the Maréchal tap did not fall into that category. Even the *Canard Enchainé* has expressed bewilderment as to how Balladur could have committed such a gross error as to assert on television that the taps were legal and then admit the next morning that they were not. My own explanation is simple: Balladur is one of those leaders to whom it is difficult to tell bad news. I suspect his staff had not dared to give him all the facts, whereupon he assumed the mantle of virtue.

Following this revelation, a high police official was made to resign, although it is obvious that he is merely a scapegoat for decisions made at a higher level. Judge Halphen is thus continuing his investigation of kickbacks in the Department headed by Pasqua, who has become an ardent supporter of Balladur, after having been for years a loyal henchman of Jacques Chirac. Balladur's poll ratings began to slip considerably after this incident, which followed another Balladur embarrassment – his having to back down from a planned University reform as a result of student demonstrations. The former image of Balladur as a wimp – expressed by the play on the word *Ballamou* – returned to haunt him. Then *Le Monde* did him and Pasqua a favor by publishing a report to the effect that French counter-espionage agents had discovered that American CIA agents had been trying to bribe French officials into giving confidential information on the French position concerning the GATT negotiations of 1993. According to the story, the American Embassy had been asked to send the agents home. This item, as if by miracle, initially took the heat off Pasqua and Balladur but, before long, every one realized that the story had been planted to divert attention from the wire-tapping scandal. Even Foreign Minister Juppé – a Chirac supporter – protested that a diplomatic incident of this type should not have been made public. Most people had no difficulty in pinpointing Pasqua, who is responsible for counter-espionage, as the one who caused the leak to be made. This can never be proved, since it is Pasqua who was asked by Balladur to discover who made the leak!

Even more serious than the contemporary wire-tapping was the revelation that President Mitterrand's "plumbers" in the Elysée Palace had set up an elaborate wire-tapping operation which lasted for three years, from 1983 to 1986, and listened to phone conversations of lawyers, journalists, politicians and even actors, such as the beautiful Carole Bouquet. In the United States, this outrageous behavior would be enough to get a President impeached but in monarchical France, there isn't the slightest indication that Mitterrand will be called to task. True, his term is about to expire, and true he is dying of cancer, but in a country which pretends to be governed by law, there should be more public outcry than has been heard. So Mitterrand, too, will beat this rap, but not the Ultimate Rap.

The first round of the presidential election will take place on April 23rd. Already there are about 10 declared candidates, including three silly ecologists, whose vanity greatly exceeds their love of nature. According to the polls, the three leading candidates – Balladur, Chirac and the Socialist Jospin – are neck and neck, each hovering around 22 percent of the vote, with Chirac actually having taken a slight lead, a major surprise. At this writing, two ambitious hopefuls, Raymond Barre and Valéry Giscard d'Estaing, are keeping their intentions secret. If either becomes a candidate, this is certain to take votes away from Balladur, who is a favorite of the same party, the UDF. The key question is who will be the two finalists after the first round. For the first time since 1969, when Pompidou and Poher were the contenders, there may be a run-off between two candidates on the Right, Chirac and Balladur. However, I suspect that Jospin will edge out one of them, most likely Balladur, if his slide continues.

Many people with whom I speak express disgust at the sorry state of French presidential politics and the régime which clearly is going nowhere. The three leading candidates are all graduates of the same school – the ENA – which selects the élite functionaries who control France. As I have said before, France is a *République de Fonctionnaires*. In reality there is but a single party, with several subdivisions, to give the illusion of diversity. Whether you talk to cab drivers or to doctors or to businessmen, every one is well aware of this lack of choice, but no one feels capable of doing anything to change the system. One doctor in the provinces, as we say, told me that he might vote for Jospin, in the hope that things would get so bad that there would be an "explosion" like May '68, which would result in a new régime. I did not have the heart to remind him that May '68 ultimately resulted in nothing but inflation, both of money and rhetoric, no more than did the Revolution of 1848. (I recommend Flaubert's *L'Education Sentimentale* for a description of the latter.)

It is time, therefore, to explain my title. Some readers express concern that I may be perceived as anti-French. Nothing could be farther from the truth. I am an incorrigible Francophile, and well aware of the ambiguity of the adjective, since I am incorrigible both in my love of France and my willingness to criticize what I do not like. As I explained a few years ago in my "Confessions of a Francophile," love of a country and its people does not necessitate admiring every institution and practice. In fact, with my populist tendencies, I feel more empathy for the so-called "common people" of every country than for its leaders. Many years ago I read Carl Sandburg's "*The People Yes*" which admirably expressed this preference. The history of all nations is the history of abuse of power and of folly, and the common people everywhere pay the price. In 1991, when I sent a memo to the government of Armenia giving my recommendations for a new Constitution, I quoted Lord Acton's famous dictum as being the first principle on which any government should be based: "Power tends to corrupt; absolute power corrupts absolutely." I would add, as a second principle, P.T. Barnum's famous remark that "A sucker is born every minute" and the corollary which I invented, "A crook is born every hour." This leads to the third principle, admirably expressed by Thomas Jefferson, "Eternal vigilance is the price of liberty."

All this to say that I write about France because I live and work here. If I lived in New York I would be just as caustic about the foibles and follies of the American élite, whether in government, business, the professions or the educational establishment. Indeed, a few of my readers have pointed out that my description of Cartesianism could apply to some of the Republican leaders of Congress! *A priori* reasoning was not invented by the French nor do they hold a monopoly on it. Its source is in the tendency of all humans to permit the wish to be father to the thought. An allied frailty of the mind is the constant temptation to confuse what *is* with what *ought* to be. That is what ideology is all about, and no government seems to be able to escape ideology. My friend and client, the late William Saroyan, once wrote that "society is based on the lies that work," a profound observation indeed. The United States does not have a philosophy of method comparable with the Cartesianism of France. To be sure, in the last century, America's greatest philosopher, Charles Saunders Peirce, invented what he called "pragmatism," a word that soon became so abused that he added a syllable to it – pragmaticism – to distinguish the philosophic concept from the word of common parlance. In Peirce's pioneer essay, *"How to Make our Ideas Clear,"* he did not even utilize the word "pragmatism" but he proposed an analytical tool for defining concepts, to wit:

> *"...consider what effects, which might conceivably have practical bearings, we conceive the object of our conception to have. Then our conception of these effects is the whole of our conception of the object."*

The idea that a concept cannot be divorced from its practical effects is a powerful insight, and much superior, to my mind, than ascertaining truth through "clear and distinct" thought. The problem with Peirce's definition is that it meets itself coming and going. While an undergraduate at the University of Pennsylvania, I attended a graduate course on the "philosophy of history" taught by Dr Elizabeth Flower, who had a sharp mind and a lovely face. She once bandied the term "rationalist-empiricist dichotomy" in an offhand way, as though all present understood it. I mustered up the courage to ask her what it meant and (as I recall), she explained that (a) thc rationalist believes that ideas precede facts, but how can one verify ideas without facts?; (b) the empiricist believes that facts precede ideas but how does he know what facts to look for if he does not have an idea to start with? Indeed, returning to Peirce's definition, if a concept needs practical effects to be understood, so practical effects need a concept to be identified.

This intellectual quandary, added to the confusion between *is* and *ought,* seems to be at the heart of America's inability to deal with its own realities. The notion of "political correctness," for example, seems to proceed from an unwillingness to deal with facts that conflict with the theory. The agonised reaction to the recent book *"The Bell Curve"* is another example of the hostility of belief to unpleasant facts – here, the proof that certain segments of the population are not as "intelligent" as others. Certain facts simply do not jibe with democratic beliefs. In the ideal world all people ought to be equal in talent and intelligence; in the real world they are not. But recognizing that they are not does not tell us what to do about it.

My problem with the book *"The Bell Curve"* is that in a democratic society there should be no categories of people, just individuals. One does not educate "blacks" or "whites"; one educates John Smith and Mary Brown. Of course, this simplistic credo has of late been tarnished in the United States by the so-called "affirmative action" movement by which individuals are not judged as such but by their membership in a category. This has led to some appalling results. It used to be that the objective of admitting disfavored persons to élite universities was to give them equal opportunity to education. Now they are demanding to decide what the curriculum is as well. The phenomenon known as "multiculturism" is in practice grotesque, based as it is on the idea that an obscure African poet, for example, is just as important as Shakespeare. The willingness of many American universities to debase their teaching is an indication that numerous academics are prey to a malady that is as bad as Cartesianism in France.

The strength of French culture stems from a respect for tradition and the maintenance of the beautiful and precise French language. A centralized government is the watchdog of this culture. In the United States, the opposite tendency seems to prevail: to disparage tradition and to treat culture as an individual option. I am not close enough to the American scene to describe these phenomena in detail but I have read enough to be amazed and disturbed. Young Americans do not seem to have any notion of grammar and word usage. I knew a Yale law graduate who used to say, "Her and me went to the movies." Another Yale law graduate occupies the White House with disastrous effect, both on prose and on policy.

The French élite are chosen for their ability to deal with abstractions: they are required to speak and write well, in an organized fashion. The American élite are chosen on the basis of multiple-choice tests, like the SAT and the LSAT, which are totally passive in nature and do not require any "affirmation action," such as writing, or any effort at organization and synthesis. I believe these tests have had a noxious effect on American culture, and some day I will elaborate on this subject.

In the meantime, let us return to Paris, the loveliest city in the world, where the food is great, mail is delivered three times a day, garbage is silently collected every morning, flowers abound in public places, and the women are the most elegant and beautiful in the world.

Vol. XVII, N° 2, March, 1995

On Lying, Liars and Monsieur Tapie

Being a child of the adventitious and craving approval, to boot, I tend to choose topics suggested to me by my loyal readers. The other day, I lunched with a recent French friend whom I met thanks to my "Montaigne and Descartes." The friend is one of the world's leading *amateurs* of Montaigne, to the point that he named his house *Les Essais*. Much to my surprise, during an agreeable lunch, my friend suggested that I write about Bernard Tapie, the rogue businessman who is a member of the European Parliament and whose legal problems are legion. I told my friend that while I had occasionally referred to Tapie in my Newsletters, I had hitherto found him too easy a target to be worthy of a whole issue. This remark puzzled my friend who opined that the *phénomène* Tapie tells a lot about contemporary France and thus is a fitting topic for my pen (actually, a word processor).

As I write this, Tapie, aged 52, has just been tried before the Tribunal Correctionnel of Valenciennes, in Northern France, along with a number of others involved in the fixing of a soccer match in 1993 by representatives of the Marseille team whose owner was Tapie. The court will announce its judgment on May 15th. Before describing this colorful case, let me first give some background about Tapie, not as a biographer would, but as a member of the public who has followed his career through the media.

It seems to be about 15 years ago that I began to hear of Tapie as a sharp operator who, having mastered the French Bankruptcy Code, would buy up insolvent companies for a song, then make a quick profit on the resale after some cosmetic improvements of the business. Following Mitterrand's election as President in May 1981, Tapie began to get more favorable coverage from the media, particularly television. Just as anti-Semites have their favorite Jew, so the Socialists, known for their hostility to business, had their favorite capitalist in Tapie. Indeed, Tapie even hosted a television show devoted to entrepreneurs. He made much of his modest origins and the fact that he was a high-school dropout. Newspapers began describing him as an *industriel,* which is the most flattering label for a businessman since it implies that he has created factories and jobs. The irony of all this was that he had never started a business in his life but rather, as indicated, made his living buying up bankrupt companies, laying off workers and shedding assets. Hardly a week went by without Tapie on television, constantly presented in a favorable light. Once he even sang a ballad, demonstrating an agreeable baritone voice. Indeed, in his youth he had embarked on a singing career, which was short-lived, although he did cut a few 45 r.p.m. records, as Bernard Tapy.

The big breakthrough in Tapie's public image occurred when, in 1986, he seized on an opportunity to take control of the floundering Marseille soccer (called *"football"* here) team. Tapie had no prior connection with Marseille, having been born and raised in a working-class suburb north of Paris. With typical gusto, he went into soccer in a big way, buying up expensive players, such as Jean-Pierre Papin, personally supervising every aspect of the team and appearing at every match. As the Marseille team started to climb to the top of the league, Tapie became the darling of the Marseille fans and much admired by many lovers of the sport. Soon, Tapie capitalized on this fame, first to take his holding company public, under the name Bernard Tapie Finance, and then to enter politics; he ran for Parliament on a Socialist label and, after his opponent's election was invalidated, won a seat in the National Assembly, representing a Marseille suburb.

Having made a bundle from the floating of his stock, Tapie purchased Hubert Givenchy's expensive town house in the fashionable St.-Germain district of Paris, acquired costly antiques and paintings, and a huge yacht called the *"Phocea."* By this time, Tapie had become *persona grata* to President Mitterrand himself, who held out Tapie as the epitome of a socially-conscious capitalist. During Mitterrand's second term, Tapie reached the height of his fame and glory when Prime Minister Bérégovoy, in April 1992, named him *Ministre de la Ville*, that is, Minister of Cities, whose main function was to make life more palatable for residents of the ghastly suburbs crammed with immigrants and their unruly children. Tapie went about this assignment with his usual verbal vigor and media attention. But, after a few months on the job, he was forced to resign when a *Juge d'Instruction* indicted him on charges of embezzlement brought by a former business partner. It took a while, but Tapie managed to get the charges dismissed by paying off the complainant handsomely. Having thus been "cleared," Tapie talked Bérégovoy into giving him back his ministerial post, but his return to government was short-lived, as the Socialists were routed from office in March 1993 when the Right won a landslide legislative election, although Tapie himself regained his own seat.

Pierre Bérégovoy committed suicide on May 1, 1993. In a way, this was the beginning of the end for Tapie. After Prime Minister Balladur named a new president of the Crédit Lyonnais, the giant nationalized bank which had been giving credit to Tapie and his companies for years, the businessman's fortunes changed for the worse. It appeared that Tapie had personally guaranteed all the loans which his companies had received. As the financial press had been reporting for some time, Tapie's companies had never really prospered. Indeed, Tapie was a poor manager. He juggled assets and played with figures, but all his companies were either bankrupt or close to it. It became clear that without the massive support of the Crédit Lyonnais, Tapie himself would have been bankrupt a long time ago. Few doubted that this support was politically dictated, based on Tapie's ties with Mitterrand and Bérégovoy and perhaps payoffs to bank personnel. Finally, the new president of the bank called Tapie's loans in 1994 and attached his furniture and art works. The French tax authorities seized Tapie's yacht, alleging tax fraud. The weaker Tapie's business situation became the more he relied on his political fortunes, taking over the Radical party – a hollow shell waiting for a providential leader – and managing to win a respectable 12-percent vote in the European Parliament elections. Tapie's support came mainly from the blue-collar workers and the disgruntled, who admired his panache in twitting the nose of the establishment while forcing his way into respectability.

Bankruptcy proceedings were finally brought by the Crédit Lyonnais, his main creditor, against Tapie and his wife. Early this year, the Tribunal de Commerce of Paris declared them both bankrupt and ordered the liquidation of their assets. The case is on appeal.

Let us now return to the bribery scandal. Tapie himself had never been charged with participating in the bribery of three Valenciennes players to throw a match, scheduled just six days before Marseille won the European championship in Milan. Instead, the number-two executive of the club, Jean-Pierre Bernès, took the rap along with a player who delivered the F 250,000 bribe money. Considering how actively Tapie ran the club, it was not difficult to deduce that he was involved in the scheme but, as no one pointed the finger at him, he managed to stay clear of a direct accusation. However, a Yugoslav, Boro Primorac, who had been the Valenciennes soccer coach, alleged that he had been invited to lunch on June 17, 1993, at Fouquet's, by emissaries of Tapie and then led to his nearby office on Avenue Hoche, where Tapie asked him to testify to certain "facts" that would help Bernès' case.

In what may turn out to be the most costly error of his life, Tapie chose to deny that he had seen the coach on that day. For a few days, Tapie tantalized the press with the promise to produce an irrefutable alibi witness. Then, lo and behold, there appeared one day on television the smiling face of Jacques Mellick, Mayor of Béthune in Northern France, member of the National Assembly and a former Socialist Minister, who claimed that he had been with Tapie in his office within the same time frame as the coach had alleged, and naturally, he had never seen the coach. Mellick knew Tapie because the businessman had purchased the Testut company established in Béthune. A lot of people, including myself, doubted the veracity of Mellick's story. But soon, Mellick reinforced the alibi by asserting that his parliamentary secretary, Corinne Krajewski, had also accompanied him to Tapie's office. She backed up this tale. So far so good, *n'est-ce pas*? But then the French police, at the behest of the pugnacious Public Prosecutor of Valenciennes, started to demolish Mellick's story.

In the first place, they produced a local newspaper photograph showing that Mellick had attended a public ceremony in Béthune at the same time as he claimed to have been with Tapie. To this, Mellick rejoined that the time reported in the newspaper was erroneous and that he had rushed back to Béthune to attend the ceremony. Whereupon, the police showed that it would have been impossible to cover the 215 kilometers by automobile in the short time between the end of the alleged meeting with Tapie and his appearance at the ceremony. Mellick then got his chauffeur to back up his story about having driven to Paris in the morning and returning to Béthune in the afternoon. But, as the chauffeur claimed to have purchased gasoline on the way, the police ascertained that Mellick's official credit card had been used the prior day but not on June 17th, to which Mellick rejoined that as this was a private trip he had paid for the gas in cash. The police produced other witnesses to the effect that Mellick was in Béthune at the time he claimed to have been in Paris. Yet, Mellick, wrapping himself in his mantle of Mayor and member of Parliament, stood by his story.

Nevertheless Tapie was indicted for this attempt to obstruct justice. I do not know why it took so long to bring the various culprits to trial, but it finally opened in March in Valenciennes. The first major surprise was provided by Bernès who admitted his own guilt and also pointed the finger at Tapie as the mastermind of the operation. Not perturbed, Tapie put on a veritable side-show in the courtroom, something that the peculiar French procedure allows, since the persons on trial can comment on the testimony of witnesses. Tapie's line was that the unfortunate Bernès had become so depressed that, despite his innocence, he was not only confessing to a crime he did not commit, but also implicating another innocent man, to wit, Tapie. That this preposterous pitch could even be uttered with a straight face says a lot about the histrionic abilities of Tapie, who has been getting away with so many lies for so many years that he has come to believe himself invincible.

But the worst was to come on March 17th, when Mellick's former parliamentary secretary testified that she had lied about seeing Tapie with Mellick on June 17, 1993. She asserted that Mellick had asked her to lie to bolster his own testimony. Moreover, she said that having told Mellick the prior day that she was going to change her testimony, the mayor threatened to fire her husband from his job in City Hall. Despite this dramatic testimony, when Mellick's turn came to testify, he maintained that he had been with Tapie, but perhaps, after all, he had been alone with him. By this time, everyone except Mellick realized that his goose was cooked, and also Tapie's, but both clung to their story.

Then, the next day, the police moved into action, arresting Mellick at his son's home at 6 am on charges of suborning perjury. A few hours later, Mellick's son read a televised statement admitting that his father had not been with Tapie on June 17th and had lied because he feared that the fall of Tapie would endanger the 300 jobs of Tapie's company in Béthune. A sorry excuse, indeed, for committing perjury. This dramatic turnabout did not faze the brazen Tapie, who appeared on the evening news with the basic message that he did not really need Mellick's testimony to prove that he had not been with Primorac! In other words, why would anyone believe a miserable Yugoslav against the word of an honorable parliamentarian?

The high point of Tapie's acting career came the following Monday when he admitted to the Court that he had "lied in good faith," while still maintaining his innocence! Surprisingly, the Public Prosecutor requested only a six-month prison sentence for Tapie, plus twelve months suspended, while asking for suspended sentences against all the other defendants who had actually participated in the bribery. As one of my friends remarked, *"Why all this hullabaloo, and spending so much of the taxpayers' money to bring these culprits to trial, if their punishment is to be so mild?"*

I have given these farcical details to indicate to readers how the French cultural and legal systems foster lying. Of course, lying exists in all cultures but each one deals with it differently. When I served as a judge advocate officer of the US Army in France, attending French trials one day and conducting courts-martial the next, I came to realize that American justice was basically Protestant in character and French justice Catholic. The difference could be illustrated by the trial of O.J. Simpson. If he were being tried in France, the judge would start off by interrogating him, but not under oath. If O.J. remained silent, something that rarely happens in France, the court would admonish him that this is proof of his guilt. If he confessed and expressed contrition, making what I call the "Othello defense" ("one that loved not wisely but too well") the jurors would weep and hand him a five-year sentence. For France is a Catholic country that looks to the salvation of souls through Confession and Absolution. Interestingly, even if the accused pleads guilty, the court conducts a full trial, because the objective is ultimately to judge the accused's state of mind and his worthiness for redemption.

In the American system, the accused cannot be forced to testify but, if he does, he must take an oath; thus he can later be charged with perjury if he lies. The fact that he confessed to the crime and expresses contrition does not count much in Protestant justice. To be sure, he can "plea bargain" with the prosecution, but the lightness of the sentence is justified merely because the guilty plea saves the prosecution time and money: it is not a reward for contrition. Thus the trial ends with the guilty plea and sentencing is left generally to a subsequent hearing.

It seems inconceivable to the Catholic judge that an accused not be interrogated, since the cleansing of guilt by confession is a basic tenet of his religion. Getting the truth is not a sufficient end, for in many cases the accused's guilt can be proved without his confession. In the Protestant system, the objective is ostensibly to get the truth but it is considered improper to force an accused to testify against himself. It is thus very interesting to note that in neither system is truth the highest value; in the Protestant system, the dignity of the individual is more important than the truth, since the system is willing to let a guilty man be acquitted if the only means to establish the truth is to force him to testify. In the Catholic system, getting the truth is not sufficient if the accused does not participate and explain his motives, and thus be given an opportunity to seek absolution.

What I am getting at in my round-about way is perhaps not a surprise to many readers but is worth stating nevertheless: contrary to the assumptions that we tend to entertain, truth is not the highest value in most societies. Several years ago, I read an article by Simon Rifkind, the venerable New York lawyer, who was once a federal judge, making the point that the American system does not always place truth-obtaining as its primary value. He gave several illustrations, not only the privilege against self-incrimination but also, for example, the rule that a wife cannot be forced to testify against her husband (and vice versa). In the French system, spouses and family members can be questioned by the court but, like the accused, they cannot take an oath, presumably because they are expected to lie in favor of the accused.

Sissela Bok, who is the best thing that happened to Derek Bok (not excluding 20 years as president of Harvard University) wrote a provocative book several years ago called "Lying." Swedish by birth and the daughter of not one but two Nobel Prize winners, Gunnar and Alva Myrdal, Sissela seems to hold that truth-telling is the highest value in society, judging by her moralistic attitude to lying. I do not doubt that she is personally a truth-teller of the first order. But most people consider that there are times when it is permissible to lie. Doctors often lie to their patients about the gravity of their malady. What husband has not lied to his wife when she asks what he thinks about her latest dress? And who does not stretch the truth when he tells a mother that "your baby is absolutely beautiful?"

Of course, so-called "white lies "are considered to be the acceptable concomitant of good relations in civilized society. But, in graver circumstances, it is also considered permissible to lie. In wartime, all governments fib about military movements, for example. And I suppose that any French patriot would have lied about the whereabouts of a Resistance member, if asked by the Gestapo. The trouble is that alongside white lies and permissible lies, millions of lies are perpetrated every day in every country for a variety of causes – getting money being doubtless the principal one, followed closely by lying to get power or even to get sex.

Having lived in both a Protestant culture and a Catholic one, I believe I can summarize their respective approaches to lying as follows: When a Catholic lies, he knows he's lying and knows he can go see a priest, confess and get absolution. When a Protestant lies, he convinces himself he has told the truth, for he has no safety valve. He continues to believe he has told the truth until his lie is proved publicly or in court. If he is not caught, the Protestant liar allows the mechanism of denial to efface his sin. As a Protestant theologian told me recently, a Protestant has to await death before he can get confirmation that his sin is forgiven, as only God can forgive. Consequently, it is comforting to let the subconscious convince you that you had not sinned after all. With this approach to sin, lying – rather getting caught at it – is taken much more seriously in a Protestant country than in a Catholic one. In the United States, for example, Gary Hart's political career was destroyed not because of philandering but because he lied about philandering. In France, a politician would be envied for his mistresses and considered gallant for lying about them. In 1974, when

Nixon was hounded out of office over Watergate, every French person I spoke with, including my wife, thought it shocking that so "great" a President could be disgraced for a mere cover-up. Nixon illustrated perfectly the Protestant approach to lying: he felt it necessary to announce *"I am not a crook"* and then being caught lying, could not be forgiven by his compatriots. It has been known for months that President Mitterrand's henchmen in the Elysée Palace had illegally tapped thousands of phone conversations for three years, but it is so obvious that he would lie about knowing of it that no one even bothers to ask him!

There is no doubt that you can have more fun with sin in a Catholic culture. In France, no politician is permanently disgraced no matter what he has done. Every seven years, after the Presidential election, the Parliament enacts a general amnesty law and lots of people get their misdemeanors wiped off the books. Indeed, it then becomes a misdemeanor to refer to a person's amnestied offenses!

To return to Tapie, he clearly owes his survival up to now to an extraordinary mastery of televised communication. It is said that he knows exactly whom to call in each television newsroom, and whenever he is in trouble he manages to get interviewed on prime time to present his clever perversion of the facts. He has a tremendous gift of gab and, like all con men, is very convincing whatever nonsense he spews. I have no doubt that a motion picture will be made some day about his extraordinary career. At this writing, I would say that he is likely to spend some time in jail before the year ends, but hitherto he has managed to avoid a single day of incarceration, whereas dozens of lesser crooks have not fared so well. I would not be surprised if he ended with a bullet in his head, not necessarily placed by him, but I hope that he will survive and write his autobiography. If he tells the truth, for a change, it is bound to be a classic social commentary of twentieth-century France.

His basic message will surely be this: a country which twice elects François Mitterrand as Chief of State certainly deserves a Bernard Tapie to entertain it.

In closing, I wish to make clear that my comments on the quirks of the two leading branches of Christendom do not proceed from animosity towards either of them. I was baptized in the Armenian Apostolic Church, commonly described as orthodox, but my parents, in addition to our parish church located at 6006 Walnut Street, frequently attended services at the Armenian Protestant church at 6027 Ludlow Street and the Armenian Catholic one at 6012 Market Street, all in West Philadelphia. And as we lived in a Jewish neighborhood, our "playground" being Sansom Street between 56th and 57th, I was blessed with an ecumenical childhood. I resurrect these addresses of yesteryear to commemorate a world that has disappeared. But what interests me now is how different religions spawn divergent attitudes towards justice. Any system has the flaws of its qualities.

Just as Socrates said that "the unexamined life is not worth living," so I hold that the unexamined society is not worth living in.

Small businessmen for sale

Vol. XVII, N° 3, April 1995

Easter 1995 – Meditations at Tilly

This is being written on Easter day at my country place in Tilly, located 65 kilometers due west from Paris. A generation ago, this was a farm house: my predecessors in title transformed it when the farmer retired. My neighbor's house across the street was also a farm building; now it shelters not only my neighbor but also a handsome pipe organ which he purchased years ago from the Count of Paris. Occasionally, I am privileged to play Bach on it.

This area once played host to history. The modest Château of Tilly, which hardly anyone notices as he drives by, belonged to Admiral de Grasse, a name every American should revere (but which most cannot recognize), for he commanded the French fleet at Yorktown. Ten kilometers away is the town of Anet: there, Diane of Poitiers held court in a château made for a woman, and what a woman! Not only was she the favorite of François I, the learned King who turned his eyes to Florence, and brought Leonard da Vinci to the Loire Valley, but also she became the mistress of his son, when he was King Henri II. Who remembers that the King of Spain had taken the two sons of François I as hostages and that Diane was part of the delegation that went to Spain to deliver them? In his dungeon, the adolescent Henri had never seen anything so beautiful as Diane, and it was love at first sight. Later, his father fixed up a de luxe marriage for Henri – to Catherine de Medicis – but Henri never forgot Diane and took her as his mistress, although she was 20 years older than he. Henri died young, in a jousting match, after which Diane retired to Anet. In case you have forgotten, this was the 16th Century.

Only a few kilometers from Anet is Ivry-la-Bataille, so named because Henri IV won a big battle there. Was it against the Huns? or the Moors? or only Protestants? Who remembers? Every schoolboy knows, however, that Henri of Navarre converted to Catholicism to become King, and uttered the celebrated *bon mot:* "Paris is well worth a Mass!" The countryside is mainly flat, suitable for farming and grazing. The staples are wheat, corn for animal feed, colza and safflower for oil. Only an occasional hill relieves the flatness. It was my late farmer neighbor, Rémy Noblet, who told me that this area was liberated by the American Army. Only a concrete bunker on the road between Tilly and Ivry serves to recall that Germans occupied this land 50 years ago.

From time to time, while traveling these roads, I remind myself that horses and carriages once preceded me carrying kings, princesses, lords and ladies back and forth from Paris. Today, people travel to do their shopping. In Tilly, there are no shops: for bread I have to go four kilometers to Berchères, a lovely village where, in the shadow of the church, a *boulangerie* is the only shop. It is, of course, a "mom and pop" operation, but as the *boulangère* is relatively young, I prefer to think of them as a husband-and-wife team. It pleases me that the French language has a feminine form for the wife of the *boulanger.* Elsewhere, she would be the "baker's wife," but here she is queen of the shop: *La Boulangère*. And a deserving queen she is, for I have never seen her without a smile on her face. Always neatly dressed and unruffled, she greets her neighbors by name. I have never bothered to tell her mine, but she did remember the name of Jules, our little dog, and she always asks to be remembered to my wife. Several years ago, they remodeled their shop to add groceries, fruit and vegetables, which the *boulangère* serves as graciously as the *pain aux céréales*.

Today, I did my main shopping in Houdan, only 12 kilometers from Tilly, to the south. Once a medieval *bourg,* Houdan still has the shops which are the glory of small towns: a *fromager,* a *poissonnier,* two *fleuristes,* two *charcutiers,* two *bouchers,* two *café-tabacs,* a *quincaillerie,* and, of course, a *Maison de la Presse*. It even has a *mercerie*, where you can buy needles and thread, a disappearing business. Sadly, one notes the closing of shops and the falling-off of trade; several *hypermarchés* lurk in the vicinity offering unbeatable prices. To compete, the Houdan shops double up. The fish vendor sells also fruit and vegetables, even cheese. The cheese man dispenses wine in an adjoining boutique. Several years ago, there were three green-grocers; one sold his lease to a realtor, another, a man in his 80s, died: his shop remains empty. Each time I go to Houdan I dread the disappearance of shops which are the *raison d'être* of this *bourg.* To buy some bulgour, I had to make a brief visit to the *hypermarché*; the cashier is as impersonal as the cash register, she doesn't even look at me as she takes my money. How can she possibly know that I have a dog named Jules?

Napoleon once heaped scorn on England as being "a nation of shopkeepers." As he was used to being catered to, Napoleon evidently never noticed that France, too, was a nation of *boutiquiers.* Without shops, Paris would lose half its charm. Outside Paris, shops are what make towns and villages livable. They play a social role, not just economic. But shopkeepers are becoming an endangered species, not only because of supermarkets but also because of the recession.

You see, France is undergoing hard times: the franc is strong but the economy is weak. Shoppers cannot be blamed for flocking to the supermarkets to save a few francs: most people have not had a raise in years, because the technocrats have finally licked inflation and at least four-million people are unemployed, living off handouts. Never since the middle ages have there been so many beggars in Paris: one sees them everywhere, not only in the Metro as before, but also at every major intersection where there is a red light. With that wonderful gift of concision, the French have given a one-word label to this situation; it is an abstract noun, of course – *l'exclusion.* In the United States, one speaks of poverty: the French speak of exclusion.

The Balladur government, in power now for two years, has basically followed a policy of *immobilisme.* Rather than stimulate the economy to reduce unemployment, Balladur raised taxes and social charges. He maintained the policy of his Socialist predecessors to favor the *franc fort.* No one points out that when you put these words together they become Francfort, which is the French spelling of Frankfurt! The symbolism is perfect, because French policy is to emulate Germany. A few years ago, I asked a French Treasury official what the thinking was behind the strong franc. His answer: "Credibility: the Germans have 40 years of credibility, we have only ten." This was all. If you decipher the code, all that is behind the strong franc is the vanity of the French technocrats who want to be able to meet their German counterparts and proudly say, "You see, we too can maintain a strong currency." The price of this vanity is four-million people looking for work.

The Germans have a visceral loathing of inflation because of the terrible experience of the Weimar Republic, whose debased currency destroyed the middle class and led to the rise of Hitler. France has no comparable reason to place deflation as the highest economic goal, particularly since the liberalization of imports, even from Asia, has made it difficult for French companies to compete, and thus has aggravated unemployment. And for the first time since World War II, France has become a country of *rentiers.* Until recently, one could earn nine percent net of taxes on fixed-income investments, with no risk of depreciation of the capital by reason of the low inflation. Why invest in business and risk losing your capital when you can get that kind of return on a safe investment?

In a week, French voters will choose among nine Presidential candidates in the first round of the elections, and the two leading candidates will then fight it out two Sundays thereafter. Whereas only a few months ago, after the pullout of Jacques Delors, it seemed that Edouard Balladur would be a shoo-in, there has been a dramatic turnaround in the polls: Jacques Chirac has a clear lead, and even the Socialist candidate Lionel Jospin is ahead of the Prime Minister. How did this reversal come about? I think that the main credit belongs to Chirac, who refused to be intimidated by the polls and concentrated on visiting people all over France. Despite the defection of a number of former henchmen, chief among them being Charles Pasqua, Chirac managed to keep tight control of his political party, the RPR, which has the most powerful organization in the country. By contrast, Balladur has no party of his own: for two years he has courted the various components of the UDF, but they have no machine comparable with that of the RPR. Another reason for Chirac's rise is that he finally learned how to avoid the hard image he used to project on television, far different from his actual personality: that of a warm and gregarious man.

Balladur assumed that he could be elected by merely relying on television. His spokesman, Nicholas Sarkozy, was so sure of Balladur's election that, in January, he even suggested that Chirac renounce his candidacy so that Balladur could be elected on the first ballot, a feat that no one has achieved since the advent of the Fifth Republic! His ratings began to decline after he capitulated once again to students who objected to a mini-reform. This reminded many people of the Balladur of 1993 who backed down over reform of Air France when the unions struck, and withdrew another measure involving students. Balladur was also hurt by revelations that for years he had received a "consulting fee" of $20,000 a month from GSI, a data-processing company which he once headed, even while he was a member of Parliament. It says a lot about contemporary France that it is not illegal for a *député* to be paid by a private company! The *Canard Enchaîné* revealed also that Balladur had made a nifty capital gain on a GSI stock transaction whose justification seemed murky indeed.

Realizing that his image as a haughty technocrat wearing tailor-made English three-piece suits needed improving, Balladur took to the huskings and tried to out-do Chirac. It was comical to see Balladur, who probably had never touched any animal other than a well-coifed Pekinese, pretending to enjoy the caressing of hogs at agricultural fairs. For a time his ratings rose. It became front-page news that Balladur had actually stood on a table to address a crowd at a political rally. Of all the lowly things one has to do to get elected, Balladur must surely believe that standing on a table is the lowest. But the main sacrifice that this noble man has had to make is to call a halt to wearing English suits. I heard his tailor being interviewed the other day on French radio: he complained that Balladur has stopped his bi-monthly fittings and is now wearing undistinguished French suits.

Jospin, the Socialist candidate, lacks charisma, doubtless a result of his Protestant background. Once head of the party and for several years Minister of Education, he represents the old guard of the Mitterrand years, and thus cannot divorce himself from discredited policies such as nationalization and invasive regulation of business. Most of his support will come from people who simply vote Left out of habit; he has no drawing card for traditional voters on the Right. According to the polls, he will have difficulty in getting more than 20 percent of the vote in the first round.

To his Left are three candidates: the Communist, Robert Hue, who is hovering at ten percent in the polls; Arlette Laguiller, the Trotskyite lady who is a permanent fixture of presidential campaigns, credited with five percent; and Dominique Voynet, the female ecologist, with three percent. The two male ecologists dropped out: Brice Lalonde, quite early, and Antoine Wechter, at the last minute, because he could not muster the 500 nominating signatures from local elected officials.

On the Right, we have Jean-Marie Le Pen, the anti-immigrant campaigner, who is credited with 13 percent in the polls, and Philippe de Villiers, who is running on an anti-corruption and anti-EC ticket, trailing at five percent. Last of the nine candidates, and certainly least, is a complete unknown, Jacques Cheminade, who managed to get 500 signatures, but has a zero rating in the polls. Altogether, the Rightist candidates total 62 percent and the Left 38 percent. Thus, barring a miracle in favor of Jospin, the next President of France is going to be either Jacques Chirac or Edouard Balladur, with the former heavily favored.

Not being a French citizen, I do not vote, but my wife's clear favorite is Jacques Chirac. Now 62, Chirac is two years younger than Balladur, but is much more experienced in politics. Chirac gives hope of a needed change in French domestic economic policies. Without a drastic effort to reduce unemployment, France may be in for rough times. Already, strikes and demonstrations are becoming commonplace, and most seasoned observers of the French scene expect another "May '68" if Chirac wins and does nothing quickly to stimulate the economy.

The question is: where will the bold new ideas come from? Chirac himself, once Mr Pompidou's "bulldozer," has never been known as an idea man but as a man of action. In the past, he has always needed a guru. In the old days, he had that improbable pair, who were Pompidou's advisers, Marie-France Garaud and Pierre Juillet, whose ideas I was never able to fathom. After breaking with them, Chirac picked up Balladur as his strategist, but their tandem in the 1986-88 cohabitation with Mitterrand led to Chirac's defeat and the

President's re-election in the last presidential election. In 1993, Balladur was supposed to content himself with the Prime Minister's job and to let Chirac become President, but Edouard double-crossed Jacques, his "friend of 30 years." So now, everyone is wondering who Chirac's guru will be. According to the *Canard Enchaîné*, the five leading advisers to Chirac are all *ENArques* like him, something which does not surprise me. To expect a new idea from an *ENArque* is like expecting Médoc wine from a turnip.

Chirac himself released a book last year, the banality of whose contents was so striking that I considered it credible that he had written it all himself. When a man has spent his whole adult life adulating "the State" and is surrounded by people of the same kind, how can he be aware that he and his companions are the problem and not the solution? Still, being an optimist by nature, I would like to believe that Chirac will be the architect of a French perestroika but the more realistic part of my brain reminds me of that exquisite saying: *Plus ça change, plus c'est la même chose.*

That Chirac is the front-runner is a tribute to his courage and determination. Perhaps, also, he knew better than anyone that the French, being Catholics, like to reward losers. Mitterrand was twice defeated in his quest for the Presidency. Even de Gaulle had been a loser; defeated in 1946 when he proposed a new Constitution, he seemed finished in the '50s until the Algerian rebellion gave him a new lease on power. Americans, being Protestants, do not like losers; to lose is to fall from Grace.

Well, my meditations are ended for the day. Tomorrow morning, Easter Monday, a holiday, I will go see my blond *boulangère* at Berchères and buy a big *brioche*. I pray that Chirac, or whoever wins the election, will allow her to survive, for without her my France would be a wasteland.

Vol. XVII, N° 4, May, 1995

Feudal France; Serial Justice

Well, Jacques the First was crowned as King of France on May 17th, while François the Last, the outgoing monarch, too sick to seek re-election, looked on benignly. Jacques Chirac, to use his street name, wasted no time in selecting his chief Baron, Alain Juppé, as Prime Minister. The other principal Baron of the new régime, Philippe Séguin, hid his disappointment and remained President of the National Assembly. Both Baron Alain and Baron Philippe had remained loyal to Jacques Chirac, the heir apparent, while the Usurper, Prince Edouard Balladur, whom many suspect of being an Armenian from Smyrna, exploited his power and patronage as Prime Minister to win the support of former Chirac loyalists in his quest for the throne.

The other Pretender to the throne, the Socialist, Lionel Jospin, did surprisingly well in the two-round election. He actually scored the most votes among the 10 candidates in the first round, a respectable 23 percent to 21 for Chirac, and got 47 percent in the second round, more than anyone would have thought possible a month earlier. As befits any Pretender, Lionel went to the same school as Jacques, the Ecole Nationale d'Administration, which selects the most worthy youth of the Nation for the sacred responsibilities of power. The televised debate, prior to the second round, showed that the two were worthy scholars of the religion of the State. When Lionel suggested that to reduce unemployment, the work week should be shortened by two hours, Jacques opined that this would not lead to more jobs in the private sector, as employers would obtain more productivity. However, both agreed that it would lead to more employment in the Public Sector, as functionaries are already fully productive, and thus more civil servants would have to be hired to make up for the lost time. That is the first principle of the ENA catechism: there can never be enough functionaries to do all the thankless work that they have to do.

As if to underline the necessity of putting people to work, Prime Minister Juppé named a cabinet of 42 Ministers, the second largest ever, including 12 women, Not only was such a large cabinet necessary to reduce unemployment, but also it was a gesture of appreciation for those who stuck by Jacques Chirac, when the going was rough or, as in the case of most Centrists, switched to him when the going got rough for Edouard Balladur. Under the French system, the number and names of ministries are not determined by law, but depend solely on the wisdom and the wit of the President and the Prime Minister. In the first government of the reign of François the Last, a wonderful ministry was created, called the "Ministry of Free Time" (*Ministère du Temps Libre*). This ministry was so successful that it was abolished after a couple of years: in 1981 there were only one-million people with Free Time but thanks to the efforts of the Socialists, the number of people with Free Time jumped to four million in 1994. Not to be outdone by the Socialists, Messieurs Chirac and Juppé created a Ministry called "Solidarity among the Generations," naming to this post a woman whose profession was that of midwife in Lille, a Socialist bastion. These gentlemen have been so busy since the new government was named that they have not found the time to tell the Minister what she is supposed to do to promote "solidarity among the generations," nor has she told them either. I certainly hope that she will keep busy delivering babies, because that certainly promotes solidarity among the generations, at least in my family. Another poetic Ministry is that of "Labor, Social Dialogue and Participation." Presumably the social dialogue for which this Minister is responsible touches people in the same generation; else it might interfere with the work of the midwife just mentioned.

Baron Alain Juppé delivered a 150-minute address to the National Assembly, setting forth his program. Commentators were unanimous in concluding that the speech lacked eloquence and poetry, but even Racine and Molière were never able to invent monologues that lasted two-and-a-half hours without losing their audiences. Juppé should be forgiven for being so boring in his maiden speech to the Parliament because his mind was elsewhere. In keeping with the selfless tradition of French Prime Ministers, Baron Alain has decided to run for Mayor of Bordeaux, a mere 600 kilometers distant from Paris where his main office is located. As Juppé explained in a radio interview which I heard, it is the duty of national officeholders to learn what life is like in the provinces, else they cannot properly perform their national duties. Thus, tiring as it must be for a Prime Minister, he reluctantly stands for office to replace the ailing Jacques Chaban-Delmas, who is retiring after 47 years as Mayor of Bordeaux, some of which included service as Prime Minister under President Pompidou. Baron Philippe Séguin, while President of the National Assembly, is also Mayor of Epinal in the Vosges mountains. This way he learns about local problems and becomes a better legislator. This is the great tradition in France, where many dozens of Ministers and members of Parliament are also Mayors of cities and towns. For example, when Jack Lang was Minister of Culture he was elected Mayor of Blois, a city where he never lived. You do not have to be a resident of a city to want to learn about local problems and thus better serve the national interest. As for Prime Ministers under the Fifth Republic, most of them have been Mayors at the same time: Jacques Chirac (Paris), Pierre Bérégovoy (Nevers), Edith Cresson (Chatellerault), Michel Rocard (Conflans Sainte Honorine), Pierre Mauroy (Lille) are among the most famous.

During the presidential debate above-mentioned, Lionel Jospin delivered a low blow by contending that if elected President he would seek to abolish the *cumul de mandats*. He made the point that it is hard for a man to fulfill both jobs satisfactorily: in practice, most national officeholders visit the cities of which they are Mayors only on weekends. Jacques Chirac, naturally, defended the status quo, repeating the standard line that it is good for such public servants to learn what's going on in the grass roots. Jospin also advocated reducing the Presidential term to five years. Despite the fact that Chirac's mentor, Georges Pompidou, tried to enact such a measure 20 years earlier, the future President dismissed the idea as not being timely. Lionel got off the best line of the debate when he said, "Five years of Jospin are better than seven years of Chirac." Coming from a Protestant, the *propos* was understandable, but Catholic France likes its Bishops and Kings to serve longer terms.

As might be expected, Lionel Jospin did not raise any ethical objection to a national official holding a local office at the same time. The notion that there might be a conflict of interest in this situation is totally absent from the French mentality. I have questioned dozens of people on this subject, including my French wife (my only one, for that matter) and they invariably reply the same way. If you ask, "Do you see any problem in a man being Prime Minister and Mayor of Bordeaux at the same time?" the answer is always, "It's good for the people of Bordeaux." That it might not be good for the people in all the other places in France never bothers the French. The other day I posed the question to a young French lawyer, and I got the same answer. When I pursued the matter by asking her, "Doesn't it bother you that the Prime Minister can favor Bordeaux over other cities?" her reply was, "They'll get their turn."

This led me to reflect on how lacking I have been in the study of ethical philosophy. I had blithely assumed that the only just system was simultaneous justice, that is, one in which society tries to be fair to everyone at the same time. It had never occurred to me that an alternate system could well be what I now call "serial justice," where fairness is achieved sequentially and not simultaneously. In its crudest terms, what the young lawyer was telling me was, "I don't mind being screwed today if I know that I'll have my turn to screw the others tomorrow." It is justice based on each person waiting his turn to be unjust.

This explains why the French are not bothered by conflicts of interest in their leaders and civil servants. If an entire country does not see an ethical problem, then there simply isn't an ethical problem. The French political landscape is like a stage on which the actors are expected to play the maximum number of roles. The watchers consider this entertainment. The name of the play is "Power and Privilege" and the watchers, like true voyeurs, have as much fun as the actors. How can there possibly be an ethical problem when they are all having so much fun? When Chaban-Delmas was Prime Minister and simultaneously Mayor of Bordeaux he straightened out Ford Motor Company, which had conceived the wild idea of building a factory near Strasbourg. He convinced them that Bordeaux would be a better site and there the factory was erected. This is not conflict of interest; this is better knowledge of sites that only a Prime Minister who is Mayor of Bordeaux can acquire. How can anyone complain about superior knowledge?

There cannot be the slightest doubt that the French population feels at home in the neo-feudal system that has blossomed during the Fifth Republic. In fact, the press openly uses the term *fief* (fiefdom) in describing the political strongholds that the various national figures have in the provinces. Thus Epinal is the *fief* of Philippe Séguin as Bordeaux will become the *fief* of Alain Juppé. When Jacques Chirac was Mayor of Paris he was simultaneously member of Parliament representing the Corrèze *département*, some 600 kilometers to the south. France is the only country I know where one learns at 30 (if he is an *ENArque*) how to run the country and at 50 how to run a city. But usually the feudal beneficiary is already a Mayor before becoming Prime Minister. However, in Juppé's case he preferred the reverse strategy: first make your name in Paris and then seek a lifetime *fief* in the provinces. This is his reward for 20 years spent in advancing the career of Jacques Chirac. It is common knowledge that Juppé hopes to succeed Chirac in 2002 but he may be surprised to discover that Chirac wants to succeed himself.

In the original feudal system the King rewarded his barons and warriors by giving them fiefdoms. They thus became local potentates while having a duty to serve the King at court from time to time and to fight his wars. By hypothesis this system was ethical since the King was the center of the system and the only players were those who got rewards in exchange for services to the King. There was a *quid pro quo*. In the modern feudal system of France, the source of power is not only the King but ultimately the People, who elect the lords and barons. The *quid pro quo* for getting all the power is entertaining the People and throwing them crumbs, a factory here, a school or stadium there. Just as pigeons wait their turn for the crumbs, so the French people wait for their serial justice. In the same way, I had always assumed that "*Liberté, Egalité, Fraternité*" were meant to be simultaneous objectives. Now I understand that they are sequential goals: first you get Liberty, then you trade it for Equality, and finally you give up Equality for Fraternity. *C'est logique, n'est-ce pas*?

For years I naively believed that because Montesquieu was a Frenchman, the concept of separation of powers was well-accepted here. I have just learned that Montesquieu did not write *L'Esprit des Lois*. Just as Bacon really wrote Shakespeare, so a Joseph Mountbank, of New Haven, Connecticut, authored "The Spirit of the Laws" and, knowing that his 18th-century American contemporaries were enamored of French ideas, conceived the bright idea of publishing the book in the name of this obscure nobleman from Bordeaux. This accounts for the fact that Americans practice the separation of powers, while the French practice the accumulation of powers.

Most French people with whom I have spoken assume that this practice goes on in other countries, but when I point out that Margaret Thatcher, when Prime Minister, was not mayor of London or Liverpool, or that Helmut Kohl, when Chancellor of the Federal Republic of Germany does not rule the city of Hamburg or Munich, or that the Mayor of New York is not a Congressman from Indianapolis at the same time, my French friends shrug their shoulders, as if to say, "What untalented people, these foreigners!"

I have little doubt that French notions will ultimately prevail throughout the European Union. One day the Prime Minister of Europe will be Mayor of Manchester, commuting every weekend through the Chunnel. Already, migration of powers exists in the Union: when fifteen heads of government get together in the Council of Ministers, they became legislators for the entire Union, whereas they were selected to be executives and cannot legislate in their own countries! I would surmise that separation of powers suits Americans because they have limited mental spans; French brains, as is well known, can handle several concepts simultaneously. Moreover, there is no ethical problem because they can concentrate so intensely on whichever problem is before them that they can disregard any conflicting interest. For example, when Juppé will sit in the City Hall of Bordeaux he will think only of local interests, and when he is in the Hôtel Matignon, he will not even remember that he is Mayor of Bordeaux. Of course, all the people who work for him will also forget.

Who am I, raised in another system, to complain about this one? To be sure, I haven't asked the four-million people in France with Free Time what they think of the system, but surely they can't complain, having all that time on their hands.

Vol. XVII, N° 5, June 1995

Golden Rule, French Style

Despite not having had much choice in the matter, I am proud of being a product of Philadelphia public schools at a time when they had remarkable teachers, most of whose names I can still recall. Among other things I owe to these schools is a modicum of knowledge of the Bible, because I grew up at a time when the United States Supreme Court had not yet abolished Bible reading in public schools, on the ground that this violated the First Amendment prohibition of government "establishing" religion. I consider this a foolish decision, not the least because the few verses that were read every morning were inoffensive; they certainly did not make me religious but did give me some inkling of the majestic prose of the King James version of the Bible, including the 23d Psalm which was my favorite. Our schools having many Jewish students, I cannot recall Jesus ever being mentioned in a Bible reading, and so I suspect that it was elsewhere that I learned of the Golden Rule, which is probably the best-known teaching attributed to Him.

I happen to believe that this rule is the best succinct rule of conduct ever invented. Sometimes, I even recommend it to my clients. Holmes, in his famous essay, "The Path of the Law," expounded on the difference between law and morality by positing that the former is the advice a lawyer can give to a "bad man." My answer is that I do not knowingly give advice to bad men.

It was a few years ago that I discovered that the Golden Rule loses something when translated into French. This occurred when I mentioned the Golden Rule to a French client, first using the English term and, on drawing a blank, then translating it to "*la Règle d'Or*," but to no avail. As my client did not understand what I meant, I expanded on it by saying, in English, "You know, the rule Jesus gave, which is commonly expressed as 'Do unto others as you would have others do unto you.' My client's face lit up and he said in French, "*Ne pas faire à autrui ce que vous ne voudriez pas qu'ils vous fassent*." I immediately noticed that he had put it in the negative. ("Do not do to others what you would not want them do to you.") When I questioned him on this, my client replied that this was the way he had learned the rule.

On subsequent occasions, I tried the same experiment on French clients and friends, and invariably the Golden Rule was stated in the negative. Puzzled by this, I wondered whether the French translation of the Bible differed from the English one on this crucial point. After all, it might have been that the original Greek version was in the negative, and that the translators of the King James Bible had preferred the positive. But when I managed to locate a French Bible I found that in both Gospels, Matthew (7:12) and Luke (6:31), the words of Jesus are stated positively, as in the English version. The Matthew verse in the King James Bible is

> "Therefore all things whatsoever that ye would that men should do to you, do ye even so to them: for this is the law and the prophets."

To my mind, it became a proper inference that the Catholic Church in France had been teaching the Golden Rule in the negative. On a recent weekend in the Cévennes, that marvelous mountainous region of the south of France, I visited a friend who was born in this Protestant stronghold, near the town of Pont de Montvert, where the War of the Camisards broke out in reaction to the revocation of the Edict of Nantes by Louis XIV, an ignoble measure that led to France losing most of its dynamic Huguenot population. Thinking that perhaps the Protestants had learned the rule differently, I tested it out with my friend and his wife, but they, too, came up with the negative version. When I told them that the Bible version was not the same, they looked at me in disbelief and brought out the old family Bible, which was published 150 years ago. I managed to locate the Matthew and the Luke verses and showed my incredulous friends that Jesus had spoken positively. All in all, I have asked at least 20 persons and they all gave the negative version, saying that it was the way they had learned it in religious instruction. None of my Catholic friends ever referred to the biblical version, apparently because they had never read it. Some told me that they had been admonished not to read the Bible, as it was the clergy's exclusive privilege to interpret it.

When I am in a preaching mood, I point out to my friends that the negative version does not have the same meaning as the affirmative. It is one thing, for example, to say, "Do not shoot your neighbor's dog if you would not want your neighbor to shoot yours." It is another to say, "Give a bone to your neighbor's dog when he's hungry if you would want your neighbor to do likewise to yours." The first is a rule of abstention from doing evil, the second is a rule of goodness. It is, if you'll pardon the expression, a rule of affirmative action. To be sure, even a negative rule can be made positive by use of the double-negative, as, for example, "Do not fail to give your neighbor's dog a bone." but why march up the hill just to march down?

I would not dwell on this discovery were it not my sense that it has some significance for my quest to understand the French character. Why does the French Catholic Church teach the Golden Rule in the negative when the Bible states it positively? The old chicken-and-the-egg dilemma is posed, of course: did French character cause the negative translation or did the translation influence French character? I am referring to the common perception that the French lack civic sense and hospitality and even pride themselves on being individualists (which I generally translate as being selfish). When a Frenchman buys a plot of land, he builds a fence around it before he even builds his house. He does not want to be bothered by neighbors, and in return he does not bother them. This is the negative Golden Rule, which is, of course, better than no rule at all. (To be fair, let me mention that the French are not the only people who believe that "good fences make good neighbors;" else, we would not have Robert Frost's immortal poem, "*Mending Wall*").

Recently, I mentioned this discovery to an American from New York who informed me that the negative version originated in the teachings of Hillel, which are part of the Talmud. I am fascinated by the notion that the French Catholic Church might have been inspired by the Talmud, a delightful idea, coming after the Dreyfus case, Action Française, and Jean-Marie Le Pen. Of course, even the rule in the negative is a great advance for civilization, and we should feel indebted to Hillel for having formulated what I would call the "Silver Rule." Indeed, it occurs to me that Jesus must have been familiar with this rule because, in the Matthew version, after stating the rule positively, He states: "for this is the law and the prophets." Is it possible that Jesus accidentally converted the rule from negative to positive? If so, it is the most glorious mistake in all scripture. If it was a deliberate conversion, one can understand why Jesus was not popular with the orthodox theologians. It is interesting to speculate that had Jesus been accepted by his peers as a Talmudic interpreter, the history of the world would have been very different but the Jews would still have been in a "lose:lose" situation. Judaism would have evolved naturally, minding its own business and, as Jews do not proselytize, they would have been the only Christians in the world. The rest of us would have been pagans or Moslems, persecuting the Jews, of course, from time to time.

So, to conclude all this rumination with the familiar dichotomy, there is good news and bad news. The good news is that French Catholics are reconciled with Judaism: the bad news is that in France the Golden Rule is made of silver.

Tapie, continued

Just in case you're wondering, Bernard Tapie was handed a one-year jail sentence by the Valenciennes court that tried him for bribing players of a rival team and for suborning perjury. The sentence was twice that asked for by the Public Prosecutor. Tapie is still a free man, as he has appealed the sentence. The colorful public figure expressed great dismay at the idea of going to jail: as he explained it, his only objective was to protect his Marseilles players from being injured in a match to be played just four days before the final of the European Cup. Had he stated this at the outset, he might not only have escaped prosecution but also been awarded the *Légion d'Honneur* by his admirer, François Mitterrand, for humanitarian works. Tapie also opined that it is unjust to send a man to jail who has had the tribulations that he has lived through. If you don't get the point, neither do I, but I think he might have been suggesting that the Valenciennes adventure was merely a peccadillo compared with what he had gotten away with in his checkered career.

Tapie's personal bankruptcy was also confirmed by the Court of Appeals of Paris. As a result, he is ineligible for public office for five years, an interdiction that deprived him of the opportunity to run for Mayor of Marseilles, where he was once a hero. Unless the forthcoming amnesty law, which will follow the election of a new President, applies to his conviction – an unlikely event – Tapie may finally see the inside of a prison cell before year-end. However, a rumor has been making the rounds to the effect that Tapie is planning to move to Brussels and thus hinder efforts to incarcerate him. If Tapie does go to jail, I have little doubt that within a week he will be immensely popular with the other inmates and will end up selling them shares in his future enterprise.

Never one to stand still, Tapie just signed on to star in a moving picture to be written and directed by Claude Lelouch, the French *cinéaste* whose most famous film is *A Man and a Woman*. Lelouch says that Tapie is a born actor, a point with which no one would disagree. All con men are born actors as are most politicians and some lawyers. To be sure, acting is a noble profession, particularly if it leads to playwrighting, as per William Shakespeare and Molière. Yet, I still hold that Tapie's ultimate contribution to civilization will be his memoirs, if he ever gets around to writing them honestly.

Juppé, continued

Well, Baron Alain Juppé, the first Prime Minister of President Chirac, managed to be elected Mayor of Bordeaux, barely garnishing a majority of the votes on the first round. Juppé also made the headlines when the *Canard Enchainé* revealed that he had a sweetheart deal with the City of Paris, under which he was able to rent a luxury apartment belonging to the City at a below-market rental. The *Canard Enchainé* also disclosed that the new Mayor, Jean Tiberi, who took over when Chirac gave up the job, had arranged for favorable rentals to his two sons, who owned apartments in the city but preferred renting them out. In a later issue, the *Canard* revealed that Juppé also had arranged favorable leases not only for all his children but also for his ex-wife. In other countries, public housing is for the poor, in Paris it is for the privileged.

These scandals aroused much discontent in a city where cheap rents are hard to find. It helped contribute to the loss of six *arrondissements* to the opposition in the June municipal elections. (In Paris, each *arrondissement* has its own mayor.) *Le Monde* published an eye-opening article revealing that the City of Paris owns 150,000 apartments, including several thousand of the best category, called "the private domain," which are let out to those who have "pull," including not only politicians and high civil servants, but also journalists.

Why a city should have a "private domain" is a mystery that has not been explained but it is obvious that in a monarchy like France, government serves mainly to foster the well-being of the élite who rule the country.

Another fascinating aspect of this issue is that although Jacques Chirac was mayor of Paris for 18 years, while these shenanigans were going on, no one has called him to task, just as no one questioned Mitterrand when it was learned that a special squad of *gendarmes* conducted thousands of illegal wiretaps under his nose. In France today, as in olden times, the King can do no wrong, even when he is called *Président de la République*.

Pizza
Hut

Vol. XVII, N° 6, July 1995

Paranoid Alley: from Paul Valéry to Pizza Hut

In my "Easter Meditations" I expressed concern about the possible loss of the *boulangerie* at Berchères, near my country house. Not long after writing that, an event even closer to home made me aware of how vulnerable France is to losses of that type.

One of the pleasures of my life is walking to work every morning. I live on rue Weber, near the Porte Maillot and the Bois de Boulogne. In my immediate neighborhood, most of the streets are named after composers. The French have a wonderful custom of naming streets after the great men and women of the past or, at least, those who were once thought great. Indeed, it is to the credit of the French that despite their reputation for chauvinism they have been generous in naming streets after foreigners, including several American presidents: Washington, Lincoln, Wilson, Franklin D. Roosevelt, Eisenhower and Kennedy. (I have yet to see a "Charles de Gaulle Boulevard" in New York City.) Americans are often more practical in numbering their streets but, with a little curiosity, you can get educated just walking the streets of Paris, for the municipal authorities have adopted recently the practice of adding to the name plates a brief description of the person whose name graces the street. However, I did not need such a plate to surmise that my street was named after Karl Maria von Weber, the early-19th-century German composer, most famous for operas, such as *Oberon* and *Der Freischütz.* In my usual itinerary (I like to vary them), I turn left off Weber to rue Pergolèse, named after the 18th-century composer (his name is spelled Pergolesi, of course, in his native Italy) whose *Stabat Mater* is, fortunately, still heard now and then. (It is worth mentioning that Perolgesi died at the extraordinarily young age of 26.) Then I pass by rue Berlioz, a private street (where Romy Schneider once lived), protected by a giant gate, and soon cross avenue Malakoff (not a composer but a battle fought by the French during the Crimean War) and take a diagonal to rue Piccini, which leads to avenue Foch.

If you think you've just spotted a typographical error, you are mistaken, for it is Piccini, not Puccini, the gifted composer of *La Tosca, La Bohème* and *Madame Butterfly,* to cite the most famous of his operas. Adding to the confusion, the city misspells Piccinni's name which, according to both my *Petit Robert* and my *Petit Larousse,* should be written with a double "n." At any rate, Niccolo Piccinni, too, was an Italian composer of operas, who settled in Paris in the 18th century and became a rival of Gluck. Now he is only a street, since no one seems to play his works. Amazingly, Giacomo Puccini has no street named after him in Paris, despite the fact that his *La Bohème* immortalized the *Quartier Latin.*

The most dangerous part of this itinerary is crossing the majestic, tree-lined avenue Foch at a place where there is no traffic light. I call it the *autoroute Foch* ("Foch freeway") because, in the morning rush hour, thousands of single-occupant cars hurry in toward the Arc de Triomphe. Occasionally, if the drivers have to slow down, they look at me with curiosity and compassion, as if to say, "What is this well-dressed man doing on his feet? Surely, his car must have been stolen."

This is the time to pause briefly in my itinerary to confess that I call my morning walk to work (whatever the route) "Paranoid Alley." Why this name? Because, years ago, I discovered that I had a tendency while heading for my office to imagine all sorts of dire things that would happen when I arrived: *e.g.,* my secretary would call in sick, the computer would fail with an important contract due, the check the client promised would not be in the mail. To be sure, once I got to the office, none of these horrid events would occur, and so I decided I needed an antidote for paranoia, which took the form of reciting poems to myself while walking to work. (Fortunately it's only a 20-minute walk, as my repertoire is thin.) I usually start off with my favorite Shakespeare Sonnet, which begins:

"When I consider everything that grows,
Holds in perfection but a little moment."

I often follow-up with my favorite Yeats poem, "Sailing to Byzantium," whose last stanza I am particularly fond of. It begins:

"Once out of nature, I shall never take
My bodily form from any natural thing."

If I'm feeling romantic, I then take on my preferred Keats sonnet:

"Bright star! Would I were steadfast as thou art
Not in lone splendour held aloft the night."

Finally, if I'm in a histrionic mood, I finish off with Othello's closing speech, a marvel of dramatic poetry, which contains the famous lines:

"Speak of me as I am
Nothing extenuate nor set down aught in malice
Then must you speak of one,
That lov'd not wisely but too well."

Back to my itinerary: safely across the broad avenue, I now take up what is my favorite section, rue Paul Valéry. This is a narrow, one-way street, named after the celebrated poet and essayist who was born in 1871 and died in 1945. On the left-hand side of the street, as I walk to work, I pass the house (number 40) where he lived. I know by heart the words on the plaque, fixed to the front of the handsome *hôtel particulier* (my translation):

"In this house
built and inhabited
by Berthe Morisot
1841-1895
Lived and Died
Paul Valéry
1871-1945"

Berthe Morisot was the most famous woman impressionist painter of her time, a friend of Manet and of Renoir, and she was the aunt of Paul Valéry's wife. This may account for Valéry's interest in painting: one of his most famous essays is called "*Degas, Danse et Dessin*." His best-known poem is *"Le Cimetière Marin,"* which refers to the sailors' cemetery of his native city, Sète, located on the south-west coast of the Mediterranean. The term "man of letters" fits Valéry to a "T." He was one of the most subtle, yet prolific and broad-ranging, intellectuals of the 20th century but I doubt that he is well-known in translation. I had never read him before coming to France, but when I discovered his essays, I found them enlightening and free of ideology. Valéry is among the writers who made me realize that the French mind itself is one of the fine arts. For years, I used to carry in my wallet this extract from his essay, *Images de la France* (my translation): "France is perhaps the only country where considerations of pure form, a concern for form in itself, have persisted and dominated in the modern era. The sentiment and the cult of form are… accompanied, in fact, by a particular liberty with regard to content, and often coexist with a kind of sense of generalized irony."

I used to get a kick out of showing this to French lawyers whenever I was met with a particularly formalistic argument. Usually, they were amazed and would blurt out, "Really, did Valéry write that?" Why not? Valéry was smart and knew his country-men. It gives me pleasure to know that I am walking the street where he lived and where he walked.

Soon, I am crossing avenue Victor Hugo. The author of "*Les Misérables*" needs no introduction. Rue Paul Valéry continues on the other side, and I go past one of my favorite restaurants, Villa Vinci, and an elementary school tucked into this narrow street. Fortunately, it is only now that I notice that I have been walking up hill, because on the right-hand side I see the massive stone wall of the only reservoir known to me in Paris. For years, I have seen only the wall, and yearn to gaze at the water from up high. I envy the apartment dwellers who have this view. On the opposite side is the grocery store run by a young Moroccan from Agadir. I enjoy stopping there, buying fruit and chatting with him about his homeland, which is one of my favorite countries, particularly because of Marrakech and the extraordinary Hôtel La Mamounia, where Churchill used to go to relax and paint.

Now, I am coming to the point of this essay. On the corner where rue Paul Valéry crosses rue Lauriston, for years I would walk past a restaurant called Le Valéry and almost every day I would tell myself, "I must try that place." It was only last year that I finally did so, and was absolutely delighted with my find: it was a "Mom and Pop" restaurant; I never saw the Pop, who always remained in the kitchen, but the Mom, a cheerful, slightly plump woman was a delightful hostess and waitress. The cuisine was *bourgeoise* and excellent. Soon after discovering Le Valéry I took my friend Dick Malyan there. Dick, an Englishman who has been all over the world, immediately summed up its charm by saying, "It's like being in the provinces." Indeed, the sedate décor, the old-fashioned food and the reasonable prices made us forget we were in Paris. Everyone I invited there just loved the place. Unfortunately, the restaurant was not open for dinner, so I was never able to introduce my wife to Le Valéry.

About two months ago, I went by Le Valéry and saw that it was closed for renovations. Thinking that Mom and Pop had decided to change the decor, I went inside and asked the workman if "Madame" was there. One of the men, in a matter-of-fact, almost harsh voice, told me: "They're gone, they've sold out: this will become a Pizza Hut." I was horrified and felt as if I had lost a friend, without even the opportunity to attend his funeral. Le Valéry was gone forever. I had eaten there the prior week and Mom had not breathed a word. I guess that she was too embarrassed to confess that they had given up the fight, that the price paid for the leasehold by Pizza Hut was more money than they could ever aspire to by staying in business. Now, the renovations are finished and Pizza Hut is operative with its complement of red delivery motorcycles parked in front. Paul Valéry's sailors must be turning over in their graves in Sète!

Moving on, I pass by another landmark that disappeared, some years ago, from rue Paul Valéry. The last functioning brothel in Paris was located at number 4, not far from avenue Kléber, in a four-storey town house whose sedate, unmarked exterior gave no clue to its prurient interior. Occasionally, when walking home (never in the morning), I would see a striking young woman emerge from the house; as she was elegantly dressed and haughty in demeanor, (she did not deign to give me a glance), I would never have guessed that she was, as the saying goes, a "pro." It was one of my French clients, a businessman who knew that sort of thing (including Madame Claude's telephone number) who alerted me to the fact that number 4, rue Paul Valéry was the only bordel which had not been closed down in the late 1940s when a puritan streak consumed France, under the prodding of the notorious Marthe Richard, who campaigned against the "degrading" of women in houses of prostitution. (Now the prostitutes degrade themselves directly in the streets, even on prestigious avenue Foch.) The reason for this exception? The good lady who ran the house had hidden Resistance fighters during the German occupation of Paris, and to reward her the authorities allowed her to stay open. However, when the Madam, having grown old, sold her house and business to a worthy successor, the police put the new Madam out of business, saying that the *tolérance administrative* was not transferable. Then 4, Paul Valéry became, of all things, a Kosher restaurant! I could hardly believe my eyes when I saw the sign on the building but, after a while, I screwed up my courage and made a reservation there to lunch with some colleagues from my firm. The dining room was on the ground floor, and we felt positively sinful eating Kosher food in such surroundings. My table had a view of the elegant staircase, and I couldn't help thinking of Clemenceau's famous remark to the effect that "the most delicious moment in sex is following the young woman up the staircase." Sadly, the Kosher restaurant lasted only a couple of years: doubtless there were too many memories haunting the place. Now, it is occupied by a division of the French company, Pont-à-Mousson. I enjoy the idea that perhaps an executive is now occupying an office which was once a bedroom he had visited in happier times!

After crossing avenue Kléber (named after a General who served under Napoleon), I continue my way for a short stretch on rue Belloy (named after an 18th-century cardinal-archbishop of Paris), and I reach Place des Etats-Unis (named after the USA), a lovely London-type square, surrounded by elegant town-houses, one of which belonged to Edith Wharton before World War II. A statue of Washington facing Lafayette is the main ornament of the square which, for me, is a haven of greenery and peace.

By this time, I have run out of poems and my journey on Paranoid Alley has ended. I cross avenue d'Iéna, named after one of Napoleon's greatest victories, to reach my office. I would prefer that my street be called avenue J.S. Bach, as I do not like Napoleon. There is a rue Jean Sebastien Bach in Paris but it is a miserable street in the 13th *arrondissement,* hardly worthy of the greatest composer of all time. But, then again, he wasn't French and didn't win any battles.

P.S.: This issue is dedicated to the memory of Enrique Vera Villalobos (1934-1995) of Buenos-Aires, Argentina. R.I.P.

Vol. XVII, N° 7, September 1995

Bernard Lewis, the Armenian Genocide and Freedom of Expression in France and Turkey

A number of friends, knowing that I am of Armenian origin, have asked me whether I was behind the recent legal action initiated in France against Bernard Lewis, the emeritus Princeton professor accused of having cast doubt on the reality of the genocide perpetrated by the Turkish government against its Armenian population in 1915. They should know better.

In an interview granted last year, Lewis, who is said to be married to a Turkish woman, was asked by a journalist of *Le Monde* to express his views on the genocide and his apparent offense was to have said that this was the "Armenian version" of history. Some Armenian organizations in France brought a criminal complaint against him, invoking a French statute that makes it an offense to deny crimes against humanity. The court dismissed the action saying that this statute only applied to World War II crimes. Then an Armenian organization, joined by a Jewish one, initiated a civil action against Lewis, based on what we would call "tort" in the common-law system, and what the French call "civil responsibility based on fault," embodied in the celebrated Article 1382 of the Civil Code. This time the plaintiffs met with more success, as the court decided that Lewis had indeed committed a tort by implying that the events of 1915 were not historical fact and awarded symbolic damages.

Civil libertarians, who seem to be congregated mainly in the United States, will no doubt wonder what became of free speech in France. I can't help but share their perplexity. Before Armenian readers begin casting stones at me, let me state my credentials as a believer in the reality of the Armenian genocide. My father, Karnig Kevorkian, was the sole survivor of a family that was massacred by the Turkish army in April 1915, along with the entire Armenian population of Chunkoush (spelled Cungus in current maps), some 10,000 souls. Three years earlier, at the age of 16, he had escaped from Turkey, and made his way to America, God knows how. Readers who have seen Elia Kazan's marvelous film, *America, America,* will have an idea of what my father's adventure must have been to leave his mountain village and cross most of Turkey, and without knowing any European language, to reach Ellis Island, the sanctuary which represented hope and a new life for millions of oppressed from all lands. But for this adventure I would not be here today. In 1915, when news of the massacres reached America, my father, along with other young Armenians whose families had been slaughtered, volunteered to join the Légion Arménienne, organized by the French Army to fight the Turks, who, it must be recalled, were allies of Germany and the Austrian-Hungarian Empire in World War I. He got as far as Tiflis in Georgia, when the war ended, and then returned to America, landing in Philadelphia, where in 1919, at the age of 24, he founded an Armenian-language weekly newspaper called the *"Groong,"* which became his life's work.

My mother, Hripcimée Hovaguimian, was born in Smyrna, now called Izmir, then a cosmopolitan Aegean port city which, like Alexandria in Egypt, had large Armenian, Greek and Jewish communities. The secret program of the Young Turks to exterminate the entire Armenian population was initially concentrated in Biblical Armenia, the ancestral land of Anatolia, extending to the Caucasus, where Mount Ararat stands, the place where Noah's Ark landed. That is why my father's town was among the earliest to be stricken. The Armenians of the port cities like Smyrna and Constantinople were saved for later extermination, but my mother's family, warned by a friendly Turk that their turn was coming, managed to escape to Marseilles. In the 1920s my mother, being an intellectual, began writing articles for my father's newspaper, the original focus being the famous trial in Berlin of Soghomon Tellierian, the young Armenian who killed Talaat Pasha, the infamous Turk who was one of the architects of the extermination of the Armenians. My father came to Marseilles in 1926 to marry Hricipmée, their correspondence having ripened into a romance between two distant refugees. Thus my brother Andrew and I were born into a thoroughly Armenian family in Philadelphia, carrying the torch of Armenian survival. The "Groong" was our life and our livelihood, our home and our language were Armenian, and only the public schools and the streets of Philadelphia made Americans of my brother and me.

If I give these personal details, it is to demonstrate that I do not need lessons in Armenian patriotism. But it must be said, and I say it often, that "my mind does not have a passport." When I discovered Bach, at age 17, I realized that my mind aspired to the universal and was not beholden to any race or tribe. And I owe to my American upbringing, and my study of law, a deep faith in the values embodied in the First Amendment of the United States Constitution. I believe in the freedom of expression, and the concept that speech and writing should not be inhibited by government action, including the courts, unless there is a "clear and present danger" of harm to society. By American constitutional standards, it would be unthinkable that a court could condemn Bernard Lewis for saying peacefully anything about a historical fact, including denying its existence. This is the standard that I would like to see applied in France.

The Libertarian View: Despite their claim to have invented "the rights of man," the French have a long history of infringing the freedom of expression. It is a criminal offense here to insult the President of the Republic and, even, a foreign head of state! It is also a criminal offense to "injure the honor of the Army"! And after World War II, a number of criminal statutes were enacted limiting the freedom of expression, including a 1990 law that makes it a misdemeanor to deny the existence of certain crimes against humanity. The same year, Jean-Marie Le Pen, head of the Front National political party, was held liable to a number of non-profit organizations for the "fault" of stating that the Jewish Holocaust was a "detail" of World War II. I have no fondness for Le Pen, but I believe that he has the right to call any historical event a detail. Indeed, the history of the world is nothing but a collection of details. The extermination of the Armenians, under cover of World War I, was also a detail, albeit a horrible one. It was important for my family, but does not seem to have bothered the Hottentots, the Chinese, or even most Americans.

In a free country, who is to say what official history is to be? Who is to say what is important and what is minor? If I want to say that Napoleon was a tyrant, or that George Washington was a mediocre general, am I accountable in damages to the Corsican Historical Society, or the Daughters of the American Revolution? The idea is absurd. By American standards, no such organization would have what the lawyers call "standing" to sue for tort in a civil action a person who denied a historical fact or insulted a historical character. In a free country, no one should be the custodian of history. The approach of libertarians is that "if you don't like his version of history, write your own." The public will judge whose version is more accurate." Indeed, the American constitutional perspective is not founded merely on starry-eyed idealism, but also on the very pragmatic consideration that society is better off when even hateful ideas are aired openly, rather than being forced to go underground where they can nurture hateful action. When a bad idea is expressed freely there is at least an opportunity to counter it with fact and persuasion, and to convince its author to change his mind. Even Saul of Tarsus, once a powerful hater, got converted.

It is for this reason that lawyers of Jewish origin, acting for the American Civil Liberties Union, went to the courts to defend the right of American Nazis to march in Skokie, Illinois, and in Philadelphia. Of course, some American Jews were deeply offended and canceled their membership in the ACLU, but I salute these lawyers for their principled and courageous stance. It is a pity that France has no equivalent organization. Several years ago, when my friend Robert Badinter was Minister of Justice, I introduced another old friend to him, Norman Dorsen, then Chairman of the ACLU, and I broached the idea of forming a French branch of this noble organization. Robert told us that it was unthinkable in France to have people on the "Left" defend the free speech of those on the "Right," and vice-versa. In other words, for French intellectuals, who have forgotten the heritage of Voltaire, your right to free speech depends on whether you say things I agree with!

But, this being said, let us return to the Armenian genocide, which occurred 80 years ago, beyond the memory of all but a handful of the living. The word "genocide" has become so banal, being applied nowadays to Bosnia and to Rwanda, that it is easy to forget that the word did not exist before World War II. When, as a child, I first learned of the unfortunate fate of my ancestors, the prevalent term was "the Turkish massacre of the Armenians" or, for short, "the Armenian massacres." Ever since the United Nations adopted the term "genocide," along with an international Convention, there has been much quibbling as to what constitutes a genocide, that is, the attempt to destroy an entire ethnic group. I detest the quibbling, because it gives bureaucrats and diplomats the occasion to indulge in their favorite sport – talking – while others indulge in their own favorite sport, killing. The Kevorkians of Chunkoush, my grandfather and my grandmother and their three young children, Aram, Hagop and Mariam, are just as dead whether you call it a massacre or a genocide. And their killing was just as inexcusable, whatever the term that is applied.

The Armenians "Left": The Turkish perpetrators (who enlisted the occasional help of the Kurds) did not take the trouble to count their Armenian victims, estimated by most historians as between a million and a million-and-a-half. The Turks were not noted for mathematics or accounting, but for centuries were effective soldiers and organizers, having assembled an enormous array of captive peoples stretching from the Middle East to North Africa and even parts of Europe, which explains, for example, why Bosnians are Moslems. Most tourists to Turkey today do not even realize that in olden days this was a Greek and Armenian land, constituting Byzantium to the West and the Christian Kingdom of Armenia to the East. The Armenians, descended from ancient Urartu, had the dubious distinction of becoming the first Christian nation, when their king, Drtad, converted from paganism in the year 301. For centuries they had to defend their faith against more powerful enemies, including first the Persians, who were Zoroastrians before becoming Moslem, and the Arabs. The Turks, of nomadic origin, arrived from central Asia only in the 11th century and were already Mohammedans. Ultimately, through conquest they made Armenia and Greece and a number of other nations their subjects in the Ottoman Empire. Fair game: in the olden days, might made right, and conquest passed good title to land and peoples.

So, as the 20th century began, Armenia had long ceased to be an independent nation, most of its territory being in Turkey, and the remainder (now the Republic of Armenia) being part of the Russian empire. Why then did the Young Turks, who had re-taken over the government in 1912, feel it necessary to eliminate this population? I do not believe that the burden is on the victims to explain the motives of their tormentors. How do the present-day Turks explain it? Very simply: they say it never happened! I have already recounted that several years ago, I visited a Turkish rug dealer in Paris. I told the smiling young salesman that my father was from Chunkoush, and he said, still smiling, "Oh Cungus, that place has never been the same since the Armenians left." I smiled, too. Was I to get angry at a 25-year-old lad who had been taught that the Armenians had simply "left?" Was I to tell him they never left, since they were slaughtered on the spot and their bodies tossed into the endless ravines that surround high-perched Chunkoush? Instead, I bought a few rugs, perhaps even one made by the Armenians before they "left." I felt no hatred for this young man, rather sympathy, even pity, for someone whose government has decreed that he must never learn the truth about its predecessor's vile deeds. This is, of course, a philosophical choice: I would rather live painfully with the truth than blissfully with falsehood. Not everyone agrees with me. Indeed it is a crime in Turkey, even today when this nation is beating on the door of the European Union to be admitted as a member, to print the "Armenian version" (to borrow Lewis' phrase) of the events of 1915. Recently, a courageous Turkish publisher was prosecuted for trying to do just that.

The Hierarchy of Horror: You see, so far as aftermaths are concerned, the big difference between the Armenian genocide and the Jewish Holocaust is that the German government officially acknowledged the latter while since the 1920s successive Turkish governments have chosen the big lie, simply denying that it took place. While I have not visited the Holocaust Museum in Washington, I am told that it reproduces Hitler's ugly remark in 1939, "Who remembers the Armenians?" Few people are aware that immediately after the defeat of Turkey, in 1919, its government actually court-martialed several of the leaders who had organized the extermination of the Armenians. Fortunately, records of these proceedings exist, and have been examined by eminent historians, including Professor Vahakn Dadrian, of the State University of New York at Geneseo. [See his comprehensive article on the genocide in 14 Yale *Journal of International Law* 221

(1989)]. Of course, the reality of the genocide was amply reported in its day, by such impartial sources as Arnold Toynbee and Lord Bryce. The American Ambassador to Turkey was the first Henry Morgenthau; son of a Jewish immigrant from Germany, and father of the second Henry Morgenthau, who served as F.D. Roosevelt's Secretary of the Treasury, and grandfather of Robert Morgenthau, who is Manhattan's outstanding District Attorney and of the third Henry Morgenthau, who made his career in public television. Despite the efforts of the Turkish Army to keep it a secret, Ambassador Morgenthau discovered the existence of the systematic program to exterminate the Armenians, and spread the word to the civilized world. His account of these ghastly events is contained in his absorbing book, *"Ambassador Morgenthau's Story."*

It is fitting that another Jew wrote the best novel on the subject of the Armenian genocide: Franz Werfel, an Austrian writer who was famous *entre les deux guerres* and had married the widow of another Austrian Jew, Gustave Mahler. Werfel's *"Forty Days of Musa Dagh,"* based on a true episode when an Armenian community in Syria (then under Ottoman rule) manages to resist the Turks in a mountain redoubt, was a best-seller in the 1930s and would have been made into a Hollywood moving picture but for Turkish pressure. A few years after writing this book on Christian victims, Werfel himself was forced to flee Austria because of Nazi persecutions of the Jews. While making his way to Spain via France, he stopped in the small town of Lourdes, in the Pyrenées, and there learned the story of Bernadette Soubirous, whose vision of the Virgin Mary and ensuing miracles brought her sainthood. Werfel was inspired to write another novel that became a best-seller during the 1940s, *The Song of Bernadette,* which was made into a Hollywood film, starring Jennifer Jones. Franz Werfel lived just long enough to discover the horror of the Shoah, from which he had escaped. Surely he must have compared the two genocides. In one, an ancient people, who steadfastly remained Christian in a Moslem land, were brutally slaughtered on their ancestral territory. In the other, an ancient dispersed people, largely assimilated, except for religion, in various European lands where they had lived for centuries, were methodically transported and scientifically exterminated. It is odious to have to erect hierarchies in horror, but if I had to express an opinion as to which is more horrible, I would select the Shoah, not only because six-million perished (as against "only" 1.5-million Armenians) but also and mainly because the perpetrators were supposedly Christian and the denizens of a race that had produced Bach, Dürer, Kant and Goethe, to name a few. The Turks were for centuries soldiers and empire-builders, and had conducted pogroms against the Armenians at various times in the preceding 100 years.

Let me confess that, from time to time, I hear words of resentment that the Jewish Holocaust gets so much "coverage" and other mass crimes less attention. Occasionally, even Armenians complain that the Israeli government does not give enough support to the efforts of Armenians to get their genocide recognized. To my mind, there can never be too much coverage of the Jewish Holocaust. Its horror is a perpetual offense to humanity. There should be no "genocide jealousy," nor pride that "my genocide beats your genocide." Most Jews and Israelis feel the call of the universal conscience and realize that unless they support efforts to force the Turks to acknowledge the Armenian genocide, the revisionists who deny the Shoah will be encouraged. Armenians, like Avis, being number two, must simply "try harder" to keep the cause alive until a Turkish government acknowledges history. Most Armenians, like myself, would gladly waive any claim to reparations or restoration of territory for this simple declaration.

Why have Turkish governments been able, for 75 years, to get away with the big lie that the Armenian genocide never took place? The answer is found in history and geopolitics. Turkey is wonderfully located. Although defeated in World War I and forced to give up its empire by the victories Allies, it benefited from the paranoia that overtook the West when Russia become Communist. England and France grabbed up mandates over the more interesting Turkish colonies, like Iraq, Syria, Lebanon and Palestine, and offered to the United States in 1919 a mandate over Armenia, which had become independent the prior year. Unfortunately, the isolationist reaction which prevailed in the United States after the war led the same Senate that was to reject the Treaty of Versailles and the League of Nations to refuse the mandate over Armenia which, faced with a resurgent Turkey led by Mustapha Kemal (later known as "Ataturk"), was gobbled up by the Soviet Union and became a satellite "Republic."

Well aware of Turkey's strategic location as a bulwark against the Soviet Union, England and France catered to the Turks during the 1920s. In World War II, Turkey managed to stay neutral, smiling in the direction of whichever side happened to be winning at the time. Of course, the advent of the Cold War again served

Turkish interests, since the country became of strategic importance for spying on the Soviet Union and housing American ballistic missiles. Constantly obtaining American military and economic aid, Turkey has played to the hilt its anti-Soviet advantage, and has used millions of American dollars to engage high-priced PR outfits like Hill & Knowlton to counter Armenian efforts to get the genocide recognized. Now, Moslem fundamentalism has provided Turkey with another winning hand for American and English sympathy: as a Moslem nation with a secular government, it is portrayed by the US State Department as a bulwark against Islamic extremism. Thus, it has been able to get away with human-rights violations galore and persecution of its greatly-increased Kurdish population, who now occupy what were the former Armenian regions.

Several years ago, the late Cy Sulzburger, the star foreign correspondent for the *New York Times* told me of a lunch he had with a fawning high Turkish official in Ankara. When the conversation got to Armenian terrorist attacks on Turkish diplomats, Sulzburger told the Turk, "Perhaps the situation might improve if a Turkish prime minister had the courage to take a cue from Willy Brandt who, when Chancellor of Germany, kneeled at the Holocaust memorial and asked forgiveness." Cy told me with grim amusement that on hearing this remark, his Turkish host got red as a beet and looked like he was getting apoplexy: he left the table, never to return, leaving Sulzberger with the check.

The Alleged Armenians: Not long after that, a French-Jewish friend of mine told me, a propos the Turkish denial of the Armenian Genocide: "I'm a peaceful, non-violent fellow, but if the Germans were to begin to deny the Holocaust I think I would go berserk and feel like killing people." I know how he felt, because the worst moment for me is not so much thinking of the atrocious death of the Kevorkians of Chunkoush but seeing the words "alleged genocide." Paradoxically, I would prefer that the Turks assert that the Armenians deserved to be killed rather than saying, as they do, that they were not killed. For example, if the Turks were to say that the Armenians of Chunkoush had taken up arms in revolt and had to be suppressed, like the Warsaw Ghetto, it would console me to think that little Mariam, aged nine, little Hagop, aged 11, and little Aram, aged 13, had died with a musket in their hands. What infuriates me is when an American newspaper or a State Department flunky uses the words "alleged," because the implication is that the "Armenian version" is a fabrication. What happened then to the Armenians of Chunkoush? Did a million-and-a-half people commit suicide? Did they flee to the moon? Were the Armenians of Turkey the first Astronauts? Denying the genocide is to deny their existence, and to deprive me of my ancestors. Was my grandmother an alleged person?

I am rarely prone to rage, but when I read statements like that my fury rises uncontrollably, and I feel like shouting at the author, "Your alleged mother was a whore." If readers fail to understand this, I can reply only with Shakespeare's immortal words: "He jests at scars that never felt a wound." Curiously, it is after being afflicted with such feelings that I see why the French have made it a crime to deny or justify crimes against humanity, such as the Holocaust. For it is better that the State intervene through the courts than that the uncontrollable anger of survivors and descendants cause them to resort to violence.

When I was a child, my father never spoke of his slaughtered parents and siblings. He preferred to create a new family, but he counted on the verdict of history to vindicate these victims. During my youth in Philadelphia, I never heard anyone contest the reality of these crimes; indeed, people from the preceding generation would occasionally embarrass me by recalling that their parents told them to eat their dinner by saying, "Think of the starving Armenians." Until a Turkish government has the courage to acknowledge these events, Armenians everywhere, except perhaps in the struggling Armenian republic, will not let up the struggle.

Paradoxically, I get less angry at Turkish denial than that of their apologists in the West who confuse ignorance with objectivity. No people willingly studies the ignominy of its ancestors, lest the current generation be tainted. Look at how reluctant the French have been to study the crimes of Vichy. And look at the reluctance of Americans to admit the hideous treatment of the American Indians, now recognized as "Native Americans," or the vileness of slavery. But in all countries, perhaps under the pressure of foreign scholars, a handful of academics can be found to explore the truth of their own nation's crimes. Turkish academics have no freedom to become part of the handful. And worse, Turkish subsidies reach academics elsewhere who do their best to adulterate the written record of the past.

If Bernard Lewis, who is alleged to have started life as a Jew, would sit down with some renowned authorities of the Armenian Genocide, such as Professor Dadrian or Yves Ternon, a French surgeon with no Armenian family, who has written several books on the subject, I believe he would end up being convinced that the "Turkish version" of these events is much further from the truth than the one that has been accepted by most historians. It would also be good for Lewis to read the extraordinary work, which so far exists only in a French version, of Raymond Kevorkian (no relation) and Paul Paboudjian, called "*The Armenians in the Ottoman Empire on the Eve of the Genocide*." This book describes hundreds of Armenian communities and is replete with photographs of Armenian schools, churches, bands, sports teams, stores, and just bystanders: there are even pictures of Chunkoush. What happened to these people in April 1915, Mr. Lewis?

To my mind, this book alone is the best testimony to the genocide. These living Armenians of Turkey did not voluntarily disappear from the face of the earth. Being an optimist, I believe that even Bernard Lewis can be persuaded one day to change his mind. I say this because I am convinced, until proof of the contrary, that Bernard Lewis is an honorable man. And I am sure that his alleged mother was a decent woman, as well.

Vol. XVII, N° 8, December 1995

The Free Lunch, the State and other French Fictions

As I write this in mid-December, France is in the throes of one of its periodic suicide parties. The railroad and other public-transportation workers, including those of the Paris subways and buses, have been striking for more than a week, joined now and then by postal workers and other government employees, including, thank God, some who work in tax offices. (May they strike forever!) And, to be sure, the university students are in unrest all over France, demonstrating almost on a daily basis somewhere.

The strikes were a *riposte* to Prime Minister Juppé's hastily-drawn plan to reform the social-security system, which included measures intended to align the more-favorable retirement benefits of functionaries with those of the private sector. Functionaries were described, properly, as a "privileged" category of workers, since they have, in practice, life-time jobs and more generous retirement benefits than the common lot of workers – meaning that they can retire at an earlier age, and that their pensions represent a higher percentage of their prior earnings. Alain Madelin was fired by Juppé a few months ago as Minister of Finances for daring to suggest that these privileges should be reduced, after having unsuccessfully tried to convince Juppé that the number of functionaries, already a staggering five million, should be pared. Yet the enormous deficit engendered each year by the social-security system – because there is no matching of benefits to receipts – forced Juppé to propose another "temporary" tax, given this time the ugly title of "contribution to the reimbursement of the social debt," whereas the last "temporary" tax, now becoming a permanent feature, was called *"contribution sociale généralisée."*

The absence of a true parliament was demonstrated by the farcical manner in which Juppé presented his plan. For two days the National Assembly purported to "debate" the social-security problem, while remaining in the dark as to what Juppé would propose. On the third day, like Christ resuscitated, Juppé appeared on the floor to announce his plan, whereupon it was adopted without debate! This is what we used to call in Philadelphia "getting things ass backwards." In normal democracies, the parliament debates a bill that is placed before it. In France, where Descartes still rules the mind, one does not need to know what one is talking about; it suffices to see things clearly and distinctly. So the legislators waxed eloquent for two days, and blithely accepted to wait for Juppé to come up with a magic solution to the country's problems in true Cartesian fashion. Since he said it was the only possible solution, it *ipso facto* became the only solution. And to prove the irrelevance of Parliament in the Fifth Republic, Juppé requested – and will get – the power to promulgate his measures by *ordonnances*, a power which is supposed to be exceptional, according to the Constitution, and which in the past has been invoked when the government enjoys a slim majority in the National Assembly, hardly the case now, considering that the RPR-UDF coalition comprises 80 percent of that body.

While barely six percent of the total French work force is unionized, it is no accident that most of the union members are concentrated in the public sector, including in state-owned utilities, enjoying a monopoly and thus the power to strangle the French economy. These include the railroad monopoly (SNCF), the Paris subway-bus service (RATP), the electricity and gas company (EDF-GDF), the air lines (Air France-Air Inter), the postal service (La Poste) and the telecommunications industry (France Telecom). Unions are also strong in the public-education system and in state-owned Renault, the car company, which the government is hoping to privatize. In the private sector, which is subject to competition, unions are basically insignificant, with exceptions, such as the printers union, powerful in newspapers.

Because of this stranglehold which unions enjoy over the public sector, it was relatively easy for the Force Ouvrière (F.O.) and the Confederation Générale de Travail (C.G.T. – close to the Communist Party, which is the only European one not to have changed its name) to paralyze public transportation. The French who are not on strike have reacted admirably to this challenge, and I lift my hat to them. In my office and elsewhere, those who live in the suburbs get up at 5:00 am to drive to work. Three women on my staff have been riding in on bicycles. Others walk long distances. A waitress at my favorite nearby bistro, the Galliera, takes an hour-and-a-quarter to walk to work from the 18th *arrondissement.* Of course, it helps to know that the boss will not pay you if you do not show up for work.

In Paris, the hardest hit are the restaurants and caterers. I was told by an employee of one caterer that the company's loss from canceled reservations reached $500,000 in one week. Some famous restaurants are virtually empty in the evening, as people struggle to get home. One popular restaurant at the Porte Maillot says its business is down by 60 percent. Even my Moroccan grocer on rue Paul Valéry complains that his business is down by 25 percent. And as Christmas approaches, the department stores are virtually empty. If this keeps up, there will be a lot of bankruptcy filings in France in January.

As to the students, their predecessors are the ones who started the famous revolt which became known as "the events of May '68," a period through which one has had to live, as I did, in order to believe what happened. My literary career, if one wants to call my desultory essay-writing that, began with those events. On May 30, 1968, de Gaulle returned to Paris after his mysterious two-day disappearance (it turned out that he was in Baden-Baden getting support from the French Army commander there) and it was announced that he would make a radio address at 4:30 pm France had been paralyzed for two weeks: no mail, no transportation, no gasoline. I felt so tense that at 2:30 pm I called in my secretary and began dictating to her whatever came to mind, terminating at the very moment that de Gaulle began his fighting speech, which announced the dissolution of the National Assembly and the holding of elections. With several members of my staff, I walked to the Place de la Concorde, and we were among the first to participate in what became a massive rally of the "silent majority" supporting de Gaulle. It took us four hours to march to the Arc de Triomphe, in total euphoria. The next day, gasoline appeared, people left for the long Pentecost week-end and the "events of May" were over.

My secretary typed up my stream-of-consciousness musings and I left them unedited, simply adding the title "The Latest French Revolution." This intense period, when social organization broke down, forced me to lift my attention to matters larger than practicing law, and I wrote, for my own edification, a few other essays, including one in French called *La France et son Etat.* The French newspapers, led by *Le Monde*, had written some of the most ludicrous nonsense ever spawned by man about these events, calling it a revolt against the "*société de consommation*" and proclaiming that "*un homme nouveau*" ("a new man") was born. The Leftist press was in ecstasy over the marvelous slogans with which the students covered available walls, such as "Il est interdit d'interdire" (It is forbidden to forbid). However, in reflecting on what had happened, I realized that all the original strikers were part of government-owned institutions: the universities, the railroads, Air France, the coal mines, Renault. People in the private sector, those who had "capitalist" bosses, did not strike. Yet the French Leftist press was portraying the movement as a revolt against capitalism!

Why are the university students demonstrating this time? Already beneficiaries of free "higher education" they want more of the same, that is, more money to hire new professors and administrators for their institutions. This at a time when the government has announced a major effort to reduce public deficits and has raised high taxes even higher!

Last year, my oldest grandchild, then 15, told me that "the Metro should be free." This prompted me to write him a short letter in French on the theme "there is no such thing as a free lunch." For readers who do not know the origin of this expression, let me explain that in the USA, during the Great Depression of the '30s, some bars would sport a sign announcing "Free Lunch Inside." But when the customer got inside, he discovered that the lunch was free only if he paid, let's say, two dollars for the beer. This lesson caused some economists to point out that nothing is free in society: either you pay in some other way, or someone else pays. This is what I explained to my grandson David, but it is obvious that there are millions of other Davids in France who still believe in the free lunch.

French universities are a joke, not only because they are founded on the principle of the free lunch, but also because they perpetuate the fiction that anyone who succeeds in his *baccalauréat* exam is capable of attending university. In olden times, the French *lycée* was itself an élite institution, and it could be said, in the 19th century, that a student who obtained his *bachot*, having studied Latin, Greek, mathematics, literature and philosophy (that is, Descartes) did possess a liberal education, and could go on to advanced studies, such as law or medicine. But in the second half of the 20th century, this notice became a farce. To illustrate the absurd pretension of the Ministry of Education, let me mention a personal experience. In the '50s I was one of the fortunate Americans to obtain a Fulbright Scholarship to the University of Strasbourg. During the enrollment process, the professor in charge of the program made us write a letter to the Ministry requesting a waiver of the *baccalauréat* so that we could take exams. A few months later we got the answer: the Ministry refused the waiver for all the Fulbright students. At that time I had degrees from two Ivy League universities – a B.A. from Penn and a LL.B. from Harvard. Thus, the French Ministry of Education was saying that seven years of university education in the United States was not the equivalent of a French high-school diploma! Of course, I was delighted to have an excuse not to take exams, but the absurdity of this decision still makes me chuckle.

As late as 1975, when I got official figures from the Ministry of Education, only 25 percent of an age group obtained the *baccalauréat* and, even then, the average age was 19, which meant that the typical student had repeated one year during his primary or secondary education. In more recent years, the government has debased the *baccalauréat*, having embarked on a policy of allowing 80 percent an age group to get the *baccalauréat*. Although the French never refer to the bell curve of intelligence (even though a Frenchman, Alfred Binet, invented the IQ test), I recall from my student days that 20 percent of a population have "subnormal" intelligence. Hence, the French goal seems to be that anyone of normal intelligence should be a *bachelier,* whereas the unstated goal in the past was basically that only the 20 percent or so with higher-than-normal intelligence should reach university level.

Anyone in his right mind would reason that if the *baccalauréat* is made available to the immense majority of high-school students, then the universities cannot be opened to all of them, particularly if university education is "free" for the students. However, the French have not had the courage to institute *sélection* (as they call it here) and have thus maintained the fiction that any *bachelier* is entitled to enter university without entrance barriers. As a result, the selection is done at the university, simply by flunking most of the people who take first-year exams. In law and medical schools, some 80 to 90 percent fail their first-year exams.

Clearly, a system with such a policy is not an educational system but an elimination system. It is a squandering of resources to crowd a thousand students in an amphitheater with the avowed goal of eliminating 900 of them a few months later. This system is utter madness, and only politicians who are utter cowards, to wit, all French politicians, would allow such a system to continue.

Paradoxically, many of the students who expect an automatic right of entry in universities accept the rigorous competition that is a barrier to admission to the so-called *grandes écoles.* These schools, led by the Ecole Polytechnique and Ecole Normale Supérieure, admit only a tiny fraction of the thousands who sit for exams after a two-year cram course of brain-breaking effort. Why it is all right to have *sélection* for a *grande école* and not for a university is an aspect of French logic which escapes me.

And why a university education which confers financial advantage to graduates should be "free," that is, paid for by the taxpayers, also escapes me. In the United States, most universities charge tuition ranging from, say, $15,000 to $25,000 a year. While the upper levels seem to be outrageous, it is obvious that much redistribution is involved there, since the expensive institutions offer a high percentage of scholarships to the less affluent. Moreover, student loans are available, and it is only normal that a student finance his higher education through his own enhanced earning power. And parents who save $100,000 to put a son or daughter through four years of college can do this only because the tax rates in the United States leave room for saving. In France, the tax rates are so high that the average "high-earner" could never save that amount of money without living like a common laborer. The other day my accountant made rough calculations showing that a professional who had, say, $225,000 of net fees, that is, gross fees less expenses, but before taxes, would pay about 65 percent to the government for various taxes, including the license tax *(taxe professionnelle)*, social security and income taxes. Thus, a man or woman having generated perhaps $400,000 in fees and "earning" $225,000 after paying all his business expenses, would net only $78,750 after all these taxes, that is, less than 20 percent.

The French system is to have the government grab through taxation the maximum of what would otherwise be discretionary income, and to let functionaries decide how the money should be spent. Years ago, when I began practicing in France, I attended a Harvard Club luncheon at which spoke a tax official who had studied in that noble university. As I happened to be sitting next to him, I asked him, naively, why the French tax system did not permit charitable deductions to non-profit organizations, as in the United States. He stared at me sternly, and replied "It's not up to the individual to decide how his money is to be spent." I looked at him in amazement, and asked, "Who is to decide, then?" His reply, "*Nous, les fonctionnaires*."

This man was by no means a Marxist or a Socialist. He doubtless thought of himself as a conservative, which is why I keep saying that the difference between an *ENArque de droite* and an *ENArque de gauche* is as minute to outsiders as the difference between a Sunni and a Shi-ite in the Moslem religion. France has been socialist well before Mitterrand came to power in 1981. Valéry Giscard d'Estaing, who masqueraded as a *libéral* (which has the opposite meaning to "liberal" in the USA) just as he masqueraded as a nobleman (his father, a commoner, bought the d'Estaing title), was the arch-type of the *fonctionnaire* who knows better than the taxpayer how the latter's earnings should be spent. He had once stated that a country whose tax and social-security bites exceed 40 percent of the gross national product ceases to have a free economy. Well, during his reign from 1974 to 1981, these *prélèvements obligatoires* rose from 36 percent to 42.5 percent, an increase of 18 percent. They are now about 45 percent, if government statistics can be believed, which means that almost one franc out of two earned is removed from the disposable income of the earner.

These dramatic increases have, of course, been accompanied by a growth in the ranks of functionaries and other protected categories, who number about five-million people, all having, as we have seen, life-time jobs and generous pension benefits, while almost an equal number are unemployed and/or receiving the dole. To illustrate what life-time jobs mean in practice, let me recount another anecdote. Many years ago I had gotten friendly with a public servant with whom I dealt professionally, and so I invited him to lunch, an accepted practice here. In desultory conversation, I mentioned that he was the only one in his bureau whom I knew, and asked if he had any assistants. "Of course," he replied, "I have ten." Surprised by this answer, I inquired why I had never encountered the others. He explained: "Only two or three are any good." So I asked, naively it turned out, "Then why don't you fire them?" He looked at me with as much amazement as if I had asked him where he had parked his space-ship. Then he said, "I can't." "Why not?" I persisted. Again an amazed look: "Don't you understand? The *administration* is supposed to know the qualities of the persons it hires; thus if the person is incompetent, it is the fault of the *administration* and not of the employee." He went on to recount that one of his assistants had gotten her job through a *concours*, that is, a civil-service exam. She was so bad that he told her to stay home and just collect her pay! My friend has since retired, but for all I know this woman may still be at home, receiving a monthly check from the *administration.*

Out of a potential work force of about 25-million people (the total population being 58-million), 15-million people in the private sector are working not only to support themselves and their families, but also to pay the salaries of five-million functionaries, as well as the payments to five-million people who are unemployed or on the dole, and perhaps 10-million retired people. Clearly the proliferation of functionaries cannot occur without their creating all sorts of constituencies: people who get handouts of one kind or another. Aside from the massive redistribution accomplished by the family-allowance system, and social security, there are literally thousands of subsidies which the various ministries administer, for culture, for sports, for industry (even the daily press received a handout two years ago), and for what passes for charity. In France, most nonprofit associations with cultural or philanthropic objectives seek money from the so-called "State" rather than from individuals, since the "State" has taken disposable income from the individuals. Of course, the "State" means functionaries when it comes to handing out money and it means taxpayers when it comes to forking up the cash.

The biggest fiction of all in France is *l'Etat.* If you read the constitution of the Fifth Republic, the word *état* is hardly mentioned. France is referred to mainly as a republic and as a nation. When Pétain capitulated to the Germans in 1940 and founded the Vichy regime, he called the country *l'Etat Français*, and changed its motto from *Liberté Egalité Fraternité* to *Travail Famille Patrie.* De Gaulle, Pétain's enemy, created the Fifth Republic. Yet, ironically, today one hears more and more about *l'Etat,* because France has become a *République de Fonctionnaires*. The word *l'Etat* serves as a mask to hide the reality that when it comes to spending the people's money it is *les fonctionnaires* who decide, and when it comes to paying it is *les contribuables* who pay. I call the former *les fons* and the latter *les cons.*

Since there is no legal impediment to *fonctionnaires* engaging in political activity and being elected to office, the Fifth Republic has witnessed the gradual monopolization of the political function by civil servants. They have, of course, taken over all the political parties except one. That is why my barber keeps telling me that there is in reality only one party in France, *le Parti des Fonctionnaires.* The lone exception is Jean-Marie Le Pen's *Front National,* the party which will benefit the most from the strike. My barber predicts that this party will get at least 30 percent of the vote in the next legislative election, slated for 1998. He told me recently, "I now understand how Hitler came to power: people are so disgusted that they will vote for an extremist." My barber, in business for himself, and working alone with a manicurist, is hurting badly. The Champs-Elysées sector, where his shop is located, is replete with empty office buildings, as companies have fled to the suburbs for lower rent. He told me that for the first time, he has had to dig into his savings to pay the rent.

There is in France a crying need for a party of non-functionaries that does not have the racist and xenophobic overtones of the *Front National.* It might be called *Le Parti des Autres.* If Le Pen were intelligent, he would change his tune, get two or three rabbis to support him, and take on *les fons.* He'd get a lot of backing from *les cons.*

The ascension of Juppé and Chirac to the highest functions in France demonstrates the validity of the Peter Principle, which holds that people rise to the level of their own incompetence. Juppé was a creditable Foreign Minister; but as Prime Minister he is totally out of place. Chirac was a good Mayor of Paris (despite his condoning of unethical practices in the housing sector) but as President he has bungled, starting with the resumption of nuclear testing, naming Juppé Prime Minister, and failing to keep his campaign promises. Most people blame Juppé and Chirac, as much as Blondel, for the present mess. They have spent their adult life in the cocoon of *l'Etat,* shielded from the reality of the world of the common people. You can get into a *grande école* by writing a beautiful *plan* in the entrance exam, but in real life you get into a mess by thinking that a plan is a substitute for dialogue and getting the facts. As I finish this, Juppé has caved in to virtually all the strikers' demands. Soon, all that will be left of the *plan Juppé* is the name and higher taxes.

The *fons* have won and the *cons* will continue to pay.

Vol. XVIII, N° 1, January 1996

The King is Dead; the Cuckolds Remain

The big news in early January was the death of François Mitterrand, also known as King François the Last, following closely on the near-death of the French economy in December.

If ever the continuity of the monarchical-Catholic tradition needed demonstrating, King Jacques the First did a masterful job of demonstrating it. Even though Mitterrand had himself ordained in minute detail what he wanted in the way of funeral services, in particular, that they take place in his home town, Jarnac, Chirac insisted on putting on a big show at the cathedral of Notre Dame in Paris, to which "the greats of this world" were summoned. Thus, simultaneously with the church service in Jarnac, where his casket lay in modest state, a grandiose Mass was held at the cathedral, attended by heads of state and government, including Arafat, Castro, Kohl, Mubarak, as well as stand-ins like Prince Charles and Al Gore.

It was obvious to cynical observers that Chirac saw in this most timely departure of his predecessor the opportunity to score points which he has sadly been lacking in opinion polls, by reason of the disastrous start of his seven-year term. Politicians are the same the world over. To get a vote they'll show up in maternity wards or funeral parlors: kissing babies and weeping for the dead are the easiest ways to get sympathy, since there is no danger that either category will talk back. Even more disturbing to some was the thought that the President might have been sincere in honoring his predecessor, considering that Chirac is supposed to be a Gaullist and Mitterrand was consistently odious in his treatment of the founder of the Fifth Republic. Mitterrand branded de Gaulle's régime a "permanent *coup d'état*," a characterization that did not prevent him from enjoying, quasi-permanently, all the trappings of power which the Constitution bestows on the elected monarchs of France.

The press and TV made a big thing of the tears shed by Helmut Kohl at the Notre Dame ceremony. I would like to believe that he was weeping not for Mitterrand, who did his best to thwart German reunification, but rather for the French people, so easily duped by pageants and hypocrisy. The Notre Dame Mass harkened my mind back to the death of President Georges Pompidou in April 1974, which gave Richard Nixon, then struggling desperately with the Watergate scandal, the opportunity to break away and play the role of the "most powerful leader in the world." He could barely conceal his contentment to be the cynosure of the ceremony, despite the somber context. Similarly, Chirac was in seventh heaven, presiding over the cathedral service, and later hobnobbing with the distinguished guests at the sumptuous lunch served at the Elysée Palace. In a television address, he delivered such a panegyric of François the Last that one would never have guessed that they had been bitter political adversaries for two decades. My wife, who remains a staunch Chirac supporter, thinks it was smart politics on his part to want to cash in on the sympathy aroused by Mitterrand's death, all the greater in that his cancer caused him considerable suffering in the past several months. Yet Chirac's eloquent tribute to Mitterrand seemed to go beyond the necessities of the situation. Is it possible, some wondered, that Chirac, having broken the promises that he made to those who elected him, thinks he can make up for these lost supporters by fishing among the hallowed "*peuple de gauche*" who elected Mitterrand? Was Chirac burying de Gaulle as well as Mitterrand?

Ever since I read Sophocle's *Antigone*, I have held to the belief that the dead belong to those who loved them. Doubtless, Mitterrand felt the same way, which is why he ordered the modest ceremony in Jarnac. Another reason for his choice was clearly that he wanted his mistress and the daughter that she bore him, Mazarine, to attend the funeral services, easier to do in Jarnac than in Notre Dame. (As Islam is the second religion of France, the Paris ceremony might have better been held in the Great Mosque, where polygamy is recognized.)

The French public thus feasted on the incredible photograph showing side-by-side the official widow, Danielle Mitterrand, *née* Gouze, with her two sons, and the unofficial widow, Anne Pingeot, with her daughter, who resembles her father more than his sons do. Some commentators pointed out that while the great Kings of France all had mistresses and some had bastards by them, the tradition was that they slink out of Versailles the day before the funeral, leaving only the official family to appear at the ceremonies. The newspapers revealed for the first time that the then 50ish Mitterrand had first noticed the then 20ish Ms Pingeot on a golf course at Hossegor (north of Biarritz), where her father, described as a "rich industrialist from Clermont-Ferrand," had a summer residence, near Mitterrand's own retreat at Latche, in the Landes bordering the Atlantic. This noticing took place apparently in the '60s, and as Mazarine was born in 1974, it is anyone's guess how long they had been lovers. What is presently clear is that while Mazarine, now 21, was growing up, the President lived basically with her mother in a residence paid for by the taxpayers on the Quai Branly, yet maintaining cordial relations with his official wife, more suitable for presentation to visiting heads of state. It has also been revealed that for the past 10 years Mitterrand spent Christmas with his mistress and daughter in Egypt at Assouan, and returned to Paris in time to spend New Year's Eve at Latche with his official family and some select friends. Courageously, despite his extreme weakness, Mitterrand hued to this tradition last month and basically bade adieu to both families on these occasions. A great soap opera this would make: "François's Other Wife." But the last chapter may still be unwritten, since the rumor is that Mitterrand's frequent visits to Venice may have left visible traces there.

Another revelation, that some considered more grave than the prominence given to the unofficial family, was that Mitterrand's prostate cancer was discovered back in November 1981, six months after the beginning of his first term and, by that time, metastases had already attacked his bones. This disclosure was made in a scoop by *Paris Match*, the picture magazine, which quoted excerpts from a book published a few days later, written by Mitterrand's long-time personal physician, Dr. Claude Gubler. The author admitted that at the President's request, he had deliberately concealed the cancer from the public, and actually signed false health "bulletins" giving a rosy picture of his patient's state, despite his prognosis that Mitterrand's life span was from three months to three years. This chicanery was in striking contradiction of Mitterrand's campaign promise to be "transparent" as to his health and to publish periodic medical bulletins reporting thereon. He did publish the bulletins, but they were false.

I remember very well the insistent rumors about Mitterrand's illness, which I heard from several sources late in 1981, but I, for one, was taken in by these official reports, as well as the later 1992 report purporting to reveal a newly-discovered prostate cancer, which was in reality then fully matured. To some observers this deception was characteristic of Mitterrand, who had spent a lifetime not only fooling people but also making hypocrisy one of the fine arts. It is one thing to say that "my health is none of your business" and another to promise "transparency" and then publish falsehoods with the help of a subservient physician. Yet, the bulk of outrage in the days following the revelation was directed not at Mitterrand but at his doctor for the wholly contradictory offenses of both revealing a "state secret" and violating his patient's right to privacy. Indeed, Mitterrand's extended family (his mistress and daughter having joined as plaintiffs) sued for an injunction against the publication of the book and quickly obtained the desired court order. Fortunately (for those who believe in the freedom of expression) the first printing of 40,000 copies was sold out before the order was issued. Now, Gubler's thin volume is a collector's item and is likely to pass "under the cloak," like the unexpurgated edition of *Lady Chatterly's Lover* during the 1920s. Gubler faces criminal charges, as violation of medical secrecy is a penal offense in this country, which claims to have invented the "Rights of Man." Moreover the medical association is considering the revocation of his license to practice, a rather harsh sanction for a man who prolonged Mitterrand's life for 14 years, with devoted and constant attendance, including daily perfusions early on.

Quite disturbing to some people was Gubler's assertion that late in 1994 Mitterrand's cancer was so acute and his pain so great that he ceased to function as President, lying in bed all day and signing papers without reading them. It should be recalled that during the last two years of his term, Mitterrand was "cohabiting" with the opposition Balladur government, and thus had only residual powers. Yet, he still bore the ultimate responsibility for foreign policy and, in particular, possessed the key to the buttons which can set off France's ample supply of nuclear weapons. Various politicians who dealt with him during this period, including Alain Juppé, who was then Foreign Minister, issued statements decrying Gubler's assertions and claiming that Mitterrand looked perfectly normal to them. They could hardly say otherwise at this late date!

I find it fascinating, but not surprising, how little indignation has been expressed about Mitterrand's fraud while so much wrath has been voiced against his physician, who says he felt it his duty to reveal the truth, with the objective of making it impossible in the future for such deception to be renewed. To say that the health of a President, or a candidate for the presidency, is nobody's business but his own is perfectly inane to me. It must be recalled that Mitterrand ran for re-election in 1988, while 71 years old, and claimed to be in good health. Obviously his health was relevant to some voters, considering that all of his opponents were younger than he. It must also be emphasized that Mitterrand did not content himself with silence about his health but affirmatively misled the public by getting his doctor to issue false statements. Thus, to assert that the doctor cannot now reveal the truth to the very public to whom he lied for 13 years is to imply that once he agreed to being manipulated by a devious patient his only duty was to that patient and not to the public he fooled. While I have not researched the question in American law, I would like to believe that an American analysis would lead to a different result, to wit, that a patient who orders his physician to publish false reports on his health has waived his privilege of confidentiality and thus cannot later prevent the physician from telling the truth. Otherwise, the implication is that physicians who sign authorized statements about the health of public figures have no duty to be truthful. Perhaps the answer will vary according to whether we are in a Protestant country or a Catholic one. It is perhaps relevant that Dr. Gubler is a Protestant!

Dr Gubler and his publisher, Editions Plon, have appealed the ruling, and I hope that the higher courts will look beyond their noses and strike a blow not only for the freedom of expression but also for the right of the public in a democracy to obtain accurate information from their leaders. France is light-years behind the United States in disclosure of all kinds. There is no Freedom of Information Act, for example. Nor is there any publishing of proposed regulations before they are issued, to give interested parties the right to make observations. Several years ago, I tried to find out how much President Mitterrand earned as President and was unable to get the information. Apparently this is also a state secret! Also, in French courts no "discovery" is permitted, that is, a party cannot obtain relevant documents and depositions from an adverse party in order to get the truth before the court.

The ease with which government officials can invoke "*secret défense*" to avoid giving testimony in court is another scandalous example of the lack of candor in this society. Several years ago, a "bug" (a microphone, for the uninitiated) was found in the offices of the *Canard Enchainé*, the weekly newspaper noted for revealing the shenanigans of French politicians. Even though the placers of the bug were identified, the examining magistrate was never able to get testimony from them as the government invoked the ridiculous claim of "*secret défense*." (It should be recalled that when "tricky Dick" Nixon tried to get the CIA to back a similar claim to prevent information from being obtained about the Watergate burglary, the courts shot down this absurd pretense.) More recently, in a scandal involving the embezzlement of public funds by officials of the Socialist government, it was revealed that Charles Pasqua, then Minister of the Interior, issued what came to be known as the "true false passport" to one of the culprits, who took it on the lam to Brazil, but Pasqua was able to beat the rap by claiming, without any proof, the privilege of "*secret défense*."

Speaking of scandals, I had heard through the grapevine that the French Prime Minister gets every year a cash appropriation which ends up being distributed to hundreds of officials in a purely discretionary fashion. Finally, this was revealed with considerable detail on television on Sunday, January 13th, in the program of Emmanuel Chaim called *Capita*l. He disclosed that the Prime Minister receives annually in cash the equivalent in francs of about $95-million and every month his chief of staff calls in the chiefs of staff of the various ministers and hands them their share of the loot. Then each minister divvies up the cash as he sees fit, all without the slightest accountability! No current minister agreed to appear on the program but two former ministers, women both of them, were interviewed. Both admitted to using part of the cash to buy clothes and other personal items and said that this fund was "black money" which they and the other beneficiaries never reported on their tax returns. Even more startling was the assertion that one former Prime Minister, on leaving office, took with him 12-million francs (about $2.5-million) left over in his safe. According to the reporter, this distinguished person did not deny the report, merely stating that he took only his share, which presumably means that as he departed in the month of May, he left enough cash for his successor to use and distribute during the remaining seven months of the year! This is what passes for honesty in France.

Amazingly (although nothing should amaze me any more about France), I did not see a word in print about the revelations made in this program. The public was doubtless too busy mourning the "congenital liar" (to use the harsh term recently employed by William Safire to describe Hillary Clinton) just buried in Jarnac to take heed of the fact that high public servants get part of their earnings in unreported cash, something an ordinary citizen can go to jail for.

To return to Mitterrand, I suspect that he once hoped to find a place in the Pantheon, where the great assassinated Socialist leader Jean Jaurès lies, not to mention Voltaire and Victor Hugo, and that he would have volunteered to be buried alive there if his successor had agreed to the deal. However, the controversy over the revelation in 1994 of his Vichy past (in the Péan book) probably persuaded him that this could not be achieved. Judging by the wide current of sympathy engendered by his death, and the gushing done by Chirac, I would not be surprised if a Pantheon burial were promoted soon by his supporters. (No one has proposed it for de Gaulle, who is buried in the church cemetery of Colombey-les-deux-Eglises, where he had his home, but he does not need the Pantheon to assure his immortality.)

The French, as befits a Latin people, are fascinated by cuckoldry. "*Cocu*" is a favorite insult of motorists (when they are not using that other and shorter word that begins with "c") and the verb "*cocufier*" is a very active one indeed. I think of this because it is clear to me that Mitterrand devoted a lifetime to making figurative (and occasionally actual) *cocus* out of a goodly portion of the French population. Many of them seem positively to enjoy that state, giving reality to that famous song of Serge Lama, *"Je suis cocu et content."*

I have already pointed out that the human brain seems in perpetual tension between two opposite tendencies, the first being to learn the truth and the second being to avoid the truth when it is too painful to face. Freud earned a good living from this insight, and while I don't think much of Freud, I do think much of the insight. The willingness of so many otherwise intelligent people to be *cocufiés* by Mitterrand is a fascinating subject of study for future PhDs. In the meantime, I can provide an outline of an explanation.

To begin with, Mitterrand discovered very young that he was a natural Janus, that is, his personality was suited to beguiling people of different origins. He could have become a first-rate con man, but being highly ambitious, saw a higher destiny for himself. Coming from a Catholic far-Right background, he found it natural when he escaped from a German prison camp to head south for Vichy, where Hitler's collaborators were ensconced, rather than north to London, where a rebel general, named de Gaulle, had organized the Free French. This choice meant that Mitterrand, like Laval, like Pétain, expected the Germans to win the war and establish a new order for decades to come. It was only in mid-1943, months after the Allies had landed in Morocco and freed all of North Africa of the Axis armies, that Mitterrand realized that he had made the wrong choice, and then he turned tail and embarked on a pseudo-*résistant* career. After France was liberated, de Gaulle reluctantly gave credibility to Mitterrand's Resistance role because, to restore the dignity of the French, the leader of the Free French opted to make believe that a majority of French had resisted the Germans whereas the painful truth was that a majority had collaborated. It must be said that the population did not show much gratitude for this fiction, since de Gaulle lost power in 1946, when his proposed constitution was rejected.

Mitterrand was clever enough to capitalize on this fantasy and enjoyed a flourishing career during the Fourth Republic, remaining on the Right while de Gaulle's political career seemed finished. When the Algerian crisis brought de Gaulle out of internal exile in 1958, Mitterrand saw that he had no future on the Right and became *un homme de gauche,* not a difficult task for a Janus of his talents. As he was eclipsed by de Gaulle's popularity, it was during this period that, to get attention for his dwindling career, he organized the phony machine-gun attack on himself in the garden of the Observatory in October 1959, which almost landed him in jail, when the gunman spilled the beans. In 1965, his lucky break came. No one on the Left wanted to run against de Gaulle, who seemed (and was) invincible, so Mitterrand jumped at the chance. He got 35 percent of the votes in the first round, and this, combined with the centrist Lecanuet's 17 percent, forced de Gaulle into a second round. In a Catholic, Latin country, this was enough to restore Mitterrand's reputation and make him a leader on the Left. In 1968, during the "events of May," when de Gaulle appeared to have abandoned power, Mitterrand actually flirted with the idea of taking power with the Communists, but as the latter demanded powerful ministries, which the Socialists refused, the Communists backed down. The full story of these secret negotiations has not been published, but I trust that some day, with the help of the usual American and British scholars, the truth will come out.

In due course, Mitterrand took over the Socialist Party, and then his Janus qualities were fantastically useful in uniting the several factions which inhabit the Socialist mansion. Although rumors of Mitterrand's involvement with Vichy abounded, including the fact that he had received that evil regime's highest decoration, the *Francisque,* from the hands of Pétain himself, Mitterrand's guile was such that he managed to convince even Jewish Socialists that he had joined Vichy only as a cover for his Resistance activity. French intellectuals rarely bother to check the facts (as Pierre Péan was to do in the '90s), so Mitterrand got away with this lie, while remaining friends with dreadful Vichy collaborators who had participated in the 1942 round-up of the Jews in Paris.

What I said above about people concealing the truth from themselves is particularly applicable to French Jews who supported Mitterrand. It is hard for them now to admit to themselves that they were taken in. The fact that Mitterrand had several Jewish friends, and even a Jewish brother-in-law, made it easier for them to be fooled. If he had lived a hundred years ago, Mitterrand would have managed to convince both the Dreyfusards and the anti-Dreyfusards that he was one of them. Mitterrand had the gift of making opposites think they had his entire attention and sympathy. Thus he could spend hours with an ardent Jew like Elie Wiesel, talking religion, and also wine and dine with René Bousquet, who had headed the Vichy police, reminiscing about the good old days. Another comparison to make is that of a double agent, equally at ease working for the KGB and the CIA, with neither being sure where his real loyalties lie. Finally, he can be compared with a consummate actor who can be convincing either as a cop or a robber, or with a bisexual. Such people are rare but they do exist.

When one considers Mitterrand in this manner, there is not much mystery left. He was supremely ambitious and supremely self-centered, like many an artist who has appeared on earth. As he could lie with a straight face, as we used to say in Philadelphia, and had the gift of gab, it was not difficult for him to fool most of the people he met. He never fooled de Gaulle, which is why Mitterrand loathed him so much. I hate to repeat myself, but only a Catholic, Latin country could have allowed a Tartuffe like Mitterrand to go so far and get away with so much. His regime was the most corrupt that France has ever seen. His party organized graft openly, and right under his nose in the Elysée Palace, thousands of wire-taps of private persons were made. He consistently used public funds for private purposes. And, of course, five-million unemployed are a living legacy of his disastrous economic policies.

One of my friends is proposing to initiate a subscription to erect a statue of Mitterrand in an ideal spot for such a commemoration: the garden of the Observatory, the scene of the phony assassination attempt in 1959. Those who believe his story can salute the good fate that spared him for better days, and those who don't can have equal satisfaction in greeting him with that famous gesture that uses two arms and no words. The ambiguity of the statue would perfectly mirror the ambiguity of Mitterrand's whole life and the ambiguity of a France that seems to treat de Gaulle and Mitterrand with equal respect. (Can there be any greater contrast than that between the monolithic de Gaulle, who "assumed France" in 1940 when it was on its knees, and the opportunistic Mitterrand, who assumed poses and disguises all his life?) And, to be sure, the statue would face south-east toward Vichy, while one arm would grandly point to the Pantheon.

Vol. XVIII, N° 3, May 1996

Happy as a God in FrancoReich

Having been blessed, or blighted, as it occasionally strikes me, with a good memory, I recall that many years ago a French friend once told me of a book called *"Dieu est-il Français?"* ("Is God French?"), making the point that the expression was a vain mistranslation of a German phrase, which is the equivalent of "Happy as a God in France." The idea, I gather, was that while it's good to be a God, particularly a German one, it's even better to be a God who gets to enjoy French food, wine and scenery.

Often while walking to work, or in my after-dinner stroll, or while playing Bach on the piano in the morning, phrases and ideas come to me and I then seek to explain to myself why they did. Perhaps, in this example, it was my mind's way of saying that only a God could be happy today in France. Certainly not the restaurant operators. The other night, I dined in one of Paris's best two-star restaurants and there were only six persons served all evening. In the old days, the restaurant would have turned away people. The event is commonplace. Virtually everyone is moaning, either about high taxes and social charges or about unemployment, which continues to increase despite the lavish promises made by candidate Chirac to treat it as his highest priority. After he named Alain Juppé Prime Minister, the latter made clear by his actions that his highest priority was getting elected Mayor of Bordeaux, while remaining head of the RPR party. Is there any other country in the world where the head of government is also mayor of a large city and directs the leading political party? Even Comrade Brezhnev was not so ambitious, and obviously not so talented, since he did not attend the Ecole Nationale d'Administration.

Once Juppé lined up his offices (he added the presidency of the Urban Community), he then made his highest priority, with Chirac's blessing, to continue the deflationary policies of his predecessor Edouard Balladur – the *franc fort* being its keystone – so much so that some people began calling him BallaJuppé. A lawyer friend of mine told me the other day about a conversation he had with a Parisian cab driver, who sighed, "I should have voted for Balladur." *"But Balladur would have followed the same policies as Chirac,"* replied my friend. *"Yes, but at least we knew that,"* was the cab-driver's lament.

To get elected, Chirac, true to his record, made whatever promises were necessary to pass Balladur on the first ballot. To middle-class audiences he proclaimed the French version of the Lafer curve: *"Trop d'impôts tuent l'impôt"* ("Too much taxes kill taxes"). Yet when he got elected, he promptly proceeded to raise taxes, professing surprise at the size of the deficits left by Balladur's government, of which Juppé was a member for two years! To working-class audiences he promised to reduce unemployment by energetic measures, but the technocratic device proposed by Juppé to stimulate hiring of those who have been out of work for two years is merely a drop in the bucket. Unemployment continues to rise.

Promises mean nothing to Chirac, who is as cynical as Mitterrand was about the credulity of the electorate. The difference between the two cynics is that Mitterrand used Delphic ambiguity to make promises he knew he would not keep, whereas Chirac, never one for subtlety, makes his blatant promises with what T.S. Eliot called "one bold stare." A man I knew well years ago was one of Chirac's henchmen in the Corrèze, the great man's fiefdom in the provinces, which he represented in Parliament while also running Paris. The man told me that Chirac had promised to put him on his party's ticket for a local election, but when the ticket was announced the man was not on it. Furious, he went to Chirac and reproached him for not keeping his promise. Not perturbed, Chirac replied, *"Mon vieux, les promesses n'engagent que ceux qui les croient!"* (*"*Old boy, promises bind only those who believe them!*")*.

Chirac is, of course, an *ENArque* (generally written "*énarque*" by the French press but I prefer for foreign readers the former version, as it makes clear that the first three letters are initials, referring to the Ecole Nationale d'Administration). Balladur and Juppé are also graduates of this school, as are virtually all the political leaders in France, including François Léotard, just elected head of the UDF party, chief partner of the RPR in the government coalition, and Philippe Séguin, president of the National Assembly, as well as most of the leaders of the Socialist Party, such as Lionel Jospin, Michel Rocard, and Laurent Fabius. I have, to be sure, described in past Newsletters the overwhelming stranglehold that the *ENArques* have over all facets of the political and economic establishments in France. A little snippet in the French press last month brought home to me how pervasive is their domination. *Le Figaro* reported that in a ceremony at the Elysée palace, Chirac awarded the Légion d'honneur to three men. One had just been named head of the French Red Cross and the two others held similar posts in philanthropic organizations. Each, it turned out, was an *ENArque*.

The school was founded 50 years ago by General de Gaulle, under the impetus of arch-statist Michel Debré, to select "the best and the brightest" to become functionaries, but the power of its graduates is such that it has become commonplace for them to hold plush jobs outside of government, whether in banks, insurance companies, industry and quasi-public organizations. As I have pointed out in prior issues, the *ENArques* pay no heed to separation of powers, and are blind to any notion of conflict of interests. They routinely take jobs in industries they were charged with regulating. On the political level, they simultaneously hold national and local offices, as illustrated by Juppé. As they keep their civil-service status on hold while occupying elective office, they have a safety net on which to fall back.

I recall these facts because I want to develop a point in this Newsletter that was merely adumbrated in my December 1995 issue, what I call the "unholy alliance" of this dominant French nomenclatura with the German Bundesbank and other economic policy-makers in Germany. It is clear that the *ENArque* class, led by Chirac, is going whole-hog ahead with the Maastricht-Treaty goal of a single currency for the European Union and, to achieve this, it is deemed necessary to keep the franc strong and inflation low even if that means continued high unemployment, oppressive taxation and the steady impoverishment of the French middle class. It used to be that the only way most people without inherited wealth could build capital was in the form of real estate, principally their own dwelling place, whether a house or an apartment. In times of inflation – the entire post-war period until the strong-franc policy was unfurled during the last years of Mitterrand's reign – the standard way of financing a home purchase was to pay 20-percent down and get a 15-year fixed-interest mortgage loan. Even if the interest rate was, say, 10-percent per annum, the inflation rate was generally about the same, so that the borrower paid back the loan with depreciated francs, while his house's value often soared to ten or fifteen times the price he had paid. For most people, this was their only "nest egg," since high taxes made it impossible to save in any other form.

Now that route to capital formation is closed. During the reign of Mitterrand, two dire trends cohabited with remarkable correlation: the decrease of inflation and the increase of unemployment. One consequence of this was that the real-estate market collapsed. Values of residential property in Paris and other large cities have been decreasing every year for the last four or five years. Thus the *nouveaux riches* have been finding out that their net worth has diminished. And their children are unable to purchase apartments and houses because high income taxes prevent them from accumulating enough to make a down payment, and interest rates remain relatively high, while interest expense is not deductible from income taxes. Even though inflation has been only two percent for several years, interest rates on mortgages start at about seven percent and it is difficult to find a lender who does not require at least a 30-percent down payment. Of my six grown-up children living in France, none can afford to buy an apartment, whereas my daughter living in New York has owned one for more than 10 years.

This situation – huge unemployment, high interest rates, depressed real-estate values – can be directly attributed to the insane strong-franc policy, which is ENA policy, since *ENArques* in both Socialist and so-called "Right" governments have continued the same policy, personified by J-M Trichet, Governor of the Banque de France. Until recently, I did not perceive the connection between the real-estate phenomenon I have just described and the revelations about the fancy city-owned apartments that Messrs Chirac and Juppé were occupying at low rentals (in addition to their official residences) but now I see that there is real significance in them. The French Civil Code contains a famous definition of ownership: it is the right "to enjoy and to dispose of property;" Indeed, the enjoyment (*jouissance*) is a distinct property interest called *usufruit.* What the *ENArques* have learned is that they do not have to hold title to real estate to enjoy the use of it and indeed to dispose of it, since by controlling city-owned apartments they can decide who the next occupant will be. Thus, they are *de facto* owners without having had to pay for their acquisitions. The present Mayor's two children, it was learned last year, own apartments suitable for their own occupancy, but they prefer to rent them out, since each enjoys a large city-owned apartment at below-market rentals. And it is not just city-owned apartments that are involved. Government-controlled insurance companies and other institutions own thousands of apartments in Paris, the cream of which are available to the *ENArques* and their favored friends: journalists, judges and others who can show proper gratitude for the favors bestowed on them. For example, last year a courageous lawyer brought a taxpayer's suit to challenge Juppé's apartment deal, but this required getting approval from an administrative court to sue in the name of the City of Paris. It turned out that the judge who denied the motion is himself the proud tenant of a city-owned apartment but this did not, said he, prevent him from being very objective, since, as I showed in "Montaigne and Descartes," a Cartesian never has a problem with conflict of interests.

It has taken me a long time to grasp the extent to which the functionary caste, led by the ubiquitous *ENArques*, have obtained an *usufruit* on the wealth of the land, enriching themselves with the fruits of ownership and privilege while conducting policies that are leading to the impoverishment of the hard-working middle class. Depending on their rank and connections, they reap all sorts of privileges. As we have seen, those who work in ministerial cabinets get cash payments which are undeclared. Because of the hundreds of state-controlled companies in France, they get directorships and other assignments. One of the choicest plums is the presidency of the Mont Blanc Tunnel Company: as the tunnel was dug many years ago, there is no work to do, but the president gets a handsome salary and the use of a chalet in Chamonix. Edouard Balladur enjoyed this one for several years. Then he got another sinecure, the presidency of GSI, a subsidiary of a state-owned company, which paid him $200,000 a year for being just a figurehead and gave him an opportunity to benefit from a stock deal that netted him a couple of million dollars.

Moreover, many members of this dominant class, which controls all the major political parties, have engaged in corruption on a large scale in order to finance their political activities. In the March Newsletter, I mentioned the journalist Jean Montaldo in my discussion of Henri Emmanuelli. Since writing that piece, I read Montaldo's 1995 book called *"Rendez l'Argent!" ("*Give the Money Back!*")*. I had previously read his best-seller, aptly called *Mitterrand and the Forty Thieves*, but the new book is almost unbearable to follow in its revelation of details of the organized racket put into place by the Socialist Party once Mitterrand took it over. A vast network of "delegates" of the party, operating under cover of dozens of companies, shook down contractors who dealt with Socialist municipalities and other government entities, collecting a percentage of the contract price in exchange for helping them get the work. Despite extensive evidence uncovered by examining magistrates, only a few were actually prosecuted, the various Mitterrand governments effectively stifling tax and police investigations. Many of the Socialist bigwigs were *ENArques*, such as Lionel Jospin, Michel Rocard and Laurent Fabius, all of whom knew and benefited from this racket.

According to Montaldo, when Balladur became Prime Minister in 1993, he blocked prosecution of the Socialist racketeers for reason of political expediency. In my opinion, Montaldo is too indulgent towards the so-called "Right" parties, who were just as guilty of illegal campaign financing, differing only as to methods. For example, it was learned last year that the *Parti Républicain* had received substantial cash from the Prime Minister's slush fund, described in my January issue. Chirac's party, the RPR, never lacks for cash in political campaigns, since it has access to the treasuries of large state-owned companies or substantial suppliers of goods and services, such as the two leading water companies, which are notorious corrupters of politicians. Several months ago, a driver for the RPR revealed to a *Juge d'Instruction* that he had conveyed large chunks of cash during Chirac's presidential campaign to a woman in Chirac's headquarters. After the initial play given to this revelation, the press has been strangely silent about this potentially-explosive case, but one day in April a strange little article appeared in *Le Figaro* relating that the driver had been interned as insane by someone at a police infirmary after he had gone to the police complaining of the threats he had received. Personally, I do not doubt for a minute that he received threats, and I consider it very disturbing, and reminiscent of what used to go on in the Soviet Union, that a man can be interned by the police for being insane, against the wishes of his family and without consultation with his own physician and lawyer.

The fact is that the French political system, dominated by *ENArques*, survives only through what I call the "equilibrium of dishonesty." When one party alone is dishonest, the others can denounce it, but when they are all dishonest, it is the same as their being all honest; there is no one to do the denouncing. This is what happened in Italy until a few courageous judges began to dismantle the system by showing that all the political parties had shared in the graft. So far, no French judge has been able to engage in the systematic investigation of the parties at the national level, and I doubt that this will be done while Chirac is President and his henchman, Jacques Toubon, a former head of the RPR(!) is Minister of Justice. No accident, that appointment, just as it was no accident that Mitterrand named Henri Nallet Minister of Justice after he served as Treasurer of Mitterrand's re-election campaign. And it is no accident that the two leading water companies, ostensibly private, which in the past have provided vast sums of money to politicians, are now headed by *ENArques*.

If we add all that was stated above to what I've previously written about the dominant functionary class, in "Montaigne and Descartes" and "Feudal France – Serial Justice," it boils down to a France which is only a pseudo-democracy and which is sadly lacking in the ethical base that should lie at the heart of any democracy. If that sounds like a strong statement, I am well aware of it, but I take comfort in the fact that increasing numbers of French commentators are beginning to discover what I began to discuss at least 15 years ago. For example, in a full-page article in the Economics section of *Le Figaro*, a professor at the prestigious Institut des Sciences Politiques, Jean-Jacques Rosa, published on February 29th, made similarly strong statements, concluding with these words: "So long as this fundamental reform [*i.e.*, separation of powers] is not undertaken, France will remain "the last communist country in Europe.'"

Increasingly, in conversations over the lunch or dinner table, I hear remarks to the effect that "France is a monarchy" or "France is not a democracy." The problem, as with Mark Twain's famous remark about the weather, is that no one is doing anything about it.

Against this background, the reader will perhaps understand why I consider it outrageous that European unity is being premised on the single currency as the most important ingredient. What the European Union needs more than a common currency is a common ethic, which, so far as France is concerned, means an uncommon ethic. A monstrous fraud is being perpetrated on the peoples of Europe by those who want them to believe that a democratic union can be achieved by means of a single currency. The Soviet Union had a single currency – the ruble – which was also a strong currency, but it did not have democracy or freedom or even prosperity. Let me make an analogy: if you were advising your daughter on what it takes to make a successful marriage, would you say that the most important factor is a joint bank account? Even if you placed economic factors at the head of the list, you would start with "marry a man who has a steady job" rather than "be sure you have a joint bank account in dollars." Europe is wallowing in unemployment. Germany admits to having more than four million out of work; France has at least that much, without admitting it, since government figures are juggled; Spain has a 20-percent unemployment rate. And so on. Yet the functionaries and politicians directing the European Union have given priority to the single currency as being the glue that will hold the peoples of Europe together. Can there be anything more stupid than basing economic policy on a single criterion, the fear of inflation engendered by the disastrous experience of the Weimar Republic? The Bundesbank is like the French General Staff in World War II, applying the lessons of an earlier war, whereas times had changed. The Bundesbank geniuses do not seem to realize that the middle class can be ruined by deflation as much as by inflation, yet this is what is happening in France for all but the blind to see.

The heart of this asinine policy is the unholy alliance welded between the German Bundesbank and the *ENArques* of France. It is my thesis that the *ENArques* have agreed to let the Germans run the European monetary system in exchange for the German agreement to allow the *ENArques* to apply their methods on the European level and, in effect, dominate the administration of the European Union. This alliance lays bare the ethical vacuum in which the future of Europe is being built.

If the Germans had any sense, they would come to the realization that no lasting society can be founded on monetary policy alone, that the ethical premises of a society are much more fundamental, and that the present power structure in France is the antinomy of any democratic union. In stating that, I am operating on the perception that German society is more pluralistic and democratic than that of France, an assumption which I hope is founded but which is not based on personal observation. It is obvious that in the post-war period, the Germans kept quiet and let the French do the talking for them, since the former were guilt-ridden over the Hitlerian episode and were too ashamed to admit openly that they yearned for reunification. The French took advantage of this guilt to assume the role of sole thinkers of the Franco-German alliance, while privately hoping that Germany would remain divided forever. Now that Germany has been reunited, almost by bodily spasms, rather than planning, the danger may be that the Germans have gotten used to not thinking, or thinking in only one dimension, to wit, monetary policy.

Let me make another analogy: the United States Constitution contains a little-known provision (Art. IV, Sec. 4) to the effect that the United States guarantees to each state a "republican form of government." What that means is that if a particular state suffered, say, a military coup and became a dictatorship, the other states and the federal government would intervene to restore democratic government to that state. There is no similar provision in the Treaty of Rome or the Maastricht Treaty. The foundation of the community, as its original title indicated – European Economic Community – was economic, not political, union. When the Rome Treaty was negotiated, in the late '50s, France still was in the Fourth Republic and Germany was still seeking respectability, under Adenauer, as a democratic state. The reign of the *ENArques* began only after de Gaulle took power in May 1958 and introduced the Constitution of the Fifth Republic, whose principal architect was none other than Michel Debré, the one who started the ENA. It is supremely ironic that Mitterrand voted against this Constitution and denounced the new regime as a "permanent *coup d'état*" in a book of the same title. The essence of this Constitution was to turn the Parliament into a rubber stamp and to give the executive real control of law-making, whether by decree or by imposing bills on the Parliament. The next major evolution was the taking over of the executive branch by the civil servants, particularly *ENArques*, who then, in view of the shocking absence of legal obstacles to their engaging in political activity, even took over the legislative branch. By the time Pompidou became President, the *ENArques* had spread their tentacles – Chirac and Balladur played key roles in his cabinet – while waiting for the "Barons" of Gaullism to leave the scene. On Pompidou's premature death in 1974, the *ENArque* Chirac abandoned the leader of his own party, Jacques Chaban-Delmas, one of the Barons, and helped fellow-*ENArque* Valéry Giscard d'Estaing get elected President. Giscard became an elected monarch surrounding himself with *ENArques* (including Chirac as Prime Minister), increasing taxes and social charges, and turning France into a welfare state while proclaiming himself a "libéral." Then Chirac abandoned Giscard, ran against him in 1981 and, by his lukewarm support in the second round, helped Mitterrand to get elected. Supreme irony: the man who had denounced the Fifth Republic as a permanent coup d'état felt very comfortable on its throne and, with the hordes of *ENArques* in the Socialist Party, ensured that the takeover of power by the functionary class was indeed permanent.

If you have followed this chronology, it is easy to understand why Chirac waxed so dithyrambic about Mitterrand after the monarch's death in January. After all, *François Dernier* had delivered up to his successor the throne intact with all its privileges and the coterie of courtiers ready to pursue the permanent *coup d'état*. I have it from a confidential source that a major revision of the Constitution was proposed to Mitterrand a few years before the end of his second term, one that would have shortened the president's term to five years and introduced other needed reforms. Mitterrand would not hear of any reform that would shorten his reign and the draft was discarded. Chirac, of course, has refused to make any major changes in the monarchical regime with which he feels so comfortable.

So this is my point: if the Germans wanted to show the world that they are devoted to democracy and pluralism, and are not just economic robots, they would strike a historic blow by refusing to go ahead with any union with France until and unless this country ends the reign of the *ENArques*. It could be done very simply by proposing a political treaty which sets minimum standards for a democratic form of government, the keystone of which would be the separation of powers, itself founded on the prohibition of political activity by civil servants. One paragraph, which I would be happy to draft, could save Europe.

The reader may well be wondering: What about the rest of western Europe: what about the British? The British performance with regard to Europe is dismal, particularly since John Major (whom I call Minor) has been Prime Minister. By reason of the Tory phobia against federalism, the British have muddled along with a Europe that is centralized, bureaucratic and undemocratic, instead of taking a firm stand against any union with nations such as France that are dominated by a single caste. And when the Labor Party comes to power, I predict that they will happily ally themselves with the French *ENArques* to perpetuate the French model of oligarchic government. The Italians, too, have just turned to a Left-leaning government, including the former Communist party, which will be willing allies of the *ENArques*.

What is the French model? Few people in Europe, I would wager, are aware that the French invented the Value Added Tax and "sold" the idea to the rest of the Community. When I began practicing here in the '60s, commentators openly called the VAT "fiscal anesthesia," since most consumers were unaware they were paying a tax when they bought things in a store. A housewife who pays F. 1,200 for a dress in France does not realize that she is paying F 200 tax, since the price sticker does not mention the tax. Two-thirds of French tax revenues come from the VAT and other indirect taxes, including the huge bites on gasoline and diesel fuel, and other automobile-related taxes. In the French model, income taxes play the role of what I call "showcase taxation," meant to punish high-earners and keep them so busy trying to cope with taxes that they have no time for protest or political activity. Only 50 percent of French families pay income taxes, and ten percent pay 90 percent of all income taxes collected. Yet the truly rich, those who have capital as distinguished from income from their work, hardly pay any taxes in France. Not only can they afford to take up residence in Switzerland or elsewhere, but also, with capital, they can purchase tax-shelter plans, helped by high-priced consultants and French banks who peddle such devices to the wealthy. Lest you think I am exaggerating, let me report that I recently attended a session at the American Chamber of Commerce in France where a tax partner in a Big-6 accounting firm made the very point that the truly rich do not pay taxes, while hard-working professionals and executives bear the brunt of income taxation.

In the French model, or rather the ENA model, this dominant caste utilizes the VAT and other indirect taxes to make "the suckers" pay and inflicts punitive income taxation on the most dynamic element of the population. In this manner, they enhance their own power by using these revenues to purchase votes from the under-classes, whom they have helped to impoverish by *dirigiste* measures that foster unemployment. I haven't the slightest doubt that this is the model that the European Union will pursue. Already billions of dollars are collected from the wealthier nations and redistributed to countries like Ireland, Greece and Portugal that, of course, just love the Community and the bureaucrats who do the handing-out. The future will see handouts galore.

The *ENArques* form a veritable aristocracy, not one based on birth, as in the past, but on their mastery, in the French educational system, of what I call the "Cartesian canon," grounded on Descartes' first principle that whatever one sees "very clearly and very distinctly" is true. They place form over substance, theory over fact, abstraction over the concrete, and *a priori* reasoning over induction. The selection process results in a homogenous class of uncreative but smooth-talking clerks, who can say banalities with brio and who contribute no added value to either the French economy or French culture. The old aristocracy, through the accident of birth or through the ennobling process, at least produced some creative geniuses, not the least of whom were Michel de Montaigne and Charles de Montesquieu, and even lesser figures who left us memorable maxims, such as La Rochefoucauld and Mme. de Sévigné. In a half century, the ENA has not even produced one *bon mot* let alone an *Esprit des Lois*.

It is a pathetic and nothing less than a looming catastrophe for Europe that France is prisoner to such a sterile yet greedy class while Germany, without a dominant class of functionaries, is prisoner to tunnel vision based on the dread of inflation. My analysis of the realities of today's Europe nevertheless leads me to the conclusion that Germany is its only hope, just as the United States of America is the only hope for the rest of the world. It is vital, if Europe is to be saved from a new tyranny, that the Germans take stock of their leadership role and cease to cower under the reminders of the evils of the Third Reich. It is time that the Germans take pride in being a more pluralistic, more democratic country than France. and insist that France free itself of its *ENArque* ruling class. The threat to democracy in Europe today is not a future Fourth Reich but rather the present Fifth Republic, which has become a feudal monarchy with a dominant class, making a mockery of the separation of powers.

To return to my title, I have been thinking of sponsoring a contest to find a new name for the European Union. Obviously, "Reich" should be in the name, in recognition of the dominant and central position of Germany, with its 80-million population. In the title, I floated FrancoReich as a suggestion, but I have also thought of ENAReich. Perhaps EuroReich will do, and the phrase would become: *"Happy as an ENArque in EuroReich."* Readers are invited to send me their suggestions as to a better name for the European Union. Please don't send in EuroMerde. As you can see, I've already thought of it.

Vol. XVIII, N° 4, July 1996

Catholic and Protestant Justice

The criminal justice system is much in the news these days in France, what with a leading company president being incarcerated by an examining magistrate (*Juge d'Instruction*), while a former minister and mayor is jailed after conviction for corruption, and President Mitterrand's former physician is branded a criminal for revealing the details of the president's bout with cancer.

Before discussing these cases and others, let me remind my readers that my introduction to French courts began 40 years ago when I was fortunate to be stationed here as an officer in the US Army's Judge Advocate General's Corps. Although no one told me I would be practicing comparative criminal law, that in fact is how I came to describe this experience. Based first in La Rochelle and then in Poitiers, one day I would be involved in a court-martial, either as prosecutor or defense counsel, applying the rules of American criminal procedure and, the next day I would hop into my Simca Aronde and drive, say, to Angoulême and be an official Trial Observer when an American soldier was tried by a French court. This lasted for 30 months, enough time for me to generalize that French justice was Catholic justice while American justice was Protestant.

The essence of the French system is inquisitorial, in the sense that judges take the lead in getting the facts in the investigative stage and conducting the actual trial, while in the common-law system, called "adversarial," lawyers develop the facts and the judge plays a neutral role. That much I knew before coming to France, but what I did not know is that the core of the French system is based on the confession and this is an eminently Catholic notion. Of course, in every system, even in Asia, the police try to wrest confessions out of suspects. But American justice requires that the police advise a suspect of his right to remain silent. The French rules allow the police to confine and grill a suspect for 20 hours before he can see a lawyer, and, even then, the lawyer is limited to 30 minutes with the prisoner and cannot participate when the suspect is again questioned.

At a later stage when a *Juge d'Instruction* is named to conduct a judicial investigation, the suspect is again grilled for hours, but he has the right to counsel if he is formally charged. It is virtually unheard-of that a suspect remain silent, because the *Juge* will slap him in jail, or keep him there, until he confesses. Again, when he appears before the *Tribunal Correctionnel* on misdemeanor charges, or the *Cour d'Assises,* for felonies, the presiding judge starts by interrogating the accused and his lawyer cannot ask questions except with the judge's permission.

When I first began attending French trials, it used to drive me up the wall to hear the judge ask the accused: "Do you acknowledge the facts?" *("Reconnaissez-vous les faits?").* "How can they be 'facts' if the accused is presumed innocent?," I would ask the French lawyer in our JAG office. I never got a satisfactory answer to what the French lawyer considered an unsatisfactory question. In other words, he could not understand why I did not comprehend that there was absolutely no problem here.

The US Senate, in ratifying the NATO Status of Forces Agreement which allowed host countries to try US military personnel for non-military offenses, had made a reservation requiring that each such trial be attended by an American officer whose duty was to report whether is was a "fair trial." My initial dilemma was how not to report that by American standards all French trials were inherently unfair, since the accused was not advised of his right to remain silent and, in effect, despite lip service to the presumption of innocence, had to convince the court that he was not guilty. Indeed, in the rare instances when an accused denied the charge, the judge would point to the voluminous file before him and tell the accused that denying the "facts" was bad faith and would be severely sanctioned. I was soon made to understand that the Army frowned on officers reporting that a trial was unfair since that was bound to result in a diplomatic incident, so, like my colleagues, I adopted a result-oriented approach. It must be said that most of the cases I attended were for minor offenses, such as brawls, indecent exposure and traffic accidents leading to bodily injury. Almost always the sentences were lenient: fines or suspended jail sentences. This was the corollary of getting admissions of guilt: the good Catholic, having confessed, is rewarded for his contrition.

The importance of the confession was brought home to me in the most serious case that I observed, that of a black soldier who was accused of raping two white women tourists at knife-point. Despite the overwhelming evidence against him, the soldier persisted in denying his guilt. While the Army had no duty to defend soldiers tried in French courts, Congress had recently enacted a law requiring the Army to pay for defense counsel in felony cases. Consequently, I had hired for him one of Poitiers' top barristers, who kept telling the soldier that if he confessed he would get a light sentence, but that if he kept denying his guilt, the court would be much more severe. This went on for over a year while the accused languished in the Poitiers prison. Then, one day, a Frenchman in that prison was tried on a similar rape charge, to which he had confessed, and got only a two-year jail sentence. The next day the black soldier called in his lawyer and agreed to confess. Sure enough, he was meted a similarly lenient jail sentence. If he had been tried by a US court-martial he would have gotten 20 years at hard labor, confession or no confession.

From such observations, I came to realize that the French courts judge the criminal while American courts judge the crime. A French *Juge d'Instruction* will spend an inordinate amount of time and effort, even when the accused has confessed, to get a psychological profile of the accused, to try to understand the factors which led to his committing the crime and to estimate the likelihood of his redemption. An American prosecutor will spend his time proving the circumstances of the crime but will leave to the defense the burden of explaining mitigating circumstances. In the French system, even if the accused admits his guilt a full trial is conducted, because it is the accused who is being judged, not just the crime. In the American system, if there is a guilty plea, no trial is held. To be sure, the judge will hold a hearing to determine what sentence will be meted out, but the emphasis remains on the severity of the crime and not the state of contrition of the criminal.

At the end of my JAG service, I generalized the pros and the cons of the two systems as follows: if I were guilty of a crime and knew that the prosecution had adequate evidence of my guilt, I would rather be tried by a French court, since by confessing and expressing contrition, I could get a lighter sentence than one given by an American court. Conversely, if I were innocent, or at least thought that the evidence was weak against me, I'd rather be tried by an American court, where the accused benefits from more safeguards, including the right not to testify, without his silence being used against him.

These fundamental differences can be illustrated by the case of O.J. Simpson, who was acquitted without ever having testified in his trial. If he had been tried in France on similar charges, it is inconceivable that he could have remained silent throughout the investigative stage and the trial and still be acquitted. In a French court, the accused's silence can be considered as evidence of his guilt. Thus, had Simpson been tried in France, his defense strategy would have been totally different: if he did commit the murders, and the prosecution had substantial proof, his lawyers would have urged him to confess and would have adopted what I call the "Othello defense," to wit, the *crime passionnel* of a man who "loved not wisely but too well." If he was not the murderer he would necessarily have had to testify and convince the judges and jury of his innocence. He could not, as in California, remain silent and let the prosecution prove his guilt beyond a reasonable doubt.

Indeed, one of the key aspects of French criminal justice is that the standard for determining guilt is merely "*l'intime conviction*," which might be translated as "deep-seated conviction," an essentially subjective notion which allows the triers of fact to convince themselves of the accused's guilt without reference to the weight of the evidence. This is a shocking concept by American standards but not in the land of Descartes who, need I remind you, held that "the things that we conceive very clearly and very distinctly are all true." The French standard is expressed in this code language which is posted in the jury room of the *Cour d'Assises* (Art.353, Code of Penal Procedure; my translation):

"The law does not ask judges to account for the means by which they convinced themselves, it does not prescribe the rules on which they must particularly base the scope and sufficiency of the evidence; it mandates that they inquire of themselves, in silence and in meditation, and to seek, in the sincerity of their conscience, what impression was made on their reason by the evidence brought against the accused, and the arguments of the defense. The law asks them only question, which encompasses the whole extent of their duty: 'Do you have a deep-seated conviction?'"

A corollary of the *intime conviction* standard is the absence of any rules of evidence in French trials. The common law developed elaborate rules of evidence designed to eliminate unreliable proofs, such as the hearsay rule, the best-evidence rule, and the exclusion of opinions except from experts. None of this in France. In one case I heard in Poitiers, involving a fatal accident between a motorcycle and an automobile, a woman testified that she was in her kitchen when she heard a crash. The judge asked her what were the circumstances of the accident and the woman replied that she had not seen it. Then the judge asked, "How did it seem to you that the accident occurred?" In other words, the judge was asking her to conjecture as to the causes of the accident. It is to the witness's credit that she refused to give her opinion, which could have been enough for the judge to form an *intime conviction.*

A lawyer might well ask at this point, "But doesn't an appeal court review the sufficiency of the evidence?" The answer, as to felony convictions in the *Cour d'Assises,* is "No." Presently, the only review is by the *Cour de Cassation,* which does not deal with the facts, only legal and procedural issues, where formalism plays a greater role than common sense. I recall a decision reversing a murder conviction on the ground that the court's decision did not recite that the doors of the court-room were open when the sentence was pronounced!

Curiously, misdemeanor convictions in the *Tribunal Correctionnel,* where three judges decide without a jury, can be appealed to the Court of Appeal (again three judges), but this is a trial *de novo,* and the same standard of *intime conviction* is applied. Unlike an American appeal which is limited to determining whether there was sufficient evidence for the court below to find guilt, the French appeal involves a fresh determination of guilt but no higher standard of proof. The government is now considering a bill to permit appeals of felony convictions, as well.

The most troublesome criminal cases for French courts are those where the accused does not confess for, no matter how conclusive the evidence of guilt, it bothers the Catholic conscience that the accused maintains his innocence. Such cases are indeed rare but inevitably create controversy and extended aftermaths, as illustrated by the famous *"Omar m'a tuer"* case, involving a Moroccan gardener convicted of slaying his employer, despite his denials. This case had a particularly bizarre *dénouement,* as the King of Morocco on a recent state visit here reportedly entreated President Chirac to show clemency, which he did by reducing Omar's sentence drastically.

Against this background, it is not difficult to interpret the first two cases alluded to in my opening sentence. A woman *Juge d'Instruction*, of Norwegian origin, with the irresistible name of Eva Joly, who has been investigating a shady investment made by the powerful oil company Elf-Aquitaine in, of all things, the Biderman clothing company which went bankrupt, slapped Elf's former president, Loik Le Floch-Prigent into jail, thereby creating quite a stir because Le Floch was president of the SNCF, France's rail monopoly. (He has since resigned.) It is quite obvious, to me at least, that the only reason for incarcerating him at this time, when he is presumed innocent, is to incite him to confess, a standard procedure in France. Of course, this is never the official reason given, since the law does not authorize torture, which is what this really is. The standard reason given is to prevent the suspect from tampering with other witnesses, but this does not hold water; the investigation has been going on for two years, ample time for Le Floch to do such tampering, had he wanted to. The man Le Floch is suspected of helping illegally, Maurice Biderman, has also been languishing in prison for weeks. The fragility of the "tampering" excuse is demonstrated by the fact that Le Floch was placed in the same prison as Biderman and, according to a report in *Paris Match,* the two men even took a 90-minute prison promenade together!

The other case resulted in the sentencing on appeal of Alain Carignon, the former mayor of Grenoble, to four-years' imprisonment for awarding a lucrative water concession to the powerful Compagnie Lyonnaise des Eaux in exchange for various valuable favors. By French standards, a four-year unsuspended sentence for a first offense is an extremely harsh punishment, but my readers will have, by now, guessed the reason: Carignon, despite a lengthy pre-trial confinement, did not confess his guilt, thereby demonstrating that he is not a good Catholic. The lesson for Le Floch is thus plain: he should take advantage of his present confinement to confess and express contrition, whereupon he will be released from prison and on trial will get a suspended sentence. Another fascinating aspect of the Carignon case is that Jérôme Monod, the Chairman of the company which did the corrupting, was never heard as a witness despite the strenuous efforts of Carignon's lawyers to have the court call him. This is all the more curious in that evidence was given that Monod had attended a lunch with Carignon at which the water contract was discussed. Monod, to be sure, is an *ENArque*, a former head of the RPR, Chirac's party and, of course, is a buddy of the President.

France is not at its first paradox when non-dangerous people are put in prison while presumed innocent and are spared prison once found guilty, provided, of course, that they have confessed. Confession is good for the soul, and if prison helps you confess, then it follows that prison, too, is good for the soul. For one trained in the common-law system, I find it curious thatthe accused, despite being expected to confess, is not allowed to take an oath to tell the truth! Doubtless, the origins of this rule are mired in Canonical logic. But as history alone does not justify the maintenance of a rule of law, I surmise that today's French logic is that an accused who lies in his defense will be punished enough if convicted and there is no need to threaten him with prosecution for perjury.

What is sad, and outrageous to me, is that hundreds, if not thousands, of less-famous people are presently crammed into French prison cells by order of *Juges d'Instruction*, who use this method to extract confessions or to assure that the suspect does not later escape punishment at the hands of tender judges. Sometimes pre-trial confinement lasts several years, while a "diligent" *Juge d'Instruction* examines the state of the suspect's soul. There is no right in internal French law to "a prompt and speedy trial" as guaranteed by the Sixth Amendment of the United States Constitution. To be sure, the European Convention on Human

Rights does have a provision requiring trial in a "reasonable time," but most French lawyers have never read this convention, and are so inured to the system that they do not dream of challenging it on the basis of foreign legal principles. In case you're wondering, the writ of habeas corpus does not exist here.

When I discussed these French practices recently with an Italian friend, he pointed out that Italian prosecutors had used pre-trial confinement of politicians and business men as a way of getting confessions that finally unveiled the large-scale corruption of all political parties in Italy. If you cram a middle-class man who has never been incarcerated into a tiny, smelly cell with nine other prisoners, it is not difficult to break his will and make him "talk." One well-known captain of Italian industry, Raul Gardini, committed suicide rather than face this ordeal. My Italian friend claimed that without such pre-trial incarceration it would have been impossible to get evidence of corruption, the implication being that the end justifies the means. This is an age-old issue. Torture is often effective as a way of getting evidence but it is considered abhorrent in all civilized societies when practiced in its most blatant forms. But I submit that depriving a person of his liberty, particularly in degrading circumstances, merely to make him confess a crime, is also a form of torture, which should not be tolerated.

The extent to which the inquisitorial system is embedded in the mentality of French lawyers is illustrated by the fact that lawyers are forbidden to interview witnesses before trial. Merely talking to a witness is considered tantamount to tampering with evidence. It is no wonder that French lawyers are so indifferent to the gathering of facts, and consider that in criminal cases their main role is to try to poke holes in the prosecution's case and to plead for leniency. It used to bother me, in my Trial-Observer days, when I would approach the defense counsel prior to the hearing to ask his opinion on the case, to get the invariable response: "Don't worry, he'll get a light sentence." I felt embarrassed even to ask the lawyer, "But did it occur to you that he might be innocent?"

In one such trial I attended, a black soldier was accused of the misdemeanor of indecent exposure, which goes by the grandiose name of "*outrage public à la pudeur*" ("public outrage to modesty"). A gendarme's wife and daughter testified that they were on the balcony of their apartment when the soldier, in the garden below, exhibited his genitals. It seemed like an open-and-shut case. Although, as indicated above, I had no responsibility to defend the soldier, I was intrigued and after the hearing I asked the soldier what had happened. He told me, "Lieutenant, I was only taking a leak." He went on to explain that he had been in the bar located at the other end of the garden and when he asked for the men's room, the owner pointed him to the garden. He had not been aware that anyone had seen him urinating under a tree. Intrigued, I asked him to show me the scene of the "crime" and, with his *avocat*, who had not bothered to investigate the "facts," we drove there and looked at the garden and the balcony, which was quite distant from the tree. Recalling that the incident had occurred in June, I asked the soldier if the trees had leaves on them at that time. He replied that they bore a full complement of leaves. It became thus evident that the women could not have seen his private parts unless they were looking for them with binoculars! I deduced what had really happened: the gendarme's family was tired of getting whiffs of urine from the garden when the wind blew in their direction and had "sicced" the gendarmes on the culprits. As none of these facts had come out at the trial, I was concerned that a miscarriage of justice would occur and asked the lawyer what he could do. He said that he would prepare a "*note en délibéré*" and give it to the presiding judge, not exactly a practice authorized by the Code of Penal Procedure. However, he did it and the soldier was acquitted.

As this case illustrates, French lawyers simply accept the inquisitorial system and the laid-back role which they themselves play, because that is the only system they know and most of them do not even realize that it is a heritage of the Inquisition. It took me about an hour to convince a friend of mine who is an outstanding *avocat* that the criminal-justice system is founded on Catholic notions, particularly the confession. He is a seventh-generation French lawyer but apparently no one had taught him that the Church had something to do with the law he was practicing. Indeed, until the separation of Church and State early in this century, every French courtroom featured a Crucifix on the front wall. Torture, as an official method of obtaining confessions of guilt, was abolished only in 1788, one year before the Bastille fell.

Against this backdrop, it might appear paradoxical that in civil cases the concept of "discovery" is anathema to the legal establishment. For non-lawyers, let me explain that "discovery" is a system prevalent in common-law jurisdictions by which adversaries are required, in advance of trial, to produce documents and give testimony which shed light on the issues in the litigation even if the evidence is unfavorable to their case. If a criminal defendant is supposed to confess his guilt, why shouldn't a civil defendant be required to produce evidence in his possession that proves his liability? To answer this question would probably require complex explanations but one common denominator in both criminal and civil litigation is the indifference of the legal profession to gathering and developing facts. More than a half-century after discovery has become an established practice in American and British courts, there is simply no movement in the French bar to institute it here.

While speaking of paradoxes, let me end with the case of Dr. Franz Gubler, who was convicted of the misdemeanor of violating the doctor-patient confidentiality obligation by writing a book describing how he treated François Mitterrand for prostrate cancer for 13 years and at his patient's request lied about it in medical bulletins. The paradox is that Gubler was punished not for having lied for 13 years, but rather for finally having told the truth! Gubler claimed that having lied for so many years he felt he had a duty to tell the truth to the French public. French law purports to hold that medical secrecy can never be waived by the patient, except when the patient accuses the doctor of malpractice. Moreover, a doctor who at the patient's request lies about his health has, by hypothesis, not revealed a secret, but on the contrary has concealed it, thus doing a good deed! Gubler, who is a Protestant, obviously did not know the logic of Catholic France: you get credit only for confessing evil deeds: confessing good ones is in bad taste.

Will Protestants never learn?

Vol. XVIII, N° 5, September 1996

The Golden and the Silver Rules, Revisited, and Platinum Added

Among the Newsletters of last year, the one that aroused the most learned responses was "Golden Rule – French Style." For new readers, let me recount that in it I related that I had once recommended to a French client that he apply the Golden Rule in a given problem, only to learn that he did not know the rule by this label. When I stated the rule in English, he gave a sign of recognition and then recited it in French, but in the negative, thus: "Do not do to others what you would not have them do unto you."

Over the years, I discovered that this negative version, which I call the "Silver Rule," is the version that the French learn in church, whether Catholic or Protestant, despite the fact that the Biblical version, in both the gospels of Matthew and Luke, is stated positively. (In case you're wondering, a reader from Athens confirmed that it is positive in the original Greek of the New Testament.) From an Italian reader, I learned that he, too, had been taught the Silver Rule; likewise a reader from Santiago, Chile, and one born in Quebec. A reader from Boston wrote me that he had found in Voltaire's writings a reference to the negative version, from which I surmise that Voltaire had learned it from the Jesuits who had educated him. It would thus appear that Christians of Latin countries have been given what appears to me to be a watered-down version of Jesus' dictum. In a word, to me the Silver Rule prescribes merely abstention from doing evil, while the Golden Rule prescribes goodness. Mind you, even the Silver Rule is a sublime rule of conduct; were it universally obeyed, there would be no crime.

Thanks to several learned Jewish readers, including a former Justice of the Israeli Supreme Court and a rabbi in New York, I have acquired a most welcome knowledge about Judaism and the origin of the Silver Rule. The only Biblical reference to it is in the book of Tobit, a book dating from about 400 B.C. and considered apocryphal, since it is not accepted in the Protestant and the Jewish Bibles, but only in the Roman Catholic one. In my Jerusalem Bible, the rule is stated thus: "Do to no one what you would not want done to you." But it was Hillel, a later precursor of Jesus, who gets the most credit for formulating the Silver Rule. The circumstances are worth recounting. A heathen told Hillel that he was considering conversion to Judaism and asked what he could learn while standing on one leg. (He had asked the same of another Talmudic scholar, Shammai, who told the heathen, in effect, to go shove it.) Hillel replied with these immortal words: "What is hateful to you, do not unto your neighbor. This is the whole Torah; all the rest is commentary. Go and study it."

According to Paul Johnson's best seller, *A History of the Jews,* Jesus had been raised in the Hillelian school of thought, and must have known this version. To my mind, he greatly improved it by eliminating the negative and making it a positive rule, but it is important to realize that Jesus was a Jew and stated, according to Matthew, that he was merely preaching what was already in the law. As my old friend from Philadelphia, Burt Caine, pointed out to me, Jews consider that the most fundamental law of conduct is "love thy neighbor as thyself" and thus the Hillelian statement must be interpreted in this light. This was later confirmed to me by Rabbi Ben Zion Gold, whom I was delighted to meet at the home of Ruth and Henry Morgenthau in

August 1995. Like most Christians, I suspect, I had associated the "love thy neighbor" dictum with Jesus, but Rabbi Gold reminded me (if I had ever learned it) that it is first stated in Leviticus, one of the earliest books of the Old Testament. Sure enough, when I waded through Leviticus, with all its tedious and precise rules of observance, I found this marvelous passage (19:18): "Thou shalt love thy neighbor as thyself."

There is, of course, a lot of ambiguity packed into this phrase; not only is "love" the vaguest of concepts, but also the phrase does not overtly require action. One can love in silence and at a distance. In practice, most French apply the notion "I don't bother my neighbor; let him not bother me," which makes it all the easier to love the unobtrusive neighbor. At any rate, the Silver Rule, as propagated by the Catholic Church, at least in the Latin Countries, appears to follow Tobit and Hillel more than Jesus. And as Catholics also stress "love thy neighbor," what differences there are between the two religions seem to relate to rules of observance and dogma, rather than rules of conduct. A rabbi from Jerusalem, whom I met in Staten Island last year at the birthday party of my old friend from West Philadelphia High, Janice Oser, told me that the essence of Judaism is in observance. (I suspect that a Catholic priest from Brooklyn might have told me the same thing about his religion.) Yet not long after that, I read an article by a rabbi in the *Sunday Times* of London, in which he stated that the essence of Judaism is in the rule of conduct, to wit, love thy neighbor. To me this suggests that there are basically two schools of thought in perhaps all religions: one which gives primacy to observance and the other which stresses conduct. The former view is obviously favored by the most conservative elements of the establishment, because it promotes the institutional aspects of the religion and assigns a greater role to the rabbis and the priests, whatever they are called. I would suspect that the same cleavage exists in the Muslim religion.

Indeed, I can't help generalizing this issue by drawing a parallel with the eternal debate over form and content, which exists everywhere, including in the law and in the Cartesian-pragmatic dichotomy on which I have often commented. There are those in every society who attach the most importance to form while others give greater emphasis to content or result. Perhaps, one day we will find that certain genes predispose people to one or the other.

Surely, by now, some readers are wondering, "Why can't you have both form and content and, in religion, observance and conduct?" Indeed, this is a good question. The sonnet is a good illustration of the wedding of form and content. If you write 14 lines based on a certain rhyme scheme, and begin with "Shall I compare thee to a summer's day?," you are likely to become immortal, but if you start with "Today is Tuesday and tomorrow is Wednesday," you are likely to remain an unknown poet. My point is that form without content is not poetry, but content without form can be poetry, as Walt Whitman and Amy Lowell, among others, demonstrated. And so, I betray my preferences by saying that in doubt I favor content over form. One is not a good Jew simply because he eats Kosher, any more than one is a good Christian simply because he goes to church every Sunday. Conversely, I would consider someone a good Jew or a good Christian who practices goodness in his daily life, even if his observance were nil. Unfortunately, not every one will agree with me!

I must concede, to state the case for the other side, that the institutionalizing of religion seems to be a practical necessity, in the sense that someone has to do the teaching of the rules of conduct, and his *quid pro quo,* so to speak, is to throw in the rules of observance, which help him earn a living and keep the faithful in line. Put another way, the form of the sonnet makes it easier to inspire most people to find good verse, but some people do not need form to create beauty or to practice goodness. I must admit that the works of my favorite composer, J.S. Bach, argue against me, since he was highly dependent on form, *e.g.,* the fugue, to create his incomparable beauty. Indeed, in his case, form seems inseparable from content, as perhaps it is with the most devout of any religion.

The grandeur of the Jewish religion is that it provides a continuity of a people with its past, thanks to the magnificent saga of the Old Testament. But its vulnerability lies in the very fact that it is tied to a people not prone to proselytizing, thus dooming it to be a minority religion except in the Jewish state, something it took a Holocaust to achieve. Neither the founders of the Catholic Church nor Mohammed tied their religion to the destiny of a single people and thus insured, by the sword, if necessary, that the majority in a given place would become the faithful. The tragic destiny of the Jewish people was that it spawned on the world a prophet whose teaching fostered the universal aspect of the Jewish message, favoring conduct over observance, but which, in practice, often led to their persecution at the hands of those whose conduct did not live up to Jesus' tenets. I must add that in my lifetime the people I have known with the warmest hearts, the most generous souls and the most open minds have mainly been Jews. This might be fortuitous but I suspect, rather, that it is the result of centuries of carrying around a book which is a saga of sin, frailty, hope and redemption and a Talmud which favors reflection and dialogue.

To return to Jesus who, one can not too often repeat, was a Jew and not a "Christian," it seems evident that his Hillelian background inclined him to be more concerned with content than with form, which, just as evidently, did not endear him to those institutionally charged with enforcing religion. He was, if you will, a poet speaking free verse rather than drafting sonnets. The genius of Jesus was to see that by converting the negative rule of Hillel to a positive one, he could do the spiritual equivalent of what nuclear fission was later to do, unleash tremendous amounts of energy, but the comparison stops there, for nuclear energy was first devoted to destruction. Doubtless, the Church fathers who came to prefer the negative version deemed this energy dangerous. It is most significant that the French Catholic Church (and others) reverted to the Tobit-Hillel formulation rather than propagate the language of Jesus.

I am impressed with the psychological insight of Jesus in converting the Silver Rule to the Golden. Over the years I have noticed that individuals tend to judge themselves, or their tribe or nation, by their good qualities, and judge others by their bad features. If you ask many a Frenchman what he thinks of the USA, you are likely to hear him speak first of poverty in the slums, but if you ask him to describe his own country, he is apt to speak of the beauty of Paris and the countryside, as though France, too, did not have slums. In a similar vein, if you determine your conduct to others only by what is hateful to you, you summon up only the negative juices, so to speak, but if you act towards others on the basis of what would be pleasing to you, you call on positive values. The same insight is contained in Jesus' celebrated dictum about seeing the beam in your neighbor's eye but not the mote in your own.

The more I think of it, the more Jesus comes through not only as a particularly good Jew but also a particularly intelligent one. He was well aware that each human being, by his very nature, is forced to judge others by his own subjectivity. Therefore, the issue becomes not how to eliminate subjectivity – an impossibility – but how to use it positively. Unlike Descartes, whose first principle in the *Discours de la Méthode* was: "The things we conceive very clearly and very distinctly are all true," the message of Jesus was "Try to see the facts through you neighbor's eyes before reaching a judgment." It is a pleading in favor of the open mind. It is only recently that I have understood the connection between goodness and intellectual honesty. Goodness opens the mind to another's point of view, thus favoring honest discourse and tolerance. A bad spirit closes the mind and favors bigotry and fanaticism.

This being said, it is my belief that Jesus would not have been crucified if all he did was to convert the Silver Rule to Gold. We must not forget that Jesus went a step further when he preached "turn the other cheek" and its corollary, "love thine enemy." The Platinum Rule, as I have dubbed it, could be stated, in parallel with the Silver and Golden ones, as "Let others do unto you what you would not do unto them." This is a far cry from Tobit's dictum. Quite understandably many contemporaries found this teaching anathema. It is one thing to turn the negative rule into a positive one; it is quite another to preach a form of masochism and self-sacrifice which the great majority of human beings find impossible to practice because it is simply unnatural. Yet, over the centuries a handful of worthy souls have found the strength to practice some form of what I call the "third stage of goodness." Ghandi's non-violence, emulated by that great American, Martin Luther King, was a form of turning the other cheek, since he and his followers allowed violence to be done to them without responding in kind. In pragmatic terms, the third stage of goodness has some educational value in arousing the support of those who witness the suffering of its practitioners and, occasionally, in converting the inflicters of the suffering to doers of good deeds, *viz.*, Saul of Tarsus who became Paul.

Before I close, let me refer to one of the most interesting letters I received in response to my Golden-Rule Newsletter, from a lawyer in Newark, New Jersey. He sent me an extract from a 1979 Louisiana Supreme Court decision, which observed that implied into every Louisiana contract was the equitable "Christian principle not to do unto others that which we would not wish others to do unto us." It is noteworthy that Louisiana, once a French colony, utilized the negative version of the rule, rather than the positive one reported by Matthew and Luke. This rule was once embodied in the Louisiana Civil Code but has since been eliminated in favor of the safer concept that "no one is allowed to take unfair advantage of another." And where the old Code stated that "no one ought to enrich himself at the expense of the other," now the Code adds the qualifier "unjustly" before "enrich," thus implying that one is free justly to enrich himself at the expense of his neighbors which is, of course, the only way my rich friends do it.

This is a long way from the extreme rule which probably earned Jesus his untimely death, to wit, that one having an extra shirt should hand it to his shirtless neighbor. (*Cf.* Tobit: "Give your bread to those who are hungry, and your clothes to those who are naked.") Moreover, Jesus opined that the rich would have a hard time going to heaven, but only the poor seem to believe this, judging by the propensity of the rich to hold on to their worldly possessions and to pass them on to their heirs.

As this is the first time that I had heard of the Golden Rule, in any form, being applied in law, it consoled me to think that I had once tried to get a client to apply it in his business dealings. In all candor, I must admit that I haven't heard from him in years! He may be in Heaven, for all I know, but more likely he's in Florida or the Côte d'Azur.

Vol. XVIII, N° 6, October 1996

October Stream of Consciousness

My readers are by now aware of my fondness for walking in Paris. In addition to my strolls to and from the office, in good weather I have taken to an evening walk after dinner, which invariably leads me, either via avenue Foch or avenue de la Grande-Armée, to what the Parisians still call the Etoile, although its official name is now "Place Charles-de-Gaulle." The other night, a balmy October evening, I let my mind wander as it willed and these were the associations that followed one another:

After a strong Newsletter, such as the one entitled "Happy as a God in FrancoReich," I get a number of letters or verbal comments from well-meaning friends expressing concern that I may be endangering myself with the powers-that-be in France. It bothers me that this bothers my friends, because I like to think that I am in a country that tolerates freedom of expression. To one such friend who made the comment in person, I asked, "If I were writing in the USA or Great Britain would you be worried about my safety?" He replied in the negative, whereupon I asserted that the fact that he thought differently about France made it all the more important that I air my criticisms. If a prominent lawyer, who is closer to the end of his days than to their beginning, does not have the courage to speak up, who will do so? A 20-year-old unemployed lad looking for his first job? A 40-year-old trying to raise a family and desperately clinging to a job which the economic situation places in jeopardy?

And so I remind myself that courage is the rarest of human virtues, not only physical courage but also, and mainly, moral courage, the courage to speak and do what is right. I recall, while at Harvard, hearing Archibald MacLeish cite these immortal words from Pericles' Funeral Oration, uttered 2500 years ago: *"The secret of happiness is liberty and the secret of liberty is courage."* As I aspire to happiness, I require liberty and I can not have it without courage. It never ceases to amaze me how lacking in courage are most of the political "leaders" of the powerful nations of the world which call themselves democracies. I put "leaders" in quotes because these people are really followers rather than leaders. They follow so-called "opinion polls" and the advice of craven courtiers whose only objective is re-election of their chosen "leader" and continuation of their sinecure. Bill, John, Jacques and Helmut are followers, not leaders. Pericles was a leader. Of all the elected officials in the world, the only one I admire is Nelson Mandela, who braved 27 years in prison to maintain the fight against apartheid and came out of jail a statesman, without bitterness, ready to lead a disparate nation.

When I talk with American friends who support Bill Clinton, people I respect for their own character, I invariably get the line that "character is not all that important; we must choose the lesser evil." It is amazing that when these same people were opposed to Nixon, character was indeed the primary quality required of a President. What is America about if not character? I no longer believe the bunk about "choosing the lesser evil." Let us remember that choosing the lesser evil is still choosing evil. I'd rather that evil be thrust on me than choose it. Who am I to know which of two potential evils will turn out the worse? Let us recall that when Lyndon Johnson ran against Barry Goldwater, the latter was billed as an "extremist" and a "war-monger." Johnson, by contrast, appeared as a moderate. But it was Johnson who turned out to be the most devious President in American history, and who stealthily enmeshed his country into its most ignominious and stupid war. My father often recalled to my brother and me an old Turkish saying: "The devil had two sons, Ullig and Bullig: to hell with both of them!"

This line of thought reminds me of my old friend John Hess, one of America's finest journalists, who deserves more fame than he has. John keeps telling anyone who will listen: "Vote for the loser each time; you're sure not to be disappointed." As to Dole, while I hold him in higher respect than Clinton (for whom I confess that I voted last time), I nevertheless believe that he is the right man in the wrong place. At 73, and inured to the legislative branch, he hardly seems fit for the arduous and novel experience of chief executive. And I am appalled by reports that he favors lowering of gasoline taxes, already ridiculously low. Gasoline costs about five dollars a gallon in France, most of which represents taxes. American consumers pay about five times less, an encouragement to waste a precious natural resource, which makes them increasingly dependent on so-called "Arab oil." And our Saudi Arabian "friends" take so-called "Arab money," which started out in American pockets, and subsidize Islamic movements all over the world which treat the United States as their primary enemy!

Thinking of political courage reminds me of Vachel Lindsay's poem, *Eagle Forgotten,* dedicated to John Peter Altgeld, the Democratic governor of Illinois who had the courage to pardon the "anarchists" who had been unjustly imprisoned after the Haymarket riot of 1886. (In Europe, where May Day is celebrated, who knows that this holiday commemorates Chicago's Haymarket Riots?) Altgeld had been considered a leading contender for the Democratic Presidential nomination in 1896, but he was so vilified by the press for his courageous decision to do right that he was denied the nomination and soon passed into political oblivion. This is what moved Vachel Lindsay to refer to him as an "eagle forgotten" and to finish his poem with this moving line: "Better to live in mankind than to live in a name."

Evoking Lindsay leads my mind to recall that I first discovered him thanks to my high-school English teacher, David Paul, one of a handful of outstanding teachers whom I was fortunate to encounter in my life. I first had him in the 10th grade at West Philadelphia High School. A trim, serious man who rarely smiled, Paul started us off with what I came to call "thought poems," as distinguished from lyrical poems,which I had never enjoyed up to then. The first one was Lindsay's *Factory Windows are Always Broken.* Another was *Fire and Ice* by Robert Frost. Paul would ask us to interpret the meaning of these poems, something I found challenging. After one class, I dared approach him and told him that I had never enjoyed reading poetry, which I tended to consider "sissy stuff," particularly as rendered by the girls in our class in elementary school who would inflict their silly rhymes on us. Paul gave me what I considered a stern look, then walked to a nearby shelf and fetched a book which he handed me, saying, "Here, read this." I waited until I reached the corridor to look at the title page; the book was *John Brown's Body* by Stephen Vincent Benét, a poet totally unknown to me. During the weekend, I devoured the book, which was a kind of epic poem recounting America's Civil War, and that converted me to the love of poetry. To this day, I marvel at the audacity of David Paul who, being told by a fallow youth that he had never read with pleasure even a sonnet started him off with 200 pages of poetry! Great teachers like that deserve to be remembered, yet most of them live in mankind rather than in a name.

In a later English class I wrote a paper on Stephen Vincent Benét, reading all his poems, including his unfinished epic, "Western Star." He came from a poetic family, having a brother, William Rose Benét, and, I seem to recall, a sister who also wrote poetry. These days, I don't see much mention of any of them in what I read. One of my favorite poems of Stephen Vincent Benét is one which begins: "I have fallen in love with American names." When driving through the French countryside, I often think of this poem, and tell myself that if I had the talent, I would write a poem called "I have fallen in love with French names." For France abounds with fascinating place names. There are 36,000 communes in France and thousands of lesser places, called *lieu dit*. Near Biarritz, there's a place called *La Négresse,* named, apparently, after a black woman from Martinique who ran a tavern there. When I lived in Poitiers and drove to Paris, I would encounter a place called *Veuves*, which means "widows," conjuring up a sad clump of houses in the Middle Ages where the men-folk had been either massacred or carted off to war, never to return. Closer to Paris, on the road to my country house in Tilly, I sometimes take a route which passes through *Boissy sans Avoir*, which literally means "Boissy without Having." I can't for the life of me imagine how a town could acquire such a name, and each time I go through it, I tell myself that I must learn the origin of the intriguing denomination. And then I think of *Les Gets,* in the Alps, which I visited in 1968. A guide-book recounted that this name was probably a corruption of *Les Juifs,* meaning "the Jews," its original name when a community of Jews trekked over the mountains coming from Italy and settled there in the Middle Ages. The Jews have long since lost their identity in Les Gets, and this leads my mind to wax ironic over the famous remark of de Gaulle, uttered in exasperation when the Israelis managed to sneak out of Cherbourg harbor some gunboats which they had purchased in France, but which de Gaulle had embargoed: "The Jews, an élite people, sure of itself and dominating." *("Les Juifs, un peuple d'élite, sûr de lui-même et dominateur.")* Did de Gaulle know of this unsure tribe lost in the snows of the Alps who not only did not dominate anything but also who lost their very name to French pronunciation?

And this brings my mind to Richard Eberhart's poem, *The Groundhog,* where the narrator recounts seeing the corpse of this animal while walking in the woods and, on later returning to the same spot, notes that nature has consumed most of its remains. At the end of the poem he thinks "Of Montaigne in his tower, of Saint Theresa in her wild lament." I pondered for years over these allusions and finally realized that the poet seemed to be saying that both the skeptic (Montaigne) and the intense believer (Saint Theresa of Avila) had to grope with death and decay and the ineffable mystery of the universe.

There's nothing like an evening walk in Paris when you started out life in Philadelphia.

More on EuroFarce

In a recent issue, I invited readers to propose an alternate name for the European Union, suggesting that "*EuroMerde*," while accurate, might be off-bounds. Several good suggestions came in, and the ones that I prefer are "EuroRacket" and "EuroFarce," as they best describes the phony democracy that is being foisted on the peoples of Western Europe by the united bureaucrats of their nations.

By way of illustration of the dangers of EuroFarce, I read in the European Edition of the *Wall Street Journal* several weeks ago that a women's organization whose main function is to lobby the European Commission for women's rights is in fact 95 percent subsidized by that very Commission! In other words, it is a front organization for the Commission's own staff. This means that taxpayers' money is being used by the European Commission to create a phony public demand for what is in reality its own agenda! Can you imagine the abuses to which such practices can lead?

Another illustration from EuroFarce: Commission staff members had information several years ago of the gravity of the "mad cow" disease but decided to underplay the issue so as not to to upset producers of this wholesome product who evidently are more important than the consumers who risk contamination with a devastating disease. The European Parliament, a farce in itself, since it masquerades as a legislative body, whereas this power is in the Council of Ministers, is purporting to investigate this cover-up but one can safely predict that no bureaucrat will be punished for endangering public health.

Make no bones about it, the so-called European Union is already an abomination and it will get worse if the Maastricht Treaty is implemented. In reality it is a union of functionaries who will control all of Western Europe just as the *ENArques* control France. Already, this caste has access to the treasuries of the richer nations, who contributed billions of dollars of their taxpayers' money each year so that the functionaries can redistribute these funds to the poorer nations such as Ireland, Greece and Portugal, and for their pet projects, wherever located. A French newspaper reported recently that local politicians in the Valenciennes region had directly lobbied the European Commission for a huge subsidy, which was granted, but fortunately never spent because French bureaucrats in Paris had not been consulted as to the projects the money was to be used for. That may be good news, temporarily, but it indicates the danger that lurks on the horizon when the European Commission becomes all-powerful. Most French people are not even aware of how much of their tax money goes to the European bureaucracy, as accountability is not a strong suit of functionaries.

For an American to understand what the EU represents, the best analogy is to imagine that the Democratic Party were enshrined in the US Constitution as the sole authorized political party, with unlimited power to tax and spend. Aside from the EuroSkeptics in the Tory Party of Great Britain, there is really no opposition in the EU to the unofficial party of the functionaries, whose fundamental technique for obtaining and maintaining power is to use regulation to make work for themselves and taxes to acquire money for redistribution, thereby buying constituencies which will keep them in power.

Vol. XVIII, N° 7, November 1996

Weeping for France

Since the subject keeps coming up as to how I find the time to write this Newsletter (people have stopped asking me "Who writes it for you?"), considering that I put in a long day, and many a night, as a lawyer, it is worth repeating what William Saroyan answered when I posed a similar question to him in 1961: *"There's plenty of time, Aram; most people don't know the usage of time."* In my case, I write mainly on weekends, in my country place, on my laptop computer, as I am doing now, but I never undertake the actual writing until I have first composed the beginning in my head, almost always while walking, as I did just now in my beloved French countryside.

Once initiated this way, the writing usually is done in two-or three-hour spurts; thus the typical six-page Newsletter is basically written in six hours, although I do tinker with the text in varying degrees before it finally goes out. In most instances, the title comes to me quickly once I have gotten the text under way. If I give these details now, it is by way of introduction to the point that the present Newsletter has not been a typical production: I actually wrote three versions, with different titles, and tried consolidating them, before I decided to discard them all and begin afresh. The reason for this is the embarrassment of riches, if you will, that have been accumulating in my head and on paper as to the sorry state of France. Here are the three titles that I had previously tried:

Fin de Siècle: Fin de France (End of Century: End of France)
The Strong-Currency Cult and Collective Suicide
Occupied and Unoccupied France.

To develop all these themes around the central topic of the sad decadence of France today would have taken more pages than the Newsletter was meant for; that is why I decided to adopt a more succinct format, merely presenting disparate items without taking the space to fit them into a coherent plan. Consider the following:

– Captain Barril and murder in the Elysée: Paul Barril was a captain in the *Gendarmerie,* a branch of the French Army charged with police functions. He served in the Elysée Palace during the reign of the man I call "François the Last," and got close to François de Grossouvre, a long-time buddy of Mitterrand, doing a lot of his boss's dirty work, including covering up for his mistress and their daughter. Barril's book of revelations, published a few months ago, alleges that Grossouvre was murdered in his office in the Elysée Palace and that the crime was covered up to appear as suicide.. He ties this murder to Gilles Menage, Mitterrand's chief of staff, who tried to get the book seized by court order, but his petition was denied. (It is interesting to note that accusing a Mitterrand henchman of murder is not ground for seizing a book whereas telling the truth about Mitterrand's concealed cancer is.) So far as I know, Barril's charges are not being investigated by the police.

– Jean-Edern Hallier blackmailing Mitterrand: The undisputed bad-boy of contemporary French literature is Jean-Edern Hallier, who is also a self-promoter of the first order. Barril's book discloses that he was the go-between when Hallier blackmailed Mitterrand by threatening to publish a book which, among other things, revealed the president's secret love life. The blackmail worked, since Hallier succeeded in getting a large tax liability written off in exchange for handing over his manuscript to Barril. Of course, he kept a copy, which was published last year after Mitterrand died. Again, no one was prosecuted for this obviously illegal transaction.

– Wire-tapping under presidential authority: It is not new to my readers that during Mitterrand's reign, officials acting under his authority conducted thousands of illegal wire taps, mainly of the conversations of people suspected of being political enemies, such as Hallier, as well as lawyers, journalists and actors. While the word got out during Mitterrand's reign, he was never questioned about it, and there has still been no prosecution of the persons responsible for the wire-tapping. Barril's book attributes this operation to Menage who, far from being punished for it, was given the choice plum of the presidency of the state electric and gas monopoly. Barril himself quotes extracts from illegal wiretaps, thus demonstrating that the fun goes on and on.

– Shenanigans at Paris City Hall: Before becoming President last year, Jacques Chirac was Mayor of Paris for 18 years, and even kept that office while Prime Minister from 1986 to 1988. During his reign, he built up a formidable cash machine to finance his political campaigns and those of his henchman, who like him, have no compunctions against holding both city and national offices simultaneously. Thus, one of his chief lieutenants, Jacques Toubon, is Minister of Justice while remaining Mayor of the 13th *arrondissement* of Paris. Perhaps the main vehicle of graft was the tremendous stock of public housing controlled by the city. I read recently that 20 percent of all lodgings in Paris are owned by the City. These include luxury apartments which were leased at below-market rents to favored politicians, like Chirac himself, as well as to journalists, judges and other influential persons. The cheaper lodgings, called "HLM," meant for the hoi-polloi, provide opportunities for graft, since contractors and suppliers were shaken down to give commissions in exchange for lucrative contracts. A courageous *Juge d'Instruction*, Eric Halphen, has been investigating these irregularities, and has latched on to the present mayor, Jean Tiberi, and his wife Xavière, who received a payoff in the amount of F 200,000, ostensibly for a report she provided on a technical subject, for which she is not exactly known to be an authority. Criminal charges were recently brought against her by an assistant prosecutor of the Essonne *département,* near Paris, who took advantage of his politically cautious superior's vacation climb in the Himalayas to initiate the prosecution. Whereupon, Toubon and Interior Minister Jean-Louis Debré, hoping to reverse the decision, hastened the return of the chief prosecutor by sending a helicopter to pluck him from the mountain-side, thereby causing another embarrassing scandal when the news leaked out.

In 1994, Chirac's men tried to get rid of Halphen by incriminating his father-in-law, a physician at the American Hospital, in a sting operation but this backfired as the courts saw through the entrapment scheme and dismissed charges against the doctor. This year, Halphen conducted a surprise search of Tiberi's private apartment but the judicial police refused to participate in the search, obviously following orders from Chirac's lieutenants, including Debré, who is none other than the son of the late Michel Debré, founder of the Ecole Nationale d'Administration. The Court of Appeals of Paris has just sanctioned the police official, Olivier Le Foll, who took the blame for refusing to cooperate with Judge Halphen, but Debré is keeping his obedient servant at his post, a decision much criticized by French judges and others.

Another mini-scandal came to light when it was revealed that the son of Mayor Tiberi had been receiving a salary from state-owned Air France for three years without doing any work there. He was ostensibly serving in the cabinet of the Minister of Relations with the Parliament, who generously reimbursed Air France for its outlay, at taxpayers' expense, of course. This is just the tip of the iceberg concerning the use of state companies and social-security organizations to pay salaries of persons "working" in various ministries and even in unions like Force Ouvrière, that are basically financed with public funds.

Le Canard Enchaîné, the French weekly newspaper that unearths most of the scandals in France, revealed several months ago that the City of Paris had for years been illegally providing free maid service to two former high national officials. After the word got out, the two agreed to refund the cost of the services but only for the period still open for claims under the statute of limitations. One of them, a member of Parliament, even borrowed from the Parliament to make the refund, thus revealing another racket for which the placid taxpayers are paying: the Parliament is also a bank! Of course, no charges were brought against any one for the illegal use of public funds.

Mr Chirac was Mayor of Paris when all these shenanigans were being perpetrated and a vast machine of graft put into place, yet the press spares him and concentrates on the current mayor, a non-entity who was merely Chirac's flunky. These cases, which are but a drop in the bucket, illustrate the ethical vacuum in which the highest French officials operate. I want to make clear that at the lower levels French functionaries are generally honest and efficient. You do not have to pay a bribe to get a birth certificate, as in some third-world countries. But the highest level of officialdom, led by *ENArques*, practices the ethics of what the French call *"une république bananière," i.e.,* a banana republic.

– Crédit Lyonnais: No better illustration of the incompetence of the *ENArques* in the economic sphere can be given than the continuing saga of the agony of the Crédit Lyonnais, once France's top bank, which was nationalized in 1946. Several years ago, a leading *ENArque*, Jean-Yves Haberer, who had held the prestigious post of Directeur du Trésor in the all-powerful Ministry of Finance, was named President of this bank. He embarked on an extravagant expansion program, made enormous investments in private companies without the slightest "due diligence" and failed to supervise various subsidiaries which made huge loans to such crooks as Robert Maxwell, Bernard Tapie and Giancarlo Perretti, the last-named having acquired MGM with the money of the Dutch subsidiary of Crédit Lyonnais. For years, the financial statements of this bank had been false, since adequate reserves were not taken for bad loans and worthless investments. When Edouard Balladur became Prime Minister in 1993, he removed Haberer as President, not for incompetence, but because it is traditional for a new government to award supposed "plums" to its favored cronies. Far from being punished, Haberer was given another plum, the presidency of the Crédit National, also a state-controlled bank. The new president, Jean Peyrelevade, lost little time in taking stock of the disastrous state of the Crédit Lyonnais, and the stink became so great that Balladur was forced to remove Haberer from his new post, although he presumably had not had enough time to do any damage there.

The Crédit Lyonnais was really bankrupt – its losses are likely to exceed $ 25-billion, a world record – but the government kept it alive by injection of billions of francs in fresh capital and by placing its worst assets and liabilities in a new entity called *"Consortium de Réalisation"* (shades of the Resolution Trust Company, a relic of the US's own Savings and Loan scandal). A parliamentary committee made a tepid investigation of the Crédit Lyonnais, which an author of one exposé called the "Crazy Lyonnais." Although there had been wholesale dishonesty in various subsidiaries, the new management of the Crédit Lyonnais and the government have done very little to bring criminal proceedings or even to recover damages from the culprits. For years, a "Big Six" accounting firm certified the false accounts of the bank, yet no action has been taken against this firm or any of the auditors of various subsidiaries. Early in August, the Minister of Finance, Jean Arthuis, recommended to the Minister of Justice that former Crédit Lyonnais executives be prosecuted for having issued false financial statements. As it is extremely rare for functionaries to be prosecuted for anything, the Ministry of Justice tried to gain time by issuing a statement to the effect that the legal basis for prosecution is not clear, ostensibly on the ground that French law does not make it a criminal offense to publish false consolidated accounts, only false accounts of the individual subsidiaries. This flimsy excuse does not hold water in the case of Haberer since he was also President of one of the most notorious subsidiaries of his bank, which issued inflated balance sheets. I suspect that if charges are brought, the investigative stage will drag out for years and that ultimately Haberer will beat the rap. He knows too much and can implicate many other members of the Caste of Functionaries, including Jean-Claude Trichet, now head of the Banque de France who, as *Directeur du Trésor,* was responsible for overseeing nationalized banks. It is obvious that Trichet did not adequately supervise the Crédit Lyonnais, but as architect of the "strong franc" policy, he is the high priest of the *Secte du Franc Fort* and untouchable.

– The Corsican Fiasco: Corsica is a permanent cancer on the French body politic. For decades, various independence movements in Corsica have been defying the law, blowing up government buildings and even tourist housing, as well as periodically killing each other. The Corsicans are really a breed of Italians and only the fact that Genoa sold their island to France in 1768 made them French subjects. Pasquale Paoli, having fought the Genoese to obtain Corsican independence, then took up arms against the French, without success. Later, Napoleon Bonaparte upstaged him by demonstrating that it was easier for a Corsican to colonize France than to decolonize Corsica. There are today as many Corsicans living and working on the mainland as on the island, and most of those who do not "emigrate" have little attachment to France. After Algeria became independent, many departing French people tried to establish farms and businesses in Corsica, but the natives kept blowing up their homes and setting fire to their crops. Successive governments have made economic concessions to Corsica, such as lower gasoline and fuel taxes, but it is a hopeless task to create a viable economy on the island. The present government, led by the Minister of the Interior Debré, has been conducting secret negotiations with the thugs who masquerade as independence-seekers. The height of ignominy was reached in January when 600 of these thugs, armed to the teeth, held a press conference in a small Corsican town while the police stayed discreetly away.. One of my waggish friends has a great idea for solving two major French problems with one fell blow: move the Ecole Nationale d'Administration to Corsica. At least two possible outcomes can be envisaged: 1) the Corsicans will blow up the school and that will solve the ENA problem radically; 2) no one from the mainland will apply to the school and only Corsicans will become *ENArques*, in which case the French would sell Corsica back to the Genoese and the ENA with it. The Genoese might be reluctant to buy it, but a soft loan from the Crédit Lyonnais might help convince them.

– Asbestos and Pollution: In the past, I have touched on the case of contaminated blood deliberately sold by a government agency with the approval of the responsible political leaders at the time, and which has cost thousands of lives. A similar scandal has been brewing for years and has finally come to light in recent weeks: that involving the continued use of asbestos in public and private buildings, including schools and universities. Whereas the cancer-causing properties of asbestos have been known for at least 20 years, the French government failed to take any effective action against its use, with the result that thousands of people, particularly construction workers, have been endangered needlessly.

Another example of official irresponsibility involves atmospheric pollution. The government is finally beginning to admit how polluted Paris is, and the main cause is the proliferation of diesel-fueled cars, busses and trucks. For many years, diesel fuel has been taxed at a lower rate than gasoline, with the result that about half of all private vehicles have diesel engines, which spew out unfiltered sulfur and other pollutants. Until a few years ago, gasoline engines were fed only leaded gasoline, but now new cars of this type have to be equipped with catalytic converters while older cars continue to pollute. Moreover, diesel engines are not required to utilize any anti-pollutant devices! The government does not have the courage to raise taxes on diesel fuel to discourage purchase of these automobiles, because both Renault and Peugeot, the only French car manufacturers, are dependent on these sales.

– Declining Cuisine: My own bell-weather of the French economy is seeing what is happening to French restaurants, once the glory of this country. In the past several months, two of the Michelin Guide's three-star – the highest ranking – restaurants have filed for bankruptcy in the provinces. In Paris several noted restaurants, including the Toit de Passy, Vancouver and Le Duquesnoy have closed their doors, and it has just been revealed that a Paris landmark, the Brasserie Lorraine, in the Place des Ternes, one of my favorite spots, has filed for bankruptcy. To add insult to injury, it has been reported that this might become a McDonald's "restaurant." Last year, in my "Paranoid Alley" essay, I lamented the loss of my beloved bistro, Le Valéry, which became a Pizza Hut. One sees more and more fast-food outlets in Paris, the suburbs and the provinces. I believe that McDonald's alone has close to 500 in this country! There must be at least a thousand American-style fast-food places (I don't call them restaurants) in France, and every day traditional restaurants are giving up the ghost, victims of high costs, prohibitive taxes and social charges and a dwindling customer base. Unlike some people, I do not blame American fast-food chains for peddling the only things they know how to sell – sugar, fat and starch – but I do blame, and severely so, the French *ENArque* ruling class for the policies which have made the propagation of this awful junk inevitable in this country, simply because more and more French people can not afford to go to traditional restaurants. And it is cheaper to eat a hamburger and fries, or a pizza, than to buy fresh produce in the market and prepare a wholesome meal at home. Most traditional restaurants, including those with Michelin stars, have lowered their prices by proposing fixed-price menus that would have been unthinkable years ago.

As I happen to believe that good food is one of the artifacts of an advanced civilization, the decline of French cuisine bespeaks a national disaster. The irony is that while increasing numbers of their compatriots are gobbling down flour, sugar and fat in the quest for cheap calories, Messieurs Chirac and Juppé are enjoying two gourmet meals a day, *arrosés*, as the French say, with the best French wines, all at taxpayers' expense. When the crowds clamored for bread, Marie-Antoinette replied "Let them eat *brioches*" (mistakenly translated as "cake"). Today, Mr Chirac says "Let them eat Big Macs!" Sadly, I predict that in a generation, one will see on French streets the same kind of ugly obesity that one finds all over America today, where vast numbers of the young and not-so-young fill their bellies with sugar-laden hamburger "buns," fried potatoes soaked in animal fat, ground beef glimmering with grease, soft drinks with sugar, candy bars containing more sugar than chocolate.

– Unemployment and the strong franc: Unemployment continues to rise but the government continues to propagate, and the obsequious French press continues to print, the fictitious figure of 12.6-percent unemployed. In reality, as a French tax official confirmed to me the other day, there are five-million jobless people which, placed against a potential work force of 29-million, puts the percentage of theoretical job-seekers at 17 percent. And if you remind yourself that France's five-million civil servants (and other state workers) are never laid off and thus that the unemployed come from the ranks of the private sector, this means that the percentage of unemployed in the private sector is well over 20 percent. Successive French governments, all dominated by *ENArques*, have disguised the real unemployment number by techniques such as not counting people in training and severance programs.

The Juppé government, which made a pretense last year of attacking unemployment through a single measure, a subsidy for hiring people who had been out of a job for two years, has now given up that pretense and curtailed even this modest boon. It is clear that the Chirac-Juppé tandem has only one objective – meeting the Maastricht criteria for deficit reduction – so as to be able to claim that the single currency can be adopted in 1999. This year the government even resorted to a gross numbers game by transferring billions of francs from the French telecommunications system, intended to fund pensions, to the general treasury.

Some commentators have taken to calling the Maastricht criteria the "Holy Grail" to indicate their awareness that this has become a religion for the functionary caste which controls France. One hears frequent references to the famous line uttered by Louis Jouvet in the film role of the quack doctor, Dr. Knock, *"You will die cured."* The French are being cured of inflation but they are dying of unemployment and high taxes, all signs of health in the cult of the strong franc. Several weeks ago, *Le Figaro* reported that the Canadian economist, William Vickrey, just named winner of the Nobel Prize, had criticized the strong-franc policy as a sure source of continued unemployment. (Sadly, Vickrey died of a heart attack only a few days after making the statement.) I have been saying the same thing for years, to no avail.

On November 22nd, *l'Express* published an article by former President Valéry Giscard d'Estaing calling for a reduction of the value of the franc with relation to the dollar. He made the wholly sensible point that achieving a single currency is dangerous if that currency is overvalued to the point of harming the European economy. (Significantly, his co-architect of European policy during the '70s, Helmut Schmidt, then Chancellor of West Germany, recently wrote a scathing criticism of the strong-mark policy, with personal attacks against the head of the Bundesbank.) Giscard's comments have been greeted with derision by Chirac's spokesmen.

– Freedom of Speech: The beleaguered government, particularly Minister of Justice Toubon, grasps at any straw to divert attention from the disastrous economy and its own corruption. Jean-Marie Le Pen, always a willing target of baiting by journalists, provided one such straw recently when, in answer to a loaded question from a reporter, he replied; "I don't believe in the equality of races." This was enough to unleash all the self-righteous hounds in France, including Toubon, who promptly sponsored an amendment to an already-restrictive law making it a criminal offense to disparage races and other groups. I hold no brief for Le Pen but I will defend his right peacefully to express an opinion without being hauled off to prison. It is shocking to me that when Le Pen was interviewed on television by Christine Ockrent, the French equivalent of Barbara Walters, he was not even given the opportunity to explain his remark. She kept baiting him rather than listening to what he tried to say. Perhaps I will be prosecuted, too, for making the observation that if all races were "equal," in the sense of identical, they would not be differentiated as races in the first place. In the only commentary that I have seen by Le Pen, he made the point that the eight finalists of the 100-meter dash in the 1996 Olympics were all black, certainly an indication that blacks might be superior, and thus unequal, to whites in running fast.

Another example of the curtailing of speech was the prosecution of two French rap singers in Toulon, who were sentenced to three-months in prison and a prohibition of singing publicly for six months, for some strong language against the French police uttered during a concert there. As their luck would have it, the judge was a former policeman. The complainants were 30 cops who officiated at the concert and claimed they felt endangered by the provocative lyrics. As Justice Holmes was wont to say, "Hard cases make bad law." Even he would have acknowledged that speech that incites violence is not protected but it should be noted that no one in the audience interpreted the anti-police lyrics as a call to attack those present. Again, Toubon, relieved to be able to divert attention from the corruption cases involving members of his party, spoke out on the issue, saying the sentence was too harsh and ordering the prosecutor to appeal. Curiously, Toubon was criticized on the Right for being soft, since the rappers have offended a lot of people by adopting the name *"Nique ta Mère."* I must confess that I had never heard the word "*nique*" but I am told by more knowledgeable people that it refers to an act which would make the perpetrator guilty of incest. I hold no brief for ugly rap singers, no more than I do for Le Pen, but the right of free speech is meaningless if it is reserved only for the speech we like.

Well-paid functionaries: Like most people in France I had shared, and propagated, the illusion that civil servants, while having lifetime jobs and better pensions, were nevertheless penalized by earning less than those in the private sector. False, it turns out: the government statistical agency, called "INSEE," just came out with a report that shows that the average pay of functionaries in France significantly exceeds that of the private sector, at all but the highest level. This is the crowning proof, so to speak, that the Fifth Republic has erected an unproductive privileged class of nomenclatura which, as in the Communist countries, lives at the expense of those who work harder, take more risks and earn lower income.

Speaking of the latter category, the last part of November witnessed another suicidal happening when long-suffering French truck drivers struck for retirement at 55, shorter hours and better pay, and not only struck but also set up 248 road blocks, paralyzing traffic all over the provinces The trucking industry is depressed because the economy is weak. The major concessions made by the operators and the government to forestall a broader paralysis of the economy will make the industry weaker and add to the taxpayers' already staggering burden.

– Summing Up: So where do we go from here? The points made above are merely illustrations of a very sick society. If I were the only one saying so, I would have hesitated to use such strong language, but when a Gaullist stalwart like Charles Pasqua, former Minister of the Interior, uses the term "*déconfiture*" (an elegant word for "bankruptcy") to describe the present situation, one need not apologize for stating the facts. Frédéric Dard, a popular novelist, used the word "stench" in a newspaper interview to describe his feelings on the subject. A French friend told me the other day that "France is bankrupt, morally, culturally, politically, economically and every which-way." Indeed, the Fifth Republic is rotten to the core and the great bulk of French people are fed up with it, even if they do not know why. The latest poll shows Chirac's approval rating at 27 percent and Juppé's at 20 percent. Most people I speak with express despair because they realize that there is no political figure or party on the horizon that can offer any hope, certainly not Le Pen and his National Front. Many productive citizens are leaving the country and vast amounts of capital have already flown the coop.

Several Frenchmen with whom I have talked recently have openly mentioned the need for a revolution. When I asked one of them, a middle-aged lawyer, not known for his levity, who could lead such a revolution, his reply was that only two people were possible: Le Pen and Tapie, and he preferred Tapie. I report this only to illustrate the depths of despair to which the French are succumbing. Imagine looking to a mountebank like Tapie to lead a revolution against the *ENArques*!

But the most significant remark I want to report is that of a young man – only 25 – who comes from a bourgeois family and whose father is a prominent politician, a member of the UDF party, which supports Chirac. Knowing that this young man works with his father, I hesitated to tell him that I was opposed to the Maastricht treaty. But when I did, he surprised me by saying that he, too, was hostile to it. I asked him whether he conveyed his views to his father. He replied "Yes," and added that his father expressed dismay, saying that "We are creating Europe for you, the young." The son replied, "The young need to dream, and there are no dreams in the Europe you are preparing."

This is, to me, the most damning condemnation of contemporary French and European policy. A regime which offers no hope to its youth is contemptible. What that rap group should be singing is *"Nique la Cinquième République; nique l'Union Européenne."* Taking a broad view of the century which is ending, I note that German-French idiocy produced two catastrophic wars. Now, a different type of German-French idiocy, personified by the fatal attraction of Jacques and Helmut, is at loose, preparing to lock future generations into a virtual gulag; one without bars but also without hope. In the real gulags, at least, people could dream of escaping. In the Kafkaesque world of the EU, they can look forward only to mysterious directives from faceless functionaries in the Brussels castle.

I weep for my beloved France, the France of my wife, my children and my grand-children, and the France of *les braves gens*, who always pay for the stupidity and cupidity of their leaders, in war as in peace.

Vol. XIX, N° 1, February 1997

To Change the Subject

A number of readers, including some who feel that I've exhausted the subject of French politics, have suggested that I write about the Good Old USA, my native land, for a change. To this I readily agree; whenever I criticize something French I invariably get letters and Email from American readers, saying, in effect, "Things are pretty bad here, too." I have an advantage in looking at France through the eyes of an outsider and, in some ways, it can be said that I am also an outsider to the USA, since I've been living in France for 35 years, although making several trips a year to the USA.

But first, I am pleased to reveal that several readers identified the poem I quoted in my last issue as being the work of Robert Frost. Being a great admirer of that poet, I am mystified as to how I forgot his name while remembering the poem. As there were a few errors in my memory, I am reproducing here the full poem, called *Dust of Snow.*

"The way a crow
Shook down on me
The dust of snow
From a hemlock tree
Has given my heart
A change of mood
And saved some part
Of a day I had rued."

No one can be objective about any subject, let alone his native country. When writing for others, one should, at least, examine his own values and try to alert the reader as to one's fundamental outlook. So-called "scholars" like to appear as having no prejudices, but that is impossible. We all have what Holmes called "inarticulate major premises" in expounding on any subject. I remember reading, many years ago, a very long article on tax policy in the *Harvard Law Review,* written by two law professors. It was only on the 37th page of the article that these "scholars" deigned to reveal what their basic value system was that led them to propose particular tax measures. Why should I have to wade through 36 pages to find out the authors are socialist, or whatever?

In the case of the USA (please note that I am trying to avoid the word "America," since we tend to forget that this term is not the exclusive trade-mark of the United States of America and, for that matter, United States is not either, since there are other United States, including those of Brazil), I would not want to hide from anyone, let alone myself, the basic gratitude that I feel to a country which in 1912 welcomed my Armenian father, an escapee from Turkey, where three years later his entire family was massacred by the Turkish army in the town of Chunkoush. My father arrived penniless in the USA and although he did not die rich 60 years later, he did have a social-security pension and lived in freedom, writing what he wanted in the Armenian newspaper he founded in 1919 and published for 43 years. The public-school system of

Philadelphia turned my brother and me, born into an Armenian-speaking family, into English-speaking Americans in less than two years, aided and abetted by the streets of West Philadelphia, a true melting pot.

With this background, I can't help but be opposed to bilingual education for immigrant children in the USA. My parents never thought that their sons were entitled to be educated in the public schools by Armenian-speaking teachers. So, of course, I am appalled by the decision of the Oakland public-school authorities to "educate" black children by using their primitive street language (called "Ebonics") in the schools. To my mind, this smacks of the kind of pseudo-thinking that leads many American universities to downgrade the basic English-language masterpieces and to treat every obscure third-world poet as though he were the equal of Shakespeare. Even the French admit that they never produced a Shakespeare, and I, for one, am ready to admit that Armenia didn't either.

Speaking of universities, let me vent my spleen at Princeton University, an institution that has produced some outstanding basketball players, like Bill Bradley, and my friend John Hummer, now a Silicon-Valley venture capitalist, but presently seems to be devoting itself to producing Turkish propaganda. Armenians are incensed at this institution's accepting a grant from the Turkish government for an "Atatürk Chair of Turkish Studies." This is surely the first time an American university has named a Chair after a dictator! Moreover, the Atatürk Chair has been bestowed on a "scholar" noted for denying the 1915 genocide of the Armenians, in the great tradition of Bernard Lewis, another Princeton professor, who calls the genocide of which my grandparents and their three remaining children were victims, along with 1.5-million other Armenians, merely the "Armenian version" of history. It is easy to downgrade historical events by labeling them as somebody's allegation. For example: "According to the English, Wellington won the battle of Waterloo." Or, "The Bnai-Brith claims that six-million Jews were killed by the Nazis." As a matter of principle, I do not believe that American universities should accept grants from foreign countries and, in particular, from countries which do not respect freedom of expression. In Turkey, no historian or journalist is allowed to tell the true story of the Armenian genocide. If Princeton had wanted to do a good deed, it would have suggested to the Turkish government that its grant money be used to endow a "Woodrow Wilson Chair of History" at the University of Ankara and allow a Western professor to teach the truth there. In the meantime, let me suggest to the gullible authorities of Princeton University that if they want to obtain grants from foreign sources, here are some potential chairs which could be endowed:

The Nicholas Ceaucescu Chair of City Planning
The Adolph Eichmann Chair of Mass Transportation
The Mao Tse Tsung Chair of Cultural Reform
The Benito Mussolini Chair of Corporate Governance

The subject of foreign money naturally brings me to Bill Clinton and the Democratic party, which broke all records in 1996 for the indecent collection of campaign contributions. Before I get into these shenanigans, let me mention that an obstacle to setting decent limits on campaign spending is the constitutional notion of free speech, particularly as it applies to television advertising by politicians. In France, where free speech is also recognized as a constitutional right, paid political advertising is not permitted on television or radio. This restriction does not seem to bother anyone, including, for once, me. Indeed, the French system is to organize free television appearances by each candidate, on an equal basis, before each presidential campaign. And the French set relatively low limits on spending for each election, the transgression of which can result in the revocation of the term of the elected official. This happened, for example, when Jack Lang's election to the National Assembly was nullified by the Constitutional Council. The United States Supreme Court held, several years ago, that a legislature could not limit the amount a candidate could spend out of his own funds, on the ground that this violates his right of free expression. I think this decision is wrong. There is a difference between spending and speaking; if you equate money with talk in the realm of human rights, you prove indeed that "money talks." I do not believe that the First Amendment was enacted to allow millionaires to buy political office. While there are theoretical limits in the USA on political contributions by third parties, these are easily circumvented, as the recent election has shown. If necessary, I would favor a constitutional amendment to limit political advertisements, particularly on television and radio.

This brings me to the outrageous excesses committed by the Clinton camp in collecting money from tainted sources, such as Asian "businessmen" fronting for foreign governments, and by foul means, such as making the Lincoln Bedroom available to large donors of campaign contributions. Mr Clinton seems to have forgotten that the White House belongs to the American people, not to its temporary occupant, and that if any money is to be made from its use this money belongs to the people. Can you imagine what would happen if the CEO of, say, General Motors, rented out the boardroom to outsiders and collected the rent for his own benefit? Just one incident like this would be enough to cost him his job. If Bill Clinton can get away with collecting money from overnight guests at the White House, what's to keep him from renting out the White House limousine, or Air Force One, to private users and using the money to send his daughter to college? Or for that matter, what's to keep him from installing a McDonald's in the White House, to be operated by Chelsea as franchisee? We used to snicker at posters showing Richard Nixon's face and asking *"Would you buy a used car from this man?"* I would not buy a used car from Clinton, for fear that it might be government property.

The moral atonality of Bill Clinton seems to know no bounds. In my view, the explanation of his all-out effort to get re-elected, even by violating the law and collecting money from Asian patrons, is that he hoped that this would put off for another four years the hearing of the lawsuit brought against him by Paula Jones. For those of my readers who are not familiar with this name, I will explain that she is the former Arkansas State employee who brought a civil suit against Clinton, alleging that during a conference held in a hotel, Bill Clinton, while governor, got a state trooper to bring her to his room, his sole greeting to her being to pull down his trousers and underpants and inviting her to do honor to his private parts. This story is, of course, inherently implausible. Despite the fact that he dodged the draft, went to Yale Law School and married Hillary Rodham, Bill Clinton is a Normal American Male (NAM) and no NAM, particularly one from the South, would pull his pants down in front of a strange woman without first saying, at least, "Hi y'all."

Of course, the basic question of American governance is how people like Clinton get elected in the first place. If I may lift my mind, for a moment, to a loftier generalization, I doubt that any so-called democracy in the age of television is governable other than by resort to demagoguery. I know of no way to avoid it under current rules of the game. When I visited South Africa several years ago, shortly before the breakthrough that turned over control of the country from the white minority to the black majority, I had an insight regarding a way to attenuate the risk of a drastic shift of power from the "haves" to the "have-nots." The idea will shock most people, I suspect, but here it is for posterity: instead of "one man one vote," citizens would have a number of votes proportional to the income taxes they pay. Every one would have at least one vote, so that no one is disenfranchised, but those who contribute more to the nation's tax revenues would get extra votes, up to a limit. After all, in a corporation a shareholder has one vote per share, not one vote per person. This system would reduce the natural tendency of all democracies to tax the most productive members of society in order to distribute goodies to those who contribute little or nothing. And it might, as a corollary, reduce the temptations towards demagogic campaign promises.

In France, for example, more than half the so-called "working population" pays no income tax. It is easy for them to vote for politicians who continue to raise taxes on the so-called "rich." In fact, in the USA as well as France, journalists and politicians confuse high-earners with the rich. Being rich is having assets that substantially exceed liabilities – what accountants call "net worth" or "net assets." For years, journalists described Donald Trump as a "billionaire" because they saw his assets, but it turned out that his liabilities were at least as large as his assets. *A fortiori,* someone can be a high earner of income from personal services and have little or no net worth after paying his taxes and living expenses. In France, the really rich, *i.e.,* those with high net assets, generally pay less income taxes than do executives and professional whose only "wealth" is their brain and their time. This used to be true also of the USA in the days of tax shelters and I suspect is still largely true.

After this aside, let me turn to another aspect of the USA that came as a surprise to me when a friend sent me Philip Howard's book called *The Death of Common Sense*. As I've lived in France for such a long time, I had not been aware of the extent to which my homeland had attained rigidity in the making of laws and regulations that produces silly and wasteful results. It is, if you will, the rule of law reduced to absurdity. Howard cites many examples, such as that of some nuns who started to renovate a four-story slum building only to be denied a building permit since they had not planned for an elevator, an item which would be too costly for this program and not really necessary. In this municipality, the regulation provided no leeway for a waiver of the elevator requirement, so this worth-while project had to be abandoned. An even more shocking illustration was that of a city which implemented the state's requirement that each child should have an education appropriate to his need, by spending $90,000 to send a mentally-retarded child to a specialized educator in Japan, just so that his IQ could be raised, say, from 70 to 75. In terms of cost-benefit analysis this expenditure is absurd, but the school board considered that the law required it.

If Philip Howard's book is a fair representation of what is happening in the USA, then it is indeed a frightening development – the rule-of-law gone berserk. Curiously, it bespeaks a kind of American Cartesianism, in the sense that *a priori* rules are promulgated which are intended to cover all situations, and therefore leave no room for discretion and judgment. It strikes me that one explanation is the desire of bureaucrats to avoid taking responsibility for individualized decisions; hence they make generalized rules which simply can not fit every case and still be just or sensible. I would be interested in hearing from readers as to what they make of this phenomenon and its causes. At any rate, my French readers should be relieved that I have found a different target for my criticisms!

Vol. XIX, N° 2, April 1997

April in *ENArchie*

The good news is that Spring has come to Paris and to all of *ENArchie*, the land of the *ENArques,* otherwise known as the Republic of France. And Spring does more than *ENArques* can to justify high taxes to man. The bad news is that nothing is being done to reduce unemployment, political and financial scandals abound, strikes continue and Jean-Marie Le Pen is gaining ground as a consequence.

I wish I had something new and exciting to report about France and Europe, but that is not the case. The casts change but the caste remains and, with it, unrest. This month it's the French interns and allied medical professionals who are on the warpath, blocking trains and roads and appearing everywhere unexpectedly like Indian, oops, Native American, raiders, dressed in white frocks. Their grievance? They have discovered that the Medicare system's drive to reduce costs includes a collective financial penalty whenever over-all medical prescriptions exceed budget. Already, newly-minted French doctors have little economic future, but the new measures will make them even more dependent on technocratic whims. Another striking category is the workforce of the once-independent airline, Air Inter, since taken over by Air France when it acquired its only long-distance rival, UTA. The pilots of Air Inter are paid better than those of Air France. Indeed, I am told, they are the best paid in the whole world. Air France, being owned by the unfortunate taxpayers of France whose ownership is disguised under the euphemism of *l'Etat*, has been losing tons of money for years, as it has been operated for the benefit of its employees rather than for its owners or customers. The personnel of Air Inter do not want to lose their privileges once they are merged fully into Air France. Thus, frequent strikes are the lot of its unhappy passengers, who are taking trains and rival airlines with increasing gusto.

The victory of the National Front's candidate in the mayoralty contest of Vitrolles, near Marseille, stunned the other political parties, particularly after the victor, Catherine Megret, who was fronting for her husband Bruno – disqualified because of a prior election irregularity – gave an interview to a German newspaper, which abounded in derogatory views on immigrants. Megret is Le Pen's leading henchman, and a likely successor to the charismatic leader of the *Front National.* Significantly, Le Pen stayed out of the Vitrolles campaign, so that Catherine and Bruno could project a more innocuous image. The polls purport to show that the Front does not have more than 15-percent support among the national population. But I am skeptical about this figure: polls are taken by telephone, and many people are unlikely to disclose sympathy for the *Front National* while talking to a stranger. I suspect that the Front will get more than 20 percent in the next legislative elections, as most people seem disgusted with the meaningless choice between the current majority and the Socialists who contributed so mightily to France's sorry economic plight. Although the elections are slated for next year, when the current five-year term of the National Assembly expires, President Chirac has the right to dissolve this body earlier, and rumors are out that he may do so this year. I suspect that Prime Minister Juppé is pushing for an early election since that would mean that he remains Prime Minister for the campaign, whereas some knowledgeable observers are predicting that Chirac will name a new head of government in May, in order for a new team to lead the legislative battle. This being said, let us not forget the old saying, "*Plus ça change, plus c'est la même chose.*"

With immigration a constant issue, the government came up with yet another amendment to the immigration law, which led to a big howl during the month of March. This turned on the so-called *"certificat d'hébergement,"* the invention of the Socialist government in 1982. This may be translated as a "dwelling certificate," a document signed by the host of an alien seeking a temporary visa to enter the country and then approved by the local Mayor. Of course, visitors from the European Union and other friendly powers, such as the USA, do not need a visa for a visit of up to three months. However, citizens of most African and Asian countries, which are richer sources for illegal aliens, do need such a visa and thus have to find a person willing to house them during their stay in France. The controversial amendment merely would have grafted onto the current regulation an additional requirement that the host inform City Hall when the foreign visitor leaves his home. This hardly seems a fighting issue, but a hundred cinema types called a press conference to protest the measure, announcing that they would engage in "civil disobedience" if the measure became law. At first, these protesters seemed courageous, conjuring up images of Thoreau, Gandhi and Martin Luther King, until one learned that the law provided no criminal penalties for not so notifying the authorities, the only sanction being a two-year prohibition of giving more certificates.

Soon, the issue took off and become a front-page item, with petitions and demonstrations all over France, including from members of the Bar. To have fun, I faxed two lawyers who had been imploring me to join the movement and asked them for a copy of the proposed law. Neither had the text! In France you don't need to know the facts to have an opinion; facts are for people who are not smart enough to have ready-made opinions. The main objection voiced against the notification requirement was that it would constitute *"délation,"* a dirty word in France signifying "snitching." When I would ask friends what was so objectionable about having to report the departure of a visitor to whom the government has granted the favor of allowing entry into the country, the universal answer was that "I am not going to do the work of the police." When I would ask the friend, "If you saw someone committing a burglary in a neighbor's house, wouldn't you call the police?," the answer was generally the same. Faced with the uproar created by the intellectuals and the Left, the government caved in and the proposed law was modified to eliminate the offending provision. Now the *certificat d'hébergement* will be issued by the *préfecture,* rather than the City Hall, and the alien himself is supposed to turn in the stub when (and if) he leaves the country. A tempest in a teapot, in the best French tradition, because the proposed law would have done nothing to reduce illegal immigration, its only purpose having been to steal the thunder of the *Front National.*

Le Pen's party held its national convention in Strasbourg at the end of March and this aroused a lot of protest movements. When I heard that Le Pen had called for a Sixth Republic, this drew from me a wan smile. Fifteen years ago, after Mitterrand had been in office several months, I gathered together one evening a number of French friends and tried to get them to begin a movement which would combat the socialization of France. My objective was simply to be a catalyst since, as a foreigner, I could not get involved in French politics. In my invitation to them, I pointed out that France had become a "republic of functionaries" and that it was abnormal that functionaries could hold political office without losing their civil-service status. After a number of meetings, the group came to realize that the Fifth Republic's constitution needed radical change, and that a Sixth Republic was necessary. The group was a highly sophisticated one, including executives of multinationals, doctors and lawyers, some of whom had studied in the USA, yet they were too close to the French scene to notice what was fundamentally wrong with their nation's political institutions. At one point I tried to get them to set up a permanent organization with at least one full-time employee to provide daily continuity for recruitment of members and diffusion of information. I knew the task was hopeless when one member innocently chirped forth, "I know just the right person for the job, he's an *ENArque.*" The movement soon died out, while everything I predicted has taken place, and now it is Le Pen who is calling for a Sixth Republic!

I have already expressed my unhappiness over the fact that there is no valid opposition in France to the political parties controlled by the *ENArques.* Le Pen is simply too stupid to realize that his real opportunity was to be an alternative to the rule of the functionaries. Instead, he has targeted immigrants as the enemy, and allowed some of his backers to cater to the anti-Semites who are found in every society. Neither Jews nor immigrants are to blame for France's economic plight. Indeed, it was the immigration of a million *pieds noirs* from North Africa, many of whom are Jews, which gave France a much-needed economic shot in the arm during the '60s. And immigrants from all climes have provided the manpower for French factories and construction sites, as well as for all the menial tasks, including night-work, that the "pure" French do not want to perform. The real enemy of France is the functionary caste which has grabbed the economic and political levers of the country and created a welfare state on which it feeds. One cannot say often enough that the main beneficiaries of the welfare state are not those who are receiving welfare but rather those who are handing it out. Handouts require bureaucrats to do the handing out and once they are ensconced in their lifetime jobs in France, there is no way short of revolution to dislodge them. In the meantime, the country becomes poorer as the economy stagnates and the most dynamic elements of the populace emigrate to more congenial places. Every new government that comes to power in France thinks up new forms of handouts, and the same phenomenon is taking place in Brussels, for the European Union. The agricultural subsidies alone are colossal and replete with fraud, but those whose jobs depend on handouts have no incentive to reduce the funds that pass through their hands, since economies might cost them their jobs. Most French and German taxpayers seem unaware that much of their taxes are siphoned off by Brussels bureaucrats who keep thinking up ways to distribute the money to poorer countries, such as Ireland, Greece and Portugal, and even to fund projects in France and Germany which hardly need the intervention of Brussels.

To return to Le Pen, his rabble-rousing has provided Chirac a convenient excuse to pose as a defender of liberty and opponent of racism, with the intention of diverting the people's attention from the real problems of France. Le Pen also provides a useful diversion from the scandals which are at the heart of French politics. Several judges are continuing to investigate the illegal campaign contributions and bribes solicited by Chirac's supporters, including the *femme fatale*, Louise-Yvonne Cassetta, who is alleged to have handled a lot of cash in the last presidential election. If she ever spills the beans, this could be a fatal blow to Chirac himself.

Another scandal that has not gone away, but rather grown, is the revelation that President Mitterrand had personally authorized the illegal wiretaps that were performed by "officials" working in the Elysée Palace during his term. Documents were discovered in the garage of a former *gendarme* working for Mitterrand, Major Christian Prouteau, which show that Mitterrand personally read these illegal wiretap reports and annotated them in his own hand! Despite this, the Juppé government has refused to lift the absurd "*secret défense*" ban on releasing information in the possession of the Ministry of Defense, to which the *gendarmerie* belongs. The prior government, led by Edouard Balladur, had also asserted this ban. It is clear to everyone that Mitterrand's wiretaps did not have a defense motive, because existing law provided a basis for legal wiretaps. Rather, Mitterrand was spying on political opponents, including Jean-Edern Hallier, the late gadfly writer, who had learned of Mazarine, the President's daughter born out of wedlock, and was preparing a book on this and other secrets of Mitterrand, including his far-Right origins. It is incredible, in a country which purports to have an independent judiciary and to abide by the rule of law, that public officials can hide behind a spurious "defense secret" label and no judge can force them to give testimony or turn over papers. No government wants to change this abusive rule because it provides the ultimate protection for officials engaging in illegal acts, as when Charles Pasqua, while Minister of the Interior, issued a phony passport to a Socialist functionary, allowing him to escape to Brazil after embezzling public money. Pasqua got away with this outrage, as did the officials who, during Giscard's reign, planted a bug in the office of *Le Canard Enchaîné*. One consequence of this stonewalling by the Chirac regime is that no one believes that illegal wiretaps have stopped.

It will be recalled that even when Chirac was in the opposition, he never took up cudgels against the Socialists on the issue of corruption. And despite all the revelations about Mitterrand, including wire-tapping, Chirac ordered a High Mass for his deceased predecessor in the cathedral of Notre Dame, a ceremony that, as some Protestants and Jews pointed out, was not called for in a Republic that professes secularity. And now, if Chirac continues to protect the memory of Mitterrand, this is not out of tenderness for a scoundrel but because he wants to establish the precedent that the President is above the law and untouchable, a precedent whose first beneficiary will be Chirac himself. And he really needs it.

To make matters worse, the press is hobbled by economic weakness and laws which make it difficult to publish the truth about leaders and institutions. Recently, *Le Monde* was found guilty of defamation of the King of Morocco, under a horrendous provision of the 1881 Press Law which makes it a misdemeanor to "offend" a foreign head of state. It is well known that Morocco has an autocratic regime, where it is impossible for the press to criticize the King. If France lends its hand to such a regime by inhibiting criticism, then what became of the "rights of man" which France claims to have invented? The other day, a French lawyer defended the law to me by making the distinction between criticizing and insulting the foreign leader. But one man's criticism is another man's insult. If I call Bill Clinton a liar, a cheat and a lecher, I cannot be prosecuted by the government of the USA, but the French courts could brand me a criminal.

Thank God I've always considered Clinton to be a saint, an honest man, and a faithful husband! And, come to think of it, Saddam Hussein isn't such a bad guy, after all.

Vol. XIX, N° 3, May 1997

Surrealism in May

My recollection is that surrealism was a French invention and it is not surprising that it has finally caught on in the political arena, judging by the current election campaign triggered by President Chirac's surprise decision to dissolve the National Assembly. Of course, this was not a surprise to my readers, since I alluded to the possibility in my April issue, based on rumors which struck my Armenian nose as being plausible. That the French President has the power under the Constitution to dissolve the lower legislative chamber any time after it has been in office a year is already a demonstration of the monarchical nature of this regime created by and for de Gaulle, yet suiting all the monarchs who have succeeded him. But for the monarch to utilize this power for crass political advantage is something that he can not acknowledge. So all his art, and this is where the surrealism comes in, is deployed to explain why it was in the interest of the country to hold elections now rather than in March of next year when the National Assembly's five-year term would have expired. Chirac found a magic word to explain the early elections: *élan*. Of course, this had to be a not easily translatable word: if the idea could readily be expressed in other languages, where then would French genius lie?

In order to explain to my worthy readers what *élan* means in French, I turned to my Roberts & Collins *French-English Dictionary*. I first found that in zoology *élan* means an elk or a moose, but I felt sure that this was not what Chirac was seeking. Then the book went on to say that in a race it means the "run-up," that is, a good start. But this is hardly what Chirac could admit. The dictionary went on to give another definition: "momentum." This seemed to be getting nearer to the idea. Further on, the dictionary added "vigor" and "a boost" as possible definitions.

So now you are getting the point. Chirac called for new legislative elections to give a boost, to add vigor, if you will, to the country. Of course, some commentators immediately pointed out that Chirac's supporters in the National Assembly – principally, his party, the RPR, and his allies, who trade as the UDF – comprise 80 percent of that body's members. As it is absolutely clear that both these parties will lose a substantial number of their seats in the Assembly, it is hard to see how a reduced majority, if he gets one at all, can possibly give vigor or a boost to Chirac's program for this unhappy nation. The real reason for the dissolution is one that Chirac can not admit, to wit, that if he waited until next year, he was sure to lose his majority in the Parliament. By holding the election now he at least has a fighting chance to keep a majority, albeit a much reduced one. This is not *élan*, it is survival.

The reason why Chirac thinks he has a better chance now of getting a majority in the National Assembly is simply that he has taken the opposition by surprise, thus depriving them of valuable months in which to prepare their programs, select candidates and, above all, raise money for the campaigns. Chirac's own party, the RPR, never lacks for money. And he appears to have been preparing this surprise since several months, in great secrecy, so that his trusted henchmen have had the time to prepare. No sooner was the deed announced than all the "notables" of the regime were out touting the party line, to wit, the need for a new *élan* and the advantage of giving the new legislature a five-year slate to accomplish its mission. These "tenors," as they are also called, included Alain Madelin, the so-called "*libéral*" who was fired as Minister of Finance in 1995, after only a few months in office, for daring to suggest that France had too many *fonctionnaires.* It is obvious that Madelin believes the press reports that he's a possible Prime Minister if Chirac does not keep Alain Juppé. Other party-liners include Edouard Balladur, the defeated Presidential candidate, and his right-hand man, Nicolas Sarkozy, as well as François Léotard, head of the UDF, who would love to become Prime Minister, too, but would settle for one of the better ministries, such as Finance, Defense or Foreign Affairs.

Trial balloons have been released suggesting that Chirac might name a non-politician to be Prime Minister, in particular Jacques Calvet, president of Peugeot S.A. or Jérôme Monod, head of the powerful Compagnie Lyonnaise des Eaux, which has just merged with the financial house Compagnie Financière de Suez. A neophyte to the French scene might assume that a French businessman might bring fresh ideas to the political arena, but surely my faithful readers have guessed already that both Calvet and Monod are *ENArques*, who got their jobs in so-called "industry" by being dutiful functionaries and laboring in ministerial cabinets. Monod, indeed, was once secretary-general of Chirac's RPR party. While Juppé, playing coy, stated on television that he was not a "candidate" to succeed himself, everyone understood that these words, when decoded, simply mean that if Chirac re-appointed him he would do his patriotic duty and accept. The conventional wisdom opines that if the "Right" gets a substantial majority in the National Assembly, Juppé will be rewarded with another term as Prime Minister. Lending support to this view is Juppé's announcement that if the present majority won the elections, the new government would do wonders in the first 40 days. Journalists are so blasé nowadays that no one asked him why, if he could do wonders in 40 days, he simply did not do them now, with his 80-percent majority in the National Assembly, instead of waiting for a reduced majority to do them.

Juppé, remaining Prime Minister and head of the RPR, obviously had to play a central role in the campaign, thus adding to its surrealism, since his poll ratings are still devastatingly bad. Despite this, the initial polls after Chirac's announcement paradoxically showed a large majority for the RPR-UDF coalition. This could mean only one or two things: either the French voting population is hopelessly conventional or the memory of the disastrous reign of the Socialists under Mitterrand is so keen that Chirac's band seems the lesser evil. Later polls show the gap narrowing between the two main camps, the Left one comprising not only the Socialists but also the Communist Party (the only European party to keep that historic name) and the Ecologists. It will be recalled that French elections are two-round affairs: in the first round a majority of votes properly cast is required for election. In the second, a plurality suffices, but generally only two candidates remain, the others either being disqualified if they did not obtain 12.5 percent in the first round or withdrawing in favor of a stronger candidate. The National Front, despite poll ratings in the 15-percent range, is unlikely to win more than a few seats, since the other parties generally gang up on it in the second round, even to the point of the RPR or UDF candidate withdrawing in favor of the Socialist when the latter is leading, and vice-versa. Because of the so-called Rightist parties' unwillingness to support his party in run-offs, Jean-Marie Le Pen made a speech which seemed to indicate that he would urge his supporters to vote Socialist in the second round, as he abhors Chirac more than he does his Socialist rival, Lionel Jospin. However, Le Pen's two main henchmen backed away from this position.

The election campaign for the first round has been greeted with apathy by most French citizens. The polls show that a large number voters are likely to stay away from the ballot boxes on May 25th and June 1st, the two successive Sundays when these surrealistic elections will take place. Chirac's strategy thus far seems to have been a smart one, since the Socialists appear lack-luster, with the same old faces spouting the same old tunes. The alliance with the Communists is an embarrassment to Jospin since they are opposed to the Maastricht Treaty and the single currency. The Socialist proposals to fight unemployment among the youth have as their main props: 1) the creation of 700,000 jobs, half for the civil service and half for the private sector, the latter by shifting unspecified subsidies, and 2) the reduction of the work-week to 35 hours, without lowering pay, which will supposedly force employers to hire new workers to make up for lost production. As any employer knows, this is arrant nonsense. If employees are to earn the same pay for fewer hours, their bosses will simply require more productivity from the same people, adding more equipment if necessary. It never ceases to amaze me that while French Socialists take as their major premise that labor creates wealth, they nevertheless conclude that by working less a nation can become richer.

This is as good an occasion as any to pay tribute to my old friend Montesquieu in whose *L'Esprit des Lois,* one can read in a little-known chapter words to this effect: "A man is not poor because he has nothing but because he does not work." This was written a century before Karl Marx wore out the seat of his pants in the British Museum. To be sure, Marx, properly indignant at the way many English workers were treated in the Industrial Revolution, added a gloss: "Even a working man remains poor if his employer apprehends most of the fruit of his labor." He made a religion out of the idea that the "surplus value" of production belonged only to labor, who would become their own employers through communism. In practice, while western countries gave labor increasingly larger shares of their own production, communism merely substituted a privileged class of nomenclatura who benefited from this "surplus value." Finally, these workers stopped doing any productive work because they were getting nothing valuable in exchange. This was pungently put by the Poles: "We pretend to work and they pretend to pay us." Now, in Western welfare states like France, with millions unemployed in the private sector (bureaucrats are never laid off), the motto of many is "We do no work but they pay us anyway." In barely two centuries of the Industrial Revolution we have evolved from a situation where the masses were exploited by a few to one where a relatively few highly productive people are being exploited by a huge bureaucracy and its constituency of welfare beneficiaries of various sorts.

Some of my Left-leaning friends are fond of repeating the old saw that "the French Right is the most stupid one in the world." I would agree if for no other reason than that the Right does not say often enough that "the French Left is the most stupid one in the world." In fact, the most stupid of all are those who fail to grasp that in France "Right" and "Left" amount basically to the same thing.

Chirac and Juppé, being the chief priests of the French bureaucracy, obviously will not dismantle the system which they and their fellow *ENArques* are committed to making the model for the European Union. While the Socialists have the frankness to admit they have no solution for unemployment other than to create more bureaucrats, Chirac's crowd does not even purport to explain how it will fight this blight. Presumably this is one of the secrets that will be unveiled during the magic 40 days following June 1st. Paradoxically, this being France, it is just possible that if Chirac's supporters gain a slim majority in Parliament, the new government might accomplish more than they could with a large majority. As a precedent, I am thinking of the 1967 legislative elections, when de Gaulle was still President, and his party barely kept control of the National Assembly. Georges Pompidou, renamed Prime Minister, obtained from the Parliament the exceptional short-term power permitted by the Constitution to legislate by decrees, called *Ordonnances.* The result was a remarkable crop of innovative measures that have stood the test of time, including employee profit-sharing in private companies, the creation of the French SEC, named the "Commission des Opérations de Bourse," and the institution of a flexible legal form for joint ventures, called the *groupement d'intérêt économique* (GIE). The mere fact that I evoke this glorious precedent demonstrates that I'm an incurable optimist. Most people would dismiss this possibility by saying that Juppé is no Pompidou, just as Chirac is no de Gaulle, and go back to sleep.

It is no wonder that most people are yawning in May, a practice aided and abetted by the prevalence of holidays in this magical month. May 1st was Labor Day, and coming on Thursday allowed many enterprises to *faire le pont* (literally, "make the bridge" to Saturday and a four-day weekend). Most French people are unaware that on May Day they are honoring the valiant American workers who were clobbered in the Chicago Haymarket Massacre of 1886. It is indeed touching to see so many French people give up a nice working day just to honor the American labor movement. As if this homage does not suffice, the French bravely took off May 8th, which old-timers will recall as being V-E Day, that is, Victory in Europe in 1945. (As Ascension Day happened to fall on May 8th this year, the French were deprived of an extra holiday.) May 8th again was the occasion to "*faire le pont.*" Then another long weekend occurred when the French celebrated Whitsun Monday on May 19th. I think another May holiday should be added for the last week: why not Michael Jordan Day?

If the Socialists win a majority, this would ordinarily lead to another period of "cohabitation," as it is called here, when the President – elected for a seven-year term – hangs on to office and "grins and bears" a Prime Minister from the opposition, whom he is obliged to name. Mitterrand, a man with much pride and no shame, endured Chirac from 1986 to 1988 and Balladur from 1993 to 1995. In 1986, when I was younger and naive, I lost a bet to my late friend Franc Ricciardi by wagering that Mitterrand would resign if the Socialists lost that year's legislative election. Since that time I do not bet on any politician doing anything out of principle.

It has been assumed that Chirac would play the game of cohabitation if his party loses, naming Jospin Prime Minister and presiding grimly over the weekly cabinet meetings, as the strange Constitution of the Fifth Republic requires. However, it is possible that Chirac might resign if his majority is defeated and this would give rise to a new Presidential election within a month, in which Chirac could be a candidate but surely not the only one on the so-called Right. However, as the new President can not dissolve the National Assembly for a year, I do not know what Chirac would gain by resigning, other than the opportunity to avoid the unpleasantness of cohabitation or to give his rival Edouard Balladur the occasion to run for the Presidency once again.

For Chirac, maybe *élan* will turn out to have been a moose, after all. One thing appears certain, however: whoever wins the election France will be the loser.

Vol. XIX, N° 4, June 1997

Élan was a Moose, After All

The French electorate dealt Jacques Chirac a humiliating defeat in the parliamentary elections of May 25th and June 1st. In my May issue, I poked fun at his purely verbal excuse for this action, to wit, the need for a new *élan*, by pointing out that the first dictionary definition of *élan* is that it is an elk or moose. I concluded by suggesting that the moose is indeed what Chirac might get from these stupidly organized elections. Someone should have told Chirac the old adage: *"If you ask a silly question, you get a silly answer."*

The basic stupidity of Chirac's move stemmed from his keeping Alain Juppé as Prime Minister to lead the so-called Right into battle, while being perfectly aware that Juppé's popularity ratings have been consistently under 30 percent for the last 18 months. What *élan* could be expected from such a deservedly unpopular politician, who is a caricature of the *dirigiste*, know-it-all *ENArque*? Chirac's strategy was as convincing as that of a psychiatrist who would advise a married woman complaining of the impotence of her husband to divorce him and then remarry him, in the hopes that this would give him an *élan.* Any sensible woman would reply, *"If I'm going to divorce, I might as well get me a new husband and try* his *élan."*

According to the *Nouvel Observateur,* the bright idea to dissolve the National Assembly originated with Dominique de Villepin, an *ENArque* of course, who serves as director of Chirac's cabinet. Villepin had held the same post in Juppé's cabinet when the latter was Minister of Foreign Affairs in Balladur's government, and Juppé loaned him to his boss when Chirac became President. It is typical of the *ENArque* mind, beholden as it is to Cartesianism, to place form over substance. So clever did the scheme seem that it never occurred to this trio of *ENArques* that it might matter to the electorate who was to lead Chirac's troops into battle and with what objective. Thus, Juppé was allowed to remain as Prime Minister without any new program. The only way the dissolution ploy could have worked would have been to ally form with substance: if Chirac had first chosen a new Prime Minister and organized a new government which presented a new program, they might have gone before the electorate with a plausible story to tell. When the first round on May 25th demonstrated that the voters were skeptical that Chirac had anything valid to sell, the President saw the error of his ways and allowed Juppé to announce that he would not remain Prime Minister no matter who won. But this was not enough to turn the tide. Chirac allowed a wishy-washy tandem of Philippe Séguin and Alain Madelin to appear as the leaders of the new government without, however, any program other than vague assurances that they were a better alternative to the Socialists. The latter, with a designated leader in the person of Lionel Jospin and some specific promises as to how to attack unemployment, to wit, creating public-sector jobs and reducing the work-week, appeared more credible to a sizable segment of the population.

Despite this, the Socialists did not obtain an absolute majority in the Assembly and require the votes of the Communists and the Ecologists to be sure of control of the lower house. (The Senate, relatively powerless, remains in the control of the RPR/UDF coalition.) Most significantly, without the help of the *Front National* (FN), the Socialists might have lost the election since, by staying on the second ballot, Le Pen's party caused the defeat of 46 candidates of the RPR/UDF coalition backing Chirac. If these seats had gone to the coalition candidates the outcome would have been different. The strange nature of French elections is seen in the statistic that with 15 percent of the votes, the FN garnered only one seat in the National Assembly, whereas with only ten percent, the Communist Party won 38 seats, and the Ecologists with four percent got eight seats. This disparity can only enhance the bitterness of the supporters of the FN, who feel increasingly alienated from the mainstream of French public life. If you listened to the crowing of the Socialists and the moaning of the losers, it was easy to forget that the Left garnered only 40 percent of the popular vote in the first round and the Right, including the FN, represented 60 percent. Respectable commentators, including Jean d'Ormesson, a regular contributor to *Le Figaro*, openly question the wisdom of the RPR/UDF's refusal to make alliances with the *Front National,* whereas the Socialists do not hesitate to ally themselves with the only Western party that still calls itself Communist.

In the week following the ignominious defeat of Chirac's scheme, the jokesters were having a good time pointing out that the President's main accomplishment so far has been to rebuild the Socialist Party, considered moribund after its disastrous defeat in 1993 and, until a month ago, showing no signs of returning to life. As a corollary, others snickered that Chirac did not so much dissolve the Assembly as dissolve the Right. Sure enough, starting on the Monday following the second round, calls were heard for Juppé's resignation as head of the RPR, and Philippe Séguin openly posed his candidacy to succeed Juppé, with the support of Charles Pasqua, once a stalwart Chiraquien, and Nicolas Sarkozy, Edouard Balladur's leading henchman. Juppé tried to hang on for dear life, while seeking to mobilize the party's machinery, but after a few days he succumbed and announced that he will not continue as head of the RPR. Thus, Séguin, the mayor of Epinal and outgoing president of the National Assembly, an *ENArque* and statist, to be sure, who opposed the Maastricht Treaty, will take over the RPR, bringing him one step closer to realizing his ambition of succeeding Chirac as the King of France. As to the UDF, François Léotard, who had shown too much enthusiasm for the dissolution ploy, yielded his presidency to François Bayrou, and offered the presidency of the *Républicains Indépendants* to Alain Madelin, who foolishly had supported the Chirac initiative but was now threatening to start his own party. Despite the overwhelming appearance of an unintended debacle, a few French friends, with that incurable taste for rationalization, have assured me that Chirac had deliberately planned it this way, so that the Socialists would inherit the impossible task of dealing with unemployment and the euro. The rest of the analysis is, of course, that next year, when the Socialists shall have made a mess of things, Chirac will dissolve the National Assembly and his supporters will return to power.

This is a good occasion as any briefly to summarize the history of the Fifth Republic and its decadence. When de Gaulle returned to power in 1958, thanks to the Algerian civil war, he quickly proposed a new constitution, principally drafted by Michel Debré, designed to eliminate the perceived flaws of the Fourth Republic, which led to unstable governments at the mercy of an all-powerful parliament dominated by political parties, none of whom could command a majority alone. In the Fourth Republic, as in the Third, the President was merely a ceremonial figure whose role, as de Gaulle sneeringly remarked, was to "inaugurate chrysanthemums." De Gaulle's constitution made the executive branch all-powerful, albeit two-headed. To suit the great man's penchant for avoiding the nitty-gritty of administration, his charter provided for both a President and a Prime Minister, but gave the President an array of powers that made him the head executive. Not only did he name the Prime Minister and other high officials but also he played the key role in foreign affairs and defense, the former by virtue of the power "to negotiate and ratify treaties" and the latter as "chief of the armies." Moreover, the President was granted the authority to dissolve the National Assembly at any time after it had been in office for a year. As to the government, led by the Prime Minister, the constitution specified that it "determines and conducts the policy of the nation." It could also legislate in certain domains by decree and, on top of that, it basically controlled the agenda of the parliament, which ended up with little initiative in making laws not desired by the executive. Article 49(3) of the constitution bestowed an incredibly powerful weapon on the government: when this provision is invoked, any government bill is automatically enacted unless the parliament votes to censure the government, which would require the government to resign. As this would lead to a major crisis, and doubtless bring on the dissolution of the National Assembly, Article 49(3) has been devastatingly effective in making the parliament subservient to the government. As added protection of the government against parliamentary encroachment, de Gaulle's constitution even introduced a constitutional court that could nullify laws that invaded the powers of the government, whereas the Council had no comparable power in the reverse case.

The crowning measure that ensured the hegemony of the President came in 1962 when de Gaulle pushed through a constitutional amendment by referendum to allow the election of the President by popular vote, whereas in the original version he was selected by a few-thousand elected officials. This amendment was bitterly opposed by all parties except de Gaulle's own, and was even decried as unconstitutional by most scholars. Yet the people voted for it and, once adopted, the amendment made the President an all-powerful figure who was said to be "legitimated" by popular will. Interestingly enough, one power that the President did not possess under the constitution was that of removing the Prime Minister, but he soon acquired this in practice whenever the two officials belonged to the same party. Debré, de Gaulle's first Prime Minister, as arrogant and as unpopular as Juppé, dutifully resigned when de Gaulle requested it, without being reversed by the parliament. Another pernicious practice soon arose which made a mockery of the constitutional provision to the effect that the government "determines and conducts the policy of the nation." Beginning, particularly, during Pompidou's presidency, the Elysée Palace came to accumulate counselors who, in effect, became a second government, seeking to make policy in place of the Prime Minister. The crucial test of this rivalry occurred when Pompidou's first Prime Minister, Jacques Chaban-Delmas, one of the Gaullist "barons" who had served with the Free French during the World War II, took seriously his constitutional mandate and announced a vast program, concocted by his chief adviser Jacques Delors, under the heading *Nouvelle Société*. This initiative incurred the wrath of Pompidou's brain trust, led by Marie-France Garaud and Pierre Juillet, who did their best to undermine the authority of the Prime Minister. Chaban, a veteran politician, thought he could remain in office by seeking a confidence vote from the National Assembly, which he easily obtained. But this did not afford him immunity from the President's *de facto* power and he dutifully resigned a few weeks later. Gaullism was effectively buried when Pompidou died in 1974 and Chirac betrayed his party's candidate for President, Chaban-Delmas, supporting instead his fellow *ENArque*, Giscard d'Estaing. Two years later, Chirac took over the party, renamed it *Rassemblement pour la République,* and the RPR became his personal vehicle for seeking the presidency.

Since Chaban's time, Prime Ministers who are of the same party as the President invariably bow to his wishes and resign when requested. The absurdity of this practice which, I repeat, has no constitutional basis, is highlighted when, as now, the two are from different parties. Why should the two situations be handled differently? The Fifth Republic is a bastard monarchy: when the President's party and allies control the parliament, the President is an absolute monarch; when the opposition controls the parliament he is a constitutional monarch. It is little wonder that the French people seem to appreciate cohabitation! But in both cases, the parliament is a rubber stamp, either for the President or for the Prime Minister. Only the French could have invented such a system.

The other principal characteristic of the Fifth Republic is, as we have seen, the domination of the functionary class, led by the *ENArques* who migrate at will from the civil service to the political-elective sphere. It is no accident that the founder of the ENA is none other than the author of the constitution, Michel Debré, who, despite his good intentions, must be rated as one of the most pernicious French leaders of the last half-century. And it would be bad enough that the functionary class wields vast powers under a monarch, but it is much worse when one of them actually becomes the monarch, as with Giscard and Chirac, and perhaps one day soon, Jospin or Séguin. I laughed when I read that Juppé, an *ENArque* himself, professed a few weeks ago to want to abolish the ENA and replace it "by something else." The joke is that the ENA is not really a school; it is an excuse for the selection process by which elite functionaries are chosen. The selection is the message, not the school. Thus, the school could be eliminated altogether since it teaches nothing, but the selection process would still produce the same type of functionary. This process eliminates those who have not mastered the Cartesian canon and selects those who have. It must be borne in mind that *ENArques* are the species and Cartesians the *genus.* The principal prep school for the ENA is Sciences Po. I have often spoken with graduates of this school and they all admit that what they learn there is only to express themselves as dutiful Cartesians, dividing all discourse into two parts. In other words, they develop the gifts of gab and oversimplification. This explains why an *ENArque* is never at a loss for words and glib solutions. The oral exam of the ENA ensures that no one who stutters ever becomes a high functionary in France, no matter how bright he is.

The new Jospin government is, to be sure, heavily populated by *ENArques*, including Jospin himself and several of his key ministers, such as Martine Aubry, Elisabeth Guigou, Jean-Pierre Chevènement, Alain Richard and Hubert Védrine, who occupy the chairs of Labor, Justice, Interior, Defense and Foreign Affairs, respectively. And their cabinets are full of *ENArques*, some of them having done a tour as members of the Brussels bureaucracy. This government is immediately confronted with the need to deal with its campaign promises, notably, the 35-hour work week, with no reduction in pay, and the creation of 700,000 public-sector jobs. These proposals run smack into the top EU priority which is the single currency, slated to become effective barely a year and a half from now, on January 1, 1999. Every day, virtually every hour, one hears of the most famous Maastricht criterion for going ahead with the euro, the limit of national budget deficit at three percent of the gross domestic product. It must be recalled that the true priority, the sole policy, of the first two years of Chirac's reign was to do everything possible to meet the Maastricht criteria And "everything possible" included playing with the accounts. Even that supposed purist, Helmut Kohl, tried to "cook the books" by re-valuing Germany's gold reserves, but got shot down by the head of the Bundesbank. The Socialists had promised to do an "audit" of France's finances as soon as they took office. *Le Canard Enchaîné* reported that the preliminary results of this inquiry are disastrous, the deficit being more than three percent, because of diminished tax receipts owing to a sluggish economy. Jospin attended an EU meeting in the first part of June and announced that he wanted the so-called "stability pact" to take into account France's concerns about *le social,* which are magic words in France. I consider it both sad and laughable that French politicians claim that they have found a "third way" of organizing society, which is neither capitalism nor socialism. The key to this imagined way is to pretend that what is merely "economic" is crass and immoral but if you baptize something as being *social*, then it is good and immutable.

Virtually the entire political class refuses to admit that the astronomic level of taxation, including social-security charges – amounting to 45 percent of the GNP – has something to do with high unemployment or the bankruptcy of thousands of small business enterprises or the flight of capital and brains Who but the children of Rousseau and Descartes could believe that *le social* can be divorced from *l'economique.* When I tell my French friends, even my own family, that the USA has achieved essentially full employment while stemming inflation, the glib response is invariably "Yes, but they are *emplois précaires,"* that is, not long-term jobs. My 18-year-old grandson – the same one who at 15 told me that "the Métro should be free" – gave me this line, which he had learned from the economics teacher in his *lycée*. When I pointed out to David that in the private sector all employment is necessarily *précaire,* in the sense that if the enterprise falters or fails, no one can be assured of a life-time job, he replied that he could not tell his teacher that, lest he fail the course! To be sure, his teacher is a *fonctionnaire* with a lifetime job, and it is wonderful to note that 30 percent of the members of the National Assembly are teachers. Thus, French youth, just like their parents, are constantly brainwashed with the party line that the American model is not one to be followed and that only a "French solution" can possibly work. As I pointed out in my French version of "Montaigne and Descartes," the Cartesians prefer a French falsehood to a foreign truth and, I would add, they prefer a French malady to a foreign cure. The latter observation was confirmed at the time of the contaminated-blood scandal when the French functionaries continued to sell blood which they knew to be tainted rather than to use the purifying system invented by an American laboratory. Better a thousand dead French hemophiliacs than to suffer the humiliation of being saved by *les Américains.* This is, of course, the mentality of the French élite, an in-group that has even organized a confidential club called *"Le Siècle,"* which meets over dinner once a month and unites everyone that counts in government, civil service, business, the press and academia. Meanwhile, the common people of France are continuing to eat Big Macs (there are now 570 McDonald's in France – count on 1,000 by the year 2000!) and watching American TV re-runs by the hundreds. Colombo has appeared so often on French TV that many viewers doubtless consider Peter Falk to be a native French speaker.

To summarize, the Fifth Republic was made by and for de Gaulle, and never should have survived him, but for the people's nostalgia for monarchy, the entrenched caste of functionaries and that most powerful of human forces, inertia. With such a model, is it any wonder that the European Union is a dictatorship of the national executives, united in the council of ministers, while a bunch of supernumeraries from each country accept money and prestige to make believe that they constitute a European parliament?

To return to Lionel Jospin, a few words are in order to introduce him to my readers. Although a Protestant, he benefits from the rule in this Catholic country that no politician is ever finished until he is buried or cremated. In the early years of Mitterrand's reign, Jospin was First Secretary of the Socialist Party and seemed to prefer that role to that of minister, but he finally became Minister of Education, a hopeless task in that monstrous bureaucracy dominated by unions, where nothing but cosmetic reforms ever get accomplished. Jospin managed to keep his image of "Mr. Pure" despite the scandals that shook the Socialist Party when it was revealed that the party had set up dummy companies to shake-down contractors for money. Jospin, like others who served Mitterrand faithfully, including Pierre Bérégovoy, never became part of the President's inner circle made up of sybaritic sycophants with whom he liked to wine and dine. The reason, of course, is that the Calvinist Jospin is not much fun to be with, at least not if you're a Mitterrand. Ironically, four years ago Jospin considered that his political career was finished when he was defeated in the legislative elections that resulted in a landslide for the Right. He decided to return to the diplomatic corps, in which he had started his career after graduating from the ENA, and humbly asked Juppé, then Foreign Minister, for an ambassadorship to Poland. As the arrogant Juppé ignored his request, it must have been particularly pleasing for Jospin to replace him as Prime Minister. What revived Jospin's career was the 1995 presidential election. Jacques Delors, just retired from the European Commission, was the great white hope of the Socialists to run against Edouard Balladur and Jacques Chirac. When Delors unexpectedly declined to be a candidate, the Socialists were desperate to find a sacrificial lamb to represent them in what appeared to be a shoo-in for the Right. Jospin and Henri Emmanuelli, also a former First Secretary of the party, were the only candidates and as the latter had been charged with campaign-financing violations, Jospin got the nod of his party. To everyone's amazement, including his own, he came in first in the initial round, and made a respectable showing in the final round against Chirac. This resurrection allowed him to take over the leadership of the Socialist Party, and it was Chirac's heavenly *gaffe* which gave Jospin the second most-coveted post in France.

While Jospin will have to contend with the demagogues in his party and the *provocateurs* in his coalition, including the Communists, the Ecologists and Chevènement's "Movement of Citizens," there is hope that he will awaken to economic realities. Personally, I would bless him if he dropped the euro and did something to stimulate the French economy. One Jospin measure which I approve is his insistence that ministers give up their other posts, particularly their mayor jobs. I have oft commented on the feudal habits of most leading French politicians, who occupy national office while holding local positions. The prime recent example was Juppé himself who, immediately on becoming Prime Minister in 1995, ran for mayor of Bordeaux, while also remaining president of the RPR party. Sadly, the French who oppose what they call the *cumul des mandats* do so only on the ground that the office-holder does not have enough time to do two or more jobs. They completely fail to see the ethical impropriety, that is, the conflict of interest. Already, Jospin's ministers who have obeyed his stricture, like Catherine Trautmann, who is Mayor of Strasbourg, have not resigned but simply delegated their duties. I heard one minister opine on the radio that the parliament should pass a law ensuring that if a Mayor does resign to became minister, he can regain his post automatically once he ceases to be minister, hardly a safeguard against conflicts of interest!

As I have been hard enough on French politicians, let me conclude with a broadside against the man I consider to be the biggest fool in all of Europe, Helmut Kohl. His failure to see that Europe needs a common ethic more than it needs a common currency is one of the most dangerous follies of European history. The 15 Soviet republics had a common currency, the ruble, but they did not have an ethical political system, without which there can be neither democracy nor prosperity. I hope the German people will be wise enough to boot Kohl out of office next year and, with him, the EuroFolly which is Kohl's Holy Grail.

Vol. XIX, N° 5, July 1997

On Ethics *à la Française*

Often I am tempted to call this Newsletter "The Interactive Newsletter," because of the many stimulating comments I receive from readers all over the world. Frequently these comments teach me more than I taught the reader and, at any rate, restore my faith in the therapeutic value of intellectual discourse. Sometimes I find myself on the defensive when Francophile readers abroad, particularly in the United States, take me to task for criticizing French institutions and remind me how bad things are in their own country. The implication of such comments is the logical fallacy which I assimilate to the Latin adage, so fondly used by American lawyers: *inclusio unius est exclusio alterius,* to wit, to include one is to exclude others. The fact that I criticize certain aspects of French civilization does not at all imply that France is the lone sinner, or that, for example, the USA is without flaws.

This leads me to make an effort to set forth what I consider to be a fundamental difference between the two countries in the realm of ethics. Let me preface the point with a personal anecdote from my tender adolescence in Philadelphia. We had a neighbor woman who, for reasons I need not go into, personified evil to my sensitive soul, and this troubled me immensely that a person could exist who appeared so committed to evil. Yet, one day when I was chatting with her, I was enormously relieved to discover that she at least paid lip service to honesty and fair dealing. The insight that struck me so deeply at the time was that it would be much worse if she did not know that these were the proper standards of social conduct but rather believed that she had no duty to others.

Essentially, this is the difference between immoral and amoral. In the former, the person knows what is right and, for whatever reason, transgresses; in the other, the person does not subscribe to the generally-accepted standard. It is one thing to adhere to the Ten Commandments and nevertheless commit sins from time to time; it is quite another not to believe that what you are doing is sinning. The point I wish to make in comparing French public life with that of the USA is not that there is less sin in the latter than in the former, but that the French do not recognize as sin many things that are so recognized in the USA.

The principal domain of ethical deviance has to do with conflict of interests. In the USA, the rule is well established that public officials can not have conflicting interests, whether they stem from personal assets or activities or from other public charges. To say this is not to claim that such conflicts never exist; it is merely to point out that the standard exists that proscribes such conflicts. In France, what is lacking is the standard. This is a fundamental difference.

The most glaring illustration of this French indifference to conflicts of interest is one that I have frequently mentioned: the practice of a person holding two or more public offices at the same time. Although this practice, called *cumul des mandats,* is occasionally criticized as not conducive to efficiency, it is never condemned for its real vice: ethical impropriety. I never cease to be amazed that 50-million French citizens who, year after year, see their prime ministers double as mayors, and their mayors double as members of parliament, do not see the ethical problem raised by the obvious conflict of interest in holding simultaneously national and local office, or executive and legislative office. In my essay, "Feudal France – Serial Justice," I recounted a conversation with a French lawyer *à propos* Alain Juppé's becoming Mayor of Bordeaux just after he was named Prime Minister (having been, I might add, Assistant Mayor of Paris while serving as Minister of Foreign Affairs, and in his city job having leased a city-owned apartment to his own son at a sweetheart rent). When I asked this lawyer if it did not bother her that as Prime Minister Juppé could favor the city of Bordeaux to the detriment of other cities, her reply was "The others will get their turn." This led me to formulate the insight that for the French justice consists of taking turns being unjust.

Recently, over a lunch table I succeeded in convincing my leading *ENArque* friend, a man of good will, that there was an ethical impropriety in the *cumul de mandats.* But why did he have to wait 30 years to see this? One of my French readers, a retired surgeon and an expert on Montaigne, gave me credit for opening his eyes to the ethical issue, which he hadn't seen in 45 years of adulthood. I mention these isolated cases not to boast, but merely to indicate the immense ethical vacuum in which most French intellectuals are educated.

An allied practice to the *cumul des mandats* is arguably more pernicious because of its virtual invisibility to the French public's conscience. I'm referring to the fact that civil servants are able to keep their functionary status, *i.e.,* lifetime jobs, while holding elective office, whether legislative or executive. When Valéry Giscard d'Estaing, to take an example, held office as member of parliament, mayor, minister and President of the Republic, he simply was on leave from the civil service, and later, on being defeated for re-election, retired as a civil servant with the rank of Inspecteur Général des Finances. Virtually all prominent French politicians holding elective office remain functionaries on leave. To name them is to recite an "honor roll" of French politics: Chirac, Jospin, Balladur, Fabius, Séguin, Rocard, Léotard, Aubry, Chevènement and so on. All these people, and the dozens of school teachers serving in the National Assembly, have a fallback position in the civil service. Thus their ultimate loyalty is to the functionary class. How can one, in good conscience, serve as legislator, and objectively decide on legislation dealing with the civil s"ervice, when one is still a civil servant? Yet 50-million people do not see the ethical problem staring them in the face.

And when functionaries are not holding elective office, they are often on leave in lucrative jobs in so-called private industry or in state-owned enterprises. For example, Martine Aubry held an important post in Pechiney which she got only because she was an *ENArque*. Louis Schweizer, another *ENArque*, got the top job at Renault only because he had been director of Prime Minister Fabius' cabinet. These functionaries in industry have little fear of getting fired, for when they screw-up they can simply return to the civil service, or to the cabinet of a minister. No matter how bad a job they do, they always land on their feet. Thus, Jean-Yves Haberer, the *ENArque* who consummated the ruin of the Crédit Lyonnais – its total losses are likely to reach $30-billion (Yes, I said "billion"!) – was named by fellow *ENArque* Edouard Balladur to head another state-controlled bank, the Crédit National. (Atypically, he was fired several months later when the Crédit Lyonnais stink became too strong, although he had done nothing wrong in his new job. Yet, so far as I know, he still holds high rank in the civil service.)

This insensitivity to conflicts of interest in France is not limited to public life. France is one of the few countries that allow accounting firms to practice law. This custom began with the "Big Six" and was quickly imitated by many of the French accounting firms, which saw the opportunity to use their leverage as auditors to sell legal and other services. It should be obvious that an auditor has a conflict of interest in certifying accounts where one of his partners has proposed or advised on transactions contained in those accounts. I had a case several years ago when a corporate client of an accounting firm which provided the statutory auditor of the company sued that firm for defective software provided by its computer subsidiary. The statutory auditor had an obvious conflict of interest, yet he did not resign his position. In another case, a "Big-Six" firm advised a client on a major restructuring which had serious tax risks, yet it provided the statutory auditor who will have to take a position on these risks. The legal divisions of the "Big-Six" firms routinely prepare contracts and give advice on matters which necessarily present ethical problems for the auditors of the same clients. Ironically, but not surprisingly, while the "Big Six" and their French emulators are busy selling other services they frequently neglect their original function, which is auditing. In the USA and Great Britain, the Big Six and their insurers have paid hundreds of millions of dollars in damages for badly done audits. In France, too, the same causes produce the same effects. It should not come as a surprise to my readers to learn that the Crédit Lyonnais' false financial statements were certified year after year by two of the "Bix Six" accounting firms!

The French Bar and the Ministry of Justice, being part of a culture which is insensitive to conflicts of interest, have been notoriously indifferent to the ethical aspects of the obvious over-reaching of accounting firms in France. The Bar is worried about the competition, of course, but does not see the ethical breaches on which this competition is based. Just as the term *cumul des mandats* hides the ethical problem, the Paris Bar defines the issue as being one of the *périmètre du droit, i.e.,* where does accounting end and law start? This formulation overlooks the conflict of interest which occurs when the same firm audits accounts of a company and gives legal advice as to the transactions involved in these accounts. But how can one expect French Ministers of Justice to get excited about conflicts of interest in accountants when they and their colleagues in the government benefit from them on a regular basis? And how can one expect the French parliament to legislate on the subject when so many of its members are practitioners of conflicts of interest? The absence of ethics in the highest spheres of government makes it easy for conflicts of interest in civil society to go unnoticed.

Whenever I try to explain to myself the origins of this ethical blindness of the French to conflicts of interest, I invariably end up with the monarchical-feudal-Catholic traditions of this country which simply did not generate any ethical standards other than those based on respect for authority and other people's property. The Church, for centuries allied with the Monarchy, was busy controlling thought and imposing religious standards but not ethical standards applicable to civil society. There simply has been no discernible countervailing civic movement that can lead to an ethical awakening as to conflicts of interest. Certainly the centralized and monstrous Ministry of Education (recently called a "mammoth" by the newly-named and unorthodox Minister, Claude Allegre) does nothing to inculcate this type of ethical awareness on French children. Indeed, many French school-teachers have been getting their ethics from Marx and Lenin.

In the United States, if a Congressman from Arkansas were to seek to be Mayor of Philadelphia simultaneously, he would likely be shipped off to an insane asylum before he could even submit his candidacy. Yet, for years Jacques Chirac was mayor of Paris while representing the distant Corrèze *département* in the National Assembly and 50-million French citizens did not bat an eyelash. As I pointed out in my essay, "Montaigne and Descartes," this ethical blindness is abetted by the subjective standard of truth which is the cornerstone of the Cartesian method, as set forth in Descartes' *Discours de la Méthode:* "The things which we conceive very clearly and very distinctly are all true." Thus, it suffices that a person having a conflict of interests convince himself very clearly and very distinctly that it does not prevent him from doing both jobs well, and *voilà,* no conflict.

The French example serves to remind us that a system of ethics is not innate with the human race but rather an acquired characteristic. The concept of conflict of interests is a rather sophisticated one, since it takes a certain involvement with society for one to detect the unfairness that results from an abuse of trust. My own education on this subject came from the late, great Warren Abner Seavey's first-year course in Agency at Harvard Law School. The basic principle of conflict of interests is embodied in the pithy phrase: "A servant can not have two masters." During the early 1980s I ran into Pierre Mauroy at the US Embassy's Fourth-of-July garden party and, as he seemed accessible, I asked him how someone could be simultaneously Prime Minister and Mayor of Lille. Evidently taking me for an American tourist or other species of ignoramus, he laughed and said, patronizingly, "It's true that in America that's not done, but here it's different." I saw that there was no use arguing with him. If I had told him that "a servant can not have two masters," and asked how he could serve the people of Lille and all of France at the same time, he might have replied: "In a hierarchical society like France, the people are not the masters but the servants, and as such can have as many masters as we can fit into the annual budget."

When I was young, I naively believed that socialism was a more ethical system than capitalism because "the people" – not selfish capitalists – owned the means of production. It is only experience, such as that of the Soviet Union and France, which demonstrates the fallacy of this belief. In socialism, "the people" are in reality a caste of functionaries who wield the real power and who have a conflict of interest between their role as operators of factories and businesses and their role as regulators and guardians of the public interest. To illustrate, when "the state" owned the Seita, the tobacco monopoly, France was one of the last Western countries to regulate tobacco advertising. Similarly, as owners of Renault, the car company, the functionary caste resisted for years the introduction of unleaded gasoline and the use of catalytic converters to reduce exhaust pollution. And the biggest scandal of all was the deliberate sale of contaminated blood by the functionaries who controlled the blood monopoly.

Yet, the French people continue to be brainwashed with the notion that *l'Etat* is the guarantor of the public interest. I am doing my modest best to educate those who listen to me that the word *Etat* should never be used but, rather, broken down into its two components: when it comes to deciding, *l'Etat* means *les fonctionnaires* (*les fons)* and when it comes to paying, it means the taxpayers – *les contribuables* (*les cons).* The French people are doing absolutely nothing about the scandalous fact, as revealed on the television program "Capital" last year, and reported here, that each month millions of francs in cash controlled by the Prime Minister, are divvied up and distributed to ministers and high functionaries in their cabinets, including high tax officials. This is money which is not reported on the tax returns of these officials, who are charged with enforcing the laws of the land. *Les cons,* indeed.

Vol. XIX, N° 6, September 1997

Diana's Last Ride and French Justice

Although I was in San Francisco when the collision occurred which cost the lives of Diana, Princess of Wales, and her lover, Dodi al Fayed, as well as the driver Henri Paul, it struck close to home, as the Alma underpass is only a few minutes walk from my office and I have often driven through it. This short, well-lit, underpass is not a dangerous one when the vehicles are not speeding, and I have never known of any accidents in it. As I complete writing this, two weeks following the burial of Diana, the main mystery about the event turns on the immediate circumstances of the crash. The lone survivor, the 29-year-old bodyguard, Trevor Rees-Jones, who alone was wearing a seat-belt, recovered enough from his facial injuries to give testimony but could not remember the crash itself. On the other hand, it is clearly established that the ill-fated driver was under the influence of a heavy dose of alcohol, mixed, apparently, with Prozac and another drug. As he is not here to defend himself, it is worth stating that no evidence has been reported in the press to the effect that Henri Paul showed any visible trace of his drinking and it is hardly likely that the bodyguard, for one, would have taken a seat alongside him if he detected anything abnormal in his bearing. The paparazzi, whose hounding of the "star-crossed lovers," (as Shakespeare said of another pair) led to the unfortunate decision to send the regular driver on a decoy mission and call back a security man who had gone home to relax, are very much on the hook. There is still a possibility that one of them may have been close enough to the car to take a flash picture that momentarily blinded the driver and/or caused him to swerve in a way that led him to crash into the 13th of the pillars which separate the opposite lanes of the underpass. Moreover, the police are investigating the possibility that another automobile had been in the tunnel and had contact with the Mercedes. However, for present purposes, I will assume the most accepted fact pattern, to wit, that the photographers were relatively far behind the Mercedes and that only the excessive speed and Paul's lack of control of his reflexes were the immediate causes of the accident, possibly abetted by the presence of another vehicle in or entering the underpass from the feeder lane on the right.

The foreign press and radio-television news organizations have assigned many top personnel to looking into the legal aspects of the case. I have been interviewed by *ABC News, CNN, Fox News, The New York Times* and *The European* so far and, having helped educate these media, I see no reason why I should not give my loyal readers a glimpse of the legal and the judicial aspects of the case under the French system.

The best way to start on this complex subject, it seems to me, is to stress what is different in the French system as compared with common-law jurisdictions, such as Great Britain and the United States. As to substance, two areas stand out: French criminalization of the invasion of privacy and of failure to assist persons in danger. As to procedure, there are again two salient differences in French law: the role of the *Juge d'Instruction* ("JDI") and the right of injured parties to become civil parties in criminal prosecutions.

Role of the French Police: Before coming to these points I believe this is a good occasion to deal with the role of the police immediately after the accident. Every civilized nation grapples with the age-old balancing act of simultaneously giving the police enough leeway to find culprits and evidence to convict them and still protect the rights and dignity of suspects. There is little doubt that in a Catholic country like France, the see-saw tips in favor of the police, doubtless the heritage of the tradition that a good Catholic should confess his sins and get on with the business of repentance. Thus, under the French Code of Criminal Procedure, the police can arrest and detain anyone, including your mother, without charges, for 24 hours and then, for another 24 hours with the consent of the public prosecutor. (Although purporting to be a Latin people, the French have never heard of the writ of *habeas corpus,* except in American movies.) During this time, the person detained has the right to phone a family member or employer to advise of the detention, and to ask to be examined by a medical doctor designated by the police. He has no right to have a lawyer present while being interrogated. He is not advised of any right to remain silent, for this right does not exist. After the first 20 hours of detention he has the right to see a lawyer of his choice, but only for 30 minutes, and then he can be questioned again without the help of the lawyer. And the lawyer is forbidden by law to tell anyone, repeat "anyone," of the detention of his client! After these 24 or 48 hours, the detainee must either be released or charged. If the latter, he can again be placed in pre-trial confinement by the JDI, often for months, sometimes for years. I betray my prejudices when I say that this system is abominable. When defending a soldier in an Army court-martial, I succeeded in throwing out a coerced confession and cited Justice Holmes' famous remark to the effect that "Better that an occasional criminal should go free than that the police play an ignoble part." This is a value judgment which not everyone shares, certainly not the French legal authorities and the political establishment. The 20-hour rule was a "reform" voted only a few years ago. Before that, a detainee could not see a lawyer, no matter how much he insisted. The only hope that I see for changing this system lies with the European Court on Human Rights, to me one of the few bright spots in a decadent European continent.

In the present case, the seven photographers found on the scene were thus arrested and detained and their cameras and film confiscated. (The legal basis for this confiscation is presumably to gather evidence but if the photos are used to incriminate some photographers, I suppose that a challenge might be made at some point.) The Public Prosecutor of Paris (*Procureur de la République)* almost immediately charged a JDI with the investigation of two possible offenses: negligent homicide and failure to assist persons in danger. Once he did so, the Procureur had no further role in the actual investigation but he still could look into other possible offenses arising out of the same events. As these offenses are misdemeanors (*délits*), the *Procureur* is not required to name a JDI in all cases. If the police report made after the accident had been sufficiently explicit and convincing as to the existence of a misdemeanor, the *Procureur* could have himself charged the accused and had them brought before the *Tribunal Correctionnel* (a chamber of the court of first instance), the trial taking place usually several months thereafter. Note that if an accused has been arrested in *flagrant délit,* that is, in the very act of committing the crime, the Procureur can have him tried immediately – another abominable practice, in my opinion, since the accused does not have the time to prepare his defense and obtain adequate legal advice, as the court commits any lawyer who happens to be standing around, and the lawyer has only a few minutes to discuss the case with the suspect. To be complete on the chapter of misdemeanors, I should mention another unique institution: the right of the purported victim to bring the alleged perpetrator of a *délit* directly into the *Tribunal Correctionnel* without the intervention of a Public Prosecutor. This is known as the *citation directe.*

When it comes to felonies (*crimes*) the Procureur has no choice: a JDI must be named, and if the latter finds that the evidence warrants a charge, the case is heard by the *Cour d'Assises,* the only French court which has a jury. As it does not appear that any felony will be charged in the present case, I will not dwell on the hoary institution of the *Cour d'Assises,* other than to point out that to ensure that juries do not go astray, the three judges deliberate and vote with the nine jurors, conviction requiring a two-thirds majority.

Judges and Prosecutors - A Single Profession: At this point, I would do well to relate how these professionals of criminal justice are chosen. *Procureurs*, JDIs and sitting judges are all part of a generic profession called *la magistrature* and its members are generically called *magistrats.* They are, in effect, civil servants and move from one assignment to another in the course of their career. The standard way to enter this profession is to apply for admission to the Ecole Nationale de la Magistrature in Bordeaux, after finishing law school. Those who are admitted undergo a three-year training consisting of theoretical instruction and practical experience in the courthouse. Graduates then get assigned generally to a small town in the provinces where they can be JDIs, *substituts* (assistants to the *Procureur*) or sitting judges alongside an experienced presiding judge. They get graded every year by their superiors and, if they do well, move up the ladder, the most ambitious ones all wanting to be assigned to Paris. Thus, for example, a person can be a Procureur in the provinces and be named a presiding judge in Paris. Because of the generally-shared desire of all to move to Paris and there rise to high station, the rank-and-file of this profession are quite conventional and sensitive to political influences. It is only a small handful of JDIs, like Eva Joly and Eric Halphen, who have the temerity to probe political corruption. Like most civil servants, *magistrats* are not paid well by private standards, but they do have a lifetime job. As a result of their modest pay, judges tend to hand out low damage awards.

Parties to the Investigation: The *Procureur* is not the only party who can have a JDI begin an investigation. The victim or his next of kin can file a complaint with the head JDI and this will also trigger an investigation. Of course, if the *Procureur* gets there first, a victim can still join in the investigation by constituting himself as *partie civile.* In the present case, Dodi's father did join in, as did, I understand, the brother and a sister of Diana. By joining as civil parties, the complainants are entitled to be represented by lawyers, who have access to the file as it develops. Similarly, when the JDI formally places a suspect under examination (*mise en examen*), he is entitled to be represented by counsel, who also can get copies of the documents in the file (but can not give them to the accused). In the Diana case, the seven photographers arrested at the scene were immediately so charged, as were three other photographers identified later. To satisfy the curiosity of lawyers in the audience, let me answer a question they are bound to ask: "Can a separate civil suit be brought by victims of a crime?" The answer is "Yes," but the suit will be stayed pending the termination of the criminal proceedings, including appeals, which can take years. Of course, if the defendant is acquitted, the victim who filed a complaint in the criminal case can not bring a separate civil suit based on the same acts.

The *Juge d'Instruction:* There is a great deal of formalism involved in the performance of an investigation by the JDI, and this accounts for the slow pace at which he moves. He is required to make written minutes (*procès-verbal*) of any witnesses or parties heard, and to keep a written record of his other actions. The judge can, of course, be assisted by the judicial police, who are administratively attached to the Ministry of the Interior but under the direction of the *Procureur,* as well as by qualified investigators of the *Gendarmerie,* who are part of the French army. As indicated above, this high-profile case warranted use of the Felony Squad for the investigation, even though the offenses mentioned by the *Procureur* are only misdemeanors. The JDI, as I have stated in prior Newsletters, is a descendant of the Grand Inquisitor of the Catholic Church. Napoleon called him the most powerful man in France, as he can put people in jail while investigating their alleged offenses. This power is often abused in order to coerce confessions, and my readers know what I think of this practice. However, it is vital to point out that the JDI is not a prosecutor; he is charged with getting all the truth about the alleged offenses and the people involved, including getting evidence of their innocence or mitigating circumstances. He can, for example, order medical and psychiatric examinations of the persons accused. The thoroughness of his mission and the formalism and paper-work involved, plus the heavy workload of most JDIs, explain why these investigations rarely take less than a year and, in serious cases, often take two or three years. It frequently happens that the poor bloke being investigated languishes in prison while the JDI takes his time adding documents to the file. Thus, in practice, the accused is often punished before his trial and, when the trial takes place, the actual sentence frequently does not require any more prison since the pre-trial confinement is credited against the sentence. Of course, if he is found innocent, as he is theoretically presumed to be, he's had tough luck but can spend another two years trying to get measly damages from the State for his unjust imprisonment.

Aware that public opinion throughout the world is impatient to ascertain the facts of the tragic end of Diana and her lover, the French judicial authorities are trying to accelerate the *instruction,* as the investigation is called. A second JDI was named to help the first one, a relatively unusual step, and dozens of police have been assigned to them. Lawyer for the parties play a relatively passive role in the i*nstruction* as they are not allowed to interrogate witnesses or potential witnesses. Of course, they can suggest leads to the JDI and request various measures, such as laboratory tests or the naming of experts. In practice, the JDI is the boss and does things with little interference from the attorneys.

Another key aspect of the instruction is that it is supposedly conducted in secrecy. It is a criminal offense for anyone involved, including the judge, to make any public disclosure of what is taking place. In practice, this is often breached, even by some judges, who discreetly leak information to favored reporters (as in the Gregory case) and often by lawyers or police who give background briefings.

According to usage, the JDI will make what is called a *reconstitution, i.e.,* a re-enactment, of the alleged crimes, which requires going to the scene with the accused and all interested parties and trying to re-enact what allegedly happened. In the present case this will be a massive undertaking, which will have to be done at night, starting with the scene at the Ritz Hotel in Place Vendôme, and then the chase which took the vehicles to the Place de la Concorde via Rue de Rivoli, and then along the Seine in the tunnel, which begins at that square and leads to the Place de l'Alma, where the road briefly resurfaces to allow the entry of vehicles from the Cours de la Reine on the right before going in the fatal underpass. This re-enactment is likely to rival a Hollywood spectacle and become a major media event in itself. Of course, the photographers, unless they change their tune, are not likely to be willing participants in any effort to show them in a bad light. Their story is apparently that they were trailing the Mercedes at a distance and reached the underpass only after the accident occurred. I don't envy the two JDIs who will have to conduct this spectacle.

If a JDI concludes his investigation with a finding that no crime was committed (*non lieu*) or by the decision to send one or more persons to trial before the *Tribunal Correctionnel* this decision can be reviewed by the *Chambre d'Accusation* of the Court of Appeals of Paris. It is relatively rare that the JDI's decisions are reversed. You may be wondering what the *Procureur*'s role is in this process. Once the judge brings charges, the Procureur must issue a *requisitoire*, which is a detailed bill of particulars of the charges as developed by the JDI. This seems a rather strange system, since the JDI has done the investigation and could make the detailed charges himself. Once the investigation is closed, the JDI has no further role in the penal process. The actual trial of a misdemeanor is, as stated above, before a three-judge panel, and the presiding judge does most of the talking and questioning. The *Procureur,* being a *magistrat,* sits on a dais to the left of the judge (if facing them), and is usually a passive observer, saving most of his efforts for the closing argument, also called *requisitoire,* in which he summarizes his view of the evidence and indicates what punishment he seeks.

The Trial: Whereas the *instruction* can last for months or years, the actual trial is a relatively brief affair, taking hours in most cases, since the presiding judge has the entire file before him and often knows what his decision will be before the trial starts. This being an inquisitorial system, the presiding judge really acts as the prosecutor, starting off by interrogating each defendant and then conducting the examination of witnesses. Even if the defendants admit their guilt the trial continues, since the object is to get a total picture of the crime, the victim and the defendant. Lawyers can ask questions only with the permission of the presiding judge. The main role of the lawyers for the defendants is to make the *plaidoirie* – the closing argument – an art form in which many *avocats* excel, by which they present the facts in the best light for their client and either request acquittal or a lenient sentence. The court often issues its decision from the bench, after deliberating in chambers, but just as often it will take from two to four weeks to announce its decision, including the awarding of damages to the civil parties. Interestingly, no stenographic report of the trial is made, and often the written decision of the court will be issued months after the judgment is announced in open court. The clerk of court makes a rudimentary summary of the events. In many cases, this is so badly written that it is difficult to know what the case is about from just reading it.

The Appeal: The decision of the *Tribunal Correctionnel* can be appealed both by the defendant and by the *Procureur.* The Court of Appeals, in effect, conducts a trial *de novo,* since it can hear witnesses and make new findings of fact and law. Its decision can then be reviewed by the highest court, the *Cour de Cassation,* but only on points of law. Of course, this appeal system pleases most defendants since they get a second crack at seeking acquittal, or obtaining a lighter sentence. The latter result occurs more often than not, as the elapsed time tends to efface the ill-feelings wrought by the original offenses. However, in some cases a person acquitted in the lower court gets convicted on appeal or, if convicted below, gets a heavier sentence if the Procureur has appealed. (Obviously, the American notion of "double jeopardy" does not exist in France.) Personally, I consider this to be a bad system. It would be preferable to do a better job in the trial court and then reserve the time and talents of the appeals court for a review of a complete record and consideration of points of law, including the adequacy of the evidence, as in the common-law system. However, the present system seems so ingrained in the mentalities of judges and lawyers that I detect no movement whatever to change it. When it comes to felony convictions in the *Cour d'Assises,* no appeal (in the French sense) is allowed but the accused can have his conviction reviewed by the *Cour de Cassation* on points of law and procedure. As I pointed out in my "Catholic and Protestant Justice," the main advantage of the French system for the accused is that if he confesses he is likely to get much a lighter sentence than his counterpart in the USA.

The Possible Offenses - Right of Privacy: It is time, now, to get into the substance of the possible offenses. At the heart of the case is the right of privacy. It should be obvious to everyone that the best protection that society affords to its members stems from unwritten rules. The typical French person is a more private individual than his or her American counterpart. I have known business executives who have worked together for 20 years and still call each other *Monsieur.* In the same vein, they have never met each other's wife and, indeed, may never have inquired whether the other is married. Certainly, they would never ask if the other has a mistress. And, of course, they would not discuss salaries together. As to public figures, the French do not expect the press to regale them with savory details of their love affairs. For example, I had known for 20 years that François Mitterrand was a "lady's man"; indeed, even before his election to the presidency in 1981, my wife had seen him in a dress shop with his then mistress. It was common knowledge during his presidency that he did not live with his wife, who was at his side only on ceremonial occasions. Yet the press never wrote about these things, out of respect for *la vie privée.* Having these unwritten rules, it is not surprising that France legislated on the subject only recently, when "international standards" began to break down the traditional discretion of the press. The Civil Code now contains an article consecrating the right to privacy and gives the courts power to enjoin violations "of the intimacy" thereof, as well as to award damages. Thus, for example, a court held a publication liable for printing a photo of the actress Isabelle Adjani strolling in a public park while pregnant. When the photo of the famous actor, Jean Gabin, on his death bed was published without permission, this was held to be wrongful. More recently, the magazine *Paris Match* was held liable for publishing a photo of Mitterrand on his death bed.

Moreover, the new Penal Code makes it a misdemeanor to breach the "intimacy of private life" by recording private conversations or taking the picture of a person in a private place without his consent. The difference between the civil offense and the penal one is thus that for the latter, the criterion is that it must take place in a private place, such as a home, an office, or even a restaurant. I have found no case dealing with the question as to whether filming someone in a private vehicle, without his consent, is a violation of the penal statute. My own view, and that of most lawyers with whom I have discussed the matter, is that it is.

This penal provision will inevitably play a role in the criminal investigation now under way. Unlike most offenses, this one can not be invoked *sua sponte* by the *Procureur,* but must be raised by the individual concerned. Thus, the mission given to the JDI by the *Procureur* did not mention this possible offense. However, it is possible that the families of Diana and of Dodi al Fayed will bring a complaint along these lines, requesting that the *Procureur* add this count to the offenses being investigated by the JDI. The Penal Code specifies that a deceased person's next-of-kin can bring such a complaint. If the *Procureur* fails to act, the families might bring a separate complaint directly to the chief JDI who can either name a separate JDI to investigate the complaint or assign it to the JDIs now investigating the accident. As it is clear that the paparazzi were trying to take pictures of Diana and Dodi in the car – a private place – and, indeed, photographed them after the accident, there are grounds for asserting that this statute was violated. Of course, the photographers will argue that Diana had consented to being photographed since, as a royal "entertainer," she had craved and solicited publicity. However, I do not see that this applies to Dodi and, at any rate, even an entertainer has a right to some privacy in living his or her personal relationships. The importance of establishing this violation is that even if the alleged drunkenness and excessive speed of the driver were the immediate causes of the accident, this would not prevent the court from holding that the photographers were also a contributing cause by following the lovers' automobile with an illicit motive, *i.e.,* invading their privacy.

Non-Assistance to a Person in Danger: Another innovation of French law, a much older one, is the misdemeanor of "non-assistance to a person in danger." This charge is typically invoked, for example, when a medical doctor fails to stop at the scene of an accident to treat the injured, or when parents do not seek medical help for a gravely-ill child. In the present case, the suspicion was that the first photographers who arrived on the scene busied themselves to take pictures, rather than to call for help, or even to seek to administer first-aid. My guess is that this charge will not hold up against most of the photographers.

Endangering Life: Another offense of recent vintage is the misdemeanor of endangering the life of a person by violation of a legal obligation. It is not necessary, to prove this offense, to show that anyone was actually injured or killed, the idea being, for example, that a drunken driver lucky enough not to have caused an accident should still be severely punished for the potential risks that his conduct promoted. However, the courts have been reluctant to find people guilty of this offense when there is no actual victim. Thus, a man driving at 125 miles per hour, well above the highway speed limit of 80 mph, was acquitted of this charge, on the ground that the actual driving conditions were such that no one was endangered. Apparently, when the photographers were first placed under arrest, this was one of the charges made by the police, doubtless on the assumption that they were exceeding the speed limit and came too near the Mercedes before the accident. Of course, Henri Paul being dead, no criminal charge can be brought against him, but it is conceivable that a charge of endangering life might be brought against other participants in this drama.

Negligent Homicide: The most serious charge is that which we would translate into English as "negligent homicide." The applicable article of the Penal code lists several ways in which this offense can be committed: "clumsiness [*maladresse*], imprudence, inattention, negligence or failure to observe safety requirements." (A comparable misdemeanor exists for negligently-caused injuries resulting in incapacity to work for more than three months.) Whether this charge can stick against the photographers merely for following Diana's car is problematic but certainly al Fayed's lawyer will contend that the pursuit is what led Henri Paul to drive so fast and to take a route which allowed him to do so. Readers should note that it is not necessary, to sustain a conviction, to prove that the defendant's conduct was what American lawyers call the "proximate cause" of the accident, nor is it a defense to show that the victim committed what we call "contributory negligence." In a recent case where several children drowned in a canyon, both the electric company which unleashed dam waters and the teacher who took the children there were found guilty of negligent homicide.

It is conceivable that charges may be brought against the manager of the Ritz Hotel for allowing Henri Paul to drive the car which the hotel had rented, as it has been suggested in the press that he did not have the special driver's permit needed to carry passengers. This is a rather tricky question. The highway code (*Code de la Route*) requires a special authorization to drive vehicles meant for public transportation, such as taxis or buses, and also for what is called *véhicules de remise.* The code does not define this term and I have found no one who knows what it really means, but the dictionary indicates that the term is a vestige of the horse-and-buggy age. Large carriages with a driver parked in a covered zone called "*remise,*" so by extension, the term seems to apply now to hired vehicles with chauffeur. But the Ritz Hotel rented the Mercedes without a chauffeur and, arguably, Henri Paul, a security man and not a professional chauffeur, did not require such a permit merely for a one-shot drive to accompany Diana and Dodi to the latter's apartment, where apparently they were headed. Another possible charge which is certainly being investigated is whether the hotel's management knew of Paul's drinking habits, or had noticed his drinking that evening, or indeed whether he should have been allowed to drive after he had gone home at the end of a trying day's work. Although unlikely, considering how badly he was injured, it is conceivable that the bodyguard could be accused of negligence for not having insisted that Diana and Dodi wear their safety belts. After all, he did have the good judgment to attach his own belt.

Corporate Criminals: Until the enactment of the new Penal Code, it was not possible to charge corporations or other legal entities with criminal offenses, since only individuals were considered as being able to commit criminal acts. Now, the Code specifies various crimes for which legal entities can be so charged. These include all the crimes mentioned above, except for non-assistance to a person in danger. Thus it is possible that the corporation owning the Ritz Hotel, a UK limited company, might be charged. This is the company of which Mohammed al Fayed and his family own the shares, and of which he is a director. It is also conceivable that the agencies for which the photographers worked could be charged for various offenses on the ground that they were responsible for the acts of their employees.

It is too early to tell where the investigation will lead, but my hunch is that because of public opinion, the JDIs will find it judicious to bring charges against various journalists and someone at the Ritz, even if the facts are murky. By doing so, they will pass the buck to the Tribunal Correctionnel and to the Court of Appeals. Unless it is discovered that another driver had collided with the Mercedes and fled the scene, no one will go to jail, and the damages awarded will be miserly compared with what a jury would grant in the USA.

In conclusion, some readers may be disappointed that I have not waxed philosophical or poetical about Diana, Princess of Wales, and her tragic last ride. So much has been written on the subject that I do not feel I have anything to add. I did like her face and demeanor and felt sorry for her suffering. With only a slight alteration, Shakespeare said it best:

"Had she been put on, she might have proved most royal."

Vol. XIX, N° 7, October 1997

Reflections on Franz Werfel, Maurice Papon and European Decadence

One might have supposed that a novelist who was twice honored with a Book of the Month Club selection, and a foreign writer at that, would be remembered 50 years after his death, but I have spoken with few people recently who can identify Franz Werfel, let alone own up to having read one of his works. For Armenians of my generation, Werfel is a cherished name because of his once-celebrated novel, *"The Forty Days of Musa Dagh,"* which recounts in fictionalized form an actual episode of the 1915 Turkish Genocide of the Armenians, the first Christian nation. The Armenian community of Musa Dagh in Syria, then part of the Ottoman Empire, decided to resist the Turkish Army rather than to be "resettled," the pretext used by the Turkish authorities to lead more than a million Armenians to their death. I won't tell you the ending, as I hope you will read the book some day!

This novel became a best-seller in the United States in 1933 but in Germany, the Nazis, who had just come to power, banned and burned it, not only because Werfel was a Jew, but also because it served to remind the German people that Turkey was its ally in World War I and used the cover of war to exterminate the Christian Armenians who had been living in their 3000-year homeland. When Werfel wrote *Forty Days* little did he imagine that he, too, would be in danger of extermination, for having been born a Jew. Once World War II began, Hitler set forth to imitate the Young Turks who had perpetrated the Armenian Genocide, making the famous remark: *"Who remembers the Armenians?"* Thus, Werfel had to flee the Third Reich and tried to make his way to Spain, via the Pyrénées Mountains. There, holed up in a little town called Lourdes, Werfel discovered the story of Bernadette Soubirous, the 14-year-old peasant girl who claimed, and convinced a skeptical Church, that she had seen the Virgin Mary in a grotto on several occasions. Werfel vowed that if he managed to escape the Nazis, he would write the story of Bernadette. With luck and much travail, Werfel and his wife, the former Alma Mahler, got to Spain and then to America. In 1942, Werfel's promised novel, *The Song of Bernadette,* translated from the German, was again a Book of the Month selection and became a runaway best-seller. It was made into a motion picture, starring Jennifer Jones. Sadly, although *Forty Days* could have become a magnificent film, MGM bowed to Turkish pressure and buried the project. I hope that some day a worthy production will be made of it.

Though I had read both books in my adolescence, I knew little about Franz Werfel, other than that he had married the widow of Gustave Mahler. Recently, my old childhood friend, Willard Aronson, who used to live around the corner from me at 56th and Walnut in Philadelphia and now resides in Oklahoma City, sent me a biography of Franz Werfel, translated from the German of Peter Stephan Jungk (Grove Weidenfeld, NY 1987). Werfel was born in 1890 into a prosperous Jewish family living in the German-speaking part of Prague. Before he was 20, he began to have a reputation as a poet and had made contact with famous writers, including Rainer Maria Rilke. Later he turned to plays and novels and received critical and popular acclaim in both genres. He had an affair with Alma Mahler while she was married to Walter Gropius, the architect who later founded the Bauhaus and ended up in the USA, one of his last works being the Harkness Commons at Harvard Law School, completed in 1950. Alma divorced Gropius and married Werfel, remaining with him until his death in 1945. They had no children together.

What impressed me in this biography was the display of the rich cultural life of the German-speaking communities, which included Austria, Prague, part of Switzerland and, of course, Germany itself. Werfel moved freely from one place to another, spending time in Prague, Vienna, Leipzig and Zurich. He was a friend of Franz Kafka and Stefan Zweig (also Jewish writers expressing themselves in German), Thomas Mann, and the composers Arnold Schöenberg and Alban Berg, to mention only a few. I regret to say that I am ignorant of the German language and have neglected much of its important literature in translation. It is evident that Jews were an integral part of the Germanic civilization until the advent of Hitler. Need we be reminded that Sigmund Freud and Alfred Adler were Jewish, and that Albert Einstein wrote only in German? I do not intend to make a catalog of Jewish contributions to German culture. The Werfel biography brought home to me the tremendous loss that European culture sustained when the scoundrels who created the Third Reich, with the willing assent of millions of German citizens, destroyed its Jewish population along with those of Eastern Europe. When thinking of the Holocaust one tends naturally to concentrate on the victims and their families, but it must be said that Europe, too, suffered an inestimable loss from this event. It is as though a vital part of the European soul was cast out of its body.

When you kill six-million Jews, you kill not only men, women and children but also you kill a myriad of neurons that were part of present and future poets, painters, philosophers, composers, architects, engineers, scientists, doctors, lawyers and entrepreneurs of all kinds. The loss to European creativity of these active neurons is colossal and, what's more, continuing. When Europe chased away its Werfels, Zweigs and Einsteins, to name only three, it maimed its own brain, to speak in collective terms. And I say "Europe" and not only Germany, because I feel that this was a collective responsibility. The villains of Europe's intellectual suicide are not only Hitler and Mussolini but also I place enormous blame on the cowards who allowed these monsters to get away with their crimes for so long: the Chamberlains, the Daladiers and the Quislings. Today the monsters are gone but the cowards remain, as the events of Bosnia demonstrated.

Yes, it is on reading the Werfel biography that things gelled in my mind, connecting my present observation of the intellectual and ethical decadence of Europe with the loss of countless neurons that once were connected to human beings, diverse among themselves, but labeled conveniently by those that hated them under a single word: Jew. To the extent that these neurons were displaced and not permanently lost, the main beneficiaries have been two nations, Israel and the USA. The latter has shown to the world that Jews thrive in conditions of liberty and equal opportunity. The former, that Jews in their own nation become like everyone else, which itself is an accomplishment. Both the USA and Israel have gained from the influx of Jews, while the loser has been Europe. Among the neurons that escaped to the United States are those of my friend and Harvard Law classmate, Gerry Gunther, who has had an outstanding career as a professor of constitutional law at Stanford and recently published the authoritative biography of Learned Hand. When Jerry was a child in Usingen in the early years of the Nazi reign, a teacher in elementary school called him a "Jewish swine," the teacher being furious that none of the "Aryans" in the class could recite the names of the early Teutonic kings, whereas Gerry could.

If Helmut Kohl and his predecessors had been really intelligent, they would have tried to bring Jews like Gerry Gunther back to Germany, even if it cost a million marks a head. One-hundred-thousand Jews would have contributed more creativity to Germany than the 20-million sovieticized citizens of East Germany, who have done little to divert that country from its post-war destiny as a soul-less, materialistic producer of chemicals, cars and machine goods. There was as much moral ground for West Germany reuniting with its Jews as for reuniting with Prussia and Saxony.

As for France, that brings me to Maurice Papon, the former Vichy functionary who is said to have ordered the rounding up of Jews in Bordeaux, now on trial in that city for complicity in a "crime against humanity." This case has created a *malaise* in France. Papon is 87 and the alleged crime dates back 55 years. Unlike the USA, which has no statute of limitation on murder, France has a ridiculously short ten-year prescription for that crime. Thus, to get at the people who participated in the wartime crimes against civilian populations, the French parliament edicted a new category, crimes against humanity, which were deemed "*imprescriptible.*" Papon, like many other Vichy functionaries, including François Mitterrand, "turned his vest," to adapt the French saying, when he saw that the Allies were going to win the war, after all. Thus, he managed to be classified as a *résistant* and got into the good graces of de Gaulle. After the liberation of France, Papon continued as a dutiful functionary, finally rising to the position of Prefect of Police of Paris and later getting named Minister of the Budget when Giscard d'Estaing was President.

About 20 years ago, rumors began circulating that Papon, while Secretary General of the Prefecture of the Gironde *département,* where Bordeaux is located, ordered the arrest and deportation of several-hundred Jews, who perished in Nazi death camps. Charges were brought and fought and, in typical French fashion, the penal system hemmed and hawed until, finally, after 13 years of proceedings, the indictment against him was upheld by the highest court so that he could stand trial in the felony court of Bordeaux, the *Cour d'Assises.* During all this time, Papon remained a free man, not spending so much as an hour in jail. But it is one of the bizarre features of French procedure that a person to be tried by the *Cour d'Assises* must be a prisoner when he appears in court. I had known of this strange rule, but had never verified its legal basis. In the misdemeanor court, the *Tribunal Correctionnel,* described in my last Newsletter, if a defendant is tried while free, the court that convicts him can order his immediate incarceration. However, the Code of Criminal Procedure contains no comparable provision for the *Cour d'Assises!* Instead, it requires that the free defendant report to jail the night before his trial begins. This situation reminds me of my favorite episode in the old radio series, "Amos 'n Andy." When Amos visits Andy in his new office, Andy explains that he has hired a secretary, Miss Blue, and installed a buzzer system, but the electrician put the buzzer on her desk and the bell on his. So Andy would call out, "Miss Blue, buzz me." Then, when she buzzed, Andy would call out again, "Now, will you please come in." The analogy is plain: instead of amending the code so that a free defendant can be arrested once convicted, the French choose to imprison him throughout the trial, when he is presumed innocent.

At least this was thought to be the hard-and-fast rule, until Papon's counsel, Jean-Marc Varaut, had the bright idea to read the Code and discover that there was nothing in it requiring that an accused remain a prisoner during his trial. So Varaut moved the court to set Papon free, making an obvious point about his advanced age and fragile health. The civil parties – families of victims and anti-racist organizations – howled in protest, but the court, after ordering a medical examination of Papon, decided to set him free, whereupon more howling ensued. The public learned for the first time about the silly rule that a convicted felon who is not detained during trial can not be put in jail until his petition for review is decided by the highest court. This is France for you: for decades non-detained defendants have been dutifully reporting to prison on the eve of their trial by the *Cour d'Assises* and French lawyers, living by the laws of inertia, have been dutifully letting their clients stay in jail during their trial. Then, all of a sudden, the lawyer for an 87-year-old man says, in effect, "My client has been free for 55 years after the events for which he is now accused. Considering that the constitution states that a person is presumed innocent until proven guilty, why should he be locked up during his trial, when he most needs freedom to defend himself?" I do not know if Jean-Marc Varaut actually said that but that is what I would have said, had I stood before the judges of the *Cour d'Assises.*

To call the proceedings in this type of case a "trial" is to mislead readers who are accustomed to the Anglo-American criminal system. It would be more appropriate to call it a "happening." People are called as witnesses (*témoins*) who have no personal knowledge of the facts and they are asked to give their opinion, not as experts but just as important people who might impress the judges and jurors. Thus, Pierre Messmer, who was a Gaullist during the war and became Prime Minister in 1973 under Georges Pompidou, "testified" that Papon should have resigned his Vichy post rather than order the arrest of Bordeaux's Jews. (My *concierge* thinks the same thing but she was not asked to testify.) As there are no rules of evidence in French courts, Messmer was also asked what he thought of Papon's role as Prefect of Police in 1961 when a demonstration of Algerians in Paris was brutally repressed and the next morning scores of bodies of dead Algerians were seen floating on the Seine. Of course, even an American school child, used to watching Perry Mason on television, would object that the 1961 events are not what Papon was being tried for. Messmer replied that Papon could not be blamed for the 1961 deaths since he was merely following orders of the Minister of Interior. But, Monsieur Messmer, why could not have Monsieur Papon resigned in 1961 rather than allow his police to kill demonstrators and throw their bodies in the Seine? Another "witness" was former Prime Minister Raymond Barre who, of course, had nothing to do with the events of 1942. Instead, he was asked whether, when he appointed Papon a minister in the 1970s, he was aware of his Vichy record. Barre replied in the negative but, as my brother Andy used to say, what has this to do with the price of beans in China?

The Papon case illustrates dramatically, yet farcically, all that is wrong with French society 50 years after the end of World War II. It demonstrates than France can never escape the errors of its past, since it is never willing to face the truth about its past. When France was liberated by the Allies, they committed the error, too, of encouraging the fiction that French forces and the résistance had played a major role in that liberation. Of course, de Gaulle just loved that fiction since he had fought hard to thwart the original Allied plan for a military government of the liberated country. Then after some showcase trials of collaborationists, including Pétain and Laval, and the shaving of the heads of prostitutes who had slept with the enemy, de Gaulle and the governments which succeeded him in the Fourth Republic, basically perpetuated the myth that only a minority of French were collaborationists and the majority were freedom fighters. Whereas the Vichy government had been voted into power by the parliament of the Third Republic when Paul Reynaud resigned as Prime Minister in 1940, and despite the fact that many Vichy laws remained on the books during the Fourth and the Fifth Republics, and Vichy officials kept their jobs in the postwar era, the fiction was maintained that Vichy was not a legitimate government and thus France was not responsible for the atrocities

it committed, including the rounding up of Jews by its police for shipment to Nazi death camps. It was only in 1995, a full 50 years after the end of WWII, that President Chirac, newly elected, made a public statement admitting that France was Vichy and thus responsible for its crimes, a position that many French leaders continue to contest.

As a believer in the rule of law, which includes the notion of equal protection of the laws, that is, treating people similarly situated the same way, I have a problem with trying an 87-year-old man 55 years after the events when a whole régime was responsible for cowardly and indecent conduct and most of the guilty persons have escaped punishment, including François Mitterrand, who served for 14 years as President of the Republic. Mitterrand, it must be recalled, was decorated by Marshal Pétain for his service to Vichy and the Péan book revealed that he had been offered the post of head of the Department of Jewish Affairs in 1942. He did not refuse it out of principle but only because he coveted another position. If Mitterrand had been opposed to Vichy's treatment of the Jews he should never have become a Vichy functionary. And while Mitterrand was President he continued his friendship with René Bosquet, the Paris police chief who rounded up the Jews in 1942 and sent them off to be exterminated. Papon is obviously a scapegoat and even guilty scapegoats can arouse sympathy.

French Jews face a dilemma: traditionally voting Socialist ever since the Dreyfus Affair, when the Right was anti-Semitic and anti-Dreyfus, they voted massively for François Mitterrand, and several prominent Jews, like Jack Lang, Robert Badinter and Georges Kiejman, served his régime and called themselves his friend. After the publication of the Péan book, many Jews openly criticized Mitterrand, but not those who were his "house Jews." It is hard to admit that you had been hoodwinked by the most Florentine of Frenchmen, particularly when, with a bit of perspicacity, you could have discovered the same facts as Péan did. Sending Maurice Papon to jail, an unlikely event, since he might be acquitted or, even if convicted, get a suspended sentence or, at any rate, expire before the *Cour de Cassation* rules on his case, is not going to expiate the crimes committed by the Vichy régime because these crimes were widespread and had thousands of authors.

To return to Franz Werfel, the Jungk biography has got me thinking about the comparative role of Germanic and French Jews in their respective cultures. I do not know enough about the former to formulate a theory but I will advance a conjecture, to wit, that the German-language Jews made a relatively greater contribution to their society and thus that their elimination has left a tremendous void. As to why this would be, the conjecture relies on the fact that the German-speaking countries were dispersed and pluralistic, thus giving rein to more diversity, whereas France's centralism and Catholic-Cartesian tradition placed French Jews in a tighter intellectual straight-jacket. I am reminded of my own *bon mot* to the effect that "in France even the Jews become Catholic." Germany, it must be recalled, was the homeland of Martin Luther, and whereas France gave birth to John Calvin, the Protestants were persecuted on and off until the revocation by Louis XIV of Henry IV's Edict of Nantes sent the Huguenots to enrich other countries, including faraway South Africa, where their descendants still produce a tasty white wine near Cape Town.

I am reminded also of a passage I read many years ago in the memoirs of Albert Schweitzer who, let us not forget, was an organist and authority on J.S. Bach before becoming an M.D. and missionary in what is now Gabon. Schweitzer relates that when his book on Bach, written in French, became successful, he was asked to translate it to German, another language in which he, an Alsatian, was fluent. But Schweitzer came to realize that he could not translate his own French, but rather had to rewrite the book in German. The passage I cite from memory went something like this. "Writing in German is like hiking through a thick German forest, whereas writing in French is like strolling in a formal French garden."

So, my conjecture goes, the Jewish intellectual tradition, rooted in the Torah and the Talmud, may have been more at home in the German language and in the more pluralistic philosophical and literary traditions of the countries where they lived than in the rigid, formalistic Cartesian canon. This, of course, leads me to my favorite theme, that it was an intellectual disaster for France to disregard the empiric and tolerant model of Michel de Montaigne in favor of the sterile, *a priori* reasoning of René Descartes. This brings me to an extraordinary letter I received recently from a reader in San Diego, Henri Charmasson, who, as his name suggests, began his life in France. With much vigor and many citations, Henri brought water to my mill, to borrow the French expression, by showing that it is no accident that so many of my French intellectual heroes, like Montaigne, Montesquieu and Pascal, came from the South of France, for that region has always been the hotbed of dissidence and resistance against the centralism and conformism imposed by the Monarchy, allied to the Church. When I wrote my French essay, "*Montaigne et Descartes*," 25 years ago, I was intuitively choosing the former over the latter, without grounding it in the historical and geographical background. Now, Henri's letter reinforces that intuition, by showing that the culture of the South, with its Greek and Roman roots, its own language, the Langue d'Oc, and the diversity of its human resources, including Jews expelled from Spain in 1492, was far different from that of the North. The Kings and Bishops brutally crushed the Cathar dissidence in religion, as they later repressed Calvinism, and destroyed the centers of learning and culture that once dotted the South of France. This reminded me that Montaigne's mother came from a family of Spanish Jews. It also brought to mind a book I had read many years ago, written by Simone Weil, the intellectual (not to be confused with Simone Veil, the politician), which extolled the diversity of French culture before it was ruthlessly suppressed by the Monarchy and the Church in their joint effort to control the minds and the bodies of all the people. Today the heirs of these Kings and Bishops are united under the banner of the Ecole Nationale d'Administration and are ruining what is left of French culture and diversity. It all ties together.

In 1973, when we moved from the Parisian suburb of Villeneuve-le-Roi to live in Paris, I took leave of the local haberdasher with whom I had become friendly. Replying to my inquiry as to his family, he told me: "Olivier is taking a preparatory course to seek entrance to the ENA." Without thinking, I blurted out, "*Mon Dieu*, what is this country coming to if even the sons of Jewish merchants want to become functionaries!" Even though I did not realize it at the time, that remark was prophetic. I do not know if Olivier made it to the ENA, but other French Jews did, notably Jacques Attali and Laurent Fabius, who also served as minions to Mitterrand. It is perhaps significant that the ENA was founded by Michel Debré, a Jew converted to Catholicism. Several years ago, I coined the word *CartésoCon* to designate the typical *ENArque* who has all the right answers but the wrong facts or to use shorthand, "the light but not the keys." One such person, Giscard d'Estaing, was elected President in 1974 and today France is run by *CartésoCons* who think up magic solutions for all problems, such as the 35-hour work-week to cure unemployment.

If a French Jew were to seek my advice as to what to do with his life, I'd offer him three choices. If he were religious, in middle age and/or attracted by his roots, I'd suggest that he go East to Israel. If he were young and inclined to pluralism, I'd recommend that he head West to the USA. And if he had a heroic bent, with a penchant for martyrdom, I'd urge him to stay in France and seek to rid it of Cartesianism and its *ENArques*, as St. Patrick rid Ireland of its snakes. *Vive Montaigne, Vive la France!*

Vol. XIX, N° 8, December 1997

The Christmas Issue: My Favorite Sayings

Several Decembers ago, a young lady visiting my office asked me, eyes wide open in expectation, "Will there be a Christmas issue of the Newsletter?" The idea that my modest musings could arouse hopes, associated with the joy of the holiday season, warmed my heart and I did indeed write a Christmas issue that year. Since then I have tried to keep it up, even if only in token fashion, as during the horrible December of 1995 when the French public-transportation workers strike practically paralyzed the economy and spoiled the Noël of many a household. Last year, I managed to find laughter in describing President Chirac's soporific television performance which, in retrospect, makes it easier to see why he is now a lame-duck President withering away after his disastrous decision in April to dissolve the National Assembly. This year, I have resolved to offer my faithful readers something in the nature of a Christmas gift by discoursing on some of my favorite sayings, in three languages.

1. "The world imagined is the ultimate good."

My first year at Harvard Law School was such a cultural shock, as I grappled with the mysteries of what is called "legal thinking," that I consoled myself often with attending lectures, concerts and other events taking place in the Yard. I continued the practice as much as possible in my second and third years, despite the limited time afforded by my Law Review duties. In the early 1950s, Harvard and I enjoyed the visits of a fantastic list of world-class cultural figures, including Robert Frost, T.S. Eliot, Bertrand Russell, Dylan Thomas, Thornton Wilder, Richard Wilbur, Aaron Copland and Wallace Stevens.

When I attended Wallace Stevens' reading of his poetry I had little familiarity with his poems, and his raspy uninspired voice – after all, he earned his living as an insurance executive in Hartford – did little to enhance my appreciation of them. Indeed, I could not understand any of the poems he read and listened, half-asleep, until, of a sudden, I heard this line which stood out like a beacon in a thick fog: "The world imagined is the ultimate good." This was the only line in the hour-long reading which I could identify as a seemingly plain declarative sentence, yet as I did not retain the rest of the poem, or even its title, I went away completely mystified as to what it was supposed to mean. For years this line lingered in my memory and whenever I would come across a Wallace Stevens collection of poems in a book store I would try to find this line, without success, until finally I bought a "collected works" and located the poem. It has the strange title, *Final Soliloquy of the Interior Paramour;*" and begins,

Light the first light of evening
As in a room in which we rest
And for small reason, think
The world imagined is the ultimate good.

This line has haunted me for more than 40 years; it is one of those incredibly rich insights that are in themselves worth a college education. The basic idea, to me, is that each human being is the maker of his own universe, his own values, his own happiness. Each person's imagination can make the world an existentialist paradise. It can also make it a Hell. I won't go any further, since I can not improve on Wallace Stevens, and I would not deprive you of the pleasure of seeking your own interpretation of this, my favorite single line in all poetry.

2. "All things fall and are built again. And those that build them again are gay."

These lines are from the poem, *Lapis Lazuli,* by William Butler Yeats, the great Irish poet who honored this otherwise dismal century. He describes a carving on lapis lazuli in which two Chinese men are contemplating the ruins of a town and he notes that they are smiling. The point is that survivors are happy when they rebuild. It was on reading these lines that I finally understood how my father who, as an adolescent, lost his entire family – massacred by the Turkish Army in Chunkoush in 1915 – could sing and be happy, despite this horrible memory and despite the hardships of the Great Depression of the 1930s in the United States. He was rebuilding, just as were the survivors of Auschwitz who went on to create new lives, after having lost their families and endured torture and starvation. The world belongs to the survivors, Yeats is saying, and they are happy if they can rebuild. I cited these lines in my Foreword to the catalog of the National Gallery of Armenia, because the thought is universal and no one can improve on it, not even an Armenian poet.

3. "Le mieux est l'ennemi du bien."

It is time for a French saying, and this pithy one attributed to Voltaire, which shows off the French language at its best, is one of my favorites because it is so useful in daily life. Literally, it says: "Better is the enemy of good," but it is not very understandable in that form. The closest English saying is, I suppose, "Let well enough alone" but this does not have the sweep of the French saying. The point is, of course, that it is often unwise, even counter-productive, to try to improve on a writing or a situation which is already satisfactory. Although as a lawyer I tend to be a perfectionist in drafting contracts and opinions, I realize that there is a point when it does not make sense to keep working on it. This thought was caricatured in Albert Camus' novel, *La Peste,* (The Plague) where one of the characters is purportedly working on a novel, but he never gets past the first line, because he keeps re-arranging the words.

4. "L'arbre qui cache la forêt."

Another French saying, literally, "The tree that hides the forest," bears a superficial resemblance to the familiar "Not to see the forest for the trees," but when you think about it they are not identical. The English expression has "trees" in the plural whereas the French one uses a single tree. To me, the former suggests that a person sees a lot of details but does not realize that these details add up to a coherent whole, an American failing, if I may interject an unkind generalization. On the other hand, the French saying implies that the person is too close to the single tree to notice that behind and around it there is a whole forest. In other words, he is blinded by a single fact and has not observed the rest of the relevant data, perhaps a French failing, as my readers know by now.

5. "What you can say later, do not say earlier."

You guessed it; this is an Armenian saying. For those of you eager to learn this wonderful Indo-European language, let me start you off with the transliteration of the original saying, which I learned from my father, Karnig Kevorkian: *"Inch vor vertche gernas essel, aratch mi esser."* There is a story behind it, or rather two stories. When I was 37 and undergoing a struggle over my departure from the firm where I had been a partner, my father visited me in Paris, and I told him about my travails. The person I had been negotiating with had gone back on the oral agreement we had reached and I realized that he used this technique to ascertain my limit, from which he would henceforth work down. I did not know how to prevent this from continuing. My father told me, "I do not know enough about your world but maybe I can pass on a bit of advice which I got from my father when I was very young." He had been on a long walk with his father, when they met a man on a donkey who asked the way to the blacksmith's shop in Chunkoush. Karnig's father told him that it was up the hill and as they were going there he would show him the way, but asked whether his son could ride on the donkey's back, to which the man readily agreed. When they got to the top of the hill, the father said, "By the way, the shop is closed today." After the man left, Karnig reproached his father, "If you knew the shop was closed why didn't you tell him right off?" His father retorted, "If I had told him earlier, you would have had to walk up the hill. What you can say later, you do not have to say earlier."

Although, like my father, I did not relish the illustration that led to the saying, I did find the maxim very useful in my negotiation and have ever since considered it an excellent rule. There is generally an optimum time to make any point. To state it otherwise, one should never lie but one can often choose the best time to tell the truth. One should always be aware of the importance of timing in any negotiation or litigation. Of course, every woman knows this rule instinctively, at least as to choosing the moment to tell her age!

6. "The Child is father of the Man."

This is another line that is worth four years in any Ivy League college. Its author is William Wordsworth, who began writing poetry in the 18th century but continued well into the 19th. This line is from a small poem called *"My heart leaps up when I behold."* It should be – but isn' t- obvious that before any person was an adult he or she was a child and that child is what shaped the adult. The child fathers the man or mothers the woman. Each time I think of this line I remind myself that whenever I meet someone new I should try to imagine what he was like as a child, for the child is key to the understanding of that person. I am assuming that you agree with the basic observation, shared by most psychologists, that one's personality is essentially shaped by the time he is four or five; but even if it is ten or twelve, the point still holds.

7. "If thou regrett'st thy youth, why live?"

While we're on English poets, let me cite my favorite line by my favorite romantic, George Gordon, Lord Byron. This handsome nobleman was forced to flee England because of the scandal aroused by his incestuous affair with his half-sister. As Mathew Arnold said (I seem to recall) Byron made his European travels "a pageant of his bleeding heart," a phrase one does not easily forget. Quite a lover, Byron spent a lot of time in wicked Venice where married women of the best families were willing preys of his amorous attentions. One reason, I must confess, why I am so fond of Byron is that he is the most famous non-Armenian to have bothered to learn the Armenian language. Despite his debauchery of the night before, Byron would get rowed the next morning to the little island of San Lazzaro in the Lagoon, where a learned order of Armenian-Catholic monks, called the Mkitarists, had been established a century earlier in a former leper colony. There, a monk taught Byron to read and write Armenian and, to prove his knowledge, Byron actually translated some Armenian writings into English, which were published by the Mkitarists after Byron's death. I ran across a copy of this slim volume on the shelves of the library of the University of Pennsylvania in 1950 when I was doing research on my senior honors thesis in American History on "The United States and the Armenian Mandate." Those were the days before the Xerox machine, but I wish now that I had a copy of this book.

To return to Byron's line, what he was saying is that if the burden of one's youth is too heavy to bear, then life is hardly worth living, the idea being, in a way, an extension of Wordsworth's line. Byron tried to redeem his youthful errors by joining in the Greek revolutionary movement to seek freedom from the Turks. He died at Missolonghi, shortly after having composed these poignant lines on his 36th birthday:

Tis time this heart should be unmoved,
Since others it hath ceased to move:
Yet, though I cannot be beloved,
Still let me love!

. "To know more and more about less and less is, finally, to know less and less."

I'm not sure who is the author of this line, which I read in an American intellectual journal many years ago. If I had to take a stab at it, I'd say the author was Dwight McDonald, who was a noted intellectual in my youth. At any rate, the subject being discussed was, I believe, the proliferation of Ph.D theses on esoteric and narrow subjects in the ostensible quest to be contributing to "original knowledge." The sentence struck me as being a major insight of general application, and reminded me of someone I had known in my undergraduate days who went on to do his Ph,D. thesis on "Minor English novelists of the 19th century." Imagine studying a novelist because you think he is minor and suddenly having to throw all your work out the window when you come to the realization that he is major after all! I suppose that since that time someone has one his Ph.D. thesis on "Unpublished English novelists of the 19th century." Of course, there is an antidote to this saying, to wit, "The Devil is in the details." But the Devil really gets around, whereas most of us get lost if we don't keep track of the big picture.

9. "Only the innocent feel guilty."

I am doubly pleased to cite this expression which gives me another occasion to mention two of my favorite people, John and Karen Hess, who personify integrity in their writings and fidelity in their friendships. They quoted this line, which did not originate with them, in their trenchant exposé of awful American eating habits, called *The Taste of America.* In my legal work, I find myself often repeating this phrase to clients who have really done nothing wrong but who nevertheless feel guilty. Over the years, I have developed the corollary, "Only the guilty feel innocent." Nixon illustrated the point with his famous plea, "I am not a crook." And more recently, in France, Georgina Dufoix, a Socialist minister immortalized herself in the contaminated-blood-scandal with the phrase "*responsable mais pas coupable*."

Well, it's time to wish all you innocents out there a Merry Christmas and a Happy New Year.

Vol. XX, N° 1, January 1998

Twenty years, *déjà*!

With this issue, my Newsletter begins its 20th year. The first Newsletter was issued in September of 1978 and, as this was late in the year, I kept Volume I open through 1979, but in retrospect I wish that I had treated the 1979 Newsletters as Volume II. The first issue went to fewer than 100 people, mainly clients and correspondents in the United States. Today I send it to about 2,000 persons, of whom more than 500 receive it by E-mail. Judging by what I am told, I would estimate that for each recipient there are at least four other readers, not only persons in the office or household but also those to whom it is re-transmitted. Thus, I surmise that each issue is read by at least 10,000 persons, a figure that I find staggering, considering that I have never sought a large audience, preferring quality and diversity of readership to quantity. At the last count, readers were located in 55 countries!

At the beginning, this Newsletter was merely intended to inform clients of the firm of new French and European legislation and legal developments. Indeed, the first four issues dealt respectively with consumer warranties, corporate control, price controls and taxation. While I wrote the first issues myself I did intend to enlist lawyers of the firm to help in the writing, and two early Newsletters were credited to colleagues, but soon I ran out of volunteers and resigned myself to writing them all. Prior to this issue, 116 Newsletters have been published, of which 114 have been written entirely by myself.

It was only in October 1980, two years after the first issue, that I summoned up the temerity to deal with a non-legal topic, to wit, the French mind, in a Newsletter called "A Word about the French Spirit." This brought me more "fan mail" than all the prior issues combined, which encouraged me to "branch out" from time to time into subjects of general interest, including French politics, particularly after the election of François Mitterrand as President of France in May 1981 and the advent of the Socialists. In recent years, the legal topic, in the narrow sense, has been the exception rather than the rule, although several of the Newsletters which have been most praised, such as the two on the Dreyfus Affair [combined in this book] and the one last year on the accident of Diana, Princess of Wales, have dealt with the French court system.

What prompted me to write the first Newsletter was an inquiry from the house counsel of an American corporate client about a new French law on consumer warranties. On reading his letter I felt a pang of guilt, telling myself that it was I who should have taken the initiative to inform clients of this new statute. Thus, the Newsletter began as an exercise in self-discipline. I used to read all the new laws and regulations published in the *Journal Officiel*, attentive to items that might interest our clients. Paradoxically, although the Newsletter continues, and my colleagues continue to peruse the *Journal Officiel,* there is hardly anything in French legislation in recent years that is worth taking seriously, at least when it is enacted. I have oft pointed out that many French laws never go into effect, whether because they require implementing decrees that are never issued, or because they are repealed or amended before they take effect, or simply because they are so silly that they are not applied. In the last category, for example, is the law allowing comparative advertising, which I vainly took the trouble to discuss in January 1992 and which contains so many asinine restrictions that no one dares to advertise comparatively. In the second category, one can cite a major revision of the Code of Penal Procedure enacted by a Socialist parliament late in 1992, which would have largely adopted the adversarial system but which was repealed several months later by the new "conservative" majority before it went into effect. As to the first category – laws awaiting implementing decrees – they are legion. The French legislative process is a farce.

This subject leads me to cite a new book that is beginning to attract attention, *Les Trente Piteuses,* by Nicolas Baverez. The title, that might be translated, "The Thirty Miserable Years," contrasts with a term which had become fashionable among French economists, *Les Trente Glorieuses* ("The Thirty Glorious Years"), referring to the three decades following World War II when France's economy made major strides. In contradistinction, Baverez asserts that the current period can be described as pitiable, with France mired in unemployment, deflation and stagnation. In the course of his analysis, Baverez delivers a devastating critique of the political institutions of the Fifth Republic, including the Parliament and the judiciary, both subservient to an all-powerful executive branch. Among the points made by the author is that "Too many laws kill law" (*Trop de lois tuent la loi* – an adaptation of the remark *Trop d'impôts tuent l'impôt*) referring, as I have often done, to the proliferation of legal texts that are never enforced.

According to the blurb on the back cover, the author was 36 years old in 1997 when the book was published. This struck me hard, because it means that he was born in 1961, the very year when I came to France to work as a lawyer. Thus, he was only seven years old in May 1968 when the student revolt triggered strikes that put all of France out of business for a month, and only 12 when the Yom Kippur war of 1973 led to a massive increase in oil prices and a transfer of wealth to many Arab nations, and only 20 when the so-called "Mitterrand generation" came to power in France. My point is that while I lived these years as an adult, observing with the eyes of a foreigner the gradual and extraordinary assumption of power by the caste of functionaries who now rule France, Baverez has learned the story largely from books, but he has learned it well, coming to the same conclusion as I have, to wit, that France is in a state of decadence.

It pleases me to note that Baverez, whom the blurb describes as a historian and economist, adopts many of the themes that I have been harping on for the past 20 years, among them being the need for a major revision of the French Constitution to institute a true separation of powers with checks and balances. Moreover, he specifically advances two of my pet proposals: that civil servants be required to resign before running for office and that no public official be allowed to hold more than one position. Throughout the book, he refers, as I have been doing for years, to the current regime as a monarchy and the functionary class as an aristocracy based on diplomas rather than birth. Regrettably, all this he recites without humor. Moreover, Baverez appears in two respects to be the typical French intellectual: first, he basks in abstraction: the book is replete with abstract nouns and adjectives and contains very few verbs and adverbs; second, this point flowing from the first, he does not indicate how the country can free itself of that aristocracy and adopt a new Constitution. I am reminded of the favorite fable of my childhood: the mice hold a general assembly to decide what to do about the cat who stealthily pounces on them without warning. One mouse suggests that the solution is to tie a bell around the cat's neck so that they can hear him coming. Everyone thinks this is a great idea and the motion is adopted unanimously. But then a little mouse chirps up: "But who is going to bell the cat*?"*

So my question is who is going to oust the *ENArques* from their monopolistic position in the French government and economy? Who is going to tell Chirac, Jospin, Rocard, Juppé, Balladur, Fabius, Séguin, Aubry, to name a prominent few, that they can not be functionaries and also elected officials and ministers? Who is going to tell the numerous *ENArques* in business, such as the heads of Renault, Peugeot, Cie. Générale des Eaux, Cie. Lyonnaise des Eaux, Air France, again to name only a few, that they can not have civil-service status and run ostensibly private companies? People in power do not give it up lightly, particularly when power conveys privilege and financial advantage.

When my French friends describe their despair over the economic situation and high taxes, they frequently say that the country needs a revolution. But when I ask them whether they will be part of it, the answer is invariably, "Why me*?"* Aside from Le Pen's Front National, there is no political movement whatever to counter the dominant parties which together make up what I call le *Parti des Fonctionnaires,* to wit, on the Left, the Socialist Party and the Communist Party and on the Right, the RPR and the UDF, all dominated by *ENArques* and other functionaries, in one guise or another.

In the last month, much media attention has been given to the purported uprising of the unemployed, who have occupied a number of quasi-official buildings, mainly those of the organizations that hand out unemployment benefits, called ASSEDIC. In reality, this has not been a grass-roots movement, but rather one organized by the Communist union, the CGT, which has many sympathizers among the journalists of TV, radio and the press. The sit-ins have gotten a lot of coverage and embarrassed the Jospin government. One does not know whether to laugh or cry when one notes that these unemployed were not asking for jobs, but rather a Christmas bonus (*prime de Noël*). And their spokesmen were not criticizing the government for the high taxes and social charges that have hobbled the entrepreneurial class (what remains of it) but rather blaming the "evil capitalists" who make money while laying off workers. Having obtained some handouts, the protesters broadened their demand to an over-all rise of F1,500 per month in the so-called *minima sociaux,* a new term for the multitude of handouts to people out of work, many of whom earn more this way than they would by working. Indeed, *chômeur* (unemployed) is becoming a recognized profession in France.

The Communist Party is supposedly an ally of the Socialists and it has four ministers in the Jospin government. But everyone knows that the two parties hate each other and that this is merely a marriage of convenience. Ultimately, the Communists would love to discredit the Socialists and, by appearing as the champions of the working class, regain the supporters that they lost during the Mitterrand era. Moreover, the Communists are opposed to the Maastricht Treaty and the common currency, which are pillars of the Socialist platform. Robert Hue, the chief Communist, has just come out firmly against the strong-franc policy, which he rightly credits as contributing to unemployment.

Until December, Prime Minister Jospin was riding high in the polls and seemed, like Edouard Balladur before him, to have mastered the art of doing nothing while appearing earnestly to deal with the nation's problems. Now, in January, his charmed life seems to have come to an end, not only because of the continuing pressure exerted by the organized unemployed but also because of a major gaffe he committed while speaking in the National Assembly on two anniversaries – the 150th of the abolition of slavery in French colonies and the 100th of the publication of Emile Zola's stirring *J'accuse* in the newspaper *l'Aurore.* Jospin took advantage of this occasion to applaud the Left for being Dreyfusard and opposed to slavery and then went on to assert that the Right had favored slavery and later became anti-Dreyfusard. On hearing these demagogic remarks, all the opposition members filed out of the Assembly in protest. The public uproar among the political class was so great that Jospin had to eat crow and present his "regrets" to the parliamentarians. Jospin also showed himself a poor student of history by referring to Léon Gambetta as one of the leaders of the Left who had supported Dreyfus, whereas this politician had died 12 years before the affair began!

This incident is not serious in itself but it indicates the state of mind of so many French politicians whose minds are mired in the clichés and shibboleths of the 19th century. The Left-Right cleavage is a joke in France and, like the word *l'état,* serves only to mask the reality there is no opposition to the reign of the *ENArques*. Juppé was "Right" and Jospin is "Left," but both raised taxes and did nothing to encourage entrepreneurs to create jobs.

The official figure of 12.4 percent unemployment is utter nonsense, yet it is repeated endlessly by journalists, and even by Nicolas Baverez, who should know better. I do not expect much from French journalists, who are being paid, in effect, by the government to be good boys, for they get an extra 30-percent deduction on their income taxes! (Juppé, to his credit, had tried to eliminate this absurd bribe paid to an entire profession, but the wily Jospin has decided to keep it.) However, the *New York Times* reporters in Paris, including the able Craig Whitney, also repeat this false figure time and again. In a recent article, the *Times* asserted that the French unemployed were 3.1-million, which, if this represents 12.4 percent of the potential work force, means that the latter figure is 25-million. However, the true number of unemployed is more like five-million, a figure that was given to me by a high tax official a year ago. A recent study, which the government tried to squelch, asserted that the total under-employed in France came to seven-million, including 1.5-million of involuntary part-time workers. Even if you take out all these part-time workers, that leaves 5.5-million unemployed. Assuming the figure is "only" five-million, that still represents 20 percent, not 12.4! Even more startling is the fact that if you take out of the denominator of the total work-force the five-million employees of the public sector who never are laid off, that means that the unemployed in the private sector represent 25 percent! One out of four in the private sector is jobless. And thousands of talented people are leaving France to work elsewhere.

So far, Jospin's only cure for unemployment has been to create thousands of new functionary posts, ostensibly under non-renewable five-year contracts, but just try to get rid of these functionaries when their contracts expire! His other long-term remedy is the absurd proposal to reduce the workweek to 35 hours, without lowering the pay of these lucky workers. The CNPF, France's leading employers' association, led by its new President, Baron Ernest-Antoine Seillière, himself an *ENArque* and self-made heir to a steel fortune, has vowed to fight the 35-hour chimera. But without this magic solution, the Socialists would have to admit that it is necessary to have five-million unemployed so that five-million functionaries can have lifetime jobs and generous retirement benefits, paid for by the 15-million in the private sector who still have work but are reeling under the tax burden.

Fortunately for Jospin, the World Soccer competition will be hosted by France in June and this is likely to divert employed and unemployed alike for a while, but days of reckoning will come in due course, perhaps when the unemployed ask for paid vacations this summer. One happy day their unemployment benefits will be paid in Euros and their troubles will end.

On Lying, Liars and Mr. Clinton

Readers may recall a piece I did, called "On Lying, Liars and Monsieur Tapie" (March 31, 1995) which dealt with Bernard Tapie, the rogue French businessman turned politician, once the darling of President Mitterrand, who named him a Minister, despite the unsavory reputation he already had. Tapie's comeuppance finally occurred when, as head of the Marseilles soccer team, he bribed players on a rival team to throw a game, and then, when the story leaked, got a fellow Socialist politician, Jacques Mellick, to lie in his favor. The latter, in turn, got his secretary to lie to support his alibi, but she finally turned state's evidence, after which Mellick admitted his guilt, finally leading Tapie to confess in open court, making the immortal defense: "I lied in good faith!" Tapie spent only six months in jail for these offenses, proving once again that it pays to confess in France.

These affairs led me to compare Catholic and Protestant attitudes toward lying, as depicted respectively in France, where it is taken in stride, doubtless because of the availability of Catholic confession, and in the United States, where it is taken seriously, doubtless for the opposite reason. I pointed out that Protestants often deal with their own lying by convincing themselves that they told the truth. An avid Moroccan reader and friend encouraged me to follow up on the theme of lying with a discussion of Muslim attitudes on the subject. According to my friend, the typical Muslim deals with unpleasant truths not by denying them but rather by portraying himself as a victim. For example, if he has arrived late for work, he does not say he overslept, but rather, *"I was betrayed by sleep."* If he missed the bus, it was because *"the bus left without me."* And if he broke a glass at work the reason is that "the glass escaped from my hand." Thus the culprit becomes the object rather than the subject of the incident. I asked my friend, "But surely there must come a time when this Muslim must face up to his own guilt?" To this my friend replied, *"To be sure: then the ultimate excuse becomes 'it was written'."* In other words, Allah had destined the transgression to take place. No wonder Islam is such a popular religion! Moreover, who can disprove the proposition that anything that happened was meant to happen?

As I write this, the Clinton-Lewinsky affair has not reached its *dénouement*, but already several readers have asked me to comment on it, particularly as it is seen through French eyes. Many, if not most, French people look on Americans as overgrown children, generally naive and often hypocritical in their attitudes towards sex and public figures. On the whole, the French do not expect their political leaders to be honest, let alone faithful to their wives. Indeed, they are rather proud to be a nation which has produced virile Kings and, now, virile Presidents. Louis XV, for example, while credited with being a good Catholic monarch, kept his courtiers busy lining up buxom females to consume his sexual appetite. More close to our time, the French love to recount the happy end of Felix Faure, one of the Presidents of the Third Republic, who died in the throes of coitus. To appreciate the following story you must know that *connaissance* in French means both "consciousness" and "acquaintance." When Faure's valet summoned a priest for the last rites, he was asked, "Does *Monsieur le Président* still have his *connaissance?"* To which the valet replied, "No, she left by the back stairway." Even closer at hand, more than one president of the Fifth Republic has been known to pursue women avidly, and I am not referring to General de Gaulle.

Most French people with whom I have spoken about Clinton's travails, women as well as men, laugh at the fuss being made over the Paula Jones affair and the most recent aftermath involving Monica Lewinsky, who signed an affidavit in that case denying a "sexual relationship" with the president. When I try to explain that lying under oath is considered a serious offense in the USA, they shrug and say, "If they did not want her to lie, they should not have called her to testify on a matter which is no one's business but her own."

One of my French friends, not known for his gravity, asserts that this is all Hillary's fault. "If she had fulfilled her *devoir conjugal* more assiduously, poor Bill would not have had to seek gratification elsewhere," explains this compassionate male. On hearing the words *devoir conjugal*, my mind reverted to the first time I heard this term, uttered by a cleaning woman in the Judge Advocate office in La Rochelle, when I was young and untutored in every-day French vocabulary. The woman was complaining about her husband's disinterest in satisfying her physical needs. For the record, I want to state that I did not rise to the occasion.

A century and a half ago, de Toqueville pointed out in his *Democracy in America* that in the USA virtually all problems end up in the courtroom. The notion that no man is above the law is a noble one and the fact that even a President of the United States can be hauled into the civil courts is the best demonstration of the meaning of the rule of law. In France, powerful people often refuse to appear when called to testify and basically they get away with it. We come back to the essential contrast that France is a vertical society and the United States a horizontal one. Yet it is patent that the legal process is abused in the United States, particularly in the area known as "discovery," a means by which a litigant can harass his adversary as well as third parties by prying into matters which are not really germane to the case. I do not understand why Ms Lewinsky was called to testify in the Paula Jones case, involving an alleged incident in Arkansas which occurred years before she met Clinton. And why did she not object to giving an affidavit? I find it ironic that Clinton, who received huge financial support for his campaigns from plaintiffs' lawyers, may now be undone by them.

Of course, the American press comes in for French criticism as well, since the French are much more respectful of the distinction between the private and public lives of their leaders. The traditional American journalistic ploy is to convert what is a private matter into a public one by asking the politician about his private life and then demonstrating that he lied. By this method, the issue becomes not one of sex but of "character." Thus, Gary Hart, once a contender for the presidency, stupidly fell into the trap by answering questions about his "womanizing," which then gave an excuse for reporters to follow him around and make a fuss about his lying. Paradoxically, telling the truth can also be fatal to presidential candidates, as when George Romney was discredited by the press for having admitted that he had been "brainwashed" during the Vietnam war. (I thought his remark both honest and courageous.) And Edmund Muskie was destroyed politically for shedding a tear about an unjust attack on his wife. American presidents are supposed to hold themselves out as paragons of virtue, strength and infallibility even though everyone knows that no one is perfect. It is little wonder that Clinton, in his 1992 campaign, chose to deny the Gennifer Flower liaison, using all the subtleties of language that he learned at Yale Law School. But most French people would say that the journalists should not have asked the question in the first place.

As there is always a silver lining in every cloud, what I find positive in the impending demolition of an American president is the demonstration that neither the country's institutions nor its vitality depend on any individual. After all, the business of America is not government but business, and there is plenty of that to keep Americans busy. As to Clinton, he might ponder, along with the rest of us, the trenchant Shakespeare sonnet that begins: "The expense of spirit in a waste of shame is lust in action."

Vol. XX, N° 2, February 1998

Sinking in the Atlantic

Sometimes – in fact, almost always – I have trouble convincing myself that it is worthwhile to begin another Newsletter, having the impression that I've said it all before. Indeed, in reviewing some past Newsletters, I become conscious that certain themes keep cropping up, such as ethics and Cartesianism. Then, I have to confess to myself that my value system is different from that of my surroundings, since I was born and bred in the United States and despite three decades of exposure to French "culture" I still have the capacity to be shocked by the value system here. At the same time, some friends who know me well tell me that if I were living in the USA I would rebel also at the prevalent standards. Realizing that this is probably true, I used to tell myself that I am half way between the United States and France, but it was only recently that it dawned on me that this half-way position puts me squarely in the Atlantic Ocean, not a good place to be if you're not a good swimmer! Hence the title: sometimes I feel that I am sinking rapidly in the Atlantic Ocean.

As one who has practiced in both legal systems, I can attest to the strengths and the shortcomings of each, particularly in the field of litigation. The fundamental difference between the two systems has to do with the approach to facts. I once wrote that after 25 years in France two mysteries remained in my mind, the first being how the French can afford the prices in the shops and, the second, how facts are proved in a French court. In French civil cases, witnesses are rarely heard, and most cases are decided on the basis of documents exchanged by the parties, as elucidated by the briefs and oral arguments of their lawyers. There is no "discovery" to speak of, which means that one party does not have access to documents or witnesses that the other party does not voluntarily produce. The documents that are submitted do not have to be authenticated nor their relevance established. Yet somehow, the courts end up assuming they have enough facts to decide the case. Fortunately, there are no juries in civil cases – for good reason, since there are no witnesses.

In an American lawsuit, the rule is that no facts are established unless they are admitted in the pleadings or proved in open court by live witnesses. But before you get to that stage of the case, months, sometimes years, are consumed by the process called "discovery," in which each party can compel the testimony of the other party's personnel and obtain documents which it would not otherwise produce. Frequently, this process results in thousands, if not millions, of pages of documents, requiring computer programs for sorting and retrieval, and making it virtually impossible for the judge, let alone the jury, to absorb the evidence and reach coherent findings of fact.

My readers will not be surprised if I say that both systems are unsatisfactory and that the best system would lie somewhere between the two extremes. The American system's key flaw is best described by the maxim I quoted in last December's Newsletter: "To know more and more about less and less is finally to know less and less." American lawyers tend to drown themselves in facts and they do not reflect enough on the facts they are gathering. Of course, as most lawyers charge by the hour, discovery for a paying client is a lucrative business, so self-interest of the legal profession tends to perpetuate this system. I have never seen a lawyer's bill which states: "Thinking about your case." Yet this is really what clients should most want to pay a lawyer for. When I was a young Wall Street lawyer, at Dewey Ballantine, engaged in major litigation,

I drifted into the specialty of just thinking about the theory of the cases. Once, the firm had inherited an important anti-trust case from an uptown firm which had already engaged in years of discovery, with no end in sight. As this was a geographic price-discrimination case under the Clayton Act, between two substantial companies, I thought about the underlying issues and convinced the partner in charge, the late Phil Scott, to make a motion for summary judgment. This was an audacious step since the rationale of such a motion is that there are no real issues of fact and, thus, the case can be decided on questions of law. My point was that there was really no need to gather more facts, since the test of an anti-trust violation is injury to competition, not to a competitor, and the lowering of prices in an area where the competitors are of equal financial strength does not injure competition. Although the judge denied the motion, he did accept our theory of the law, which prompted the other party to settle the case quickly. The problem had been that the lawyers who had been "handling" the case were having so much fun and profit gathering "facts" that they were not thinking about the law applicable to the case.

The abuse of discovery in the United States is largely a result of the reluctance of the lawyers and the judge to spend time thinking about the case at an early stage, whereas this is the stage when thinking is the most productive. Instead, judges indulge in the shibboleth that "the policy of this jurisdiction is to encourage liberal discovery," a hollow statement because unless you know what the case is about you can not know whether discovery is necessary or useful, let alone worth the cost it entails.

The French judicial system is guilty of the other extreme, since in civil cases it allows parties to conceal facts that are relevant to the issues of the case and permits judges to remain indifferent to the enormous factual gap which results. French commentators do not seem to focus at all on the vast contrast between the role of the judge in criminal and in civil cases. In the former, the judge acts as the Grand Inquisitor, directing the police inquiry in the investigative stage and badgering witnesses, sometimes putting them in jail to make them confess and, in the trial itself, conducting the interrogation of the accused and the witnesses. Yet, in civil cases, the judge acts as an indifferent bystander, not even looking at the documents which one party gives to the other until the case is called for oral arguments or thinking how best justice would be served. Ultimately, this contrast reflects French-Catholic attitudes: where sin is involved, that is, in criminal cases, the judge is an activist, wanting to ferret out the truth and, in particular, wanting to find a guilty party who will confess his sin. Where the matter concerns only private interests, that is, basically, money and property, the judge says, in effect, "Don't bother me with your crass facts, you are both unworthy before God."

Of course, few French judges would admit to the validity of what I've just written, since they take for granted the values of their system, just as few American judges, particularly as they come from the Bar, would admit that they are accomplices to the abuse of the fact-gathering process. Paradoxically, my half-way remedy for the flaws of each system – let's call it the "Atlantic Ocean compromise" – would be for judges to become more activist in both countries. In the United States, judges should get more involved earlier in the legal issues that set the framework for the factual issues, and in France, judges should be more activist in the fact-development process. Of course, inertia being what it is, there is fat chance of this type of reform taking place in either country, so I will continue to sink in the Atlantic.

Ultimately this dilemma – France giving preference to theory over fact and America getting lost in facts and failing to theorize enough – reminds me of the insight that I got from Professor Elizabeth Flower, in a course I took at Penn on the "Philosophy of History." Speaking of the "rationalist-empiricist dichotomy," she explained (my paraphrasing) that the rationalist believes that ideas have a life of their own but the problem is that he can't verify them without ascertaining facts, while the empiricist says, in effect, that facts induce theories, but the problem is that he can't know what facts to look for unless he starts with a theory. The truth, again, is somewhere in the middle: we need both facts and theory and there must be a constant interplay between the two. We keep improving the theory with the discovery of new facts and we discover new facts because we have theories. I hope that I will not be surprising any reader if I say that every intellectual discipline, whether it be law, history, journalism, medicine, or science, involves the same process, getting facts, fitting them into a coherent theory, which in turn leads to getting more facts and sometimes modifying the theory. Any intellectual system will break down if theory becomes dogma, so that the believer refuses to consider further facts, or if facts remain unconnected and do not become part of a theory. A child starts life with disparate facts and begins the process of maturing by fitting the facts into a coherent concept. Religious and political fanatics commit the opposite error of abstaining from confronting theory with facts, because they already have the "truth."

Years ago, I read a book of correspondence between Locke and Leibnitz on the issue of so-called "innate ideas." Locke, of course, was the proponent of the *tabula rasa* theory, that is, each person begins life with a clean slate and develops ideas from the facts discovered through his senses. Leibnitz espoused the cause of innate ideas. From what I've read more recently, it would appear that Leibnitz was closer to the truth, in that it seems to be admitted now that people are born with the innate ability to organize facts into coherent patterns and this includes, as Chomsky has expounded, the ability to acquire language skills. However, individuals end up being different as to their degree of theorizing and nations also seem to have differing propensities in this domain. I remain intrigued by the question as to why the French have, as a people, taken to Cartesianism, which favors *a priori* theorizing over facts. A friend of mine, a psychiatrist from another Latin country, claims that this is ingrained in French genes. While I am reluctant to believe that human genetic material differs with geographic borders, particularly within Europe, others are just as reluctant to accept my explanation for French Cartesianism, which ties the phenomenon to the Catholic-Monarchical tradition of France, both of which tend to promote simplistic, authoritarian rules of conduct.

A case in point: the legislation proposed by the Socialists to reduce the workweek to 35 hours in order to promote employment is a perfect illustration of Cartesianism in the political-economic sphere. The idea is simplistic, static and mathematical: if, say, 20-million employees now work 39 hours a week, that makes 780-million hours worked. If you divide this figure by 35 hours, the result shows that 22.2-million people are required to produce the same number of hours. Ergo, employment will be increased by 2.2 million! This theory is on the same level of realism as "belling the cat," related in my last Newsletter. In the first place, the legislation will require employers to pay the same amount for the reduced workweek as they did for 39 hours, obviously no incentive to hire more workers. In the second place, it is so difficult to fire workers that sensible employers would prefer paying overtime, if 39 hours are really necessary, to taking on new heads. In the third place, employers will seek ways of improving productivity through new equipment rather than hire more workers. Indeed, it was announced recently that industrial investment is up for 1998, a sign to me that employers are already preparing to reduce dependency on labor.

The final irony of the 35-hour panacea was the announcement, played down by the servile French press, that it would be applied to the public sector, *i.e.,* to functionaries. Is the idea to encourage the growth of an already-bloated bureaucracy? This would require raising taxes, already astronomic, and further heighten the exodus of present and future entrepreneurs from France. An economist was quoted in *Figaro Magazine* of February 28th to the effect that 50,000 highly-qualified people are leaving France every year, while 100,000 mainly unqualified and illicit immigrants are flocking in, aggravating the social and budgetary problems of France.

Every time I take a taxi in Paris, I ask the driver how many hours he works a week. The answer is invariably 11 hours a day, for six or even seven days a week. That means 66 to 77 hours. Then I ask, "Why don't you work only 35 hours?" and the reply, accompanied by a sardonic laugh, is "I wouldn't eat at 35 hours." Nor would I, nor would the other independents in France – doctors, dentists, restaurateurs, trades-people. The French system is destroying the middle class and, in particular, the self-employed, who have to work double time to help pay for the functionaries and those who do not work. The European Union, following the French model, is designed for two classes, functionaries and employees of large entities, on the one hand, and the unemployed, the retired and handout receivers, on the other. The system is thus making life easy for the multinationals, more and more concentrated in all the major industries and commerce and able to pass on increased costs to their customers.

Despite these problems, the French press is having a good time playing up the "Monicagate" and Iraq issues, not necessarily unrelated, and both starring Bill Clinton. There is general relief here that the Pentagon has put off bombing Iraqi sites and the press is giving some of the credit to Jacques Chirac, whose popularity has risen in the polls, as has Prime Minister Jospin's, who has been more convincing in that role than the hapless Alain Juppé.

As to the Monica Lewinsky scandal, the conventional wisdom coming from the American press is that presidential sex capers are less important than presidential lying or inciting to lie, while a minority say that even lying is all right if it is meant to conceal private sexual conduct. I take a view that has more nuances. When Anthony Lewis, in the *International Herald Tribune,* opines that what public officials do “in the bedroom” should not be of public concern, he conveniently forgets that the escapades of Clinton with Lewinsky, if they happened at all, took place in or adjoining the Oval Office, not in either of their bedrooms. In other words, this was workplace sex and as such is a legitimate concern of those who pay the workers, in this case, the taxpayers of the USA. Would not the shareholders of General Motors object if their Chairman was inviting into his carpeted office a receptionist for a bout of fellatio every now and then? Is this any way to run a company or a country? Of course, if the allegations are not true, that’s another story, but it’s not right to say that if true, they are irrelevant. Perhaps this is not an impeachable offense but it is surely relevant to Clinton’s place in history to know that he was ejaculating while he should have been cerebrating about what to do about Saddam Hussein.

Of course, Clinton might contend that, unlike Gerald Ford, he is capable of doing both simultaneously, in which case I can assure him that his place in history is indeed secure.

Vol. XX, N° 3, April 1998

French Contrasts: Maurice Papon, Pierre Julitte and Others

The month of April, though hardly begun as I write this, is running true to tradition with blustery rain showers interspersed with sunshine. Fittingly, the political-judicial events suit the weather. The six-month marathon trial of Maurice Papon, the former Vichy functionary accused of "crimes against humanity" by ordering the arrest and deportation of French Jews, ended as the month began, and Jean-Marie Le Pen, founder of the right-wing National Front, was also in the news.

In last October's Newsletter, I described the Papon trial in Bordeaux – then a month old – as a "happening." Subsequent events did not belie this description of a trial where there were no rules of evidence and a flock of lawyers had many a field day plying an 87-year-old man about events which took place 55 years earlier in conquered France. Probably the most dramatic moment of the trial occurred on January 27th when Arno Klarsfeld, the upstart son of the intrepid couple, Serge and Beate Klarsfeld, who have made it their lifetime work to seek justice for the Jewish victims of the French collaboration with the Nazis, announced to the press that the presiding judge, Jean-Louis Castagnède, had Jewish relatives who could themselves be plaintiffs in the case, since members of their family had been deported under Papon's orders. This startling revelation seemed for a moment to be the bombshell that could put an end to the trial. Klarsfeld's fellow counsel, representing other civil plaintiffs, were furious at this grandstand play which seemed to be coming from the wrong party. Papon's lawyer, Jean-Marc Varaut, castigated Klarsfeld, saying that he had no objection to the judge, who made it known that he had been unaware of the possible connection to the case of family members, with whom he had lost touch. After threatening to seek recusal of the judge, Klarsfeld backed down and, as the family members had not joined in the suit as civil parties, there was no technical ground for the judge recusing himself.

Later, when the time for closing arguments arrived, Arno Klarsfeld again offended his co-counsel by taking the position that, after all, Papon was only a minor criminal who did not deserve the maximum sentence of life imprisonment but something like ten years. The general view of the other plaintiffs' lawyers was that any crime against humanity is, by hypothesis, *le crime des crimes* for which only the maximum sentence is fitting. The Public Prosecutor took the middle ground, asking for a 20-year sentence. Of course, Varaut and his fellow defense counsel demanded acquittal on the grounds that Papon was merely following orders and, at any rate, was not aware of "the final solution" which awaited the Jews who were deported under orders bearing Papon's signature as Secretary-General of the Gironde Prefecture, where Bordeaux is located. During the last week of closing arguments, Papon's 88-year-old wife died and the case was interrupted for 24 hours so that he could attend her funeral.

The *Cour d'Assises*, which hears felony cases, is the only tribunal in France with a jury, but the nine lay jurors deliberate in the presence of the three judges who hear the case and who also vote. As a majority of eight votes is necessary to convict the accused, this means that if five of the jurors side with the three judges, the requisite majority is obtained. It took less than 24 hours for these triers of fact to return with a verdict that satisfied virtually no one. Papon was acquitted of the various counts of complicity to murder the deported Jews, but nevertheless was found guilty of complicity in several crimes against humanity and given a ten-year jail sentence. Papon's lawyers quickly filed a petition for review of the verdict by the Cour de Cassation, the highest judicial court in France, and announced that they would appeal, if necessary, to the European Court of Human Rights, based in Strasbourg. As Papon was free during the trial, he can not be imprisoned until his case is heard by the highest court which, in theory, can "break" the decision only for procedural defects.

It should be recalled that after World War II, Papon led a very respectable life as a professional French functionary, right under de Gaulle's nose, so to speak, since Papon rose to the exalted rank of *Préfet de Police* in Paris and later became a minister under Giscard d'Estaing. Many people have forgotten, or never knew, that the Americans and the British had planned for a military government of liberated France. It was only de Gaulle's proud obstinacy that gave France a military role in the Allies' victory and allowed him to form a provisional government in 1944. But, in order to show that he could effectively govern France he had to rely on the very Vichy functionaries, like Papon, who had been his enemies in 1940 when the Vichy government sentenced de Gaulle to death in absentia for defying the armistice. This explains why post-war France conveniently overlooked the less-egregious actions of relatively minor Vichy functionaries or of those who managed to get close to the Resistance when the Allied victory seemed assured. Thus, what was remarkable about this case was the late bringing of charges against a pillar of the French civil service. Of course, these charges became possible only after the enactment by the French parliament in 1964 of a law punishing "crimes against humanity," including genocide, and declaring at the same time that such crimes are "*imprescriptible*," that is, not subject to a statute of limitations. Although there is nothing in the law stating that it applies retroactively, that is the way it has been interpreted. I would have thought that, as an original matter, this feature of retroactivity would have troubled some sensitive spirits but that does not seem the case. At the time of the Nuremberg trials, some voices were heard – notably, that of Senator Robert Taft of Ohio – claiming that the prosecution of Nazis for war crimes violated the rule against *ex post facto* laws, but the trials were conducted by the military occupants of Germany and, since time immemorial, victors have gotten their way against the vanquished.

The case of Vichy functionaries being tried by civilian courts is far different. Immediately after the war, thousands of collaborators were tried and many executed but the idea was that they had betrayed their country by acting under color of an illegal regime. At any rate, amnesty laws were enacted in 1951 and 1953 wiping the slate clean for those who had not been tried. Thus, by creating a new but retroactive crime against humanity in 1964, the Parliament made it possible to get at those who had participated in the genocide of the Jews even though "ordinary" traitors who had killed only French Catholics or Communists because they were, say, in the Resistance could no longer be brought to justice. Many will say that it is a good thing that genocide is treated in this special way. As an Armenian whose paternal grandparents were murdered by the Turkish Army in the 1915 genocide of the Armenians – a genocide which the Turkish government and its paid apologists say never took place – I can not quarrel with the idea that genocide, in effect, violates natural law and must perforce be treated retroactively since, by hypothesis, it is carried out by governments who are not acting illegally under their own laws.

This being said, many French people, among them some Jews with whom I have spoken, did not think it was wise to try an 87-year-old man for offenses committed 55 years earlier. The very idea of statutes of limitation is to prevent the bringing of stale claims when the passing years make it difficult for the accused to gather and conserve evidence necessary to defend himself. This rationale applies as well to crimes against humanity as to any other crimes. Papon surely committed the error of living too long while preserving a vigorous mind. If he had contracted Alzeimer's disease, like Ronald Reagan, he surely would not have been put on trial. Under the French inquisitorial method, where the accused is the principal witness against himself, being bombarded with questions by the judges, the prosecutor and the complainants' lawyers, it is a decided handicap to have an alert mind at 87. Had I been Papon's lawyer, I would have been tempted to urge him to remain silent throughout the whole proceeding, rather than answer questions about events and documents dating from 1942. In my view, Papon's demeanor aggravated his case: he came through as an arrogant, unrepentant bureaucrat who never considered the option of resigning or asking for transfer rather than participate in the odious process of depriving men, women and children of their liberty, simply because they were Jews. Paradoxically, by being so defiant, by defending his right to be the dutiful functionary doing business as usual, as though laws about Jews were no different from laws about work permits, Papon made it easier for the jurors to convict him.

On balance, I am favorable to this trial having taken place: it stands as a precedent for the rule that functionaries can not hide behind orders or laws that violate fundamental decency. Let us not forget that the Vichy regime on its own initiative enacted a law creating a "Status of Jews" which, among other things, eliminated them from public positions. Thus, it must not have appeared outlandish to Papon to do the Nazis' bidding by signing orders for the arrest and deportation of Jews. Yet, Papon knew, or should have known, that the basic traditions of the French republic did not permit racial or religious persecution. The verdict apparently accredits Papon's assertion that he did not know that the Jews would be killed but, by finding him guilty of other crimes against humanity, the court implicitly found that Papon's administrative role made him an accomplice to a "hegemonic" scheme of the Nazis to victimize a group of people merely for their race or religion. In other words, even if the Jews had not been killed, merely deporting them would have satisfied the 1964 definition of crimes against humanity.

In writing this, I am reminded of another act of deportation for which no one has been punished, that of American citizens of Japanese ancestry living on the West Coast who were forcibly taken from their homes and placed in concentration camps, ironically, in the same year, 1942. This measure is a permanent blot on President Roosevelt's record and that of the United States Supreme Court which initially upheld its constitutionality. True, these citizens were not exterminated but they were unjustly deprived of their liberty for years. It is interesting to think that if the American Congress enacted a measure comparable to Article 212-1 of the French Penal Code, the Papons of the US bureaucracy could be prosecuted.

As I pointed out in my October Newsletter, the main argument against the Papon trial is its highly selective nature. Hundreds of functionaries, including police and gendarmes, participated in the arrest and the deportation of Jews and other victims of Nazism. A friend from San Francisco recently sent me a book called "Surrender on Demand" written in 1945 by Varian Fry, recounting his mission to Marseille in 1940 to save European intellectuals (including Franz Werfel) as well as labor and political leaders who were earmarked for extermination by the Germans. Fry managed to get quite a few Vichy officials to help him or at least not to hinder him, but generally these officials would tell him that when the chips were down they would not hesitate to arrest these refugees and turn them over to the Germans. These officials were not anti-Semitic; they were simply scared, and did not have the stuff of heroes like the handful of functionaries who refused to do the Nazis' bidding and sometimes paid with their lives. The reason why so many French people today do not approve of the Papon trial is obvious: they would do as Papon did if similar circumstances would arise again. There are few heroes in any society and when it comes to good deeds it is easier to help "one's own kind" than the people on the other side of the tracks. To illustrate: Robert Badinter's recent book shows that when the Vichy regime instituted a rule limiting the number of Jewish lawyers to two-percent of a given bar, the various bar associations dutifully applied this rule without protest and, it is sad to relate, even the "lucky few" among the Jewish lawyers who were selected graciously accepted this distinction. Another example: some brave journalists have been reporting on French involvement, during Mitterrand's reign, in a more recent genocide, that committed by the Hutu regime of Rwanda against the Tutsi tribe. The Papon case might serve as a precedent for charging the French officials who abetted the genocide with arms and logistical help. But don't bet on it happening before 50 years.

Speaking of heroes, it is time to mention Pierre Julitte, who was the only authentic Gaullist hero whom I had the privilege of knowing at close hand, but who lived and died basically unknown to the French population. I met Julitte in the late '60s when he had just been named non-executive chairman of the French subsidiary of Arthur G. McKee & Company, then a major American engineering company. At first, all I knew of him was that he had retired as a functionary of the Ministry of Agriculture and through a connection had obtained this sinecure. Tall and stiff, with a trim mustache, Julitte struck me at first as a formalistic gentleman of the old school, with a tendency to prolixity. Sometimes he would submit for my review a draft of several pages and I would end up whittling it down to two paragraphs. Pierre had the humility to see that I was right and, after a few weeks, he paid me the supreme compliment of saying that he wished he had met me twenty years earlier.

It was only then that he gave me a novel he had written, called *L'Arbre de Goethe* ("Goethe's Tree" – published by Doubleday in 1971 as *Block 26: Sabotage at Buchenwald*) which, I was to discover, was an autobiographical account of Julitte's experience in the dreaded concentration camp of Buchenwald. The book's title stemmed from the legend that Goethe had studied under a tree that was within the precincts of the camp. Buchenwald contained another, deadlier, camp, called Dora, in which able-bodied prisoners were forced to work in a factory until they died of exhaustion. The novel recounts how Alain (Julitte's name in the book) and a few fellow prisoners gradually came to realize that they were producing part of a sophisticated rocket, which the outside world came to know as the V2. They managed to get word out to the Allies in London, who bombed and destroyed Dora in the Spring of 1945. While many prisoners died, Julitte was lucky to survive this bombing which helped to shorten the war. When the American Army liberated Buchenwald, Julitte weighed only 65 pounds and could hardly walk.

After reading this novel, I looked on Julitte in a totally different way and eagerly pumped him with questions about his war-time experiences. A functionary in the Ministry of Agriculture, he had been mobilized as a Lieutenant in the French Cavalry when war was declared in September, 1939. After France capitulated in June, 1940, Julitte actually went to London before de Gaulle issued his famous "call of June 18th." I asked Pierre how he knew that de Gaulle was organizing the Free French movement. He answered, "I didn't know of de Gaulle at all. I just decided it was my duty to go to London. I figured that someone would be organizing a resistance." Pierre was already 30, married, with two young sons, and had every excuse to join the two-million French soldiers who simply surrendered and were either made prisoners or demobilized. Yet he chose duty to his country before self-interest. And instead of seeking a desk job in London, Julitte volunteered to be parachuted to France to work with a resistance network in Southern France. He was arrested on a train by the Gestapo late in 1942 and sent to Buchenwald. I asked Pierre if he ever saw his family before his arrest. He told me of a poignant scene when he managed to get word to his wife to go to a certain café in Angers with their sons; Pierre sat at another table merely gazing at his family, not daring to speak to them. Later his family went into hiding to avoid reprisal by the Nazis, but his parents and sister were jailed by the Gestapo until Pierre himself was arrested.

On being liberated from Buchenwald, Julitte insisted on keeping his ragged prisoner's garb and organized a march with fellow-prisoners on the Champs-Elysées so that the Parisians could see what some of their compatriots had endured. De Gaulle decorated him with the highest distinction: *Compagnon de la Libération.* After the war, he became part of the civil administration of the French zone of occupied Germany. I asked Pierre how he could stand returning to Germany after all he had endured in Buchenwald. His answer was characteristic of his idealism. "I felt that I had to contribute to a fresh start in Franco-German relations. Three wars were enough." Julitte's idealism was such that unlike many Gaullist followers who cashed in on their wartime experiences by getting plush political plums, he stayed out of the limelight and was virtually unknown to the man in the street. He died as he lived, choosing the worst possible time to go, on August 15, 1991 – Assumption Day – when Paris was void of Parisians. Very few journals took note of his passing, let alone his heroism.

Another person I knew who went to London – at the age of 17 – was my wife's brother, the late Jean-Paul Eve. He ended up in the celebrated *Deuxième D.B.* (Second Armored Division), led by the dashing General Philippe Leclerc, which participated valiantly in the war effort, first in Italy, then in France and Germany. Men like Pierre Julitte and Jean-Paul Eve were among the small minority who saved the honor of France during World War II. The contrast between these men and functionaries like Maurice Papon and François Mitterrand could not be greater. Julitte, too, could have joined Vichy, since he had been a functionary before being mobilized. But he chose to go to London, leaving behind wife, children and parents, and he chose to risk his life to serve the cause of liberty. Both Papon and Mitterrand served Vichy assiduously but, after the American invasion of North Africa, when it appeared for the first time that the Allies would win the war, they dabbled on the fringes of the Resistance to save their skins. Mitterrand perpetrated a monumental fraud – one among many – by claiming to have been in the Resistance throughout the war, whereas he had served Vichy so well that he received its highest decoration, the *Francisque,* directly from the hands of Pétain. That such a scoundrel could have been president of France for 14 years and the darling of the "caviar Left" phonies who invented the term *le peuple de gauche* is testimony to the moral decadence of France in the last half of the 20th century.

This brings me to Jean-Marie Le Pen, the pugnacious Breton who founded the *Front National* (FN), which scored 15 percent of the votes in the March regional-council elections and thereby disrupted the harmony of the traditional so-called Right parties. French elections must appear mysterious to many of my readers and understandably so, since there are so many of them. France being a highly centralized country, the only significant subdivision prior to 1982 used to be the *département*, of which there are 95. The reason why there are so many Departments in a relatively small territory is that during the French Revolution the Convention designed them so that a citizen could reach the administrative capital on horseback within a day. France being what it is, the horses are gone but the Departments have remained. Then in 1982, when the Socialists were in power, Gaston Defferre, the Mayor of Marseille and Mitterrand's first Minister of the Interior, who had a bug about decentralization, fashioned a law which created 22 Regions, each grouping several Departments. Thus, he simply added another layer of administration whereas the daring thing to do would have been to eliminate the *départements*. The Region is administered by an elected council, headed by a president and several vice presidents, who naturally need a handsome Palais de la Région in which to meet. No one knows what the Region's powers are and no one cares since everything is decided in Paris by the *ENArques*. But it is hard to turn down the perks which come with the office.

Where the plot thickens is that the regional-council elections are based on proportional representation, unlike those of other elections. Thus, in the regions where the Front National (FN) is strong, mainly in the South of France, its members have what politicians call the "swing vote." By siding with the RPR and UDF they could ensure the election of a Rightist president in several regions. Despite the fact that the national leaders of these parties, Philippe Séguin and François Léotard, respectively, adjured their members not to make deals with the FN, several local political bigwigs did the opposite and got elected with FN support, thereby creating a national scandal. In the meantime, the Left has proudly been using a new label – *la gauche plurielle* – highlighting the fact that the Socialists can not rule without the support of the Communists and the Ecologists. Many people on the Right have been wondering why the Left is allowed to be "plural" but not the Right. This issue has created a furor, which is far from being resolved. It should be obvious that 15 percent of the population are not Fascist or Right-wing extremists. Despite the verbal excesses of Le Pen and some of his key henchmen, the majority of people who vote FN do so as a protest against the traditional parties whose policies have led to high unemployment, high taxes and the usurpation of power by a caste of functionaries, bent on creating the European Union on the French model. So long as the RPR and UDF are led by the same caste, it is sure that the protest votes will continue.

Mitterrand was very clever in allying with the Communist Party to gain power and he succeeded in reducing the latter's following from its high of 20 percent to a low of seven percent. There is unfortunately no one on the Right who has the art to do what Mitterrand did, that is, make an alliance with the FN and ultimately reduce its constituency to a hard-core of five percent. Le Pen is certainly an obstacle to such an alliance, simply because he can't resist the temptation to make outrageous remarks, like calling the Holocaust "a detail" of World War II, or to engage in ruffian tactics against a political opponent, as when he physically assaulted a woman candidate. For the latter offense, he has just been sentenced to two-years ineligibility to run for office. In the USA, a court can not inflict a punishment of this sort but, judging by certain egregious cases, *e.g.*, Mayor Barry of Washington DC, it might not be a bad idea to introduce this concept there.

I have stated it before, but can not repeat it enough: the tragedy of France today is that the Fifth Republic is morally bankrupt and the only real opposition to the various pseudo-parties that make up what I call *le Parti des Fonctionnaires* is Le Pen's FN, which President Chirac just labeled as "racist and xenophobic." This absence of constructive opposition explains why 42 percent of the eligible voters stayed home in the regional election and another three percent cast blank ballots. As with the former Eastern Block, many French people, among them the most industrious, are voting with their feet, leaving what a friend of mine calls "Goulag-sur-Seine." The French today fit Yeats' famous remark about an earlier time in Ireland: "The best are without conviction while the worst are full of passionate intensity." France needs another Joan of Arc, but even a Margaret of Grantham would do the trick.

Vol. XX, N° 4, May 1998

The Merry Mythic Month of May

It never ceases to amaze me how crazy the month of May is in France. This is my 37th May in a row, so you'd might think that I should have gotten used to it by now. What I'm referring to are all the holidays. We started out with May 1st, which fell on a Friday, thus heralding a long weekend. As I have pointed out previously, this commemorates the 1886 Haymarket Riots of Chicago, and is thus a sacred day for the labor movement.

Then, a week later, we had May 8th, also a Friday, and gracing another long weekend. This commemorates the Allied Victory in Europe in 1945, over "our friends the Germans." The French had stopped celebrating this day during Giscard's reign but, in 1981, Mitterrand reinstated it in the euphoria following his May victory, feeling, doubtless, that the French had to be reminded of their heroic efforts to endure the Vichy regime which he served so gloriously, as well as the German occupation. Having created a Ministry of Free Time (*Ministère du Temps Libre*) in the first Mauroy government, Mitterrand must have thought that the French did not have enough leisure, so he added a fifth week of vacation, to which anyone with a year's seniority is entitled, and reduced the work week to 39 hours. It wasn't long before a lot of people discovered that they had plenty of free time on their hands, as unemployment soared during Mitterrand's reign, which ended only in 1995.

So now, I've related two holidays, in case you've lost count, but there's more to come. Thursday, May 21st was Ascension Day, a Catholic holy day. This provided an excuse for bridge-building, since in France everyone is an engineer when it comes to abstaining from work. You guessed it; taking Friday off after a holiday on Thursday is to *faire le pont*, that is, to bridge to Saturday, and thus have a four-day weekend. You wouldn't have known that this is a religious commemoration, since the churches were empty, but the super-highways and trains were full of devout pilgrims going to their country houses for prayer.

Three long weekends in one month are not enough for the tired French, who live under so much stress, worrying whether airline pilots and trainmen of their nationalized transportation companies will go on strike and deprive them of their justly-acquired leisure. So to top off this glorious month, it will end in the Pentecost (Whitsun) Sunday on May 31st and, as it is unjust that a holy day fall on Sunday, the lay republic of France grants the next day, Monday, June 1st, as a holiday. So that makes four long weekends in 32 days. If you've followed closely this narrative, you'll have detected that there was one week which did not have a holiday and this is the real purpose of this issue of the Newsletter, to propose that the perfectionist French fill this ignoble gap by declaring May 15th as a holiday. This will commemorate what, you might ask. The answer is simple and straightforward: it will mark "Middle of the Month Day." Brilliant, *n'est-ce pas*?

For employers, having so many holidays, not to mention having to deal with people taking one of their five weeks of vacation in May, is very disruptive of the work schedule. In my office, I do not allow "making the bridge." In fact, we spread our staff out on both days, just so that clients from unlucky countries that work on Ascension and Pentecost will have someone to talk to when they call our office. But most companies, while complaining of their lack of productivity and measly profits do *faire le pont*.

As if this disruption of the economy does not inflict enough pain on people like me, we have had to put up this year with the commemoration, all month long, of the 30th anniversary of that notorious fiasco, which lovers of barricades and mythology call simply "the events of May '68." Throughout the month, most Parisian newspapers, including *Le Monde* and *Le Figaro* have been carrying articles memorializing these events that wrought havoc on the French economy. I lived through this period in Paris, having started my law firm barely 18 months earlier, and so I would like to present here a somewhat personal account of them, based on my recollections and prejudices.

The events began rather inauspiciously with the student strike at the newly-minted university in Nanterre, a miserable suburb west of Paris which had been ruthlessly "modernized" with unsightly high-rise buildings, including those of the university. Having been a student in a French university 15 years earlier, I knew how irrelevant these institutions were. New buildings do not change old habits. I sympathized with the students, who crammed into overcrowded amphitheaters to listen to a professor deliver a *cours magistral* which they were expected to learn by heart. Whether they attended lectures or went on strike made no difference, since they learned nothing in either case.

Then the unrest spread to the Sorbonne in Paris, on the Left Bank, and the weakness of the government led to the students occupying the university premises, setting up barricades on nearby Boulevard Saint Michel. As the government wanted to avoid loss of life, no effective police action was taken against the barricades, which conjured up the "heroic" uprisings of the past. Seeing the government's continued weakness, the Communist union, the CGT, decided to politicize the situation and got the workers of the state-owned Renault factory in Paris to go on strike, in feigned support of the students. Soon virtually all state-controlled utilities went on strike, including the rail lines, Air France, airports, the postal service, the Paris Metro and buses. In a matter of days, gasoline could no longer be found. Determined to keep coming to the office from my suburban home, despite the lack of public transportation and lack of fuel, I managed to reserve a small car from Hertz at Orly Airport with a full tank of gasoline, but to get the vehicle I had to enter the terminal which was occupied by burly union members. This was a harrowing experience but I told them I was a tourist and they let me in. Thus, I was able to go to work during the last two weeks of May.

My most illuminating experience during this period was to visit, one afternoon, the Odeon Theater in the Latin Quarter, which was occupied by the "students" (in fact, this included anyone who joined the crowd). The setting could only be described as a permanent "happening." People sat around simply haranguing each other, with no one moderating the discussion and no discernible subject. A would-be Danton in the first balcony made fearsome oratory, while a timid woman who described herself as a housewife spoke of her domestic problems. It was like a college "bull session" with the janitor joining in. But at least I got a taste of what the French Revolution must have been like in Paris. The walls of Paris were littered with pompous slogans like "It is forbidden to forbid" and the asinine intellectuals writing for *Le Monde* and *Libération* were proclaiming that *un homme nouveau est né* ("a new man is born"). Oh, really? If he was born, he must have been still-born.

Aside from a few leaders who pictured themselves as future Lenins, the students clearly had no agenda, but the unions did: money and power. The Pompidou government engaged in a crash negotiation with the unions at the Ministry of Labor, on the rue de Grenelle. To get them back to work, Pompidou agreed to an across-the-board wage increase of 10 percent, something which a month earlier no one had even dreamed of demanding. Yet, sensing blood, the union members refused to ratify these agreements, which became known as *les accords de Grenelle*. On Friday, May 24th de Gaulle made a *faux pas* by appearing on TV and proposing a referendum, but the unions made it known that they would prevent the referendum from taking place, by blocking the printing of ballots. This only aggravated the situation by making de Gaulle himself appear ineffective.

The last week of May, despite the balmy, sunny weather, was a period of intense stress for most people in France, as de Gaulle and his government seemed powerless to end the strikes. The left-wing political parties held a rally at Charlety Stadium and it seemed that the Socialists, led by Mitterrand and Mendès-France, and the Communists were perilously near to seeking to take power "from the street." Then on May 29th the most incredible rumor of all emerged. It seemed that de Gaulle had disappeared: he was no longer in Paris and no one knew where he was. During this time I was witnessing these events in disbelief, telling myself, "This can't be happening," and also, "Now I know what revolutions are like."

On the morning of May 30th, a Thursday, the radio announced that de Gaulle was back and would address the nation on radio at 4:30 in the afternoon, after which there would be a demonstration of his supporters on the Champs-Elysées. (It turned out that he had gone to Baden-Baden where his tough friend General Massu commanded a crack unit of French paratroopers.) I was so tense that to distract myself, I called in my secretary at 2:30 pm and began dictating to her, in a stream of consciousness, ending only when the radio announced that de Gaulle was ready to speak. His talk was electrifying, short but to the point: he announced that he would resist all efforts to topple the government, and that he was dissolving the National Assembly, calling for new elections. This was the old de Gaulle. With a few people from my office, then on rue Galilée, I walked to the Place de la Concorde, which was still virtually empty, and I saw former Prime Minister Michel Debré and other notables lining up side by side. We joined the cortege and soon an incredible mass of a million Parisians – the hitherto "silent majority" – was at our sides, as we wended our way at snail's pace towards the Arc de Triomphe, singing the Marseillaise and shouting slogans. It took us four hours to cover the four kilometers but, by the time we got there, it was clear that de Gaulle had won the battle. This was the most fantastic improvised, peaceful demonstration that I ever expect to see in my lifetime.

The next day Paris was crammed with automobiles and I got caught up in the biggest traffic jam that I've ever been in, even abandoning my rented car on the Boulevard des Italiens, but it was a joyful occasion. Suddenly, in the afternoon, a "miracle" occurred, service stations had gasoline once more and the word got out that the strikers were returning to work. It was clear that the unions and the left-wing parties had capitulated, deciding that the jig was up. As the Pentecost weekend was on the horizon, everyone left Paris for three days of *détente*. *Voilà*, the events of May had ended. It was only later, when I had lunch with a friend who was then close to Mitterrand, that I learned a key fact which, so far as I know, has still not been published, to wit, that Mitterrand and the Communists had been negotiating the formation of a "provisional government" that would take over, but the Communists had demanded four powerful ministerial portfolios, including that of the Minister of the Interior, who controls the police. Mitterrand refused and so the Communists put an end to the strikes.

Of course, when the legislative elections were held in June, de Gaulle's party and his allies won an overwhelming majority in the National Assembly. May '68 had accomplished nothing except a general wage hike which naturally led to inflation and devaluation of the franc. For once, I had some foresight and, sensing the prices would soon rise, I hastened to complete the purchase of a new Mercedes sedan which I had been looking at. Believe me, when I say that the 280 SE that I purchased had a sticker price of exactly FF 29,800 (about $6,000). Today, the comparable model costs 12 times as much in France, a good indicator of the inflation of the past 30 years.

It was during these events of May, which even de Gaulle found baffling and called *insaisissable*, that he purported to find the solution to what was missing in French society: *la participation*. I did not find this convincing at the time and still do not. Yet, de Gaulle pursued his notion that a referendum was needed to alter French institutions. This took place a year later, with de Gaulle asking for a single "yes or no" answer to two questions, one calling for abolition of the Senate in favor of a new amorphous body composed of economic and social representatives and the other instituting various aspects of "participation." This again was bad strategy, to ask two questions but require a single answer. Most people would have voted for "participation" but were not convinced that abolishing the Senate was a good idea. A solid majority voted No, and de Gaulle made good his threat to resign. And so, a new era was born: a Fifth Republic without de Gaulle, who had designed the constitution for himself. Ironically, now the Socialists are talking of reforming the Senate, a conservative body.

If I dwell on this chronology, it is because I am recurring to a favorite theme, that the Fifth Republic has been a fiasco without de Gaulle. Chirac, who is no more worthy of being a successor to de Gaulle than I am of replacing Michael Jordan on the Chicago Bulls, demonstrated the fatefulness of the month of May last year by making one of the most stupid decisions in the history of France: dissolving the National Assembly despite having, with his allies, an 80-percent majority in that body. This led to the not-surprising victory in May 1997 of the Socialists and their allies and placed Lionel Jospin in the Prime Minister's mansion, a place that he would not have bet a *sou* on his chances of occupying when 1997 began. De Gaulle, also, had let a massive majority become meaningless by insisting on a referendum whose utility appeared dubious to most people. There the comparison with Chirac ends.

To return to May '68, there was one by-product for which I am personally grateful: after a period of intense practice of law and thinking of little else but work and raising a family, these events got me to reflect on the broader issues of society and the problems of France. I wrote several essays for my own edification, including that stream-of-consciousness one I had dictated to my secretary, which I entitled "The Latest French Revolution." In a way, this beginning of non-legal writing led ultimately to this Newsletter, which emerged a decade later. One of the essays I wrote, in French, was called *La France et son Etat*, in which I pointed out what French commentators had failed to do, that the strikes were not directed at capitalistic, private enterprises, but rather were concentrated in state-owned universities and enterprises. France was not suffering from capitalism but really from the excessive power of the functionary class, masquerading as *l'Etat*. The blindness and vacuity of French journalists and intellectuals is such that in 30 years most of them have still not seen the point.

What France needed in '68 and needs even more in '98 is a cure made up of that old-fashioned substance called "liberty." But to get that, what is needed is not long weekends but, as Pericles told the Athenians, courage.

Vol. XX, N° 5, June 1998

Nobody Here but Us Turks

This issue is prompted by the historic decision of the French National Assembly to recognize the reality of the Armenian Genocide of 1915. But first let me relate one of my favorite hoary jokes of the past: A farmer, hearing noises in his chicken coop, comes out with his shotgun, and asks "Who's in my chicken coop?" Then a voice is heard saying, "There's nobody here but us chickens!"

I have often used this story in my law practice to illustrate the point that in some circumstance the very fact of protesting is an admission of guilt. Now back to the Armenian Genocide: the full text of the resolution voted by the French lower chamber was this: "The French republic acknowledges the reality of the Armenian Genocide of 1915."

You will notice that this resolution does not mention Turkey, nor the Ottoman Empire, nor Taalat Pasha nor Enver Pasha, the Turkish initiators of the genocide. Indeed, if one did not know the context and read the statement "cold," he might infer that it was the French who had committed the genocide in days bygone, since generally the person who acknowledges an act is the one who committed it. Yet, who protested, and loudly at that? The present Turkish government. Like the man in the chicken coop, they were saying: "Nobody here but us Turks."

Recently a dear friend from San Francisco sent me by Email a clipping about the commemorative cross on a hill in that city that an Armenian association plans to buy, and the friend made a comment to me to the effect that this is just another example of never-ending enmity between peoples. In my reply, I took my friend, who is Jewish, to task and he quickly saw the point. How would the Jews of the world feel if the present German government protested every memorial to the Holocaust?

For that is the point: what is news about the Armenian Genocide is not that it occurred in 1915 but rather than the present Turkish government, like most of its predecessors, continues to deny that it ever took place. This is what makes it a current issue and this is why the French parliament went to the trouble of passing a resolution about it.

It is easy for those who never suffered a genocide to say, "Let bygones be bygones: forgive and forget." But as someone said, "I forgive only those who ask forgiveness." Shakespeare, as usual, expressed better than any one else the difference between a victim and an indifferent bystander: "He jests at scars that never felt a wound." The continued Turkish denial of the horrible extermination of the Armenian people living it its territory is for today's Armenians a present wound and each new denial is to rub salt into the wound. There is hardly an Armenian alive today whose family did not suffer in the 1915 events. Indeed, most Armenians in the USA, in France, in Lebanon, in Argentina – places where Armenians tend to concentrate – are descendants of survivors of the Genocide.

In my case, my father's whole family – his mother, father, two brothers and a sister, were massacred, along with all the 10,000 Armenians in the town of Chunkoush (now spelled Cungus by the Turks). Throughout Turkey and Syria, then part of the Ottoman Empire, Armenians were systematically exterminated, either directly in their towns, whenever there were no foreign diplomats or missionaries present to witness the events, or in the guise of deportation, where Armenian men, women and children were forced to march hundreds of kilometers without food or water and were prey to bestial brutality at the hands of the

Turkish army or marauding Kurds. It is estimated that more than a million Armenians died – some say 1.5-million – and those who managed to survive, sometimes by playing dead, or hiding under the bodies of their dead relatives, were, of course, permanently severed from the land which had been the home of the Armenians for 3,000 years. Today all of Anatolia, in eastern Turkey, is barren of Armenians and only the ruins of churches and monasteries stand as reminders of what was a living civilization.

You might ask, "But why did the Turks commit this genocide?" It is not for the victims to explain their assassins' motives. Why did the Nazis of the Third Reich exterminate the Jews? Both peoples had in common the fact of being of a different religion from that of the dominant population and both were disproportionately prominent in business, finance, the professions and the arts. In Turkey there was at the time a "Pan Islamic" movement and the Christian Armenians constituted an obstacle to this union, much as Israel today is an enclave in an Arab region.

My father had managed to escape from Turkey in 1912 and make his way to the United States. Of course, he never saw his family again. From his native Chunkoush there were a few other survivors in Philadelphia, men who had been orphaned by the Turkish Army: Harry Krikorian, Sarkis Bogosian, Nishan Androian and Mardiros Klijian. For them, and for us, their children, there was no doubt of the reality of the Armenian Genocide: we did not need a resolution of any parliament to become convinced that the Turkish government had sought, and largely succeeded, in exterminating a whole nation. And, of course, Chunkoush was but one of the towns whose Armenians had been massacred or deported to their deaths. In Philadelphia alone, we knew survivors from Malatia, from Kharpet, from Diarbekir, from Sebastia. Look at a map of Turkey and you'll find these towns, but if you go there you will not find any Armenians and the Turkish guides will not even mention that the ruins of churches you see were once Armenian churches, the worship places of the first Christian nation in the world.

It must be recalled, for those who are rusty in both history and geography, and some of my readers have candidly acknowledged these lacunae so far as Armenia is concerned, that what is now Turkey was once a Greek and Armenian land. Today's Istanbul was once Constantinople, which was the capital of the Byzantine Empire, a Christian empire, most of whose emperors were Greek, but some of whom were Armenians. When Yeats, the Irish poet, writes of "Sailing to Byzantium," he is speaking of this land, not of Turkey. And to the east of Byzantium was the Armenian kingdom, mentioned in the Greek and Roman chronicles, visited and conquered by such stalwarts as Alexander the Great and even Marc Anthony. So how did these lands become Turkey? By conquest, simply. The Turks, the Tartars of Central Asia, came west in the 12th century AD and, being tough soldiers, not troubling themselves with the effete pre-occupations of Christian Greeks and Armenians, ultimately won the land and made its occupants their subjects. The Crusades were about the Christian peoples of Western Europe trying to dislodge the Turks from their conquered territories. It is probably hard for most people today, so pummeled by television and movie "culture," to realize that the Ottoman Empire included a substantial part of Europe – the Turks almost reached Vienna – the Middle East and North Africa. If the Arabs today hate the Turks, it is because they remember all too well that they were under Turkish dominion for centuries.

And people rusty in history probably do not remember that Turkey was an ally of Germany and the Austro-Hungarian Empire in World War I. It was because Turkey lost the war that it lost its empire, its once-occupied territories becoming objects of mandates given by the League of Nations to the British and the French, including what was once known as Palestine. And how many people ever knew that the first government of Turkey after its defeat actually tried by court-martial the Turkish leaders who had caused the annihilation of the Armenian people? Unfortunately this government fell and its successors adopted the denial line, but the court-martial records still exist. So how can the Turkish government today deny an event which one of its predecessors acknowledged was a crime?

The answer has to do with power politics or, if you will, geopolitics, and describes a situation which has lasted for three-quarters of a century. The big event which helped restore Turkey in the good graces of the Western Powers who had defeated it was the Russian Revolution of 1917. Czarist Russia had been an ally of France and Great Britain in World War I, but when Lenin took over, he made peace with Germany in the treaty of Brest-Litovsk and went about his merry way of sovietizing Russia and its vassal nations. Thus, the USSR became a potential enemy of the West, whereas the Russia of the Czars had been its ally. In this new power shift, Turkey, bordering on the USSR and controlling its access to the Mediterranean through the straits of the Dardanelles, occupied a crucial geographical location. Thus, after the War and into the '20s, England and France, with the benign blessing of isolationist America, supported Turkey's re-establishment as a regional power, and among other things, went back on their commitments to Greece and to Armenia, the remnants of which had become an independent republic in 1918. Assaulted by the Turkish Army, led by General Mustafa Kemal, this republic lost its independence in 1920 when the Soviets took over and made it part of the USSR. In 1922, the British and French watched idly as the Trukish army committed the rape of Smyrna, destroying its Greek and Armenian populations.

Later, Mustafa Kemal, who came to be called "Ataturk," became the dictator of Turkey and by "modernizing" that country ingratiated himself with the Western Powers, who conveniently forgot how much blood he had on his hands. Because Turkey, a Moslem nation which had destroyed its Christian population, now purported to become a secular country, abandoning the veil for its women and adopting the Latin alphabet in place of the Arabic, the West closed its eyes to the fact that it was a military dictatorship. When World War II came, Turkey managed to stay neutral, despite its traditional sympathies for the Germans and, after the war, the Cold War made it an indispensable ally of the Americans, who were bent on "containing" the Soviet Union. Turkey, in exchange for money and arms, allowed American bases on its territory and the planting of missiles directed at the Soviet Union. During the Korean War, Turkey even provided soldiers for the United Nations forces.

All this explains why subsequent Turkish governments, after the one that tried the perpetrators of the Armenian Genocide, have been emboldened to deny that the Genocide ever took place. And these governments have used American aid money to buy the services of Hill & Knowlton, the leading US public-relations agency, to propagandize the American people, and to visit the editorial rooms of leading American newspapers, like the *New York Times* and the *Wall Street Journal,* which have constantly downplayed the Armenian Genocide and adopted a favorite editorial line to "our allies the Turks." The American State Department, conveniently forgetting the tons of archives in its possession which leave no doubt of the reality of the Genocide, now refuses to use that word in association with "Armenian," for fear of offending the Turks. I find it ironic that Madeleine Albright, who wanted to deny to herself that she was born a Jew, is now head of an unprincipled State Department which denies the reality of historical events that are amply documented in its own files. Need I remind her that the first Henry Morgenthau, who was Jewish himself, was the American Ambassador to Turkey in 1915, and reported extensively on the massacres and deportations taking place, which the government of Turkey tried to keep secret, under the cover of war. His book, *Ambassador Morgenthau's Diary,* reports these horrible events in graphic detail, with photographs of Armenian victims. Of course, the archives of the *New York Times* are themselves replete with news reports of these events in 1915 and of subsequent relief efforts by a number of American organizations. This makes it all the more reprehensible that this newspaper adopts the Turkish party line while at the same time never losing an opportunity to remind its readers of the Jewish Holocaust. In October last, the *Times* waxed indignant that the European Union refused to admit "democratic Turkey" as one of its members. I wrote a "Letter to the Editor" against this editorial, which naturally was not printed. Then, a few weeks later, when the Turkish military, who really run the country, forced the stooge civil government to ban the Islamic party which had won the last election, the *Times* finally acknowledged that Turkey was not a democracy after all.

And it is sad to relate that Israel, for reasons of expediency, has chosen to make a military alliance with Turkey, and thus tends to withhold its support for recognition of the Armenian Genocide, which, of all countries in the world, Israel has the most moral grounds for acknowledging. Not long ago, the Turkish government refused to accredit the new Israeli Ambassador to Turkey, since he had written an article referring to the Armenian Genocide.

When as an undergraduate at the University of Pennsylvania, I wrote my senior honors thesis in History on the "United States and the Armenian Mandate" (for the League of Nations had offered such a mandate to the USA, which the Senate refused), the library stacks were replete with books about the tragic events of 1915, including a book by the world-class English historian Arnold Toynbee. So, you might ask, how is it possible for the Turkish Government to deny historical events?

Well, part of the answer lies in semantics. You see, the word "genocide" did not exist in 1915 and for decades thereafter. It was coined only in 1944, by Raphael Lemkin, and later made the subject of an international treaty. When I was a child, we referred to these events as "the Armenian massacres," since there simply was no word to describe a government-operated program of extermination of an entire people. So today the Turkish position is to quibble about whether what took place satisfies the legal definition of "genocide" contained in the United Nations Convention of 1948, which made genocide a crime under international law. This definition reads as follow:

Art. 2. In the present Convention, genocide means any of the following acts committed with intent to destroy, in whole or in part, a national, ethnical, racial or religious group, as such:

(a) Killing members of the group;

(b) Causing serious bodily or mental harm to members of the group;

(c) Deliberately inflicting on the group conditions of life calculated to bring about its physical destruction in whole or in part;

(d) Imposing measures intended to prevent births within the group;

(e) Forcibly transferring children of the group to another group.

Clearly what happened to the Armenians of the Ottoman Empire in 1915 satisfies that definition. However, as the word "genocide was not used at the time, you can not point to a contemporary account that calls it by this term, thus giving the Turks the leeway to argue about it. For example, they used to say, "Sure a lot of Armenians were killed by Turkish soldiers but that was not government policy." This is a lie, since documentation exists showing that the orders to exterminate the Armenians came from the highest levels of the Turkish government. The current party line of the Turkish government and its paid lackeys, including, sad to say, some American academics who will do anything for money, is that there were some "unfortunate events" that took place in wartime, indeed even a "civil war," which made some victims among both Turks and Armenians, but in no event can these events be described as a "genocide." When the French resolution mentioned above was passed the first article I saw on it in the *International Herald Tribune* reflected this party line, referring to the alleged "civil war" and carrying the Turkish assertion that 45 of its diplomats were killed by Armenian terrorists during a phase that stopped about 15 years ago.

This is merely an illustration of how easy it is to distort and falsify history. With few exceptions, journalists are the most gullible and lazy people who live from writing. Always pressed by deadlines, they have no time to do research and their knowledge of history ends with yesterday. So it is easy to plant "stories" and "themes" in their minds and once these are planted they tend to get repeated over and over again. The idea that Armenians were engaged in a "civil war" in Turkey during the first World War is a myth: it is an example of the "big lie" technique which Hitler made so fashionable. If you read contemporary news accounts on the microfiches of the *New York Times* and other papers, as I did for my college thesis, you'll not see a single reference to a "civil war." The idea is preposterous. The residents of Chunkoush and other towns where Armenians were concentrated were unarmed and peaceful. The mountains of Anatolia where Chunkoush, Kharpet, Diarbekir are located were not a war zone. But even supposing, for the sake of argument, that there had been a "civil war" in which Armenian fighters were protagonists, is this any excuse to massacre the entire civilian population of Armenians? The United States had a civil war but the North did not embark on the systematic extermination of the civilian population of the South, even if there were necessarily civilian casualties because of military operations and blockades. No, the "civil war" concept, now being bruited by Turkish propagandists, is simply an invention, as they have no valid historical data to contradict the overwhelming weight of the evidence.

Of course, these efforts are abetted by the passage of time, since most people alive today have no personal knowledge, not even based on newspaper reports, of events which took place eight decades earlier. When I was young, I used to be embarrassed by people telling me that their parents forced them to eat their dinner by saying "Think of the starving Armenians." This term was a household phrase in the '20s because, as stated above, many relief organizations raised money on that theme to feed the orphans and other survivors of the first "death march" of the century. These survivors were huddled in refugee camps throughout the Middle East. It was because Franz Werfel, the great Austrian-Jewish writer, visited one such camp, that hewas inspired to write his historical novel, *The Forty Days of Musa Dagh* which, transmated into English, became a best-seller in the United States.

The sad yet inevitable consequence of contemporary Turkish governments' denying the reality of the Armenian Genocide is to make them accomplices of that atrocious event. Why do they persist in the denial? In my view, each successive government is stuck with the lies of its predecessors and would fear public opinion which has been "brainwashed" on the subject of the Armenians. I've previously recounted that when I told a young Turkish salesman in a Parisian rug shop that my father was an Armenian from Cungus, his smiling reply was that "Cungus has never been the same since the Armenians left." That's what he had been taught: the Armenians "left," not that they were massacred or deported but that they emigrated to more attractive places like the USA. It would take a very courageous Turkish government to renounce decades of lying on this subject. Another reason, doubtless even stronger, is the fear that Armenians would seek reparations for the losses suffered by their ancestors. After all, the Kevorkians and their neighbors in Chunkoush had homes, furniture, businesses, jewelry, money and other assets, all of which they were forced to abandon. Personally, I do not give a hoot for reparations, but other Armenians do not feel that way, and why should they? After all, the postwar German governments paid reparations to Jewish survivors and descendents of Holocaust victims, and even today Swiss banks are forking up money that belonged to Holocaust victims.

I repeat, I would gladly give up any claim for reparations in exchange for a simple acknowledgement by the Turkish government that the regime in power in 1915 engaged in a deliberate program of extermination of the Armenian people. Personally, I wouldn't care if the government avoided the word "genocide," as the word "extermination" is good enough for me.

To me the most disturbing aspect of the Turkish government's efforts to squelch the truth of the Armenian Genocide is its enlisting of some American universities as allies. I have earlier commented on the disgusting action of Princeton University in accepting money from the Ankara government to endow an "Ataturk Chair in Turkish Studies" and to name a notoriously negationist professor as the first occupant of that chair. The very idea that Princeton, which once had Woodrow Wilson as its president, a man who had no doubt as to the reality of the Armenian Genocide, would name a chair for a dictator and allow an undemocratic, military regime to pay for it, is a good indication of how venal American universities have become. I wonder when Princeton will change its name to "Ataturk University of Princeton, New Jersey." The Turks have tried to foist their money on other universities as well. The History Department of UCLA just barely voted, by a one-vote margin, to refuse the Turkish Government's proposal for a chair there.

The other day my oldest grandson, David, age 19, who is only one-quarter Armenian, expressed his indignation over the continued Turkish denial of the 1915 realities. This touched me immensely because he had not been raised as an Armenian. My wife not being Armenian and my children not having married Armenians, I had become inured to the idea that the Armenian-ness of my roots would gradually disappear among my descendants. What I saw in David's spontaneous disgust was that so long as the Turkish government continues to deny the genocide, it will have to reckon with one-eighth, one sixteenth, and one-thirty-second Armenians. For what counts here is the denial of truth, which amounts to injustice. You can kill Armenians, you can dilute their blood, but you can not eliminate from the human race that most ancient of quests, which began when the first man became aware that he was not just an animal: the quest for truth.

Vol. XX, N° 6, July 1998

"The Tainted Source," by John Laughland

Having just read one of the most illuminating books of recent years has led me to the wholly unprecedented step of devoting an entire Newsletter to John Laughland's *"The Tainted Source."* To whet the reader's appetite, I will reproduce a quote found in this book and ask you to guess the author:

Above and beyond the concept of the nation-state, the idea of a new community will transform the living space given us all into a new spiritual realm... The new Europe of solidarity and co-operation among all peoples, a Europe without unemployment, economic and monetary crises, a Europe of planning and division of labor, having at its disposal the most modern production techniques and a continent-wide system of trade and communications developed on a joint basis, will find an assured foundation and rapidly increasing prosperity once national economic barriers are removed.

Sounds like Jacques Delors (once head of the EC Commission) you might say? Keep guessing, while I give you another quote, from a different author: "There must be a readiness in certain cases to subordinate one's own interests to those of the European Community."

While you're guessing, here's another quotation, this one from two famous authors: "The destruction of the Bolshevik danger and of plutocratic exploitation will create the possibility for a peaceful and harmonious co-operation between all the peoples of the European continent, in the political as in the economic and cultural domains."

All these quotes sound like the pronouncements we've been getting from the proponents of the European Community and the single currency, *n'est-ce pas*? Well, let me give you the authors. The first quote was penned by an Austrian Nazi, Arthur Seyss-Inquart, in 1940, when he was in charge of the occupation of Norway. The second is from another Nazi, Walter Funk, who headed Hitler's Finance Ministry. And the third has as co-authors none other than Adolph Hitler and Benito Mussolini, in a 1941 joint communiqué!

The reader will now understand the excitement I felt on discovering the second chapter of Laughland's book, entitled "Fascists and Federalists." It is startling to learn that much of the language currently being deployed to justify the dirigiste model of European union currently in fashion was utilized by the Nazis, who were the ultimate dirigistes. Indeed, Laughland reveals that the first conference under the banner of the "European Economic Community" was held under the auspices of the Third Reich in 1942.

Before I return to the book, let me say a word about the author. Several years ago, I began to admire an occasional op-ed article in the European Edition of the *Wall Street Journal* written by John Laughland. The author was described merely as an Englishman teaching at the prestigious Sciences Po school in Paris. What struck me then was Laughland's remarkably mature and critical grasp of the French political scene. I assumed that the author was a man in his 40s or 50s and wondered why I had never noticed his existence before. Then, last year, I met a young American lawyer practicing in Brussels, who spoke to me of his circle of friends there, and the name of John Laughland cropped up. To my amazement, the lawyer told me, and I made him repeat it, that John was in his early 30s. Later last year, I met John in Brussels at a gathering which marked the beginning of a monthly discussion group. Earlier this year, I read his first book, *"The Death of Politics,"* which is a devastating critique of the Mitterrand years and the régime which represents contemporary French government. So many of the points and facts had been treated episodically in my Newsletters that I marveled at how someone so young could have, in a much shorter time frame than mine, absorbed and digested so much about France.

John Laughland is a political and moral philosopher with a point of view that he would describe as "liberal," not in the US usage, but in the etymological sense, that is, a believer in liberty. And he employs the word "politics" in the noble sense, as per Aristotle's "Man is a political animal," not in the pejorative way most people use today. His heroes include Edmund Burke and Friedrich von Hayek. After reading "*The Death of Politics*" I chided John, gently to be sure, for giving a title to a book about France which does not immediately convey the drift of the work. I suspect that John enjoys the use of mysterious titles because "*The Tainted Source*" is also one. It is only at the end of the second chapter of this book, after one has read a number of citations such as those I quoted above, that Laughland explains his title, to wit, that both "Nazi and pro-Europeanism" currents of thought have "antecedents... that reach back into European intellectual and geopolitical history." These antecedents are the tainted source.

Laughland then launches into these antecedents with two complex chapters, the first entitled "Holding the Center." This deals essentially with the Germans' historic fear that their geographic position in the middle of Europe makes them vulnerable to attack on several sides and the resultant strategy which German regimes have adopted to achieve hegemony in a larger European "space," including the customs union among a multitude of German states organized by Prussia early in the 19th century. Laughland explains that German ideologues have always preferred this type of hegemony to the concept of "balance of power" long favored by the English and the French, which supposes the existence of "nation-states" based on sovereignty. In addition, the Germans, according to the author, have attached more importance to "economism" and administration than to politics. The implication is therefore that having failed in two World Wars, Germany is now at home in the type of ersatz European union which it has since helped to organize and which allows it to assert hegemony without this appearing too blatant.

We begin to see where Laughland is heading in his crucial next chapter on "The European Ideology" in which his own value system is revealed. In the course of discussing law, he excoriates Kelsen's concept of law as being "commands" issued from on high, preferring the notion that in a free society, that is, a democratic state, law results from the interaction of free citizens living their normal lives and pursuing their aspirations. He makes the key point that freedom is antithetical to a planned society governed from above. Thus Laughland's ideal is a state which provides a rule of law and judges to resolve the inevitable conflicts which result from people enjoying liberty. The author concludes this chapter with an illuminating discussion of Saint-Simon, the French philosopher who, in 1803, proposed that a "Council of Newton," composed of scientists and mathematicians, be elected by all of mankind to rule the world. Later, he proposed other crackpot schemes, including one for a banking corporation to control all of industry. According to the author, Saint-Simon believed that: "In a completely industrialized society there would be no more governments, only administrators. He thought that the principal activity of politics was balancing the budget, and that meant that the essence of politics was administration." After Saint-Simon's death, his followers came up with an even more hare-brained scheme for a "unitary, directing bank" which was to plan everything. Let us read and weep:

The social institution of the future will direct all industries in the interests of the whole society and specially of the peaceful workers. We call this institution provisionally the general system of banks.

The system will comprise in the first instance a central bank, which constitutes the government in the material sphere: this bank will become the depository of all wealth, of the whole productive fund, of all the instruments of production, in short, of everything that today makes up the whole mass of private property.

No comment, other than to say that if you wonder where Frenchmen like Jacques Delors get their ideology, you need look no further. Speaking of Delors, Laughland recounts (page 324) that Delors told the "European Parliament" in 1991 when the USSR shed its communist regime: "We cannot unite the states of Western Europe and at the same time encourage the breakaway of Soviet republics." Delors is also quoted as having complained to a senior Russian official about the abandonment of the Soviet clearing system. He exclaimed: "But how can you have abandoned something like that, when we drew inspiration from your system by introducing the ECU!"

In another chapter, Laughland attacks the underlying assumptions of the single-currency project and advances his own theory of the role of a sound currency in a democratic society founded on the gold standard and the rule of law. He then devotes a long chapter, called "The Third Rome," to Russia, which German strategists want to include in a "common European home." He shows that Russia has essentially reconstituted its empire, exercising control over the former Soviet republics, a movement that satisfies the EU's repugnance to encourage the self-determination of small nations.

Throughout this book, Laughland contrasts the technocratic, undemocratic character of European institutions with the rule of law, politics and parliamentary government. Laughland asserts that France and Germany have abandoned (if they ever had it) a system of government based on the rule of law and parliamentary law-making and, instead of reforming their internal systems, the leaders of these countries have designed and implemented a supranational system based on executive, bureaucratic power. As I have oft pointed out, the so-called "European Parliament" is a farcical front, with no legislative power, while the real law-making power is in the European Commission, the Council of Ministers and now the Central Bank, all of whom represent the executive power. Just as there is no separation of powers in France, there is none in the European Union.

In his very short concluding chapter, entitled "A Continent in Decline," Laughland laments the disappearance of effective parliamentary power in Europe and takes a parting shot at proportional representation which, by reason of the party-list system, deprives the citizen of local representation. His ultimate paragraph becomes a credo for the free society: liberty implies uncertainty, so that "any attempt to remove uncertainty by artificial political means is self-defeating and contrary to human nature." Here we are at first principles, and the problem is that not everyone agrees on first principles. Experience teaches that man craves security as much as he craves liberty, and if man is a political animal he is also an economic one or, as the French might say, "*un animal, tout court*," that is, nothing but an animal. It is this duality of aspiration that makes for the vital conflicts of our time. Planners and dirigistes cater to man's need for security, a much easier "sell" than arguing the virtues of striving in a sea of uncertainty. Where Laughland is right is in the fact that technocratic planners never succeed, except in feathering their own nest.

The educational value of "*The Tainted Source*" for the current generations can not be overestimated. I lived through World War II, the enemies being Hitler and Mussolini and, like most people, I had retained only the popular image of them as madmen bent on conquest and genocide. It is important to be reminded that these dictators professed ideologies that denoted a grand plan for the Europe which they once virtually commanded. One easily forgets that the term "Nazi" was an abbreviation for "National Socialist" and that Mussolini's regime was based on corporatism, that is, a highly organized and concentrated economic system directed from on high. Petain's Vichy government followed the Italian model of corporatism. The dictators are gone but the ideologies and adherents have remained and, some would say, the EU is rapidly becoming a "Fourth Reich" dominated by German power and policies, with the complicity of the functionary caste in France. I was fascinated to learn from Laughland's book that Robert Schuman, who is considered one of the "fathers of Europe" and who gave his name to the "Schuman plan," that is, the European Coal and Steel Community, which was a government-organized cartel, was born in the Lorraine when it was part of Germany, was educated in Germany, and became French only after World War I. He was one of the French parliamentarians who, in June 1940, voted full powers to Pétain and he served, albeit briefly, as a Minister in the first Vichy government.

Although Laughland, ever the philosopher and ever the Englishman, refrains from *ad hominem* attacks and concentrates on ideology and ideas, I will not show such restraint. When the "events of May '68" got me thinking on serious topics, I had the insight that the ultimate subject is sociology, because this is the study of what people do in groups. I have long believed that man is not what he says but what he does. In this connection, stressing ideology tends to lead one to overlook the facts of the quest for power by groups. Hitler was an individual but the Nazis were a group. The most interesting study of contemporary France would be to investigate how the functionary class came to acquire the immense, dominant power that it possesses today and, as a corollary, how the non-functionaries let it happen. Ideology alone does not explain the acquisition of power. To get that you have to study people and groups, a painstaking inquiry that I hope will be undertaken soon with regard to France and Europe.

In my "Montaigne and Descartes," I advanced a theory as to the use of what I call "the Cartesian canon" to select the élite functionaries in France, in particular, the *ENArques* and *Polytechniciens*, but a much vaster subject is how this was allowed to happen by other groups which possessed power before the new caste took over. In this century, de Gaulle bears huge responsibility for the advancement of the functionary class. He had such contempt for French politicians and the parliamentary system in which they operated during the Third Republic that on taking power after the liberation of France he acceded to the proposal of his arch-dirigiste lieutenant, Michel Debré, to create a school to select top functionaries, which became the Ecole Nationale d'Administration. Then, when he returned to power in 1958, he let the same Debré draft a constitution which thoroughly subordinated the parliament to the executive branch. And, by not erecting any legal barrier between the civil service and the political realm, he set in motion the process by which the functionary class gradually took over political power, the most important milestone being the 1974 election of an *ENArque*, Valéry Giscard d'Estaing, as President of the Republic. The crowning blow in the effacement of the separation of powers came with the election of François Mitterrand, who cynically embraced the constitution of de Gaulle's Fifth Republic, which he had labeled as a "Permanent *Coup d'Etat*" in a book with that title. Sixty percent of the members of the National Assembly elected in the Socialist landslide following Mitterrand's election in 1981 were civil servants who, of course, conserved that status while holding elective office. Is it any wonder that today the functionary class is the most privileged class in France? Recent statistics show that the average functionary today earns more salary than the average employee in the private sector. Yet the former has a lifetime job, while the latter is subject to the risk of being laid off. Moreover, functionaries can retire with a pension of 75 to 80 percent of their last salary, while retirees of the private sector average 30 to 35 percent. Much as I admired de Gaulle, particularly for his wartime role in leading the "Free French," I've reluctantly come to believe that if people of the ilk of John Laughland and myself subsist in the 21st century, their history books will judge de Gaulle severely for having led the way in turning over France and Europe to the functionaries.

On the European level, this occurred because of de Gaulle's hostility to a federal Europe and his advocacy of "*l'Europe des Nations*." As a result, he let the existing EEC institutions, based on the bureaucratic mechanisms of the Treaty of Rome, continue to grow and to enhance their power. What has resulted is not a "Europe of Nations" but of mandarins, one increasingly devoted to unitary law and centralism. In the United States, after two centuries of experience under the federal constitution, Congress still does not have the power to dictate to state legislatures what laws they will enact. Each state still has reserved domains of power, and makes its own laws governing such diverse subjects as business organizations, marriage and divorce, education and gambling. By contrast, the Council of Ministers, acting on the prodding of the European Commission, can edict "directives" which then become binding on the member states, obliging the parliaments of each country to enact conforming legislation. Thus, a handful of government executives and bureaucrats legislate for 300-million pseudo-citizens.

When in 1991 I visited Armenia, for the first time, while it was still part of the Soviet Union, I was asked by President Levon der Petrossian and Edvard Yegorian, his then chief advisor on the project for a new constitution, to convey my ideas on the subject. In my paper, I stated that the first principle of government should be that "Power tends to corrupt, absolute power corrupts absolutely," which is Lord Acton's immortal phrase. I still hold that to be the key to any analysis of society and it is applicable to any form of social organization, including business corporations and families. It is worth stating that the word "corrupt" in the phrase does not just refer to bribes and personal advantage but also must be understood in the larger sense of "abuse." Lord Acton's words could be paraphrased, "Power tends to be abused, and absolute power leads to horrendous abuse."

It is because of the danger of abuse of power that the system of "checks and balances" was installed in the United States Constitution. Although the intellectual basis for the separation of powers was best expressed by a French author, Montesquieu, in his *L'Esprit des Lois,* it has never been practiced in France, and least of all in today's France. Nor is it applied in the European Union. Thus, France and the EU represent egregious cases of abuse of power by the functionary class, who are accountable to no one but themselves. In Lord Acton's terms, therefore, the EU is a corrupt entity. And Tacitus' famous phrase takes on new meaning: "Never were there so many laws as when the state was the most corrupt."

To return to *The Tainted Source*, if I have any criticism of Laughland's book, it is thus that he lingers too much in the realm of ideas and does not delve into the realm of power and its abuse, which is a study of people acting in concert, a study of groups. The iron grip which the functionary class has on European institutions will not easily be relinquished. This class has at its disposal the vast taxing powers of the member states and wields that power for its own aggrandizement and even gratification, since EU functionaries pay no taxes anywhere, yet use other people's taxes to build constituencies through subsidies, consultancy fees, advertisements and other ways of molding public opinion. As Chief Justice John Marshall once remarked, "The power to tax involves the power to destroy." But in Europe it is also the means to build and maintain a power base for the functionary class. By reason of high payroll charges and the Value Added Tax, a French invention which its proponents cynically described as "fiscal anesthesia," the functionary class makes the common people of Europe unwittingly pay the bulk of taxes while at the same time imposing punitive and confiscatory levels of income taxes on the most dynamic individuals in the society, with the result that they are so busy working to pay taxes that they have no time to revolt against the functionary class. The middle-class and independent tradesmen and professionals are being destroyed or exiled by these policies, while industry and commerce are increasingly concentrated, and rife with cartels and monopolies, whose existence is favored by the caste of functionaries. In France the *ENArques* often end up managing these enterprises.

Ideas can, of course, be weapons in a struggle for power, but it is going to be very difficult to organize constituencies that can resist, let alone overcome, the power of the functionary caste in the European Union. When I saw John Laughland recently in Paris, he handed me an incredible document which demonstrates how far EU technocrats are willing to go to perpetuate their power. Presently, the various governing treaties of the EU, that is, principally, the Treaty of Rome and the Maastricht Treaty, do not confer any penal jurisdiction to EU institutions. Even antitrust violations give rise only to civil fines. Yet, this document, a report from a panel of EU-subsidized stooges, which has been meeting secretly for months, recommends the creation of the first "European crime," to wit, a crime "against the financial interests of the European Union." This crime is to be enforced by a "European Public Prosecutor," but in the courts of the member states. The following extract, which begins the report, is edifying: "The budget, defined as 'the visible sign of a true patrimony common to citizens of the Union,' is the supreme instrument of European policy. To say this emphasizes the extreme seriousness of any crime which undermines this patrimony." Can you believe that this was written in 1997 and not by Saint-Simon in the early 19th century? Can there be anything more grotesque than describing the budget as "the supreme instrument of European policy?" What is the function of the budget in the EU? Essentially, to pay the salaries and perks of EU functionaries, and provide subsidies, grants and loans by which these functionaries enhance their power and longevity. Can there by any more dramatic proof that the spirit of Saint-Simon lives on, and with it, the tainted source?

When the United States Constitution was drafted in 1787, the main obstacle to its adoption by the 13 colonies was the absence of provisions guaranteeing the liberties of their citizens and their own prerogatives. It was only when the proponents of the draft made a commitment to adopt a "Bill of Rights," by way of amendment, that the Constitution was adopted after a lengthy and edifying public debate. Contrast that process with the insidious and stealthy way that the European technocrats go about their business of grabbing power and privilege and, above all, contrast the priorities: the United States gave precedence to the rights of citizens while the EU gives priority to protecting its budget! I knew that these people had no sense of humor, but now I see that they have no sense of shame.

Several years ago, in commenting on the Maastricht Treaty, I stated that it is more important for Europe to have a common ethic than to have a common currency. It is to my mind one of the most subtle obscenities of the 20th century that the Maastricht Treaty purported to create a common citizenship of the European Union, which is not a state, and this, purely on an economic model. The discourse was, in effect: "People using the same currency have sufficient ties to be considered citizens of the same entity." Thus, what unites people is money, not values. Do you want to be a citizen of a monetary club?

There is no way that I could do justice to Laughland's book other than to reproduce it entirely. So the point is that you should go out and buy it. The first edition was published by Little, Brown in Great Britain in 1997 and a pocket version (on which this review is based) was published there this year by Warner Books. Fortunately, John Laughland is here today to exhort us that economic *dirigisme* and bureaucratic centralism will lead to a spiritually bankrupt Europe, one in which the liberty of the individual is necessarily imperiled.

Vol. XX, N° 7, September 1998

Comparative Clinton

As I like to start my Newsletters with a bit of humor, let me adapt the old vaudeville joke. Someone asked Hillary Rodham Clinton the other day, "How's your husband?" and she replied, "Compared with what?" Let us compare, indeed. It is a telling commentary on the decline of American civilization that the most famous four-minute speech uttered by an American President since Lincoln's Gettysburg Address is Clinton's sordid pseudo-confession of Monday, August 17th. After promising to tell the truth (once Monica Lewinsky had spilled the beans), Clinton took a week to decide what "version" of the truth he was going to tell. I happened to be in the USA when he appeared on television and can attest that the public reaction was not only heavily negative but also heavily spiced with sarcastic humor, much of which can not be repeated in polite company. This was a contrived speech, satisfying the famous definition of a camel, to wit, a horse designed by a committee. Whereas Lincoln drafted his immortal address alone, while on the train taking him to Gettysburg, Clinton had many advisers helping him concoct his "confession," and one report I heard on TV stated that every line was tested by public-opinion polls.

Three days later, when Clinton announced that he had ordered missile attacks on supposed terrorist targets in Afghanistan and Sudan, several friends with whom I spoke alluded to the motion picture "Wag the Dog," in which an American president, beset by scandals, concocts a phony war in order to divert attention away from his problems. Now, more than a fortnight later, as I write this, there is increasing skepticism about Clinton's claim that the Sudanese pharmaceutical factory was producing an ingredient for a deadly nerve gas. Indeed, the latest report I read in the *International Herald Tribune* of September 4th stated that the Pentagon did not even know that the target was a pharmaceutical factory! If this is intelligence, then give me guesswork.

Americans begat a republic with a President who was "first in war, first in peace, first in the hearts of his countrymen." As a child in a Philadelphia public school, I was taught that when little George Washington was given a toy hatchet by his father, he cut down a cherry tree. When asked about it, he gave this now-mythical reply: "Father, I cannot tell a lie. It is I who cut down the cherry tree." (Note that he spoke correct English, too). If Bill Clinton had been asked by his father the same question, he would surely have replied, "Dad, will you please define what you mean by a cherry tree?" And after quibbling for hours about the definition, Clinton would have denied the deed on the inarticulated ground that what he cut down was not a tree but only a sapling. Thus, to use Clinton's famous phrase, his reply would have been "legally accurate." However, accuracy is not a matter of law but of fact. This is so obvious that it would be redundant to say "factually accurate."

Like all interesting issues, the Clinton case marks the intersection of two fundamental tenets of the American-Protestant psyche: an aversion to lying and the protection of privacy. Not only did Clinton lie more than once in his testimony in the Paula Jones case, but also he made a grievous error in answering questions on his relationship with Lewinsky and in urging her to submit an affidavit of denial. The only rational explanation I can conceive is that they thought these false statements would strengthen Clinton's defense against Paula Jones. As it turned out, the judge in that case ruled that other affairs were not germane to the case, so the statements were unnecessary. The judge later dismissed the case on what used to be called a "demurrer," to wit, that the allegations, even if true, do not constitute sexual harassment. Thus, for purposes of her ruling, the judge took as true that Clinton, while governor of Arkansas, had spotted Paula Jones, a state employee, at a conference held in a hotel and dispatched a State Trooper, that is, a police officer, to summon her to his hotel room, where he pulled down his trousers and under-shorts, exposed his penis and invited this woman, whom he had never met, to perform what the press calls "oral sex" on him, but what medical books call *fellatio*.

I was dismayed to read in Judge Wright's decision that she calls this conduct merely "boorish and offensive." According to my dictionary a "boor" is a "bumpkin," a person of "little refinement." If "unrefined" is the worst that a lady in Arkansas can say about a man who exposes himself and solicits *fellatio,* I wish I had been born in Little Rock rather than in prudish Philadelphia. In most places in the world, such conduct is a crime, known in English as "indecent exposure" or in France as *outrage public à la pudeur.* I believe that Judge Wright's decision is wrong, and should be overruled in the pending appeal. That the top public official in a state can use the police to summon a lowly state employee to his room and solicit a sexual act with his exposed penis should be considered sexual harassment and a lot more. Also disgraceful in my view is the opprobrium that Clinton's caviar crowd in Hollywood and New York has been heaping on Paula Jones because she has "big hair," a big nose and a big mouth. The implicit rationale is that a female who looks like her and, to boot, once lived in a trailer, had no right to refuse Clinton's naked advances, whereas a neatly coifed lady wearing a Donna Karan dress would have been entitled to do so, and sue afterwards. And I find it interesting that Monica Lewinsky also has "big hair" and looks somewhat like Paula Jones. As Monica did go along with the President's penchant for *fellatio,* Clinton, to use baseball jargon, was batting.500 with the "big hair" category. Of course, he was president by that time, not the governor of the most modest state in the Union, and he had the Oval Office as a romantic setting. I suspect that the reason Clinton felt that it was "legally accurate" to claim that he had never been alone with Monica Lewinsky was that portraits of George Washington and Thomas Jefferson were part of the décor. After all, the interrogator did not define "alone" as meaning only that no other living persons were present.

If I dwell on these sordid details, it is to drive home the point that the "public-private" distinction which Clinton defenders have been making is too facile and does not fit the facts. The assumption of many people is that sexual conduct is necessarily private, but this does not withstand serious scrutiny. To take an easy example, if Clinton were a pedophile and benefited from sexual favors of an 11-year old, would anyone sane say that this is a private matter? What makes sexual conduct private is that it is performed in circumstances which make it no one's business but the participants'. No one has asked Bill what kind of sexual relations he has with his wife: that is private. But what he does in his office with a government employee is public business, and the fact that supposedly consenting adults are involved does not alter that conclusion. To take another example, if two of my employees had sex in our law library during business hours, that is certainly my business, to say the least, and this would justify their dismissal. Both the Paula Jones case and the Monica Lewinsky episodes illustrate clear abuse of office by a senior public official.

Thus, I do not agree with the off-stated assertion that it is not the sexual misconduct which is deplorable but only lying about it. Whether Clinton's actions constitute "high crimes and misdemeanors" sufficient to warrant his impeachment and conviction is another kettle of fish, but I agree with William Pfaff, the incisive columnist of the *International Herald Tribune,* that Mr. Clinton ought to resign from the high office which he has disgraced and in which he is no longer credible.

Despite the voluminous press coverage, the quality of reporting and commentary has been deplorable. The press has allowed itself to be manipulated by both camps, but mainly by the Clinton crowd. To give an illustration, most newspapers carried the obvious Clinton plant to the effect that even if he did discuss Lewinsky's future testimony with her, "he did not direct her to lie." But any journalist with brains who took the trouble to think this out would have seen the fallacy in these words. The issue in obstruction of justice is not whether an official "directed" someone to lie but whether he conspired with another to conceal the truth. When Clinton discussed this matter with Monica, she was no longer a government employee and thus Clinton had no power to "direct" her to lie. And if he had possessed such power while she was working for him, he also would have had the power to direct her to have sex with him, thus removing the defense that this was a consensual relationship.

Even more striking is the failure of the press to point out that the consensual argument is irrelevant to the dereliction of duty committed by both the President and the intern in having sex on the job. After all, as Monica's chief supervisor, it was Bill's duty to train her for government service and not for servicing his sexual cravings. Yet another aspect has been ignored by all journalists, to wit, the fact that these escapades constituted a serious security risk. When I was in the US Army, officers with top-secret security clearances would routinely be drummed out of the service when sexual peccadilloes made them vulnerable to blackmail. Even if Monica Lewinsky was not an agent of the Mossad or the KGB, would not Clinton be vulnerable to a future plant of a "big hair" girl in the White House by a foreign government? Finally, it should be pointed out that during Clinton's tenure as commander-in-chief of the armed forces, several officers have been discharged for acts of adultery. Why should lesser officers be held to a higher standard of moral conduct than the commander-in-chief?

As this is a Legal Newsletter, it might be instructive to examine some of the legal niceties by which Clinton has artfully dodged telling the whole truth in the past. The leading US Supreme Court case on perjury involved a Hollywood producer who, when testifying as to charges of fraudulent bankruptcy, was asked, "Did you have a Swiss bank account?" He answered, "My company had a Swiss account." Later, when it was discovered that he, too, had such an account, he was tried for perjury and convicted. But the Supreme Court overruled the conviction, holding that giving a truthful, albeit incomplete, answer, does not constitute perjury. Going even further back into the common law, there used to be a doctrine known as the "negative pregnant." If John Doe were charged with slaying Thomas Roe with an ax and Doe answered "I did not slay Thomas Roe with an ax," this was considered an admission that he did slay Thomas Roe but not with an ax. The negative answer was pregnant with an admission. Clinton, doubtless having discovered these fine points at Yale Law School, has mastered the art of what I call the "negative barren." For example, when a journalist asked him in 1992 whether Gennifer Flowers' allegation of a 12-year affair with him was true, he replied *"No."* This answer would have been truthful if his affair had lasted only 11 years or, indeed, had lasted 13 years! Similarly, when once asked if he had had an affair with Flowers, he replied, "There is no affair." Thus, by answering in the present tense a question posed in the past tense, he was being truthful while really avoiding a responsive action. In his Paula Jones deposition he finally admitted that he indeed did have sexual relations with Flowers, but he denied it as to Lewinsky by toying with the silly definition of "sexual relations" adopted by the court. As only *fellatio* was involved, Clinton had the "out" that he was a passive beneficiary of Lewinsky's activities. In other words, she was doing the work and he was merely an innocent bystander. After all, Clinton does not have a "relation" with his barber when he gets a haircut. Of course, these examples show the importance of formulating good questions and following up on evasive answers.

Some of my American friends disagree with me on the seriousness of Clinton's derelictions, contending that he has been "a good president" and that this is all that counts. This of course raises the question as to what is meant by the term "a good president." For most Americans, it apparently means that the economy is strong and they are earning a decent living. That was the underlying campaign assumption of Clinton's camp in 1992, to wit, "It's the economy, stupid." But if Jesus were around today and speaking modern jargon, He might say, "Bread alone ain't enough, stupid." For certain women's lobbies, the fact that Clinton has appointed women to high posts makes him a good president, even if the women, like Janet Reno and Madeline Albright, are incompetent hacks. By my criteria, Clinton has not been a good president. I voted for him in 1992 because I was utterly disgusted with George Bush's decision to leave Saddam Hussein in power after the allied forces crushed the Iraqi army. This was certainly the most asinine decision an American president has ever made. Keep in mind that before the Gulf War, Bush had stated that "Saddam is worse than Hitler." This was in itself a ridiculous utterance, since no one in the 20th century, with the possible exception of Stalin, was worse than Hitler. But if Bush believed it, how could he have left this horrible person in power? In 1945, had Bush been president, would he have kept Hitler in office, on the ground that the allies needed a counterweight to the Soviet Union?

If I bring up this point, it is to highlight the fact that Clinton won in 1992 only because Bush was washed up and another mediocrity, Ross Perot, was a candidate on his Right. It is deplorable that American politics produce presidential candidates who are lightweights with no sense of history and no vision of the future. In 1996, I abstained from voting because Clinton's inadequacies had already come to light. It was bad enough that he turned over half his domestic agenda to his non-elected wife, and allowed her to propose her disastrous health-care reform. But in foreign policy, his waffling on the atrocities being committed in Bosnia cost thousands of unnecessary deaths and untold suffering. And during Clinton's cosmetic African tour last year, he admitted that he had allowed a genocide to take place in Rwanda, which could have been avoided by forceful intervention. Today, with Saddam Hussein thwarting weapons inspections, the Middle-East peace process stymied, the Russian economy in shambles and Asian nations in financial turmoil, we see what it means to have a feckless American president representing the only superpower in the world, who is simply not up to his responsibilities. Clinton decides what is right by opinion polls and his personal credo seems to be "elections and erections are what I have lived for."

Thus far, Clinton has managed to avoid punishment for his disgraceful role in financing his 1996 election campaign, in which he made as many solicitation phone calls from the Oval Office as a bucket-shop huckster from Canada. He degraded the White House by turning the Lincoln Bedroom into a motel suite for campaign contributors and allowed foreign agents easy access to him in exchange for enormous gifts of money. He dragged his Vice President, Al Gore, into this game as well. And the abuse of so-called "soft money" contributions can still lead to criminal charges. I'm convinced that this all-out effort to raise money in disregard of decency and legality was motivated by Clinton's desire to stave off the day of reckoning in the Paula Jones case, because he had hoped that the courts would rule that the case could not proceed while he sat as President. As it turns out, the Supreme Court wisely ruled otherwise, and it is the "big hair" woman who has unraveled his Presidency, just as it was a lowly black janitor who caused the arrest of the Watergate burglars, which led to the ouster of Richard Nixon in 1974.

I do not agree with commentators who decry the loss of prestige suffered by the United States because of the judicial inquiry into Clinton's conduct. On the contrary, this case demonstrates the soundness of American political institutions founded on the rule of law, the separation of powers and a strong, independent judiciary. In the ideal democracy, leaders are worthy of worthy institutions, as in the Golden Age of the United States, when Washington, Adams, Jefferson and Madison were its first Presidents. But if I have to choose, I much prefer a country with sound institutions whose leaders are occasionally unworthy, to one with worthy leaders whose institutions are unsound. If Clinton is forced to resign or, better yet, has the decency to resign, the United States will survive and be strengthened, by showing that its political credos and institutions require high standards of conduct from elected officials.

This naturally leads me to the French reaction to the Clinton scandal, which is incredulity that the sexual exploits of an American president can be the subject of a judicial inquiry. As I've previously reported, my French friends love telling the story of President Felix Faure who died while exerting himself in "gallant company." The circumstances of his demise did not prevent the admiring Paris municipality from naming a broad avenue after him, in the 15th *arrondissement.* (Now, the ENA alumni association wants to change the name of the avenue to honor Captain Alfred Dreyfus, who was unjustly convicted of espionage in December 1894, a month before Faure became President and resisted efforts to overturn the conviction even after Emile Zola sent him his celebrated *"J'accuse."*) I must confess to having little sympathy for the French view, which stems from the outmoded tradition that "the King can do no wrong." Monarchs like Louis XIV had mistresses galore, and Louis XV, considered a "good Catholic King," had an insatiable sexual appetite which kept his courtiers scampering for fresh maidens to deflower. Basically, the French have the opposite view to that I expressed above: they admire a great King even if the institutions stink.

In the last month, French *juges d'instruction* have targeted several prominent politicians for criminal investigations, including former Prime Minister Alain Juppé and former Defense Minister François Léotard. The allegations involve illegal financing of political parties. Juppé, while the number-two official in Paris City Hall, under Mayor Jacques Chirac, is accused of having padded the city's payroll with about 20 employees who were working only for the RPR party. In a public statement, Juppé did not deny the allegations but used the excuse that there was then no public funding of political parties. It is clear that Juppé is willing to take the rap for Jacques Chirac who, as the first elected mayor of Paris, obviously was responsible for the illegal use of public funds, as well as the many other financial abuses committed during his tenure. Chirac stalwarts were quick to claim that as President he is immune from any prosecution, other than for High Treason. However, several months ago, the Socialist Minister of Justice, Elisabeth Guigou, opined that the President was subject to prosecution for offenses committed before his term began. In retaliation, the RPR fired a warning-shot at Prime Minister Jospin by pointing out that he had been paid a salary and bonus for three years by the Ministry of Foreign Affairs even though he had no assignment there. Naturally, Chirac, Jospin, Juppé and Léotard are all *ENArques*.

As to Léotard, he is suspected of having, while head of an allied party called *Républicains Indépendants,* financed the acquisition of the party's headquarters building by means of a phony loan from an Italian company, backed up by a cash deposit of five-million francs in a Luxembourg bank. The most astounding aspect of this case is that Léotard's defense against a charge of "money laundering" is that the cash came from the so-called "secret funds" which the Prime Minister gets every year from the budget, and which top government officials utilize for their private ends, without paying taxes on the income. Most non-French readers will react with disbelief when I say that this is a defense, one which the juge d'instruction wants to refute by showing that there was another, illicit source for the money. French newspapers, which for decades have remained silent about this outrageous practice of officials divvying up among themselves funds supposedly intended for secret intelligence operations, have been going along with the assumption that if Léotard can show that the cash deposit in Luxembourg came from these public funds then he is not accountable to anyone for their use. In the past, ministers have often refused to testify before the civil courts by raising the unsupported claim of "*secret défense.*"

I had previously alluded to this shameful abuse in my Newsletter of January 1996, when I reported that a French television program called "Capital" had the temerity to expose this misuse of the taxpayers' money. Emmanuel Chaim interviewed two former female ministers who candidly admitted that they had received each month an envelope containing cash, which they did not report as income, even though they used the money for personal purposes, such as buying clothing. Having heard about this practice from insiders, but never having seen any public reference to it, I was so amazed at this TV exposé that I did not have the reflex to record it. Later I tried to obtain a copy or a transcript of the program but without success, and no newspaper, not even the *Canard Enchaîné,* reported it. I suspect that Chaim was warned that he had treaded on forbidden ground.

When the investigation of Léotard became headline news, *Le Monde* finally published a story about *les fonds secrets*, but it accepted, without indignation, the standard line, which has no legal basis, that the Prime Minister, who receives and allocates the funds, is not accountable for their use. Recently, one of my French friends told me that an old buddy of his, who just retired as a senior tax official, complained that his pension did not take into account the cash that he had received every month! My friend claims that he told this man that it took a lot of gall to expect the taxpayers to include in his retirement pay a percentage of his unreported income. Several months ago, a French acquaintance in the know told me that during Mitterrand's reign, these "secret funds" were used to finance the Socialist Party's failing newspaper, called *Le Matin.* Every month for a year, two motorcyclists from the French Customs would bring four-million francs to the newspaper's office. The paper failed anyway. As you might guess, no one has been prosecuted for this abuse of public funds.

It is interesting to compare American and French practices in the realm of financing political parties. French politicians tend to steal directly from the taxpayers while Americans resort to getting funding from pressure groups. Knowing the *ENArque* mentality and, in particular, their pretense of serving the public good, I am sure they feel it is more virtuous to steal public funds than to become beholden to private interests. In the States, stealing from the Treasury is frowned upon, while accepting contributions from private pressure groups is considered legitimate, so long as no specific promises are made. That's comparative culture.

To return to Clinton, it is amusing to speculate that had he been born Guillaume Clinton in Brittany, he would surely have become an *ENArque* and ended up as President of France, with fewer headaches than he has now, and with neither Ken Starr nor Hillary Rodham on his tail. Perhaps it's not too late for him to sign up for a Berlitz crash course.

Vol. XX, N° 8, October 1998

Les Misérables: Clinton, Tripp, Lewinsky, Starr, the Congress

Although we have all reached the nausea level, I can't let my September Newsletter stand as the last one I'll have written on the Clinton mess. As my readers know, it was composed before the so-called Independent Counsel Kenneth Starr, sent his report on the Lewinsky matter to Congress, and all hell broke loose. Although Starr took pains in his cover letter to the House to point out that the report contained sensitive material which should be kept under lock and key, the House committed one of the most outlandish acts in American history by releasing the report on Internet. This was followed by the even more outlandish decision to release for television the video tape of Clinton's testimony before the Grand Jury, a supposedly secret proceeding. After this, virtually all the evidence before the Grand Jury was made public.

The fact that I was critical of Clinton does not mean that I approve of the actions of his adversaries. As a child in Philadelphia, I learned that "Two wrongs do not make a right." It is, as lawyers say, an *a fortiori* case that multiple wrongs do not make a right, nor do they reflect glory on the nation that gave the world "the American dream." Let us make a catalog of all that is wrong in this sordid affair.

• Clinton, President of the United States, has sex with a fellow employee of the American people, in the immediate vicinity of the hallowed Oval Office.

• The young lady in question does not even have the good sense and decency to protect the confidence of the immature sinner to whose animal needs she catered.

• One of her "friends" secretly and illegally records their intimate phone conversations and turns her in to the Independent Counsel, who wires the "friend" for more squealing.

• Clinton testifies under oath in the Paula Jones civil suit and lies about his sinning.

• A goon squad of prosecutors and FBI apprehends the young ex-intern, as though she were Public Enemy Number 1, and prevents her from calling her lawyer.

• The Independent Counsel forgets that he was hired to investigate a land scandal in Arkansas and makes the Lewinsky case his first order of business.

• When the scandal hits the press, Clinton vehemently lies about it on television and his wife also denies the liaison and claims that it is all a Right-wing plot.

• The prosecutor threatens the young ex-intern with criminal prosecution and she accepts immunity in exchange for testifying against the President.

• Despite this, the President lies again before the Grand Jury and the same day delivers a miserable, evasive speech on television.

• The Congress, on receiving the prosecutor's report asserting that there is substantial and credible evidence of impeachable offenses, makes the report public before it has even considered the evidence.

And there we stand today with a grotesque litany of events that has made the United States of America not only the laughing stock of the rest of the world but also, and foremost, has raised legitimate concern that the most powerful nation on earth has lost its head.

Of all the events listed above, the most outrageous are the decisions of the House of Representatives to publish the Starr report and then the evidence in the Grand Jury proceeding. The House received this report and evidence in furtherance of its constitutional function to decide whether the President should be impeached, that is, charged with "High Crimes or misdemeanors." When the House acts in this capacity it is serving a judicial function, and the Senate also performs a judicial function in holding a trial and deciding, after all the evidence is in, whether the President should be convicted and removed from office. The impeachment process is not a referendum nor is it an election or a poll-taking operation. If this function had been assigned by the Constitution to the Supreme Court and the Independent Counsel had been responsible for presenting the indictment, would it be conceivable that he could disclose all his evidence to the public before it were presented to the court? Of course, not. This would be considered a violation of one of the most fundamental guarantees contained in the Constitution, that no one can be convicted of an offense without due process of law, which requires an impartial tribunal not pressured by public opinion.

Justice Oliver Wendell Holmes, Jr. was fond of saying, "We need education in the obvious." It should have been obvious to the House of Representatives that due process of law demands that any accused be given a fair trial, and a fair trial can not be had if the persons responsible for the prosecution release all the evidence so as to inflame the public against the accused. This is trial by a mob, not by a court. That Congressmen on the House Judiciary committee can be so indifferent to the basic principles of due process of law is in my opinion a much worse offense that perjury about one's sexual peccadilloes. The only justification that I have seen mentioned in the press for this flagrant abuse was the fear that the Starr report would be leaked to the press. But this is hardly an excuse for the wholesale leaking which the Committee itself perpetrated. By analogy, would any person in his right mind deal with a leak in his cellar by flooding his entire house?

As indicated, this violation of the basic principles of American law dwarfs the offenses which Clinton is alleged to have committed. I have no love lost for him, but I believe that, like anyone in the United States, he has a right to a fair trial. What the Congress did fills me with disgust similar to that I felt when I saw the filmed "trial" of Nicolai Ceaucescu and his wife in Romania. That this couple was detestable and doubtless committed many crimes is no excuse for degrading the judicial process by means of a kangaroo court.

Part of the "education in the obvious," I would remind us all, is that justice is bifurcated: one element is substantive, that is, whether certain acts, if proven, merit punishment, and the other is procedural, whether the process by which one is tried and punished is fair. I believe that this double sense of justice is innate in most humans. Even a child knows that it is unfair to be punished without being given an opportunity to defend himself, or to be punished by an angry parent who has been inflamed with unverified reports. This obvious distinction was often forgotten by people – invariably white – who commented to me on the O.J. Simpson case. They would say, "He's obviously guilty," as though that were the only consideration. The fairness of the process itself is also a consideration. Justice Holmes once wrote in a case involving wiretapping, "We have to choose, and for my part I think it a less evil that some criminals should escape than that the government should play an ignoble part." Applying this principle to the Clinton case, it is clear to me that the Congress has played an ignoble part, and the reaction of most people throughout the world is the healthy one of revulsion. If Clinton succumbed to animal instincts and reacted in shame by denying it under oath, the members of Congress did not have the same excuse. They were not tempted by Lewinsky's thong underwear (whatever that is) and I see no excuse for their complete disregard for the most fundamental principle of due process of law. If anyone deserves impeachment, it is the Republican majority on the House Judiciary committee.

As an American living in a country of Catholic traditions, I have often commented on the effects of religious differences on the institutions of the two countries I know best. The USA has an essentially Protestant culture and this has both good and bad aspects. As my old friend, Judge John Noonan, a Catholic himself, has pointed out in his splendid new book, called *The Lustre of our Country,* we owe much in the way of religious freedom and tolerance in the USA to the proliferation of Protestant sects. This factor and the easy mobility of people in an expanding country made it impossible for States to maintain established religions, as several had done at the outset of the Republic. But one drawback, at least culturally, of Protestantism, is that it does not have the confessional and absolution. As a consequence, Protestants often resort to denial, that is, denying to themselves that they have sinned. I am persuaded that much of Clinton's playing with the definition of sexual relations was part of this denial process and, thus, in his mind when his answers became "legally accurate" they also became factually accurate. Catholic countries, like France and Italy, which have separated Church and State, tend to be more tolerant of sin and lying, since the confession is available and no sin is a permanent bar to entering the gates of Heaven. In France, an accused in a criminal matter or a party in a civil case does not even take an oath!

The Clinton-Starr duel represents two sorts of Protestants, one, the Elmer Gantry type, a charming preacher-sinner resorting to denial to save his soul, and the other, the implacable Calvinist ferreting out the damned soul who has found worldly success but not Grace. Starr has been compared with Inspector Javert in *Les Misérables,* the relentless police officer who pursues the ex-convict Jean Valjean, now a reformed, respectable citizen. Clinton is no Jean Valjean nor is he an evil man, just a weak one. I have hitherto refrained from commenting on Kenneth Starr because, frankly, I did not know what to think of him and his mission as Independent Counsel. However, I am ready now to come down hard on him and on the Congress that voted him unlimited time and money to fish up damaging charges against the Clintons, for matters that arose before they together became President. Even if the Sixth Amendment principle of a "prompt and speedy trial" does not technically apply here, nonetheless there is an element of unfairness in conducting never-ending investigations. No one should be under a permanent cloud in a fair-minded society. Moreover, the very essence of being a prosecutor in the American tradition carries with it the notion of "prosecutor's discretion." The State's Attorney does not have to prosecute every offense he has uncovered, even if the evidence is there. Nor does he have to grant immunity to one offender to get evidence on another. And if he had to choose offenders, why did he not give immunity to Clinton to testify against Lewinsky? After all, she lied, too, under oath, and even threatened the President, a federal offense.

On balance, I think Starr is a genuine villain in this piece. How he got from Whitewater to White House sex is still a mystery to me. Among other disgusting actions, he wires Linda Tripp to obtain evidence on Lewinsky and even gets the latter's doctors to reveal her confidences. He might have taken the time to read a bit of Shakespeare and remind himself that "The quality of mercy is not strained." It would have taken a bigger man than Kenneth Starr to send a one-sentence report to the House of Representatives, to wit, "My investigation has not revealed any impeachable offense which I feel should be brought to your attention." This would have spared the country a humiliating spectacle. Again, to quote Holmes, "Hard cases make bad law." To which I would add, "Hard men make bad prosecutors."

My catalog of *Les Misérables* would not be complete without commenting on Hillary Clinton. I find it sardonic that the press has portrayed her as the "wronged woman," as though she were unaware of her husband's philandering. It is obvious that the Clinton marriage is nothing more than a business partnership, the business being to acquire and share political power. As Holmes might also have said, *"Hard women make bad wives."* It is sad that part of Clinton's comedy act had to be to apologize to her publicly. As a French woman commented to me, "Every married woman knows that if her husband has a healthy sexual appetite to which she does not cater, then he will go elsewhere for gratification." It is unfortunate that Americans are not ready for a President with an official mistress, as in the golden age of the French court at Versailles, or an unofficial one, as in the brass age of the Fifth Republic under Mitterrand. With such a mistress, Clinton would not have had to engage in furtive sex with a silly sophomore like Monica Lewinsky. And he would not have had to waste a good cigar. As Kipling wrote: "A woman is only a woman but a good cigar is a smoke."

Seen from abroad, this American version of *Les Misérables* is a failed novel, there are no good people in it. How can one feel any sympathy for a woman who secretly records intimate telephone conversations and then turns in her "friend" to the prosecutor? And how can one appreciate this "friend" who expects a high-paying job in New York without having "to work for it" and then negotiates immunity in exchange for ratting on the President? With a loftier sense of her mission in life, she could have earned the plaudits of the entire world by braving prosecution rather than revealing the intimate details of her liaison.

No, this version of *Les Misérables* reveals Washington at its worst, where there is no decency, no love, nothing but vultures preying on each other. This is a tale with many a Judas but no one resembling Christ. Overlooked in this mountain of filth is the fact that, as a *New York Times* editorial courageously pointed out, a pharmaceutical factory in a foreign country called Sudan was bombed by United States missiles with no justification. To bomb a foreign country is an act of war, and only Congress can declare war, under the Constitution. If there is an impeachable offense committed by Clinton, it is rather this one, yet no one in Congress has suggested that he be impeached for it. Nor is anyone suggesting that the word "Intelligence" be taken out of the name of the CIA and "Fiction" substituted for it. In other words, serious matters are not being discussed in a country which purports to be the leader of the "free world," a world which is in a mess all over.

To return to Bill Clinton, I still think he should resign, as a service to the country. While a number of respectable people have contended that for a President to resign is to establish a "dangerous precedent" for the United States. I don't buy that argument. The truly dangerous precedent is for a President to escape accountability for his errors of judgment and his misconduct. There is still ringing in my ears the phrase of George Washington which I learned from my junior-high-school history teacher, Mary Williamson: "Let us build a standard to which the wise and the honest can repair."

The wise and the honest are absent today both in the White House and in the halls of Congress. The vulture has replaced the American Eagle. That's something to worry about.

Vol. XX, N° 10, December 1998

The Christmas Issue: Paul Gitlin, Harold Robbins and William Saroyan

It has been my sad duty over the years to write eulogies of friends who have died. Among these were the Newsletters I devoted to John Laughton, the Anglo-French lawyer who was our beloved colleague, Larry Fleisher and Franc Ricciardi, who both died in May 1989, to Vittorio Cassoni and Georges Bret, who were 1992 losses and to Arletty, the great French actress, who also died in 1992. After the last, painful, tributes I told myself that I should not wait until my friends died to honor those whose lives had enriched mine since I began practicing in Paris in 1961, and I made up a list of people who deserved a living tribute. I never got around to this project, perhaps because of the fear that I might jinx my friends if I sang their praises.

High on the list I had drawn up was Paul Gitlin and now it is too late to pay him a living tribute, as he passed away suddenly in New York the week before Christmas. Paul was one of the lawyers I admired most in the world, because of his acuity, honesty, creativity and tenacity. He was still in active practice right up to the end, at the age of 83. Readers familiar with the publishing industry would recognize the name of Paul Gitlin as that of one of the leading copyright and literary lawyers in the United States. Among his clients, at one time or another, were William Saroyan, Harold Robbins, Cornelius Ryan, Irving Wallace and Senator Bill Bradley. This is a very incomplete list.

In April 1961, two days after my arrival at Coudert Frères in Paris, there occurred one of the great events of my life: meeting William Saroyan, the Armenian-American writer from Fresno who was then a client of the firm and who became an instant friend when I introduced myself to him with: "My name is Aram and, what's more, my son's name is Aram." It turned out that Bill's New York lawyer was Paul Gitlin, of the firm of Ernst, Cane, Berner & Gitlin, with offices on 45th Street. It was Paul who had referred Bill Saroyan to Coudert, and when I took over Bill's account I corresponded with Paul. Later in the year, Gitlin came to Paris and I discovered a burly, vigorous, straight-talking man of 46 who wasted no time in getting to the point. His devotion to Bill Saroyan was immense, despite the fact that Bill's days of glory were long past. At age 26, Saroyan had burst upon the literary scene in the '30s with his collection of short stories, headed by "The Daring Young Man on the Flying Trapeze," soon followed by a dazzling array of books and plays, including the novel "The Human Comedy," which was made into a movie starring Mickey Rooney, the Broadway hit "The Time of Your Life," which won the Pulitzer Prize in 1940, and an endearing collection of short stories about his Fresno childhood, called "My Name is Aram." World War II was Bill's undoing, as he would tell it: he was drafted as a "buck private," shortly after his marriage to Carol Marcus, and when he returned to civilian life he found that both he and the world had changed. His writing was no longer in style. He now had two children, Aram and Lucy, and he discovered that his non-Armenian wife had ambitions other than to become an Armenian mama. He drank a lot and gambled. He divorced his wife, only to remarry her and then divorce again. His post-war novels, such as "The Adventures of Wesley Jackson," and "Rock Wagram," were not commercial successes, nor was his major effort to return to Broadway with "The Cave Dwellers." Bill's gambling losses led him to get behind in his taxes and his publishers received tax liens. Saroyan decided to move in Paris in 1959 at a time when the USA did not tax "earned income" of Americans residing abroad. When I got involved with him, one of the missions that Paul Gitlin assigned me was to negotiate with the IRS a settlement of Saroyan's past tax liabilities, a task which took a long time but which was finally accomplished.

In the meantime, however, Bill Saroyan parted company with Paul Gitlin. I did not know the reason at the time but I was later to hear the versions of both parties which basically coincided. In those days, most authors had both an attorney and a literary agent. To the former they paid fees and to the latter they paid commissions on advances and royalties from book contracts, generally ten percent. Paul Gitlin had the bright idea of proposing to his clients combining both roles and charging merely the commission. He was apparently the first lawyer to propose serving in this dual capacity, now commonplace. Bill Saroyan angrily rejected the proposal and severed his connection with Gitlin. But another of Paul's clients jumped at the idea and became rich as a consequence. His name was Harold Robbins.

Because of Saroyan's leaving Gitlin, I had lost touch with Paul, but in 1969 our relationship revived. What brought this on was my one fleeting moment of fame when I became the subject of a New York Times article, replete with pictures, on the first page of the second section. In the Spring term of that year I became a Visiting Professor of Law at New York University, thanks to the support of my friend and classmate Norman Dorsen, who was, and still is, one of the leading lights on the faculty. I had wanted to get teaching out of my system but, having started my own firm in Paris only two years earlier, and with a wife and seven children, I saw no way both to teach in New York and practice law in Paris unless I commuted back and forth. So I hit upon the crazy solution of taking the Air France flight to New York on Sunday, teaching International Law and Corporations on successive Mondays and Tuesdays and, when my Corporations class ended at 8 PM, I would dash to Kennedy Airport and take the 10 PM Olympics Airways flight to Paris, arriving Wednesday morning, when I would bathe and shave, and then work through Saturday, and resume the routine. These were, of course, the days before the Concorde and the fastest plane was the Boeing 707, the first major jetliner. John Hess, the Times correspondent in Paris, thought this would make an interesting story and suggested to the home office that I be interviewed. The result was the article above mentioned, written by a young reporter, fresh out of Harvard College, David Andelman, who got his first byline and who thereafter became a friend for life. This story created a minor sensation and was carried by the International Herald-Tribune, as well as by dozens of newspapers throughout the United States. Incidentally, it was thanks to this story that I made other life-time friends: Merrill and Sybil Conn. The Times article mentioned that when in New York I liked to find someone who had a piano as I missed playing Bach when away from home. A few days later I got a letter from a complete stranger, saying that they had a brand-new Steinway baby grand in their Manhattan apartment and inviting me to visit. This was Merrill Conn. I phoned and was quickly invited to their United Nations Plaza high-rise apartment, where I not only played Bach but also enjoyed a delicious dinner and warm conversation Now the Conns live in San Francisco and are among my dearest friends.

Another person who read the article was Harold Robbins, who was living it up in his villa located on Avenue Victoria at Le Cannet, a suburb of Cannes on the Côte d'Azur. He spoke with Paul Gitlin about it and the two of them contacted me in Paris, about Harold's project to acquire rights to a French television serial called "Yao," on an African subject. And so it was that Harold Robbins became my client and friend, and my relationship with Paul Gitlin resumed and blossomed into friendship. My first meeting with Harold occurred in June 1969 when he invited me to Cannes to discuss the deal. He put me up in the luxurious Carlton Hotel on the Croisette, a place in which I had never before set foot. The morning after my arrival, Harold sent a chauffeur to drive me to his villa, located in the heights above Cannes, with an unencumbered view of its magnificent bay. I did not know what to expect to find in Robbins, as I had never read any of his novels or seen a picture of him. Harold received me on his immense terrace overlooking the bay and turned out to be a bald man in his early 50s, with a round face and a soft, hesitant speech. Only the smart sunglasses suggested the Hollywood type. He told me that he had fallen in love with Cannes several years earlier and acquired the property, demolished the existing house and built one to his taste. What struck me immediately about it was that it was air-conditioned, a feature which was simply unheard of in France in those days. Harold introduced me to his wife, Grace, and their young daughter Adriana, and then we got down to business.

While watching French television Harold had been struck by the nightly series called "Yao" (the hero's name), which Claude Vermorel had shot in Africa solely with native actors and extras and which told a story entirely involving Africans. Detecting my puzzlement as to why an American novelist whose fame had been achieved writing about power and sex, would get involved in such a subject, Harold explained that the newly-developed interest of black Americans in their origins should provide a market for this type film. He therefore wanted to acquire the series and convert it into a full-length motion picture suitable for theater projection. Soon the French director, Claude Vermorel and his wife arrived at the villa and we began our discussions, with me acting as Harold's spokesman, as he spoke very little French. After lunch on the terrace, Harold called Paul Gitlin in New York to report on the day's negotiations, and it was not long before I came to realize how good a deal Robbins had made in accepting Paul's offer to be both lawyer and agent. I was to discover that Paul handled Harold's money, paid his bills, filed his tax returns, negotiated with the IRS and, in sum, assumed all the worries while Harold had his fun.

To return to "Yao," one of Gitlin's assigned worries was getting financing for Harold's project and he managed to do so. In due course, I prepared contracts with Vermorel, which I sent to Paul for approval and from his comments and questions I saw that he was still an excellent technician of the law of copyright. It was later that year that Harold visited my office in Paris for the first time. We had just moved into 46 avenue d'Iéna and I was quite pleased with our layout and furniture. When Harold sat down in front of my desk in my oval office, his eyes coolly made the rounds and he said, "Beautiful office, Jack, there's just one false note," and he pointed to one small item which, indeed, did not fit in with the antique English furniture that I had just acquired. I was very impressed with the way Harold had quickly sized up my large office and displayed impeccable taste. Beneath his brash exterior, Harold was a refined and sensitive man.

It was during this stay that I met James Baldwin, the black American writer, who was living in France. Harold tried to enlist him to do a screenplay for "Yao." Baldwin came to my office and then the three of us had lunch at Fouquet's on the Champs-Elysées. Baldwin, who was small and ascetic-looking, spoke as though every word gave him pain. He brought up his favorite subject, the plight of his black brethren in the USA, and at one point he said, "You're all guilty, man." I asked him, "Whom do you mean?" and he replied, "All you whites." This aroused my truculence and I told him, "Look here, Mr. Baldwin, my father came from the mountains of Armenia and I don't think he ever saw a black person before coming to America and he certainly never persecuted one. Indeed, the Armenians were persecuted by the Turks. So I don't personally feel guilty about the blacks. The Armenians had nothing to do with slavery in the United States." Baldwin listened calmly and when I'd finished, he said, "You're still guilty, man, you're all guilty." And so, I learned something about the collective responsibility of all whites from the lips of a militant black man.

As it turned out, Baldwin declined the project and Harold hired various technicians to try to turn the disparate 26 episodes of "Yao" into a coherent full-length feature. I wish I could say that he succeeded but when I saw the first projection in a Paris studio, I had trouble following the plot and I could not see why 20-million black Americans would be any less confused. As I recall, the film got virtually no distribution in the USA. Harold returned to what was his forte, churning out quickly-read novels of lust and action, inspired by the lives of real people, such as Howard Hughes, Porfiro Rubiroso and Henry Ford. Early on, I admitted to Harold that I had never read any of his novels, a fact which he accepted graciously and he prevailed on Paul Gitlin to send me a collection of his paper-back productions which sold by the millions in airport lobbies. They were ideal novels to read on airplanes, as the chapters were short and crammed with action and sex. I used to jest that a Robbins novel had at least one orgasm per chapter but, aside from the sex, I admired the skill with which he told his stories and moved the action along. It takes art to do this. I am reminded of an essay I read a long time ago about a writer's experience during the depression. He made the point that while working on his "great American novel," he imagined that he could easily earn a living dashing off short stories for popular magazines such as The Saturday Evening Post and Colliers. But after constant rejections he realized that the greater did not include the lesser, i.e., that writing pot-boilers was a separate art which serious writers did not necessarily possess. On this theme, I recall also that Brahms once signed an autograph with the words, "J. Brahms, who wishes that he had written 'The Blue Danube.'"

Truly, Robbins pioneered and excelled in a 20th_century popular art form that has since attracted a ream of imitators. He knew that he would never win the Nobel Prize for Literature but he was proud of the fact that, after the Bible, no collection of books of a single author had achieved as wide an audience. I believe that some 700-million Robbins books have been sold throughout the world. It might be mentioned that despite the fact that Robbins spent so much time in France, his novels met with little success here, perhaps because the action was too American and the sex too explicit. About 15 years ago, when Laffont published one of his novels, Robbins was invited on the television literary talk show on prime time, Apostrophes, hosted by Bernard Pivot, a very French Frenchman. Harold invited me to be among the background spectators and he, dressed in a white suit, did his best to play his part as a debonair Hollywood type. Pivot questioned Robbins as though he had come from outer space. It was clear there was no common ground between them.

Having written an essay in 1969 called "Quantitative and Qualitative Truth," I once told Harold of my theory that there were essentially two types of people, qualitative and quantitative. Without hesitation, Harold retorted, "I'm quantitative." Although I rarely mentioned Saroyan to Robbins, I could not help contrasting the two writers who became my clients thanks to Paul Gitlin. While Robbins was getting million-dollar advances before writing a single word of a planned novel, thus forcing the publisher to make a big promotion of the book when it finally appeared, Bill Saroyan was moving from publisher to publisher getting measly advances on finished works which rarely sold more than 5,000 copies. Saroyan was qualitative. He was dwelling frugally in a rickety fifth-floor walk-up on rue Taitbout in the unfashionable 9th arrondissement of Paris, while Robbins was living high on the hog on the Riviera moving from villa to yacht to Carlton, spending money faster than he earned it. In those days in France he had several automobiles, including a hand-made English Jensen. He had bought for Grace a "little" Rolls-Royce in California and when she balked at driving French cars in Cannes, he had her Rolls flown over by Air France freight at the then costly price of $2,800. Robbins would spend a fortune on parties and entertainment. As we were in Cavalières in August of 1969, Harold invited my wife and me to a dinner party at the Carlton to watch the annual fireworks contest There were 20 people at his table and Russian caviar was served in a bucket, with the best champagne flowing. My wife and I had never seen so much caviar in one place. Paul Gitlin, who was there with his vivacious wife Zelda, also a straight-talking New Yorker, told me that this price-tag was modest compared to Harold's Hollywood parties, when he would fly in show-girls from Las Vegas and easily spend $100,000 in an evening.

A few years later, when Harold wanted to buy a yacht and summoned me south to help him negotiate the purchase, he asked me to call Paul in New York to advise him of his intention. Paul replied dourly, "We can't afford it. He hasn't even paid last year's taxes." When I reported this to Harold, he was unperturbed and wrote out a check to firm up the deal, letting Paul do the financial scampering. He named the yacht "Graziana," a combination of Grace and Adriana and hired a four-man crew to operate it. The next summer, my wife and I attended a big party on the yacht which included, with typical Hollywood flourish, a woman jumping fully-dressed into the Mediterranean. My French wife does not go for this sort of hi-jinx and although she liked Harold in more intimate settings, vowed never again to attend a Robbins party, thus depriving me of further presence at his Riviera escapades.

In 1980, Harold bought land overlooking a canyon in Los Angeles and built a $3.5- million mansion. In April of 1981, I visited Los Angeles and had lunch with him at the Polo Lounge at the Beverly Hills Hotel, after which he drove me in his fancy Maserati to visit the house, which had only three bedrooms and two Rolls-Royces. That night he had the housewarming, which I attended. There was a fancy sit-down dinner for 24 people at an elaborately decorated table, and then a party for a larger crowd, with musicians. Among the celebrities I met there were Cyd Charisse, Buddy Hackett and the then supreme Hollywood producer, Joe Levine. Of course, several of Harold's novels were turned into motion pictures but in general they were not as successful as his books.

Two days later, I flew to Fresno for the first time and visited the dying William Saroyan, who was living in a simple tract house with minimum furniture. The contrast could not have been greater. Yet, in their origins both men had more in common than one would have suspected. Both had lived in orphanages early in life: Saroyan because his father had died young and his mother had placed their four children in an orphanage so that she could work for a living; Robbins because he had been abandoned at birth with the name of Francis Kane. Later he lived with a foster family named Rubin and it was this name which he later converted to Robbins. He left that family and school at age 15 to begin his own struggle to the top. Saroyan left school at age 14 and worked at a number of odd jobs, including a Postal Telegraph messenger, and took up writing seriously at 18, much to the dismay of his doubting family. Both had unsuccessful first marriages. Saroyan never married again, while Robbins did, more than once.

Harold's luck changed as the '80s evolved. His lavish life-style finally took its toll. He had to sell his villa and yacht in France, and then his Hollywood mansion. He suffered a stroke and hip injuries from a fall, which made him an invalid. He and Grace divorced, another costly event. His books met with less success as various imitators of his formula provided novelty to the publishing world. As he no longer came to France I had lost touch with him, but I kept sending him my Newsletters. A few years back, I was delighted to get an e-mail message from him and his new wife Jann, saying that they were avid readers of my Newsletters and were living in Palm Springs. In February 1996, I visited Los Angeles and prevailed on my old friend from Philadelphia, Leonard Monroe, and his wife Suzette, to accompany me on my first visit to Palm Springs, to see Harold. As luck would have it, we went on Valentine's Day, which was their fourth wedding anniversary, and were invited to the dinner party they were throwing at one of the local restaurants. We visited Harold's home during the afternoon, and found him in a wheelchair but cheerful and hospitable. He was watching a film called "Showgirls" which he was enjoying immensely, despite the panning it received from the critics. That evening we attended the dinner party and I was pleased to find among the guests Harold's friend and physician from Cannes and a French producer I had met years earlier. Harold was in his 80th year but aside from the wheelchair still resembled the man I had met a quarter-century earlier. All Harold's friends were happy that he had found in Jann a woman who loved and cared for him. At someone's request, I improvised a toast to both of them. At the end, Harold quipped, "Don't forget to pay your share of the bill" but, of course, it had been paid for.

Paul Gitlin was not at the party because Harold and he had a falling out, but when I later saw Paul I detected that his affection for Harold was still there, just as it had been for Bill Saroyan despite their also parting company. In October 1997, 18 months after I last saw him, Harold passed away. It is too bad that he did not write the one book that would have been his best, that of his own life.

Paul Gitlin was born in Brooklyn in 1915 to a devout Jewish orthodox family. He got his undergraduate degree at NYU and then moved north to Harvard Law School, where he developed an early interest in copyright law, even winning a coveted prize for the best essay in that field. After his graduation in 1938, he was not able to land a law job. When W.W.II arrived, he entered the military service and saw action in the South Pacific. After the war he found a position at Ernst Cane, which finally become his own shop when the other partners died. Thus his whole career was with a single firm and in the field that he loved.

On many occasions when I visited New York I was privileged to be invited to lunch with Paul. There was no use in asking, "Where shall we meet?" because Paul lunched in only one restaurant, the Four Seasons in the Seagram Building, and at only one table, beside the pool. Paul drank copiously in those days a clear white liquid which was not water, but he never lost the keenness of his mind. He would speak fondly of his son Jonathan, who had become a lawyer but decided not to follow his father's footsteps as a literary lawyer. We would often reminisce about Bill Saroyan. Paul told me that he had once invited all his stable of writers to his home in the Hamptons and that Bill not only out-drank them all but also stole the show in conversation. I was not surprised, because I have never known a more striking and fascinating talker than Bill Saroyan when he was in a good mood. Paul Gitlin could have given him a run for his money, but being the wise lawyer that he was, he knew that it does not pay to outshine a client in conversation! It is unfortunate that Paul Gitlin did not write his own memoirs but perhaps he felt that his duty as a lawyer was to carry the foibles of his famous clients with him to his grave. At least he had the satisfaction of surviving most of them.

HAPPY NEW YEAR to all my faithful readers.

Vol. XXI, N° 1, January 1999

Euro and Crime in *ENArchie*

The year in France began with a lot of hype about the introduction of the euro as the official future currency of 11 of the 15 nations now comprising the European Union. The press started calling the 11-nation block "Euroland" but this English-language title did not please the august Académie Française which opted for the more prosaic *zone euro.* To be sure, the franc still is the currency of the man in the street, who buys his baguette with it, and the several-million unemployed still get paid in francs. About the only practical significance of the arrival of the euro, besides freezing the exchange rates among the 11 countries, was that the Paris bourse, to wit, the stock exchange, now quotes in that currency. It is not until 2001, if we live that long, that paper money and coins are slated to bear the euro imprint, although it seems possible that the switchover date will be moved up.

The official propaganda of the French government, which is an emanation of the functionary class that rules the country, proclaims that the euro is a panacea which will bring prosperity and stability to the EU. The virtue of proclaiming "truth" is that you do not have to explain the why and wherefore by which you got to it. I seem to be the only person in France who remembers that the Soviet Union had a single currency. The ruble was the only valid currency in Russia, the Ukraine and Kazakhstan, just to name three of the 15 nations making up the USSR, and yet this currency did not bring either prosperity or stability, because the underlying economic and political systems were rotten. What will determine the prosperity of France and the rest of the EU are the same factors. The *raison d'être* of the new European Central Bank, led by a Dutchman who could be a clone of the faceless Bundesbank fathers, is premised on the German credo that inflation is the only devil known to economic man. The fact that German unemployment is at its highest level since the end of World War II – ditto for France – is not their official concern, since economic and fiscal policies are still within the province of the individual countries making up the EU. The biggest time-bomb facing both France and Germany is the astronomic cost of future pensions to be paid to an increasing number of retirees and to be financed by a decreasing number of working people.

Since the '80s, every French government, whether labeled as "Right" or "Left," has professed that "unemployment is our highest priority." Curiously, the facts have borne them out, in the sense that keeping unemployment high has indeed been the top priority. The primary objective of the functionary class, led by the ubiquitous *ENArques*, is to maintain its own political power and economic privileges. They are the equivalent of the *nomenklatura* which ruled the Soviet Union and led it to its ruin. But unlike the Soviet Union, where the "working class" could say, "We make believe we're working and they make believe they're paying us," the French-functionary solution for unemployment is simply to pay people without the pretense of working. Not only are there generous unemployment benefits, pseudo-training programs and early retirements, but also the infamous RMI for people who have never worked or who have exhausted their unemployment benefits. "RMI" stands for *revenu minimum d'insertion* which literally means "minimum insertion revenue" and if this is incomprehensible to you in English, don't feel bad because it's equally incomprehensible in French! This handout was invented by an *ENArque*, to be sure, Michel Rocard, one famous for being incomprehensible in all circumstances, who served as Prime Minister for the first three years of Mitterrand's second term, beginning in 1988. The idea was that, starting at age 25, everyone who was not working should get a basic minimum payment in exchange for agreeing to be "inserted" into the work force. In theory, this handout was to be managed by municipalities which were supposed to develop schemes for inserting these unfortunate dole receivers into the world of the employed. As with everything else in *ENArchie,* where theory is an end in itself, once the RMI got rolling no one bothered to do the inserting. This dole amounts to F 2,502 ($455) per month for a single person and rises with each dependent.

Let me recount two conversations of the past week which illustrate the nefarious consequences of the RMI. A young woman lawyer I know related that her baby-sitter had applied for a job with Euro-Disneyland but when she got the offer, she refused it. Asked why, she replied: "I'm going to be 25 soon and will be eligible for the RMI. With that and occasional odd jobs, undeclared, I'll earn as much as I would with a regular job for the minimum wage." A similar refrain was heard from a potential nanny of one of my friends; with the RMI she is eligible for a housing allowance and other benefits she would lose if she worked. "Why should I work for the minimum wage when I can get the same benefits while staying in bed all day?" The monthly minimum wage, called SMIC, is F 6,797 ($ 1,236).

The other panacea for unemployment, promised by the *ENArque* Lionel Jospin when he campaigned in 1995, after President (and *ENArque*) Chirac's inane decision to dissolve the National Assembly, is the 35-hour work week, which is being implemented by another *ENArque*, Martine Aubry, minister of solidarity and all that. The theory of shortening the work week from 39 hours to 35 was that this would create more jobs by spreading the available work among more people. After laboriously drafting a silly law to this effect, which programmed an initial period of voluntary compliance in exchange for subsidies for new jobs, before the shorter workweek becomes compulsory, the self-assured Aubry sat back waiting for major employers to negotiate agreements with unions, which would supposedly create 600,000 new jobs during 1998. Well, guess how many new jobs have been created? Only 8,000, and these only because the taxpayer is footing the bill. Most companies merely agreed to give overtime pay for the extra four hours per week in exchange for flexible working hours. Any sensible person could have predicted that the 35-hour week plan would be a fiasco.

Is it that the *ENArques* who rule France are not sensible people? Certainly, in this context they are not, because they are blinded by their own self-interest, propped up by their near-religious belief that they are "protectors of the public interest." They can not afford to propose sensible solutions, all involving more liberty for the entrepreneurial class and lower taxes and social-security charges, because these solutions would loosen their hold on the reins of power and the privileges which go with it. The power base of the *ENArques* is found not only among the five-million civil servants in France with lifetime jobs and 1.5-million employed by state-owned enterprises but also among the many millions of people who receive handouts from the so-called "State." About ten years ago, I read in the *Wall Street Journal* an article by a Swedish economist explaining why the welfare state of Sweden was irreversible: more than half the voting population consists of civil servants with lifetime jobs or persons receiving more benefits from the government than they are contributing to the tax coffers. This point-of-no-return has now been reached in France and explains why the only choice offered to the French electorate is voting for functionary-dominated parties calling themselves "Right" and functionary-dominated parties calling themselves "Left," both mainly led by *ENArques*. The only difference between the two is that the former get their statist inspiration from Louis XIV and Colbert, while the latter are descendants of 19th-century dreamers of the likes of Saint-Simon, Proudhon and Marx. Even among royalists or Communists or Islamists there are rival clans, and if you allow yourself to be diverted by these rivalries, you can forget that your life is being dominated by people offering you little choice or freedom.

The main difference between the Soviet *nomenklatura* and the French variety is that the former remained in power by physical oppression, gulags and propaganda, abetted grandly by the inertia which rules all people, while the latter have taken over the political sphere and created permanent constituencies of functionaries and welfare-beneficiaries. Whereas the Soviets turned their frontiers into prison walls, the French rulers, until now, have not prevented their citizens from leaving the country, and many thousands of persons with money or ambition have flocked to places such as England, Switzerland, Florida, Silicon Valley and even Belgium, whose tax system is more favorable to persons of wealth. Dozens of show-business personalities, including Alain Delon, Charles Aznavour and Jean-Paul Belmondo, live in Switzerland, as do hundreds, if not thousands, of the rich French families, who are fleeing the wealth tax and the confiscatory income-tax rates. The 1999 *Loi de Finances* includes two pernicious, but little-discussed, provisions designed to make it more costly for the wealthy to leave the country. One provision imposes the capital-gains tax on unrealized profit on shareholdings of persons who leave France. Thus, if a shareholder moves, say, to Switzerland, he must pay the tax (or post security) on shares which have appreciated in value but have not been sold. The other provision subjects to the gift and inheritance tax gratuitous transfers of personal property if the beneficiary is resident in France, whereas previously these taxes were applicable only when the donor or decedent was a French resident or the property was located here. Unlike in the United States where tax laws are drafted by Congressional committees, in France the functionaries do the drafting and the Parliament puts a rubber stamp on the measures. No explanation was offered for the modification of a fundamental principle of taxation. In my view, the reason for the change is to get at families where the parents have left the country but their children have remained in France, often to finish their schooling. This measure will encourage the children to leave, too.

A concomitant of the proliferation of handouts is, of course, high income taxation on the so-called "rich" (in reality, people who work hard, whereas the real rich – those with high net worth – easily escape prohibitive taxation by leaving the country or using tax shelters). An often overlooked consequence of the steep taxation of the most industrious citizens is that they are effectively prevented from engaging in politics, either because they leave the country or are so busy working to pay taxes that they have no time for anything else. Hence the near-monopoly of the functionary class over the political process, made possible, of course, by the scandalous absence of any law prohibiting civil servants from engaging in politics. As taxpayers are not allowed to deduct substantial charitable contributions from income, another long-term effect of the system, is that it is virtually impossible to establish non-governmental centers of political and economic research and proposition. There is no Brookings Institution in France, let alone a Harvard University. Another reason for the lack of independent not-for-profit institutions is the inheritance system which provides for "forced heirship" in favor of descendants and even ascendants. Thus, a French resident with, say, three children, must leave three-fourths of his estate to his children, no matter how wealthy he is. This explains why there are no equivalents to the Ford Foundation or the Rockefeller Foundation in France. Indeed, thousands of private associations are dependent on governmental subsidies. And the wealthy who have already left France are not inclined to create foundations to save the country from the functionary class. The late Jimmy Goldsmith became a political non-conformist and was opposed to the current trends of the European Union. Yet, I see no signs that he left any part of his colossal fortune for the creation of a foundation that could be a counterweight to the French functionary class.

As I have oft pointed out, the only opposition to the functionary party in France has hitherto come from Jean-Marie Le Pen's National Front, which stupidly grounds its platform on xenophobia. Now, that party has been split in two by the open conflict between Le Pen and his once chief lieutenant, Bruno Mégret, who, having been given the position of *Délégué Général*, had the opportunity to control much of the party apparatus. Thus there are at present two parties vying to use the same label, *Front National.* What apparently triggered the schism was Le Pen's decision to have his wife stand in for him in future elections if he were barred from becoming a candidate by reason of his criminal conviction for striking a political candidate in an earlier election. Mégret believed that as number two in the party, he should have been the front-runner. The two parties will be squaring off in the elections, later this year, for members of the so-called European Parliament. The traditional "Right" parties, the RPR and the UDF, are also squabbling, because the RPR wants to present a single list led by, you guessed it, the *ENArque* Philippe Séguin, whereas the centrist UDF is against his heading the list because he once opposed the Maastricht Treaty.

The Socialists and their allies are also split on a number of issues, and the coming elections merely aggravate the tension. The only acceptable pluralism in France, it would seem, is within the Left camp, which now openly calls itself *la Gauche plurielle.* The Green party, led by Dominique Voynet, the Environmental Minister, strangely decided to have Daniel Cohn-Bendit – formerly "Danny-the-Red" during May '68 – lead the list for the European elections. This is all the more bizarre in that Danny was a member of the German parliament until recently, and he is not even a French citizen!

One of the issues dividing the Left majority is what to do about the appalling rise of criminality throughout France. I got a taste of this personally on November 24th last, when I was attacked in my garage, in the 16th *arrondissement,* by three young men who stole my car and left me with a broken and dislocated shoulder. Paris is decidedly a very unsafe place these days. One does not have to be a statistician to observe that the police are not there when you need them, but this impression was recently confirmed by the leaking of a report to the effect that of the 89,000-strong police force in France (not counting the gendarmes, who are part of the French Army), only 5,000 are on the terrain at any given time! They are notably absent from the Parisian suburbs (unlike most US cities, the well-to-do live in Paris and the poorer people in the banlieues) which are dominated by sizeable street-gangs. Jean-Pierre Chevènement, the Interior Minister (also an *ENArque*), who amazingly recovered from a coma caused by an allergy to anesthesia during an operation, returned to his post early in January and immediately caused a stir by proposing some sort of banishment for youthful troublemakers. It would be better to banish the *ENArques*.

The French elite, who pride themselves on having a "French solution" for all problems, do not like to notice that the crime rate has diminished in the United States – doubtless correlated to the diminution of unemployment – whereas it is reaching disastrous levels here. I would confidently guess that the three men who attacked me have reached the age of 25, are on the RMI and have no desire to be "inserted" into the work force so long as they can supplement their handouts with an occasional heist in the 16th *arrondissement.* Of course, I was to blame for having a luxury car in the first place and I'll try to behave better in the future.

One thing is sure about France – the coming millennium will be no Millennium.

Vol. XXI, N° 2, March 1999

Tainted Blood, Tainted Justice

On February 8th, there began in an unusual locale – the former Hotel Majestic on avenue Kléber – one of the strangest trials in French history, that of three former ministers accused of involuntary homicide in connection with the transfusion in 1985 of contaminated blood to various victims who contracted AIDS or hepatitis C. The court, pretentiously called *Cour de Justice de la République,* was a special one set up pursuant to a 1993 constitutional amendment, and is composed of three professional judges from France's highest court and twelve parliamentarians, all elected by their respective peers.

On several occasions in these Newsletters, starting in 1991, I have recounted the sorry saga of one of the worst state crimes – war and genocide excepted – of the 20th century, which involved the knowing sale, mainly to hemophiliacs, of blood tainted with the AIDS and/or hepatitis-C virus by the government agency which enjoyed the monopoly of collecting and selling blood in France. When young hemophiliacs began dying, the government, as all governments do, tried to stonewall the tragedy, but ultimately the stink became so great that a judicial investigation was undertaken and resulted in charging the head of the government agency, Dr. Michel Garretta, with the misdemeanor of selling mislabeled merchandise. He and three others were convicted in 1992-3 and Garretta actually served some time in prison. While admitting that he was aware that his entire stock of blood was dangerously contaminated, he nevertheless had allowed the blood to be sold for transfusing unwitting patients, just to get rid of the inventory. However, Garretta and the others protested that they had been a scapegoat for decisions taken at a higher level of government. In the meantime, the victims' lawyers pressed for prosecution of all culprits under a more serious charge, the felony of poisoning. The highest civil court, the *Cour de Cassation,* ultimately held that this charge could be maintained and a *Juge d'Instruction* was named to investigate 32 potential culprits. To complicate matters, attempts to prosecute the then Ministers of Health and Social Affairs and the then Prime Minister ran into the obstacle that under the constitution only a special court, called the *Haute Cour,* could try them for offenses committed in their official capacity. This court had never been convened during the Fifth Republic and its procedure was considered so unwieldy that the government sponsored a constitutional amendment which led to the new court above mentioned. A special panel of three judges from the *Cour de Cassation* was appointed to investigate and draw up charges against the three ex-officials: former Prime Minister, Laurent Fabius, Georgina Dufoix and Edmond Hervé, the latter two having been ministers of Social Affairs and Health, respectively.

It was Georgina Dufoix who became notorious when the scandal came to light by replying to journalists' queries as to whether she felt responsible for what happened: "Responsible but not guilty." The indictment, which I have read, turned out to be devastating, accusing all three politicians of having failed to enforce rules dating from 1983 which called for selection of blood donors, in particular, by avoiding inmates of French prison – a favored source – it being known that 16 percent of them carried the AIDS virus. Moreover, the bill of particulars cited evidence that the politicians had been responsive to lobbying efforts of Diagnostics Pasteur, a private enterprise jointly owned by Institut Pasteur and Sanofi, a subsidiary of ELF, the notoriously-corrupt oil company controlled by the government, to block approval of an American blood-testing product developed by Abbott Laboratories, until Pasteur's own product could become commercially available. While the judicial panel rejected the charge of poisoning, for lack of intent to kill, it did find that the ministers had been negligent in performing their duties at a crucial time in 1985 when all health authorities were aware that blood transfusions transmitted the AIDS virus. To back up its charge of involuntary homicide and negligent injuries the panel cited seven cases of persons who were infected during this period from contaminated blood knowingly administered to them from the government agency's inventory. One of the victims was a new-born infant who had been given a transfusion and who died of AIDS at the age of six.

Several weeks before the trial was to begin, a well-orchestrated campaign of pro-accused articles began to appear throughout the French press, clearly the work of PR and crisis-management specialists providing "background" information to cooperative French journalists and to a number of big names among the French establishment. One would have thought that the forthcoming trial was the biggest frame-up since the Dreyfus case. The theme was "How dare anyone accuse serious government officials of penal offenses when they were merely doing their best to deal with a novel situation created by the sudden discovery that the AIDS virus was conveyed in blood." To make matters worse, articles began appearing about how unwieldy the new court's proceeding would be. Many of the witnesses to be called were themselves facing criminal charges and it was not thought fair to require them to take an oath, in view of the peculiar French rule that parties in penal (and even civil) proceedings can not testify under oath, it being openly admitted that they are free to lie in their own interest. (Wouldn't Bill Clinton be at home in France?) Finally, adding to the surreal nature of this trial, its venue was not the imposing Palais de Justice on the Ile de la Cité, but rather a right-bank former hotel which housed the Gestapo during the German occupation, and which has since become a conference center. When the trial actually opened, the worst fears were realized, since the presiding judge, Christian Le Guhenec, who had risen to the top of the French judicial hierarchy mainly by serving as a functionary in the Ministry of Justice, gave the appearance of not having mastered the facts and technical details in the file. He was roundly (and atypically) criticized in the press for being incompetent.

French criminal trials apply the inquisitorial system, which means essentially that the presiding judge interrogates all the witnesses, as well as the accused, and to do this well must have an intimate knowledge of the copious file before him, which contains the entire history of the case from the initial police investigation through the judicial investigation. From the first day, the press began reporting that the judge had not done his homework and was unfamiliar with the facts, including the technical terms and the names of key persons. Despite this lack of preparation, the judge had placed an added burden on himself by ruling that the parliamentary judges could not ask questions directly, but must submit their questions to him in writing. Another flaw in the proceeding was that the victims were not represented, as the constitutional procedure did not allow them to become civil parties, an exception to the usual French rule in criminal cases. Aggravating this flaw, the *Procureur Général* (a term we might translate as "Attorney General") had recommended dropping the charges against the accused. Indeed, at the end of the trial, he and the *Avocat Général* (which we might translate as "Solicitor General") each spoke in favor of acquitting all the defendants!

What kind of prosecution is this, you might ask, if the prosecutors are against bringing the charges and then plead for acquittal? A good question, I would say, but one which can only be elucidated by harking back to the inquisitorial system prevalent in France. The *Procureur* can prosecute misdemeanors alone but, in most cases, and necessarily in felony cases, the charges must be investigated by a *Juge d'Instruction,* who in effect brings the indictment, if there is one. Once the trial is held, the Prosecutor is free to oppose the charges verbally, even though he can be ordered by the Ministry of Justice to support the charges in writing. The elegant phrase which describes this duality is *"La plume est serve mais la parole est libre."* ("The pen is subservient but the word is free.")

As I once pointed out, a major overhaul of penal procedure had been enacted early in 1993 by the Socialist-dominated parliament, which would have brought it closer to the adversarial system, the judge remaining neutral, and the accusation being presented by the Prosecutor, with defense counsel having the right of cross-examination and the right to examine their own witnesses in defense. This law was supposed to go into effect on January 1, 1994, but in the meantime the May legislative election produced a Right majority led by Chirac's RPR, which simply repealed the new law! Now, no one even mentions this aborted reform, not even the Socialists, as though it were a bad dream which had been infused into the French mind by telepathy from the United States. When people say that the French Right is the most stupid in the world,

I heartily agree, and to the extent that Mr Chirac can be considered to be on the Right, he certainly is no exception to the rule.

No one can understand French politics if he analogizes the Right to economically conservative parties such as the Tories in the UK or the Republicans in the USA. The model of the French Right is not Edmond Burke but rather Louis XIV. They are Statists and so are not inclined to favor any measure which gives the individual an even break against the State. The French Left has a more ambiguous heritage: its components are also Statists but many of them have a tradition of defending civil liberties, at least of those who vote for them.

To return to the trial, all three defendants vigorously contested the charges, disclaiming any personal responsibility for what happened, generally on the ground that they had delegated authority to underlings, who did not inform them of crucial facts. Hervé was himself an underling of Dufoix since his Health Ministry was part of her larger Ministry of Social Affairs. Not surprisingly, Hervé was also an active mayor of Rennes, in Brittany, while he was purporting to serve as Minister of Health. As for Fabius, he contended that when he was informed of the situation by his subordinates, he acted promptly to order testing of all donors. Many talented barristers were at their side. No one was surprised when this politician-dominated court came in on March 9th with a verdict of acquittal for Laurent Fabius. Georgina Dufoix was also acquitted but a mild surprise occurred when Edmond Hervé was found guilty in connection with the contamination of two of the complainants.

This surprise became more intense when the court announced that Hervé was "dispensed of punishment" invoking but not quoting a rarely-used provision of the Penal Code (Article 132-59) which allows the court to waive any punishment when "it appears that the re-employment of the guilty person is assured, that the injury caused is repaired, and that the disturbance resulting from the infraction has ceased." Instead of citing these grounds, the court justified its decision on the basis that the charges were old and moreover that: "Mr. Hervé did not totally benefit from the presumption of innocence in being subject before the judgment to excessive opinions." Lawyers and judges, and the press in general, have heaped scorn on the court for this part of its decision. Some pointed out that Maurice Papon, at the age of 87, was tried 55 years after the fact, but this did not lead to his being dispensed of punishment. Others argued that the presumption of innocence means only that the prosecution must sustain the burden of proof. And how can professional judges, sitting without a jury (the parliamentarians were judges here, not jurors), take into account prejudicial press coverage at the same time that they find the accused guilty? *"Ce n'est pas logique,"* as Descartes would say.

In reality the conviction of Edmond Hervé seems clearly to have been a political decision to propitiate public opinion, which had been skeptical from the start as to the likelihood that three Socialist politicians would be found guilty. As Hervé was the lowest on the totem pole, and his demeanor during the trial was rigid, he was the obvious scapegoat. By the same token, the court did not want to punish him. This half-baked compromise pleased no one, not even Hervé, who fiercely criticized the court's decision and announced that he would seek review before the supreme court, the *Cour de Cassation,* but he later changed his mind. Whatever happens, he will remain famous in the annals of French justice as a convicted criminal whom the court has found undeserving of punishment. Along with Georgina's "responsible but not guilty" we now have Edmond's "guilty but not punishable."

As the messy Clinton-impeachment farce demonstrates, politics and justice do not mix well. It is relatively easy to convict government officials of crimes which breach their trust, such as bribery or embezzlement, but to hold that an official act or omission which results in loss of life, without a specific intent to harm particular persons, can be a criminal offense is thought by some to render public service very perilous indeed. Yet, we learn in American law that "one intends the natural and inevitable consequences of one's actions." In Hervé's case, the court found that he should have ordered the destruction of the inventory of contaminated blood and also recall the transfused for testing. If he failed to do this, knowing that the blood would inevitably transmit deadly viruses to innocent victims, why should he be immune from criminal penalties?

For Laurent Fabius, who is President of the National Assembly, getting acquitted was supposed to represent an opportunity to stay in the contention for the supreme position which every ambitious politician in France covets: President of the Republic. Yet Lionel Jospin, the current Prime Minister, is clearly the front-

runner among potential Socialist candidates for the presidential elections slated for 2002. But as a lot can happen in three years, Fabius is surely hoping that Jospin will stumble, even if it takes a little pushing on his part. On hearing the verdict Fabius proclaimed that "truth had finally prevailed." But the aftermath of the trial has soured his victory. After all, if the verdict represents truth, then it means that one of his ministers was guilty of criminal negligence under his watch. In other times and other places a Prime Minister would have resigned for less than that. But, as Clinton and Mitterrand, among others, have shown, successful politicians seem to be born without shame.

Fabius was Mitterrand's "fair-haired boy" (a figure of speech, as he is bald), during the '80s when he was named Prime Minister at age 37. To be sure, he is an *ENArque*, and he is also a graduate of the prestigious Ecole Normale Supérieure, which produces academics in literature and science. As Prime Minister, he was undistinguished and spent most of his energy trying to stay clear of the scandals which inevitably cropped up during the reign of his unscrupulous mentor. The most international of these was the sinking of the Greenpeace ship, "Rainbow Warrior," in New Zealand by French undercover agents. Fabius managed to pin blame for this on his Defense Minister, Charles Hernu, who obligingly resigned. Soon, *Le Figaro*'s famous cartoonist, Jacques Faizant, began portraying Fabius always carrying an open black umbrella. The only memorable remark Fabius made during his tenure as Prime Minister was, in replying to a journalist's question as to the difference between Mitterrand and him: "He is he and I am I" (it sounds slightly better in French: "*Lui c'est lui et moi c'est moi.*"). Now he can say: "He is dead and I am innocent." But who will believe him?

It appears virtually certain that the so-called "Court of Justice of the Republic" will not survive this disastrous beginning. The name itself is silly: aren't all courts supposed to be courts of justice? And why should parliamentarians be judges of criminal offenses? This was not a matter of removing ministers from office but rather of judging actions of persons no longer in place. The incongruity of this special court just for ministers will become more apparent when the 31 underlings who worked for them, including Louis Schweitzer, Fabius' chief of staff, stand trial for their role in the blood scandal. It is not yet known whether the forum will be the *Tribunal Correctionnel,* which tries misdemeanors, or the *Cour d'Assises,* which has jurisdiction over felonies, or both. At any rate, this is likely to turn into farce, with each defendant disclaiming responsibility and pointing the finger at either an underling or a superior. But at least the victims will be represented in the proceedings as civil parties.

As Justice Holmes was fond of quoting, "Hard cases make bad law." Among the many questionable aspects of this case is the fact that Dr Garretta will have to stand trial again, since the new charges against him, based on the same facts, will be for poisoning or administering dangerous substances. This sounds like "double jeopardy" to me but the Bill of Rights is not part of the French system. Nor is the notion of "prompt and speedy trial." After all, the facts have been known since 1993, at the latest, but the *Juge d'Instruction* still has not made her report. Why should suspects have to wait six years to find out whether they will have to stand trial? Maybe Ken Starr can answer.

While the French press has been unusually frank in criticizing the trial and the court itself, virtually no one gets to the heart of the institutional and cultural vices that brought about this disgraceful process by which thousands of people were infected, 600 of whom have already died. Chief among them, in my view, is the Statism prevalent in France which led to the government having a monopoly over the collection and distribution of blood. When the State both runs and regulates a business, it has a conflict of interest – invariably the business interest prevails. This is a fundamental ethical flaw which permeates Statism everywhere whether it be the Socialist variety or the Fascist one. Another flaw is the chauvinism which leads the elite in France to prefer a French malady to a foreign cure, just as it prefers a French falsehood to a foreign truth. We hear every day that whatever the problem there must be a "*solution Française*." Better the patient die of a French virus than be cured by an alien drug.

Put these two factors together and you have a tainted system of governance which leads to tainted blood and many other abuses, including tainted justice. When 35 officials are considered responsible for a major scandal, you can be sure that it is the system which is bad, not just individuals.

Sequel to Paranoid Alley

If I were asked to name my sentimental favorite among the Newsletters I have written over the past 20 years, I would doubtless choose "Paranoid Alley: from Paul Valéry to Pizza Hut," which dates from July 1995. What inspired that essay was the discovery, two months earlier, on my daily walk to the office, that Le Valéry, a restaurant I was fond of on rue Paul Valéry, had closed, only to be replaced by a Pizza Hut outlet. I lamented the fact that the closure had been so sudden that I did not have the opportunity to bid adieu to the "mom and pop" who ran this delightful restaurant which, as my friend Dick Malyan pointed out, had an air of the French provinces about it. I mentioned also that having discovered Le Valéry only the prior year I had not taken my wife there because the restaurant was not open in the evening. Since that time, during my morning walk each time I passed the Pizza Hut store, a take-out and delivery place, I felt a pang for the good-old-days of Le Valéry.

Last month, when I was in the States, my wife told me on the phone that thanks to our oldest son, Reynold, she had discovered a wonderful little restaurant, called Villa Pergolèse, on rue Pergolèse, very close to our house on rue Weber. It was reasonably priced, she said, and featured old-fashioned cooking, hard to find these days in Paris. She insisted that I try it out when I returned to Paris. On Friday evening, March 5th, my wife reserved a table there for several members of the family. As I arrived the last, the others were already seated and having their aperitifs, and I was pleased to note a plate of pistachio nuts as accompaniment for the drinks. The lone waitress brought me a single-malt Scotch and I settled down with the pistachios while looking at the menu, which offered a wide choice of à la carte platters, plus a prix fixe dinner of three courses for F 145 (about $25). When the waitress came back to take the orders, I found myself blurting out (in French, of course): "You know, your restaurant reminds me of a place I used to go to, called Le Valéry, on rue Paul Valéry." The woman stared at me, eyes wide open, and replied: "Le Valéry? That was our restaurant!" Indeed when I got over my initial shock, I recognized her as the "mom" of Le Valéry. I simply had not noticed the resemblance when I first saw her, as I could not have imagined that the former owners of Le Valéry were now in business only 200 yards from my home. She said that she thought she had recognized me but had not wanted to risk an error.

When we got over this joyous rediscovery, I told her about the Newsletter I had written on the transformation of their restaurant to a Pizza Hut and how saddened I had been. She explained that Pizza Hut had been soliciting them for months to buy out their leasehold, because of its corner location which facilitated access for the red delivery motorbikes. Her husband kept refusing but finally he told her, "Well, if they want the place they'll have to pay my price." So he proposed a price which he thought steep but which Pizza Hut accepted immediately, on condition that they vacate the premises quickly. Thus, the couple had no opportunity to inform their patrons of their departure. They then spent nine months looking for another location in which to establish a restaurant, and finally found one on rue Pergolèse where the prior owner had gone bankrupt. As this unattractive stretch of the street is located between avenue Malakoff and avenue de la Grande Armée, whereas rue Weber, where I live, is on the other side of avenue Malakoff, I rarely stroll there and had never noticed the restaurant, which does not have a flashy exterior. I confessed to the lady that I did not even know her name. She wrote down on a card her husband's name, Claude Brouard, and on my insistence, revealed that her first name was Lucette. I told her that I had never actually seen her husband as he had always remained in the kitchen when I used to frequent Le Valéry. "True," she replied, "my husband is timid and never meets the customers." I retorted that tonight would be an exception because I would not leave their place until I met Monsieur Brouard. And so, as we were leaving, after a delightful meal, the bearded chef-owner came out of the kitchen and with his wife greeted us with a warm smile.

Naturally, I am happy to share this good news with my readers, many of whom have lamented with me the disappearance of good traditional restaurants in Paris. Villa Pergolèse is located at 17, rue Pergolèse, 75116 Paris, and the phone is 01 44 17 99 88. It is open in the evening only on Thursday and Friday. The prix fixe at F 145 is one of the best bargains in Paris! Hurry: while McDonald's is not likely to locate on rue Pergolèse, one never knows!

Vol. XXI, N° 3, April 1999

In Memoriam: Howard Goldfarb (1929-1999)

As a member of the entering class of Harvard Law School in September 1950, I discovered that we enjoyed two distinctions: ours was the first class to admit women – a dozen or so out of 500 – and also the first to use the spanking new Harkness Commons and dormitories designed by the celebrated Bauhaus architect, Walter Gropius, who, let us not forget, himself had the distinction of being the second husband of Alma Schindler, better known as Alma Mahler, widow of the great Gustav. Alma ditched Gropius for Franz Werfel,the Austrian-Jewish author, later to become famous for the novels *The Forty Days of Musa Dagh* and *The Song of Bernadette.*

Attending an open house for our class in the ground-floor lounge of the Harkness Commons, I noted a Steinway baby-grand piano there for the playing. As I had never touched a Steinway, I overcame my natural timidity and sat down to play the first Bach piece I had learned, the *Allemande* of the *sixth French Suite* in E major. When I finished I noticed a young bespectacled man standing besides the piano, to my left, who said, matter-of-factly, "That's nice. What was it?" I identified the Bach composition and he identified himself as Howard Goldfarb of Washington, Pennsylvania, and a graduate of Washington & Jefferson College, located in the same town. In turn, I told him my name and alma mater, the University of Pennsylvania, and confessed that although I was from Philadelphia, I had never been farther west than Chester and hadn't the faintest idea where Washington was in the state of Pennsylvania. He replied that it was about 30 miles south of Pittsburgh. Thus began a friendship which lasted until March 24, 1999, when Howard Goldfarb succumbed to leukemia, a month after having attained the age of 70.

As it turned out that Howard and I were assigned to Section One (out of the four into which the first-year class was divided), we organized in the ensuing days a study group which came to include Raymond Falls, of Youngstown, Ohio; Bud Gibbs, of New York City; and Gustave Hauser, of Shaker Heights, Ohio. All five of us became buddies and remained so after graduation. Ray Falls, who was elected President of the Harvard Law Review, went on to become a litigating partner at Cahill Gordon in New York but was the first of our group to die, seven years ago. Bud Gibbs still practices law in New York City in his own firm. Gus Hauser had the good sense to give up law for business and became a pioneer in cable television, founding Warner Cable and then his own company, Hauser Communications. His foundation, headed by his dynamic wife, Rita Hauser, who had an outstanding law career as a partner at Stroock & Stroock & Lavan, has made major contributions to Harvard Law School and NYU Law School, among others. Howie Goldfarb, after stints in Europe, which I will describe below, ended up back in Washington, Pa., practicing in the firm his father had founded. He chose the life of a small-town lawyer.

While I am on the subject of Harvard Law, let me pass on an insight that I acquired from the great Warren Abner Seavey, one of the top professors in our day, a master of Torts and Agency. I was fortunate to be assigned to the Seavey Club for the Ames moot-court competition, which brought me into social contact with this wise mentor, and I acquired almost as many *aperçus* from his off-hand remarks as from his classroom teaching. One such remark was that the greatness of the law school came not from the faculty but from the student body. Surprising as it first appeared, this insight was confirmed by my experience: indeed, many of the professors were mediocre, some so dull that students abjured their courses, even if the subject was important. Thus I never took Evidence because a superannuated bore named Maguire was the only one to teach it, and I never took Antitrust because another bore named Bowie was its lone expounder in our day. Later, I needed both Evidence and Antitrust in my practice and easily acquired the fundamentals from reading a few basic texts. Even professors of great reputation in the outside world, such as Zechariah Chaffee (Equity), Manley Hudson (International Law) and Sheldon Glueck (Criminal Law), were panned by those who took their courses. In our day, only a handful of professors merited the top grades as teachers: Seavey, Austin Scott, Lon Fuller, Ben Kaplan, Paul Freund, Henry Hart and Barton Leach are those I would name, even though I did not have all of them. The ability of the school to attract some of the brightest students in the land, from diverse backgrounds and geographical origins, and the ensuing interaction and competition of these students are what made the three-year experience so enriching. Our first-year study group and my later experience on Law Review exposed me to fine minds and taught me that rubbing heads together is the best way to learn law.

It is difficult for me to accept that almost a half-century has elapsed since I entered Harvard Law School and met Howie Goldfarb. In my mind's eye he is still the young man who listened to me playing the piano and, to be sure, I am still that youthful piano-player. For my readers, most of whom were probably not even alive in 1950, these reminiscences must seem those of the distant past. The world has changed a great deal in five decades: in the early '50s, air travel, for example, was a luxury, television was still a novelty, there were no computers, no E-mail, no fax machines, no photocopiers, not even telexes. Long-distance phoning was costly and most people used the mail to communicate, while those in a hurry sent telegrams and cables. Even feminism was in its infancy; none of us thought it unusual, at the time, that Harvard Law School waited until 1950 to admit a dozen women.

But the most difficult part for me is to try to put in words why Howard Goldfarb meant so much to me. How to describe his reality? Physically, he was over medium height, with a trim built. His bright eyes and close-cropped hair were brown, and his complexion light. He was always neatly dressed without appearing dapper. His voice was strong yet suave and musically nuanced. He spoke rapidly, in a confident manner but was never overbearing. What was it about him that made us instant friends and kept us united in friendship over the years despite the distance that separated us? I have had to pause in the writing of this eulogy to think about this question. J.P. Morgan replied to a *nouveau riche* who asked him what it takes to afford a yacht, "If you have to think about it, you can't afford it." So, as to friendship, if you have to think about whether someone should be your friend, the answer is that he shouldn't. In 1950, I never thought about it: friendship with Howie came naturally. It flowed from his first step in walking over to the Steinway to inquire about the Bach piece. Now, I have to think about it only because I want to explain to persons who never knew him why he was so special.

In reflecting on that question, I realize that friendship itself is a form of ego-gratification. By hypothesis, a friend is someone who likes you, as you like him and, presumably, like yourself, the latter being a thought one does not often articulate, at least not I. In Howie, I felt instant comfort: he was never threatening or harsh, he laughed at my jokes, he respected my silences as I respected his. Perhaps that is one definition of a friend: someone you can be silent with, without offending him. Another quality Howie possessed was the ability, at any time, to move from anecdote to generalization, from the concrete to the abstract: in short, his mind was philosophic. He gobbled up the present but was always mindful of the broader lessons that the present contained. And he saw the humor in these lessons, or at least the irony. He was tolerant, much more than I at the same age. Rarely was he vehement. I suppose that is why I felt comfort in his presence. When I would get excited about something he would express sympathy but his own calm would help me settle down.

It is said that to learn about a person's character one should either play cards with him or travel together. With Howie, I never played cards but we did a lot of travelling, with never a quarrel or an unpleasant moment. For, as fate would have it, the first person I met at Harvard turned out to be the one I saw most often after graduation in June 1953. We both obtained Fulbright Scholarships to study in France, Howie in Grenoble under Prof. Tunc, and I in Strasbourg, ostensibly to study the new Court of Justice set up under the Schuman Plan. As I had never been to Europe, I was eager to take advantage of my free trans-Atlantic travel, and arranged to leave during the summer so as to tour Europe before the academic year commenced. Howie made the same decision and we resolved to meet on the continent to travel together. I embarked in mid-July on the SS Georgic, a Cunard liner, planning to disembark at Southampton, but when I discovered that the ship would first land in Cobh, Ireland, I decided to get off to tour the Emerald Isle. From Dublin, I took a ferry to Glasgow, visited Edinburgh and the Western Highlands, then took a train to London, which was still rejoicing in the coronation of Queen Elizabeth II. In mid-August, I took a ferry from Dover to Rotterdam, and then set off by train to Brussels, where I met another classmate, Randy Warner, a tall, soft-spoken Arkansan from Fort Smith, whom I had gotten to know on the Law Review. Randy had won a Sheldon Fellowship, a more lucrative scholarship than our Fulbrights, with a cash grant that permitted him to buy a new Volkswagen Beetle. As we had planned to meet Goldfarb in Frankfurt, Randy and I set off in that direction, stopping first in Liège, Belgium, to see a young student I had met on the Georgic. In Cologne, we discovered that the devastation wrought by WWII was still visible, while in Kassel we were utterly shocked by its vast scope: block after block of what were once homes were represented by rubble. On the way to Frankfurt, we stopped in Usingen to take a picture of the house where our classmate Gerry Gunther once lived. Arriving in Frankfurt, we soon found Howie and that evening attended a performance of Stravinsky's ballet, "The Fire-Bird," in the new opera house.

None of us had ever been to Europe before; everything was to be discovered. We quickly agreed on an itinerary that would take us north to Denmark, Norway and Sweden. Ours was lackadaisical touring: we made no advance reservations, merely showing up in a town and looking for a cheap hotel, preferably with three beds. We often bargained with the hotel-keeper, a chore that most often fell to me, because of my Armenian roots. The three of us knew no German, but I quickly learned *"Haben zie ein zimmer für drei personen?"* We visited the university town of Göttingen, where Gauss and Rieman once reigned, and moved on to Hamburg where, thanks to Randy's nautical skills, we sailed on the lovely lake. In Denmark, we drove up the peninsula to Aarhus, saving Copenhagen for our return from Sweden. In a little restaurant where the waitress spoke no English we found a customer who purported to know the language but he was nonplussed by Randy's southern accent and we ended up eating whatever we saw. From Jutland, we took a ferry to Oslo and spent a few days in that capital of Norway. In a restaurant I was amazed to run into a couple I knew in Philadelphia: Norma (now a federal Judge) and Bernie Shapiro. The highlight of our trip was the road to Bergen via Odda; the mountain scenery was gorgeous, everywhere waterfalls graced the hillsides. Near Odda, we stopped to watch reindeer being shot, not a pleasant sight but a memorable one.

Nearing Bergen, we finally discovered the magnificent fjords which are the pride of Norway. On the deck of a ferry boat, Howie and I struck up an innocent conversation with two cheerful English girls in their early 20s. Suddenly I saw a steely-eyed woman heading straight for me, and when she was at talking distance she said, "Young man, I don't want you to speak with my daughter." Flabbergasted, I blurted out, "But why not? I was doing no harm." She replied, sternly, "Because you're Jewish and I don't want my daughter frequenting Jews." I replied, "Lady, it so happens that I'm not Jewish but besides, we were only chatting." She insisted, "Oh yes, you are Jewish, but your friend over there [pointing to Goldfarb] is not." I glanced at Goldie (as I sometimes called him); he was laughing uproariously, enjoying the idea that he, the grandson of a rabbi, was taken for a *goy* while his Christian friend was being singled out as a Jewish pariah. It was an instructive experience for me to feel the sting of anti-Semitism without being a Jew. Of course, it illustrates the utter stupidity of anti-Semites, who hate an abstraction but in real life can not tell the difference between a Jew and a Gentile, let alone have the discernment to judge people on their own merits as individuals.

After touring Sweden and returning to Denmark via Copenhagen, Howie and I parted company with Randy in Amsterdam, as September was ending, and we took a train to Paris, arriving in the evening at the Gare du Nord and staying at a dingy hotel nearby. The next morning we hastened to change money on the black-market based on a tip an American had given us in Frankfurt: "Go to the Café Sportif on the rue des Rosiers and ask for Max." Knowing nothing about Paris, we were unaware that this street was in the heart of the Jewish quarter, and we were bemused to find that Café Sportif was a Kosher restaurant! When we asked for Max, the owner eyed us suspiciously but in a jiffy Max appeared, ushered us into a hallway and whisked francs from an inner pocket as fast as any prestidigitator could have done it.

On October first, our official indoctrination session began at the Sorbonne. Howie and I found rooms at the Cité Universitaire and we would take the Métro every morning to the Gare de Luxembourg, close to the building where we had conversation sessions with a sympathetic instructor named Michel Gauthier, who was writing a thesis on Paul Valéry. Howie was more adept at speaking French than I was, but I could understand it better. This led us to a funny routine when we would ask for directions of a passing stranger. Howie would spout out, for example, *"Monsieur, pourriez-vous nous indiquer le chemin pour aller à la Sainte Chapelle?"* and the Frenchman, hearing his language spoken so well and so quickly, would respond with elaborate instructions at a fast pace, whereupon Howie would turn to me and ask, "What did he say, Jack?" We both got a big kick out of this mutual dependency.

Later that month, after Howie began dating one of our fellow Fulbright students, he related to me an amusing incident. One evening they had entered a restaurant on the Ile de la Cité to have dinner, but after being seated by an imposing Maître d'hôtel, Howie studied the menu and saw that the prices were astronomical, considering the meager Fulbright stipend of $100 a month. After much soul-searching about what to do in this embarrassing situation, Howie, as he told it to me, found courage by asking himself, "Now, what would Jack Kevorkian do in this situation? Surely he would walk out, saying that he had made a mistake." And that's what he did. Naturally, I was amused and flattered at being taken for a role model by a friend whom I considered more sophisticated than I, but I did not dare tell him that I would not have had the nerve to walk out of a fancy restaurant where I had taken a date.

Soon, October in Paris came to an end and Howie and I separated to go to our respective universities, he to Grenoble and I to Strasbourg. But we had hardly settled there before the Christmas recess arrived and, in mid-December, we met again with Randy Warner and his Beetle in southern France and headed for Spain. This was a joyful time, and instructive, for Spain in 1953 was still showing the scars of the Civil War; Franco was in command and the ominous Guardia Civil were ubiquitous in their green uniforms, with rifles slung over their shoulders. Two memories stand out. On the road leading to Burgos, we stopped on a hillside to have a picnic; below in the sun-bathed valley a happy farmer was plowing on foot behind an ox and singing in a beautiful baritone voice a haunting Spanish song, oblivious of our presence, while sheep in a nearby field accompanied him with their soft bells. I told Howie, "This is truly a pastoral symphony," and I wanted the moment to last forever. Being young, I assumed that I would enjoy other such occasions, but I have never again heard a farmer singing in a field. In Seville, Howie disappeared for a few minutes and returned with an old man he had managed to find, who took us discreetly to an unmarked synagogue in a narrow street. I thought it uncanny that Howie had been able to unearth one of Spain's rare Jews. It was a moving moment for Howie: his face was pensive and his silence eloquent as we visited this small synagogue.

Back in our respective provincial universities, Howie and I turned our thoughts to military service. We had been too young to serve in World War II but, in July 1950, the Korean War jolted our generation which had assumed that war was a thing of the past. We were almost drafted in our first year but Congress voted a student-deferment program allowing us to get our degrees, and our Fulbrights entitled us to a further deferment. Howie and I learned that there was a Judge Advocate General's office in Heidelberg where the US Army had its European headquarters. So we got our papers together and went there to be interviewed for a commission as First Lieutenant, which would require us to serve three years rather than the two years faced by draftees. In due course, we each learned that we had been accepted.

But there was still touring to do. On Easter day, 1954, Howie and I were together in St. Peter's Square and saw the Pope bless the cheering crowd. The next day in Rome, when Howie was on his own for a few hours, he was taken in by a con man masquerading as an airline pilot who had contraband Swiss watches (then a luxury) on his hands, and abetted by a confederate posing as a bystander and would-be buyer. The upshot was that Howie, not an easy man to fool, ended up with a worthless imitation of an Omega watch, but instead of worrying about his loss of money, he took pleasure in dissecting the elaborate scheme. In Rome, of course, we took in art and antiquities; Howie was a discerning seer and he could put in words why he liked something he saw. After Rome, we traveled by train to Naples and Pompeii, then north to glorious Florence, ending up in Venice where, after some memorable days, we took leave of each other.

In January 1955, Howie and I met again, this time in Fort Benning, Georgia, to learn how to be Infantry Officers. At the time, the JAG Corps was headed by a major-general who had once been an infantry officer and he felt that all Army lawyers should have a dose of basic training. It was quite an experience for Howie and me, relatively effete and spoiled civilians, to don an officer's uniform and live in an ordinary barracks like enlisted men, making our own beds and passing inspections. We learned how to assemble and fire a rifle, do map reading, and the rudiments of infantry tactics. I still have the pictures that Howie and I took of each other for posterity one Saturday afternoon, carrying our rifles and trying to look like ferocious warriors.

When our two months in Fort Benning ended, a more enjoyable experience awaited us: the JAG School at the University of Virginia in Charlottesville, where we were supposed to learn military law and regulations. After three years at Harvard Law it was hard to take this instruction seriously, but we had to make an effort to appear studious, because we knew that our future assignment would depend on it. Howie and I were together virtually every evening, strolling from our dormitory into town and inhaling the luscious odor of the magnolia trees which blossomed in the glorious Spring of Charlottesville. We had the good fortune to find our classmate Wayne Barnett in Charlottesville, as he had entered the JAG a year before us and was assigned there to write a legal bulletin. We spent many an evening playing pool with Wayne in Charlottesville and drinking beer. As this idyllic time came to an end, Howie and I began to worry about our future assignments. The idea of going to Korea itself was dreaded by our entire class. Each officer was asked to fill out a preference form with an indication of why he wanted a specific assignment. I recall that Howie and I actually hesitated to put France as our first choice, because of the Army's notorious tendency, particularly in World War II, to give perverse assignments: if you knew Chinese they might send you to Germany to be a radio operator but then draft a civilian radio operator and ship him to language school to learn Chinese. However, we decided to take a chance that the Army had become more rational; thus, we put down France as our first choice, noting that we knew French and had been Fulbright Scholars in French universities. Our only other worry was that we might have antagonized one or more of our instructors by appearing too lackadaisical in class. Fortunately, some members of our class were more unpopular than we with the instructors, and Howie and I learned that we were among three officers assigned to France, the third being Marion Harrison, now a distinguished Washington lawyer and still a friend.

After a home leave, we reported in June 1955, to Fort Dix, New Jersey, to prepare for our departure, which meant, among other things, getting shots at the Army dispensary for our supposedly perilous overseas assignment. Then we were transported to Maguire Air Force base, also in New Jersey, and flown to Frankfurt, where we learned that Howie and Marion would serve in Orleans, while I would go to La Rochelle, on the Atlantic coast, a fishing port which in olden times was the focus of historic attention because of the blockade organized by Cardinal Richelieu to overcome the Protestant population of that city. After getting established in La Rochelle, I began to get worried that I had no news from my friend Goldfarb. Finally I learned that he had come down with a bad case of hepatitis and was in the Army Hospital located at La Chapelle-St. Mesmin, near Orléans. This was apparently due to the shots he had received at Fort Dix because, in those days, no one used disposable needles. After purchasing a Simca Aronde automobile, I visited Howie at the hospital on one of my trips to Paris and found him philosophical about the bad luck which had spoiled his arrival in Orléans and prevented him from enjoying the nearby Loire Valley chateaux and restaurants, not to mention Paris, only 120 kilometers to the North. Howie's hospitalization lasted almost a year, as I recall, but finally he turned to active duty at the JAG office and, like me, spent much of his time as a Trial Observer when American soldiers were tried by French courts under the NATO Status of Forces Agreement.

After our military service ended in December 1957, Howie returned to Washington, Pa., to practice law with his father, and I went to New York to resume work in a Wall-Street firm. During the summer of 1958, Howie came to New York with his bride, Sally Heymann, and we had a joyful reunion in our apartment, joined by the other members of our Harvard study group and their respective wives. Much to my surprise, Eve, my French wife, hit it off perfectly with Sally despite their sharply different backgrounds. The chemistry of this friendship, it turned out, was founded on the frankness that Sally and Eve had in common.

Unfortunately, Eve took less kindly to New York and in three-years time we were back in Paris, where I began work at Coudert Frères. Howie and Sally made annual pilgrimages to Paris, principally at Christmas time, and they spent a good part of their time and money eating first-class meals, often with me present. On one of these trips, they brought their daughter Nancy along and she stayed with our kids in Villeneuve-le-Roi, while the adults celebrated New Year's Eve.

In the mid '60s, I received a rare letter from Howie, in which he expressed restlessness about being stuck in Washington, Pa. and inquired as to the outlook for doing as I had done, transplanting to Paris. Although he did not use the term, I conjured up the phrase "lives of quiet desperation" as I read his letter. Yet, I knew how difficult it must have been for Howie to envisage leaving his father's firm and his home town to live abroad. In my reply, I gave encouragement for the idea but told him that finding an opening would be no easy task, as it had taken me a year to land a job, despite my Wall-Street credentials. I never heard from him again on this particular topic and I surmised that he had abandoned the idea. About a year after that, Howie wrote me that in looking at a map of Europe he had hit on the idea of taking a vacation in Corsica, with a view of buying property there as an investment. He reasoned that land must be cheap there and asked me what I thought of the idea. I replied that I had no specific knowledge of property values in Corsica, but was of a mind that if he, Goldfarb, could deduce in faraway Washington, Pa. that there were bargains to be had in Corsica, then Rothschild in nearby Paris was likely to have thought of it already. A few weeks later I got a Corsican post card from Howie, saying only, "You were right, Rothschild thought of it first!" When Sally and Howie came to Paris from Corsica, we had a big laugh about his thwarted investment plan.

Later the Goldfarbs began vacationing every summer on the Côte d'Azur at the Hotel Metropole in Beaulieu-sur-Mer, not far from Monaco. This became an annual ritual, and they were so fond of this Riviera escape that they would rarely stop in Paris. One summer, when we rented a house in Vallauris, Eve and I drove over to Beaulieu to have lunch with Howie and Sally. Their daily routine was to bask in lounge chairs beside the pool, read and enjoy the good food at lunch and dinner. This sedentary vacationing was not at all to the taste of Eve and me, but I surmised that during their cold, dark winters in Washington, Pa., the thought of their annual sun-feast in Beaulieu must have helped Howie and Sally survive.

In the early '70s, I finally was able to go to Pittsburgh on business and made it a point of visiting the Goldfarbs in Washington. Seeing for the first time their charming but simple wood-frame house on McKennan Avenue, with an open porch, gave me an inkling of the pleasures they could derive from small-town living. Sally organized a dinner party in my honor, attended by some professor-friends at Washington & Jefferson, the local college which provided an intellectual environment for those who sought it, as the Goldfarbs clearly did. Other occasions for me to see Howie and Sally were our law-school class reunions in Cambridge, Mass., which occur every five years. In September 1977, when I visited Pittsburgh on a round-the-world business trip which took me to New Caledonia, Howie and Sally came to have dinner with me in my hotel and, over a drink, Sally broke the news that she had been diagnosed with breast cancer; despite an operation, metastases had occurred. She was calm and smiling as she told me this, as though the most important consideration in her mind was to avoid upsetting me. I looked over at Howie; his facial expression was impassive. Sally fought bravely against this dreaded scourge. At one point, years later, when Eve and I saw Sally and Howie in Paris, she was in remission and we were encouraged to think that she had been cured. But finally Sally succumbed to lung cancer in September 1991, ending her 33-year marriage with Howie.

After Sally's death, Howie stopped coming to France, turning his sights instead to Los Angeles where Nancy was living with her lawyer-husband Jim Shalek and their children. Whenever I would speak with Howie, he showed pride in Nancy's professional doings and his grand-children's exploits. Since our first times together at Harvard I had been so accustomed to my friend's stoical, uncomplaining character that it was an unspoken pact between us that I would never inquire as to his state-of-mind and he would never speak of his loneliness or suffering. Professionally, Howie had become the outstanding local lawyer, excelling in real estate and banking matters, and respected by all for his fair-mindedness and integrity. After his father's death, he had taken on a partner and had more time for travel and community activities, such as serving as trustee of his alma mater. A few years ago, I learned from Jim Shalek that Howie had a new, happy relationship with a person Jim described only as "an Italian woman." I was pleased for Howie and wondered when we would have the occasion to meet this mystery-woman.

As Howie was not a prolific letter writer, I felt very flattered when he would take the time to send me a one-page note to compliment me on one of my Newsletters. About a year ago, I received a note with less pleasant content: he had contracted leukemia. The note was so upsetting to me that I filed it away and sublimated its contents. Later I received word from him that he was going to our 45th reunion at Harvard Law School in October 1998, and I replied that I would attend, too. At the opening Friday dinner, I finally met Phyllis, whose soft, sensitive face immediately warmed me to her. But the harsh truth about Howie's leukemia was written all over him and was confirmed by the side comments that I was able to glean from Phyllis. The next day, I made a point of staying close to Howie when the class picture was taken and after lunch we ambled over to Harvard Square and had ice cream in a shop on Brattle Street. There Howie gave me a grim account of his battle with a rare form of leukemia, the early wrong treatment in Pittsburgh and the better one in New York when in desperation they turned to another specialist. True to himself, there was nothing maudlin in Howie's words. The hours we spent together that Saturday afternoon, while Phyllis discreetly steered herself away from our conversation, were the most tender moments in our 48-year friendship. It became clear to me that coming to Cambridge for a last look at Jack and his other classmates had required tremendous physical effort and courage on Howie's part. After this afternoon talk, Howie said he needed to rest in order to summon up the strength to attend the evening dinner at the Boston Art Museum.

When I arrived there during the cocktail hour, I sought out Howie and Phyllis. An ensemble was playing classical music, barely audible in the din of conversation. I led Howie to the Steinway piano and managed to persuade the young woman at the keyboard to yield her bench to me for a few minutes. And then, despite the din, I played for Howie the *Allemande* of Bach's *sixth French Suite.* As I finished, I looked up at him standing beside the piano: he was smiling broadly, his eyes were staring off at distant space: his expression was ethereal. After the dinner, I joined Howie and Phyllis on the bus which took us back to our Harvard Square hotels. I sat beside Phyllis while Howie chatted with our classmates. She told me of the desperate battle they had been fighting to keep Howie alive, while praying for a miracle cure. In December the whole family took a vacation in the Caribbean. Secretly, Howie had arranged for a wedding ceremony to take place and thus Phyllis became his wife, with the Shalek family in joyful attendance. Alas, the New Year brought a fatal relapse.

In reading the above, I am not satisfied with what I have written. I fear that I have failed to make Howard Goldfarb come alive to people who did not know him. If I'm publishing it nevertheless, that is because there is a lesson to be learned: if we cherish a friend, or think we do, then while he is alive we should take the trouble to put down on paper the traits and attributes which constitute his reality. By doing this we would also learn something about ourselves. In one of my favorite books of William Saroyan, *Short Drive, Sweet Chariot,* there is a passage in which the writer, replying to a question from his cousin as to the aim of life, replies: "The full-time work of any mind should be to discover as complex a truth about itself as possible." Later, in another great book, *Obituaries,* Saroyan wrote "My real work is being" (later to become the title and theme of David Stephen Calonne's perceptive study of Saroyan). In reflecting on the secret of Howie Goldfarb's existence, I suspect that early on he had discovered a complex truth about himself and concluded that, rather than seeking fame and fortune, his real work was being. He cultivated his interior life, partook of immortality in Bach's music, basked in art, read and reflected, and provided love and comfort to his family and friends, while abstaining from inflicting pain on others. He worked at being. And so, Howard Goldfarb was and, for me, still is.

Vol. XXI, N° 4, May 1999

Serbs, Kosovars: The Agony of Little Nations

Several readers have asked me to write about the current "war" in and about Serbia, one reader even asserting that I must have special knowledge about the Balkans, which I do not. What I do know something about is how it feels to be born into an ethnic group having its roots in one of the little nations of the planet, Armenia in my case. The Armenians have in common with the Serbs the fact of having been conquered by the Turks in the Middle Ages and yet having remained Orthodox Christians. But whereas the Serbs finally got rid of their Turkish masters when the Ottoman Empire began to crumble, the Armenians remained a subjugated people within the boundaries of Turkey and it is the Turks, under cover of World War I when they were allied with Germany and Austria-Hungary, who got rid of the Armenians in 1915, by exterminating 1.5-million and driving the remaining Armenians from their homeland. The irony, if you will, is that today it is the Christian Serbs who are driving from their homes the Moslem Albanians, descendants of a ancient, non-Slav, people who accepted conversion to Islam under Turkish rule.

My heart goes out to the Kosovars, as it does to the Serbs, both victims of their own past and of their present leaders, as well as of the incompetent and cowardly leaders of the Western Powers now masquerading as the North Atlantic Treaty Organization. Just as the people of Iraq are victims of Saddam Hussein, so the Serbs are victims of Slobodan Milosevic and his communist cronies who are continuing the oppressive regime which ruled Yugoslavia for 45 years but at least kept all the ethnic groups in tow. Bombs always fall on the common people, not on their dictators. I once saw a television interview of Saddam Hussein in which, when asked whether he was worried for his safety, he replied sardonically, "Since the beginning of time, have you known of a single instance when a head of state was killed by overhead bombing?" Slobodan has his shelters, but the people in buses and trucks have none and when an American pilot drops bombs at 15,000 feet, he can't tell the difference between Serbs, supposedly the enemy, and Kosovars, whom the pilot is reportedly out to protect.

This war is ostensibly designed to strike at "ethnic cleansing," a form of racism, but the American president, a draft-dodger himself and a spineless self-indulgent opportunist, is so afraid of being unpopular that he does not want to lose a single American airman. Thus, our pilots drop bombs at an altitude where they can not see the target. In effect, Bill Clinton is telling the world that the life of one American pilot is worth more than the lives of a hundred or a thousand (what is the limit?) undifferentiated people on the ground who may be Kosovars as well as Serbs. If that isn't a form of racism, then what is?

How can the United States be a "superpower" if it is not willing to risk the lives of military personnel who are, after all, volunteers? And how can it have moral authority as an international policeman if innocent people are put at great risk because the policeman wants to take no risk? So if you care to know how I feel about this mess, the first answer is that I feel disgust that the United States of America, of which I am a citizen, has a nerd as its President. Here is a man who smokes marijuana without inhaling, who gets sex without penetration and now conducts war without soldiers on the ground. Clinton is said to be constantly concerned with the judgment that future historians will pronounce on his presidency. In my view, when the future Edward Gibbon writes his *Decline and Fall of the American Republic*, interesting comparisons will be made between the type of decadence represented by Nero and Caligula and the American type represented by the successive presidencies of Bush, the flabby patrician, and Clinton, the Arkansas hulk. In Rome, the Praetorian Guard made and unmade emperors; in the USA, pollsters, fund-raisers and hype professionals turn hollow men into presidents, under the indifferent gaze of a majority of Americans who do not even vote and who know virtually nothing of the history and the geography of the other nations of the planet, whose destinies the USA will influence while its politicians pander to the present.

It is obvious that Clinton and his shameless stooge, Madeline Albright, whom he summoned in January 1998 to bear witness that he "did not have sex with that woman," have botched up the Kosovo crisis. That same month, according to the *New York Times*, a crucial policy meeting on Kosovo took place in the White House but Clinton did not attend, as he was too busy preparing his artful dodges about Monica Lewinsky. The end result was a half-baked negotiation at Rambouillet where Madeline used blunderbuss and threats to try to force an agreement which neither the Serbs nor the Kosovars wanted. When Milosevic refused to go along, Clinton felt that he had to make good on his bombing threat and, to do so, pull out the Western observers in Kosovo, thus making it easy for the Serbian army to drive out the ethnic Albanians. As I write this, NATO bombers are doing their best to return Serbia to the Dark Ages while a million displaced Kosovars are enduring untold hardship. Bravo, Bill.

Now, if you want me to be more constructive, I will do so. The "logic" of the situation where a purported superpower does not want to risk the lives of its military men is that the United States should set up a Foreign Legion. I am serious about this. The French have had a Foreign Legion since 1831, made up essentially of troops who are not French citizens but commanded by French officers. It is the most prestigious corps of the French Army: when they parade, along with other units, on the Champs-Elysées on Bastille Day, the soldiers of the Foreign Legion receive the most applause. Every French officer worth his salt wants to serve in the *Légion Etrangère.* They have a tremendous *esprit de corps* and are the first to be called into action in an emergency. In recent years, they were in the Chad, in Lebanon, in Bosnia and in Mururoa, for the atomic testing. I know all this because Pascal Kevorkian was in all these places. And when he served in dangerous areas, his mother and I did not write to our French *député,* saying, "What is our boy doing in harm's way?" He was doing what he was paid to do. Contrast this attitude with the fawning and hand-wringing because three American soldiers, not even combatants, were captured by the Serbs. Bill Clinton's servile black friend, Jesse Jackson, went all the way to Belgrade to "rescue" them. How touching. Why didn't the good Reverend rescue some Kosovars while he was there, or lay wreaths on the graves of the victims of American bombing? I'm sure Bill calls his friend "Uncle Jesse" in sheer gratitude for the services he renders, in peace (Monica Lewinsky) as in war.

Yes, the United States needs a Foreign Legion and the quicker the better. It should be a requirement of recruitment that the volunteers have no relatives in the United States and the American officers who lead them should also be volunteers for that particular assignment, thus reducing the risk that tearful relatives will complain to their Congressmen when their "boys" see action. Preferably the American Foreign Legion should not be based in the continental USA, just as the French one was based in Algeria until France gave up that territory in 1962. If this idea seems startling at first, just remind yourself that America won its independence in the 18th century with the use of mercenaries, including the young Marquis de Lafayette who was made a Major-General at the age of twenty! There would be no lack of foreigners who would join an American Foreign Legion for the money and the adventure.

This being said, I still want to make the point that the Kosovo-Serb conflict should never have become an American problem. The Balkans are in Europe, after all. It has become an American problem only because the Western Europeans, now pretending to be the "European Union," have not been willing in the past 50 years to devote adequate manpower and resources to acquiring real military power. I was in France in 1954 when the treaty for the European Defense Community was rejected by the French parliament. Pierre Mendès-France, a strange man who was idolized by many of the non-Communist élite of France, was head of government when the treaty came up for a vote, but he refused to take a stand in support of it, on the ground that it had been negotiated by the preceding governments. Edouard Herriot, a relic of the pre-war Third Republic, made an emotional speech in the National Assembly about how terrible it would be for the valiant French Army (which had ignominiously collapsed in 1940) to serve under German commanders. Mendès-France stood by impassively, refusing to submit his government to a vote of confidence. He survived this cowardly stance but in a matter of weeks was ousted anyway. This was 45 years ago but the effects of this rejection are clearly visible today in the dependence of France, Germany, Italy, Benelux and Great Britain – nations which together have as great a population as the USA – on American military power and logistical support. The French and the German governments devote a much smaller percentage of their GNP on defense than the USA, preferring instead to indulge their populations in welfare-state goodies, five-week vacations and early retirements.

Recently I listened to an interview of Jacques Delors, former head of the European Commission. When asked why the European Union has taken a predominantly economic hue, he very succinctly explained that in the '50s, the visionaries had tried to start with a defense community but, as this was shot down, they turned to an economic route. This was a telling remark. It should be obvious that no nation or group of nations can claim to be a power on this dangerous planet if it lacks the military power not only to defend itself but also to prevent genocide in its surroundings. From the beginning of the mess created by the breakup of Yugoslavia, France, Germany and Great Britain reacted in cowardice to the massacres and deportations (of Serbs, too) being perpetrated before the eyes of millions of television viewers, simply because they lacked the military power and the will to intervene. They sent food, blankets, bandages, singers and politicians rather than troops. Finally when the stink got too bad, this became an American problem and dealt with in typical Clintonian manner, dilly-dallying and glossing over difficulties by means of cosmetic solutions. With the so-called Dayton Accord, Clinton strengthened the butcher Milosevic simply by dealing with him. It's a wonder he didn't give him some atomic-bomb secrets in exchange for campaign contributions.

So, to summarize, my second point is that the Serbian conflict demonstrates the utter bankruptcy of the European Union as a major power. What good does it do to have a common currency without a common army? Today, the French press is replete with articles criticizing the United States while at the same time complaining about Europe's total dependence on American military power. Charles Pasqua has bolted from Chirac's RPR party to campaign on his own list for the coming European Parliament elections on the theme that the NATO action demonstrates that France has lost its sovereignty. Even Raymond Barre, who was Prime Minister under Giscard d'Estaing, has opined that it is time to plan for a European Defense Community. Oh really?

So as not to be misunderstood, let me make clear that I believe the USA should intervene whenever necessary to prevent genocide. My point is simply that if the Western Europeans had done their job, American intervention would not have been necessary.

The third point will not be long in coming. For many years, I have held the view that the United Nations is a farce, a "thing," as de Gaulle called it (his term was *machin*). I was alive, alas, in 1945, when the UN Charter was signed in San Francisco, based on the illusion that the powers which joined to defeat Hitler, Mussolini and Tojo (I'm being nice to the late Emperor Hirohito) would remain united in the Security Council to prevent future wars. Because of this premise of unity, five nations – USA, Great Britain, France, USSR and China – were each given a veto power on resolutions. It was only because the USSR had stupidly boycotted the Security Council in 1950 that President Truman was able to get its blessing for the United Nations to intervene in defense of South Korea when it was attacked by North Korea. Had Stalin not withdrawn his delegate at that time, we would have been in the same situation as now with the Kosovo crisis, to wit, the United States would have had either to back down or intervene unilaterally, hoping to enlist support among its allies. In retrospect, this would have been a good thing, as it would have forced early recognition that the UN system could not work when the Security Council is made up of nations with disparate aims and political systems. Today, the situation has worsened because "Red China" (as it was called then) has long since taken over the Security Council seat that Taiwan once possessed. Thus, two members out of five would likely have vetoed UN intervention in the Serbian crisis, which explains why Clinton circumvented the "thing" and relied instead on NATO, an organization which by treaty is supposed to intervene only when one of its members is attacked, a situation that does not exist here. (Need I remind my readers that only Congress can declare war, under the American constitution?)

So, what am I proposing? Quite simply that the United States withdraw from the United Nations as presently constituted and start all over again in an organization whose membership is strictly limited to real democracies. More on that another day as I still haven't made my most important point, which derives from the title of this Newsletter.

The Agony of Little Nations is a phrase I got from the radio, from a speech by Winston Churchill. Now, the only nation, little or big, is the nation of the human body, with the human spirit in it, and the only agony of that nation is the agony known to that spirit. No matter what the current feeling may be, politics is not going to improve the condition of the human body or relieve the agony of the human spirit. War is not going to do these things. Politics may be necessary, war may be inevitable – at least the present war is now far beyond the state of something merely inevitable – but other and finer things are more necessary and always more inevitable than politics and war.

Dear reader, I cheated a little bit. I would urge you to re-read the preceding paragraph and put quotation marks around it, because the language is not mine. It was written in 1942, when another war was going on, and the author was none other than William Saroyan, then a young man of 33. Although only an adolescent, I was fortunate to have read at the time the extraordinary book from which this quote is derived – *Razzle Dazzle* – a collection of one-act plays, each with a dazzling preface, which Saroyan had written in the preceding three years. (These plays include *Hello Out There* and *The Ping-Pong Players* often performed by amateur theatrical troupes.) What struck me then, and still does, is that after reading the preface to *The Agony of Little Nations* you find that the play itself is simply about three boys, two white and one "colored" (the term then used) who are about to race their box-cars down a hill in San Francisco when a man of 35 appears, calls the "colored" boy a "nigger" and pushes the two protesting white boys, whereupon the black boy stabs him to death. That's all there is. Saroyan understood at a much earlier age than most of us do, if ever, that the agony of nations begins with the agony of individuals, and this agony is of the human spirit. In the play, the young man has hatred in his heart and the target of this hatred has violence in his heart. That's all it takes for murder to take place. Multiply this by any number you want and you have the Serb-Kosovar conflict. Why the hatred? Why the violence? Let us examine the questions.

William Butler Yeats spoke in one of his poems of "the eternity of soul and of race." He was alluding, I believe, to the fact that most persons feel two identities, that of their individuality (which, to complicate matters, yearns for immortality), and that of the race or nationality into which they are born and which they also would wish eternal. Those who are members of an ethnic category which has been oppressed by more powerful neighbors, such as the Irish, the Jews, the Greeks, the Armenians, the Kabyles – the list is long – are particularly sensitive to this double identity and are conscious of their vulnerability to the risk of extinction. And extinction means not being able to pass on their language, their culture and their traditions to their descendants. Oppressed people have long memories: without independence, without territory they can call their own, it is only memories which allow them to survive as a people.

It has been fashionable for at least a half-century to decry "nationalism," that is, the urge of small nations to be self-governing rather than subsumed within a larger entity. In "olden times" – in fact, only yesterday as compared with the age of fossils – the only law applicable to international relations was the law of conquest. Once-flourishing kingdoms were overrun by invading armies, and their populations, if not utterly destroyed, became known as "subject peoples." This was considered fair game since it was the only game around. On occasion, subject peoples changed masters without conquest, as for example through marriage of royalty or even by purchase. The United States used the purchase method in obtaining the Louisiana Territory (and its populations) from Napoleon and, of course, it did not disdain conquest either, in trampling over the Native Americans, once known as Indians, or provoking war with Mexico to win Texas. Today, satisfied with its conquests, the USA is a champion of settled borders, which it calls international law, as is Turkey, whose entire territory once constituted the Byzantine Empire and the Kingdom of Armenia. Now Turkey is doing its utmost to disguise or destroy the monuments and artifacts of these conquered Christian civilizations.

In the first part of the 20th century, Woodrow Wilson set forth an idealistic view of international relations by publishing his famous "Fourteen Points" in January 1918 while World War I was still going on. As a schoolboy in Philadelphia, I identified Wilson with the phrase "self determination of peoples" – the credo under which subject peoples, such as those which lived in the Ottoman Empire, were held entitled to become independent nations – yet on re-reading the "Fourteen Points" I note that Wilson did not use this term. The closest he came to it was the reference to "autonomous development" in two of the points. Even then, he was aware that "territorial integrity" and "sovereignty" were precious words for nations which wanted to be sure that their former conquests would not be called into question. Today, it is still unclear as to what it takes for a people to be entitled to nationhood. Monaco, with only 5,000 citizens, is a member of the United Nations, whereas 30-million Kurdish people, spread over Turkey, Iraq and Iran, are not considered worthy of nationhood. The Serbs, who have known centuries of oppression, feel they are entitled to be a nation while denying that status to the so-called "ethnic Albanians" within their borders. Putting it another way, the Serbs say to the Kosovars, "Go join the Albanians and you can be a nation with them, but you've got to leave the territory behind." The language is not that unusual; indeed, Croats told hundreds of thousand Serbs the same thing a few years ago. And to move a bit east, some Israelis told the Palestinians, "Go be a nation with the Jordanians but not on our lands."

While I believe that the "common people" everywhere simply aspire to peace and security, the fact is that rabble-rousing leaders, often including men of the cloth, succeed everywhere in provoking a significant part of any population to hatred and violence. What is particularly poignant about this type of situation is that past injustice suffered by one group is generally used to justify present injustice against another. The Serbs cling to Kosovo because it contains relics of their great, but losing, battle against the Turks in the 14th century, although, in the meantime, the population has become predominantly Moslem Albanians. Some Israelis lay claim to lands now occupied by Palestinians because their ancestors lived there in Biblical times. And the horrible injustice of the Shoah is relied on to justify present injustice to Palestinians who, after all, did not operate the German death camps.

I personally felt the poignancy of the double identity when I visited Armenia, for the first time, in March 1991. Invited to dinner at the home of an Armenian activist, I was moved to tears when his 11-year-old daughter recited a beautiful Armenian poem: every word was like a pearl dropping from her lips. This brought home to me the ineffable beauty of the language which I had learned from my mother and father. Yet, that same evening I was moved to depression when I heard an Armenian priest from Karabagh speak with utmost bellicosity about how it was necessary to strike at the Azeris in that predominantly Armenian territory. I told myself, "If that's the way a priest talks, what do the soldiers sound like?" Several years after that, over a lunch table in Los Angeles, when I told a few Armenian-Americans that I felt sorry for the Azeri villagers who had been driven out of their homes in Karabagh, one of them replied, "After all that the Armenians have suffered over the past 1,000 years I can't feel sorry for anybody else."

Sadly, I see no way out of this dilemma for the majority of the human race. Racial identity is all about remembering the past and if that past contains injustice, then too often this becomes the motivation for present injustice. As I once wrote, "man is memory" and, in many people, memory triggers action. A handful of individuals in every generation reject memory and identity, in order to avoid the spiral of hate and vengeance. Michael Arlen, the father, author of *The Green Hat* deliberately kept from his son of the same name his Armenian heritage but, at age 37, the son nonetheless discovered it and felt the pain of being the descendant of a martyred people. On the other hand, in the '50s, Gary Davis, son of the Jewish band leader, Meyer Davis, tore up his American passport and tried to move from country to country as "a citizen of the world." How many people are there who would give up their racial identity in this way? In theory, it should not be necessary to do so, if the identity is confined to memory alone and is not utilized to justify present injustice.

Men of good will see in others what is common to the human race; the majority see only the differences. Saroyan practiced what he preached. When I saw him in Paris in 1965 after his visit to Turkey and the home town of his parents, Bitlis, now devoid of Armenians, I asked him, "What about the Turks, Bill?" He looked at me earnestly, paused and replied, "Aram, they're our people, they're just like us." Many other Armenians would have seen only the differences. Substitute any nationality you want for "Armenians" in the preceding sentence and you have a statistical truism about the human race. Indeed, what was the Colorado high-school massacre about, other than two boys seeing the differences (*e.g.*, athletes) and not the similarities?

We should all despair that Kosovo is not only in the Balkans but also in Colorado and everywhere. The agony of little nations is the agony of each of us, born into the world of Cain and Abel, and using our double identity both as a shield and a sword.

Vol. XXI, N° 5, July 1999

A Lovable France, An Unlovable Corsica

From time to time I remind my readers, who are inured to my sometimes savage critiques of French governments and the ruling *ENArque* caste, that I am a confirmed Francophile. And, on occasion, I confess, I have to remind myself of that, too, particularly when I have been in Paris too long and have neglected *la province*, as the French call any area which is not Paris and its suburbs, and which is not to be confused with *la Provence*, in the south of France, as in Aix-en-Provence.

In May, over the Whitsun weekend, I bathed my soul with the charm of the French provinces by attending the wedding festivities of a Parisian lawyer whose roots are in the heartland of France, in the region extending from Limoges to Vichy. The marriage ceremony took place in a village near Vichy, called Deneuille-lès-Chantelle, where the lawyer has a 200-year-old family house. In France, the only legal marriages are the civil ceremonies performed by the mayor of a commune where one of the parties has a residence. Deneuille-lès-Chantelle has only 90 inhabitants but it has a mayor and a municipal council of its own. The town is next to Chantelle itself, which has a thousand inhabitants. One of the saving graces of France is that it has 36,761 municipalities, a majority of which have a population of fewer than 1,000. As I pointed out in my Newsletter, "Confessions of a Francophile," it is in the commune that democracy is best practiced, whereas, at the top, France is a monarchy, with a functionary ruling class which offers little choice to the people. I'm convinced that the non-functionary Parisians put up with this system only because they can escape to the provinces where most of them have real or imagined roots.

When I entered the small City Hall where the wedding ceremony was to take place, I was greeted by the Mayor, wearing the traditional blue-white-red sash which is the symbol of his authority. He began the ceremony by telling the bridegroom, a sly smile on his lips: "Voilà, on other days you give the orders, but today I am the boss." (I later learned that the mayor is the lawyer's part-time gardener!) The entire ceremony was conducted with the same *bonhomie*. When it ended, the guests retreated for drinks and dinner to their friend's property, overlooking a 15th-century convent which is still occupied by Benedictine nuns. On Sunday morning, a Mass was performed there, after which we drove to a nearby village, Charroux, where, in another 15th-century church, a string quartet, composed of amateur-but-talented musicians among the bridegroom's friends, played Mozart and Beethoven quartets.

The music and the surroundings lent themselves to musings about this France in which I have spent most of my adult life, while remaining *un étranger:* in French the word means both a foreigner and a stranger and I am both. Virtually every village has its own church. In olden times each church had its own priest and was crowded for Sunday-morning Mass. Now there are more churches than priests, so the priests alternate Sunday services among several churches in the area. Indeed, it is becoming so difficult to recruit French youth for the priesthood that many parishes now resort to foreign priests. Regular church-goers make up only 10 percent of the French population. Until the 16th century, the Catholic Church, ally of the Monarchy, ruled supreme over the minds of the people. And it had the real estate to go with its ideology. Then came along the

German Martin Luther, a priest himself, who objected to the sale of indulgences by the Pope – wiping out sins for a price – to finance the building of St. Peter's Cathedral in Rome. John Calvin, a Frenchman born in Picardy, joined the assault on the Church, and a number of people, including nobles, became Huguenots, ready to do battle with the King's soldiers to protect their right to be different. Montaigne in Bordeaux, also a man of the 16th century, was friendly with both Catholics and Protestants, and was enough of a skeptic to know that one should not kill for religion.

Musing in the church, I tell myself it's all about power. Did the people at the top really believe? Those at the bottom surely did but the more they believed the more they stayed at the bottom. The smart ones are ambitious and rise to the top but the more they rise the more they are aware that their preoccupation has to be about power and money and not about faith.

With the Revocation of the Edict of Nantes by Louis XIV in 1685, France finally got rid of most of its Huguenots, who took their industry and talent to many other countries, including South Africa where they created vineyards. According to Max Weber's famous thesis, the rise of Capitalism is correlated with Calvinism. Now, there are fewer Protestants in France than there are Muslims or Jews, and even fewer capitalists. At the height of the French Revolution, after the King and Queen were decapitated, the Church got its comeuppance: the traditional God was proscribed and the Goddess of Reason instituted. Churches were defaced or razed. But the Goddess did not last long. With Napoleon Bonaparte, a Corsican opportunist who used his military prowess to achieve supreme power in the aftermath of the Revolution, the Church returned to favor. Who but a Pope could crown him Emperor? It was only in 1905 that Church and State were separated in France. Now the church buildings belong to the State, that is, to the taxpayers.

Even in the mid-19th century, the conventional wisdom had been that centralism was a by-product of the Revolution and of Napoleon, until Alexis de Toqueville published his *L'Ancien Régime et la Révolution,* and convincingly demonstrated that it dated back to the Monarchy, giving the famous example of a *curé* in southern France who had to get the approval of the King in Versailles to repair his belfry. In the same way, today's intelligentsia in France like to believe that the present-day institutions of France are secular and republican in origin – the slogan being *la France laïque et républicaine* ("secular and republican France") – whereas it is clear to this *étranger* that the Catholic and the Monarchical traditions, both anchored in authority and hierarchy, are still dominant.

In June, I again immersed myself in a lovable province, this time in the Dordogne area, thanks to my friend Francis Pottiée-Sperry, who has frequented for years a delightful small hotel there, nested against a cliff and facing a gentle tree-lined stream, where ducks ply back and forth, occasionally harassed by the owner's dog. For once, I will be totally selfish and not disclose the name of the hotel. As it has fewer than 20 rooms and an exquisite cuisine, I fear that the propagation of the hotel's identity will lessen the likelihood of my getting a reservation in the future! I met Francis via this Newsletter, when one of my readers in the USA sent him a copy of "Montaigne and Descartes." Francis, a retired surgeon, has had a life-long passion for the essays of Montaigne, to the point that his home is called *Les Essais.* I soon discovered that Francis has also a gift for friendship. With his wife Odile and four of their friends, who quickly became my friends, we spent a week of complete *dépaysement,* visiting several of the innumerable medieval towns and villages, with their Romanesque churches, that constitute the man-made treasures of the Dordogne area. Its prime treasure is the meandering Dordogne river itself, considered by many to be the loveliest stream in France, its banks unspoiled by constructions. On any day-trip, one crosses the Dordogne several times because of its leisurely meandering. And from the terrace of the medieval town of Domme one has a breathtaking view of the Dordogne valley below.

It is not enough that a place be lovely for it to be lovable. What makes so many of the French provinces lovable is the juxtaposition of people and places. In short, it is the French people who make the places lovable for me. Whether in the Limousin or in the Dordogne, the current custodians of the places are amiable and attentive to visitors, and whatever their station in life, aware of the history which surrounds them, a history often marred by plagues, persecutions and wars, none worse than the first World War which virtually emptied many villages of men, as evidenced by the ubiquitous *Monument aux Morts*. Today these *provinciaux* are fighting for the survival of their way of life against the assaults of economics, centralization, standardization, and the flight of their youth, like Balzac's Rastignac, to Paris.

What would happen if a government, in the name of efficiency, tried to reduce the number of communes in France and required the small ones to join together, perhaps merging with a larger neighbor? In the first place, I don't think any government would try it in the foreseeable future. Keeping 36,761 municipalities alive, each with its mayor and elected council, is an illustration of the age-old formula: divide and conquer. The conquerors are not, as in olden time, the King and the aristocracy of birth, but a new breed, an aristocracy of functionaries, led by the *ENArques*, who choose their monarch and their successors, the latter based on the Cartesian canon. It suits them to keep the *status quo,* as the fusion of communes into larger units might unleash energies and resources which would challenge their entrenched power. But more importantly, in the second place, the inertia in France is so strong that any reform of this type would create enormous resistance. It is hard, virtually impossible, to change anything in France, other than cosmetically. Perhaps this is a good thing, after all.

It is this paradox that I find so tantalizing: the very dispersion of France into a large number of under-populated communes, many with a deserted church and all with a *Monument aux Morts,* is what makes the countryside so charming and France so lovable; yet this dispersion is also what helps perpetuate the power élite in Paris. True, you can flee the central power by moving *en province* but you can't chase the powerful from Paris unless, of course, you are an exceptional man of history, of the ilk of Napoleon.

Which brings me to "unlovable" Corsica, an island that has been much in the news in France but whose travails do not interest the rest of the world, particularly alongside the events of Kosovo. I have touched on Corsican problems from time to time, mentioning on occasion that the island was purchased from the City-State of Genoa by the French monarchy in 1768. In those days, indeed even into the 19th century, as the American purchases of Louisiana from Napoleon and of Alaska from the Czar of Russia illustrate, a nation could acquire for cash not only a territory but also its people. Today, it would be unthinkable for nations to buy people whereas corporations still manage to do so. The problem with Corsica is that its people were not French, but Italian, with some Greek mixed in, and many of them did not like the idea of having been bought. Pasquale Paoli, for one, led a revolt in the 18th century, seeking independence for his island, as later did Toussaint l'Ouverture in Haiti. Paoli was the most famous Corsican of his time and he was admired wherever courage and liberty were prized; many towns were named after him, including one in Pennsylvania, near Philadelphia. However, Paoli failed in his endeavor, but another Corsican, to wit, Napoleon, demonstrated that it was easier for a Corsican to subjugate France than to de-colonize Corsica.

Ever since that time, Corsicans have had that basic choice: stay on the island and resist being French or move to the mainland and join them. Corsicans have always achieved prominence on the mainland: today, Jean Tiberi, for one, is Mayor of Paris, and Charles Pasqua, for another, is one of the most powerful political figures in France, particularly after his strong showing in the recent European parliamentary elections. But among those who have stayed in Corsica are to be found many seeking independence for the island and who are willing to blow up government buildings and foreign tourist developments to make the point. For years, successive French governments have had to deal with these terrorist groups and invariably they have ended by placating the Corsicans, granting subsidies and tax breaks, winking at the innumerable rackets on the island and even releasing from prison those who have been convicted of violent acts. Polls purport to show that 85 percent of the Corsicans want the island to remain French but that does not deter the hotheads who make up the membership of a dozen or more independence movements.

In February 1998, the unthinkable occurred when the Prefect of Corsica, Claude Erignac, was shot to death in Ajaccio. This was the first time that the chief representative of the State was murdered, and it led to the naming of a powerful Prefect, Bernard Bonnet, with instructions to restore law and order on the island. Bonnet was assigned a special unit of *gendarmes* (police who are part of the Army) to fulfill his mission. It was not long before a number of rackets were uncovered and powerful local politicians arrested. The local branch of Crédit Agricole, France's largest bank, organized as a mutual association, turned out to be a bottomless well, making loans to politicians and their cronies which were never repaid. It turned out, also, that dozens of restaurants had been built on public beaches without authorization. These *paillotes,* as they are called, led to the undoing of Prefect Bonnet. He had obtained court orders requiring their demolition but was unable to execute the orders because of legal obstacles and political interventions. One night in April, a famous paillote, Chez Francis, frequented by the rich and powerful of the island, burned down. Gendarmes investigating the scene found a walkie-talkie on the beach which clearly came from their own gendarmerie. The next day a badly burned *gendarme* received treatment in a hospital. Before long, it became clear that a unit of *gendarmes* had set fire to the paillotte. A zealous young *Juge d'Instruction* soon charged Colonel Henri Mazères, the chief *gendarme* of Corsica, with being the instigator of the arson. Mazères finally admitted the foray and, with colleagues, pointed the finger at the Prefect. The intrepid judge then called in Bonnet for interrogation and had him incarcerated, an unheard-of event in France. The Judge, in line with Inquisitorial tradition, kept him jail for two months to induce him to confess, but to no avail.

The Jospin government was badly shaken by this turn of events, particularly since Bonnet reported directly to the Prime Minister's cabinet. Whereas in a year, the murderers of Prefect Erignac had not been found, suddenly the police activated the investigation and arrested several Corsicans alleged to have plotted the assassination. The government is back at square one in trying to make Corsica an isle of law and order. I am convinced it is a hopeless task, and so I reiterate my inspired suggestion: to kill two birds with one stone, the government should move the Ecole Nationale d'Administration to Corsica and then give Corsica back to the Genoese. Corsican *ENArques* are just what Italy needs.

What more can I do to show my love of France?

Vol. XXI, N° 6, August 1999

My Life with Computers, or Where are the Screens of Yesteryear?

If anyone has been determining my destiny since birth, He surely decided quite early that I did not have the stuff to become rich. The hard evidence came as early as my ninth year, when my brother Andy and I were among the first purchasers of Superman comic books, soon to be followed by Batman and Captain Marvel, and I kept nary a one of them. Of course, these little monthly publications, which cost ten cents then, are now worth thousands of dollars each. What brought up this painful memory of my early lack of flair for the long-term profit was a more recent, and more inexcusable, proof of this failing, to wit, I was one of the early users of small computers and had I kept a sample of each model that I discarded I would have the makings of a potentially valuable computer museum. A mere 20 years ago, who could have believed, other than a person with vision, that the computer industry would witness such a dizzying evolution, leaving behind hundreds, if not thousands, of computer models that, if collected in one place, would make an impressive museum for future generations to admire?

To make amends for my failure to keep physical specimens of my involvement with computers, I at least want to memorialize them because memory is something I do have, for what it is worth. This subject may seem prosaic today but posterity, at least mine, might find it interesting to discover what their ancestors were concerned with in this bottom quarter of the 20th century. Technical evolution (I avoid the word "progress") has been so rapid that I find it hard to believe that I started my career as a lawyer in a Wall-Street law firm, in the mid '50s, before the era of photocopiers and computers. Most lawyers practicing today have never known the time when secretaries used carbon paper to make copies of the letters they typed and, in any high-quality firm, the slightest error required them to retype the whole page. What an ordeal! As to copies of documents received, how was this handled? Well, if they were really important, we sent them out for Photostats. They were simply photographed, a costly and time-consuming process. If image reproduction was not required, a secretary retyped the document, a practice which continued well into the '60s. Carbon paper began to disappear with the Xerox copier when secretaries learned that it was easier to type only an original and then make photocopies, but the word-processor finally killed carbons.

Before discussing computers, I need to describe the historical setting which gave them particular importance for me. When I was at Dewey Ballantine in Wall Street, my most dreaded chore was billing. As low man on the totem pole working on the Du Pont – General Motors antitrust case, it was my duty to prepare the quarterly "memorandum of services" – the verbal description of the work done by the firm – to justify the huge fee that was justly charged. The billing department would send me a thick envelope filled with small yellow slips on which each lawyer (there were sometimes six or seven working on the case) had described the work he did on the matter each day during the quarter. I had to read each slip, most of them hand-written, sort them out, and try to make sense out of the writing of lawyers with whose work I was unfamiliar and draft a coherent memorandum. This was sheer agony for me and, often, it involved guessing and praying that I was not too far afield. When I arrived at Coudert Frères in Paris in 1961, the billing system was even more primitive. Each secretary typed the lawyer's daily "entries" (as they were called) on letter-sized paper and then the billing lady cut them up, sorted them and glued them to a paper which represented the work done for each client. Then a lawyer had to study these sheets and draft a detailed "memorandum of services."

I give this background because, for me, the main boon of the advent of computers and word-processors has been to ease the dreaded chore of doing monthly bills, the bane of any decent lawyer's existence. My first contact with a word-processor in Paris occurred while I was still at Coudert Frères, probably in 1966, shortly before I left to start my own firm, when I went to an IBM office which, I seem to recall, was located on rue Réaumur, to see one in operation. It seemed so complicated and expensive that we did not follow up on the idea. In my firm, the first word-processor we acquired was in reality an electric typewriter with a correction feature; this was the Xerox "Marguerite," so-called because of its daisy-wheel printer. This was in the mid '70s. The machine had no screen and was horribly complicated to use. To correct a text, the user had to create markings by special symbols and type over the erroneous text. I had an excellent secretary at the time, whom I'll call "Louise," and when we acquired the Marguerite, I sent Louise to be trained on it. However, Louise never was able to master this intricate machine and occasionally this otherwise sweet woman who I had never heard raise her voice or use profanity, would scream at the machine until her face got red as a beet, and would call Marguerite a *putain* (whore). Finally Louise gave me an ultimatum: either I got rid of this whore or she would resign. Reluctantly, I opted for the whore.

Ultimately, one of our secretaries learned to use Marguerite well and we kept her for years. In a while there came on the market more advanced word-processors, having screens of various sizes, some minuscule. In the late '70s we looked at, and purchased, two models which are now part of history, the Vydec and the IBM 6. Vydec was a small company which had developed a fantastic machine for its time. Its main virtue was a large screen which represented a full page of standard letter paper. In other words, this was the first WYSIWYG. (If you don't know what that means, dear reader, you are way behind the times! "What you see is what you get.") Our secretaries loved the Vydec because of this feature. Of course, it used large 8 inch vinyl disks, having two usable sides, each storing 15 pages, I seem to recall. The Vydec had such success that the company was purchased by EXXON, a move that one might have thought would mean access to unlimited capital for development of new improved models. Instead, this acquisition was the kiss of death for Vydec. EXXON, an oil company, did not have the faintest idea what to do with a computer company. It might as well have purchased the Curtis Institute of Music. In a few years the Vydec was outmoded, no new models came out, and Vydec died, a harbinger of things to come in the computer industry.

The other word-processor that we purchased at the same time as the Vydec was my favorite: the IBM 6. Because of its small screen and the need to paginate, our secretaries liked it less, but it had a feature which attracted me more and which, in fact, changed my life. This was the "file" capacity. In addition to word-processing, the machine allowed the user to create data files. At first, I did not know how to exploit this feature, but I soon learned that I could put on it my firm's entire mailing list. At that time, we kept client and other names on a Rolodex, a rotary card file, which was, of course, manual and kept in alphabetical order. It was a devilish task to keep this file up to date and the Rolodex was of little use if one wanted to obtain information by other than alphabetical order. I remember that one summer I hired a college girl to make a geographical duplicate of the file, so that I could know, for example, who my contacts were in California. It took her all summer to do this. Today, a computer can sort such a file in a minute!

One of the smartest decisions I ever made was to pay a service company FF 2.5 per card on my Rolodex to put this data on the IBM 6 word-processor. To do this, I improvised a file format, containing basic data, not only such necessities as addresses, phone and telex (there were no faxes then) but also such information as occupation, how I met the person, names of personnel (for companies) and the like. This basic format has served me in good stead, although it has been expanded on with successive machines. As we had 2,800 cards on the Rolodex at that time, it cost us FF 7,000 to transcribe all the names to the IBM 6, but that was one of the best investments we ever made. (Today, we have 27,000 names on our data base, which is, of course, much more sophisticated in its format and applications.) We later acquired from a client a larger model of the IBM 6 having a huge, but unique, printer which had a module for printing names and addresses on envelopes in large quantities. It was way ahead of its time, in fact, so far ahead that until recently we had no printer that could print directly on envelopes, as distinguished from making labels for them.

Let me return to billing chores. At that time, our firm did its accounts through an outside service company called CCMC, which had been organized by various large French accounting firms to do clients' accounts on a standardized program using an IBM main-frame located in Lyon. This used the so-called "batch" method. We prepared the monthly account data by hand in a special note-book (later, printed on special paper for optical readers) and delivered it to a local CCMC office, which then processed the data and after a few days gave us printouts. However, our actual recording of time sheets was done manually, on little yellow slips which were tabulated manually and transcribed to the billing memoranda. One day, it occurred to me that the CCMC standard accounting program could be adapted to billing, by putting hours in the place of money, and using our billing text in the space where comments on the accounting item were inserted. Although it had never been done before, the CCMC technicians were intrigued by the idea, and soon we developed this concept and processed our monthly billing data through this service. Of course, once the printouts came back from CCMC we had to retype the billing memorandum and the actual bill, but at least the sorting of entries and the calculation of fees and disbursements were done by their computer.

A defect of this method was inherent in the "batch" method. If there were errors in the figures or text they could not be corrected until the next month. One day, it occurred to me that I could use the file feature of the IBM 6 to record our "entries" and do our billing memoranda, since this was a word-processor. It sounds easy now, but it took me a while to figure out how to organize the files and set up the system of billing. One flaw was that the IBM 6 did not do calculations; it merely stored and sorted data. Thus we had to do our calculations manually, but nevertheless the tremendous advantage was that we could produce our final billing memoranda without retyping the basic data.

We used this system for years until we acquired in 1981 a marvelous IBM machine, called the "Datamaster" or "System/23" in the USA, and "Système 23" in France. This was IBM's first microcomputer for use by small business and was sold with a built-in operating system, and a built-in computer language, to wit, advanced Basic. In addition to the word-processing function, relatively easy to use, it could utilize a specially-designed series of programs, called BRADS (Business Reports and Development System), which cost about a thousand dollars and which turned out to be invaluable, once I learned how to use it.

Although I had become a user of both the Vydec and the IBM 6, I had no experience with real computers and computer languages. The IBM 23, as I'll call it here, turned out to be an enormous challenge for me. The glib IBM salesman (almost a tautology) had assured me that it was very easy to use, and when I asked what I was supposed to do with it, he replied, "Just read the manual." Well, it turned out that the "manual" was in reality seven thick volumes, plus two volumes for the BRADS and spread-sheet applications! When the machine was delivered, I soon realized that I had a tiger by the tail.

An enormous defect of IBM strategy, so far as customers were concerned, was that once the customer outgrew a model, he had to move up to a completely new system and could not transfer the programs from one machine to the next. Thus the billing system I had developed on the IBM 6 could not be used as such on the IBM 23: I had to redesign the file formats. Fortunately, the basic data, in particular, our mailing list, which had now reached about 4,000 names and addresses, was transferred from the 6 to the 23 by IBM technicians.

When it came to billing, I had to start from scratch. Using BRADS to create a file format, I was able easily to translate the verbal part of the time-recording system from the IBM 6 to the IBM 23. However, calculations were another kettle of fish. The BRADS manual explained that the user had to write his own "code" (as computer program instructions are often called) using the Basic language, but I hadn't the faintest acquaintance with this inpetly-named language. Turning to the Basic language manual provided by IBM, I would stare for minutes at terms like "A=A + 1," wondering how such a thing was possible. In school I had been good at mathematics, and one thing I was sure of was that whatever was on the left side of the equal sign had to add up to whatever was on the right side. After a week of staring, I came to realize that one must ignore the mathematical sense of the equal sign and interpret this operation as meaning: *"Whatever value A represents, add one to it."* Thus, if A had been equal to seven, this instruction made its value become eight.

"A" in this example represents a "variable" in computer language, and it took me a long time to understand how to use this fundamental concept. Another mystery, which gave me many sleepless nights was the difference between a numeric value and what is called a "string" in computer jargon. It was easy to understand that a word like "hello" was a string, but difficult to comprehend that a date like "1982" could be a string also. My forgetting this distinction led to many hours of dismayed puzzlement, often in the wee hours of the morning, trying to figure out why the computer was giving erroneous answers. It seems obvious that the number 1982 is greater than 982, but if these figures are used as strings, then 982 is greater than 1982. This is because the convention of computer language, in using Boolean logic, is that in comparing two strings, the program starts by comparing the first character on the left. Thus as nine is greater than one, the computer stops there and decides that 982 is greater than 1982. Of course, if these figures were declared as numeric values, the computer would find that 1982 is greater than 982. In other words, in dealing with what is declared as a string, the computer treats numbers like letters: just as the word "nine" is greater than "hundred," because "n" comes after "h" in the alphabet, so 982 is greater than 1982 because 9 is greater than 1.

I will spare the uninitiated reader further details of this sort, but will ask his sympathy over the wrenching learning process I had to undertake with the IBM 23, keeping in mind that I was in my 50s when I started! IBM did not provide any training course for this system, giving only a telephone answering service, called a "hotline," which turned out to be a cold line for me; I am still awaiting some of the answers I was promised. I soon acquired an extra set of manuals which I kept at home and spent hundreds of hours poring over them, trying to penetrate the abstruse world of computer programming and the Boolean logic which it applies. It was in this process that I discovered the difference between patience and persistence. I really had no patience to learn computing systematically, that is, starting with chapter one, mastering it, and then moving to chapter two. I would plunge right into a difficult program, encounter errors galore, which often appeared insurmountable, but after many a moment of despair, I would return and try a new approach and finally would solve the problem. This was persistence. That was the same way I had taught myself to play the piano 40 years earlier, but the objective, music, was a pleasure, whereas the computer for me had a merely utilitarian role, to simplify my administrative tasks at the office. My wife, who had to put up with my travails, never could understand that the computer had become for me an enemy. Every time the bell rang to indicate an error in the code I had written, this was a defeat. I came to dread these moments in front of the screen itself, when the bell would toll my defeats, whereas, while working at home conceiving solutions on paper, I felt some moments of exaltation, only to discover the next day that I had again made errors.

By stubborn persistence over a period of years I came to master the IBM 23 and its advanced Basic language. The time came when I stopped using BRADS to create programs and simply wrote them directly in the 23's Basic. One of the mysteries I conquered was the multi-linear function, which was like an elaborate sub-routine that performed whenever the machine saw the special label, such as "FNtick$." Over time, I became so proficient that I could simply sit before the screen and compose a program without advance preparation. Thus, our entire billing process was done in-house. Later I learned to use the spread-sheet feature of the IBM 23 to do our payroll. Prior to that, our accountant would take two days to calculate the payroll manually. With my program she produced mechanized pay slips in an hour.

The IBM 23 was a slow machine by today's standards. It was an "8 bit" system, using the prevalent 8 inch disk on its stand-alone machines. Later we acquired a hard disk having 30 megabyte capacity, and able to connect four microcomputers to it. After a few years, I discovered another marvelous feature of the IBM 23, the capacity of connecting the word-processing function to the data files. The IBM programmers, geniuses in their own right, invented a system by which a model word-processing document, say, a letter to clients about overdue bills, could contain Basic code which would open the data files and select relevant data and do calculations to be included in the body of the individualized letters. Thus I was able to send reminder letters to clients, giving details as to their unpaid bills.

Another extraordinary feature was the ability to use a Basic program to create what the IBM 23 called a "source file," which other systems call a "batch file," that is, a set of instructions to the computer to perform various steps. It all seemed utterly miraculous to me at the time, but I ultimately was able to create a program which created a source file which then returned and modified the program itself! I used this, for example, to write into the program the date it was last used. A feature of the IBM 23 which I particularly appreciated was that if the machine discovered a bug while running the program, a window would open at the bottom of the screen; you could modify the program right then and there and resume the program. However, if the program was modified too much, the machine would ultimately ask you to redo the source code. Later, I learned that this process was known as "compiling."

Over the years I became so adept at the IBM 23 that I was able to read the machine's programs, in Basic, and find bugs in them. It may sound like boasting, but I believe that I knew more about the IBM 23 programs than anyone except the geniuses who had written them. I pay tribute to these anonymous and unsung heroes, because this machine was soon forgotten by IBM which got caught up in the success of its Personal Computer, a much inferior product that nevertheless revolutionized the computer industry.

The story of the IBM PC is the story of one of the most monumental errors ever made in the business world since the beginning of time. In the early '80s IBM was "King of the Hill." It was so dominant in the computer industry that the US antitrust authorities wanted to break it up. At that time, the key computers were main-frames, a field where IBM was dominant, and minicomputers were still a novelty, with Digital Equipment, Hewlett-Packard and Data General making inroads, which IBM met with its highly successful mini, the IBM 36. Computers were mainly used for business, and only the Apple was beginning to penetrate the home market, which the "big boys" in the industry considered only a toy. IBM finally turned to the home market and decided to produce a rival for the Apple. Employing thousands of engineers and programmers, IBM could have easily developed the machine in-house. Instead, and I guess this fateful decision was born of arrogance, IBM gave a budget of $50-million to a task force, sent them to Boca Raton, Florida, and told them to produce a 16-bit personal computer. Rather than use IBM's own software writers to produce an operating system, IBM gave a contract to a small service company called Microsoft to develop the system. The result was MS/DOS, which simply means "Microsoft Disk Operating System." Instead of merely buying the program outright – indeed, IBM could have bought Microsoft itself for a song – the task force agreed to pay the small company one dollar for every computer installed with the system, which was far inferior to the operating system IBM had itself developed for the IBM 23. The rest is history, as the saying goes. The lowly PC was hugely successful, not because it was a brilliant machine, but simply because IBM was marketing it, and because, unlike its own proprietary machines, IBM created the PC with so-called "open architecture," allowing software companies to write and sell programs usable on it. In time, other companies imitated the PC, constructing so-called "clones," each one using Microsoft's operating system. Today, thanks to IBM's stupidity, Bill Gates, founder of Microsoft, is the richest man in the world, and his company is worth more on the stock exchange than IBM, which nearly folded.

IBM's error was to make an open-ended deal with Microsoft. It would have been easy, considering their relative bargaining power, for IBM to obtain an option to buy the operating system for a lump sum when, say, sales reached one-million units. Ray Kroc, the founder of McDonald's played it much smarter when, after having taken the first franchise from the two McDonald brothers, he negotiated an option to buy them out for a million dollars each, net of taxes. So it was Kroc who became a billionaire and not the McDonald brothers. The IBM-Microsoft deal reminds me of another stupid open-ended deal, the one Drexel Lambert made with Michael Milken, allowing him one-third of profits without a cap. In one year Milken earned more than $500 million! One man's stupidity becomes another man's genius, and wealth. IBM ultimately realized what a costly error it had made in allowing Microsoft to own the PC's operating system and it developed its own system for its PCs but MS/DOS's hold on the market was so strong that it became the industry standard. To be sure, if IBM had owned MS/DOS it would have obtained the monopoly that Microsoft now holds, and the likelihood is that the US Department of Justice would have instituted action to break up IBM.

To return to the IBM 23, it soon disappeared from the market, as IBM did nothing to upgrade it. At that time, IBM's arrogance was so strong that when I asked a salesman, "Our 23 is saturated, where do I go from here?" he blithely replied, "Discard the 23 and start over with a 36, or the new IBM 38," This meant that all the programs I had written for the 23 were obsolete and that we would have to write new programs from scratch. That was when I decided to drop IBM and turn to Wang Computer Inc., a company started by an immigrant Chinese engineer, which had become dominant in the office market. Wang had developed a minicomputer line called VS, which in theory would never become obsolete because as a customer outgrew one model he could upgrade to a more powerful one and keep the same programs. I was seduced by this feature, and we first acquired the VS 15, soon replaced by a larger model, the VS 75, which combined Wang's efficient word-processing system with a data-processing feature. Users had "dumb terminals," that is, a keyboard and screen, connected to the minicomputer. We engaged a computer programmer to convert my Basic programs to the COBOL language suited for the Wang. This ended my programming career because I did not find the Wang at all congenial for my style and I did not want to learn COBOL. However, I continued to be the customer for the programmer and we made many improvements on the programs used in our offices, thanks to the larger capacity and speed of the Wang VS.

In time, the Wang company made the same type of error that IBM had made. It failed to see that minicomputers, too, would be supplanted by the personal computer, becoming increasingly powerful and rapid every few months. Wang itself finally marketed a PC, but it was too little, too late. Wang even came out with a portable PC, which I found very useful, but which Wang did not promote enough, although it was the only portable PC on the market with a built-in printer. This proud company, whose computers were once to be found in virtually every law office, ultimately "went down the tube."

The next big step which revolutionized the PC world was networking, that is, tying PCs together so that they could share information and programs. Novell was the innovator in this domain, and it was PCs with networking that ultimately toppled the minicomputer and put Wang and others out of the hardware business altogether. It also led to the ouster of Ken Olson, long considered a visionary of the business world, from Digital Equipment Company (DEC), the company he founded. Indeed, DEC, once a proud company and darling of Wall Street, was gobbled up by Compaq, which started life as a measly IBM-clone maker.

In 1995, we followed the PC-in-network evolution and got rid of our Wang computers, replacing them with Dell PCs, using a so-called "4th-generation" programming language developed in France, called "Abal," for the programs. Later in the year, Windows 95, which we were testing, came out officially and our own programs were adapted to the Windows environment, including Word 7. Now we use Windows 98.

Windows has become ubiquitous but it should be noted that Microsoft was not a real innovator in this domain. Just as many automobile drivers never have known gear-shifts, so most of today's computer users do not recall the days before the mouse, and clicking on icons. We old-timers, of course, gave instructions to computers by typing in words and figures after the so-called "C prompt" appeared. The computer mouse was invented by the Xerox Research Laboratory in Palo Alto, California, but it was the Apple company that first developed its use commercially with icons. Microsoft merely copied Apple and how it got away with that is one of the unsolved mysteries of the century.

The aberrations of the Xerox company with respect to computers rank along with IBM's errors as monuments to the tunnel-blindness of huge public companies. I recall that in the '80s, Xerox, enjoying a virtual monopoly in the copier market, purchased for $900-million (then a huge sum) a company called Scientific Data Systems, supposedly important in data processing. This turned out to be a fiasco and before long Xerox wrote off the entire investment. Another booboo of Xerox is worth mentioning: it set up a 50/50 joint venture in Europe with The Rank Company, and allowed the venture to be called Rank-Xerox instead of vice-versa. The enormity of this error in trade-marking came to my attention when I once asked a French secretary, "Please Xerox this document," and she looked at me with a blank stare. Then I asked her, "What do you call your photocopier?" and she replied, "It's a Rank."

Another fundamental computer development is, of course, the Internet and the World Wide Web, which I have been using since 1994. Here again, Microsoft has not been an innovator with respect to browsers but, as shown by the current antitrust case brought by the US Department of Justice, it has used its monopoly power with respect to its Windows operating system to foist its Explorer browser on the public.

Computers have become an integral part of my life. I have two PCs at my desk in the office, one which I use mainly for keeping track of my appointments and time-recording (I developed a program which uses my appointment calendar to record time), as well as finding and entering data on our data-bases, and the other, mainly for Internet, intra-office messages, and miscellaneous software. I also have a PC at my home, and a laptop for travel, so that my office and e-mail addressees are never far away. Both the laptop and the home computer are equipped with a program called "PC Anywhere," which allows me to connect to the office computer, obtain data and download or transmit word-processing documents. Having now almost 1,100 readers of this Newsletter who get it via Internet, I have been enriched with many new friends through our cyberspace correspondence.

If I finally decided to write this account and send it out, my main motivation has been to encourage those recalcitrants who are afraid to tackle computers to rise to the challenge. This can be done at any age. I was in my 50s and totally ignorant when I started, and now it's much easier to learn to use computers than it was then.

When I see the fortunes made on the stock market with hardware, software and Internet stocks, I realize that the time, effort and resources I devoted to data processing, merely as an adjunct to my law practice, could better have been spent as my principal occupation, with law as the adjunct. But, as indicated at the outset, God surely never intended for me to be rich and I am dutifully following His orders.

Vol. XXI, N° 7, October 1999

Quantitative and Qualitative Truth

This month's trip to the USA took me to New York, Philadelphia (my home town), Los Angeles and Miami, all places where I have friends and professional contacts. I hate the term "personal friend," which I first heard from the lips of Dwight Eisenhower, who must have had some impersonal friends to boast about, not excluding his Vice-President, Richard Nixon. Among my old friendships dating from my Harvard Law School days, none is more precious to me than that of Bert Fields, the peerless Los Angeles lawyer, who is also a humanist, that is, a thinking and feeling man. My daughter Corinne and I spent a delightful evening with Bert and his wife, Barbara Guggenheim, a very special person in her own right, in their rented house in Malibu. While relaxing over a drink, Bert mentioned the exquisite sunsets that he enjoys at this house facing the Pacific Ocean and his poignant realization that death would one day put an end to this appreciation of beauty.

I told Bert that this remark triggered memories of an essay I had written 30 years ago, shortly after man first walked on the moon in July 1969. I called the essay "Quantitative and Qualitative Truth." It began:

For some time now I have been preoccupied by the antinomy of the quantitative and qualitative. The conquest of the moon struck me as the triumph of the quantitative. An allied trend of inquiry thereafter occurred to me – the different usages of the word "truth." The scientist seeks truth in unraveling the nucleus of the atom. The poet speaks of truth in contemplating a Grecian vase: "Truth is beauty, beauty truth."

I first began exploring the quantitative-qualitative dichotomy after my first visit to France, as a Fulbright "scholar." The French seemed much more preoccupied than the Americans with what we now call "the quality of life," a term which was not prevalent in the USA during the '50s, when *Time* and *Life* hailed post-war prosperity and two-car families. French tomatoes still tasted like the Jersey tomatoes which I relished in my childhood, whereas American tomatoes and fruits had lost their taste. And the man-made beauty of Paris, contrasted with the ugliness of most American cities, made me realize that esthetics is a parameter by which any society can be judged. I began to describe the United States, where people's worth was measured by their earnings, as a "quantitative society" and France as a "qualitative society." I began also to categorize people under these two broad headings. I have already related that when I told Harold Robbins that people could be classified as one or the other, he quickly replied "I'm quantitative." I'm not sure he was, though.

In 1971, after reading Lewis Mumford's monumental work entitled "The Myth of the Machine – The Pentagon of Power," I added reflections to the earlier essay and formulated what I call "the qualitative equation." This involves putting together two great poetic insights, that of John Keats, cited above, and that of Wallace Stevens: "Death is the mother of beauty." For if death is the mother of beauty and beauty is truth, then by substituting one term for its equal, we obtain, as in mathematics, death is the mother of truth or, stated less poetically, death is the source of truth.

When I formulated this equation 28 years ago, I had never seen in print anything like it, and I still haven't, but I will be modest enough to posit that I am not the first person since the beginning of time to have noticed the connection between death and truth. The point of my earlier essay was that there are in common usage two broad concepts of truth, the one quantitative, that of science, and the other qualitative, that of art, philosophy and religion. A scientist would never say that death is the mother of *his* truths; the law of gravity, for example, is supposedly independent of the life and death of humans. Why then, if you accept my qualitative equation, would poets consider that death is the source of *their* truths?

The scientist would likely answer, "That's rather obvious; *our* truths are objective, they describe events and data that exist outside of our minds, while the poet's truths are subjective; they exist only in his mind, for beauty is in the eye of the beholder." To this the poet might reply, "Objectivity is an illusion and what good are your truths if they are not apprehended by individual minds? Truth is a communication. Moreover, *our* truths are not merely subjective: the beauty of Bach's music is recognized even by people who are not attuned to Western music, like the Chinese and the Japanese. There is a universal quality to it."

I don't want to enter into the subjective-objective debate nor the related spiritual-materialist dichotomy which have bewitched many a philosopher. This essay would not have been written if Bert Fields and I had not pursued our discussion into the realm of science's attempts to vanquish death. In my 1969 musings I had written this:

Mumford's stress on the machine civilization fails to point up this hidden motivation in man's attachment to the machine – prolonged motion is a defiance of death. Those who sought to build a perpetual-motion machine were emulating the continuity of the universe. It is man's way of saying: "If my own machine (i.e. body) cannot keep going forever, at least I will do the next best thing – build something that will!"

Now, there are scientists who believe that, some day, man can be kept going forever. If my analysis is right, then their success would mean the end of qualitative truth. It follows from my equation (death is the mother of truth) that there would be no truth without death.

Bert who, of course, had not read my essay, made a similar point, which I paraphrase: "If I were immortal the sunset would not be beautiful to me, for its beauty depends on my consciousness of the ephemeral nature of life."

There ensued a discussion of what is becoming a frequent object of discussion: the prediction that science will one day vanquish death. Not long ago I read a statement by a promoter of a new scientific enterprise who boldly predicted the demise of human death by the last quarter of the 21st century (too late for him to be immortal but surely not to die rich, having gone public in a bull market). Bert seemed to be of the same opinion; that the rapid strides in cell research and artificial organs would permit medicine to replace any organ, the only really difficult challenge being to replace the human brain.

I have long felt that the path of science has followed two parallel lines which ultimately will converge: one is making machines which will be human in their performance and aspirations, and the other tinkering with humans to make them as predictable as robots. The final convergence would make one indistinguishable from the other. In 1969 I wrote:

Unless we stop it, the path of science is relentlessly heading toward the quantifying of the qualitative, the materialization of the spiritual, the "objectivizing" of the subjective. Science is not only trying to make robots write music, but also will some day try to make a robot which will like music. To do this it will seek the origin of the physical and chemical reactions of the human body which are associated with the appreciation of music. Then it will seek to reproduce these reactions. If you ask why, the scientist will reply, "One, I want the truth about music appreciation and, two, I want to help the world by making music available to the inapt. Take someone who now doesn't appreciate Bach; perhaps we will find some day that this is due to a hormonal deficiency of the inner ear. Perhaps an injection or a transplant will make this patient love Bach."

Thus far, I have refrained from editorializing, but the passage above quoted did raise the question indirectly with the phrase: "Unless we stop it." The idea of stopping science is itself one which places the person who expresses it among the Neanderthal men of the present. Scientists cloak themselves with the robes of truth-seekers, and who can be opposed to scientific truths, other than medieval Popes or contemporary Ayatollahs? During my recent trip to the States I viewed on television a popular Sunday-morning religious program in which the host, a prosperous Protestant minister, welcomed with unstinted praise a medical researcher who is tinkering with human genes, all for the good of humanity. It struck me as, if not strange, at least novel, that a man of the cloth, being of an ilk that traditionally resists the tendency of science to insert itself in "God's way," would so avidly welcome a scientist who does not hesitate to interfere with fundamental bodily processes. But, of course, one of the most troubling aspects of believing that "God knows best" is to explain why He chooses to allow certain babies to be born blind, or otherwise infirm, or afflicts them with, say, brain tumors before they reach adulthood and can be blamed for whatever evil happens to them. Thus, it is hard to quarrel with the desire of medical men and women to correct birth defects and allow the born to lead more or less normal lives. These are the easy cases.

The harder cases arrive when one asks, as lawyers are wont to do, "Where does it stop?" or "Where do you draw the line?" If it is meritorious to inject genes into a human to correct, say, dyslexia, why is it not valid to find a way to inject genes that would improve a child's IQ or give him a "musical ear" which is lacking? The most unfair practice of nature is surely the unequal distribution of talents and beauty. Why, then, should science recoil from seeking to correct this injustice?

This raises a slightly different issue from the question whether science has a right to seek immortality for man, but surely you'll agree that the issues are related. For if a man is born an idiot, keeping him alive forever is hardly doing him or humanity a favor. But if you can turn an idiot into a genius by injecting the right genes, and then make him immortal, to boot, we're on the path of perpetual glory for the human race.

Up to now, I haven't expressed my own opinion as to whether immortality for the human race is on the horizon, let alone desirable. What makes me broach the subject is that there are serious people around town who do believe that it is possible and generally, the way of science is to hold that whatever is possible is desirable. Of course, some scientists do accept limitations when it comes to destructive items such as neutron bombs and germ warfare, but in countries which do not have arsenals of such weapons scientists can always be found to work on them for "the good of their country." I, for one, do not believe that science will ever defeat death, other than perhaps keeping an isolated individual alive artificially in, say, cold storage while he is dead for all practical purposes. To be sure, the lives of some, even many, may be prolonged by science beyond what is today's norm for the very old: 100 to 120 years. But in my view death will always await our posterity unless, as suggested above, man is transformed into a machine. But who would do all that transforming? Is it conceivable that a world population of six billion could all transformed by injections, transplants and the like? Surely not. At most the rich nations might try it on their own people, leaving the majority of the earth to their historic fate. That sort of inequality would dwarf the present cleavage between rich and poor nations. I can imagine scenarios in which mortal invaders attack the immortal peoples and cut them up into pieces.

Even if we admitted, for the sake of argument, that death from so-called "natural causes" could be abolished some day, how can science prevent accidental death caused by earthquakes, fires and tidal waves? Indeed, how can murder be eliminated? Or, are we to posit that future humans will be exempt forever from murderous urges by means of tinkering with the brain? Will there be no jealous husbands because there will be no adultery? What will become of the fun and daring that are the lot of today's philanderers? So long as death will occur through accidents or natural catastrophes, it would follow that man would be reminded of his possibly tragic end and thus qualitative truth would survive in some measure.

If there is any practical point I am raising in these unusual musings, it is to question the almost unlimited allocation of resources to science among the richer nations, particularly the United States. We accept that many billions of dollars of our tax money be devoted to space exploration, merely to find out, for example, whether there is water on Mars or how far the universe is said to be expanding. And when you ask an astronomer, as Bert Fields tells me he once did, "How can the universe expand; wasn't there space into which matter enters, and wasn't this space part of the universe?," the question is regarded as impudent and not worthy of answer. To this I would add, "Who cares if it expands? If it costs me money to find out, please count me out." Personally, I would prefer that my tax dollars be used to keep my belly from expanding or, even better, for cities to be kept from expanding into the countryside.

Looking at the ugliness of so many American cities and their sprawling suburbs clogged with cars on various Interstate 95s and Freeway 405s, I am dismayed that in the last 50 years public transportation has been so starkly neglected in the United States, with the result that cities are made for automobiles rather than for human interchange and conviviality. The allocation of resources to improving the quality of life for today's humans, through better city planning and public transportation, for example, should have priority over space exploration and other scientific boondoggles designed to satisfy the curiosity of physicists. Expenditures on education, art and music would improve our children's minds and souls more than atomic accelerators can. Ultimately, the allocation of resources is the fundamental issue of public life. Scientific expenditures are unthinkingly viewed with almost the same sense of inevitability as arms and intelligence expenditures were during the Cold War.

But only death and taxes are inevitable. And if death is the mother of beauty, we can use our taxes to favor death's child, whom I call qualitative truth.

Vol. XXII, N° 1, January 2000

The Great Millennium Hoax

When I took up last month the matter of the starting date of the new millennium, the subject was treated lightly as befits a "Christmas Issue." In my inveterate naiveté I supposed that the journalists of the *New York Times* and the *Wall Street Journal* who wrote that the 21st century was to begin this month represented isolated cases of sloppy thinking. It was only as the year closed that I came to realize that these papers, as well as most of the media, including TV news services, such as ABC News, had adopted a deliberate "party line" of ignoring the historic Anno Domini chronology in order to foist on the world the mistaken notion that the third millennium AD begins with the year 2000. This was collective premature ejaculation.

This realization dawned on me when I noted that the named newspapers were ignoring Letters to the Editor, from myself and surely from others, that pointed out their error. In other words, they were stonewalling the issue and suppressing dissent. I know journalists at the *New York Times* and wrote to them individually but their answers indicated that they were powerless to influence their own bosses. I wrote also to a man I know at the European Edition of the *Wall Street Journal* and he gave me a sassy reply, the gist of which was that as millenniums are arbitrary, you can start counting a 1,000 years from any point in time. An acquaintance at ABC News similarly foiled my criticism by replying that, "We repeatedly stated during our broadcast that many people truly believe that the millennium starts next year" but as "most of the rest of the world decided to celebrate this year" ABC News had to cover these celebrations. This is journalistic "double-speak" at its best, which conceals the truth by stating it as a belief. By the same token, I could say that "many people truly believe that George Washington was the first President of the United States" and thus give the impression that he wasn't. And, of course, the "coverage" excuse is itself a cover-up for a self-fulfilling prophecy. The media first misled the public into believing that the new millennium was at hand and then dutifully "covered" the story of the celebration. It was the media themselves making the news. Any new year is a cause of celebration, and the year 2000 – a nice round figure – was itself sufficient cause to make a special event of it. There was really no need to fool the public by making believe that the year 2000 starts a new century and millennium.

For readers who missed my December Newsletter, let me repeat the simple explanation that the present numbering system of years AD began with year 1. Thus the first century ended on December 31, 100, and each successive century ended on the hundred or thousand year. I would add that the 6th century monk, Denis the Little (said to be an Armenian) placed Christ's birth as occurring on December 25th of the 753rd year of the founding of Rome. He then took the January 1st immediately following as the beginning of 1 AD and as there was no year zero, he in effect put Jesus' birth in the last days of 1 BC. Most scholars now date that birth a few years earlier, in 4 BC. But, for present purposes, it doesn't matter when Christ was born or indeed that he was born at all. What counts is that the count began with year 1. This was confirmed by the Encyclopedia Britannica, whose web site (britannica.com) specifies that the year preceding 1 AD was 1 BC. It helps to know that the mathematical term "zero," whose roots are in Hindu and Arab culture, was not even known in the West when the Christian calendar was conceived. The web site of the Royal Observatory at

Greenwich also reports that the 20th century will end only on December 31, 2000, as does the site of the United States Naval Observatory. This official US source did not carry weight with the "commander-in-chief" of the US military, Bill Clinton, whose New-Year statement parroted the fiction that the new millennium began on January 1st. Of course, we do not expect Bill Clinton to be concerned with facts, since he gets his truth from opinion polls or simply invents them.

An old friend of mine, a Harvard law professor, has engaged in playful Internet correspondence with me on this issue. He thinks it neater to begin the third millenium AD with year 2000, but to reach this conclusion he proposes saying that the first century ended with year 99. In other words, to suit his fancy, he would rob the first century of one year, and thus the subsequent centuries would have begun on the "100" years and ended on the "99" years. Those who think it "logical" to begin a century with a zero year are just not thinking about the real magic of numbers in the decimal system. When a count begins with 1, the last figure represents the number of items counted, *e.g.,* 1 to 10, but if you count from 0 to 9, the last figure does not represent the total of the items. In the proper system for counting centuries, the first two digits of the last year of the century represent the number of the century, *e.g.,* 2000 will be the last year of the 20th century whereas all the prior years began with 19. If, as the media are now asserting, 1999 was the last year of the century, why not call it the 19th century and re-baptize all the centuries back to the first one, which would become the zero century? I prefer giving a zero to those who think that way.

Of course, one can adopt any convention that one chooses, provided that the premises are stated. Americans can start their first millennium with the year 1776 but, presumably, this would require an Act of Congress, or a constitutional amendment. The problem is that the *Times* and other media players chose not to be honest with the public and adopted the "one bold stare" approach, to use T.S. Eliot's famous description from *The Wasteland.* I caught the *New York Times* with its pants down, so to speak, when the lead review of its Sunday Book Review section, on January 2nd, featured a book by J.M. Roberts, appropriately entitled "*The Twentieth Century"*. The *Times* reproduced the first chapter on its web site, and in it I found the following sentence: "The twentieth century is properly the name for 100 years which began on 1 January 1901 and will end when 31 December 2000 gives way to New Year's Day 2001.*"* As the reviewer, a Yale professor, did not take issue with this statement, I again sent an email "Letter to the Editor" of the *Times,* pointing out that its Book Review section puts the lie to its Editorial section's brazen efforts to mislead the public as to when the new millennium begins. To be sure, the paper did not print my letter, or any other on the subject. *The International Herald Tribune*, half-owned by the *New York Times*, likewise followed the party line and did not print my letter or any other contradicting its proclamation of the new millennium. *Time* also ended the 20th century a year early and decided that Albert Einstein was its "Person of the Century." I suppose that if someone found a cure for cancer this year, *Time* would report that he is well on his way to becoming the "Person of the 21st Century."

To be sure, *The London Times*, now owned by sleaze-merchant Rupert Murdoch, has us already in the 21st century, despite the fact that two centuries ago, its editors strongly asserted that the 19th century would begin in year 1801. Fortunately, some of the French newspapers have been more circumspect. *Le Monde* clearly stated that the new millennium was a year off and *Le Figaro*, while wavering, did reproduce its front page from January 1, 1900, which contained an item to the effect that the 20th century would not begin until a year later. Ironically, Fidel Castro, not a hero of mine, particularly after I read Armando Valladares' painful account of his 23 years in Cuban prisons, was one of the rare world leaders who refused to hew to the Anglo-American media's fiction that the 20th century ended last December 31st. I would add that when this issue arose in the court of Louis XIV at the end of the 17th century, the Sun King also came up with the right answer, which goes to show that one can be a tyrant without being stupid.

Virtually all the responses I got to my December Newsletter agreed with my position, but one reader wanted to take issue with my point that a decade also ends in the zero year. Another reader tried to rebut my point that President Kennedy was wrong in ending his decade in 1969, but this reader's error lies in equating "the '60s" with a decade. To be sure, the '60s go from 1960 to 1969, just as the "teens" span thirteen to nineteen, or "the F.D. Roosevelt years" run from 1933 to 1945. One can define any period of years in a particular way, but when I refer to "the first decade of my life" I can only be speaking of my first year through my 10th year, not years 0 to 9. There is no year 0. No one counts from 0, except software programmers who can choose to start an "array" with 0 rather than 1.

Some readers have expressed the view that they don't care when the new millennium starts. I would reply to this with an analogy. I don't care whether it rained in Milwaukee during the last week of December, but if the *New York Times* deliberately misrepresented the weather in Milwaukee, I would care because it would be purveying false information and destroying its credibility. Along this line, I have been receiving a weekly economic forecast from a serious economist, whose final 1999 report ended with good wishes for the "last decade, year and century of the millennium." I replied by pointing out that he was off by a year on all these "lasts" and asking him why I should take all his charts and analyses seriously if he couldn't figure out when the century ends. In his reply, he acknowledged his error but mentioned that his seven-year-old daughter believes the millennium is at hand and he did not want to contradict her. Of course, this is good-natured banter, but it does remind us that millions of children throughout the United States and elsewhere have been fed misinformation by the media as to what century they are in. I do think that this is a serious matter in an age that purports to be one of science and enlightenment. What we have here is obscurantism.

A similar type of nonsense was propounded by most of the press in referring to the so-called "Y2K" problem as "the millennium bug." Leaving aside the fact, now evident, that this problem was grossly exaggerated, thereby lining the pockets of software and hardware purveyors, as well as accounting firms which insisted that their clients and suppliers correct this bug, the Y2K bit has nothing to do with the millennium. This problem arose because in the '80s, when computer memories were short, years were referred to by their last two digits, *e.g.,* 1985 was merely 85, and no one worried about the year 2000, when 00 could be confused with 1900. But if computers had existed in the 19th century, the same problem would have arisen when 1900 came around, thus demonstrating that the problem is not one of the millennium but merely of the century.

Again, you might say, "Who cares?" and my answer is that "I care about mind control not to mention sloppy language and muddled thinking." I am incensed that news media have been deliberately lying to the public about the millennium. It is not my wont to look for conspiracies, but in view of the pervasive misinformation in the American press and their refusal to publish contradicting views, I am inclined to believe now that the major news services did get together to adopt a common "party line" on the false millennium. As I once respected the *New York Times*, I am particularly aroused at its meretricious deception of its readers. I would love to see an enterprising lawyer bring a class action against the *Times,* alleging that it sold newspapers under false pretenses. After all, if a paper advertised that it would publish a series of articles on "the Second Coming of Christ" and got gullible readers to buy the paper, wouldn't this be common-law fraud? Hoping to find allies on the Web, I found a site called NewsWatch, which supposedly reports on misinformation conveyed by the press, but it, too, has joined the hoax. It published a report on the 10 worse news distortions of the 20th century, stating that the century is now past. I sent them a letter, asking who is going to watch NewsWatch while it supposedly watches the press. I guess the answer is "yours truly."

If you're wondering why I am taking this hoax so seriously, one reason is that I am a child of the 20th century and I was looking forward to closing out this century with some leisurely reflection on its significance. Thus, I feel offended that crass press-peddlers are trying to rob me of this final year. However, a plus has already resulted: I have found a name for the 20th century: "The Fraudulent Century." It has been a century of unimaginable hypocrisy, violence and deception. Consider: two World Wars took the lives of millions; two major genocides occurred, that of the Armenians in 1915 by the Ottoman Empire, and that of the Jews by the German Nazis in the '40s, as well as some lesser ones, including that of the Tutsis in Rwanda; the fraudulent ideology of Communism served to stultify and enslave millions of human beings for 70 years, while Fascism and Nazism used the techniques of propaganda and the "big lie" to beguile and oppress many millions more in countries that were considered civilized. And as the century ends we are finding that the human race is facing a more subtle, if less violent, form of tyranny and stultification, that of the mass media and gigantic business enterprises (*cf.* merger of AOL and Time Warner) that can brain-wash the public with false information and make a mockery of democracy by using money to buy politicians. I fear that "the Great Millennium Hoax" is just a foretaste of the manipulations that will face us in the coming century.

The Great Storms

Sadly, I must record the havoc wrought by the extraordinary windstorms that struck France by surprise on successive days, the 26th and 27th of December. The loss of about 60 lives is deplorable in itself, and Notre Dame Cathedral suffered damage to its sculptures and roof, while the electric power infrastructure was destroyed in many places and several-hundred-thousand homes were without current for an extended period. The most devastating damage was done to the trees of France. Even in Paris, century-old trees were uprooted or snapped at their base, on stately Avenue Foch and in the lovely gardens that grace the city, such as Parc Monceau and the Luxembourg Garden. The Bois de Boulogne and even more, the Bois de Vincennes, suffered huge losses of trees. In the grounds of the Palace of Versailles 10,000 trees fell. Even the oaks and beeches of the elegant suburb of Le Vésinet were hit hard. Everywhere the larger, older trees were the most vulnerable, their rigidity and bulk giving no choice to the vicious winds other than to uproot them or snap them at their base. In the provinces, few areas were spared. Southwestern France, including the Dordogne, Corrèze and Charente areas, suffered enormous damage, as did the Vosges area in Eastern France. *Le Journal de Dimanche,* of Sunday, January 9th, reported that 300-million trees were destroyed throughout France and that it may take a century to restore French forests to their former glory. This figure seems incredible and even if the true count has one or two zeros less, the loss is still colossal.

Years ago, Joyce Kilmer wrote: "I think that I shall never see a poem lovely as a tree." Alas, I shall need many poems to console me for the loss of so many trees, which have been man's constant, yet oft-ignored, companions in good times as in bad.

Vol. XXII, N° 4, May 2000

18,263 Days

Fifty years seems like a long time in a person's life, but I made a paradoxical observation some time ago, that if you translate your life into days, it does not seem very long, even if the number is bigger. The number above represents 50 years, a quantity which is in the forefront of my consciousness because I am about to return to Philadelphia to attend the 50th-year reunion of my class at the University of Pennsylvania. Strangely, when I was graduated in June 1950, I paid no heed to the fact that the year coincided with the completion of half the 20th century. It was just another year for me. And never did I conceive that I might be alive 50 years thence, when the century terminates. Moreover, let me confess that for most of my life I was not conscious of the fact that the century marks the end of the second millennium AD. Who thought of millennia in West Philadelphia in my day?

I am sure, by now, that most of my readers agree that this is indeed the last year of the century and millennium, despite the blatant attempts of the American media, led by the *New York Times*, the *Wall Street Journal,* the Associated Press, ABC, *et al.*, to hoodwink the American people into believing that the 3rd millennium began on January 1, 2000. Fortunately, the French have not bought the American propaganda on this subject. Recently, I spoke before a class of law students at the University of Nanterre and, out of curiosity, asked them in what century we were: not one asserted that it was the 21st century. If I attach so much importance to this subject, it is not only because I am concerned about the dangerous power of mass media to brainwash an entire nation but also because I had looked forward to this last year of the century as a time for reflection.

That brings me back to my days at the University of Pennsylvania, which we call "Penn" for short (not to be confused with Penn State, a university in central Pennsylvania). When I entered Penn in September 1946, fresh out of West Philadelphia High School, it was barely a year that World War II had ended with the capitulation of Japan in August 1945, following the dropping of two atomic bombs, on Hiroshima and Nagasaki. In my naiveté, I was so sure that the atomic bomb would rule out war altogether that I bet my brother Andy, one year older and, evidently, much wiser, $1,000 that there would be no more wars in our lifetime. The US Congress must have been as naive as I was because it demobilized 11-million soldiers and sailors in record time. I wonder how many of my readers can decipher the term "52-20 Club." Well, I'll explain it. To make palatable the transition of so many demobilized military personnel to civilian life, Congress had voted a payment of $20 a week for up to 52 weeks for those who had not yet found a job. Many ex-soldiers felt that they were entitled to some leisure after four or five years in the service and so took advantage of this subsidy for the maximum period; hence, the term "52-20 Club." If $20 a week does not seem like a lot of money, let me remind you that the pay of the "buck private" during most of World War II was only $21 a month! In 1946, tuition at Penn was only $400 a year, a tidy sum in those days, which I did not have to pay, having won a Mayor's Scholarship.

Another boon voted by a grateful Congress for returning veterans was known as the "GI Bill of Rights," that is, entitlement to a college education paid for by the taxpayer. Thus, the entering class of September 1946 was made up heavily of men who were in their late 20s or 30s, whereas I was not yet 18. I consider myself fortunate to have been among older men during my college years, but at the same time regret that I was too obtuse to take full advantage of their knowledge and experience. One thing I did take advantage of, however, was the ability to drink beer at Smoky Joe's, despite being under age.

In Europe the University of Pennsylvania is best known for its Wharton School, an undergraduate as well as graduate business school, but I am proud to have been in the College, as it was known then, that is, the Liberal Arts school. Penn is, of course, in the élite Ivy League, and College Hall was indeed covered with Ivy. However, the campus lived in uneasy cohabitation with the city. Living at home, at 56th and Walnut Streets, I commuted every day on the 42 trolley, situated on Spruce Street. I had my first cup of coffee at the Horn & Hardart's Automat, on Woodland Avenue, which then cut through the campus. Now, enriched by huge donations, Penn has enlarged its campus considerably and eliminated many of the eyesores which surrounded it. I suspect that most Penn alumni will have forgotten that in the '40s, the University had seriously considered moving its campus to Valley Forge.

The student body was fed heavily by the "Main Line," a name given to the fancy western suburbs where the rich WASP (White Anglo-Saxon Protestant) families lived. Without shame, Penn permitted fraternities and sororities to be divided along religious lines, that is, they were either "Gentile" or "Jewish" with no mixing. Being a commuter, I did not even consider joining a fraternity and felt none the worse for that. It was well known that the Medical School had quotas for Jews and this disgraceful practice was accepted by all, including its victims. In those days, most students, reflecting their parents' credos, were conservative, that is, mainly Republican. In 1948, an election year, the principal issue was which Republican should get the nomination: Robert Taft, Thomas Dewey or Harold Stassen. As my father published an Armenian weekly newspaper, we obtained press passes to the three political conventions which were held in nearby Convention Hall. I thus observed closely the nomination of Tom Dewey by the GOP, never imagining that I would one day work for him when we both become Wall Street lawyers. (Stassen, ironically, became President of Penn!) Despite efforts by some Democrats to unseat Harry Truman, then seemingly unpopular, he pushed through his nomination, and insisted on giving his acceptance speech at 3am when most Americans were asleep. I was present with the cynical press corps who laughed heartily when Truman, with his nasal Missouri accent, twined: "There's gonna be a Democrat in the White House next January and you're lookin' at him." Dewey was considered a shoo-in that year, all the more so that the former Vice President, Henry Wallace, whom Roosevelt had ditched in 1944, became a candidate of the Progressive Party, a "third party." A stubborn Truman, refusing to be discouraged by the polls, conducted his famous "whistle-stop campaign," imprecating against the "do-nothing 54th Congress," and, to everyone's surprise but his own, won the election. Congressman Hugh Scott, who had led Dewey's campaign, spoke to Professor Carter's Political Science class shortly after the election and brought down the house with the remark that the Republicans "had snatched defeat from the jaws of victory."

In the second semester of my freshman year, I tried out for the *Daily Pennsylvanian,* the college newspaper, which was closely supervised by the Dean of Students. At the *DP* (as we called it) I made some lifelong friends, including Alan Oser, who went on to become a real journalist, becoming the Real Estate editor of the *New York Times*, and Daniel Murphy, who went to Yale Law School, and returned to Philadelphia to practice law. Other friends of the *DP* epoch, such as John Batz, a brilliant student and the first Ukrainian I ever met, and Jim Reichley, a gifted writer, of whom I had lost track, have been relocated thanks to this newsletter. It was at the *Daily Pennsylvanian* that I first become aware of McCarthyism, which was then rearing its ugly head. At that time, women students at Penn, housed in Bennett Hall, had their own newspaper, the *Bennett News* and its liberal editor Lisa Aversa (now Judge Lisa Richette) became the object of an attack by a nasty McCarthyite columnist on the *Philadelphia Inquirer,* Ivan Cy Peterman. I wrote a piece in the *Daily Pennsylvanian* criticizing Peterman, whereupon he attacked me in a new column, saying that I sounded like "a Balkan correspondent for Tass," an obvious reference to my foreign-sounding name. In those days, a smear like that could ruin a man's career. The Managing Editor, Herb Fogel, decided to consult the Dean of the Law School, Owen J. Roberts, a retired Justice of the United States Supreme Court, about what to do. I sat in on the meeting, totally in awe at being in the same room with a former Supreme Court Justice. Roberts' advice – to do nothing about the Peterman case – was conveyed in this pithy phrase which I had never heard before: "Never get into a pissing contest with a skunk."

In my senior year I became City Editor, but my most notable contribution to the paper was writing a weekly column, called "Peeks and Punches." The thing I am proudest of in connection with the student newspaper, however, is being largely responsible for the naming of its first Jewish editor-in-chief. I have never before told this story. The tradition was that the current editor-in-chief name his successor, after consultation with the senior editors. Dan Murphy, a phlegmatic Irishman from the Main Line, was the Managing Editor. In an Italian restaurant on Woodland Avenue, we had a lunch session with the editor-in-chief, a WASP who was planning to become a clergyman and, with some difficulty, Dan and I convinced him that the best man for the job was Maurice Kramer. A couple of weeks later we met officially to confirm the nomination, and then the editor-in-chief announced to Dan and me that he had decided to name someone else, a WASP, to be sure. I asked him why he had changed his mind, and he explained glumly that he had been to see the Dean of Students who told him in so many words that there was a "tradition" at the University that a Jew could not head the newspaper. I saw red and undertook the most strenuous and desperate advocacy of my life, with Dan calmly but firmly supporting me. It was 11:30 in the morning when we started arguing and the new editor-in-chief was to be announced at noon. I can not remember everything that I said but surely the most telling blow was to ask the editor-in-chief how he, a future man of the cloth, could condone such a blatant act of discrimination for which he would be ashamed the rest of his life. By now, it was noon, and the junior editors were beating on the door, eager to learn the name of the new editor-in-chief. Finally, the future minister sighed and said, *"OK, it's Maury Kramer"* and thus an ignoble tradition was ended. About 20 years later, a Jew, Martin Myerson, became President of the University! Maury Kramer went on to become Head of the English Department at Brooklyn College. I never told Maury how close he came to being rejected as editor-in-chief, because I did not want him to feel beholden to me. My satisfaction came from knowing that an Armenian and an Irishman had joined forces to shield a Jew against injustice.

The summer after my graduation I worked as a night-order clerk in the Supplee Ice Cream factory on 34th Street, near the campus. There again, I was to discover rampant anti-Semitism among the so-called "working class" men who made up the permanent staff. One of the staff, who held a menial position, was called "Sam" by other members and so I assumed that was his real name. But one evening when I was alone with him, and addressed him as Sam, he told me plaintively, "Please don't call me Sam: my real name is Joe." Flabbergasted, I inquired, "Then why do they call you Sam?" He replied, "Because I'm Jewish and they think that a Jew should be called Sam." The next night, when Joe came into the main room where all the order clerks worked, I said "Hello, Joe" and the dominant clerk, a nasty fellow, chided me, "Call him Sam, that's his name here."

These events took place five years after the horror of the Shoah became known to the world, but they indicate that not everyone had learned the right lesson in that time. When I started working in Wall Street, in the '50s, major firms were still lined up as being "Gentile" or "Jewish" with only token exceptions. Dewey Ballantine, for example, had only one Jewish partner but he kept a low profile. Since then, the need for talent has eroded these distinctions and most former "white shoe" firms are now heavily staffed with Jewish partners.

But to return to Penn, one notable experience of my senior year was a brief encounter with the notorious Dr Albert Barnes, who had accumulated a fabulous collection of impressionist and post-impressionist paintings earlier in the century, after having made a fortune selling his company whose main product was Argyrol. Barnes was a curmudgeon and a recluse, who felt that he had been snubbed by the Philadelphia Establishment and got even by restricting access to his museum in Merion, a suburb of Philadelphia. Barnes had become friendly with the celebrated philosopher John Dewey and professed to apply his theories to the appreciation of art. Thus, he would allow access to his collection only to those who had been properly "trained" to view them. My involvement with Barnes came about because the famous novelist James Michener had written to Barnes a courteous letter asking permission to visit his museum with his new wife, a painter. Barnes replied with a scornful vitriolic letter, and for reasons which I do not recall, sent the correspondence to the *Daily Pennsylvanian.* One day in the Spring of 1950, Dan Murphy received a call from Barnes' secretary asking for a reporter to speak with the great man, and so Dan took me along to see him. As we entered the building, great paintings were visible all over. Barnes met with us in his second-floor board room, along with the two women who were his trusted aides. His conversation was larded with incomprehensible references to Dewey and his objective was to get the paper to join in his campaign against Michener and Penn. Diplomatically, Dan said that we would study the matter, but that was the end of it. Barnes died in a car accident a year later, having bequeathed control of his Foundation to a little-known college for Negro students but still with restrictions on access. It took many years for the collection to become visible to the general public, but that is another story.

These reminiscences would not be complete without a mention of some outstanding professors. In my first semester I had signed up for a course in "Logic," assuming naively that it would help me think straight. The soft-spoken instructor, Nelson Goodman, demolished this assumption on the first day, almost daring us to abandon the course before it was too late. The famous "ruptured duck" insignia, proof of an Honorable Discharge, in his lapel, indicated to us that Goodman, too, had just returned from the war. This Logic course turned out to be highly technical. Goodman ignored the Churchman textbook that we had been asked to buy, and filled the blackboard with formulas, the simplest of which was "if p then q." Though he never used the term, I learned much later that we had been learning Boolean logic, a bewildering subject. I can't resist the temptation to be immodest, for a change, and report that when I looked at the posted grades after the final exam, which consisted of dealing with intricate formulas full of "p's and q's," I saw that I had an "A" but there was an asterisk beside my name. Fearful and puzzled, I slowly descended to the footnote; it stated "highest grade in exam: 98.5." Clearly, Goodman had been as astounded as I with this result. Later, I discovered that this soft-spoken man was one of the foremost logicians in the world. He went on to become a member of the Harvard faculty. One of my main regrets in life (and by stating this I am inviting young readers not to emulate me) was that I was too timid and self-effacing, when young, to approach outstanding men like Nelson Goodman and seek their guidance. When I left Harvard Law School for Europe on a Fulbright Scholarship, one of my professors kindly wrote about 20 letters of introduction to high-level contacts there. Incredibly, it seems now, I did not dare use any of them. My approach then was "what I can possibly offer this person, why would he waste his time with me?" Whereas, the right approach should have been, "What can I learn from him?" Surely, people who know me now will have trouble believing that I was timid when young, but that's the truth.

Another great teacher I had, one whom I have mentioned in an earlier Newsletter, was Conyers Reid, professor of English History, and an authority on the Tudors. He was not a flashy lecturer but one day he gave us an unforgettable lesson, by stating that students of history should seek to make broad generalizations about the subject. He illustrated this point with the remark that someone had opined that history might be summarized as an alternation of liberty and order, giving as an illustration the French Revolution and the reaction that followed. The final exam in his course threw me into a panic because there was just one question: "With your knowledge of English history, how can you explain that England had its 'glorious revolution' with the advent of William and Mary in 1688, whereas France at the same time was an absolute monarchy under Louis XIV?" Keep in mind that we had not studied any French history in the course and this broad comparison was not even hinted at. If ever there was a "thought question" this was it. I contrast this type of question with the propensity of French professors to require their students to learn the course by heart and simply regurgitate what the teacher said. One reason I have so little respect for French universities dates back to my Fulbright days at the University of Strasbourg when we were given an indoctrination session and told that the right way to answer an exam is to repeat word-for-word what the professor has taught. Based on what my grandson David, now studying law at the Sorbonne, tells me, this practice continues.

Another great insight I acquired at Penn came, surprisingly, in a course on Counterpoint, which, along with Harmony, I had taken as a lark, being the only non-music-major in the class. It was fun to be among music majors (I majored in American History) and I quickly became friendly with three of them; Jim Krayer, a trombonist; John West, a violinist; and Morris "Moose" Charlap, a bouncing pianist and budding composer. Moose was the first person I had met who was diabetic and he suffered much from this condition. He regaled us often at the piano in the Houston Hall lounge, playing and singing songs of his composition. Charlap went on to write musicals for Broadway, his most successful work being *Peter Pan.* Sadly, he died while still in his 40s. To return to the insight, I did not get it from the professor, the very Germanic William Happich, who was as pedantic and humorless as they come. Rather, it came from the process of learning to write fugues. There are two types – strict fugues and free fugues. From the names, I had assumed that strict fugues were the more difficult to compose but I was to learn that the truth was the opposite. In a strict fugue, you keep repeating the theme in various intervals, whereas in a free fugue, there are periods between the appearances of the theme when you are on your own. What is difficult is exploiting this freedom, for there are no rules: if you want the fugue to be interesting, you must have talent, something I was not surprised to learn that I did not have. But I did go away from the course with the insight that freedom is a burden for the untalented or, to put it another way, to make the most of freedom you must work at it. A few years later, while at Harvard Law, where I often sat in on Archibald MacLeish's course in the Yard, I heard him give Pericles' version: "The secret of happiness is liberty and the secret of liberty is courage."

Perhaps the most important fact I learned at Penn came in the Psychology course I took in my first year. At that time, we were required to choose at least one science course; as I had no interest – why? – in the so-called natural or physical sciences, I satisfied this requirement by taking Psychology I, which dealt mainly with the characteristics of the nervous system that affect our personality and behavior, as well as individual differences, such as in intelligence. I am still puzzled as to why I found the teachings on "individual differences" so startling. Doubtless, it was the democratic faith with which we had been inculcated in public school. Learning about the "bell curve," which summarizes the distribution of intelligence in a given population, was a revelation, in particular, the fact that about five percent of the people are morons, idiots and imbeciles (all technical terms, not imprecations), while another five percent are exceptionally intelligent. There seemed then, and still now, to be a taboo against making any public use of the former statistic. No law prohibits a moron from voting or, indeed, from running for office. Can you imagine a politician addressing his audience: "My fellow citizens and fellow morons"?

In the wake of Darwinism, a movement had developed to apply the principles of selection so as to improve the human race, as breeders had been doing with animals for centuries. One rarely sees in print the word given to this movement: Eugenics. Well before World War II, in 1927, to be exact, the US Supreme Court upheld a Virginia statute which allowed the state to sterilize women who were mentally defective. Justice Holmes, who was, after all, a product of the 19th century, recited that Carrie Buck was not only mentally deficient but also had a similarly deficient mother, and had given birth to an illegitimate, mentally defective child. He concluded that "Three generations of imbeciles are enough." His reasoning was simple enough: "It is better for all the world, if instead of waiting to execute degenerate offspring for crime, or to let them starve for their imbecility, society can prevent those who are manifestly unfit from continuing their kind."

But Hitler's pretensions to make Germans into a super race and to exterminate allegedly "inferior" races decisively put an end to the respectability of Eugenics. Yet mentally defective men and women continue to commit crimes, and in the United States they are often executed for them. I read recently that some 250 people have been executed in Texas alone during George W. Bush's tenure as Governor. Americans seem to have opted for this more radical method of insuring that "degenerates" do not reproduce, while most of the rest of the civilized world looks on in horror. To make matters worse, it appears that mentally defective lawyers are oft appointed by courts to defend the penniless accused in capital cases.

Despite the emphasis of the advocates of Eugenics on hereditary transmission of characteristics, the dominant school of American psychology in the first half of the 20th century was Behaviorism, propounded by John B. Watson, who once boasted that if given a child early enough he could turn him into anything he wanted. In other words, training and the environment were all that shaped human beings. I tended to doubt this teaching at the time, and since then, as a father of seven, I'm convinced that heredity plays as much a role as environment in shaping personality and character. The Penn faculty was heavily into Behaviorism in my day, which is one reason that I elected not to major in Psychology – the other being that all the instructors seemed to have ticks that made them unbearable to watch.

One thing that I came to realize as lacking in my Penn education was a synthesis that would tie together psychology, philosophy, history, art and my other studies, but I guess that's what the last 18,263 days were supposed to provide!

Vol. XXII, N° 5, June 2000

Back from Penn

Some readers, I trust, will be curious to get my reaction after I attended my class reunion at the University of Pennsylvania, in my hometown Philadelphia. In short, it was disappointing. For one thing, very few of the classmates I was closest to attended (Dan Murphy and Jim Reichley, whom I mentioned in my last issue, being happy exceptions), but most of all, I felt a kind of alienation which is doubtless a consequence of my having lived so many years in France. If this did not lead to some generalizations about American civilization I would not have bothered to devote this issue to the subject, but the generalizations are in me and I hope to express them to my readers, particularly since, from time to time, I am asked, "Where do you prefer living, in France or in the United States?"

To start with food, there is no contest. I remain appalled at the indifference of even educated Americans to the food they eat, especially in group gatherings such as the Friday evening dinner-dance which marked the beginning of the reunion, held at a hotel owned by the university. The food was awful, and made all the more painful by the cost of $90 per person. The main course was an overcooked steak combined with an unidentified fish! What hope is there for a people who combine meat and fish in the same plate, particularly when they are both inedible? To make matters worse, a loud orchestra pounded unwanted decibels into my brain. Another source of bewilderment for me is how Americans can find it pleasurable to eat meals in noisy restaurants, where one can hardly hear what the person seated next to you is saying. From time to time, I would escape to the hallway but this was of little relief, since the raucous festivities of another class added to the cacophony. What can one say about organizers of class reunions who do not even conceive that a quiet environment might be conducive to renewing acquaintance with people one has not seen in decades?

This purported dinner reminded me of another disastrous one I attended several years ago, to commemorate the 100th anniversary of the *Harvard Law Review.* Distinguished guests from all over the country paid $75 per person for a hideous meal that the lowliest factory worker at Renault would send back to the kitchen. At my table of 10 or 12, I seemed to be the only one who minded the fare, but I did get a laugh when I suggested that we go out to a Jewish delicatessen and come back with some sandwiches. At the head table, a sophisticated Harvard professor serving as toastmaster made witty remarks, impervious to the fact that hundreds of guests, including the élite of the legal profession, were swallowing food hardly worthy of a strip joint. On such occasions, I am reminded of the extraordinary book that my old friends Karen and John Hess wrote more than 20 years ago, called *The Taste of America,* excoriating the poor eating habits of Americans. Since that time, some progress has been made; one finds good restaurants in major cities, but food served at large gatherings such as I have just described remains poor. Once, when visiting Harvard during the tenure of my old friend Derek Bok as President, I remarked to him that the food I had eaten in a student residence was awful. Derek was taken aback by this observation and pointed out to me that Harvard had just won an award for its student food, whereupon I rejoined with a key point in the Hess book to the effect that "nutritionists are not cooks." You can get plenty of vitamins and proteins and still have a bad meal, from the point of view of taste. I sent Derek a copy of the Hess book but never got a reply. Surely, in his mind, he had more important things to do than to improve the quality of the food that Harvard students eat.

To return to Penn, the "highlight" of the dinner was the brief appearance of the university's president, Judith Rodin, a Philadelphian by origin, who congratulated the class for donating four-million dollars to the university. As her speech lasted four minutes, I surmised that her going rate is one minute per million dollars. The next day, at College Hall, we were honored with a virtuoso performance by Ms Rodin, a former professor of psychology at Yale, who boasted that the incoming freshman class was the best in Penn's history, and then described the new buildings and renovation projects which were improving West Philadelphia. On the first point, I made a mental note to myself to write a Newsletter some day on what I call "American Cartesianism." Here we were in May and the new class is to arrive in September but already she knows it's the best. What characterizes Cartesianism is *a priori* concepts: you don't need facts to make a generalization. What Ms Rodin was really saying is that by test scores and grades the incoming class has the highest numbers. Of course, she made no allusion to the undeniable evidence that test scores and grades have undergone tremendous inflation over the past generation. It used to be that an "A" was an exceptional grade. Now it's expected by any student who stays awake in class. The other day I read an article by a professor at Santa Clara University in which he confesses that he has reluctantly joined the bandwagon of high-graders, while deploring the phenomenon. The hypocrisy and deception prevalent in American education have reached epidemic proportions. Another recent news item reveals that in a state that imposes an achievement exam for potential graduates of high school, teachers and administrators have been helping their students cheat. It has also become fashionable to require college applicants to submit a "personal essay," but from what I have been told, these essays have become collective works, with teachers, college counselors, family and friends pitching in to make the essay into a masterpiece. Surely the universities know what's going on, but they are willing accomplices to a hokum process.

In thinking about Ms Rodin's speech, my mind returned to a banquet I attended several years ago at the Abbaye de Royaumont, sponsored by a French bank for its customers. When the bank's president got up to make a speech, I expected him to make a pitch for his bank, but No, he devoted his whole talk to the history of the monastery and the accomplishments of the monks there. The contrast with Ms Rodin's performance could not be more striking. Here she is, a professor of psychology, speaking to graduates of the class of 1950, but it does not occur to her to discuss, say, the main developments in psychology over the past five decades. Or, for that matter, to show any recognition that in that time frame the world has undergone the Korean War, the Cold War, the Vietnam War and a revolution in technology and morals. Basically, her message is that of a real-estate developer and a fund-raiser.

This non-intellectual content from a university president is by no means atypical. The week after my Penn reunion I read in the *New York Times* about the resignation of Neil Rudenstine as President of Harvard University. The author of the article was hard-pressed to attribute any accomplishments to Rudenstine, once an authority on Renaissance literature, other than as a fund-raiser. He was virtually invisible on the campus, according to the article, because he was constantly on the road making pitches to alumni groups, and had brought in an average of one-million dollars a day over a ten-year period at Harvard. His parents had brought him up to be a scholar but he ended up as a travelling salesman. I can just picture his future tombstone :

Here lies
Neil Rudenstine
Who raised a million dollars a day
For Harvard University and
Kept none of it for himself.
Virtue is its own reward

The same phenomenon prevails at Harvard Law School, whose fatuous dean, Robert Clark, had no discourse for alumni who, like me, attended the last three class reunions, other than self-congratulatory messages about his school. In his talks there was no recognition that a world might exist outside Harvard. Lately he has taken to sending me "personal" birthday greetings, obviously churned out by a computer and untouched by human hands, including his. Some day, perhaps next December, I expect to receive a letter from him, thus couched:

"Dear Mr. Kevorkian,

"Greetings once again from Harvard Law School and a Happy Birthday to you.

"I hope you don't mind my pointing out that according to our actuarial studies, this may well be your last birthday. Accordingly, the time would seem fitting for you to review your Will and ascertain whether it contains a large bequest to Harvard Law School.

"For $15-million, we will name a building after you, provided, however, that you are willing to retouch your name so that it will fit into Harvard's cultural landscape. Our linguists have concluded that 'Kevork' means 'George' and 'ian' means 'son of.' Thus, Georgeson Hall would be a recognizable rendering of your awkward Armenian patronymic.

"If you can not afford such a large gift, keep in mind that for $10,000 we will plant a tree in your honor on the lawn in front of 107A Dane Hall, where you spent your first glorious year at Harvard Law School. For an additional $1,000 we will add an elegant sign stating 'Please do not pee on Kevorkian's tree.' (Note that for a tree your name need not be changed).

"Well, Mr. Kevorkian, enjoy your birthday and rest assured that at Harvard you and your assets are constantly on our minds.

"Sincerely,
Robert Clark
Dean"

What irritates me the most about all this is the underlying assumption of American universities that their graduates are merely "fat cats" whose only function in life is to give money to their alma mater. While they're in college they are the "best and the brightest" but once outside they cease to have brains and knowledge but are merely pocketbooks. And, unfortunately, most graduates – my readers excepted, to be sure – seem to accept that image of themselves. I find it a glaring paradox that the United States lavishes funds on plant, equipment and professors for college students, yet expects them to act as intellectual boobs for the remainder of their lives, interested only in making money, playing golf, buying boats and expensive cars. Recently, on a web site I found a listing of the "best" American universities. The principal criterion for determining quality, it turns out, is how much money the institution spends per capita on its students. As I pointed out in my Newsletter called "Quantitative and Qualitative Truth," the USA has essentially been a quantitative society and seems bent on remaining that way. That is why I find it so distressing that American universities expect their Deans and Presidents to be money-raisers and real-estate developers rather than intellectual and moral leaders of the community.

As readers of my last Newsletter know, the best insights I obtained at Penn did not stem from high investments in plant and equipment. Nelson Goodman laid out his "p's and q's" on an ordinary blackboard and Conyers Reid opined on history without electronic gadgets. American universities have been notoriously deficient in producing graduates with a knowledge of history, geography and foreign languages, subjects which are not costly to teach but which are indispensable if Americans are to live up to their responsibilities to the rest of the world. When I was a Visiting Professor at NYU Law School in 1969, I was dismayed at how rare it was to have an stimulating conversation with most of the tenured professors there, whose talk turned mainly on their stock-market portfolio, their golf score and the country house they were buying or selling. For stimulation I turned to the students, who were then agonizing over the Vietnam War. Now, I suspect they talk about jobs at Goldman Sachs and Wall Street law firms. Per capita, there are surely more boobs with university degrees in the United States than any other country. Just look at the men who are running for President and the one in the White House.

Listening to President Rodin, I had the dread thought that the same attitudes which led to "the best and the brightest" conducting the Vietnam War as though it were a mere matter of "problem-solving" are still prevalent in the United States and are likely to produce similar disasters in the coming decades. Today's Americans, by and large, seem to live only in the present and feel no need to consult the past for guidance as to the future. Which political leader in the past 50 years could have written anything comparable with a single chapter of the Federalist Papers? Where are the Hamiltons, the Jays, and the Madisons?

This brings me naturally to the subject of the anti-Americanism that is so prevalent in the world today. Whereas in the '50s and '60s – the days of "US Go Home" – anti-Americanism was largely a product of Communist propaganda, today, in France at least, I find it pervades all segments of the political spectrum. To be sure, envy plays a role. Even *Le Figaro* writes of "the insolent health of the US economy." But, beyond that, I detect a perception that the American model of materialism and quantitative values begets a society prone to violence and aggression and indifferent to spiritual and cultural values. Certainly, American movies and TV shows exported to Europe do not portray a society worthy of emulation. And the shallowness and ignorance of American political leaders do not encourage Europeans to feel confidence that the country has the wisdom to use its power well.

To me, the worst aspect of the American political system today is its total subservience to money. The rich can buy office, as Mr Corzine is trying to do in New Jersey, or buy the candidates, as Clinton demonstrated in 1996, and both Gore and Bush are doing now. I have often criticized the French system as an oligarchy dominated by the functionary class, whose elite are chosen by co-optation. In the USA, it is money that buys power and office, while the most deprived citizens stay away from the polls, knowing they have no real choice as to who governs them. Both systems make a mockery of democracy.

Where is one to turn for a better system? I wish I knew.

Vol. XXII, N° 6, July 2000

Back to Paris and Corsica

As my last two Newsletters dealt with my *alma mater* and other things American, it is high time that I return to the theater of my principal operations, that is, Paris, in France, in Europe. Much is going on here as the century and millennium draw to their close. The European Union has to face a major choice, whether to expand geographically to the East by taking in such eager candidates as Poland and the Czech Republic, or to give priority to creating what amounts to a democratically-structured federation of its core members, as both France and Germany now seem to advocate, although they eschew the word "federation." Four years ago Jacques Chirac promised the Poles that they would become part of the EU in 2000. Like other "promisees" of this inveterate promisor, the Poles will have to learn this famous *bon mot* of Chirac: promises bind only those who believe them.

In May, Germany's Foreign Minister, Joschka Fischer, tossed a bombshell into the lethargic European community by proposing that the core members of the EU adopt a constitution that would drastically change the nature of its institutions. President Chirac, not to be outdone by a mere German, particularly on the eve of France's taking the helm of the EU for six months, then made a speech in June before the Bundestag in Berlin to propose that a "pioneer group" of nations reinforce the nature of their union by adopting a constitution with new institutions. The use of the word "constitution" raised eyebrows among the French politicians who cling to de Gaulle's vision of a *Europe des nations.* Let me remind my readers that the legal framework of the EEC and now the EU has been in the form of treaties, first the Treaty of Rome and more recently the Maastricht and Amsterdam treaties. Nations make treaties while peoples make constitutions. Those who follow de Gaulle's concepts, and there are many of them on the Left, too, can not accept that the EU become a nation in itself, for then France would cease to be a nation, but rather a component of a nation, as California is within the United States.

The idea of a "United States of Europe," while an acceptable dream for many, still appears to be a pipe dream for most people I talk to in France. The peoples of the 13 states that created the USA spoke the same language and shared essentially a common origin. The 15 peoples who presently form the EU speak 11 official languages (and many more dialects) and have a lot of history to forget if they are to feel part of the same nation. Moreover, Americans are a mobile people compared to Europeans: they are willing to uproot themselves and move to other cities and states, as evidenced by the millions of Easterners who have gone West and South. One finds few Germans in France and vice-versa: yet these two countries purport to be the "hard core" or now, to use Fischer's term, the "center of gravity" of the EU. True, many Spanish and Portuguese have immigrated to France to find work but most of them dream of, and save up to return to, their beloved homeland, at the wheel of a Mercedes or BMW. In other words, the people of Europe are not ready to mix with each other to form a new race known as Europeans.

At any rate, Chirac's speech is sure not be followed by any concrete steps in the next two years, for a simple reason: he is up for re-election in 2002 and his chief rival is his Prime Minister Lionel Jospin, whom Chirac had to name when the Socialists and their allies garnered a majority in the National Assembly in 1997, after Chirac's stupid decision to dissolve that body despite the enormous majority his coalition enjoyed. If they can avoid it, neither Chirac nor Jospin want to "make waves" about controversial issues before the election.

Until Chirac's Bundestag speech, the main item on the political agenda was the proposal to reduce the President's term of office from seven to five years. A bit of history will place this issue in context: When de Gaulle returned to Paris in 1958, propelled by the impasse over the Algerian civil war, he easily put through a new constitution for the Fifth Republic, which greatly strengthened the Executive Branch, but maintained the seven-year Presidential term of the earlier Republics, as well as the indirect method of electing the President, via elected officials, the so-called *grands electeurs*. He was himself elected the first President of the Fifth Republic by this method. However, in 1962 he startled the country by proposing a constitutional amendment for the direct election of the President by popular vote. Despite the hostility of much of the political class, he pushed through this amendment by referendum even though most constitutional scholars contended that parliamentary action was a prerequisite. He was re-elected by this method in 1965, but resigned in a huff in 1969 when another proposed constitutional amendment – to abolish the Senate and promote "participation" – was rejected by referendum. His successor, Georges Pompidou, who had a serious illness, proposed to reduce the presidential term to five years, and the amendment was actually approved by both houses of Parliament, but as Pompidou feared that he risked defeat in the next step – approval by a 60% vote of the joint houses – the amendment remained in limbo until Pompidou's premature death in 1974. His successors, Giscard d'Estaing and then Mitterrand, both loved power too much to think of reducing their term of office. In the 1995 debate between the two runoff candidates for President – Chirac and Jospin – the latter advocated a five-year term but the former (despite having been Pompidou's disciple) rejection the notion. The best (indeed, the only!) laugh of the debate was when Jospin wryly commented: "Five years of Jospin is better than seven years of Chirac."

Earlier this year, the issue was rekindled by none other than Giscard d'Estaing, who introduced a bill in Parliament calling for a constitutional amendment to shorten the term to five years. This time everyone jumped on the bandwagon, including Chirac, whose conversion to the *quinquennat* (as the five-year term is ungraciously called in French) is not based on principle but, as usual, on politics. In 2002, he will be 69 years old, and as he has already been around for too long, in the opinion of many, the thought of his remaining president until he is 76 might turn off enough voters to ensure the election of Jospin, who is running neck-to-neck with him in the polls. In Chirac's TV interview announcing his change of mind, he made clear that he would block any attempt to change anything else in the Constitution on this occasion. As Jospin was already committed to the shorter term, the Socialists in the Parliament dutifully complied, as did Chirac's own party members, and so the measure was enacted by both chambers. While it could have been easy for Chirac to let the amendment be adopted by the united chambers, he chose instead recourse to a referendum, to be held on September 26th. A large number of abstentions is expected, since the issue does not excite the population.

One of the main arguments advanced for the shorter term, aside from the fact that seven years is too long in itself, particularly since the President is eligible for re-election (as happened with Mitterrand), is that the term should coincide with the five-year term of the National Assembly. Traditionally, when a new President is elected, he dissolves the Assembly and generally gets a majority to support him. Foolishly, Chirac failed to do this in 1995 and, with his even more foolish decision to dissolve the lower house in 1997, one year before its term expired, he ended up being stuck with "cohabitation," that is, having a hostile Prime Minister. While he could have dissolved again at any time after May 1998, he has been afraid to do so, since Jospin is popular and the Right is seriously divided, not to say in disarray. Even without premature dissolution, moreover, there is no guarantee that the terms of office of President and National Assembly will coincide. If the President should die, for example, there is no Vice-President to serve the remainder of his term; thus a new election must be held and a new seven-year term begins.

It is noteworthy that Chirac vetoed in advance any additional tinkering with the Constitution, doubtless fearing certain other measures that have been bandied about, such as eliminating the President's power to dissolve the National Assembly, and limiting the President to a single term. Long-term readers of this Newsletter are aware that I am in favor of scrapping the Fifth Republic altogether and starting over again with a constitution that guarantees real separation of powers, in particular by preventing *fonctionnaires* from running for office while keeping their civil-service status and prohibiting members of Parliament from holding other offices. To Jospin's credit, it must be said that he tried to enact the latter measure but was thwarted by both houses which are, to be sure, full of members holding Mayor's seats. The former measure is one he would never propose because he is, like Chirac, an *ENArque*, and thus a *fonctionnaire,* who is sure of returning to the public payroll if booted out of office. Indeed, when this happened in 1993, Jospin was paid for three years by the Ministry of Foreign Affairs, his home corps, without doing any work.

Jospin has been on the hot seat lately over the thorny Corsican issue. Last year, in "A Lovable France, an Unlovable Corsica," I recounted the fiasco inflicted on the Prime Minister when Bernard Bonnet, his choice of tough Prefect to rule the island after the murder of the prior Prefect, Claude Erignac, was himself jailed for allegedly having ordered the night-time arson of an illegal beach restaurant. Determined to solve the Corsican quandary once and for all, Jospin's lieutenants have been meeting regularly not only with elected Corsican officials but also with leading factions favoring independence or autonomy, some of whom have engaged in terrorist acts. As the negotiations approached their culmination, word leaked out that Jospin's team had proposed a number of major concessions to the Corsican dissidents. This included compulsory teaching of the so-called Corsican language, more tax derogations, to be sure, and granting a degree of legislative power to a new Corsican assembly, to wit, the power to adapt laws of Parliament to suit Corsican particularities.

This roused the ire of a key member of Jospin's government, the outspoken Jean-Paul Chevènement, who gave a surprising interview to *Le Monde* criticizing the proposal and indicating that the was prepared to resign over this issue. (He had resigned from Mitterrand's government in 1991 because of his opposition to French participation in the Gulf War.) Unperturbed, Jospin did not respond to this provocation but brought the negotiation to an end with some cosmetic changes in language and vague descriptions of the proposed new regime for Corsica. Keeping in mind that Corsica consists of two *départements* which are part of France, critics were quick to point out that other parts of France which have independence movements, particularly the Basque country, Brittany and the Savoy region, would be sure to claim similar rights. And as the Corsicans reached the negotiating table by committing murder and destruction, this arrangement seemed to be an open invitation to the others to follow the Corsican precedent.

To return to the subject of European integration, it is noteworthy that many commentators predict the demise of nation states in favor of regional components based on ethnic homogeneity. The Catalan area, for example, straddles both Spain and France, as does the Basque country. And the Bretons, being Gaelic, can claim kinship with the Irish. The irony of this vision is that far from uniting Europe in a common nationality the EU would end up Balkanizing it. The painful fact of life is that Corsica, for example, suffers from economic underdevelopment; its leading industry, tourism, can be helped more by teaching Corsican children English rather than the Corsican dialect, which is not much of a language.

As the main innovations of this proposal will not go into effect until after the 2002 election, Jospin is obviously hoping that he can hold his government together until then and not become too large a target for the opposition parties. If there is any issue that could bring on the downfall of Jospin's government the Corsican "solution" is surely it. Already, the most famous Corsican politician in mainland France, Charles Pasqua, has come out against the notion of giving legislative power to the Corsican assembly. This is in keeping with Pasqua's strong attachment to the Jacobin concept of a highly centralized France. Pasqua, once a staunch ally and co-founder of the RPR, bolted from that party because of his opposition to the Amsterdam Treaty, which he claimed diminished French sovereignty. He joined with another former RPR leader, Philippe de Villiers, to form a rival movement, called the *Rassemblement pour la France* (RPF) but they quickly became known as the *souverainistes.* From the standpoint of human chemistry this was an unlikely combination: Pasqua is a rough and tumble Corsican politician, who rose from the ranks as a *pastis* salesman, while Villiers is a Viscount from the heavily Catholic Vendée area on the Atlantic Coast, and an *ENArque* to boot. When they tried to organize a political party, which would have sponsored Pasqua to run for President in 2002, there was so much jockeying to place their minions in key positions in the provinces that they ended up squabbling in public, and recently the party died without a whimper.

One aspect of the Corsican negotiation that has not been mentioned in the latest press releases is the demand that will surely be made for a general amnesty of Corsican offenders, including those who murdered Prefect Erignac. Several of those who allegedly plotted this assassination are behind bars, but the one who is said to have pulled the trigger is in hiding. In the past, convicted Corsican terrorists have been benefited from early release, when French governments have sought to placate their followers, and so it is not at all unlikely that this will happen again, much to the indignation of those who believe in equal justice for all.

On this subject, it is edifying to consider the methods used in July by striking workers at the Celletex textile factory in the town of Civet, near the Belgian border. They poured 5,000 liters of sulfuric acid in the stream next to the plant, which is slated to close, and threatened even more dire actions. As a consequence, they got their way, obtaining a generous layoff indemnity and the guarantee of maintaining their wage level for two years. And, to be sure, the public prosecutor decided not to bring charges against the polluters. The negotiations were conducted by *l'Etat,* to be sure, not by the employers. My readers know by now that when it comes to negotiating, *l'Etat* means *les fons* (*les fonctionnaires*) and when it comes to paying, *l'Etat* means *les cons* (*les contribuables*, that is, the taxpayers).

Crime pays in France, because there is no politician with the courage to do what Ronald Reagan did when he fired the striking air-traffic controllers, that is, uphold the law. And he taught the American *fons* a lesson, to wit, that there is a limit to what the *cons* will accept. But Reagan, for all his faults, was not an *ENArque*.

Vol. XXII, N° 9, October 2000

Soon the Century Ends, and Good Riddance

As relativity is one of the discoveries of this century, I don't mind remarking that many, if not most, Americans have been brainwashed into believing that we are already in the 21st century, whereas most people in continental Europe believe and know otherwise. One US reader chided me recently for harping too much on the role of the *New York Times* and other media in propagating this false conception of chronology. While agreeing with me on the merits, he said (I paraphrase) that as a resident of Washington DC he is so inured to hype and government deception that he attaches little importance to this particular example. To explain my concern one last time, let me make the point that communication among peoples of different countries requires some consensus on basic concepts of time and place. Recently, I read a squib in an American paper about a medical discovery that was stated to be "one of the most important of the last century." As no dates were given and the context was thin, I was uncertain as to whether the writer was referring to the 19th century (which, today still, is for me the "last century") or to the 20th which, for the *New York Times,* deserves that honor.

The subject of lying naturally brings me to what is becoming a subject of pathological inquiry: the propensity of Al Gore to invent tales. I have taken to calling him "Fibber McGore," after the hero of the radio show that was popular in my youth, "Fibber McGee and Molly." It is disturbing to me that this "chronic liar," to use the term that F.D. Roosevelt once applied to the journalist Drew Pearson, has reached such a high station in American politics, but it surely is not an accident that he was chosen as running mate by the master liar that is Bill Clinton. However, Clinton's lies seem to be of a different type, mainly to cover up his peccadilloes. He never claimed, for example, that he invented the Internet. Gore seems to live in a dream world where fiction becomes fact if it helps to make a point. This may be the sign of a creative intelligence that could help him earn an honest living some day, say, in continuing the Harry Potter series, if the present author retires or expires.

This being said, I hasten to add that I am no admirer of that other character who would be President of the United States, George W. Bush, who calls the Greeks "Grecians" and, presumably, if he met a Martian one day, would call him a "Marsk." While I am not given to predictions, I find some delight in being able to affirm that whatever happens on November 7th, the first American President of the 21st century will be a genuine, certifiable dolt. Another thing Gore and Bush have in common, besides being *fils à papa,* is their salability to the rich. Some of my friends don't like my criticizing one of the candidates when they happen to think he is preferable to the other. The underlying assumption is a defensible one, to wit, that when both candidates are pretty bad, the business of the voter is to choose the lesser evil. With all due respect to my devoted readers who feel that way, I choose to disagree. I am mindful of a phrase I read years ago in a book by Harvard Law Professor Charles Fried to the effect that choosing the lesser evil is still choosing evil. To which I would add that, based on past experience as a voter, I do not feel either a duty or an ability to decide which of the two bad candidates is worse. I recall that in the 1964 campaign, Barry Goldwater was labeled a dangerous "extremist," yet his purportedly "moderate" opponent, Lyndon Johnson, deviously embroiled the USA in the disastrous Vietnam war. My friend, John Hess, the intrepid former *New York Times* reporter, once advised: "Vote for the loser, you're sure not to be disappointed." To be sure, a protest vote is possible in the forthcoming election by voting for Ralph Nader or Pat Buchanan, but most American voters like to feel they're choosing a winner. It has been said that the 20th century is "the American Century." If so, it began with a bang with the assassination of William McKinley and his replacement by the dynamic Theodore Roosevelt, and is ending in a whimper with the likes of Gore and Bush. Who knows, maybe the next century will belong to the "Grecians."

In France, perplexed or disgusted voters often go to the polls and "vote blank" (*voter blanc* being the French statement), that is, cast a blank ballot. These votes are not officially counted as being "expressed," much to the disgust of those who vote that way. In the recent referendum called by President Chirac to reduce the term of the presidential office from seven to five years, two-million people took the trouble to enter a voting booth and cast a blank ballot, while almost 70 percent of eligible voters simply stayed away. It is years since I have been in an American voting booth, but I gather that no mechanism exists there to vote for "none of the above," a possibility which seems restricted to so-called educational tests.

As I write this, the violence occurring in Israel and the occupied Palestine territories overshadows all local politics. I wish I had something original to say on the subject of Jerusalem, which was the spark that kindled the explosion. John Whitbeck, an American lawyer I met in Paris years ago, has proposed a bold solution, on which he has written extensively, to wit, joint sovereignty, under which both parties can claim that Jerusalem is their capital. I gather that Israel rejects this idea out of hand, while the Palestinians have shown some attraction to it. It remains a mystery to me why Barak allowed Sharon to put on a show of force on that esplanade which the Moslems consider sacred (and many Israelis, too). It is difficult for a non-Jew to make any comment on Israeli actions without running the risk of being accused of anti-Semitism. Years ago, when Menahim Begin was prime minister of Israel, I made that very point to a French Jew with whom I was having lunch, and asked this question: "If I told you that I saw Begin in the street and noted that his shoe-laces were untied, would you suspect me of anti-Semitism?" My friend thought a while and replied, "Probably."

France has been affected by the Middle East crisis in that several synagogues have been the target of attacks, including arson and other acts of vandalism. While no culprits have been arrested, to my knowledge, it seems likely that the persons responsible for these acts can be found among the six-million or so Moslems who live here, most of them originating in North Africa, once a stronghold of French colonialism. An article by Ivan Rioufol in *Le Figaro* of October 16th, makes the assertion that as the Moslem population of France doubles every 20 years, in 2060 they will not only number 50-million but also will constitute "two thirds of the French population"! Fortunately for the sleep of followers of Jean-Marie Le Pen, who probably do not read *Le Figaro*, this extraordinary prediction has gotten very little attention in the media. As I will not be around in the year 2060, I can only amuse myself by picturing Notre Dame de Paris transformed into a mosque, as were many Byzantine churches when the Turks conquered Constantinople, now called Istanbul. This wild prediction reminded me of Herman Kahn's best-seller of the 1970s, now mercifully out of print, called *Japan, the Emerging Superstate*. The fallacy of such predictions is the assumption that growth will continue at the same rate as in the past. When I read Kahn's book, I pointed out the fallacy to a friend, telling him it is like saying, "If my son continues to grow at the same rate, he'll be 26 feet tall in 2010."

It is common knowledge that the Israeli government is concerned about the relatively high birth rate of its Arab population, now constituting about 20 percent of its population. The dominant majority in any country usually worry about maintaining the homogeneity of its population but the problem is thorny when the minority have as much right to be there as the majority (*cf.* American "Indians" and blacks). As to immigration, it is welcomed to a certain extent in the expectation that newcomers will be "assimilated." France has done a good job in absorbing various types of immigrants, particularly those from other Latin countries, such as Italy, Portugal and Spain, who easily become French in a generation, if they choose to remain here. But Moslem immigrants are generally more recalcitrant to assimilation because of the differences in religion, language and culture. Ironically, French leaders were quick to stigmatize Austria when its new government made a coalition with Haidar's party, which has been concerned about Moslem immigration. France's "caviar Left," as it is called here, is reluctant to admit publicly that a disproportionate number of North Africans are responsible for most of the crime in this country. One is not supposed to notice a person's race or color unless one has something good to say about him. But such lofty sentiments lead to "political correctness" and stifle public discussion of real problems, which often have something to do with the poverty and mistreatment of immigrants and minorities.

Fortunately for Jacques Chirac, the Middle East crisis has tended to marginalize the scandal that erupted late last month when *Le Monde* published (and displayed on its web site) excerpts from a "confession" taped in 1996 by Jean-Claude Méry, a professional "bag man" for Chirac's party, the RPR. Among other revelations, Méry, who died of cancer last year, stated that he solicited payoffs from contractors dealing with the city of Paris, whose mayor was Chirac, and, in 1986, when Chirac was also Prime Minister, handed five-million francs to his cabinet director in Chirac's presence. At first, Chirac's spokesmen denounced the tape as a fake and a "manipulation" but later this line was abandoned when the independent producer who filmed it in presence of Méry's lawyer vouched for its authenticity.

Unexpectedly, a day later, the heat was taken off Chirac and placed on Dominique Strauss-Kahn, because the lawyer (who had worked for him) disclosed that he had given him the original tape last year when he was negotiating with the Socialist Finance Minister a reduction in the tax assessment of another client, none other than the famous *couturier*, Karl Lagerfeld. The inference was inescapable that the lawyer was trading juicy information that could be used for political advantage by the Socialists, in exchange for a tax favor to another client. Strauss-Kahn, who is already facing criminal charges over a fee he received from a student-insurance company close to the Socialist party, admitted receiving the tape but claimed that he had never viewed it, and could not remember what he did with it! Not many observers are buying that story, and Jospin is now almost as embarrassed about the tape as Chirac is, particularly since Méry claims on it that he gave money to the Socialist Party when it was headed by Jospin.

Shortly after the scandal erupted, Patrick Devedjian, official spokesman for Chirac's RPR, sent up a trial balloon, suggesting that another amnesty law be enacted to put an end the numerous "affairs" involving party financing. In 1990, the Socialist-controlled parliament enacted such a law to protect politicians against prosecution except where "personal enrichment" was involved. If you shake down a contractor on a municipal project for the good of the party, that is all right, but if you deduct a five-percent commission for yourself, that alone is heinous. But what if the party rewards you with a government post, paid for by the taxpayers? Isn't this personal enrichment? And what if the contractor overcharged the taxpayers and did a shoddy job? The excuse for the amnesty was that the same law provided for public financing of political parties, in proportion to their electoral success. This supposedly was to do away with illicit financing, but as politicians never feel they have enough money, the illegal practices continue.

At any rate, Devedjian's trial balloon was quickly shot down by Socialist spokesmen and it became apparent that an amnesty was not politically acceptable. Although the courts have ruled that the President is immune from prosecution while in office, except before the High Court of Justice, voices have been heard to suggest that there is nothing preventing an Investigating Magistrate (*Juge d'Instruction*) from calling Chirac merely as a witness. Others have been saying that Chirac should "explain himself" to the public about the allegations on the tape. There can be little doubt that during Chirac's 18-year tenure as the first elected Mayor of Paris, his party utilized the resources of City Hall to finance itself, including placing party officials on the city's payroll and accepting payoffs from contractors for housing projects and other city works. It is impossible to believe that Chirac was unaware of this, just at it is impossible to believe that Jospin was unaware of how the Socialist Party was financed when he was its top official. So far, only underlings have been prosecuted for these doings: Alain Juppé, who was Chirac's right-hand man at the City Hall, while also serving as a minister, is to be tried for the payroll-padding; and in the case of the Socialists, Henri Emmanuelli, the party's treasurer, took the rap and was punished with two years' ineligibility to hold public office.

It is amusing to compare the differing techniques used by the two major parties. During Mitterrand's reign, the Socialists, borrowing from their comrades, the Communists, created "consulting companies" (called *bureaux d'études*) which received commissions from contractors. The money then was used to cover party expenses, such as printing posters, paying party workers and so on. Chirac's RPR seems to have preferred the good old cash-in-a-paper-bag method, placing the burden on contractors to find a way to account for cash taken out of the company's accounts. Just last month, Louise-Yvonne Cassetta, considered the unofficial treasurer of the RPR party, was tried on charges of having received bundles of cash from grateful contractors. A foreign reader might wonder what a political party does with all that cash. I am obviously not an expert on the subject, but I have been around long enough to guess what parties do with cash. For one thing, it is used to pay volunteer campaign workers who have other jobs and have little incentive to work for the party if they must pay taxes on their earnings. For another, cash comes in handy if you want to persuade an unwelcome candidate not to run against a party nominee. It also is useful in paying off journalists and publishers to back your party, or in hiring private eyes to get compromising information about rival candidates. And, of course, it pays for transportation and lodging during campaigns, and perhaps a new coat for the candidate's wife. One thing it is not used for in France is TV advertising for, unlike the USA, France prohibits paid political commercials. For presidential campaigns, candidates get free time on the government-owned TV stations.

While the next Presidential election in France is slated for May 2002, it is already clear that the main contenders will be the two *ENArques* now leading France – Chirac and Jospin – despite repercussions from the political-financing scandals. Thus, the new Millennium in France will continue to give credence to Alphonse Karr's brilliant maxim: *"Plus ça change plus c'est la même chose."* To which I add, "and the same people."

Vol. XXII, N° 10, November 2000

"Lucky Jews, Lucky Arabs"

It was while playing Bach on my piano one morning last month that this title came to me, in the height of the violence in and about Palestine, or the occupied territories, call it what you will. Since the beginning of the crisis I have been inundated with Email from Jewish sources explaining that the Arabs calling themselves Palestinians are to blame for the crisis, that parents send their children to the barricades so that they can become martyrs, that there was never a Palestinian homeland in the past, that only Jews have a historical claim to the Holy Land, that Sharon had every right to visit the Temple Mount, sacred to the Jews, that Arafat is not a democrat and can not be trusted, and so on. The very few Arab readers that I have do not seem to want to influence me, but the newspapers and TV present, from time to time, the point of view of the Palestinians, to wit, that Sharon, accompanied by a thousand soldiers, profaned the "third holiest site of Islam" in order to disrupt the "peace process," that Israeli armed forces used "excessive force," that Jewish settlements in occupied territories are an attempt to deprive the Palestinians of their rightful territory, and so on.

Why do I call the Jews and the Arabs "lucky" despite all this? Because most people on each side seem to be worried only about their own victims. But what about the rest of us, those who are neither Arabs nor Jews, and who worry about the victims on both sides? We are the unlucky ones, because we weep for the little boy crouched besides his father frantically trying to avoid the bullets that will soon kill him, and we weep for the two Israeli soldiers who got lost and ended up in a Palestinian town where they were savagely lynched. Many a Jew can apparently refrain from pitying the Arab boy by blaming his father for bringing him to a battle zone, and many an Arab can apparently feel no pain for the two lynched Israeli soldiers by blaming Sharon for the provocation. We who are in neither camp but rather in that amorphous category once known as "lovers of humanity" (a term hardly heard these days) get no solace from such ratiocinations. Do I feel any less sorry for the little boy because his father was stupid enough (if that's the case, for one version is that he went out to buy a used car) to take him into a battle zone? And am I to say "well deserved, learn to read a map" about the two hapless Israeli soldiers who were not harming anyone when they met their horrible end?

No, the hardest thing these days is to partake of humanist ideals and thus to be among those who do not hate either Arabs or Jews and want justice to prevail in the Middle East. There do not seem to be many people worrying about informing us objectively of the facts in this unfortunate part of the world and hardly any "neutral" observers seeking to guide us to a perception of what might be a just solution to a conflict between two Semitic peoples. Indeed, I wonder if it is possible for anyone to be truly "neutral" in a conflict of this type. What are the criteria by which one may appraise the "neutrality" of an outsider? Must he be so far removed from the scene, both geographically and culturally, that he is exempt from prejudices or attitudes that will deprive him of complete objectivity? Must he, for example, be Chinese or Japanese, and indifferent to both Judaism and Islam? Yet, even such a person would have a value system that might cause him to "tilt" in favor of one or the other.

As for myself, I have been examining my own attitudes in an attempt to reach as detached a view of the justice of the situation in the territories that were once called "the Holy Land." Let me start with a major insight that hit me when I visited Egypt in January 1981 and took a glorious boat ride on the Nile from Luxor to Aswan, stopping every morning to explore a temple or two that were remnants of a civilization that goes back 5,000 years, that is, 3,000 years before the Christian era. It was clear that the ancient Egyptians were superb architects and builders, excelling in engineering and science, and were also great artists, as the treasures of the Cairo Museum prove. Compared with the Egyptians, the ancient Hebrews have left nothing tangible worth speaking of, except for a Wailing Wall. So what was the insight? When it came to religion and written language, the Egyptians made a mystery of things, their hieroglyphic inscriptions being a secret language of the priest caste, with the result that the common people were excluded from their own history. The Jews, by contrast, told the story of their own tribes, beginning, to be sure, with fanciful accounts of creation but reaching into the relatively recent history of the first millennium BC, and told it in understandable language. The saga of the Jews was interspersed with moralizing and law giving; yet the authors did not try to cover up evidence of sin and crime, even in the highest circles of society. When Jesus, a dissident Jew but a Jew nonetheless, came along, his story was told by other Jews, and the success of Christianity in the Roman and the Greek worlds ensured that Jewish history would become universal history, at least to the West of Asia and to the North of Africa.

That was the insight: by making their story available to their own people and using that story to preach a moral code, the Jews gave to humanity a priceless gift that was far more valuable than all the pyramids, temples and treasures of Ancient Egypt put together. For centuries their book, the Bible, was the only book in town, so to speak. The Armenians are also an ancient people, their roots going back 3,000 years, almost as long as the Jews. Yet the Armenians left no written record of their history before their conversion to Christianity in the year 301, when they foolishly destroyed whatever pagan artifacts they had. And by making the first vernacular translation of the Bible a century later, the Armenians incorporated Jewish history into their own tradition. Unlike other ancient peoples who left, to use Yeats' words, "monuments of their own magnificence," the Jews, by unsparingly telling the story of their own transgressions, willingly presented themselves as anti-heroes, constantly failing to live up to the high standards their noblest prophets had set for them. Instead of showing gratitude for this incomparable legacy of honesty and humility, the Christian world alternately shunned and persecuted the Jews for well nigh two-thousand years.

The inspiration for Theodor Herzl to begin a movement for a Jewish Homeland was his witnessing the horrible ceremony in the parade ground of the Ecole Militaire in Paris when Alfred Dreyfus was stripped of his Captain's insignia and made to parade before an ugly crowd that was shouting "Death to the Jews." Herzl saw that it did no good for a Jew to convince himself that he was assimilated into the mainstream of his country, if others saw him as different enough to be a natural candidate for treason. This was in 1895, when Palestine was part of the vast Ottoman Empire, which encompassed most of the Arab world in the Middle East and North Africa. Herzl actually went to Istanbul to try to convince the Caliph to make land available for a Jewish homeland, but never got to first base. Later the British government floated an amazing proposal to settle the Jews in Uganda, of all places, and it is a sign of Jewish desperation that some Jews took this idea seriously! On November 2, 1917, Lord Balfour, head of the British Foreign Office, wrote a letter to Lord Rothschild, which become known as the "Balfour Declaration." Its key sentence is this:

> *"His Majesty's Government view with favour the establishment in Palestine of a national home for the Jewish people, and will use their best endeavours to facilitate the achievement of this object, it being clearly understood that nothing shall be done which may prejudice the civil and religious rights of existing non-Jewish communities in Palestine, or the rights and political status enjoyed by Jews in any other country."*

When the Ottoman Empire was dismantled after its defeat in World War I, the British took over the governing of Palestine under a mandate granted by the League of Nations. This made it easier to prepare the way for a Jewish homeland, but already the Arabs of Palestine resisted every effort of the British to instill cooperation between Arabs and Jews in view of a joint state. Immigration of Jews to Palestine and the purchase of land became fighting issues, even then. In less than a quarter century Europe was again engulfed in a frightful war, which allowed the mad leaders of a country whose Jews were the world's most assimilated to prove Herzl right in his pessimistic appraisal of the Jew's future in Europe. And only a few years after the extermination of most of Europe's Jews, Herzl's dream was realized by the creation of Israel. Whereas Herzl hoped that this homeland would be created by a political process, without bloodshed, and the British partition plan for Palestine, endorsed by the UN General Assembly, might have been such a process had the Arab states accepted it, the fact is that it was only by military force that Israel upheld its right to statehood. And it is only by military force that Israel has maintained its independence against Arab onslaughts, greatly abetted by the United States, with whom Israel has close ties.

The irony of all this deserves attention. A French friend recently observed to me that to understand the situation in what was Palestine one must realize that the Jews of Israel have become the Romans of the Middle East, and that their brother Semites in the occupied territories are closer to what the Jews once were, a bedraggled, powerless people chasing after an identity. By this quixotic logic, today's anti-Semites are the Israelis themselves. And isn't it interesting that while Herzl's inspiration was seeing an innocent Jew wrongly convicted of espionage, the state that resulted from his dream, like all states, has genuine spies and genuine criminals? When I recently saw filmed scenes of Israeli helicopters sweeping down on Palestinian towns, firing highly sophisticated missiles at pin-pointed targets, I thought of the motion picture *Apocalypse Now;* all that was lacking was Wagner's music – "The Ride of the Valkyries" – rigorously banished from Israeli concert halls because of that composer's anti-Semitism. And isn't it ironic that the stone thrower is no longer David but a youngster named Mohammed, while Goliath is a tank?

While I personally am wholly in favor of Israel as a Jewish homeland, and admire its many accomplishments, it is more important to say that the lesson I have learned from a study of history is that rights are generally established by might. Conquerors, not the conquered, make the laws and write the history books. When William the Bastard defeated King Harold at Hastings, his status not only rose from Bastard to Conqueror, but also he set up a legal and military system that protected his hold on the territory of England. The United States established much of its territorial expansion by trampling over the Indian tribes, who themselves were the first to be aware that only weapons and courage establish rights to land. When Great Britain was developing for internal use the sublime concepts of due process of law and parliamentary democracy, its navy and army were ruthlessly subjugating other peoples in Asia and Africa. And who remembers that all of Turkey today was once Greek and Armenian kingdoms, which fell to the invading hordes from Asia? Justice Holmes, in his letters to Pollack and Laski, scoffed at the notion of "natural law" and "the rights of man." He would relate that he heard of a town in Bavaria where the population would revolt if the price of beer went up by one pfennig. If so, he concluded, then the price of beer at the established price is one of the rights of man, provided, I would add, that the revolt succeeds. Nonetheless, exceptional leaders with vision and spirituality, like Ghandi and Martin Luther King, have demonstrated that rights can be established by non-violent means as well. If I were a Palestinian I would prefer such leaders to one who never takes off his military garb.

Israel's valid right to statehood has had to be vindicated by force and those who contested its right to be there have, fortunately, lacked the force to evict it. Many thousands of Arabs, now known as Palestinians, fled or were driven out of their homes in the process and became the "wandering Jews" of the Middle East. In 1967, Israel occupied more territory, in particular, East Jerusalem and the Golan Heights, by the force of conquest. Today, according to Thomas Friedman of the *New York Times,* who can hardly be accused of anti-Semitism, Israel is continuing to confiscate Arab land to make way for Jewish settlements in occupied territories. Superior force is the only lawgiver that many Israeli leaders seem to believe in at the present time. And why should they believe otherwise, since it is the central lesson to be learned from history? My answer to that question is that Jews, more than any others, should know that humiliated people do not willingly march to the negotiating table.

Some of my Jewish friends seem genuinely to be hurt and even surprised that so many Arabs of Palestine hate the Israelis, and they claim that the Western press is unfair to Israel in reporting the violent scenes taking place in that region. Is there any better way to respond to these friends than to point to the words of Hillel who, when asked by a pagan to sum up Judaism in a single phrase, replied: "What is hateful to you, do not unto your neighbor." The key words in this sentence are "hateful" and "neighbor." If a Jew would find it hateful to have his land confiscated to allow others to settle there, then his code of conduct should forbid him to do that to his "neighbor." So then the question becomes to define "neighbor." If all it means is the Jew next door, then Hillel's teaching does not prevent an Israeli from using force to seize land from an Arab in the next village. If "neighbor" is defined in an extended sense, then it does. And moreover, Leviticus would require him to love that very neighbor. Alas, for most of us, whether Christian, Moslem or Jew, "neighbor" has a narrow sense, and it will be that way for a long, long time, despite the efforts of a minority to extend its scope.

Of course, some Israelis might go further and point out that they are not bound by the teachings of Leviticus and Hillel, for not all Israelis are believers. Many of the early settlers, particularly among the Kibbutzim, were atheists, more influenced by European utopian socialists than by the Torah. On my first trip to Israel in June 1973 I visited such a kibbutz, near Haifa, established by Jews from Eastern Europe, and I happened to be there the evening when they celebrated a secular coming-of-age ceremony in lieu of the religious *bar mitzvah* and *bat mitzvah.* These kibbutzim were nonetheless patriotic Israelis and provided many soldiers in Israel's wars. Yet it is apparently not these kibbutzim who are the most rabid settlers on Arab lands but rather those who profess to be religious and believe that the Bible, aided by conquest, gives them title to the ancient provinces of Israel. Of course, fanatics see no ironies anywhere but the rest of us might consider it ironic that at a time when legal actions are being brought in the United States and France to recover Jewish property confiscated by the Nazis and the Vichy regime, comparable arbitrary actions have been committed against the Arabs by the Israeli state and are still continuing, under the benign eyes of the US government.

André Malraux, a professional pontificator, is oft quoted as saying that "the 21st century will be religious or will not be." I believe he was wrong on both counts. The 21st century will surely come and it will not be any more religious than the 20th; only one principle will prevail: might makes right. One can only pray, nonetheless, that the mighty will lean towards righteousness from time to time, for surely the truly righteous will never be mighty.

Vol. XXII, N° 12, December 2000

Christmas Issue: Bach the Healer

If I needed an excuse to write now about Johann Sebastian Bach, the easiest one is to remind my readers that the year 2000 marked the 250th anniversary of his death, which occurred on July 28, 1750. Another reason would be to nominate him as the greatest composer of the millennium that is about to end. A third, in an age of anxiety and stress, would be to urge the use of Bach's music as a form of therapy, hence my title. I do hope that this essay will encourage readers who are not familiar with Bach's music to listen, as a starter, to the pieces that I will mention below, and even to take up playing the piano or another instrument, for it is never too late to come into direct tactile contact with Bach.

Music and Me: Of course, you could not have expected to get a heavy dose of Bach in this essay without a substantial dose of Kevorkian, so we might as well begin with my own involvement with music. In the Andrew Hamilton Elementary School in West Philadelphia, we did much singing, starting in the first grade. I have been blessed with a good memory of melodies, and I can still remember the tune of a haunting song we sang in Miss Elizabeth Church's first grade, whose words began with "The leaves had a party one autumn day." In later grades we learned the rudiments of musical notation, beginning with the treble clef and base clef. I still recall the mnemonic device that the teacher taught us to remember the letters which indicate the lines and spaces of each clef. The treble lines were "Every Good Boy Does Fine"; the treble spaces were "FACE"; the base lines were "Good Boys Do Fine Always"; the base spaces were "All Cows Eat Grass." So, if you did not learn the same thing in your school, you at least are getting free musical pedagogy from me. (Note that in France they do not use letters, but rather do, re, mi, fa, sol, la, si – the "do" corresponding to C.) When I was eight or nine, my mother forced me to take piano lessons from an earnest Armenian named Elijah Yardumian, in exchange for a small ad he placed in my father's Armenian weekly newspaper. I never got further than playing Ol' Black Joe by Stephen Foster, because my mother, a proud and irascible woman if ever there was one, insisted on my being placed in the middle of the front row for the photograph of Elijah's pupils at the second annual recital. As he had put me at the end of the row, where I belonged, and refused to change it, my mother pulled me away in a huff, and not only was I not immortalized in that photo but also, much to my delight, there ended my piano education, which I had concealed from my buddies on Sansom Street, whose simple view was that only sissies took piano lessons.

One summer evening, when I was 14, I glued my ears to the archaic Atwater Kent vacuum-tube radio in our parlor and heard a mellifluous tenor voice singing the most marvelous melody that had ever entered my ears. It was love at first sound, lightning striking. At the end, the announcer identified the music as Schubert's *Serenade*. The next morning, still haunted by the melody, I searched in a trunk where my mother kept the musical pieces that she had brought with her from Marseilles. Luckily, in a large volume of standard classics I found Schubert's *Serenade*, but the music appeared daunting. I had never played anything so difficult, particularly in the left-hand accompaniment. Here, now, comes a necessary disquisition on the benefits of poverty. In the summertime, my brother Andy and I were alone, as all are buddies went to summer camp for two months. My proud mother claimed that the reason we, too, did not go to camp was that she had learned that the food they ate there came out of "tin cans," as we called canned goods in those days. But the real reason, we knew, is that we could not afford the $250 that it would have cost for each of us to spend the summer in the healthy air of the Poconos. So I had all summer to teach myself to play Schubert's *Serenade* while my buddies were learning to swim, row, ride horses and talk about sex. There were many discouraging moments when it seemed impossible for me to coordinate the two hands, but by the end of the summer – hot and unbearably humid as Philadelphia summers were in the days before air conditioning – I had mastered this lovely music, and began to tackle other pieces in the big book. From that experience I learned that enthusiasm is the best teacher.

Another disquisition is timely here, on the benefits of radio and luck. Our hoary vacuum-tube radio was issuing its dying gasps when my mother got lucky and won a small $9.95 radio in a church raffle. That radio, primitive as it was – FM had not been invented – was the source of my musical education for years, since we had no phonograph (as it was called then). Luckily, as disk jockeys had not yet invaded the airwaves, radio featured a lot of serious music. WDAS had a Morning Musical Hour and an Evening Musical Hour, which I listened to with fervor. Every Monday evening, on prime time, there was the Firestone Hour with Richard Crooks, the lyric tenor who sang operatic arias and songs by the great composers. Sunday night brought me the Celanese Hour, with another great tenor, Jan Peerce, who became a star at the Metropolitan Opera. And, speaking of opera, every Saturday afternoon I would listen to Texaco's presentation of opera at the Met, with the inimitable Milton Cross as the commentator. Thanks to Texaco, I heard virtually all of the great singers of the '40s, such as Lily Pons, the coloratura, whose Mad Scene from Donizetti's *Lucia de Lammermoor* would make Milton Cross weep; Licia Albanese and Bidu Sayao, each an unforgettable Mimi in *La Boheme*; Jussi Björling, the Swedish tenor, who became my favorite Cavaradossi (*La Tosca*); Ezio Pinza, the bass, in *Don Giovanni*; Helen Traubel, the Wagnerian soprano and Lauritz Melchior, the *Heldentenor*, her constant companion for *Tristan und Isolde*. I could go on for pages, but the point I'm coming to is that Bach was absent from my world, which was that of opera and romantic music. I also loved a type of music that has disappeared from our hearing: operetta, as it was called. My favorite operetta composers were Sigmund Romberg (*The Student Prince*), Victor Herbert (*Naughty Marietta*) and Rudolph Friml (*The Chocolate Soldier*).

The turning point came at age 17 when I became friendly with one of my classmates at West Philadelphia High School, Maurice Fraser, who had taken up the harmonica, emulating the great virtuoso, Larry Adler, the first to play the classics on that modest instrument. Maury asked me to accompany him on the piano; we would practice together after class was over, first tackling Sarasate's *Gypsy Airs.* One day, I walked Maury home, and he asked me to step in to listen to music on his phonograph. He played a Bach choral work that I listened to politely, not really "getting" it, since it was too massive for me to appreciate at a first hearing. Fortunately, I walked Maury home the following day and he again played this work, which then hit me right between the eyes. It was Bach's *B-Minor Mass*, in a version by the Robert Shaw Chorale, on the 78-rpm vinyl disks of that time. The opening *Kyrie Eleison* was the most stirring music I had ever heard. In the ensuing days I discovered the splendor of this entire work. Later, Maurice Fraser played for me a record of harpsichord music, an instrument that was new to me. The performer was none other than the great Wanda Landowska. One piece she played particularly appealed to me: it was the *Allemande* from the *sixth French Suite.* I went to the Free Library on Benjamin Franklin Parkway, borrowed the score, and learned to play it, the first Bach composition in my repertoire. (It is to this piece that I owe my friendship to the late Howard Goldfarb, as described in my Newsletter of April, 1999.) Later, Maurice acquired Landowska's recordings of the *Goldberg Variations* and the *Well-Tempered Clavier*, incredible discoveries that convinced me that Bach was meant for me. Indeed, Bach reached so deeply into my soul that I couldn't help wondering what it was about his music that affected me so profoundly. My parents – both Armenians from "the old country," as we used to say – had never listened to Bach. My genes came from a long line of Armenians. Could the first Bach have been Armenian? As this did not seem likely, I concluded that there was something universal about Bach's music and that my soul had universal aspirations. When I learned, more recently, that the first Bach came from Hungary to Germany in the 16th century, I amused myself with the fantasy that an earlier Bach (Bachian?) had emigrated from Armenia to Hungary, when the Armenian kingdom fell to the invading Turks. Would Yo Yo Ma believe the first Bach was Chinese?

By now, I hope my readers will have understood why this newsletter on Bach is so personal. For one thing, I have an enormous debt to Maurice Fraser for having introduced me to Bach, and I feel that the only way to repay the debt is to introduce Bach to others. For another, this passion for Bach leads to self-analysis. Why does he mean so much to me? Is it in the genes? All my sons are Bach-lovers, but regretfully not my wife or my daughters, which leads me occasionally to the heretical question, for which I ask forgiveness even before uttering it, to wit, is it possible that Bach appeals more, statistically, to the masculine psyche than to the female? My wife says that "*Bach est mathématique*." She senses his music as mathematical whereas I perceive Bach as a romantic and a lover, another heretical thought, no doubt, considering that musicologists steadfastly place Bach in the so-called "Baroque" period, whereas Romanticism in music supposedly arrived in the 19th century. I hate the term "Baroque" in music and, in particular, when applied to J.S. Bach. It's a meaningless label, and I would urge my readers to pay no attention to it. Bach's music is flourishing today all over the world because its beauty is timeless, as well as universal. It will never be dated, so long as the human ear and the human brain, and the emotions they engender, remain what they are.

Bach's Music: When I discovered Bach at 17, I knew nothing of musical concepts such as counterpoint, harmony and modulation, an understanding of which is not necessary to appreciate Bach's compositions. Rather, they are useful after the fact, if you want to know why you like the music. If a single musical term should be identified with Bach, it is "counterpoint" which, according to one dictionary definition, means "the combination of two or more independent melodies into a single harmonic texture in which each retains its linear character." I like this definition because it contains the word "harmonic" and thus shows the relationship between counterpoint and harmony, the latter having to do with notes sounding well when played simultaneously, *i.e.,* in what is known as a chord. Thus, if you're looking at a printed page of music, harmony is vertical, or instantaneous, while counterpoint is horizontal, or linear, as the definition indicates. Harmony can exist without counterpoint, but not vice-versa.

Bach's ultimate quest was to combine voices, anywhere from two to six, so that they would sound well together. I am deliberating stating this in a prosaic, non-exalted, manner, to stress that Bach started out as a craftsman who learned his craft the same way as thousands of other musicians in Germany and elsewhere. What raised him above all other composers of his time was turning his craft into a passionate pursuit to find the best combination of voices that his brain could conceive at any given time. He would never give up the quest. Even when he had made a lovely four-part ("part" is synonymous with "voice") arrangement of a hymn, he would often return to it over and over again and concoct other variants. (He did six versions of *Jesu Meine Freunde.*) Yet the basic objective was the same, making each voice interesting and making the combination sound beautiful together, which required being conscious of the harmonic cohabitation of the voices. A Bach remark that has survived is that his counterpoint is merely conversation. If you hear and enjoy the conversation, you've become a Bach lover.

This brings me to modulation, which, in music, is what separates the men from the boys. Modulation simply means moving from one key to another in the same composition. If you change keys abruptly, particularly if you move to an unrelated key, it is jarring to the ear. In Bach's time, the change had to be done artfully, so that the ear would not be offended but rather gratified. Again, you do not need to know this to enjoy Bach's music, but it will help to explain why you enjoy it. To give an example, I always loved the opening chorus of what many people, including myself, consider Bach's greatest work, the *St. Matthew Passion,* but I didn't know why I loved it until I realized that starting out in a minor key Bach swiftly switches to the major key in the same bar! Minor is sad, major is happy. Had Bach stayed in minor, as countless composers would have done, the music would have been acceptable. Modulating so quickly makes the music glorious. All the great composers of the Western World, such as Mozart, Beethoven, Chopin, and Verdi, to name but a few, were masters of modulation, because they knew that this is what makes their music interesting, even to the untrained ear. There is a scene in the film version of "*Amadeus*"where Mozart takes a banal composition of Salieri and "jazzes" it up, with a heavy dose of modulation, leaving Salieri bewildered. Unfortunately, this can not be taught: that's why the great composers, like great couturiers, are so rare.

From my readings of Bach's life, I deduce that the decisive event which allowed Bach to make the quantum leap from craftsman to creator was his walking 250 miles from Arnstadt, where he was the church organist, to Lübeck to listen to Dieterich Buxtehude, the Danish organist, perform his own compositions. Bach was only 20 and needed a role model to liberate himself from the stern Germanic notion that music was simply following rules. Bach had taken a month's leave to make this trip but he stayed four months in Lübeck, wallowing in Buxtehude's fresh and innovative approach to organ playing and composition. His creativity was also stimulated by French (*e.g.,* Couperin) and Italian (e.g., Vivaldi) models, as evidenced by compositions such as the *French Suites* and his *Italian Concerto.* Yet, what is amazing about Bach is that while the German in him liberated his spirit by absorbing the mellifluous, sprightly style of the Latin countries, he did not let this lower his standards and deter him from his ultimate quest to produce musical beauty through counterpoint. As a result, he became a superannuated man in his own lifetime, insisting on composing polyphonic music (another term for voices being heard contrapuntally) while the more stylish composers, including his own sons, were developing a simpler, "more pleasing" style.

But let's continue with the *genus* counterpoint and Bach's two favorite species of it: canons and fugues. When someone asked Dr. Johnson to define terms during an argument, he said, in effect, "Nonsense, we all know what light is, even if we can't define it." In the same way, everyone knows what a canon is without defining it. One need only think of *Frère Jacques* or *Row, row, row your boat.* It's someone starting out singing a tune, and another joining in later, with the same tune, while the first continues on his merry way. Even assuming the two have good voices, the canon will not sound good if the staggered tunes do not fit well together harmonically. Bach developed to the highest point the art of finding tunes that fit well together, sometimes even when they were played upside down, so to speak. My favorite piece in Bach's supreme tribute to counterpoint, *The Art of the Fugue*, is an inverted canon, that is, wherever the first voice goes up, the second one goes down, and vice-versa, but follows the first one exactly, finishing the way the first voice began. It's so sublime that when I first heard it I did not even notice that it was a canon, let alone an inverted one. That's the ultimate in art: to create content that makes one overlook form. If you hear someone reciting Keats' *Bright star, would I were as steadfast as thou art,* the content is so breathtaking that you might not notice it is a sonnet of 14 lines with a given rhyme scheme. Who worries about rhyme when he hears "Pillowed upon my fair love's ripening breast, To feel forever its soft swell and fall, Awake forever in a sweet unrest, Still, still to hear her tender-taken breath…"?

Bach's superb keyboard composition, formally called *An Aria with Thirty Variations,* but universally known as the *Goldberg Variations* (after Johann Gottlieb Goldberg, who first performed it for his master, Bach's patron, Count von Keyserling, who paid for it) features nine canons, each on a different interval, that is, in the first canon the second voice comes in on the same note as the first voice, and in each successive canon the second voice jumps an interval, while two of them are inverted, and all but the ninth one have a third voice in the left hand, just to show that Bach gave von Keyserling his money's worth. Playing some of these canons and other variations, including the sublime 25th, in minor key, is one of the great joys of my life. In fact, they are the surest cure I know of for depression. I used to call the *Goldberg* "my Valium"; now, keeping up with the times, I call them "my Prozac." While my piano technique is very limited, one talent (perhaps "need" is a better term) I have is the ability to learn by heart the pieces that I love. Thus I play them with my eyes closed and have a sense of communion with Bach. His counterpoint lends itself to playing with the eyes shut, since the voices generally do not hop around. By contrast, when you play, for example, Chopin's *Nocturne in E-flat,* where the left hand jumps an octave or more to accompany the melody in the right hand (I call this "ump ba ba" music), you have to look at your hands, or risk playing the wrong notes. If you don't know the *Goldberg Variations,* drop everything, including this newsletter, and go out and buy a CD. Glenn Gould's piano version is the best known, but I prefer the recent recording of Murray Perahia, and one sent to me by a gifted pianist who deserves to be better known, Craig Sheppard, as well as the harpsichord version of Ralph Kirkpatrick. To be sure, if you can find a Landowska recording grab it! Joel Spiegelman has done an audacious digital version and Uri Caine a brilliant jazz rendition. All this demonstrates the universality of this unique music.

Fugues, an even more sophisticated form of counterpoint, are the *ne plus ultra* of Bach's keyboard music, including his organ compositions. In his youth, while serving Prince Leopold at Cöthen, Bach wrote the first book of the *Well-Tempered Clavier* (WTC), consisting of a prelude and a fugue on each of the 24 major and minor keys, starting with C-major and moving up the scale. Later, while in his last job at Leipzig, he did a second series of 24 preludes and fugues, which some music-lovers commit the heresy of considering even better than the first, as though one could improve on perfection. Most fugues have three to five voices. The first voice presents the theme and the others takes up the theme but at a different interval; the second voice starts a fifth above, or a fourth below the first voice, which then does something else. If you are new to fugues, you may be beginning to get a glimmer of the art it takes, first to find a suitable theme, and then to make several voices sound well together as the theme is repeated over and over again. To me, there is a magic about fugues. When I play one of my favorite fugues, such as the 8th, in E-flat minor, of the first book of the WTC (which was Wagner's favorite fugue), I have a feeling of eternity. It seems like it was never meant to end, like making love. What is it about a fugue that does this? Well, you won't find the answer in this free-of-charge newsletter!

Mozart, who was born six years after Bach's death, was more influenced by Carl Philipp Emanuel Bach (who did not like counterpoint) than by his father. However, late in his short life, Mozart visited St. Thomas Church in Leipzig in 1787 and listened to the choir rehearsing a motet. He was so startled by the originality of the counterpoint that he cried out, "What is this?" Then he went up to the Church library and studied Bach's score with the parts spread out on the floor, saying that "I'm finally learning something new." One can detect traces of this new education in Mozart's *Requiem.* Beethoven first made his fame, while an adolescent, playing the *Well-Tempered Clavier* in public, but in his youthful compositions he emulated Emanuel Bach, Haydn and Mozart rather than J.S. Bach, who was, as indicated above, out of style and most of his works unpublished and unknown. It was only in his late years that Beethoven rediscovered the fugue and wrote some amazing ones, including in the *Opus 110 Piano Sonata,* the original last movement of the *13th String Quartet* (which he later published as a separate work) and the opening movement of the *14th String Quartet*, my own favorite quartet.

Bach's Life: For composers of an earlier time, Bach lived longer than most, reaching the age of 65, whereas Beethoven died at 57, Mozart at 36, and poor Schubert only 31. Bach was born on March 21, 1685 (a fateful year that saw the birth of Handel and Domenico Scarlatti). His birthplace was Eisenach in Thuringia and he spent his entire life in the same general area of Germany, dying in Leipzig, in Saxony, where he worked for 27 years as Cantor of St. Thomas Church and composed the bulk of his Cantatas, the *St. Matthew Passion* and *St. John Passion* (and two others whose scores have been lost), the *Goldberg Variations*, the marvelous *Double Violin Concerto*, the *Art of the Fugue* and the *Musical Offering* and other works.

The problem with Bach is that his work dwarfs his life. Musicologists, a fatuous bunch, on the whole, have incredible blind spots about Bach. Because his compositions are so sublime, musicologists tend to ignore the tragedies of his life. One French book on Bach has a chapter called *Un Homme Heureux* ("A Happy Man."). If Bach was happy most of his life, then he would have been an even bigger fool than the musicologists who write about him. Let's enumerate some of the "happy" events in his life: When Sebastian (his second name is the one commonly used) was only nine, his father died; a year later his mother died, and he was sent to live and study with an older brother, a musician, to be sure, like most of the Bachs. At 18, Sebastian was already a professional musician: not much time for enjoying youth! At 22, he married Maria Barbara Bach, a cousin, and quickly became a father, but three of the seven children that she bore died. Worse still, at 35, when he returned from an extended stay at Carlsbad with Prince Leopold, he discovered that his wife was dead and buried, leaving him with four young children to care for. Can you imagine the shock and guilt that Sebastian must have felt on that occasion, that "happy" man? But so far as loss was concerned, the worst was yet to come. The next year, in 1721, he married Anna Magdalena Wilcke, a court singer who was only 21, while Bach was 36. The next 21 years would be a litany of pregnancies, births, baptisms, and deaths. Of 13 children that Magdalena bore, only six survived childhood, and one of these six, Gottfried Heinrich, their second child, was dim-witted. Their first child, Christiana Sophia Henrietta, died at the age of three, when Magdalena was pregnant with their third child, Christian Gottlieb, who also died at three when, again, Magdalena was pregnant, this time with Regina Johanna, their sixth child, who died at four in the same year as Christian Gottlieb died; their fifth child, Ernestus Andreas, died a day after baptism; their seventh child, Christiana Benedicta Louise, died at two, while their eighth child, Christiana Dorothea, lived only a year; their tenth child, Johann August Abraham, died shortly after birth. In addition to all these losses of children at birth or in early childhood, Bach suffered a hard blow in 1739 when his youngest son from the first marriage,

Johann Gottfried Bernhard, a wayward son, died at the age of 24. While a musician, Gottfried was apparently unstable and a spendthrift and had caused his father much anguish.

I can hear some readers saying now, "But in those days parents were inured to the loss of children and, besides, the Bachs were devout Lutherans, so they had their faith as consolation." That is true, but I can not believe that the hurt was any less than it would be now, and only the grief-stricken need consolation. Any parent knows the joy of seeing a three-year-old child discovering life before his eyes, and keeps within the unspoken fear of losing the child. Parents live the daily cycle of joy and anguish. How could it have been any different for Sebastian and Magdalena? Unfortunately, neither of them left a diary or letters detailing the anguish and joys of their married life. (Indeed, while some portraits of Bach survived him, there is no drawing or even verbal description to show what Magdalena looked like.) Bach's music, with its celestial, timeless quality that makes the listener forget that its composer was a suffering mortal, has had the effect of obscuring the tragedy that constantly stalked both Sebastian and Magdalena. Yet, it does not take much imagination for anyone who has had to cope with the anxieties of parenthood to realize that for Bach, work, that is, performing and composing music, was a form of escape, whereas Magdalena must have suffered intensely with only the solace of having to care for the surviving children and to keep being a wife and homemaker. I am reminded of the trenchant poem by Robert Frost, *Home Burial*, where the wife, who has just lost a child, observes through a window her husband digging a grave and resents his evident sense of release in physical effort. For years, Magdalena went through the cycles of pregnancy, suffered the loss of her flesh and, Yes, dealt with the sexual appetite of her sensual husband, who evidently gave her little respite. Surely, she too must have resented his ability to escape the realities of life by writing fugues and canons. And Bach himself must have felt guilt over the role of his animal presence in the life and pains of Magdalena. (*Cf.* Shakespeare's sonnet, *The expense of spirit in a waste of shame.*) Is it any wonder that we see eternity in a Bach fugue? In French, *fugue* means "flight" and Bach was fleeing the animal world with its constant reminder of death and decay. In his counterpoint, Bach often resorted to dissonance, that is, sounding simultaneously a jarring combination of notes. It is my speculation that in dissonance, Bach was reminding himself that death, which he discovered at nine, was always stalking him, and in ending always on the tonic major chord he was placing his faith in God, in eternal life.

Less tragic, but still an immense frustration for Bach, was his job in Leipzig. In Cöthen his boss had been a young music-loving bachelor, Prince Leoplold, who paid for a talented 18-man orchestra, and encouraged Bach's creative genius, which produced such masterpieces as the *Brandenburg Concertos,* the six *Suites for Unaccompanied Cello*, and six *Sonatas and Partitas for Unaccompanied Violin.* His masters at St. Thomas Church and School were stern and stingy Lutheran elders, who expected Cantor Bach not only to make music every Sunday, which involved composing a cantata every week for several years, rehearsing with orchestra and choirs, playing the organ and conducting the heavily musical part of a five-hour church service, but also to teach individual students music during the week! And these elders did not particularly appreciate Bach's music, which was daring and ahead of its time. When the *St. Matthew Passion* was first performed, in 1727, one parishioner complained, "But this is opera!" By 1730, after seven years at Leipzig, Bach was fed up with the job and wrote a plaintive letter to his friend Erdman, asking help to find a new post. This rare letter shows how difficult it was for Bach to earn a decent living, with so many mouths to feed. He complains that whereas he had been able to supplement his salary by playing the organ at funerals, the last winter was so mild that there were fewer deaths than usual! This job search did not pan out and Bach remained another 20 years in Leipzig, until death found him.

Why, then, had Bach left Cöthen for Leipzig? Again, the musicologists are blind. They give as reasons that Leipzig was a university town where Bach's growing sons, Friedemann and Emanuel, could get a decent education and also, that Prince Leopold, having married a woman who did not like music, had to spend money on her and reduced his music budget. Yet the musicologists – males, to be sure – ignore an obvious reason that any woman would understand: surely Magdalena must have dreaded living in the same surroundings as her dead predecessor, Barbara, and must have nagged Sebastian: "Let's go somewhere else." That a wife might have influenced a major career decision does not occur to male musicologists.

Adding to Bach's woes was the fact, as I have indicated above, that his music had grown out of style. Even his sons balked at continuing the contrapuntal tradition of their father. Emanuel went to Potsdam in

1740 and become the harpsichordist of the young King of Prussia, Frederick II, known to posterity as Frederick the Great. The King played the flute and liked the new easy music where, basically, only one voice carried the melody and the rest was accompaniment. In 1740 Sebastian was already 55, considered old age in those times. It was too late for him to get another full-time position. To make matters worse he was losing his sight, although he apparently kept this to himself. Very few of his compositions were published in his lifetime. His fame was more as a fantastic organist and improviser than as a composer. In May 1747, Bach went with Friedemann to visit Emanuel in Potsdam and as soon as Frederick heard that "old Bach" was in town he commanded him to appear in court. The King was eager to hear him perform and, particularly, to improvise. Frederick gave him a complicated melody, with descending chromatic notes in the middle, and asked Bach to improvise a six-part fugue. Sebastian replied that the melody was too difficult and improvised on another tune.

On his return to Leipzig, Bach set to work writing canons and fugues, as well as a flute sonata, on what he called "the Royal theme." In early July he had completed and printed this extraordinary work, which he called *The Musical Offering*, and sent it to the King. To the two fugues he gave the Italian title, *Ricercar,* to show they were very special; one was a three-part fugue and the other an extremely rare six-part fugue. There is no indication that the King ever had the music played in court or even thanked Bach for the *Offering*! Yet all the accounts that I have read fail to point out this affront. Nor does it occur to the musicologists that by this visit and the *Offering,* Bach, now 62, was hoping for a royal appointment or some sort of sinecure that would free him of his ungrateful and unappreciative employers at Leipzig and provide some security for Magdalena and him. This trip had been his last hope. He set about getting his *Art of the Fugue* ready for publication, which meant that he would have to pay for the engraving and printing. Doubtless he hoped that this could provide him with some income. Already, the elders of Thomaskirche made no secret of the fact that they were looking for a replacement for the fading Cantor. In 1749, he had one brief period of joy when his daughter Elisabeth Juliana Friderika married his student, Johann Christoph Altnickol, she being the only Bach daughter who found a husband. The next year, 1750, with his sight almost completely gone, Bach accepted the desperate gamble to have operations – presumably for cataracts – performed by a visiting English quack, John Taylor. The operations failed, and now Sebastian was completely blind. Soon he suffered a stroke and, on July 28th he died. Although Bach had not finished the last fugue of the *Art of the Fugue*, one in which he wove his initials, Emanuel went ahead and had the work published, adding a hymn that Bach dictated on his deathbed. Only 30 copies were purchased, and Emanuel then sold the engravings for scrap metal! The children divided up Bach's modest estate, the sons taking away all his musical instruments, and left Magdalena with virtually nothing. The Town Council continued Bach's salary for six months and that was it. She had to give up the large apartment that came with the job at St. Thomas School. The feeble-minded son went to live with the sister who had married Altnickol. Magdalena became a pauper and received alms from the town. She died ten years after Bach, with nothing left but memories of a husband who was already forgotten by all but a few connoisseurs.

It took 79 years for Bach's magnificent choral music to be rediscovered, thanks to Felix Mendelssohn, who performed the *St. Matthew Passion* in 1829. The *B-minor Mass* waited until 1835 to be heard again.. Little by little, other works were unearthed, performed and published. Only a century later, in 1927, was *The Art of the Fugue* performed in public for the first time. As indicated, two of his Passions, *St. Mark* and *St. Luke,* seem to be lost forever.

The next time you hear a work of Bach, it would make me happy to know that you gave a thought to the mortal man who composed this celestial, timeless music, who toiled to the end to give us a glimpse of eternity, and to Anna Magdalena, the long-suffering wife he failed to protect despite his love for her.

The heaven for such losers is in our hearts.

Printed in France
by Imprimerie Roques et Fils, 75020 Paris
November 2002